4498300

INDUSTRIAL MARKETING RESEARCH

RONALD SERIES ON MARKETING MANAGEMENT

Series Editor: FREDERICK E. WEBSTER, Jr.
*The Amos Tuck School
of Business Administration
Dartmouth College*

GEORGE S. DOMINGUEZ, *Marketing in a Regulated Environment*
ROBERT D. ROSS, *The Management of Public Relations: Analysis and Planning External Relations*
VICTOR WADEMAN, *Risk-Free Advertising: How to Come Close to It*
FRANK H. MOSSMAN, W. J. E. CRISSY, and PAUL M. ISCHER, *Financial Dimensions in Marketing Management*
JACOB JACOBY and ROBERT W. CHESTNUT, *Brand Loyalty: Measurement and Management*
WILLIAM E. COX, Jr., *Industrial Marketing Research*
FREDERICK E. WEBSTER, Jr., *Industrial Marketing Strategy*

Industrial Marketing Research

WILLIAM E. COX, JR.

A RONALD PRESS PUBLICATION

JOHN WILEY & SONS, New York • Chichester • Brisbane • Toronto

•354002

658.8
C 878

Copyright © 1979 by John Wiley & Sons, Inc.

All rights reserved. Published simultaneously in Canada.

Reproduction or translation of any part of this work beyond that permitted by Sections 107 or 108 of the 1976 United States Copyright Act without the permission of the copyright owner is unlawful. Requests for permission or further information should be addressed to the Permissions Department, John Wiley & Sons, Inc.

Library of Congress Cataloging in Publication Data:

Cox, William Edwin, 1930-1978.
  Industrial marketing research.

  (Wiley series on marketing management)
  "A Ronald Press publication."
  Includes bibliographies and index.
  1. Marketing research. 2. Marketing research
—United States. I. Title.

HF5415.2.C68   658.8′3   78-11480
ISBN 0-471-03467-3

Printed in the United States of America

10 9 8 7 6 5 4 3 2

Foreword

Professor William E. Cox, Jr., died April 22, 1978, after a nine-month illness with cancer. This volume is his legacy to the world of industrial marketing. It might not have been completed were it not that Bill, hedging against his perennial optimism, requested a leave of absence in 1976–1977 to put it together. His malignancy had been detected several years earlier.

For twenty years, Bill Cox was a teacher, researcher, and consultant at this University. The utility of this volume, which many have described to me as being "uniquely useful," is a product of the questioning of thousands of students, the practical demands of dozens of clients, and an extraordinary and inquiring intellect. The reader should find a fine marriage of scholarly research and practical awareness in the selection of material Bill has surveyed and on which he has commented. For such was Bill's unique currency, which he spent freely on us all—the ability to understand and communicate with the worlds of research, and to practice and effect a useful wedding of both. Shortly after his operations last fall, when Bill was still expected to return to work, we talked about this volume and Bill's eyes lit up. "Putting that book together was the greatest learning experience I have ever had," he exclaimed. As you read through his work, I hope and trust you will share, in some measure, the exciting learning experience that Bill Cox was to all of us who knew him.

Several individuals warrant particular citation for their selfless contribution. George V. Havens, President of The Jayme Organization, Inc., a student, colleague, and client of Bill's, had often discussed the volume with him. Earlier Bill had realized that he would be unable to complete the final and summary chapter by himself. Fortunately he had discussed the volume thoroughly with his colleagues and he asked Dr. Luis V. Dominguez, Associate Professor of Marketing in the School of Management, to work with him in its completion. Professor Dominguez has devoted long and loving hours over these past few months to complete the final chapter so that it would have the character and emphasis that marked Bill Cox's special competence. Betty Bates did most of the typing and proofreading. Susan Ranney prepared the bibliographies and indexes. To all of them the Cox family expresses its gratitude.

> THEODORE M. ALFRED, DEAN
> *School of Management*
> *Case Western Reserve University*

Cleveland, Ohio
December 1978

Series Editor's Foreword

Marketing management is among the most dynamic of the business functions. On the one hand it reflects the everchanging marketplace and the constant evolution of customer preferences and buying habits, and of competition. On the other hand, it grows continually in sophistication and complexity as developments in management science are applied to the work of the marketing manager. If he or she is to be a true management professional, the marketing person must stay informed about these developments.

The Wiley Series on Marketing Management has been developed to serve this need. The books in the series have been written for managers. They combine a concern for management application with an appreciation for the relevance of developments in such areas of management science as behavioral science, financial analysis, and mathematical modeling, as well as the insights gained from analyzing successful experience in the market-place. The Wiley Series on Marketing Management is thus intended to communicate the state-of-the-art in marketing to managers.

Virtually all areas of marketing management will be explored in the series. Books now available or being planned cover advertising management, industrial marketing research, brand loyalty, sales management, product policy and planning, public relations, overall marketing strategy, and financial aspects of marketing management. It is hoped that the series will have some effect in raising the standards of applied marketing management.

Hanover, New Hampshire FREDERICK E. WEBSTER, JR.
June 1977

Preface

In preparing this book, I have been guided by two principles: (1) there is a need for a marketing research book that emphasizes industrial marketing research as practiced in the United States, and (2) there is no need to incorporate materials that deal with marketing research methods in general, for they are well covered in a number of existing books.

There are numerous marketing research books that provide a good general background on research methods and practice, oriented toward consumer goods and markets. I have concentrated on industrial goods and markets, while minimizing duplication of the general materials that dominate the existing books. This volume therefore is offered as a complementary product to the existing books and not as a substitute. It is assumed that the reader has access to one or more of the general books on marketing research, and Suggested Readings are provided in the chapters to facilitate this access. The text material is based on the objective of synthesizing widely scattered materials on current principles and practice in industrial marketing research, as well as presenting previously unpublished materials.

This book responds to the legion of practitioners, teachers, and students who have long lamented the absence of a balanced treatment of consumer and industrial goods and markets in existing marketing research books. The lack of balance is due to a variety of reasons, and is likely to persist. Just as it has been necessary to develop specialized books on industrial marketing to rectify the lack of balance in general marketing books, it appears that the solution to the imbalance in marketing research books is best met by a specialized work on industrial marketing research.

In preparing this book, I have drawn upon more than twenty years of teaching and consulting experience in industrial marketing research. My list of obligations to fellow academicians, former students, and consulting clients is long indeed, but foremost among them is to the late Dr. Donald R. G. Cowan, Professor of Marketing at the University of Michigan. His teaching and guidance have had a lasting effect on my life and this book is dedicated to his memory.

WILLIAM E. COX, JR.

Cleveland, Ohio
December 1977

Contents

PART I INDUSTRIAL MARKETING RESEARCH: NATURE, SCOPE, AND DATA METHODS

1. Industrial Marketing Research: Nature and Scope, 1
2. Exploratory Research, 17
3. Secondary Data Sources, 29
4. Research Designs and Primary Data Methods, 76

PART II THE PRINCIPAL RESPONSIBILITIES OF INDUSTRIAL MARKETING RESEARCH

5. Sales, Cost and Profitability Analysis, 95
6. Market and Industry Analysis, 119
7. Market and Sales Potentials, 144
8. Market and Sales Forecasting, 177
9. Input-Output Analysis, 227

PART III SURVEYS IN INDUSTRIAL MARKETING RESEARCH

10. The Place of Surveys in Industrial Marketing Research, 241
11. Sampling in Industrial Survey Research, 267
12. Analysis of Survey Data, 296

PART IV QUANTITATIVE AND BEHAVIORAL MODELS IN INDUSTRIAL MARKETING RESEARCH

13 Product Analysis, 335
14 The Buying/Selling Interface: Purchasing and Promotion Analysis, 374
15 Overview of Industrial Marketing Research, 416

APPENDIX, 440
AUTHOR INDEX, 455
SUBJECT INDEX, 460

INDUSTRIAL MARKETING RESEARCH

CHAPTER ONE

Industrial Marketing Research: Nature and Scope

Mention the term "marketing" to most people and a great many images emerge, diverse yet similar: Grand Prix, Wheaties, Cheer, MacDonald's, Ford, Korvette, Safeway. The products and firms in these images have one common characteristic, they are all associated with consumer goods and services. Most marketing and marketing research textbooks generally reinforce these perceptions by their emphasis on consumer goods and services. However the volume of transactions in industrial goods and services is more than twice as large as the volume of transactions in consumer goods and services. This reversal of emphasis is probably explained by the greater availability of consumer information and the public's awareness of it. The reason industrial marketing and marketing research practices have restricted visibility is that they concentrate on relatively few customers and prospects. One of the primary purposes of this book is to discuss many of these industrial practices, especially those involved with research.

Definitions and Comparisons

Above all this is a book about marketing research. The most widely cited definition of marketing research is that prepared by the American Marketing Association:

> The systematic gathering, recording, and analyzing of data about problems relating to the marketing of goods and services.[1]

Marketing research therefore focuses on data acquisition and analysis for the purpose of identifying and solving marketing problems. In recent years the term "information" is often substituted for "data" to stress that only facts relevant to specific marketing problems and decisions should be included. This distinction has been suggested by those interested in information systems; they classify as "noise," data not used currently or not scheduled to be used in decision-making processes.[2]

It was once fashionable to portray marketing research as an integral part of problem solving, however the writings of Peter Drucker have influenced many to broaden the scope of marketing research to include both problems and opportunities. In seeking to restore the norm, problem solving is a matter of efficiency and, at best, can produce only ordinary results by "doing things right." However, successful organizations, those that produce extraordinary results, emphasize effectiveness which is defined as "doing the right things." Effectiveness focuses on opportunities, on the products and markets that will produce optimum results.[3]

Both the Kellogg Company, the leading manufacturer of breakfast cereals, and Republic Steel Corporation, a major producer of steel and steel products, have strong commitments to marketing research. Kellogg's products are purchased by individuals and households for personal use, whereas Republic's products are bought by organizations for the purpose of producing other goods or for resale. Thus Kellogg is a manufacturer of consumer goods and Republic Steel is a producer of industrial goods. This classification of goods and services into consumer and industrial is based on buying and use characteristics rather than on the nature of the product or service. Since it is about industrial marketing research, this then is a book for Republic Steel, not Kellogg's.

---

[1] *Report of the Definitions Committee of the American Marketing Association.* Chicago: American Marketing Association, 1961.
[2] Thomas R. Prince, *Information Systems for Management Planning and Control,* rev. ed. Homewood, Ill.: Irwin, 1970, p. 16.
[3] Peter F. Drucker, *Management: Tasks, Responsibilities, Practices.* New York: Harper & Row, 1974, p. 45.

NATURE AND SCOPE

We can now define *industrial marketing research:*

The systematic gathering, recording, and analyzing of information about problems and opportunities relating to the marketing of industrial goods and services.

There are additional dimensions to this definition. Marketing research is frequently classified as a subsystem of marketing information systems, with its primary activity organized on a project basis in order to deal with specific problems and opportunities. Kotler, in his treatment of marketing information systems, has four subsystems:[4]

1. *Internal accounting system*—based on the order-shipping-billing cycle of the firm.
2. *Marketing intelligence system*—methods for monitoring changes in the firm's environment.
3. *Marketing research system*—project studies of specific problems and opportunities.
4. *Marketing management-science system*—models of marketing processes.

Industrial marketing research, as defined and described in this book, includes all four subsystems noted by Kotler. We shall also examine the issues and practices involved when the information produced by the subsystems is combined to provide a basis for marketing decisions. If the reader concludes that this is a treatise on industrial marketing information systems, fine. The key point is that a broad definition of marketing research encompasses all of the activities that some choose to call marketing information systems.

Differences between Industrial and Consumer Goods Markets

The principal rationale for separate and independent investigation of industrial marketing research methods and practices is that they differ from those of consumer marketing research. There are, of course, many similarities. However there are significant differences that have been obscured in general treatises on marketing research. These are a consequence of the differences between the *markets* for consumer and industrial goods and services. Often there are differences in the characteristics

---

[4]Philip Kotler, *Marketing Management,* 3rd ed. Englewood Cliffs, N.J.: Prentice-Hall, 1976, Chap. 19.

of the goods and services that are purchased in consumer and industrial markets, such as the dollar value of the average purchase or the service requirements associated with a sale, but many identical products (typewriters, calculators, sandpaper) are sold in both markets. By adopting buyer and use behavior as the basis for classification, the resulting *market* classification provides: (1) an unambiguous assignment of goods and services to the appropriate classification, and (2) an approach consistent with the marketing concept that emphasizes the market rather than the product.

Among the most important differences between industrial and consumer goods and services markets are the following:

1. *Derived demand*—The demand for industrial goods is ultimately dependent upon the demand for related consumer goods and is thus considered as derived demand. In many cases there is a "chain of derived demand" in which the demand for a given industrial good is derived from the demand for a number of other industrial goods as well as the ultimate consumer good.[5] The longer the chain of derived demand, the greater the prospect that demand will be characterized by a "boom-bust" cycle, stemming from changes in inventories and expectations. Industrial marketing researchers must identify the links in the chain of derived demand and analyze the demand at each link, a far more complicated process than the direct analysis of consumer goods markets.

2. *Demand concentration*—Wilson has noted that industrial markets are marked by three types of concentrations: geographic, industrial, and purchasing.[6] Geographic concentration refers to the tendency for firms in many industries to cluster spatially, based on supply proximity. Industrial concentration results from the inherent characteristics of industrial goods and services, leading to relatively limited markets for such products. Purchasing concentration stems from the structure of many industrial markets, whereby a few firms account for a high proportion of total market demand. These three forms of concentration permit industrial marketing researchers to identify their markets more accurately than their consumer goods counterparts.

3. *Demand volatility*—Shifts in business conditions, financial considerations, and prices affect the behavior of industrial buyers, resulting in

---

[5] Aubrey Wilson, *The Assessment of Industrial Markets*. London: Hutchinson and Co., 1968, Chap. 1.
[6] *Ibid.*, pp. 8–9.

sharp variations in demand level at times.[7] Buyers respond to actual and expected shifts in these factors by varying the level of inventory accumulation and postponing or advancing the timing of their purchases. Marketing and sales forecasts for industrial goods and services are then subject to much larger errors than expected for consumer goods and services.

4. *Purchasing procedures and organization*—The presence of multiple and varying buying influences in industrial firms is another important influence on industrial marketing research. More individuals are generally involved in an industrial purchasing decision than in consumer purchasing decisions, with greater variation in the composition of the "influential" group from product to product. As a result, measurement of attitudes, motivations, and relative influence on purchasing decisions is much more complex in industrial marketing research. On the other hand, those involved in industrial purchasing decisions are far more knowledgeable about products and can consequently provide better information than the average consumer.

5. *Manufacturer-Buyer relationships*—Trade relations between producers and buyers of industrial goods and services tend to be closer, stronger, and more continuous than those for consumer goods and services. Relationships tend to be closer because of the greater tendency for industrial goods and services to be sold direct rather than through intermediaries. They tend to be stronger because of more frequent, personal contact between producers and buyers. Continuity of relationship is increased by the greater use of long-term purchase contracts for industrial goods and services.

All the differences between industrial and consumer goods markets cited are important but the most significant differences are those associated with demand concentration, particularly industrial and purchasing concentration. The manifestations of demand concentration for industrial marketing research will be revealed repeatedly throughout the book.

Development of Industrial Marketing Research

Although there is no question that consumer marketing research activity is more extensive and commands more corporate resources than industrial marketing research, the reasons for the different levels of develop-

[7] Richard M. Hill, Ralph S. Alexander, and James S. Cross, *Industrial Marketing*, 4th ed. Homewood, Ill.: Irwin, 1975, pp. 47–53.

ment are not so clear. Among the factors offered in explanation are: (1) market differences, particularly demand concentration and trade relationships, (2) gross margin and value added differences, enabling consumer goods firms to spend more for marketing research, and (3) management differences, in which executives of consumer goods firms are alleged to be more oriented to the importance of monitoring consumer needs and wants. Shankleman has suggested that the rate of development of marketing research is directly related to ". . . how adequate one considers existing channels of communication to be."[8] He contends that consumer goods firms have recognized the inadequacy of their channels of communication with their customers, and have therefore relied on marketing research to fill the communications need.

Industrial marketers often claim that their sales force provides for good communication with customers and markets. Shankleman provides a charming example of this practice in a nineteenth-century English textile mill:

> The grand old man of the firm of its nineteenth-century heyday, used to hold a conference every Saturday with his assembled travellers after their weeks journeying. John Bonney heard their reports himself, the tale of their successes and failures, the comparison between their samples and goods produced by other firms. Then, if it was found that a rival firm had turned out something better in a particular line, the brains and energy of the Dewhurst Mill were mobilised and kept in action until once again the rival had been outstripped.[9]

The primary communications problem in most industrial goods firms today is that their John Bonneys do not have either the same regular contact with all members of their sales force nor the same management follow-up on the outcomes of those contracts. Consequently in large-scale industrial enterprises there is a greater need for marketing research than is often recognized.

Other writers have proposed additional factors to explain the relative lack of development of industrial marketing research. In a 1964 article, de Koning lamented the lack of theory and literature in industrial marketing research, and blamed the concern for secrecy and confidentiality of firms and consultants.[10] His review of Western European and United States

---

[8] Eric Shankleman, "The Development of Industrial Market Research and Marketing," *Commentary* (Journal of the Marketing Research Society), Vol. 9, no. 1, January 1967, p. 22.
[9] *Ibid.*, p. 23.
[10] Co de Koning, "Effective Techniques in Industrial Marketing Research," *Journal of Marketing*, Vol. 28, no. 2, April 1964 pp. 57–61.

activity emphasized the need to develop better methods for collecting primary data. Wilson concluded in 1969 that Great Britain was ahead of the rest of the world in industrial marketing research practice.[11] He attributed Britain's leadership to the need to develop effective and efficient primary data methods because of a lack of adequate secondary data. The United States with much better secondary data had less incentive to develop better methods of collecting primary data. Wilson also noted considerable growth in industrial marketing research worldwide during the 1960s as a result of the development of corporate long-range planning, which placed ". . . new and important demands on industrial marketing research to provide the information inputs."[12]

Determinants of the Importance of Industrial Marketing Research

The central role of marketing information in the management of all industrial organizations provides the basis for their adoption of some form of marketing information collection, tabulation, and analysis. It appears that the adopted form is primarily due to two factors: organization size and value added to products. The level and sophistication of the marketing information processing activity is generally related to organization size. In small organizations industrial marketing research is usually conducted on a personal, informal basis by the company officers, while large organizations tend to organize, formalize, and specialize the activity. It also appears that the importance of industrial marketing research is directly related to the value added to the various goods and services produced by the organization. Thus a firm producing both basic metals and specialty chemical products would normally invest more resources for marketing information on specialty chemicals because of the greater value added associated with these products.

Organization for Industrial Marketing Research

Our knowledge about the nature, extent, and importance of marketing research activities among producers of industrial goods and services has been enhanced in recent years by the availability of periodic surveys conducted by the American Marketing Association. Some of the findings of these surveys are presented here.

In 1973 it was determined that 59% of the responding industrial goods firms had formal marketing research departments and that 19% had one

---

[11] Aubrey Wilson, "Industrial Marketing Research in Britain," *Journal of Marketing Research,* Vol. 6, February 1969, pp. 15–27.
[12] *Ibid.*, p. 16.

person assigned to marketing research.[13] The total of 78% was close to the figure (83%) reported for consumer goods manufacturers. As might be expected, the presence of formal marketing research departments is related to sales volume. More than 75% of industrial goods manufacturers with annual sales in excess of $100 million have formal marketing research departments, while only 9% of the firms with sales under $5 million have formal departments.[14] The size of industrial marketing research departments is also related to sales volume. The average (median) number of employees in all departments is four, but firms with annual sales of $500 million and over have an average of seven full-time employees.[15] Similarly, the average number of full-time employees in formal marketing research departments in all firms surveyed is four.[16]

Out of a total of 312 industrial goods firms responding to the AMA survey, 33% had formed their marketing research departments within the past five years (1968–1973). An additional 18% had set up their departments between 1963 and 1968.[17] It is evident that the marketing research function is still a relatively new activity for most industrial goods manufacturers. The rapid economic growth of the 1950s and 1960s brought industrial goods manufacturers into line with consumer goods firms in the acceptance of this function.

Marketing Research Budgets

Although industrial goods manufacturers have been actively establishing marketing research departments, they have not been particularly generous in setting budgets. Among those manufacturers having formal research departments, the average expenditure for marketing research in 1973 was only $168,000. By comparison, manufacturers of consumer goods spent an average of $672,000.[18] It should be noted, however, that these averages are arithmetic means and thus strongly influenced by expenditures of a few large firms, for most firms budgets are actually smaller.

The survey also indicates that manufacturers of consumer goods spend more money for marketing research than industrial goods companies within every size classification. Industrial companies with annual sales of

---

[13] *1973 Survey of Marketing Research.* Chicago: American Marketing Association, 1973, p. 11.
[14] *Ibid.*, p. 15.
[15] *Ibid.*. p. 18.
[16] *Ibid.*, p. 18–19.
[17] *Ibid.*, p. 23.
[18] *Ibid.*, p. 28.

NATURE AND SCOPE

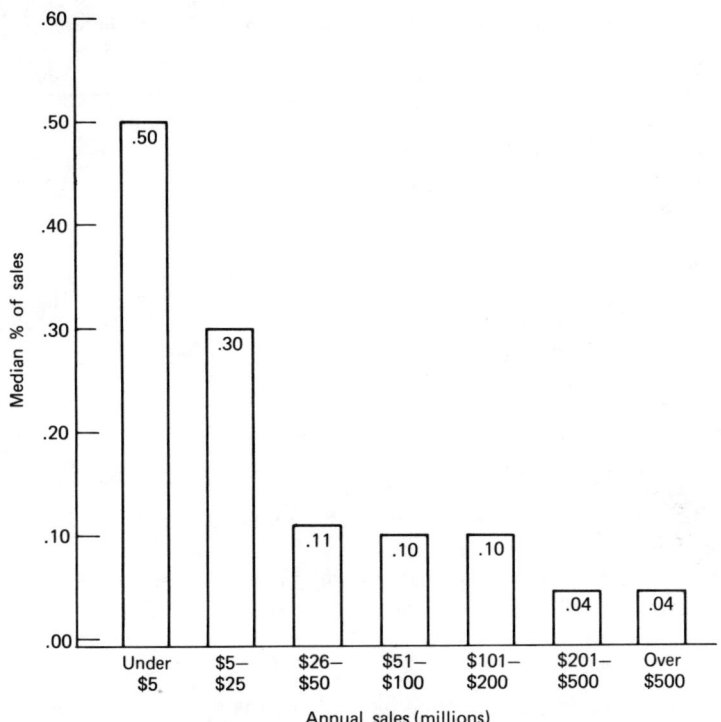

Figure 1-1   Percent of sales spent for marketing research. Base: 312 reporting firms. Source: 1973 Survey of Marketing Research. Chicago: American Marketing Association, 1973, p. 32.

less than $5 million have a median budget of only $14,000, while those with annual sales of more than $500 million report a median budget of $298,000.[19]

Expenditures for marketing research as a percent of sales tend to decline as annual sales increase for industrial goods firms, with a median figure of 0.1% for all companies.[20] Figure 1-1 shows that the largest firms (over $500 million sales) spend only 0.04% on the average for marketing research, far below the 0.5% spent by the smallest companies (under $5 million sales) in the survey.

Larger industrial goods companies showed a much greater tendency to purchase outside research services in 1973 than in 1968, but overall, the 1973 figure of 24% of the total marketing research budget allocated for this

[19] *Ibid.*, p. 30.
[20] *Ibid.*, p. 32.

Table 1-1. Major Research Activities of Industrial Companies

Type of Research Activity	% Doing
Sales and market research:	
Measurement of Market Potentials	75%
Market share analysis	75
Sales analyses	75
Determination of market characteristics	74
Establishment of sales quotas, territories	73
Forecasting and trend studies:	
Short-range forecasting (up to 1 year)	75
Long-range forecasting (over 1 year)	73
Studies of business trends	73
Product research	
New product acceptance and potential	73
Competitive product studies	73

Base: 436 industrial companies. All research activities conducted by 70% or more of the reporting companies are listed above.

Source: *1973 Survey of Marketing Research.* Chicago: American Marketing Association, 1973, p. 43.

purpose was identical to the 1968 figure.[21] Firms with annual sales of $100 million and less spent less on outside services in 1973 than in 1968, offsetting the tendency for firms with sales of more than $100 million to spend more. The 24% figure for industrial goods firms was far below the comparable figure of 49% for consumer goods companies in 1973.

Marketing Research Activities

The most common marketing research activities of the 436 industrial goods companies reported in the 1973 AMA Survey are shown in Table 1-1. More than 70% of the firms reported that they conducted sales and market research, product research, and forecasting and trend studies. The same was true for consumer goods companies.[22] Consumer goods companies, however, tend to be more active than industrial companies in: (1) advertising research, (2) test marketing, (3) consumer panels, and (4) sales promotion research.

Although industrial and consumer goods companies tend to engage in similar marketing research activities, the lower budgets in industrial com-

---
[21] *Ibid.*, p. 38.
[22] *Ibid.*, p. 43.

NATURE AND SCOPE

panies result in significant differences in research practice. The most visible difference is in the budget for outside research services. As a consequence, the industrial marketing researcher must spend a high proportion of his time on information *collection,* while the consumer goods researcher spends relatively more time on *analysis* of purchased information.

PROBLEM/OPPORTUNITY FORMULATION

There is one overriding basis for the existence of industrial marketing research activity: to improve industrial marketing decisions. Specific marketing research activities are frequently the result of requests for information by executives seeking to reduce the uncertainty surrounding a problem or opportunity and thereby make a better decision. Boyd, Westfall, and Stasch have noted that researchers should not accept a request for information as the starting point for a research study, but first should seek to understand the elements of the problem/activity.[23] These elements are:

1. *Identification of the decision maker*—Requests for information are often made by individuals other than the actual decision maker. The researcher should seek to identify and meet with the prospective decision maker to understand the environment of the decision.
2. *Objectives of the decision maker*—The translation of the objectives of the decision maker into research objectives is one of the most critical steps in the research process and one of the most difficult. Problems and opportunities are often recognized by the decision maker on an intuitive basis or with little evidence. There is recognition that something may have to be done but the objectives are unclear. It is the task of the researcher to help the decision maker in the clarification of objectives as a prelude to formulating the research objectives.
3. *Various courses of action*—There are usually a number of approaches to the solution of a problem and the discovery of opportunities. Exploratory research is perhaps the best vehicle for examining such approaches and is discussed in Chapter 2.
4. *Consequences of various actions*—In order to evaluate the consequences of different courses of action, it is important that the researcher and decision maker jointly assess the probable outcomes of

[23]Harper W. Boyd, Jr., Ralph Westfall, and Stanley P. Stasch, *Marketing Research,* 4th ed. Homewood, Ill.: Irwin, 1977, pp. 206–209.

each action. Consideration of the research parameters (time, money, personnel, objectives) is also important.[24]

Most general books on marketing research methods stress the same elements of the problem/opportunity formulation process as those outlined. This view of the process is grounded in decision theory. Different courses of action are identified, and the range and value of the outcomes of each are specified. Ramond, however, noted,

> If a manager can cram his problem into this eminently logical but often unrealistic framework, then the researcher will be happy to try to estimate the probabilities of those outcomes.[25]

Too often, marketing researchers are reluctant to use decision-theory frameworks because they consider them "unrealistic" or fear that managers will be threatened by such an approach. An alternative approach that may be less threatening to some managers and researchers is summarized in Figure 1-2, in which a list of management questions and research actions in the problem/opportunity formulation process is presented. Our position is that decision-theory frameworks are particularly useful for specifying and evaluating other courses of action. Several books have useful sections on the use of decision theory in the problem formulation process.[26] The checklist in Figure 1-2 may be helpful in understanding the problem formulation process; neither the decision-theory approach nor the checklist, however, deals specifically with techniques for identifying problems/opportunities. The identification of problems/opportunities is an important activity in all types of marketing research, but it is particularly important for industrial marketing research, as a result of relatively low budgets and emphasis on information collection. Industrial marketing researchers must accordingly concentrate on effective identification of problems/opportunities to maximize the use of their limited budgets and the value of their collected information.

A good exposition of techniques and strategies for identifying problems is offered by Ramond, who presents several decision rules to guide managers and researchers in these activities:

---

[24]Wilson, *op. cit.*, Chap. 3.
[25]Charles Ramond, *The Art of Using Science in Marketing*. New York: Harper & Row, 1974, p. 160.
[26]Boyd, Westfall, and Stasch, *op. cit.*, pp. 184–204; Paul E. Green and Donald S. Tull, *Research for Marketing Decisions*, 3rd ed. Englewood Cliffs, N.J.: Prentice-Hall, 1975, Chap. 1.

NATURE AND SCOPE

Management Questions	Research Actions
1. What problem faces us? (What are the opportunities or obstacles to meeting objectives?)	1. Obtain and analyze performance feedback information. Examine research conducted on other problems to find insights that indicate location and nature of information that points to new or unsolved problem(s).
2. What is the present environment of the problem?	2. Obtain background information on various factors that affect the problem and its solution.
3. What significant changes in the environment should be expected (by the time a solution is put into effect)?	3. Project the background data, with historical trends, to forecast the future situation.
4. What alternative courses of action might solve the problem and thereby reach the final objective?	4. Make an exploratory study: a. Seek and report likely ideas unearthed in past research and experience. b. Obtain clues and ideas from persons who would be in an advantageous position to provide them.
5. Which alternative courses of action merit final consideration?	5. Confer with decision maker in weighing the worth of the results of research and its costs against the risk reduction that would probably be gained.
6. What uncertainties would be reduced, in the final choice of hypothetical solutions, if formal research was conducted? Would such research be justified?	6. Work out probability estimates of "go" or "no go" on conclusive research.

Source: David J. Luck, Hugh G. Wales, and Donald A. Taylor, *Marketing Research,* 4th ed. Englewood Cliffs, N.J.: Prentice-Hall, 1974, p. 64.

Figure 1-2 Management Questions and Research Actions in the Problem/Opportunity Formulation Process.

1. *Respond first (or only) to declining outputs*—Offering the dictum, "Never change a winning strategy; always change a loser," Ramond suggests that the manager concentrate on declines in output measures such as profits, sales, awareness, and so on.
2. *Where possible, localize the decline in output*—Try to determine if the decline is short-term or seasonal, limited to selected market segments, the result of significant changes in competitive behavior, or a combination of these factors.
3. *Work on the biggest decisions first*—Select the problems that offer the highest potential benefit-cost ratios.[27]

[27] Ramond, *op. cit.,* pp. 156–161.

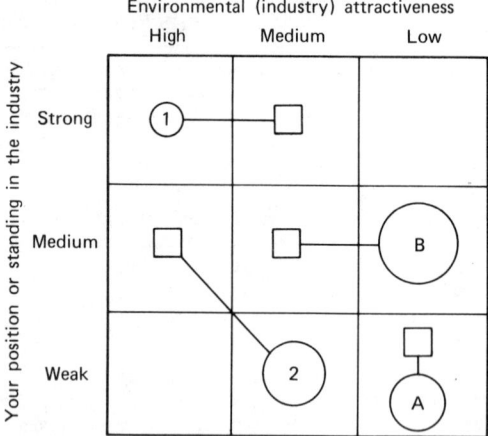

Key: Circles show the relative positions in a given industry of the products (1 and 2), the market segments (A and B), and the relative sizes in terms of sales.

Rectangles show the future relative positions of the firm and industry given the continuation of present strategies and trends.

Figure 1-3 Decision matrix for opportunity identification and evaluation. Source: William E. Rothschild, Putting It All Together: A Guide to Strategic Thinking. New York: AMACOM (American Management Association), 1976, pp. 151-156.

Identification of opportunities may best be carried out through the organized process of evaluating the attractiveness of the industries in which a firm participates, as well as its position or standing in the industry. Rothschild has shown how the General Electric Company and other organizations have organized the process.[28] Figure 1-3 shows a decision matrix in which several products (1 and 2) and market segments (A and B) of a given industry are positioned. A similar, more specific approach is provided by the "product portfolio strategy" system developed originally by the Boston Consulting Group. This system measures industry attractiveness by the growth rates of the markets in which the industry participates, and the firm's position is measured by its market share.[29]

After the problems/opportunities have been identified, the next step in the process is to identify the various courses of action that may solve the problem or provide the opportunity that will meet the firm's objectives.

[28] William E. Rothschild, *Putting It All Together: A Guide to Strategic Thinking*. New York: AMACOM (American Management Association), 1976, Chap. 8.
[29] William E. Cox, Jr., "Product Portfolio Strategy: A Review of the Boston Consulting Group Approach," *Proceedings,* American Marketing Association, 1975, pp. 465-470.

NATURE AND SCOPE

SUMMARY

In the minds of most people, marketing research is associated with consumer goods and services even though the volume of transactions of industrial goods and services is more than twice as large. Part of the reason is that industrial marketing and marketing research activities are marked by restricted visibility. Another reason is that consumer marketing research activity is more extensive. Various reasons are offered for the differences in visibility and extent of industrial and consumer marketing research. The most important factor is the higher degree of geographic, industrial, and purchasing power concentration of the industrial markets.

This book deals with industrial marketing research which may be defined as the systematic gathering, recording, and analyzing of information about problems and opportunities relating to the marketing of industrial goods and services. The book examines the four subsystems of marketing information systems—internal accounting, marketing intelligence, marketing research, and management science—and the issues and practices involved when the information produced by these subsystems is combined for decision-making purposes.

Marketing research activities are more formal and extensive among larger firms and among those with a high value added. Industrial marketing firms spend less on marketing research than firms of a similar size that deal in consumer goods and services. This is particularly true of advertising research, test marketing, customer panels, and sales promotion research. It is especially true of expenditures for outside research services.

The fundamental reason for doing marketing research is to improve decision making. This includes improving both the efficiency of marketing decisions ("doing things right") and the effectiveness of decision making ("doing the right things"). To this end it is important that the research springs not merely from a request for information but from a thorough understanding of the problem/activity that prompted the request for information. The two basic approaches used to gain this understanding are the decision-theory approach and the problem/opportunity analysis approach that underlies the "product portfolio strategy" system developed by the Boston Consulting Group.

SUGGESTED READINGS

American Marketing Association, *1973 Survey of Marketing Research*. Chicago: AMA, 1973.

Boyd, Harper W., Jr., Ralph Westfall, and Stanley F. Stasch, *Marketing Research*, 4th ed. Homewood, Ill.: Irwin, 1977, Chap. 6.

Green, Paul E., and Donald S. Tull, *Research for Marketing Decisions*, 3rd ed. Englewood Cliffs, N.J.: Prentice-Hall, 1975, Chap. 1.

Hill, Richard M., Ralph S. Alexander, and James S. Cross, *Industrial Marketing*, 4th ed. Homewood, Ill.: Irwin, 1975, Chap. 3.

Koning, Co de, "Effective Techniques in Industrial Marketing Research," *Journal of Marketing*, Vol. 28, no. 2, April 1964, pp. 57–61.

Luck, David J., Hugh G. Wales, and Donald A. Taylor, *Marketing Research*, 4th ed. Englewood Cliffs, N.J.: Prentice-Hall, 1974, Chap. 4.

Ramond, Charles, *The Art of Using Science in Marketing*. New York: Harper & Row, 1974.

Shankleman, Eric, "The Development of Industrial Market Research and Marketing," *Commentary* (Journal of the Market Research Society), Vol. 9, no. 1, January 1967, pp. 22–29.

Stacey, Nicolas A. H., and Aubrey Wilson, *Industrial Marketing research*. London: Hutchinson and Co., 1963, Chaps. 1–6.

Wilson, Aubrey, *The Assessment of Industrial Markets*. London: Hutchinson and Co., 1968, Chaps. 1, 2.

Wilson, Aubrey, "Industrial Marketing Research in Britain," *Journal of Marketing Research*, Vol. VI, February 1969, pp. 15–27.

CHAPTER TWO
Exploratory Research

Most marketing researchers devote a significant portion of their working days on informal projects that arise from spontaneous requests for marketing information. These informal projects, which are frequently characterized as "quick and dirties," must be completed quickly with a minimum of the scientific niceties. It is important to note that many of these informal projects never go beyond this stage—the findings are used as the basis for marketing decisions without any further investigation. If the informal project is merely the prelude to further research, it is usually considered to be exploratory research. In this context, exploratory research is concerned with problem definition, while subsequent research is focused on problem solutions. We shall define exploratory research broadly in order to encompass both problem definition and solution.

Industrial marketing researchers will probably find exploratory research more applicable and rewarding than their consumer counterparts. The reasons are: smaller industrial budgets and demand concentration. Since there is a relatively small amount of money available for research on most industrial goods and services, there is a tendency for researchers to spread it across many products and markets. As a result, pressures often force the industrial researcher to limit the scope of each project and to seek to close it out as soon as possible.

Demand concentration for industrial goods and services results in relatively small, well-defined markets typically dominated by a few major firms. It is frequently possible to obtain the required marketing information regarding these firms through exploratory research methods, as opposed to the more costly and time-consuming conclusive methods that dominate consumer marketing research practice.[1]

Exploratory Research Method

Since exploratory research is important in industrial marketing research, it is appropriate to examine the approaches available to the researcher. There are two basic methods for conducting exploratory research: (1) review of secondary data, and (2) survey of knowledgeable persons. Secondary data (see Chapter 3) refer to information available at the outset of a project. In relation to the research department, this information may have originated either externally or internally and may be in either published or unpublished form. Ready availability is the distinguishing characteristic of secondary data. Therefore industrial marketing researchers should develop a ready reference system for access to secondary data on all products and markets of interest to their firm.

Marketing Intelligence Systems

Development of a ready reference system for access to secondary data is best carried out within the context of a marketing intelligence system. Marketing intelligence systems involve the *continuous organized* monitoring of changes in the firm's environment, and are thus distinguished from marketing research systems, which are *discrete* and usually more specific in orientation. Aguillar has noted that all executives are engaged in various forms of environmental scanning, ranging from undirected viewing to formal search.[2] Casual processes of collecting intelligence by reading, listening, and talking to people inside and outside the firm provide useful background information and knowledge. Marketing executives, to a greater extent than others in the firm, are responsible for scanning the market environment of the firm, and are thereby engaged in the collection of marketing intelligence. Marketing decisions are often made on the basis of the casual intelligence acquired through personal monitoring of the marketplace, even though such intelligence is usually

---

[1]Harper W. Boyd, Jr., Ralph Westfall, and Stanley F. Stasch, *Marketing Research,* 4th ed. Homewood, Ill.: Irwin, 1977, pp. 42–47.
[2]Francis J. Aguilar, *Scanning the Business Environment.* New York: Macmillan, 1967.

incomplete and outdated. Such decisions are obviously not all bad, but there is a growing tendency for executives to enlist the assistance of marketing research personnel to acquire marketing intelligence as a basis for at least the more important decisions.

Pinkerton has documented how he helped to develop, organize, and implement a marketing intelligence system for the Ansul Company, a Wisconsin manufacturer of chemicals and fire-extinguishing equipment.[3] He portrayed the system as being designed on the basis of the "intelligence cycle," as shown in Figure 2-1. Each stage of the cycle required that specific procedures be developed to place the system in operation. In the direction stage, key executives were interviewed to determine: (1) major decision areas, (2) information requirements, and (3) outcomes of specific prior decisions. On the basis of these interviews, the "Elements of Essential Information" (EEI) were determined. To the extent that information requirements can be anticipated, the marketing intelligence system should be developed and organized to meet such requirements. The system must also be responsive to changing, unanticipated information needs. This requires that the collection of intelligence be broad enough in focus to signal new opportunities and to respond to the unanticipated problems.

In the collection stage of the intelligence cycle, the sources of information are identified. The primary source for the Ansul Company was the field sales force. Many industrial marketing executives still resist the idea that salesmen can be an effective source of information and intelligence. The key to Ansul's success was training and feedback. Training sessions were conducted for all field selling personnel. There was prompt acknowledgement of all information furnished as well as disbursement of information gained from others. Webster has reported similar success in using salesmen as a source of marketing information,[4] as have Stern and Heskett.[5] Other personnel within the firm, such as product and market managers, financial analysts, purchasing agents, engineers, and research personnel, may also be a source of raw information about the marketplace. They should be incorporated into the intelligence cycle by encouraging them to submit information on a standardized form.

External secondary data sources will be covered in detail in Chapter 3,

---

[3]Richard L. Pinkerton, "How to Develop, Organize, and Implement a Marketing Intelligence System," *Industrial Marketing,* April–August 1969. (A series of five articles in successive issues.)
[4]Frederick E. Webster, Jr., "The Industrial Salesman as a Source of Market Information," *Business Horizons,* Vol. 8, no. 1, Spring 1965, pp. 77–82.
[5]Louis W. Stern and J. L. Heskett, "Grass Roots Market Research," *Harvard Business Review,* Vol. 43, no. 2, March–April 1965, pp. 83–96.

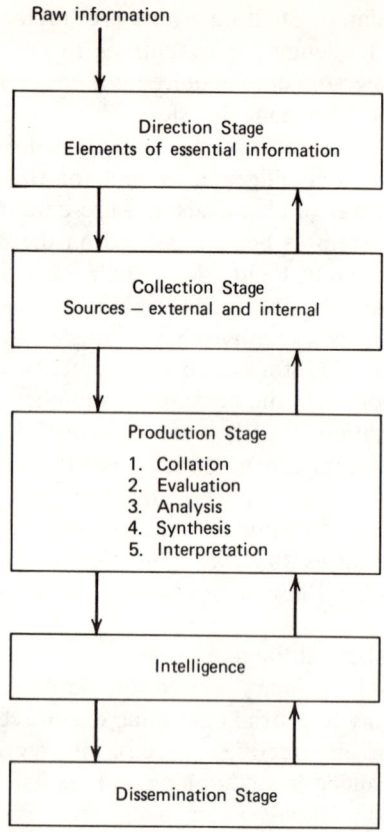

Figure 2-1 The intelligence cycle in marketing intelligence systems. Source: Richard L. Pinkerton, "How to Develop, Organize, and Implement a Marketing Intelligence System," Industrial Marketing, *April 1969, p. 42.*

but it is important to note that there is a vital need in most firms for an intelligence library with a filing system that provides ready access to such sources. The ability of the industrial marketing researcher to respond quickly and usefully to information requests may be substantially enhanced through the establishment of such a library and filing system.

It is in the production stage of the intelligence cycle that raw information is transformed into intelligence. Information is collated by subject, evaluated in terms of reliability and credibility, analyzed for potential value, synthesized with other information, and interpreted in terms of meaning and information requirements. The result of information processing in the production stage is intelligence. The resulting intelligence is

EXPLORATORY RESEARCH

then disseminated to the right people in the firm. A "suspense system" was established at Ansul to ensure that the intelligence was received, acknowledged, and used. Emphasis on feedback in the dissemination stage of the intelligence cycle is critical to insure that the intelligence output of the system is useful and is used, as well as triggering the feedback process through each of the other stages of the intelligence cycle.

The primary focus of most marketing intelligence systems appears to be competitive intelligence, particularly in highly competitive industries. IBM has long required its sales representatives to report all competitive computer installations to its Commercial Analysis Department, considered by many to be a model marketing intelligence operation.[6] The electronics industries are noted for their development of competitive scenarios in which pieces of intelligence from scientific papers, patent filings, hiring of engineers and scientists, and a variety of other sources are fitted together to estimate long-term competitive strategies regarding products, technology, and markets. Cleland and King have developed a model competitive intelligence system that provides a comprehensive program for collecting, evaluating, and disseminating information about competitive firms.[7]

Occasionally, the quest for competitive intelligence results in unethical or illegal activities. A recent survey suggested that there has been an increase in industrial espionage over the past 15 years, that executives are much more interested in competitive information today, but that ethical standards regarding competitive intelligence have not changed.[8] There is actually no need for questionable intelligence activities if a marketing intelligence system is effective, but the absence of such systems have led some firms to seek shortcuts. Perhaps the most common technique is to hire away the personnel of competitors and debrief them immediately; others advertise non-existent jobs in order to interview competitive personnel. All such techniques are temporary expedients and poor substitutes for an effective, efficient marketing intelligence system.

Surveys of Knowledgeable Persons

One of the most important differences between industrial and consumer marketing research is found in the relative importance of surveys of

[6] Business Sharpens Its Spying Techniques," *Business Week,* August 4, 1975, p. 60.
[7] David I. Cleland and William R. King, "Competitive Business Intelligence Systems," *Business Horizons,* December 1975, pp. 19–28.
[8] Jerry L. Wall, "What the Competition Is Doing: Your Need to Know," *Harvard Business Review,* November–December 1974, pp. 22–23.

knowledgeable persons. Industrial marketing researchers should devote considerable time and effort to identify those very special persons who qualify as most knowledgeable about the products and markets of primary interest to the firm. Such persons may be found in many organizations, including:

1. Customer and prospect firms
2. Industry consultants
3. Trade journal editors
4. Trade association executives
5. Government officials
6. University professors
7. Own company personnel

Just as demand concentration is a distinguishing feature of industrial markets, information concentration is a vital element to be considered in surveys of knowledgeable persons in industrial marketing research. It is not uncommon to find that less than 1% of the "knowledgeable" persons associated with an industrial market possess virtually all of the relevant information about the market. Figure 2–2 illustrates the generalized dis-

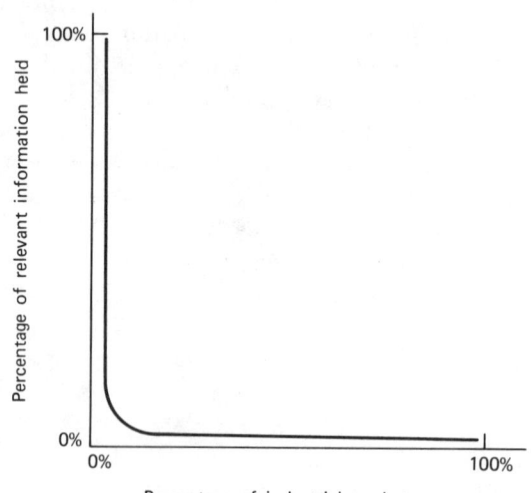

Figure 2–2 Distribution of relevant information among industrial market sources.

EXPLORATORY RESEARCH

tribution of relevant information about industrial markets. This highly skewed distribution requires that careful attention be given to the selection of knowledgeable persons, using judgment samples rather than any random sampling method.

Knowledgeable persons may therefore be either internal or external to the firm. Internal persons generally considered as product "experts" tend to be diverse, depending upon the specific nature of the information required: if technical information is needed, persons in research and development, engineering, and manufacturing may be helpful; service managers and salesmen may prove knowledgeable regarding technical applications information. Market "experts" are usually found within the marketing organization of the firm but there is no assurance that the person in any given position is the most knowledgeable person. The key to selecting the most knowledgeable persons internal to the firm is either a good memory or a formal record of the predictions and opinions of those contacted in the past. Most of the time knowledgeable persons tend to be right in their field of expertise and this fact is evident to their associates. The industrial marketing researcher may therefore seek the advice of a number of people within the firm to identify the "experts" within the organization on any particular matter. In time the researcher will find that the repeated use of exploratory research will lead to the identification of a core of "experts" who can be counted upon for reliable information.

Identifying knowledgeable persons external to the firm is initially a more difficult operation than internal identification, but with experience there is essentially no difference. The problem is that the population of potential "experts" is much larger and less known to the researcher. One common technique for identifying external "experts" is a variant of sociogram analysis, an internal "expert" is asked to identify one or more other external "experts." Those "experts" most often mentioned by their peers are then asked to consent to an interview or to serve on a panel of "experts." Cooperation is sought by stressing the value of information exchange to both the supplying and acquiring firm, as well as the recognition of the individuals as "experts" in their fields.

Another approach to the identification and use of "experts" is the key informant technique traditionally associated with the field of anthropology. Houston has noted that the key informant technique is appropriate in three general situations:

1. When the scope of data to be gathered is such that it would be difficult, costly, and time-consuming to collect using representative sampling
2. When the need for a precise estimate is low.

3. When the content of inquiry is such that complete or in-depth information cannot be expected from representative survey respondents[9]

Among the marketing applications of the key informant technique are: international marketing, in which key informants would be asked to provide a generalized profile of the social structure of a foreign country; industrial marketing, in which the firm is the sampling unit and key informants are needed to provide either broad assessments of the firm or specialized knowledge about specific issues; forecasting, in which salesmen's estimates and executive opinion are used; and exploratory research in which it is an early step in a multi-stage research process.[10]

Kotler has developed a very useful guide to obtaining information from experts.[11] He examined three important problems: (1) methods to obtain data from a single expert, (2) methods for pooling estimates from a group of experts, and (3) approaches to understanding how expert estimates are produced. In obtaining data from a single expert, Kotler identified four types of data that may be gathered: (1) point estimates, (2) sales response functions, (3) probability estimates, and (4) ratings and weights. For each type of data, the general approach recommended is to use a "bounding" process of questioning in which boundary estimates are established and closure sought through repetition.

When estimates from two or more experts are to be pooled, Kotler suggests three methods:

1. *Group discussion*—Experts are assembled and are asked to discuss the issue collectively and produce a group estimate.
2. *Pooling individual estimates*—The same as group discussion except the experts are asked to produce individual estimates and an analyst pools the estimates to produce a single estimate.
3. *Delphi method*—A group of experts provide individual estimates and assumptions which are reviewed by an analyst who modifies them and requests new estimates. The process continues until convergence is reached.

Another approach to pooling the estimates of individual experts has been suggested by Turner. He used nonmetric multidimensional scaling to

---

[9]Michael J. Houston, "The Key Informant Technique: Marketing Applications," in Thomas V. Greer, ed., *Conceptual and Methodological Foundations of Marketing*. Chicago: American Marketing Association, 1974, p. 306.
[10]*Ibid.*, p. 307.
[11]Philip Kotler, "A Guide to Gathering Expert Estimates," *Business Horizons*, October 1970, pp. 79–87.

pool estimates of customer characteristics made by ten salesmen of industrial packaging equipment.[12] A comprehensive review of the application to the Delphi method to marketing issues has been provided by Fusfeld and Foster.[13]

Kotler also suggests that the estimation process used by experts may be better understood and estimates may be improved by having an analyst work with the experts during the estimation process, using one or more methods to explore how estimates are produced. As Kotler has noted:

> The use of judgmental data (expert estimates) in decision making is hardly avoidable today, and is rapidly becoming the foundation of many of the more advanced and sophisticated decision models appearing in marketing. The marketing research profession should devote more attention to developing concepts and techniques that will improve the gathering and use of such data.[14]

Perhaps the most important area in which concepts and techniques have been developed recently for obtaining information from experts is that of key informant technique. In addition to the study of Houston, Seidler has provided a very useful review of applications, measurement problems, and methodological issues associated with the use of key informants.[15] Although specifically concerned with the use of informants in organizational analysis, the study provides valuable insights for marketing researchers.

An Industrial Application of the Key Informant Technique

An example of the use of key informant technique in industrial marketing research is provided by a study conducted by the author for an industrial service firm. After several years of declining revenues followed ten years of revenue and profit growth, the firm's board of directors questioned the advisability of continuing with one line of business. A review of internal sales records revealed that their market for the service line was limited to approximately thirty large packaged goods manufacturers. No significant

---

[12] Ronald E. Turner, "Market Measures from Salesmen: A Multidimensional Scaling Approach," *Journal of Marketing Research,* Vol. 8, May 1971, pp. 165-172.
[13] Alan R. Fusfeld and Richard N. Foster, "The Delphi Technique: Survey and Comment," *Business Horizons,* June 1971, pp. 63-74.
[14] Kotler, *op. cit:,* p. 87.
[15] John Seidler, "On Using Informants: A Technique for Collecting Quantitative Data and Controlling Measurement Error in Organization Analysis," *American Sociological Review,* Vol. 39, December 1974, pp. 816-831.

external secondary data sources were located. Executives of the firm were then asked to identify the three most knowledgeable persons in the country with respect to the service line characteristics, its market, and the capabilities of competitive suppliers. All three persons nominated were executives of present or past customers of the firm. Appointments for personal interviews were made with each nominee by telephone, using the firm's president as a reference.

Each of the three personal interviews were conducted at the informant's place of business, and lasted from 1 ½ to 3 ½ hours. A checklist of topics and questions were prepared in advance, but a questionnaire was not used and the interviews were unstructured. A tape recorder was used, with the permission of the informants, to record portions of the interviews. The sessions ranged over a wide variety of topics. Informants were asked to assess the past, current, and probable future developments of the service line, the market, and the comparative strengths and weaknesses of the major suppliers of the service line, including the research sponsor. At the end of each interview, the informants were asked to nominate three other possible informants. This produced six new names and three duplicates.

Three of those nominated (two duplicate nominees and one single nominee) were interviewed next, using the same procedures as before. After the first interview of the second round, it was felt that the response patterns had converged and that a reasonably clear picture of the situation was available. Nevertheless, the remaining two interviews of the second round were conducted and as expected, they confirmed the pattern that had emerged earlier.

The findings of this exploratory research study based on the key informant technique revealed that there had been no decline in market activity during the past two years. There had been however a concerted effort by a number of the packaged goods manufacturers to divert business to two new service suppliers during the period. This was done to assure additional sources of supply and capacity in order to handle a significant expansion of demand that was expected to occur within two years. As a result established suppliers were allocated less business during the period but could expect a resumption of their previous growth in the near future. The manufacturers were reluctant to divulge these plans to the established suppliers for fear they would add excess capacity and act to limit the competitiveness of the new suppliers. The exploratory research study sponsored by one of the leading suppliers indicated to the manufacturers (at least those interviewed) that it was necessary to divulge their past actions and plans in order to preserve their relations with the supplier, even though the possibility of the supplier leaving the business was never mentioned. The board of directors of the industrial service firm were therefore encouraged to remain in the service line business and to prepare for sufficient expansion to maintain or slightly increase their share of the market.

The recommendations were based on a judgment sample of six respondents. It could have been limited to four. The four informants were also not a representative sample, but they were all clearly experts in their field. Additional interviews and further study would have produced higher costs and relatively little additional information. Thus no further research was conducted and subsequent events supported the recommendation to the board. Some members of the board were initially reluctant to make an important decision on the basis of six interviews, but finally agreed after the logic of the key informant technique was explained. It is not uncommon for executives to be wary of small sample sizes, but they also tend to respond favorably after the logic, time savings, and economic advantages of using a few selected experts are presented.

SUMMARY

Exploratory marketing research is the informal analysis of quickly available information from secondary data sources or from surveys of knowledgeable persons. Smaller industrial marketing research budgets and greater demand concentration put pressure on researchers to limit the scope and duration of each project to a much greater extent than is true in consumer marketing firms.

Exploratory marketing research can be conducted with secondary data or by means of surveys of knowledgeable persons. Such surveys are particularly useful in industrial marketing research because high demand concentration spells a high degree of information concentration among a very limited number of sources.

As Kotler indicates, the use of expert judgmental data is becoming more extensive and sophisticated. The two keys to successful use of experts is to identify who they are and to achieve a convergence of expert judgments. The trademark of an "expert" is an excellent track record on past predictions and opinions. Once a group of experts is secured, a variety of methods for converging to a common assessment are available.

The development of a marketing intelligence system is vital to the ready availability of the information needed for exploratory research. A marketing intelligence system involves continuous, organized monitoring of the firm's environment. This requires that key executives determine the key kinds of information needed for decision making and the key external and internal information sources that the marketing intelligence system must tap.

SUGGESTED READINGS

Boyd, Harper W., Jr., Ralph Westfall, and Stanley F. Stasch, *Marketing Research*, 4th ed. Homewood, Ill.: Irwin, 1977, Chap. 2.

Fusfeld, Alan R., and Richard N. Foster, "The Delphi Technique: Survey and Comment," *Business Horizons*, June 1971, pp. 63–74.

Houston, Michael J., "The Key Informant Technique: Marketing Applications," in Thomas V. Greer, Ed., *Conceptual and Methodological Foundations of Marketing*. Chicago: American Marketing Association, 1974.

Kotler, Philip, "A Guide to Gathering Expert Estimates," *Business Horizons*, October 1970, pp. 79–87.

Pinkerton, Richard L., "How to Develop, Organize, and Implement a Marketing Intelligence System," *Industrial Marketing*, April–August 1969. (A series of five articles in successive issues.)

Seidler, John, "On Using Informants: A Technique for Collecting Quantitative Data and Controlling Measurement Error in Organization Analysis," *American Sociological Review*, Vol. 39, December 1974, pp. 816–831.

Stern, Louis W., and J. L. Heskett, "Grass Roots Market Research," *Harvard Business Review*, Vol. 43, no. 2, March–April 1965, pp. 83–96.

Turner, Ronald E., "Market Measures for Salesmen: A Multidimensional Scaling Approach," *Journal of Marketing Research*, Vol. 8, May 1971, pp. 165–172.

Webster, Frederick E., Jr., "The Industrial Salesman as a Source of Market Information," *Business Horizons*, Vol. 8, no. 1, Spring 1965, pp. 77–82.

CHAPTER THREE
Secondary Data Sources

Secondary data refers to information available at the outset of a project. Such data may be either internal or external to the firm and may exist in published or unpublished form. In both formal and informal research projects, activity should begin with an analysis of relevant secondary data.

Internal Secondary Data

Every firm, in the course of its operations, generates internal secondary data in the form of invoices, shipment reports, customer records, operating statements, budgets, corporate and marketing plans, and a myriad of additional information. Most industrial companies utilize internal secondary data to conduct sales and market analyses for forecasting purposes and in the development of market potentials.[1] These uses of secondary data are explored in detail in subsequent chapters.

The major challenge to industrial market researchers concerning internal secondary data lies in knowing what information is available within the firm. Much of the secondary data that the researcher will find useful is organized and maintained outside the marketing department. The re-

[1] *1973 Survey of Marketing Research*. Chicago: American Marketing Association, 1973.

searcher must therefore make a special effort to talk with people in the accounting, finance, manufacturing, and credit departments to ascertain the availability and location of information within those departments.

As information of value is located, the researcher will frequently find that the data are collected or presented in a manner that poses problems in terms of research use, or that vital data are not collected. The problems faced by a primary metals company and its subsequent actions will help to illustrate this common situation. In an attempt to improve the sales analysis system of the company, the marketing research department sought to have each salesman provide additional information about the customer, the products sold, and the salesman himself. This required the use of an expanded order form that would have taken more time to complete. Subsequently a systems analyst in the company developed a program in which each customer, product, and salesman was assigned a code number, and files were established for each number. These contained the identifying data the marketing research department sought. Thus for each customer the Standard Industrial Classification (SIC) numbers, the potential annual volume, and the type of account (original equipment manufacturer or distributor) were all maintained in a file that could be accessed when required for sales analysis. The files were updated as required and the program made it possible to carry more complete analyses, simplify the order form, reduce the time required to fill in the form, and provide more accurate identifying data than before.

External Secondary Data

Virtually every question or problem confronting industrial marketing researchers can be illuminated, at least partially, by external secondary data. These data, which are collected outside the firm for purposes other than the question or problem at hand, are so ubiquitous that the principal challenge for the researcher lies in knowing where to look for information in the face of so many possibilities.

STANDARD INDUSTRIAL CLASSIFICATION SYSTEM

In order to utilize the abundance of information available, it is important that the industrial firm adopt a classification system for its accounts and products. Unless there are some extremely compelling reasons, the firm should adopt the SIC system developed by the federal government. Most economic data published by United States government agencies are organized on the basis of the SIC system and, to an increasing extent, so are

SECONDARY DATA SOURCES

data available from state and local governments as well as trade associations, publishing firms, and other private organizations engaged in the collection and publication of economic statistics.

The SIC system covers all economic activity within the society, divided into the following divisions:

Agriculture, forestry, and fisheries
Mining
Construction
Manufacturing
Transportation; communication; electric, gas, and sanitary services
Wholesale trade
Retail trade
Finance, insurance, and real estate
Services
Public administration

Within each economic division, there is a further breakdown into industries and products. Figure 3-1 illustrates the relationships among the manufacturing division, an industry (composed of major groups, groups, and industries), and products within an industry.

The basic reporting units in the SIC system are establishments and products. Establishments may be:

1. *Operating units*—Each plant of the Diamond Shamrock Corporation is classified as a separate establishment.
2. *Central administrative offices and auxiliary units*—The corporate headquarters of the Diamond Shamrock Corporation in Cleveland would be an establishment as would the Diamond Shamrock Technical Center in Painesville, Ohio.

Based on their primary activity, establishments are classified into 4-digit industries. Related 4-digit industries are combined into 3-digit groups, in turn these are combined into 2-digit major groups. The industrial marketing researcher can therefore move freely between 2- and 4-digit classifications, depending on the nature of the problem. Figure 3-2 shows an excerpt from the *Standard Industrial Classification Manual* in which the 2-, 3-, and 4-digit levels are displayed.[2]

Products are classified on the basis of five or more digits; the first four

---

[2] Executive Office of the President, *Standard Industrial Classification Manual*. Washington: U.S. Government Printing Office, 1972.

Division	Major Groups (2 digits)	Groups (3 digits)
A. Agriculture	20. Food	341. Metal cans
B. Mining	21. Tobacco	342. Cutlery, hand tools
C. Construction	22. Textile mill	343. Heating equipment
D. Manufacturing	23. Apparel	344. Fabricated structural metal
E. Transportation	24. Lumber and wood	345. Screw machine products
F. Wholesale trade	25. Furniture	346. Metal forgings and stampings
G. Retail trade	26. Paper	347. Coating, engraving
H. Finance	27. Printing	348. Ordinance
I. Services	28. Chemicals	349. Miscellaneous
J. Public administration	29. Petroleum	
K. Nonclassifiable	30. Rubber	
	31. Leather	
	32. Stone, clay, glass	
	33. Primary metal	
	34. Fabricated metal	
	35. Machinery	
	36. Electrical machinery	
	37. Transportation equipment	
	38. Instruments, etc.	
	39. Miscellaneous	

Figure 3–1 Organization of the standard classification system.

Industries (4 digits)	Products (5 or more digits)

342. Cutlery, hand tools → 3421. Cutlery
3423. Hand and edge tools →
3425. Handsaws and saw blades
	34231. Mechanics' hand service tools
	    34231 11. Pliers
	    34231 21. Ball peen hammers, etc.
	34232. Edge tools, hand operated
	    34232 11. Agricultural edged handtools
	    34232 31. Axes, adzes, hatchets, etc.
	34233. Files, rasps, and file accessories and other handtools
	    34233 11. Shovels, spades, scoops, telegraph spoons, and scrapers
	    34233 21. Light-forged hammers (under 4 pounds), excluding ball peen hammers etc.

Figure 3–1 (Continued)

Source: Executive Office of the President, *Standard Industrial Classification Manual*. Washington: U. S. Government Printing Office, 1972.

Major Group 34.—Fabricated metal products, except machinery and transportation equipment.

The Major Group as a Whole

This major group includes establishments engaged in fabricating ferrous and nonferrous metal products such as metal cans, tinware, hand tools, cutlery, general hardware, nonelectric heating apparatus, fabricated structural metal products, metal forgings, metal stampings, ordnance (except vehicles and guided missiles), and a variety of metal and wire products not elsewhere classified. Certain important segments of the metal fabricating industries are classified in other major groups, such as machinery in Major Groups 35 and 36; transportation equipment, including tanks, in Major Group 37; professional scientific and controlling instruments, watches and clocks in Major Group 38; and jewelry and silverware in Major Group 39. Establishments primarily engaged in producing ferrous and nonferrous metals and their alloys are classified in Major Group 33.

No. Group	No. Industry	
341		**Metal cans and shipping containers**
	3411	**Metal Cans**

Establishments primarily engaged in manufacturing metal cans from purchased materials. Establishments primarily engaged in manufacturing foil containers are classified in 3497.

Beer cans, metal
Cans, aluminum
Cans, metal
Containers, metal: food, milk, oil, beer, general line
Food containers, metal
General line cans, metal
Ice cream cans, metal

Milk cans, metal
Oil cans, metal
Packers' cans, metal
Pails, except shipping and stamped: metal
Pans, tinned
Tin cans

Figure 3-2 Standard industrial classification manual—example of 2-, 3-, and 4-digit levels. (Source: Executive Office of the President, Standard Industrial Classification Manual. *Washington: U.S. Government Printing Office, 1972, p. 153.)*

SECONDARY DATA SOURCES

digits are based on the industries in which the products are primarily produced. Industrial marketing researchers should obtain a copy of the *Numerical List of Manufactured Products* compiled for each *Census of Manufactures*. Figure 3-3 shows that each product is coded to seven digits, and is classified within its product class (5-digit code), industry (4-digit code), group (3-digit code), and major group (2-digit code). In addition, the units of measurement for each product are shown.[3] The successive use of the *SIC Manual* and the *Numerical List of Manufactured Products* will enable the researcher to ascertain the nature of the information available in the *Census of Manufactures* and thereby utilize this important resource in an efficient manner. These sources also provide a good illustration of the way in which products are classified in the SIC system.

Although the SIC system is an extremely valuable tool, it has some limitations. Hummel has noted four major problems:[4]

1. *Multi-product establishments*—If an establishment produces two or more products that are classified into more than one 4-digit industry, the establishment will be assigned to a single industry, based on its primary activity. Primary activity, in turn, is determined by the principal product or group of products produced by the establishment, and is measured by the production value of the products in the case of manufacturing establishments. The practice of assigning establishments to a single industry therefore leads to a tendency to overstate statistics for principal products and to understate statistics for secondary products. Hummel illustrates this problem with an example of a New England firm that manufactures grinding machines and special gauges. Grinding machines are the principal product, so the establishment (and in this case the firm) is classified in SIC 3541, Machine tools, metal cutting types. The secondary products, special gauges, are classified in SIC 3345, Machine tool accessories and measuring devices. Data relating to the special gauge line, such as employment, value of shipments, and so on, are combined with data for grinding machines and classified in SIC 3541, the primary activity of the firm.[5]

2. *Captive plants*—An establishment may have a "captive" operation that produces components for its primary and secondary products, although the components are also produced by other firms as a final

---

[3]U.S. Bureau of the Census, *Numerical List of Manufactured Products—1972 Census of Manufactures* (MC 72-1.2). Washington: U.S. Government Printing Office, 1973.
[4]Francis E. Hummel, *Market and Sales Potentials*. New York: Ronald, 1961, pp. 74-76.
[5]*Ibid.*, p. 75.

MAJOR GROUP 34—FABRICATED METAL PRODUCTS

Code	Check digit	Industry and product description	Quantity measure	Data collected
342		CUTLERY, HANDTOOLS AND HARDWARE		
3423		HAND AND EDGE TOOLS, N.E.C.		
34232		EDGE TOOLS, HAND OPERATED		
34232 31	4	Axes, adzes, and hatchets		SV
34232 51	2	Cutting dies, for use in cutting cloth, paper, leathers, etc., excluding dies for cutting metal		
		Machine knives, except metal-cutting		
34232 56	1	Veneer knives and chipper knives		
34232 58	7	All other machine knives		
34232 61	1	Can openers, except electric can openers		
34232 71	0	Auger bits	Thousands	S
34232 81	9	Planes	do	
34232 83	5	Chisels	do	
34232 98	3	Other edge tools, including agricultural edged handtools		SV
34233		FILES, RASPS, AND FILE ACCESSORIES AND OTHER HANDTOOLS		
34233 11	4	Shovels, spades, scoops, telegraph spoons, and scrapers	M units	S
34233 21	3	Light forged hammers (under 4 pounds), excluding ball peen hammers	do	
34233 31	2	Heavy forged tools, sledges (4 pounds and over), picks, pick mattocks, and mauls	do	
34233 41	1	Steel goods (forks, hoes, rakes, weeders, etc.)	do	
34233 65	0	Woodworking and metalworking files and rasps, including precision files	do	
34233 81	7	Soldering irons (electric)	Thousands	
34233 98	1	Other handtools, except edge tools		SV

3425			HANDSAWS AND SAW BLADES		
34250			HANDSAWS, SAW BLADES, AND SAW ACCESSORIES		
			Power saw blades		
			Woodworking		
			Circular		
34250 11	8		Solid tooth	Ft	S
34250 13	4		Inserted tooth	do	SV
			Band		
34250 15	9		Under 2 inches	Ft	S
34250 17	5		2 inches and over		
34250 18	3		Teeth for inserted saws, sold separately		
34250 19	1		All other woodworking power saw blades (scroll, jig, etc.)		
			Metalworking		
34250 31	6		Circular	Number	
34250 35	7		Hack (power only)	M units	
34250 36	5		Band (flexible back, spring temper metal-cutting and high-speed metal-cutting)	Ft	
34250 39	9		Other metalworking saw blades (saber, reciprocating, etc.)		SV
			Hand operated saws		
34250 43	1		Hacksaw blades (hand only)	M units	S
34250 45	6		Carpenter crosscuts and ripsaws	Number	
34250 49	8		Other handsaws (heavy handsaws, including crosscut and buck, miter, coping, pruning, compass, etc., including handsaw frames, and handsaw blades sold together, or handsaw blades sold separately)		SV

Note: In the "Data collected" column: S = Shipments (quantity and value) SV = Shipments (value)
Source: U.S. Bureau of the Census, *Numerical List of Manufactured Products—1972 Census of Manufactures* (MC72–1.2), Washington: U.S. Government Printing Office, 1973, p. 118.

Figure 3–3. 1972 Numerical list of manufactured products.

product. Thus Hummel notes that the Bassick Company has a captive operation producing ball bearings (SIC 3562) for use in its principal product, furniture casters (SIC 3429).[6] The presence of captive operations results in statistical underestimates for 4-digit industries producing such products and overestimates for industries in which principal products are backed up by captive operations.

3. *Varying production and purchasing methods*—There are some industries in which establishments have varying production and purchasing methods, making in more difficult to identify potential customers and to estimate market size. Thus if manufacturers of furniture casters vary in their "make or buy" policies regarding ball bearings, analysis of the total market for ball bearings becomes more complex. Similarly if there is variation in the use of centralized purchasing, whereby some firms have their corporate headquarters buy all of the product requirements for several plants, estimation of regional potentials will be more difficult.

4. *Need for finer classification*—The practice of classifying establishments at a 4-digit level results in an aggregation of data that is sometimes dysfunctional for firms interested in specific product markets within the industry. Consider the mixture of establishments classified in SIC 3662, Radio and television transmitting, signaling, and detection equipment and apparatus: cyclotrons, radio broadcasting equipment, satellites, electric traffic signals, and so on. If data on electric traffic signals, for example, are not published beyond the 4-digit level (and some data are not available beyond this level), the information at the 4-digit level may be useless because it contains such a mixture of products unrelated to the product in question.

Problems associated with the SIC system may be at least partially controlled by the use of either census ratios or surveys of establishments.

Census Ratios

For manufactured products, the *Census of Manufactures* provides two ratios: the primary product specialization ratio and the coverage ratio. These indicate the level of product homogeneity within each 4-digit industry and provide the researcher a means of resolving the problems created by the census practice of assigning multi-product establishments to a single industry.

The primary product specialization ratio can be illustrated by examining the data for SIC 3425, Handsaws and saw blades. Figure 3–4 shows

[6]*Ibid.*, p. 75.

An establishment is assigned to an industry based on the shipment values of products representing the largest amount considered as primary to an industry. Frequently the establishment shipments comprise mixtures of products assigned to an industry (primary products), those considered primary to other industries (secondary products of a given industry), and receipts for activities such as merchandising or contract work. This product pattern for an industry is shown in columns A through D and the primary product specialization ratio in column E. The extent to which the given industry's primary products are shipped by establishments classified in and out of the given industry is summarized in columns F through H and shown as a ratio in column I.

		Value of Shipments				Primary Product Specialization Ratio Col. B	Value of Primary Product Shipments			Coverage Ratio Col. B
1972 Code	Industry & Census Year	Total	Primary Products	Secondary Products	Miscellaneous Receipts		Total Made in All Industries	Made in This Industry	Made in Other Industries	Col. F
		(million dollars)	(million dollars)	(million dollars)	(million dollars)	Col. B & C (%)	(million dollars)	(million dollars)	(million dollars)	(%)
		A	B	C	D	E	F	G	H	I
3411	Metal cans 1972	4510.8	4181.3	151.7	177.8	96	4224.4	4181.3	43.1	99
	1967	2890.6	2533.9	276.4	80.3	90	2585.7	2533.9	51.8	98
3412	Metal barrels, drums, and pails 1972	461.3	438.2	13.3	9.8	97	509.4	438.2	71.2	86
	1967	370.7	331.4	28.8	10.5	92	378.2	331.4	46.8	88
3421	Cutlery 1972	427.5	379.0	35.5	13.0	91	403.9	379.0	24.9	94
	1967	378.5	293.5	77.2	7.8	79	308.9	293.5	15.4	95
3423	Hand and edge tools, n.e.c. 1972	1233.1	979.4	118.6	135.1	89	1114.0	979.4	134.6	88
	1967	813.5	661.1	51.1	101.3	93	775.1	661.1	114.0	85
3425	Handsaws and saw blades 1972	194.3	154.5	26.8	13.0	85	201.8	154.5	47.3	77
	1967	154.3	112.8	28.8	12.7	80	138.0	112.8	25.2	82
3429	Hardware, n.e.c. 1972	3243.8	2923.0	190.3	130.5	94	3099.9	2923.0	176.9	94
	1967	2368.3	2073.6	202.4	92.3	91	2188.2	2073.6	114.6	95

Source: U.S. Bureau of the Census, *Census of Manufacturers—1972. Industry Series: Metal Cans, Cutlery, Handtools, and General Hardware* (MC72(2)–34A), Washington: U.S. Government Printing Office, 1975, p. 16.

Figure 3-4 Industry-product analysis–specialization and coverage ratios.

that the primary products of the establishments assigned to SIC 3425 accounted for one hundred fifty-four point five milion dollars in shipments in 1972, while secondary product shipments totalled twenty-six point eight million dollars. The specialization ratio is eighty-five%, based on the following calculation:

$$\frac{\text{Primary Product}}{\text{Specialization Ratio}} = \frac{\text{Value of Primary Product Shipments}}{\text{Primary + Secondary Product Shipments}}$$

$$85\% = \frac{\$154.5}{\$154.5 + \$26.8}$$

Using the same example (SIC 3425), the coverage ratio for handsaws and saw blades in 1972 was 77%:

$$\text{Coverage Ratio} = \frac{\text{Value of Primary Product Shipments}}{\text{Value of Primary Product Shipments and Other Establishments}}$$

$$77\% = \frac{\$154.5}{\$154.5 + \$47.3}$$

The specialization ratio of 85% for SIC 3425 is relatively low for an industry and suggests the need for adjustment in dealing with industry data. In addition, the coverage ratio of 77% is also low in comparison with other industries and indicates the need to determine the sources of the shipments from other industries.

If we probe further in the census data for insight into the structure of the handsaw and saw blades industry (SIC 3425) to understand more about the relatively low specialization ratio, Figure 3–5 shows that the entire industry was composed of 91 establishments with 82 establishments having a specialization ratio of 75% or more. The nine diversified establishments (10% of the total) accounted for $63.6 million of the industry shipments (32.7% of the total = 194.3 − 130.7/194.3), for an average shipment value of $7.1 million per establishment. By comparison, the 82 establishments with specialization ratios over 75% had an average shipment value of $1.6 million. The size distribution of establishments in the industry may next be examined in Figure 3–6. There is a misprint in Figure 3–6 indicating that $90.6 million in shipments was associated with the 4 establishments having 250–499 employees; the shipments figure actually includes the 2 establishments with 500–999 employees as well, so that the average shipment value for all establishments with more than 250

SECONDARY DATA SOURCES

employees was $15.1 million. The next largest group of 9 establishments, with 100–249 employees, had total shipments of $54.9 million, for an average of $6.1 million. Since the 9 diversified establishments had an average shipment value of $7.1 million, it follows that they must include some but not all of the largest establishments in the industry. Specific identification of the 9 diversified establishments would require that additional secondary data sources outside the *Census* be used, such as various industrial directories to be discussed later.

The relatively low coverage ratio of 77% for SIC 3425 may also be examined further with the aid of census materials. Figure 3–7 presents an industry-product analysis tabulation that helps to unravel the various outputs. All establishments classified in SIC 3425 on the basis of their primary product output had total shipments of $194.3 million, divided into primary products ($154.5), secondary products ($26.8), and miscellaneous receipts ($13.0). The relationship between primary and secondary product shipments formed the basis for the specialization ratio calculation. However the coverage ratio seeks to measure the proportion of the total primary product output made by establishments specializing in the primary product, and therefore classified in SIC 3425. We find that $47.3 million in shipments of handsaws and saw blades were made by establishments classified in other industries with the result that the total shipments of handsaws and saw blades from all establishments totals $201.8 million. In order to find the other industries shipping handsaws and saw blades, Figure 3–7 may be consulted. It shows first that the $47.3 million in shipments from all other industries was divided into:

SIC 3421—Cutlery	$ under 2 million
3423—Hand and edge tools, n.e.c.	5–10 million
All other industries	38.1 million

Next, the $38.1 million in shipments from all other industries may be traced from those industries that shipped more than $2 million in hand saws and saw blades:

SIC 3541—Machine tools, metal cutting types	$2–5 million
3545—Machine tool accessories	5–10 million
3546—Power-driven handtools	17.4 million
3699—Electrical equipment and supplies, n.e.c.	5–10 million

Further tracing of the output of other industries must shift to sources outside the *Census*.

This table presents selected statistics for establishments according to their degree of specialization in products primary to their industry. The measures of plant specialization shown are (1) industry specialization—the ratio of primary product shipments to total product shipments, primary plus secondary, for the establishments, and (2) product class specialization—the ratio of the largest primary product class shipments to total product class shipments, primary plus secondary, for the establishment. Statistics for establishments with specialization ratios of less than 75% are included in total lines, but are not shown as a separate class. In addition, data may not be shown, for some industries, product classes, or specialization ratios for various reasons; e.g., to avoid disclosure of individual company data.

Industry or Product Class Code	Industry or Product Class by % of Specialization	Establishments (number)	All employees Number (1000)	All employees Payroll (million dollars)	Production workers Number (1000)	Production workers Man-hours (millions)	Production workers Wages (million dollars)	Value Added by Manufacture (million dollars)	Cost of Materials (million dollars)	Value of Shipments (million dollars)	Capital Expenditures, New (million dollars)
3411	Metal cans										
	Entire industry	396	68.5	740.7	58.7	123.7	611.3	1815.8	2711.9	4510.8	138.1
	Establishments with 75% or more specialization	359	58.2	634.3	49.9	105.3	525.0	1592.3	2355.3	3932.6	119.0
34111	Steel cans and tinware end products (primary product class of establishment)	301	59.4	643.3	51.0	107.2	532.5	1597.2	2361.6	3950.0	104.2
	Establishments with 75% or more specialization	275	51.7	560.7	44.4	93.4	464.2	1418.7	2074.1	3483.6	90.2
34112	Aluminum cans (primary product class of establishment)	32	8.5	92.1	7.2	15.5	74.7	207.1	338.4	537.3	31.0
	Establishments with 75% or more specialization	25	6.0	70.1	5.1	11.2	58.1	165.7	271.0	430.7	26.9
3412	Metal barrels, drums, and pails										
	Entire industry	157	10.2	98.9	8.1	16.7	71.2	188.8	273.5	461.3	8.4
	Establishments with 75% or more specialization	133	7.1	63.8	5.6	11.2	45.7	130.1	188.0	317.2	5.9
34121	Steel pails (12-gal. capacity and under) (primary product class of establishment)	26	2.0	18.6	1.7	3.6	13.9	40.0	46.1	85.9	2.2
	Establishments with 75% or more specialization	23	(D)	(D)	(D)	(D)	(D)	(D)	(D)	(D)	(D)
34122	Steel shipping barrels and drums (over 12 gals) (primary product class of establishment)	73	7.0	70.2	5.5	11.3	50.4	126.1	205.1	330.7	5.1
	Establishments with 75% or more specialization	58	4.6	42.6	3.6	7.1	30.5	84.2	136.7	220.4	3.5

34123	All other metal barrels									
	(primary product class of establishment)	14	.8	6.6	.6	1.3	4.5	16.3	15.5	31.4	.7
	Establishments with 75% or more specialization	12	(D)	(D)	(D)	(D)	(D)	(D)	(D)	(D)	(D)
3421	Cutlery										
	Entire industry	134	13.4	102.6	10.9	22.3	73.0	322.3	112.9	427.5	11.7
	Establishments with 75% or more specialization	128	12.0	89.9	9.8	20.2	64.6	290.6	96.9	378.6	10.5
34211	Cutlery, scissors, shears, trimmers, and snips										
	(primary product class of establishment)	69	9.0	64.1	7.5	15.2	48.1	122.0	66.6	183.4	3.2
	Establishments with 75% or more specialization	61	8.1	56.8	6.9	13.8	43.0	106.0	56.1	157.1	2.7
34212	Razor blades and razors, except electric										
	(primary product class of establishment)	6	4.0	35.1	3.0	6.3	22.7	190.7	42.8	231.0	8.0
	Establishments with 75% or more specialization	5	(D)	(D)	(D)	(D)	(D)	(D)	(D)	(D)	(D)
3423	Hand and edge tools, n.e.c.										
	Entire industry	626	39.3	343.0	31.1	62.0	240.7	780.0	473.3	1233.1	33.5
	Establishments with 75% or more specialization	574	31.4	267.1	25.1	49.6	190.7	637.1	375.1	998.4	27.3
34231	Mechanics' hand service tools										
	(primary product class of establishment)	133	20.2	180.8	15.9	32.4	126.4	405.3	269.7	662.0	20.1
	Establishments with 75% or more specialization	101	14.6	127.8	11.6	23.8	91.9	310.6	197.6	501.3	14.4
34232	Edge tools, hand operated										
	(primary product class of establishment)	81	5.2	50.2	4.1	8.3	34.9	110.9	52.3	162.6	2.1
	Establishments with 75% or more specialization	62	2.5	21.7	2.0	4.0	16.5	41.5	18.2	59.4	.8
34233	Files, rasps, file accessories, other handtools										
	(primary product class of establishment)	91	10.8	88.6	8.8	16.8	62.9	214.9	121.1	331.0	7.6
	Establishments with 75% or more specialization	68	6.4	50.3	5.3	10.4	37.5	125.6	68.4	192.4	4.
3425	Handsaws and saw blades										
	Entire industry	91	6.6	56.7	4.9	10.0	37.5	127.5	70.6	194.3	6.4
	Establishments with 75% or more specialization	82	4.7	41.4	3.5	7.3	26.8	88.5	43.9	130.7	5.0

Note: (D) Withheld to avoid disclosing figures for individual companies.
Source: U.S. Bureau of the Census, *Census of Manufactures—1972. Industry Series: Metal Cans, Cutlery, Handtools, and General Hardware* (MC 72(2)–34A), Washington: U.S. Government Printing Office, 1975, p. 34A–15.

Figure 3–5 Data for establishments by industry specialization and primary product class specialization.

Item	Establishments (number)	All employees Number (1000)	All employees Payroll (million dollars)	Production workers Number (1000)	Production workers Man-hours (millions)	Production workers Wages (million dollars)	Value Added by manufacture (million dollars)	Cost of materials (million dollars)	Value of shipments (million dollars)	Capital expenditures new (million dollars)	End-of-year inventories (million dollars)
3425—Handsaws and saw blades											
Establishments, total	91	6.6	56.7	4.9	10.0	37.5	127.5	70.6	194.3	6.4	46.4
Establishments with an average of											
1– 4 employees (E8)	13	(Z)	.2	(Z)	(Z)	.1	.4	.2	.7	(Z)	.2
5– 9 employees (E6)	11	.1	.6	.1	.1	.4	1.0	.6	1.5	(Z)	.3
10– 19 employees (E1)	15	.2	1.6	.2	.3	1.0	2.9	1.5	4.4	.1	.6
20– 49 employees	23	.7	5.8	.6	1.1	4.0	11.9	6.8	18.6	.8	3.4
50– 99 employees	14	1.1	8.6	.8	1.6	5.8	17.3	7.0	23.6	.5	4.5
100–249 employees (E1)	9	1.5	13.3	1.1	2.3	8.8	37.2	19.6	54.9	3.0	13.3
250–499 employees	4	3.1	26.7	2.2	4.5	17.3	56.8	34.9	90.6	1.9	24.2
500–999 employees	2	(D)	(D)	(D)	(D)	(D)	(D)	(D)	(D)	(D)	(D)
Establishments covered by administrative record[a]	16	.1	.5	.1	.1	.3	1.0	.5	1.4	(Z)	.4

44

3429—Hardware, NEC										
Establishments, total	1054	100.2	903.9	79.1	160.3	634.1	2026.2	1265.7	3243.7	91.5	536.5
Establishments with an average of											
1– 4 employees (E8)	287	.5	3.7	.5	.7	2.6	10.2	7.4	17.7	.5	3.3
5– 9 employees (E5)	156	1.0	8.2	.8	1.5	5.2	19.5	14.9	34.1	.8	5.7
10– 19 employees (E2)	128	1.9	14.8	1.4	2.7	9.4	30.3	24.9	55.2	2.0	7.7
20– 49 employees (E1)	187	5.9	45.5	4.7	8.9	29.5	95.1	81.1	174.0	4.2	40.9
50– 99 employees	108	7.6	58.3	5.9	11.8	37.9	122.8	94.9	214.8	5.3	41.6
100– 249 employees	102	16.3	129.0	12.9	25.9	86.2	288.2	221.0	497.5	17.5	95.4
250– 499 employees	47	15.9	121.8	12.6	26.4	83.6	246.9	169.2	410.3	10.9	79.1
500– 999 employees	20	13.6	121.5	10.1	20.1	80.0	266.8	173.5	432.5	14.1	90.7
1000–2499 employees	15	<u>37.5</u>	<u>401.1</u>	<u>30.3</u>	<u>62.3</u>	<u>299.9</u>	<u>946.4</u>	<u>478.8</u>	<u>1407.7</u>	<u>36.1</u>	<u>172.2</u>
2500 employees or more	4	(D)	(D)	(D)	(D)	(D)	(D)	(D)	(D)	(D)	(D)
Establishments covered by administrative record[a]	317	.9	7.5	.8	1.4	5.1	18.5	12.9	31.4	.8	5.9

Note: The payroll and sales data for small establishments (generally single-unit companies with less than 10 employees) were obtained from administrative records of other government agencies instead of from a Census report form. These data were then used in conjunction with industry averages to estimate the balance of the items shown in the table for these small establishments. This technique was also used for a small number of other establishments whose reports were not received at the time the data were tabulated. The following symbols are shown for those size classes where administrative records data were used and account for 10 or more of the figures shown:

(E1) 10–19% (E3) 30–39% (E5) 50–59% (E7) 70–79% (E9) 90–99%
(E2) 20–29% (E4) 40–49% (E6) 60–69% (E8) 80–89% (E10) 100%

(D) Withheld to avoid disclosing figures for individual companies. Data for this item are included in the underscored figures above.
(Z) Less than half of the unit of measurement shown (under 50 thousand dollars or man-hours; under 50 employees).

[a]Report forms were not mailed to companies that operated only one establishment—generally single-unit companies with less than 10 employees. Payroll and sales for 1972 were obtained from administrative records supplied to other agencies of the Federal Government. These payroll and sales data were then used in conjunction wih industry averages to estimate the balances of the items shown in the table. Data are also included in the respective size classes shown for this industry.

Source: U.S. Bureau of the Census, *Census of Manufactures—1972. Industry Series: Metal Cans, Cutlery, Handtools, and General Hardware* (MC 72(2)–34A), Washington: U.S. Government Printing Office, 1975, p. 14.

Figure 3-6 Data for establishments by employee size.

In millions of dollars. This table shows where products of an industry (referred to as primary) are made and what products are made by establishments classified in an industry. *Read down* an industry column to find what products are produced in an industry. *Read across* to determine where the products of the industries are produced. To the extent that some of the primary products are made by industries not included, the value of such shipments is shown in the "other industries" column. The specified other industries are listed at the end of the table if they account for more than $2 million of the products primary to this chapter.

Product code	Industry, class of products, and miscellaneous receipts	All industries	Metal cans (SIC 3411)	Metal barrels, drums, and pails (SIC 3412)	Cutlery (SIC 3421)	Hand and edge tools, n.e.c. (SIC 3423)	Handsaws and saw blades (SIC 3425)	Hardware, n.e.c. (SIC 3429)	All other industries
	Total shipments and miscellaneous receipts	(X)	4510.8	461.3	427.5	1233.1	194.3	3243.8	(X)
3411–	Metal cans	4224.4	4181.3	(5–10)	—	—	—	—	(20–50)
34111	Steel cans and tinware end products	4202.2	4160.8	(5–10)					(20–50)
3423–	Hand and edge tools, n.e.c.	1114.0	—	—	7.1	979.4	19.9	(2–5)	102.7
34231	Mechanics' hand service tools	601.2	—	—	(2–5)	529.3	(2–5)	4.0	62.1
34232	Edge tools, hand operated	160.1	—	—	(2–5)	121.3	(10–20)	(under 2)	18.7
34233	Files, rasps, file accessories, and other handtools	274.7	—	—	(under 2)	252.8	1.0	(under 2)	19.9
34230	Hand and edge tools, n.e.c., n.s.k.	78.0	—	—	—	76.0	—	—	2.0
3425–	Handsaws, saw blades, and saw accessories	201.8	—	—	(under 2)	(5–10)	154.5	—	38.1
3429–	Hardware, n.e.c.	3099.9	—	—	—	(2–5)	(205)	2923.0	170.7
34292	Furniture hardware	205.0	—	—	—	—	—	197.1	7.9
34293	Vacuum and insulated bottles, jugs, and chests	85.4	—	—	—	—	—	(50–100)	(10–20)
34294	Builders hardware	928.3	—	—	—	(under 2)	(under 2)	897.1	28.2
34296	Motor vehicle hardware	1180.3	—	—	—	—	—	1131.2	49.1

Product code	Industry, class of products, and miscellaneous receipts	Other industries	Product code	Industry, class of products, and miscellaneous receipts	Other industries
	Listing of other industries with over $2 million shipments of the primary products			Listing of other industries with over $2 million shipments of the primary products—Continued	
3411–			3425		
	2023 Condensed and evaporated milk	(2–5)		3541 Machine tools, metal cutting types	(2–5)
	2037 Frozen fruits and vegetables	(2–5)		3545 Machine tool accessories	(5–10)
	2086 Bottled and canned soft drinks	(10–20)		3546 Power-driven handtools	17.4
	2899 Chemical preparations, n.e.c.	(2–5)		3699 Electrical equipment and supplies, n.e.c.	(5–10)
	3079 Miscellaneous plastics products	(2–5)		3714 Motor vehicle parts and accessories	12.8
	3714 Motor vehicle parts and accessories	(5–10)		3728 Aircraft equipment, n.e.c.	(2–5)
	3799 Transportation equipment, n.e.c.	(2–5)			

Note: Data shown parenthetically are ranges expressed in millions of dollars.
—Represents zero. (X) Not applicable.
Source: U.S. Bureau of the Census, *Census of Manufactures—1972. Industry Series: Metal Cans, Cutlery, Handtools, and General Hardware* (MC 72(2)–34A), Washington: U.S. Government Printing Office, 1975, pp. 16–18.

Figure 3–7 *Industry-product analysis–shipments by product class and industry.*

The important point in these examples is that census data *are* available for the purpose of offsetting some of the problems associated with the SIC system. It may take a bit of digging to use these data but the results are usually worthwhile.

Surveys of Establishments

In cases where census data are unavailable or inadequate, a survey of establishments may be conducted. Hummel cites a survey by a manufacturer of extruded metal parts among all manufacturing establishments in SIC 363, Household appliances, to determine their requirements for extruded metal parts. The survey revealed the number and percentage of establishments that could use the manufacturer's product.[7] As long as the objectives of the survey are limited, as in this case, surveys of establishments can be useful in controlling some of the problems associated with the SIC system.

Census of Manufactures

The most important source of external secondary data for industrial marketing research is the *Census of Manufactures*. All manufacturing establishments with one or more paid employees are included in the *Census* and classified into 450 4-digit SIC industries. The first *Census of Manufactures* was taken in 1810 in connection with the dicennial census of population, and continued at 10-, 5-, or 2-year intervals until 1939. Resuming publication after World War II, the *Census* has been conducted for the years 1947, 1954, 1958, 1963, 1967, and 1972. It is now scheduled to be taken for each year ending in "2" and "7" in the future. Annual surveys of manufactures are conducted on a sample basis for the interim years.

Statistics gathered in the *Census of Manufactures* are published in a series of final reports, which are eventually assembled and bound into five volumes. The 1972 publication program included the following final reports:

> *Industry series*—A total of 81 reports, each providing information for a group of related industries (Series MC 72 (2)–20A to 39D). Figure 3–8 provides an example of some of the information available from one of 81 reports. Emphasis is placed on United States totals in these reports, although limited regional and state data are included.

[7]*Ibid.*, p. 77.

SECONDARY DATA SOURCES

Area series—Each state and the District of Columbia is represented in this series (Series MC 72(3)-1 to 51) of reports. Statistics for smaller geographic units in each state are included.

Subject and special report series—Individual subjects, such as capital expenditures in each industry, are treated in reports in considerable detail.

One of the principal problems associated with the use of the *Census of Manufactures* is the delay in publication of the reports. As an example, Industry Series (MC 72(2)-34A) from the *1972 Census* was issued in January 1975. If the census data are viewed as benchmark sources however with the *Annual Survey of Manufactures* and other sources providing current data, the publication delays of the *Census* become less important.

Annual Survey of Manufactures

The *Annual Survey of Manufactures* plays a vital role in providing current data for the intercensal years, thereby permitting the development of time series for many important manufacturing statistics. In 1973, the *Annual Survey* reports were:

1. *General Statistics for Industry Groups and Industries (M 73 (AS-1)*—statistics on employment, man-hours worked, payrolls, value added by manufacture, capital expenditures, cost of materials, and value of industry shipments, for the total United States.
2. *Value of Product Shipments (M 73 (AS)-2)*—presents data on the value of product shipments for the specified year and the percentage change from the previous year.
3. *Value of Manufacturers' Inventories (M 73 (AS)-3)*—provides data on beginning and ending inventories for the specified year, broken down by finished product inventories, work in process, and materials, supplies, and so on. Includes the percentage changes from the previous year.
4. *Fuels and Electric Energy Used by Industry Groups (M 73 (AS)-4)*—provides estimates of the total cost of fuels and the quantity and cost of electric energy generated and used in manufacturing plants.
5. *Expenditures for New Plant and Equipment (M 73 (AS)-5)*—presents total expenditures for new plant and equipment, together with a breakdown between expansion and replacement expenditures.
6. *General Statistics for Divisions and States, Standard Metropolitan Statistical Areas, Large Industrial Counties, and Selected Cities (M 73

General Statistics by Geographic Area: 1972 and 1967

Industry and geographic area	Establishments Total (number)	Establishments With 20 Employees or More (number)	1972 All employees Number (1000)	1972 All employees Payroll dollars	1972 Production workers Number (1000)	1972 Production workers Man-hours (millions)	1972 Production workers Wages (million dollars)	1972 Value added by Manufacture (million dollars)	1967 Cost of Materials (million dollars)	1967 Value of Shipments (million dollars)	1967 Capital Expenditures New (million dollars)	1967 All Employees (1000)	1967 Value Added by Manufacture (million dollars)
3423—Hand and edge tools, N.E.C.													
UNITED STATES	626	255	39.3	343.0	31.1	62.0	240.7	780.0	473.3	1233.1	33.5	35.9	509.4
Northeast Region	223	102	15.8	139.8	12.4	24.9	97.5	296.6	187.5	467.1	11.8	15.0	187.1
New England Division	92	44	6.8	62.4	5.1	10.2	40.6	143.0	97.1	231.3	4.1	5.5	72.5
Massachusetts	48	26	(D)	(D)	(D)	(D)	(D)	(D)	(D)	(D)	(D)	2.7	35.1
Connecticut	26	14	3.7	36.1	2.5	5.1	19.9	86.7	51.9	132.5	3.2	2.3	33.1
Middle Atlantic Division	131	58	9.0	77.4	7.3	14.7	56.9	153.6	90.5	235.8	7.7	9.5	114.6
New York	57	24	4.5	39.8	3.6	7.3	30.0	70.7	41.4	108.7	2.4	4.8	59.9
New Jersey	29	14	1.6	12.3	1.3	2.5	8.4	30.5	19.0	47.9	3.1	1.7	17.5
Pennsylvania	45	20	2.9	25.3	2.4	4.9	18.5	52.3	30.0	79.3	2.2	3.0	37.1
North Central Region	250	106	16.1	147.1	12.6	25.2	100.4	344.3	202.4	540.8	(D)	14.9	230.0
East North Central Division	192	78	12.4	114.7	9.5	18.8	76.9	282.9	164.7	444.8	(D)	11.8	195.4
Ohio	58	27	5.2	48.7	4.0	7.9	33.6	112.4	59.8	172.6	2.2	5.1	83.6
Indiana	20	6	(D)	(D)	(D)	(D)	(D)	(D)	(D)	(D)	(D)		(D)
Illinois	53	23	3.6	36.2	2.8	5.8	24.7	92.1	44.6	133.9	3.5	3.3	56.1
Michigan	40	16	1.0	8.8	.8	1.4	5.3	19.8	16.5	36.0	2.4	.9	14.9
Wisconsin	21	6	(D)	(D)	(D)	(D)	(D)	(D)	(D)	(D)	(D)		(D)
West North Central Division	58	28	3.7	32.4	3.1	6.4	23.5	61.4	37.7	96.0	1.6	3.1	34.6
Minnesota	16	8	1.6	14.8	1.4	2.8	10.0	26.1	18.5	42.5	.6	1.2	12.0
Iowa	7	2	(D)	(D)	(D)	(D)	(D)	(D)	(D)	(D)	(D)	.2	2.2
Missouri	17	10	(D)	(D)	(D)	(D)	(D)	(D)	(D)	(D)	(D)		(D)
Nebraska	7	5	(D)	(D)	(D)	(D)	(D)	(D)	(D)	(D)	(D)	.3	56.1
Kansas	9	3	(D)	(D)	(D)	(D)	(D)	(D)	(D)	(D)	(D)		4.0

South Region	50	3.4	24.5	2.8	5.5	18.2	63.3	43.8	101.7	(D)	3.2	47.6
South Atlantic Division	22	2.6	20.0	2.2	4.1	14.5	47.5	24.5	69.5	1.2	2.8	40.5
West Virginia	4		(D)	(D)	(D)	(D)	(D)	(D)	(D)	(D)		(D)
South Carolina	1		(D)	(D)	(D)	(D)	(D)	(D)	(D)	(D)		(D)
East South Central Division	12					(D)	(D)	(D)	(D)	(D)		(D)
Kentucky	5		(D)	(D)	(D)	(D)	(D)	(D)	(D)	(D)	(NA)	(NA)
Tennessee	3		(D)	(D)	(D)	(D)	(D)	(D)	(D)	(D)	(NA)	(NA)
West South Central Division	16		(D)	(D)	(D)	(D)	(D)	(D)	(D)	(D)		(D)
Arkansas	2		(D)	(D)	(D)	(D)	(D)	(D)	(D)	(D)	(NA)	(NA)
West Region	103	3.9	31.6	3.3	6.4	24.7	75.7	39.5	123.4	6.3	2.7	44.8
Mountain Division	18	.9	6.8	.8	1.6	4.8	16.8	6.3	23.2	3.0	.3	4.7
Colorado	7		(D)	(D)	(D)	(D)	(D)	(D)	(D)	(D)		(D)
Pacific Division	85	2.9	24.8	2.5	4.8	19.9	59.0	33.2	100.2	3.3	2.4	40.1
Washington	6		(D)	(D)	(D)	(D)	(D)	(D)	(D)	(D)	(NA)	(NA)
Oregon	7		(D)	(D)	(D)	(D)	(D)	(D)	(D)	(D)		(D)
California	72	2.5	21.3	2.1	4.1	17.2	53.5	29.3	90.2	3.2	2.1	36.0
3425—Handsaws and saw blades												
UNITED STATES	91	6.6	56.7	4.9	10.0	37.5	127.5	70.6	194.3	6.4	6.3	97.1
Northeast Region	29	2.9	24.9	2.2	4.4	17.3	61.7	37.1	96.9	2.2	3.3	50.2
New England Division	7	1.7	16.2	1.2	2.6	10.9	43.6	23.0	65.1	1.8	2.2	39.5
Massachusetts	3		(D)	(D)	(D)	(D)	(D)	(D)	(D)	(D)	1.5	31.7
Connecticut	3		(D)	(D)	(D)	(D)	(D)	(D)	(D)	(D)		(D)

Note: (D) Withheld to avoid disclosing figures for industrial companies. (NA) Not available.
Source: U.S. Bureau of the Census, *Census of Manufactures—1972. Industry Series: Metal Cans, Cutlery, Handtools, and General Hardware* (MC 72(2)–34A), Washington: U.S. Government Printing Office, 1975, p. 11.

Figure 3-8   Census of Manufacturers data by geographic area.

(AS)–6)—includes most of the statistics provided in the *General Statistics* report (M 73 (AS)–1) for the geographic divisions noted in the above title.

7. *Additional reports*—There are other reports published in the *Annual Survey* series varying by year. For 1973, the following were available:

M 73 (AS)–7 Book Value of Fixed Assets and Rental Payments for Buildings and Equipment
M 73 (AS)–8 Employment and Labor Costs for Operating Manufacturing Establishments
M 73 (AS)–10 Industry Profiles

Current Industrial Reports

Many industrial marketing researchers find that the reports issued in the *Current Industrial Reports* series are indispensable sources of information on current activity. Monthly surveys are conducted by the Bureau of Census to supplement data collected in the *Census of Manufactures* and the *Annual Survey of Manufactures*. These survey reports for all manufacturing industries include:

Manufacturers' shipments, inventories, and orders
Manufacturers' export sales and orders
Shipments of defense-oriented industries

Quarterly and annual reports are issued for selected industries and products including:

Processed foods (SIC 20)
Textile mill products (SIC 22)
Apparel and leather (SIC 23, 31)
Lumber, furniture, and paper products (SIC 24–26)
Chemicals, rubber, and plastics (SIC 28, 30)
Stone, clay, and glass products (SIC 32)
Primary metals (SIC 33)
Intermediate metal products (SIC 34)
Machinery and equipment (SIC 35, 36, 38)

Interest in the *Current Industrial Report* series centers around two attributes: (1) currency of information, and (2) continuity of information. Currency of information is well demonstrated by the *Current Industrial*

SECONDARY DATA SOURCES

Report for Metalworking Machinery for the Third Quarter 1976 (MQ-35W (76)-3), which was issued in December 1976, only two months after the close of the reporting period. Figure 3-9 shows a sample page from this report. It should be noted that the report also contains detailed statistics on shipments of numerically controlled machines at the 7-digit level. Continuity of information is demonstrated in Figure 3-10 in which a *Current Industrial Report for Pumps and Compressors 1974,* is linked to the *1972 Census of Manufactures* and the *1973 Survey of Manufactures.*

County Business Patterns

There are a number of situations in which employment data are very useful in industrial marketing research. The best single source of employment data, based on the SIC system, is *County Business Patterns.* The data cover all employees participating in the Social Security program, and include statistics on employment, taxable payrolls, and the number of establishments distributed by employment size. Figure 3-11 provides an example of the information available from *County Business Patterns.* Several uses of these data are developed later in the book.

Other Bureau of Census Sources

The Bureau of the Census now conducts an integrated economic census program that includes a number of censuses in addition to the *Census of Manufactures*:

Census of Retail Trade—enumeration of retail establishments.

Census of Wholesale Trade—enumeration of wholesale trade establishments with employees.

Census of Selected Service Industries—enumeration of selected service establishments.

Census of Construction Industries—enumeration of construction establishments operating as general contractors and operative builders, special trade contractors, or land subdividers and developers.

Census of Mineral Industries—enumeration of establishments primarily engaged in the extraction of minerals.

Census of Transportation—includes three surveys of transportation activity: (1) Truck inventory and use survey, (2) National travel survey, (3) Commodity transportation survey.

Total shipments, shipments of numerically controlled machines, unfilled orders, and exports by class of product

Third Quarter 1976

Product Code	Class of Product	Total all Machines Quantity Number of Units	Total all Machines Value Thousand Dollars	Numerically Controlled Only Quantity Number of Units	Numerically Controlled Only Value Thousand Dollars	Export Shipments Only Value Thousand Dollars	Unfilled Orders End of Quarter Value Thousand Dollars
	Metalworking Machinery, Total	60,931	470,265	(D)	(D)	63,843	1,549,241
	Metal Cutting Type, Total	49,069	342,771	853	107,080	40,740	1,135,900
3541100	Boring machines	111	15,613	25	9,031	2,113	70,497
3541200	Drilling machines	9,090	25,063	50	3,197	1,323	37,663
3541300	Gear cutting machines	102	12,001	—	—	(D)	46,001
3541400	Grinding and polishing machines (except gear-tooth grinding, lapping, polishing, and buffing machines)	20,842	47,179	(D)	(D)	11,340	160,752
3541500	Lathes	2,825	87,484	262	41,316	8,587	303,347
3541600	Milling machines	2,275	28,884	(D)	(D)	(D)	78,822
3541800	Other metal cutting type machines (except those designed primarily for home workshops, laboratories, garages, etc.)	13,824	126,547	266	38,160	13,510	438,818
	Metal Forming Type, Total	11,862	127,494	(D)	(D)	23,103	413,341

Second Quarter 1976

Code	Description						
3542200	Presses, including forging	3,505	51,112	(D)	(D)	(D)	182,207
35423PT	Forging machines (except presses)	139	14,872	—	—	(D)	67,516
35421PT	Punching and shearing machines	1,969	23,484	(D)	(D)	2,873	71,180
35421PT	Bending and forming machines	4,963	21,897			4,001	49,892
35423PT	Other metal-forming type machines	1,286	16,129			3,553	42,546
	Metalworking Machinery, Total	65,042	521,633	(D)	(D)	102,101	1,414,881
	Metal Cutting Type, Total	53,031	386,500	1,013	134,174	71,878	1,023,081
3541100	Boring machines	154	20,235	31	9,050	(D)	75,956
3541200	Drilling machines	9,045	21,967	53	3,336	3,029	40,988
3541300	Gear cutting machines	113	11,250	—	—	4,878	33,446
3541400	Grinding and polishing machines (except gear-tooth grinding, lapping, polishing, and buffing machines)	21,600	65,149	(D)	(D)	17,048	137,964
3541500	Lathes	2,927	103,430	343	54,704	13,732	310,021
3541600	Milling machines	2,658	36,314	(D)	(D)	(D)	61,896
3541800	Other metal cutting type machines (except those designed primarily for home workshops, laboratories, garages, etc.)	16,534	128,155	319	48,970	27,114	362,810
	Metal forming type, total	12,011	135,133	(D)	(D)	30,223	391,800
3542200	Presses, including forging	3,489	58,267	(D)	(D)	(D)	145,612
35423PT	Forging machines (except presses)	114	11,215	—	—	(D)	78,241

55

Figure 3-9 (Continued)

Total shipments, shipments of numerically controlled machines, unfilled orders, and exports by class of product

Shipments Domestic and Export

Product Code	Class of Product	Total all Machines Quantity Number of Units	Total all Machines Value Thousand Dollars	Numerically Controlled Only Quantity Number of Units	Numerically Controlled Only Value Thousand Dollars	Export Shipments Only Value Thousand Dollars	Unfilled Orders End of Quarter Value Thousand Dollars
35421PT	Punching and shearing machines	2,071	26,445	(D)	(D)	5,009	71,404
35421PT	Bending and forming machines	5,014	22,263			3,876	47,234
35423PT	Other metal-forming type machines	1,323	r16,943			5,799	49,309
		Third quarter 1975					
	Metalworking Machinery, Total	64,202	541,271	(D)	(D)	92,765	1,721,199
	Metal cutting type, total	52,204	414,317	886	116,182	68,427	1,257,537
3541100	Boring machines	183	18,688	34	8,784	2,303	81,963

Note: — Represents zero. (D) Withheld to avoid disclosing figures for individual companies. r Revised by 5% or more.
Source: U.S. Bureau of the Census, *Current Industrial Reports: Metalworking Machinery—Third Quarter 1976* (MO-35W(76)-3), Washington: U.S. Department of Commerce, December 1976, p. 2.

Figure 3-9 *Metalworking machinery—third quarter 1976.*

SECONDARY DATA SOURCES

Census of the Outlying Areas—covers economic activity in Puerto Rico, Virgin Islands, and Guam.

Space limitations prohibit the illustration of examples of each of these censuses, but Figure 3-12 summarizes the major data items collected in each economic census. Additional information regarding the data available in the 1972 economic censuses is presented in a *Mini-Guide* available from the Bureau of the Census.[8]

Other Government Sources

There are many other government sources of data that may be of interest to industrial marketing researchers. Some of the more important sources, listed by publishing agency, are:

Bureau of the Census

Enterprise Statistics publications—Census data for establishments are regrouped under owning or controlling firms to provide data on the economic characteristics of the enterprises.

Concentration Ratios in Manufacturing—A special report developed from the *1972 Census of Manufactures* that shows concentration ratios and other data for the largest companies in 450 manufacturing industries.

Foreign Trade Statistics—Detailed statistics on imports and exports by commodity, country of origin and destination, and method of transportation are available.

Statistical Abstract of the United States—Annual compilation of economic, industrial, political and social statistics.

Historical Statistics of the United States, 1789–1954—Provides data on approximately 3000 time series dating back to their origin with descriptions and sources for each series.

Department of Commerce

Survey of Current Business—a monthly publication that contains data on gross national product and component series as well as a number of

---

[8] U.S. Bureau of the Census, *Mini-Guide to the 1972 Economic Censuses*. Washington: U.S. Department of Commerce, 1973.

			1973		1972	
Product Code	Description	1974, MA-35P	MA-35P	Annual Survey of Manufactures	MA-35P	Census of Manufactures
33611	Industrial pumps, except hydraulic fluid power	843.6	723.2	770.6	615.5	611.9
35612	Hydraulic fluid power pumps and motors	[c]420.3	[c]338.3	344.2	259.2	[a]261.6
35613	Domestic water systems	128.6	157.7	167.6	140.9	[b]51.1
35631	Air and gas compressors, except refrigeration compressors and vacuum pumps	[c]664.0	[c]553.7	578.8	[c]437.0	[d]480.8
35615	Pumps and compressors, n.e.c., except refrigeration compressors, total	(NA)	(NA)	224.4	(NA)	186.4
	Oil-well and oilfield pumps (except boiler-feed)	[e]82.0	[e]65.6	(f)	[e]50.5	178.8
	Other pumps (except automotive circulating pumps and measuring and dispensing pumps) including oil burner and appliance pumps, fire engine pumps, laboratory pumps, sump pumps, etc.	[e]101.3	[e]102.7	(f)	[e]85.3	
	Value of drivers	30.9	24.6	(f)	22.0	
	Pumps and compressors, n.e.c.	(g)	(g)	(f)	(g)	7.6
33635	Industrial spraying equipment	(g)	(g)	104.8	(g)	93.5

Note: (NA) Not available. n.e.c. Not elsewhere classified.

[a]Includes value of vacuum pumps.

[b]These data include domestic sump pumps, 1 hp. and under, pedestal type, product code 35615 73 and submersible type, product code 35615 76.

[c]The value of drivers for vacuum pumps are included in product class 35612 and excluded from product class 35631.

[d]Excludes value of vacuum pumps.

[e]Excludes value of drivers.

[f]These products collected only at the product class level in the *Annual Survey of Manufactures*.

[g]Separate data on these products are collected only in the *Census of Manufactures*.

Source: U.S. Bureau of the Census, *Current Industrial Reports: Pumps and Compressors—1974* (MA–35P(74)–1), Washington: U.S. Department of Commerce, 1975, p. 2.

Figure 3–10 Value in millions of dollars of shipments of pumps and compressors by class of product: 1974, 1973, and 1972.

Excludes government employees, railroad employees, self-employed persons and so on. Size class 1 to 3 includes reporting units having payroll during first quarter but no employees during mid-March pay period. (D) denotes figures withheld to avoid disclosure of operations of individual reporting units.—Represents zero.

SIC code	Industry	Number of employees, mid-March pay period	Taxable payrolls, Jan.–Mar. ($1000)	Total reporting units	1 to 3	4 to 7	8 to 19	20 to 49	50 to 99	100 to 249	250 to 499	500 to more
	Franklin (continued)											
287	Agricultural chemicals	241	514	6	1	—	1	2	2	—	—	—
2871	Fertilizers	(D)	(D)	2	—	—	—	2	—	—	—	—
289	Miscellaneous chemical products	292	736	13	7	1	2	1	1	1	—	—
2891	Adhesives and gelatin	267	657	4	—	—	1	1	1	1	—	—
29	Petroleum and coal products	(D)	(D)	8	1	2	2	3	—	—	—	—
30	Rubber and plastics products, n.e.c.	1766	4125	23	2	2	5	6	4	3	1	—
307	Miscellaneous plastics products	(D)	(D)	22	2	2	5	6	3	3	1	—
31	Leather and leather products	1831	2846	10	2	1	1	5	—	1	—	—
312	Industrial leather belting	(D)	(D)	1	—	—	—	—	—	—	—	—
314	Footwear, except rubber	1454	2465	6	1	—	—	—	2	2	1	—
3141	Shoes, except rubber	(D)	(D)	5	1	—	—	—	2	2	—	—
3142	House slippers	(D)	(D)	1	—	1	—	—	—	—	—	—
32	Stone, clay, and glass products	4410	11327	50	4	5	15	16	6	2	2	—
322	Glass and glassware, pressed or blown	(D)	(D)	4	1	—	—	—	—	1	1	1
3229	Pressed and blown glass, n.e.c.	(D)	(D)	4	1	—	—	—	—	1	1	1
325	Structural clay products	224	361	4	—	—	—	2	2	—	—	—
3251	Brick and structural clay tile	(D)	(D)	2	—	—	—	—	2	—	—	—
327	Concrete, gypsum, & plaster products	727	2021	27	1	2	10	10	—	1	—	—
3271	Concrete block and brick	191	429	6	—	—	1	—	5	—	—	—
3272	Concrete products n.e.c.	377	812	15	1	2	5	5	2	—	—	—
3273	Ready-mixed concrete	159	781	6	—	1	4	1	—	—	—	—
329	Misc. nonmetallic mineral products	(D)	(D)	5	1	1	1	1	—	—	—	—
3291	Abrasive products	(D)	(D)	2	1	—	1	—	—	—	—	—
33	Primary metal industries	3426	8423	26	7	5	4	4	2	1	—	2
331	Blast furnace & basic steel products	(D)	(D)	1	—	—	—	—	—	—	—	—
3316	Cold finishing of steel shapes	(D)	(D)	1	—	—	—	—	1	—	—	—
332	Iron and steel foundries	(D)	(D)	3	1	—	—	—	—	—	—	2
3322	Malleable iron foundries	(D)	(D)	1	—	—	—	—	—	—	—	—
3323	Steel foundries	(D)	(D)	2	1	—	—	—	—	—	—	—
335	Nonferrous rolling and drawing	(D)	(D)	4	1	1	—	—	1	1	—	—
3352	Aluminum rolling and drawing	(D)	(D)	2	—	—	—	—	1	1	—	—
339	Miscellaneous primary metal products	187	374	7	—	—	3	3	1	—	—	—
34	Fabricated metal products	9792	27293	97	16	14	25	13	13	10	4	2
341	Metal cans	176	445	3	—	—	—	1	2	—	—	—

SIC	Industry	Employees							
342	Cutlery, handtools and hardware	(D)	8	—	—	—	2	—	1
3423	Hand and edge tools, n.e.c.	(D)	2	—	1	—	—	—	—
3425	Handsaws and saw blades	101	4	—	—	1	2	—	—
3429	Hardware, n.e.c.	(D)	2	—	—	1	—	—	1
343	Plumbing and heating, except electric	(D)	2	—	—	—	—	2	—
3433	Heating equipment	1617	37	7	5	14	—	2	—
344	Fabricated structural metal products	3992	12	1	1	4	1	—	—
3441	Fabricated structural steel	722	3	—	—	—	5	4	—
3442	Metal doors, sash, and trim	(D)	3	1	2	5	2	3	—
3444	Sheet metal work	1176	13	2	—	2	—	—	—
345	Screw machine products, bolts, etc.	463	3	—	—	1	—	—	—
3452	Bolts, nuts, rivets, and washers	(D)	2	—	—	—	1	—	—
346	Metal stampings	372	7	—	—	2	—	1	—
347	Metal services, n.e.c.	263	10	3	3	—	2	—	—
3471	Plating and polishing	(D)	7	2	—	—	2	—	—
348	Misc. fabricated wire products	358	8	1	—	1	2	3	—
349	Misc. fabricated metal products	2005	13	2	1	—	3	2	—
3491	Metal barrels, drums, and pails	1084	2	1	—	—	—	—	—
3494	Valves and pipe fittings	(D)	3	—	—	—	—	2	1
3499	Fabricated metal products, n.e.c.	(D)	5	1	1	—	2	—	—
35	Machinery, except electrical	140	5	—	—	—	—	—	—
		8132	129	30	11	41	21	10	2
352	Farm machinery	200	4	—	—	—	2	—	—
353	Construction and related machinery	1862	13	—	—	—	5	—	3
3531	Construction machinery	510	4	—	—	1	—	—	—
3532	Mining machinery	(D)	1	—	—	—	—	—	—
3535	Conveyors and conveying equipment	(D)	3	—	—	—	1	2	1
354	Metalworking machinery	385	19	7	1	4	4	—	—
3542	Machine tools, metal forming types	(D)	1	—	—	—	—	1	—
3544	Spec. dies, tools, jigs & fixtures	(D)	16	6	—	4	4	—	—
355	Special industry machinery	186	5	—	—	3	—	1	—
3559	Special industry machinery, n.e.c.	(D)	4	—	—	2	1	—	—
356	General industrial machinery	2424	15	2	—	4	2	3	—
3561	Pumps and compressors	(D)	4	1	—	1	—	—	—
3562	Ball and roller bearings	140	1	—	—	—	—	—	—
3569	General industrial machinery, n.e.c.	337	3	—	—	1	—	2	—
357	Office and computing machines	536	5	2	—	—	1	1	—
3573	Electronic computing equipment	(D)	3	2	—	—	—	—	—
3576	Scales and balances	(D)	2	—	—	—	—	—	—

Source: U.S. Bureau of the Census, *Coounty Business Patterns—1973, Ohio* (CBP-73-37), Washington: U.S. Government Printing Office, 1974 p. 74.

Figure 3-11 County business patterns, Ohio, 1973.

Item	Economic censuses					
	Mineral industries	Manu-facturing	Wholesale trade	Retail trade	Selected services	Construc-tion
Number of employees						
Production (construction) workers—quarterly	X	X				X
All other employees	X	X				X
Total	X	X	X	X	X	X
Payrolls						
Production (construction) workers' wages	X	X				X
All other employees	X	X				X
Total	X	X	X	X	X	X
Operating expenses including payroll			X			
Supplemental labor costs						
Legally required	X	X	[a]X	[a]X	[a]X	
Voluntary programs	X	X	[a]X	[a]X	[a]X	
Total	X	X	[a]X	[a]X	[a]X	
Production worker man-hours quarterly	X	X				

Cost of materials, etc.					
Materials, supplies, etc.	X	X	^{a}X		
Specific materials	X	X			
Products bought and resold	X	X	^{a}X		
Fuels consumed	X	X	^{a}X		
Specific fuels consumed	X				
Purchased electricity	X	X			
Contract work	X	X			X
Total	X	X			X
Inventories					
By state of fabrication		X			
Total		X	X		
Capital expenditures					
New structures and additions	X	X	^{a}X	^{a}X	X
New machinery and equipment	X	X	^{a}X	^{a}X	X
Used plant and equipment	X	X	^{a}X	^{a}X	^{b}X
Mineral development and exploration	X				
Total	X	X	^{a}X	^{a}X	X
Quantity of electricity					
Purchased	X	X			
Generated	X	X			
Electricity sold	X	X			
Gross value, fixed assets					
Buildings and other structures	X	X			X
Machinery and equipment	X	X			X
Mineral properties	X	X			
Total	X	X	^{a}X	^{a}X	X

Figure 3-12 (Continued)

Item	Economic censuses					
	Mineral industries	Manu- facturing	Wholesale trade	Retail trade	Selected services	Construc- tion
Total sales (receipts)			X	X	X	X
Merchandise (commodity) lines			X	X		
Value of shipments or products	X	X				
Specific products	X	X				X
Legal form of organization	X	X	X	X	X	X
Water use	X	X				
Rental payments, total		X	[a]X	[a]X	[a]X	
Building and structures		X	[a]X	[a]X	[a]X	
Machinery and equipment		X	[a]X	[a]X	[a]X	X

Note: [a]Data collected on a sample basis only. Totals will be available only at the U. S. level. For the census of wholesale trade, sample includes merchant wholesalers only.
[b]Used plant and equipment collected separately.
Source: Bureau of the Census, *Mini-Guide to the 1972 Economic Censuses*. Washington: U. S. Department of Commerce, 1973, p. 13.

Figure 3-12 Major data items collected in the 1972 economic censuses.

SECONDARY DATA SOURCES

economic and industrial statistics of interest to industrial marketing researchers.

Directory of National Trade Associations—lists more than 2000 trade associations with their size, headquarters location, and principal activities.

Input-Output Structure of the U.S. Economy: 1967—a supplement to the *Survey of Current Business* presenting relationships between economic input and output for 367 detailed industries.

Business Conditions Digest—a monthly report containing approximately 600 economic time series from 1953 to the latest available data. For use in the analysis of business conditions.

U.S. Industrial Outlook—a yearly report that examines current activity in more than 200 industries and their outlook. Covers most major manufacturing industries.

Federal Reserve Board

Federal Reserve Bulletin—a monthly publication that contains the FRB index of industrial production as well as a number of other statistics on manufacturing activity.

Bureau of Labor Statistics

Monthly Labor Review—includes the "Wholesale Price Index" and the "Index of Primary Market Prices" as well as numerous other statistics on prices.

Wholesale Prices and Price Indexes—a specialized monthly publication devoted exclusively to wholesale price movements.

Securities and Exchange Commission

Form 10-K Reports—an official business and financial report must be filed annually by all companies with publicly held stock. A 10-K report should be obtained for each major customer and competitor and it is usually sufficient to ask only for Part I, Items 1-3, which contains the following information:

    Principal products and services
    Principal markets and methods of distribution
    Competitive conditions and position
    Backlog of orders and expectation of fulfillment

Raw materials—sources and availability
Importance of patents, licenses, and franchises
Expenditure on product research
Number of employees
Line-of-business sales and income for each line accounting for 10% or more of sales or income
Summary of operations for last five years
Location and character of principal plants, mines, and other physical properties

Private Sources of Information

Although the federal government is the major supplier of secondary data for industrial marketing research purposes, there are many important private sources of information. Among the more valuable sources are:

Dun and Bradstreet, Inc.

Dun's Market Identifiers (DMI)—computer-based records of 3 million United States and Canadian business establishments. Figure 3-13 shows a sample DMI report with explanations of the entries.
Middle Market Directory—list of companies with a net worth of $500,000 to $1 million with information on SIC categories, number of employees, and names of key personnel.
Million Dollar Directory—list of companies with a net worth of $1 million or more with the same type of information as provided in the *Middle Market Directory*.
Metalworking Directory—a comprehensive list of metalworking plants (20 or more employees) as well as metal distributors. Same type of information as provided in the *Middle Market Directory*.

Thomas Publishing Company

Thomas Register of American Manufacturers—a directory of manufacturers, classified by products, enabling the researcher to identify most or all of the manufacturers of any given product.

Sales Management

Survey of Industrial Purchasing Power—an annual survey of manufacturing activity in the United States by geographic areas and SIC industry groups. Reports the number of plants with 20 or more and 100

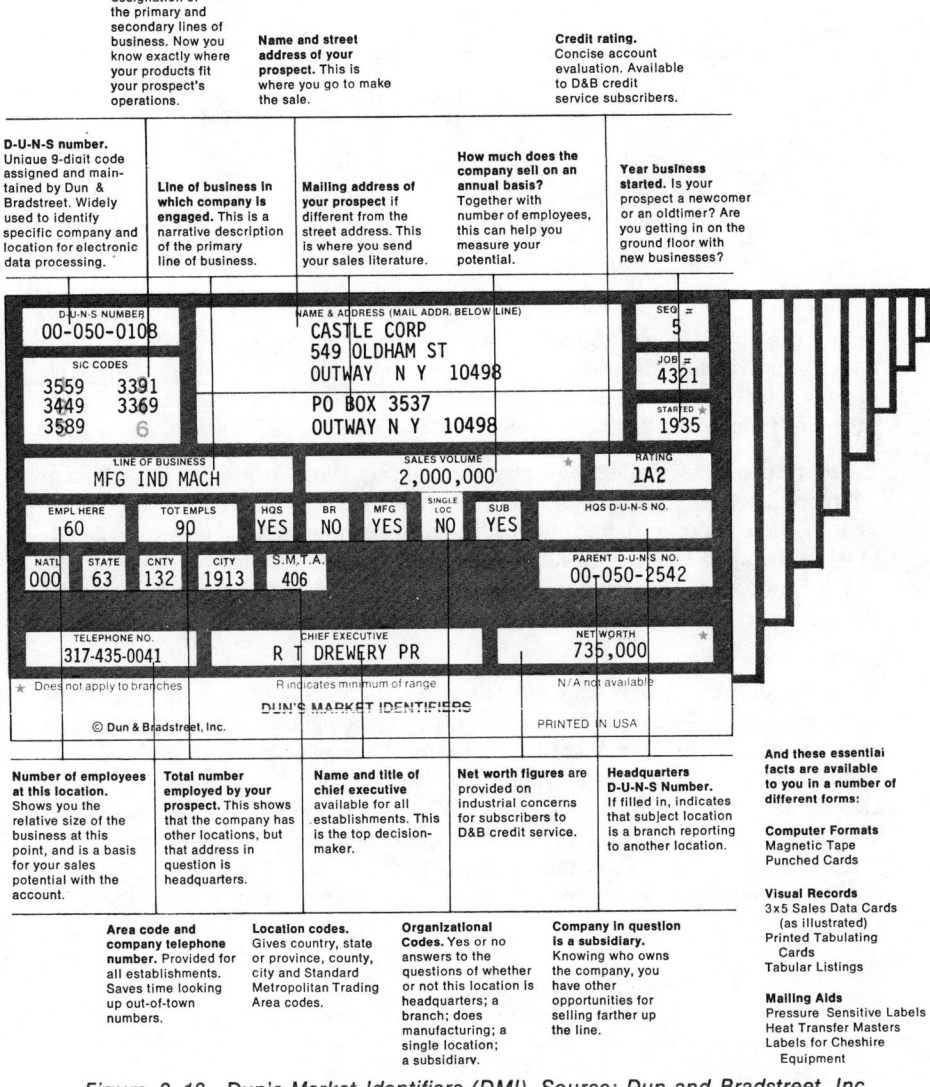

Standard Industrial Classification Codes (S.I.C.). A numerical designation of the primary and secondary lines of business. Now you know exactly where your products fit your prospect's operations.

Name and street address of your prospect. This is where you go to make the sale.

Credit rating. Concise account evaluation. Available to D&B credit service subscribers.

D-U-N-S number. Unique 9-digit code assigned and maintained by Dun & Bradstreet. Widely used to identify specific company and location for electronic data processing.

Line of business in which company is engaged. This is a narrative description of the primary line of business.

Mailing address of your prospect if different from the street address. This is where you send your sales literature.

How much does the company sell on an annual basis? Together with number of employees, this can help you measure your potential.

Year business started. Is your prospect a newcomer or an oldtimer? Are you getting in on the ground floor with new businesses?

```
D-U-N-S NUMBER        NAME & ADDRESS (MAIL ADDR. BELOW LINE)      SEQ #
00-050-0108              CASTLE CORP                                 5
                         549 OLDHAM ST
   SIC CODES             OUTWAY  N Y  10498                        JOB #
 3559    3391                                                      4321
 3449    3369            PO BOX 3537                             STARTED
 3589      6             OUTWAY  N Y  10498                        1935

     LINE OF BUSINESS            SALES VOLUME                    RATING
     MFG IND MACH                 2,000,000                       1A2

 EMPL HERE   TOT EMPLS   HQS    BR    MFG  SINGLE  SUB    HQS D-U-N-S NO.
    60          90       YES    NO    YES   LOC    YES
                                             NO
  NATL  STATE  CNTY   CITY   S.M.T.A.              PARENT D-U-N-S NO.
  000    63    132    1913    406                     00-050-2542

     TELEPHONE NO.       CHIEF EXECUTIVE             NET WORTH
     317-435-0041        R T DREWERY PR              735,000
```

★ Does not apply to branches   R indicates minimum of range   N/A not available

DUN'S MARKET IDENTIFIERS

© Dun & Bradstreet, Inc.   PRINTED IN USA

Number of employees at this location. Shows you the relative size of the business at this point, and is a basis for your sales potential with the account.

Total number employed by your prospect. This shows that the company has other locations, but that address in question is headquarters.

Name and title of chief executive available for all establishments. This is the top decision-maker.

Net worth figures are provided on industrial concerns for subscribers to D&B credit service.

Headquarters D-U-N-S Number. If filled in, indicates that subject location is a branch reporting to another location.

Area code and company telephone number. Provided for all establishments. Saves time looking up out-of-town numbers.

Location codes. Gives country, state or province, county, city and Standard Metropolitan Trading Area codes.

Organizational Codes. Yes or no answers to the questions of whether or not this location is headquarters; a branch; does manufacturing; a single location; a subsidiary.

Company in question is a subsidiary. Knowing who owns the company, you have other opportunities for selling farther up the line.

And these essential facts are available to you in a number of different forms:

Computer Formats
Magnetic Tape
Punched Cards

Visual Records
3x5 Sales Data Cards (as illustrated)
Printed Tabulating Cards
Tabular Listings

Mailing Aids
Pressure Sensitive Labels
Heat Transfer Masters
Labels for Cheshire Equipment

Figure 3-13 Dun's *Market Identifiers (DMI).* Source: Dun and Bradstreet, Inc.

(A)	(B)	(C)	(D)	(E)	(F)	(G)	(H)
STATE County SIC Metro Area		Industry	Number of Plants Total Plants	Large Plants	Total Shipments ($ Mil.)	% of U.S. Shipments	% of Large Plants
CALIFORNIA							
Alameda		**246 All mfg**	**556**	**158**	**2900.3**	**.4088**	**75**
2051		Bread & related prod	8	6	36.4	.6109	94
2052		Biscuits & crackers	5	4	87.5	5.3438	96
2653		Corrug. fiber boxes	11	6	53.4	1.2354	80
2711		Newspapers	5	4	40.3	.6569	98
3221		Glass containers	4	4	91.8	4.3714	100

A All the 2,748 counties with at least one manufacturing establishment of 20 or more employees are included, sequenced alphabetically by state. In each county, individual industries whose establishments have an aggregate employment of 1,000 or more are listed. These industries are at the four-digit level of the Standard Industrial Classification (SIC) system used by the federal government.

B In response to reader requests, we indicate when a county is part of a metropolitan area with a numerical code that refers to the 300 SM-designated metropolitan markets. To find out in which metropolitan area a county is included, look up the appropriate code number on the list of metropolitan areas and their component counties that appears on pages C-3 through C-6 in the *1974 Survey of Buying Power*.

C The "All mfg" line, which appears in boldface type, refers to the over-all totals for all the manufacturing plants in the county with 20 or more employees The names of the 4-digit SIC industries, appearing in lightface type, are shortened in some instances because of space limitations. A complete listing of all SIC-coded industry titles is in the *1972 Standard Industrial Classification Manual* (U.S. Government Printing Office, Washington, D.C. 20402; $6.95). The four-digit code used here conforms with that in the *1973 County Business Patterns* series of state reports. In a few instances, the coding is different from that used in the *1972 Census of Manufactures* reports because those publications employ the 1967 classifications.

D The total number of manufacturing plants with at least 20 employees.

E Because large plants (100 or more employees) account for a greater share of a county's manufacturing than is indicated by their numbers, a separate total of such establishments is provided. They can be considered key selling prospects—the ones that merit special selling emphasis.

F The dollar value of all goods produced by the manufacturing establishments. This figure is a reliable indicator of the county's buying potential because, over all, 54% of the dollar amount is expended on equipment, supplies, and materials (an

SECONDARY DATA SOURCES

additional 3% goes for capital expenditures). However, the ratio will differ from industry to industry; an industry's particular ratio can be obtained from the *1972 Census of Manufactures* reports. The shipments figure includes interplant shipments between establishments of a common ownership; however, they make up a very small share of the over-all total. Also, where a four-digit SIC industry is concerned, if a plant produces goods that fall into more than one classification, all its output is credited to the "primary" industry that describes the largest share of its output.

G The county's share of U.S. shipments indicates its importance relative to other counties. This year, SM provides the same ratio for four-digit industries, making it easier for the sales executive to determine those counties that are the most important markets for his products. However bear in mind that the percentage figure in boldface type pertains to a county's share of total U.S. shipments, the percentage figure in lightface type to the county's share of the U.S. total of a particular industry. Thus the lightface percentages, when totalled, will not be the same as the boldface percentage figure.

H The portion of a county's manufacturing output produced by the large plants will suggest the necessary level of sales coverage. Normally, the higher the percentage figure, the fewer the salesmen required because proportionately fewer prospects will account for relatively more of the purchases.

Figure 3-14 Guide to using SM's Survey of Industrial Purchasing Power. Source: Sales Management, *April 21, 1975, p. 44.*

or more employees as well as total shipment value. Figure 3-14 provides a guide to using the *Survey* for marketing research activity.

Predicasts, Inc.

Predicasts, F & S Indexes, and other services—a series of statistical abstracts are offered, based on forecast, capacity, and market data appearing in more than 1000 sources. Indexes collect information about companies, products, and industries. The Predicasts Terminal System permits access to the abstracts through a time-shared computer terminal. Figure 3-15 illustrates some of the data available from *Predicasts* and the *F & S Index.*

Standard and Poor's Corporation

Register of Corporations, Directors, and Executives—published annually in three volumes. Volume 3 indexes corporations by SIC number and geographic area. Used in conjunction with Volume 1, permits

GROWTH RATE

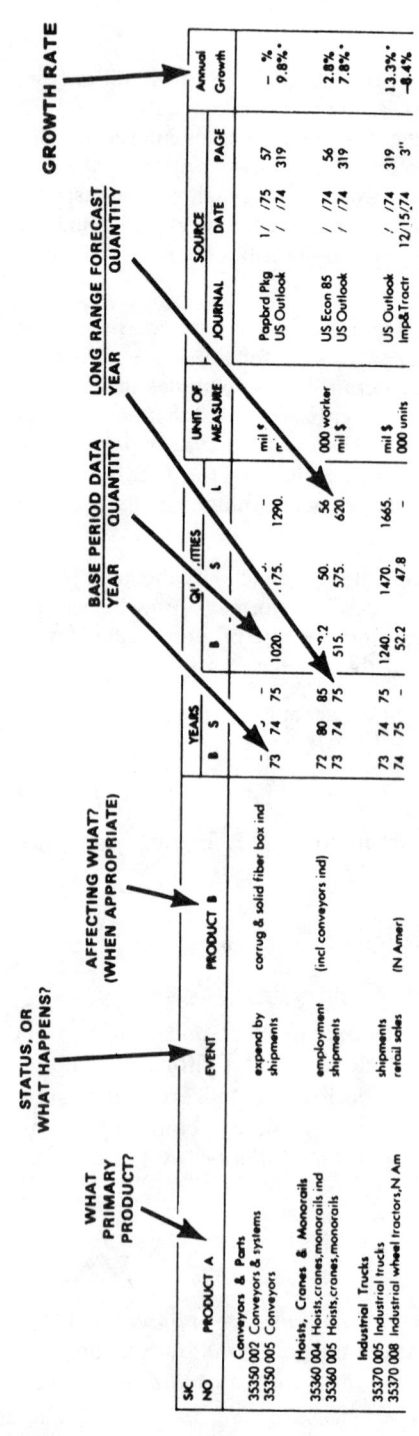

SIC NO	PRODUCT A	EVENT	PRODUCT B	YEARS B $	QUANTITIES B $	UNIT OF MEASURE	LONG RANGE FORECAST YEAR QUANTITY	SOURCE JOURNAL DATE PAGE	Annual Growth
	Conveyors & Parts								
35350 002	Conveyors & systems	expand by shipments	corrug & solid fiber box ind	73 74 75	— 1020. —	mil $	1290.	Paprbrd Pkg 1/ /75 57	— %
35350 005	Conveyors				.175.			US Outlook / /74 319	9.8%
	Hoists, Cranes & Monorails								
35360 004	Hoists,cranes,monorails ind	employment	(incl conveyors ind)	72 80 85	~.2 50. 56	000 worker		US Econ 85 / /74 56	2.8%
35360 005	Hoists,cranes,monorails	shipments		73 74 75	515. 575. 620.	mil $		US Outlook / /74 319	7.8%
	Industrial Trucks								
35370 005	Industrial trucks	shipments		73 74 75	1240. 1470. 1665.	mil $		US Outlook /. /74 319	13.3%
35370 008	Industrial wheel tractors,N Am	retail sales	(N Amer)	74 75 —	52.2 47.8 —	000 units		Imp&Tractr 12/15/74 3"	-8.4%

STATUS, OR WHAT HAPPENS?
AFFECTING WHAT? (WHEN APPROPRIATE)
BASE PERIOD DATA YEAR QUANTITY
WHAT PRIMARY PRODUCT?

NEW PLANT AND EQUIPMENT EXPENDITURES

ITEM	1957/9	1960/2	1963/5	1966/8	YEARS & QUANTITIES 1969/71	1972	1973	1974	1975	1976	1980	1985	ANNUAL GROWTH 85/72-74
					--- Millions of Dollars ---								
NEW PLANT & EQUIPMENT EXPENDITURES	34440	37016	47286	68580	78836	99740	112400	113390	123000	184400	252300		8.0%
MANUFACTURING	13886	14826	19466	26360	31706	38010	46010	48200	51900	71200	95600		7.9%
DURABLE GOODS	6420	6776	9436	14080	15303	19250	22620	22100	22800	34300	44200		7.6%
Stone, Clay & Glass Products	666	716	780	993	970	1490	1440	1450	1650	2200	2950		6.6%
Blast Furnace													
Nonferrous / Primary													
Other Prima													
Machinery exl													
Electrical Mad													
Transportation													
Motor Vehicl													
Aircraft & Pa													
Other Transp													
Other Durable													

NONDURABLES AND ENERGY

ITEM	1957/9	1960/2	1963/5	1966/8	YEARS & QUANTITIES 1969/71 1973	1974	1975	1976	1980	1985	UNIT OF MEASURE	ANNUAL GROWTH 85/72-74
FOOD, BEVERAGES & TOBACCO												
Meat Production	23.2	25.3	28.5	31.0	34.7 33.5	36.3	35.0	36.0	41.5	45.5	bil lbs	2.7%
Fluid Milk Production	123.3	125.0	125.5	118.7	117.3 115.4	115.4	115	114	112	110	bil lbs	-.5%
Frozen Foods Production	8.7	11.5	12.2	15.0	17.3 21.9	23.5	24.2	26	32	40	bil lbs	5.3%
				107.4	121.9 128.5	145.5	149	155	178	204	mil bbl	3.3%
									545	481	mil w gal	4.5%

70

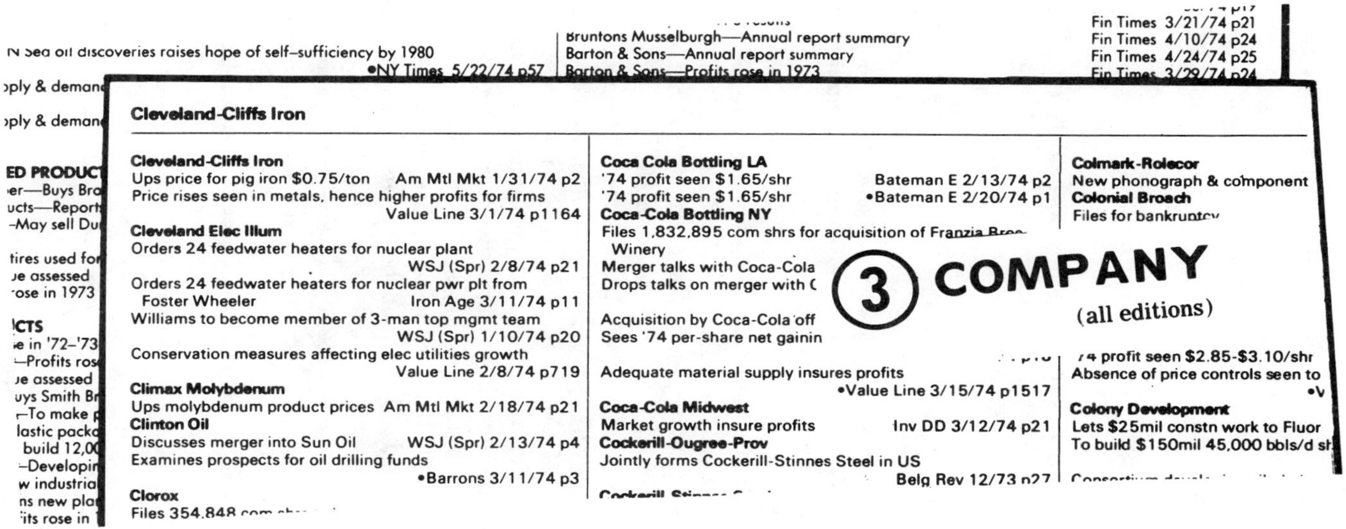

N Sea oil discoveries raises hope of self-sufficiency by 1980
•NY Times 5/22/74 p57

Bruntons Musselburgh—Annual report summary
Barton & Sons—Annual report summary
Barton & Sons—Profits rose in 1973

Fin Times 3/21/74 p21
Fin Times 4/10/74 p24
Fin Times 4/24/74 p25

Cleveland-Cliffs Iron

Cleveland-Cliffs Iron
Ups price for pig iron $0.75/ton Am Mtl Mkt 1/31/74 p2
Price rises seen in metals, hence higher profits for firms
Value Line 3/1/74 p1164
Cleveland Elec Illum
Orders 24 feedwater heaters for nuclear plant
WSJ (Spr) 2/8/74 p21
Orders 24 feedwater heaters for nuclear pwr plt from Foster Wheeler Iron Age 3/11/74 p11
Williams to become member of 3-man top mgmt team
WSJ (Spr) 1/10/74 p20
Conservation measures affecting elec utilities growth
Value Line 2/8/74 p719
Climax Molybdenum
Ups molybdenum product prices Am Mtl Mkt 2/18/74 p21
Clinton Oil
Discusses merger into Sun Oil WSJ (Spr) 2/13/74 p4
Examines prospects for oil drilling funds
•Barrons 3/11/74 p3
Clorox

Coca Cola Bottling LA
'74 profit seen $1.65/shr Bateman E 2/13/74 p2
'74 profit seen $1.65/shr •Bateman E 2/20/74 p1
Coca-Cola Bottling NY
Files 1,832,895 com shrs for acquisition of Winery
Merger talks with Coca-Cola
Acquisition by Coca-Cola off
Sees '74 per-share net gainin
Adequate material supply insures profits
•Value Line 3/15/74 p1517
Coca-Cola Midwest
Market growth insure profits Inv DD 3/12/74 p21
Cockerill-Ougree-Prov
Jointly forms Cockerill-Stinnes Steel in US
Belg Rev 12/73

Colmark-Rolecor
New phonograph & component
Colonial Broach
Absence of price controls seen to
Colony Development
Lets $25mil constn work to Fluor

3 COMPANY
(all editions)

Figure 3-15 Illustrates some of the data available from *Predicasts* and the *F & S Index.*

identification of industry and market structures with sales and employment data for 36,000 corporations.

Industry Surveys—an annual survey with useful reviews of selected industries. Valuable for industry and market studies.

USING SECONDARY DATA SOURCES

Industrial marketing research depends so heavily on the effective and efficient use of secondary data sources that it would be difficult to overstate the importance of knowing the sources and uses of secondary data. In this chapter, many of the most important sources have been identified and discussed, but there are many other sources that have not been mentioned. Boyd and Westfall provide a useful listing of guides, indexes, and periodicals of value to marketing researchers.[9] A recent article by Goeldner and Dirks offers additional sources, including a list of trade publication statistical issues.[10]

In addition to the published sources of secondary data, industrial marketing researchers also rely heavily on personal contacts for secondary data. Many of the persons discussed in Chapter 2 as "knowledgeable persons" are also valuable sources of information about the availability of secondary data. Among those most important in this regard are: editors of trade and business publications, trade association executives, industry consultants, and university professors. Another important resource is the U.S. Department of Commerce field office in your area. Field office personnel can help researchers locate government documents and, more importantly, can provide the name, address, and telephone number of the individuals in Washington working on the "industry desk" that compiles data on the industry that you are interested in. These individuals are usually very knowledgeable about their industry, data sources (particularly unpublished government data), and data limitations. Most of these persons are ready and willing to talk and work with industry people because it helps them to do a better job of collecting and presenting data of value to the industry.

There is a need to evaluate all sources of secondary data and the resulting data. Boyd and Westfall have noted:

No source of information should be treated as Calpurnian—a persis-

---

[9]Harper W. Boyd, Jr., Ralph Westfall, and Stanley F. Stasch, *Marketing Research,* 4th ed. Homewood, Ill.: Irwin, 1977, pp. 150–161.
[10]C. R. Goeldner and Laura M. Dirks, "Business Facts: Where to Find Them," *MSU Business Topics,* Summer 1976, pp. 23–36.

SECONDARY DATA SOURCES

tant skepticism is an essential posture when it comes to successful marketing research.[11]

They suggest that the researcher should evaluate secondary data sources on the basis of four criteria:[12]

1. Pertinency of the data
2. Who collects and publishes the data—and why
3. Method of collecting data
4. General evidences of careful work

Government sources of secondary data tend to be the most accurate but even these sources are subject to error. Two studies by the author demonstrated that there are significant errors in the enumeration of retail and service establishments in both the United States and England.[13] Whenever possible, it is desirable to conduct validity checks on secondary data by using independent sources.

Secondary sources do not provide sufficient or appropriate data for all marketing decisions, and there is often a need to collect primary data. Primary data collection should be conducted in the context of an appropriate research design. Chapter 4 is devoted to a consideration of research designs and primary data sources for industrial marketing research.

SUMMARY

Secondary data are information available at the outset of a research project. They can be internal or external to the firm. This chapter has focused primarily on external secondary data. The major problems with regard to internal secondary data are knowing what information is available and organizing it in a manner that is compatible with the needs of the marketing research department as well as those of other departments.

External secondary data are plentiful. The challenges lie in knowing where to look for information among so many possible sources; in evaluating the pertinence of the data; in ascertaining the credibility, trustworthiness, and purposes of the data collector; and in checking the

---

[11] Boyd, Westfall, and Stasch, *op. cit.*, p. 150.
[12] *Ibid.*, pp. 150.
[13] William E. Cox, Jr., "The Census of Business: Some Contrary Evidence," *Journal of Marketing*, July 1967, pp. 47–51; Cox, "The Census of Distribution: A Critique," *Journal of the Market Research Society* (England), Vol. 10, no. 4, 1968, pp. 225–233.

data for accuracy. Errors are often found, therefore verification is always warranted.

The starting point of secondary data collection efforts should be adoption of a classification system. Unless there are compelling reasons not to do so, the firm should adopt the Standard Industrial Classification (SIC) System that is the basis for all federal data organization and most state, local, and private data bases. The SIC system divides all economic activity into eleven divisions, broken into major 2-digit groups with 3-digit groups within each major group. Groups are further broken into industries (4 digits) and products (5 or more digits). Although the SIC system is extremely valuable, it is subject to several major problems. In many, but not all, instances judicious use of the SIC data can overcome those problems.

The major federal statistics are covered by the censuses of manufactures, retail trade, wholesale trade, selected service industries, construction industries, mineral industries, and transportation. These are conducted every five years. However for major economic activities there are also periodic updates which can be yearly, quarterly, or even monthly. Prominent among these are the *Annual Survey of Manufactures,* the *Current Industrial Report,* and *County Business Patterns.* A variety of other sources report on economic conditions, demography, foreign trade, and the detailed characteristics of publicly held corporations to name just a few.

Government data usually must be complemented with private sources. Prominent among these are Dun's *Market Identifiers, Million Dollar Directory,* and *Middle Market Directory, Thomas Register of Manufactures,* and Sales Management's *Survey of Industrial Purchasing Power.*

Extensive as secondary data are they may need to be complemented with expert judgment or primary data. The chapters that follow will deal with those as well as with the use of secondary data in more detail.

SUGGESTED READINGS

Boyd, Harper W., Jr., Ralph Westfall, and Stanley F. Stasch, *Marketing Research,* 4th ed. Homewood, Ill.: Irwin, 1977, Chap. 5.

Britt, Steuart H., and Irwin Shapiro, "Where to Find Marketing Facts," *Harvard Business Review,* Vol. 40, September–October 1962, pp. 44–52.

Carpenter, Robert N., *Guidelist for Marketing Research and Economic Forecasting.* New York: American Management Association, Research Study no. 73, 1966.

Cox, William E., Jr., "The Census of Business: Some Contrary Evidence," *Journal of Marketing,* July 1967, pp. 47–51.

Cox, William E., Jr., "The Census of Distribution: A Critique," *Journal of the Market Research Society* (England), Vol. 10, no. 4, 1968, pp. 225–233.

Frank, N. D., *Market Analysis: A Handbook of Current Data Sources.* New York: Scarecrow Press, 1964.

Goeldner, C. R., and Laura M. Dirks, "Business Facts: Where to Find Them," *MSU Business Topics,* Summer 1976, pp. 23–36.

Uhl, Kenneth P., and Bertram Schoner, *Marketing Research,* New York: Wiley, 1969, pp. 390–412.

CHAPTER FOUR
Research Designs and Primary Data Methods

Generations of marketing research students and practitioners have completed courses and studied textbooks that basically treated primary data methods as the essence of marketing research. A perusal of virtually all modern textbooks on marketing research will reveal that primary data methods continue to be the focus of these books, in spite of the fact that most firms engaged in marketing research activities spend much more time and money on the analysis and interpretation of secondary data than on primary data. What accounts for this disparity? Do these authors have a knowledge gap, or do they believe that primary data methods are more complex and more important than other marketing research activities? Without the benefit of secondary or primary data to provide adequate evidence, it is suggested that the fundamental explanation for the disparity may be traced to tradition. Early courses and textbooks in marketing research emphasized the use of primary data methods because secondary data sources were scarce and usually inadequate. It was not until after World War II, with economic recovery and the growth of electronic data processing, that both internal and external secondary data sources became important in marketing research practice. In addition the use of internal secondary data in the form of sales analysis was generally considered to be a clerical task unworthy of collegiate discourse, a bias which persists to this day.

DESIGNS AND DATA METHODS

The foregoing should not be interpreted as a denial of the importance of primary data methods but as another explanation for the different balance between secondary and primary data sources and methods found in this book. It is hoped that a similar shift in balance will eventually occur in all marketing research books, for the situation is the same regardless of emphasis by type of goods and services. Primary data methods are important in industrial marketing research and will be examined from a research design perspective in this chapter.

Chapter 1 concluded by emphasizing the importance of problem/opportunity identification as a critical step in the marketing research process. Chapters 2 and 3 focused on the use of exploratory research and secondary data sources as approaches to the specification of different courses of action and the evaluation of these differences. Research and management objectives may be satisfied by either exploratory research or by secondary data, in which case there is no need to consider the use of primary data methods. It is only after concluding that research and management objectives are not met by the use of exploratory research or secondary data that the researcher should begin a review of the various primary data methods that may be employed to meet the management and research objectives that triggered the marketing research process.

Exploratory research has therefore been presented as one of two general types of research design; the second general type of research design may be termed conclusive research. Green and Tull have defined research design as ". . . the specification of methods and procedures for acquiring the information needed to structure or to solve problems."[1] The distinction between exploratory and conclusive research is often fuzzy, but exploratory research tends to be relatively informal and directed toward the structuring of problems/opportunities, while conclusive research tends to be relatively formal and directed to problem solution and opportunity decisions. We have already noted however that exploratory research may produce conclusive outcomes and similarly, conclusive research may ". . . have byproducts which are in effect new exploratory studies leading to new hypotheses."[2]

Conclusive research, as a general type of research design, may be subdivided into descriptive and causal. Descriptive research designs, in contrast to exploratory research, are more structured, rigid, and based on higher levels of prior knowledge. Emory has suggested that descriptive

---

[1] Paul E. Green and Donald S. Tull, *Research for Marketing Decisions,* 3rd ed. Englewood Cliffs, N.J.: Prentice-Hall, 1975, p. 68.
[2] Harper W. Boyd, Jr., Ralph Westfall, and Stanley F. Stasch, *Marketing Research,* 4th ed. Homewood, Ill.: Irwin, 1977, p. 43.

research designs tend to be used when the research objectives include: (1) descriptions of phenomena or characteristics of a subject population, (2) estimates of the proportions of a population that have these characteristics, and (3) discovery of associations between different variables.[3] Causal research designs seek to ". . . discover and measure cause-and-effect relationships among variables,"[4] subject to the limitation that empirical research can never "prove" causality but at best infer it. Selltiz, et al. note that the criteria for inferring causality include:

1. Covariation between the presumed cause and presumed effect
2. Proper time order: the cause precedes the effect
3. Elimination of other plausible explanations for the observed relationship[5]

Descriptive Research

In those marketing research studies that go beyond exploratory research and may therefore be appropriately considered as conclusive research, the overwhelming majority are descriptive research designs. The reasons for the dominance of descriptive research are: (1) the dominance of research objectives associated with descriptive research designs (as noted by Emory), and (2) the widespread belief among researchers that causal research designs are excessively complex, costly, time-consuming, and basically impractical.

Modern marketing strategy is often based on market segmentation, requiring that characteristics of the market population be determined through marketing research. Kotler provides an example of this research objective, based on the assumption that International Harvester, a large manufacturer of earth-moving equipment, adopts the management objective ". . . reach a position of shared leadership with Caterpillar in the earthmoving industry by 1982."[6] After noting that Caterpillar is the dominant firm in the industry and seemingly invulnerable, Kotler suggests that International Harvester could employ a strategy of market segmentation. The construction equipment buying market can be segmented in several ways:

---

[3] C. William Emory, *Business Research Methods*. Homewood, Ill.: Irwin, 1976, p. 86.
[4] *Ibid*.
[5] Claire Selltiz, Lawrence S. Wrightsman, and Stuart W. Cook, *Research Methods in Social Relations*, 3rd ed. New York: Holt, Rinehart and Winston, 1976, p. 115.
[6] Philip Kotler, *Marketing Management*, 3rd ed. Englewood Cliffs, N.J.: Prentice-Hall, 1976, pp. 56–58.

1. *Geographical segmentation*—Kotler recommends that International Harvester ". . . study the construction budgets and growth rates of different regions and nations, find out where Caterpillar is relatively weak but the growth strong, and give top consideration to these markets."
2. *End use segmentation*—Construction markets may be classified into "residential housing, business and institutional building, road and highway development . . . [and] analysis must be made of the character, growth, and potential profitability of these different segments of the market."
3. *Buyer description segmentation*—The construction market could be segmented on the basis of (1) types of buyers: private contractors, government units, and so on, (2) customer size, (3) customer class: buying motives, buying influences.
4. *Specific products*—Demand for construction equipment varies between specific products such as front-end loaders, motor graders, and so on, within the market segments noted previously.

International Harvester, like all other industrial marketers seeking to employ a market segmentation strategy, should base that strategy on the findings of descriptive research regarding the characteristics of the market segment populations. In addition to determining the characteristics of these populations, International Harvester should also be interested in a second research objective associated with descriptive research: the estimation of the proportion of a population that has particular characteristics. Thus International Harvester should be interested in knowing what areas of the world construction market are expected to have an annual growth rate in excess of 10% annually, what proportion of the construction market in these areas will be for road and highway development, what proportion of the buyers will be government units, and so on.

One of the most important management problems in industrial marketing involves the allocation and direction of industrial salesmen. Lambert conducted a study of sales operations for a refiner and marketer of an industrial petroleum product which illustrates another research objective associated with descriptive research designs: discovery of associations between different variables.[7] He found that the firm's share of purchases in buyer firms appeared to be interrelated with, and partially dependent upon, the level and purpose of selling effort. The salesmen,

---

[7]Zarrel V. Lambert, "An Approach to Evaluating Competitive Effects and Selling Behavior in an Industrial Market," in P. R. McDonald, Ed., *Marketing Involvement in Society and the Economy*. Chicago: American Marketing Association, 1970, pp. 226–231.

"... seemed to reduce the overall level of effort expended on a buyer as their share of his business rose and ... altered the purposes of their calls as their share of a customer's business increased."[8]

Causal Research

Statisticians seem to be continually reminding their clients and the general public of the distinction between association and causality, probably because of the frequency of the misuse and confusion that surrounds the two concepts. Ramond has summarized the matter by noting: "To observe a consistent relationship (association) between two variables over time, or over cases at one point in time, does not prove that one causes the other. In its simplest slogan 'correlation is not causation' or 'correlation is not necessarily causation.'"[9] Thus it is one thing to discover that sales levels are related (associated) with the number of sales calls, it is quite another to maintain that sales calls cause sales. It may be that sales cause sales calls, or that many other factors cause sales as well as sales calls. Establishing causality therefore requires that we reduce (and hopefully eliminate) other explanations of the observed relationship between two or more variables. If the research objective is to discover and measure cause-and-effect relationships among variables, causal research designs are required.

PRIMARY DATA METHODS

Following the decision to use conclusive research designs and, more specifically, descriptive and causal research designs as a basis for marketing research activity, the researcher must review the available methods for collecting primary data. The term "primary data" refers to data not available at the time of problem/opportunity definition, and thus primary data are always collected specifically for the problem/opportunity at hand.

Collection Methods

The methods used for collecting primary data in industrial marketing research are the same as those used in other forms of marketing research:

---

[8]*Ibid.*, p. 231.
[9]Charles Ramond, *The Art of Using Science in Marketing*. New York: Harper & Row, 1974, p. 21.

DESIGNS AND DATA METHODS

1. *Surveys*—the process of asking questions of people believed to possess the required information.
2. *Observation*—the process of noting and recording information about people or behavior without asking questions.
3. *Experimentation*—the manipulation of one or more variables in order to test hypotheses regarding cause-and-effect relationships.

Although surveys are the most important, most common method for collecting primary data in all forms of marketing research, they are relatively even more important in industrial marketing research because of the virtual absence of the use of the other two methods. The reasons for the relative use and non-use of each method are now explored, using the relationship between research objectives, research design, and primary data methods as a framework within which the procedure for selecting the appropriate method may be examined.

Procedure for Selection

Figure 4-1 illustrates a procedure for selecting methods of collecting primary data. Assume that the Warner & Swasey Company, a major producer of machine tools, is considering whether to expand its tool-leasing program in order to increase sales and smooth the cyclical swings in new orders for machine tools. These management objectives have led to the specification of a research objective: to determine the extent and magnitude of awareness and interest among potential machine tool buyers in tool-leasing programs. Assume further that Warner & Swasey has conducted exploratory research and reviewed the available secondary data, thereby learning that the research objective can be met only by conducting conclusive research.

The choice among conclusive research designs is made on the basis of the research objective(s); Warner & Swasey's research objective is basically concerned with estimating the proportion of the population (potential machine tool buyers) who are aware of and interested in tool-leasing programs, and determining the magnitude of their awareness and interest. We have noted that this objective leads to the choice of a descriptive research design, so the next step is to review the characteristics and selection criteria for each primary research method associated with descriptive research designs. The alternatives are the survey and observational methods. Table 4-1 summarizes the characteristics and selection criteria for each primary research method in the context of industrial marketing research, showing that the observation method is not appropriate in this case. The survey method is therefore selected as the basis for

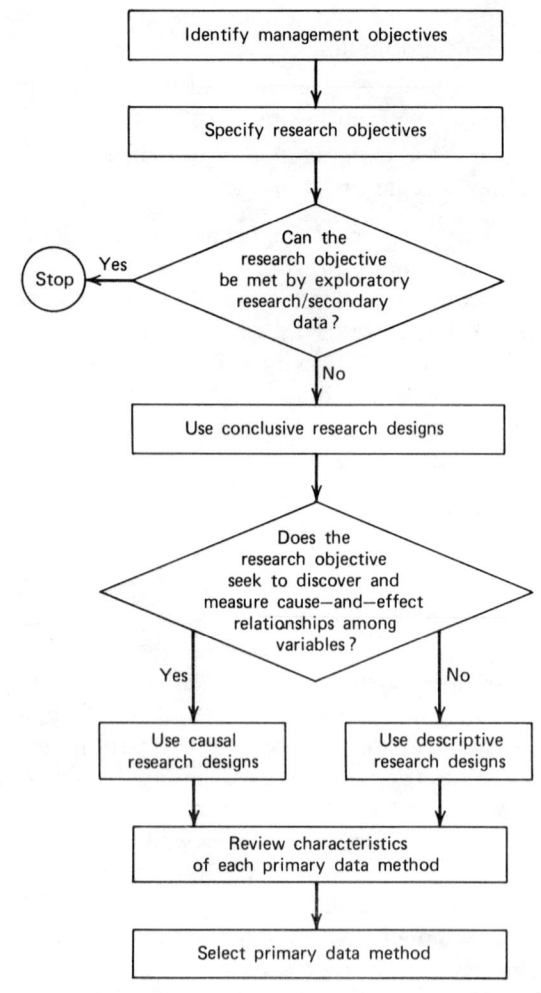

Figure 4-1 Procedure for selecting primary data methods within research objectives and designs framework.

collecting the primary data needed to meet the research objective. In Part III we shall consider the role of surveys in industrial marketing research and survey techniques.

Survey Methods

In order to select the most appropriate method for collecting primary data, it is necessary to match the selected research design with the

Table 4-1. Characteristics and Selection Criteria Associated with Primary Data Methods in Industrial Marketing Research Practice

Primary Data Methods	Type of Information Sought	Control over Variables	Data Accuracy	Cost and Time Factors	Personnel Skills Requirements
Survey Method	Current behavior Past behavior Intentions Awareness or knowledge Attitudes and opinions Motivations Demographics	Relatively high	Relatively low	Relatively low	Relatively high
Observation Method	Current behavior Results of past behavior	Relatively low	Relatively high	Relatively low	Relatively low
Experimentation	Current behavior	Relatively very high	Relatively high	Relatively high	Relatively very high

83

primary data methods available. Figure 4-1 illustrates that this matching process is conducted by reviewing the characteristics of each primary data method. In addition it is useful to establish selection criteria so that the methods and their associated characteristics can be readily compared. In cases where such discrimination is required, the selection criteria and characteristics of the methods should be set in the context of industrial marketing research.

We may open the consideration of the selection criteria by examining the characteristics of the survey method as a means of collecting primary data. Five selection criteria are utilized as the basis for evaluating each primary data method:

1. Type of information sought
2. Control over variables associated with method
3. Data accuracy associated with method
4. Cost and time factors associated with method
5. Personnel skills requirements associated with method

The survey method is the most widely used method for collecting primary data, basically because of its superior characteristics within two of the selection criteria. The most important characteristics of the survey method are those associated with the first criterion, type of information sought. The survey method is the only means of collecting primary data on most demographic characteristics of populations, attitudes and opinions, motivations, intentions, and awareness or knowledge. Since these types of information are those most commonly sought by researchers, it is to be expected that the survey method would be dominant. An additional contributing factor is that the survey method is *relatively* fast and cheap in comparison with other methods. The key word here is "relatively," for surveys can be both time-consuming and costly, but there are usually a number of ways in which the time and cost factors can be controlled and limited with the survey method, while observation and experimentation methods tend to have time and cost factor thresholds above that of the survey method. In other words, we have the option of conducting "quick-and-dirty" surveys if needed, but that option does not exist for the other primary data methods.

We can use the Warner & Swasey example again to illustrate how and why the survey method may be selected as the means of collecting primary data to reach a specified research objective. Since the research objective was to determine the extent and magnitude of awareness and interest among potential machine tool buyers in tool-leasing programs, a

DESIGNS AND DATA METHODS

descriptive research design would be needed to estimate the characteristics of the population. Descriptive research designs call for the use of either the survey or observation method, but data on the extent and magnitude of awareness and interest can only be collected by the survey method. Thus in this case, as in most that call for conclusive research designs, the selection of the survey method is made on the basis of a single criterion. Given the type of information sought, there is only one primary data method that will satisfy the research objective. Since the survey method can also be relatively quick and inexpensive, the second criterion of cost and time factors would not limit the selection of the survey method and might indeed reinforce it.

The three remaining selection criteria rarely influence the choice and use of the survey method, except indirectly through their effect on the research objective. With regard to the criterion of control over variables, the survey method is classified as relatively high because carefully drawn sampling designs can provide good control over such variables as the sampling unit (potential machine tool buyers) and the characteristics of the potential buyers selected for inclusion in the sample.

Survey methods are classified as relatively low with respect to the criterion of data accuracy since there are a number of possible sources of error. Potential machine tool buyers may be unwilling to respond to questions about tool-leasing programs, particularly if they are not interested in such programs. Other potential buyers may be unable to answer questions about tool-leasing programs because they do not have sufficient information about such programs. Still other potential buyers may feign awareness or interest in tool-leasing programs. In fact they may have little or no awareness or interest in such programs, either because they wish to please the interviewer (who may assume that the potential buyer is aware or interested) or because they reason that a positive response will maximize their choice opportunities at little or no cost. In spite of these possible errors and their effect on data accuracy, the survey method is widely used, presumably because researchers believe that they can minimize these errors to the point that the resulting primary data are sufficiently accurate for management decision.

The final criterion, personnel skills requirements, is rated as relatively high for the effective use of the survey method. Collecting accurate primary data on the extent and magnitude of awareness and interest among potential machine tool buyers in a tool-leasing program requires a high order of research knowledge and skill. For the past thirty years, marketing researchers have been trained extensively in the survey method (to the detriment of other required skills, it might be added) with the result that most researchers believe that they have the skills required to use the survey method. They do not view this criterion as a limiting factor in the use of the survey method and perhaps they are right.

Observation Methods

There are very few reported cases of the use of systematic observation as a means of collecting primary data in industrial marketing research. The reasons for this situation should be evident as we review the characteristics of the method and apply the five selection criteria to it. Since the observation method does not, by definition, permit questioning, it is limited to the collection of primary data on current behavior and the results of past behavior. In terms of the criterion of the type of information sought, the observation method is quite restricted, particularly in comparison with the survey method. Most of the reported cases of the use of the method focus on situations in which needed behavioral data were deemed to be unavailable from surveys. Wilson, for example, has noted that it is possible to measure product output for certain manufacturers' products such as machine tools by comparing the serial numbers applied in the period between one purchase (or observation) and another.[10] He also notes that the level of business activity in a firm may be measured by a comparison of invoice numbers used by the firm over a period of time.

The cost and time factors associated with the observation method are assessed as being relatively low based on the potential use of simple direct observation techniques. Examples of simple direct observation in industrial marketing research include:

1. The use of comparison shoppers by retailers to observe prices on selected items in competitive stores
2. Observing salesmen's behavior on sales calls
3. Observation of the behavior of visitors to trade show exhibits by noting systematically the number of visitors who examine different displays, their interest in various products shown, and the amount of sales literature distributed. Primary data on these behaviors can be collected quickly and cheaply, so their relative lack of use and importance must be explained by other considerations.

One criterion that helps to explain the relative lack of use of the observation method in industrial marketing research is that of control over variables, in which the method is classified as relatively low. The

---

[10] Aubrey Wilson, *The Assessment of Industrial Markets*. London: Hutchinson and Co., 1968, p. 213.

DESIGNS AND DATA METHODS

problem is that most observation techniques are inherently unobtrusive in nature, thereby denying the researcher the opportunity to control the variables of interest.[11] Additional insight into the reasons for the relatively low use of observation methods in industrial marketing research is provided by Stacey and Wilson.[12] In their analysis of the reasons why panels and audits, two of the most popular observation methods in consumer marketing research practice, are so rarely used in industrial settings, the authors note a number of limitations associated with each method when applied to industrial products:[13]

PANELS	AUDITS
1. Buying influences and authority are diffused.	1. Wide variations in products; lines are relatively wide.
2. Frequent personnel changes disrupt continuity.	2. Relative absence of branded products.
3. Managers unwilling or unable to contribute required time.	3. Unimportance of inventories for many industrial products.
4. Infrequent purchases of many industrial products.	4. Relative stability of prices for many industrial products.

Data accuracy is rated relatively high for observation methods, since observations of current and past behavior are generally free of errors. It should be noted that perceptual error does occur, in that different observers often have different perceptions of the same behavior, and there is always the danger that there will be errors in recording behavior. Nevertheless the observation method tends to produce more accurate data than the survey method, and should therefore be considered when data accuracy is particularly important in a research design.

Although the observation method is classified as relatively low on the criterion of personnel skills requirements, based on the nature of the skills required as an observer in most observation studies, there are situations in which high-level skills are required. One such situation is that of observing salesmen's behavior in complex selling circumstances; another is the evaluation of differences in product design and quality among industrial products being exhibited at trade shows. Finally, it seems that one of the major barriers to the greater use of the observation method is

---

[11] One of the most interesting books on research methods ever written is: Eugene J. Webb, Donald T. Campbell, Richard D. Schwartz, and Lee Sechrest, *Unobtrusive Measures: Nonreactive Research in the Social Sciences*. Chicago: Rand McNally, 1972.
[12] Nicholas A. H. Stacey and Aubrey Wilson, *Industrial Marketing Research*. London: Hutchinson and Co., 1963.
[13] *Ibid.*, pp. 167–168.

the difficulty of discovering creative ways to use unobtrusive measures of behavior, a task that may be aided by reading Webb, et al., *Unobtrusive Measures: Nonreactive Research in the Social Sciences.*

Experimentation

There are very few reported cases of experimentation being used to collect primary data in industrial marketing research, despite the fact that Banks, in his pioneering book, announced that, "Experimentation, the hallmark of the scientific approach, is now feasible in marketing and advertising."[14] Although Banks included many published reports of marketing experiments in his book, not one dealt with industrial goods and services. Subsequent books and articles on marketing experimentation have basically followed the same pattern, with only an occasional reference to the use of experimentation with industrial goods. There is no compelling reason why experimentation cannot be used in industrial marketing research, so the explanation for its lack of use may be revealed by the application of the five selection criteria and by the inherent characteristics of the method.

In Figure 4-1, it was shown that following the decision to use conclusive research designs to meet a research objective, the next step is to ask: Does the research objective seek to discover and measure cause-and-effect relationships among variables? If the answer is yes, causal research designs should be used. At this point it is important to note that experimentation is probably the most commonly used type of causal research design, but it is not the only method available. Ramond offers a well-reasoned argument, replete with examples, to show that appropriately analyzed historical data collected by nonexperimental methods may be effective as experimentation in eliminating other explanations of relationships between variables.[15] Although Ramond is persuasive in his brief for the value of "well-planned analysis of unambiguous data," our task here is to review experimentation as the principal method for carrying out causal research designs.

Myers and Mead have noted that,

> The essence of the experimental method is the *control* that is exercised by the researcher over the variables or factors of interest.[16]

[14]Seymour Banks, *Experimentation in Marketing*. New York: McGraw-Hill, 1965, p. v.
[15]Ramond, *op. cit.*, Chap. 4.
[16]James H. Myers and Richard R. Mead, *The Management of Marketing Research*. Scranton, Pa.: International Textbook Co., 1969, pp. 92-93.

DESIGNS AND DATA METHODS

One of our selection criteria is the control over variables; experimentation is classified as relatively very high in this regard, for it allows a maximum degree of control in comparison with other methods of collecting primary data. Virtually all reported cases of the use of experimentation in industrial marketing research appear to stem from the desire of the researcher to measure the effects of controlled variation in sales call levels, product features, and price.

Experimentation is also ranked as relatively high with respect to data accuracy since the ability to control the variables of interest tends to produce relatively error-free data. One of the early uses of experimentation in industrial marketing research was reported by this author in a study of the effects of various sales call levels on sales of threaded fasteners to industrial distributors.[17] The Ferry Cap and Set Screw Company, a Cleveland fastener manufacturer, agreed to allow the author to draw a stratified random sample of industrial distributors and vary the levels of sales-call efforts made during a one-year period by the Ferry Cap salesmen, based on the specifications set within a Latin Square experimental design. The Ferry Cap management agreed to sponsor the experiment because of their desire to obtain accurate data on the relationship between sales-call levels and sales. Earlier studies of this relationship, using historical data, suggested that it was very weak, and it was suspected that salesmen were saturating the industrial distributor accounts with calls. It was hoped that relatively accurate data on the relationship would enable management to specify optimal sales-call levels by type of account.

The report of the experimentation findings, one of the earliest reported uses of the method, had another somewhat dubious distinction. It is the report of a research failure, a novelty indeed in a literature that rarely displays anything other than success, while real-world marketing research is filled with unsuccessful research efforts. Analysis of variance of distributor sales showed that 98% of the variation in sales was "within call" variance, only 2% of the variation was accounted for by the variables that were controlled in the experiment. After much searching and testing of other variables as well as the use of data transformation functions, it was concluded that sales-call levels and sales were grossly related, but that further specification of the relationship was not justified. Although control over the important marketing variables was accomplished and accurate data were obtained, the research objective of establishing a specific

---

[17] William E. Cox, Jr., "An Experimental Study of Promotional Behavior in the Industrial Distributor Market," in Raymond M. Haas, Ed., *Science, Technology, and Marketing*. Chicago: American Marketing Association, 1966, pp. 578–586.

cause-and-effect relationship was not met. One important insight that did result from the study was that marketing experimentation will only be successful when sales forecast errors are less than the expected effect of the controlled variables. Much of industrial marketing is characterized by (1) relatively high errors in the ability to forecast sales to particular sets of accounts, and (2) the relatively small effect of promotion and price and product changes on behavior, however measured. In such situations, the use of experimentation is unlikely to be useful.

Other reasons for the relative lack of the use of experimentation is provided by the application of the three remaining selection criteria. Experimentation is limited to the collection of primary data on current behavior and is therefore the most restricted primary data method in flexibility and applicability. There are reports however of experimentation being used in the form of test marketing to collect primary data on current behavior. A 1967 National Industrial Conference Board study of methods used to appraise markets for new industrial products concludes:[18]

> The most commonly reported objectives of market tests for industrial products are to accomplish the following:
>
> 1. Determine the acceptability of the new or modified product.
> 2. Determine the effectiveness of its accompanying marketing program.
> 3. Derive some evidence of likely sales volume.
> 4. Reveal shortcomings and defects in either the product or the marketing program.
> 5. Discover uses or markets for the product that had not previously been anticipated.

A review of the cases offered to illustrate the use of test marketing shows that none of the cases were controlled experiments, their only resemblance to test marketing was that they all involved the trial distribution or sale of new industrial products on a limited scale. Confusion and emotions run high on the subject of test marketing. Wilson has noted that,

> Some confusion exists between test marketing and product field testing, and this inadvertently has led to over-optimism as to its (test marketing) effectiveness.[19]

[18] Morgan B. McDonald, Jr., *Appraising the Market for New Industrial Products*. New York: National Industrial Conference Board, 1967, p. 105.
[19] Wilson, *op. cit.*, p. 275.

DESIGNS AND DATA METHODS

This confusion is evident in the Conference Board study in which several of the "test marketing" cases are actually product field test examples. Regarding the first objective listed in the Conference Board study, Boyd and Westfall have written, without reference to the study, that,

> It is important to note that test markets are seldom used to test whether a product is acceptable or not acceptable to the consumer. This can be determined more inexpensively through the use of (other) kinds of tests. . . .[20]

Part of the confusion arises from a lack of agreement as to the definition of test marketing; observe the lack of agreement in the following:

> *Boyd and Westfall*—"Test marketing is a procedure by which a company attempts to test a new product marketing plan by introducing it on a miniature basis before committing the product to the entire market."[21]
>
> *National Industrial Conference Board*—"Test marketing involves the trial distribution and sale, on a small or limited scale, of a new or modified product or material."[22]
>
> *Aubrey Wilson*—"Experimental measurement of the effect of single variables in a marketing situation."[23]
>
> *Alvin Achenbaum* (our preference)—". . . a controlled experiment, done in a limited but carefully selected part of the marketplace, whose aim is to predict the sales or profit consequences, either in absolute or relative terms, of one or more proposed marketing actions."[24]

Ramond has captured the attraction and dismay associated with test marketing in a pithy, instructive chapter that begins,

> Test marketing has commanded more attention, wasted more money, and frustrated more product managers than any other task for which they are responsible.[25]

---

[20] Boyd and Westfall, *op. cit.*, p. 715.
[21] *Ibid.*
[22] Morgan B. McDonald, Jr., *op. cit.*, p. 105.
[23] Wilson, *op. cit.*, p. 385.
[24] Alvin R. Achenbaum, "Market Testing: Using the Marketplace as a Laboratory," in Robert Ferber, Ed., *Handbook of Marketing Research*. New York: McGraw-Hill, 1974, pp. 4–31 to 4–54.
[25] Ramond, *op. cit.*, p. 118.

Although his examples are all drawn from consumer goods, they serve to indicate dramatically the opportunities and problems associated with the use of test marketing in industrial marketing research.

Churchill has noted that the cost and time required to conduct test marketing is relatively high, and his reasoning is equally applicable to other forms of experimentation in marketing.[26] A good way to appreciate the high costs required for test marketing is to recognize that in addition to the direct research costs associated with all primary data methods, experimentation often requires that additional costs be incurred for promotion, pilot products or product variations, and distribution. If repeat purchases must be measured and seasonal variation in purchase rate taken into account, the time required to conduct experimentation will be long indeed.

In the discussion of experimentation, no distinction has been made between field and laboratory experimentation. The basic difference lies in the environment in which experimentation is carried out, and most of our examples have been field experiments. There is a growing interest in the application of laboratory experimentation in marketing, growing out of the work of Professor Robert J. Holloway and his students at the University of Minnesota.[27] We are beginning to use laboratory experimentation in the study of organizational buying behavior, and Chapter 14 will review several of these studies. Laboratory experimentation appears promising because it offers the possibility of reducing the cost and time of field experimentation while increasing the control over the experimental variables and setting. Cox and Enis provide a useful summary table and discussion of laboratory and field experimentation, comparing the data generated, data validity, and costs associated with each approach.[28]

A final criterion that helps to explain the relative lack of use of experimentation in industrial marketing research is that the personnel skills requirements are relatively very high. The research design, statistical analysis, and overall research knowledge and background required to employ experimentation effectively are of a very high order, and many organizations simply do not have sufficiently qualified personnel. Over time however we can expect that more researchers will become familiar with experimentation and that applications in industrial marketing research will increase somewhat. The rate of increase will depend primarily

---

[26] Churchill, *op. cit.*, pp. 109–112.
[27] M. Venkatesan and Robert J. Holloway, *An Introduction to Marketing Experimentation*. New York: Free Press, 1971.
[28] Keith K. Cox and Ben M. Enis, *Experimentation for Marketing Decisions*. Scranton, Pa.: International Textbook Co., 1969, pp. 106–108.

DESIGNS AND DATA METHODS

on the ability and cost of research to reduce uncertainties in marketing decisions. Since these uncertainties are greatest in the area of new product introductions, it is likely that we will see experimentation used relatively more frequently in such situations in industrial marketing. Further consideration of these issues is presented in Chapter 13, Product Analysis.

SUMMARY

Virtually all modern textbooks on marketing research treat primary data research as the essence of marketing research even though more time and money are spent on secondary data. This disparity can be traced to the inadequacy of secondary data prior to World War II and to the traditional belief that secondary data research is a clerical task unworthy of detailed treatment.

Primary data research is typically conducted for conclusive purposes, for example, for problem solution and opportunity decisions. It should be employed only after it has been determined that exploratory or secondary data do not meet research and management objectives. Primary data research can be descriptive or causal. Descriptive research is far more prevalent, especially in industrial marketing, than causal research.

The three chief methods of primary data collection are surveys, observation, and experiments. Surveys are especially popular in primary data industrial marketing research because they are the only means of collecting demographic, attitudinal, motivational, and awareness or knowledge information about customers, and because they are relatively inexpensive and quick. They do suffer from potential error and require extensive skills. However marketing researchers have developed an extensive experience in dealing with those problems.

Observational methods are especially rare in industrial marketing research. This is in good part because the conditions that make their chief forms, panels, and audits popular in consumer research do not exist in industrial markets. Experimental research, the typical approach to causal analysis, affords the researcher a high degree of control over the variables whose effects he wishes to gauge. However experimental research is pointless unless the forecast error of the dependent variable is small in relation to the effect of the independent variable. Also experimental research can be costly and complex. Laboratory as opposed to field experimentation offers some promise of alleviating those problems. Experimental research would be particularly useful for the test marketing of industrial goods and services.

SUGGESTED READINGS

Achenbaum, Alvin R., "Market Testing: Using the Marketplace as a Laboratory," in Robert Ferber, Ed., *Handbook of Marketing Research,* New York: Mc-Graw-Hill, 1974, pp. 4–31 to 4–54.

Banks, Seymour, *Experimentation in Marketing,* New York: McGraw-Hill, 1965.

Boyd, Harper W., Jr., Ralph Westfall, and Stanley F. Stasch, *Marketing Research,* 4th ed. Homewood, Ill.: Irwin, 1977, Chap. 2.

Cox Keith K., and Ben M. Enis, *Experimentation for Marketing Decisions.* Scranton, Pa.: International Textbook Co., 1969.

Cox, William E., Jr., "An Experimental Study of Promotional Behavior in the Industrial Distributor Market," in Raymond M. Haas, Ed., *Science, Technology, and Marketing.* Chicago: American Marketing Association, 1966, pp. 578–586.

Emory, C. William, *Business Research Methods.* Homewood, Ill.: Irwin, 1976.

Green Paul E., and Donald S. Tull, *Research for Marketing Decisions,* 3rd ed. Englewood Cliffs, N.J.: Prentice-Hall, 1975.

Lambert, Zarrel V., "An Approach to Evaluating Competitive Effects and Selling Behavior in an Industrial Market," in P. R. McDonald, Ed., *Marketing Involvement in Society and the Economy.* Chicago: American Marketing Association, 1970, pp. 226–231.

McDonald, Morgan B., Jr., *Appraising the Market for New Industrial Products.* New York: National Industrial Conference Board, 1967.

Myers James H., and Richard R. Mead, *The Management of Marketing Research.* Scranton, Pa.: International Textbook Co., 1969.

Ramond, Charles, *The Art of Using Science in Marketing.* New York: Harper & Row, 1974, Chap. 4.

Stacey, Nicolas A. H., and Aubrey Wilson, *Industrial Marketing Research.* London: Hutchinson and Co., 1963.

Venkatesan, M., and Robert J. Holloway, *An Introduction to Marketing Experimentation.* New York: Free Press, 1971.

Webb, Eugene J., Donald T. Campbell, Richard D. Schwartz, and Lee Sechrest, *Unobtrusive Measures: Nonreactive Research in the Social Sciences.* Chicago: Rand McNally, 1972.

Wilson, Aubrey, *The Assessment of Industrial Markets.* London: Hutchinson and Co., 1968.

CHAPTER FIVE
Sales, Cost and Profitability Analysis

In this and the succeeding chapters in Part II, the focus is on those activities that constitute the principal responsibilities of industrial marketing research. Based on a AMA survey,[1] these activities are:

1. Development of market potentials
2. Market share analysis
3. Determination of market characteristics
4. Sales analysis
5. Short-range forecasting (up to one year)
6. Long-range forecasting (over one year)
7. Studies of business trends
8. New product acceptance and potential
9. Competitive product studies
10. Establishment of sales quotas, territories

Among industrial companies with research departments that were included in the AMA survey, more than 90% of the companies were conducting each of these activities. (No other activities registered 90% or

[1] *1973 Survey of Marketing Research.* Chicago: American Marketing Association, 1973.

more.) It is appropriate therefore to organize Part II around these activities, along the following lines:

1. Sales analysis for individual firms, together with cost and profitability analysis
2. Determination of market characteristics, market share analysis, and industry studies
3. Development of market potentials and establishment of sales quotas, territories
4. Short-range forecasting, long-range forecasting, and studies of business trends
5. New product acceptance and potential, and competitive product studies

Scope of Sales Analysis

If reliable data were available regarding the allocation of corporate resources among the various kinds of research activities of industrial companies, it is likely that sales analysis would rank first, far above all other activities. The reason for this emphasis is that this activity provides the information necessary for the continuing evaluation of marketing performance. Since the terms "sales analysis" and "market analysis" are sometimes used interchangeably and also differently, it may be useful to adopt the following definition for sales analysis:

> A subdivision of marketing research activity which involves the systematic study and comparison of sales data of the individual firm.

We shall focus initially on sales analysis in the narrow sense of the term (revenue data derived from internal accounting records), and then expand the concept to include other data sources as well as cost and profitability analysis which may be considered as part of a comprehensive sales analysis program.

SALES ANALYSIS

Sales Analysis as Problem-Solving

The primacy of sales analysis as the preferred approach to problem solving in industrial marketing is based on a number of factors:

SALES, COST AND PROFITABILITY ANALYSIS

1. Sales analysis uses internal secondary data as its information base.
2. "Analysis of your own sales records is a *basic first step* in any program of marketing management based on facts. The results of that analysis have an important bearing on the amount and kind of external research you are likely to need."[2]
3. Sales analysis is versatile, since it can be used by all firms, and it is relatively inexpensive and easy to apply.

In his emphasis on sales analysis, Crisp cites each of these factors ". . . as the most important part of the total program of getting and using marketing facts."[3]

In Chapter 1, we noted the decision rules offered by Ramond as a guide for identifying marketing problems:[4]

1. Respond first (or only) to declining outputs.
2. Where possible, localize the decline in output.
3. Work on the biggest decisions first.

These decision rules will serve as the framework for our further consideration of sales analysis. Although Ramond phrased the first decision rule in general terms by using the term "outputs," initially we shall limit our consideration to sales outputs, and later expand it to cover costs and profits. Much of all marketing research activity arises from the response of marketing executives to perceived declines in sales. The initial perception of a sales decline usually occurs at an aggregate level: sales for the most recent accounting period are lower than sales for a comparable earlier period. The emphasis on responding first, and perhaps only, to declines in outputs is a matter of setting priorities, based on the belief that the greatest payoffs (in terms of cost/benefit ratios) are likely to come from reversing sales declines rather than stimulating sales that are lagging.

One of the basic tasks of a good sales analysis program in an organization is to provide an effective early warning system regarding sales declines, permitting the earliest possible identification of emerging problems. This requires that sales data be organized and presented in disaggregate form, so that sales declines may be spotted early and appropriate action initiated as soon as possible. The disaggregation of sales data is therefore the response to the second decision rule to localize the decline

---
[2] Richard D. Crisp, *Sales Planning and Control.* New York: McGraw-Hill, 1961, p. 42.
[3] *Ibid.,* p. 41.
[4] Charles Ramond, *The Art of Using Science in Marketing.* New York: Harper & Row, 1974, pp. 156–161.

in output. The preferred logical sequence to follow in localizing the decline is treated later in this chapter.

The third decision rule, work on the biggest decisions first, is again a matter of setting priorities. This task, perhaps the ultimate test of the effective executive, involves managerial judgement of the highest order. Sales analysis can help provide information regarding potential costs and benefits associated with the decision and, as such, reduce the uncertainty in the decision.

Sales Analysis as a Means of Identifying Opportunities

In Chapter 1 the importance of using industrial marketing research to identify opportunities as well as to solve problems was emphasized. Sales analysis is also useful in identifying opportunities, for it provides the factual base upon which new opportunities are spotted and acted upon. Drawing upon the decision rules formulated as a guide to solving problems, we can create a series of decision rules to aid in identifying marketing opportunities:

1. Look for situations of comparatively high sales results.
2. Comparisons of sales results should be with relevant information segments, including geographic, customer, product, time, and sales performance measures.
3. Narrow the choice of opportunities to be pursued, based on appropriate choice criteria.

The search for marketing opportunities through sales analysis initially involves devising procedures for isolating significant changes in sales results. Exception reporting systems are the preferred approach to identify departures from norms. Although they are generally based on deviations from plans or budgets, the application of the principle of management by exception may be applied to variations from any standard. In the special case of spotting opportunities, emphasis is placed on the early identification of comparatively high sales relative to the standards being used.

A successful program of spotting marketing opportunities early depends heavily on the use of a number of information segments. Just as negative sales deviations from standards are the basis of problem solving, positive sales deviations are the basis for identifying opportunities. It is not enough however to limit the search for positive sales deviations from single traditional standards, such as sales plans, sales budgets, sales potentials and quotas, or earlier sales as is so often done. A computer-

SALES, COST AND PROFITABILITY ANALYSIS

based sales analysis program using an exception reporting system can be readily programmed to highlight positive sales deviations from *all* of the standards (control units) used in sales analysis. Thus a single sales result may produce all of the following comparisons:

Information Segment or Standard	Actual Sales ($)	Expected Sales ($)		Sales Deviation ($)
Budget and quota	160,000	120,000	+	40,000
Year ago sales (same period)	160,000	110,000	+	50,000
Southern territory	80,000	50,000	+	30,000
Georgia customer #1	40,000	20,000	+	20,000
Product #	20,000	10,000	+	10,000

In this disguised example, one product line of a given division of a large industrial goods manufacturer had sales of $160,000 in a recent quarter. Most conventional sales analysis programs would show the $40,000 positive sales deviation against the sales budget and the $50,000 increase over the year-ago sales for the same quarter. Carrying the exception reporting system further however reveals that $30,000 of the increase occurred in the Southern territory, that $20,000 of the $30,000 increase came from Georgia customer #1, and that $10,000 of the increase came from Product #A. It should be stressed that this is not a "nested" result based on sequential sorting and searching for the explanation of the positive sales deviation by successively working through a hierarchy of standards of segments. Instead the use of an exception reporting system with all segments and standards provides for a maximum degree of sales disaggregation and may identify opportunities that otherwise would go undetected. This procedure also tends to encourage the use of sequential analysis by aggregation or disaggregation from the original, flagged sales exception, often without the need for additional special computer runs requiring special programs.

Exception reporting systems require that criteria be established for flagging sales deviations, and the establishment of these criteria poses a number of questions.[5] Should a single criterion be set for all segments and standards? Some firms use +/− 5% as a universal criterion, others tailor each criterion to the segment/standard. What figure should be used, if a universal criterion is adopted? The 5% figure seems to have grown out of

---

[5] Stanley J. Po Kempner, *Information Systems for Sales and Marketing Management*. New York: National Industrial Conference Board, 1973, pp. 14–15. Provides useful insights into the establishment of criteria for exception reporting as well as reasons for the continued reluctance of managements to use exception reporting systems.

empirical experience and an assessment of how many opportunities can be selected for further study.

Defining the Sales Units

In planning a sales analysis program for an industrial organization, one of the first issues to be resolved is the matter of defining the term "sales." Most firms find it desirable to define sales in terms of both orders (bookings) and shipments. The reason of course is that there is usually some delay in filling orders after they are received so that orders and shipments vary at any given point in time. Industrial firms that primarily ship from inventory may find that it is sufficient to use either orders or shipments when the order-filling time is generally less than the analysis period. When sales analysis employs a calendar month as the analysis period and most orders are shipped in the same month either measure will be adequate.

Sales data, whether in the form of orders or shipments, may be expressed in product units or dollars (or both), depending on the nature of the product and the availability of comparable secondary data. As a rule the greater the unit value of the product, the greater the tendency to plan and control sales on the basis of product units. Product units may be measured in terms of items, volume, weight, type of container, or a variety of other measures. Some of the problems associated with the use of product units as a sales measure include: comparison (in a multiproduct firm) of unrelated units (such as pounds and carloads) may be meaningless; price and profitability differences between products and overtime are ignored; and quality differences between products are not represented. Expressing sales data in terms of dollars (revenue) provides at least a partial solution to each of these problems and is probably more widely used than product units, largely because of the need to make valid interproduct comparisons. However a study by the Conference Board notes that,

> . . . such figures should be net of trade discounts and allowances in order fairly to compare the items (products, customers, etc.) under study.[6]

In periods of rapidly changing prices, it may be useful to adjust revenue data with a price index, thereby permitting the comparison of revenue (sales) in constant dollars.

---

[6]*Sales Analysis,* Studies in Business Policy, no. 113. New York: National Industrial Conference Board, 1965, p. 39.

Defining the Information Segments

After defining the sales units, the next step in planning the sales analysis program is to define the information segments that will be used. Horngren has defined an information segment as,

> Any line of activity or part of an organization for which a separate compilation of costs or sales is sought.[7]

The typical information segments for sales analysis in most industrial firms are: (1) territories, (2) customers, and (3) products.

The key to territorial sales analysis is the selection of the control unit, which may be defined as the smallest geographic unit for which company sales data are reported.[8] Crisp and subsequent authors have indicated that control units should be as small as practical, self-contained in terms of marketing practices, and compatible with external secondary data control units. Most industrial firms use counties as control units and their sales territories are based on aggregations of counties. In the largest metropolitan areas there is often a need to use a smaller control unit than the county. The usual choice is to select the central city as a control unit; thus the city of Chicago would be used in addition to Cook County, Illinois.

Sales territories tend to change too frequently to be used as control units. It is important that control units be stable over time so that valid time series comparisons may be made. By organizing sales territories along county lines, it is possible not only to compare performances over time even though territory boundaries change, but also to utilize external secondary data for territory analysis. If only one salesman is assigned to each territory, there is no need to have a separate salesman information segment. If multiple salesmen are assigned to territories, it is desirable to divide the territories by counties (and cities, if necessary) so that each salesman is identified with a unique set of control units.

The tendency for industrial sales to be concentrated among relatively few accounts indicates the need for the use of customers as information segments. Many industrial firms still use an "*A, B, C* system of classifying customer accounts: *A* accounts are the 4 (or 8) largest customers of the firm, *B* accounts are the next (twelve or sixteen) largest customers, and the *C* accounts are all of the remaining customers. In such systems the *A* and *B* accounts are also analyzed individually.

---

[7] Charles T. Horngren, *Cost Accounting: A Managerial Emphasis*, 2nd ed. Englewood Cliffs, N.J.: Prentice-Hall, 1967, p. 299.
[8] Richard D. Crisp, *Marketing Research*. New York: McGraw-Hill, 1957, p. 144.

Customers should also be classified on the basis of their primary product output, using SIC numbers, so that customer market segments can be developed. Sales analyses based on customer market segments classified by SIC numbers can be related to external secondary data sources in studies of sales performance.

Sales concentration also occurs by product line and individual products in most industrial firms, resulting in a need to establish products as an information segment. Sales data are usually disaggregated for key product lines and products and aggregated for less important lines and products. New products are often isolated early in their life cycle to facilitate sales tracking and analysis. Figure 5-1 shows an output page from the sales analysis program of an industrial goods manufacturer. Each of the three information segments (territories, customers, and products) are included in the program.

In addition to the primary information segments noted above, many industrial firms use other information segments in their sales analysis programs. These segments include:

1. *Channels of distribution*—Firms using multiple channels of distribution, such as those in the truck aftermarket, will analyze sales through each major channel.

Territory # 14	1974 Sales	Current Qtr. 1975 Sales	Y-T-D 1975 Sales
Canton, Illinois			
Canton Iron Works			
13 Flat Head Std	233		
16 Square Head Set	312	7	7
41 Lo Carb Special	494	515	515
Total	1039	522	522
Chicago, Illinois			
Midwest Metal Products			
1 Lo Carb Std Hex	146		
28 Ferraloy Hex	123		
39 Spec Hicarb Hex	6349	1066	1066
Total	6618	1066	1066

Figure 5-1 Sales analysis output—industrial goods manufacturer.

SALES, COST AND PROFITABILITY ANALYSIS

2. *Types of customers*—Many industrial firms sell to both OEM (Original Equipment Manufacturer) and industrial distributor accounts, treating these account classifications as separate information segments.
3. *Method of sales*—Firms that use both leasing and outright sales will usually treat these different methods as separate information segments for sales analysis purposes.

For additional ideas and details about information segments used in sales analysis programs, consult a book on distribution cost accounting, such as Heckert and Miner.[9]

Influence of Concentration on Sales Analysis

We have noted the importance and prevalence of concentration in industrial marketing but its effects are so pervasive that additional consideration is warranted. Concentration is a fact of economic life in the United States at every level of economic activity. A popular expression for the prevalence of concentration in marketing activities is the 80–20 principle: 80% of the sales volume and net profit of a firm comes from 20% of its territories, customers, salesmen, products, and orders. There is nothing magical about the 80–20 relationship, of course, for it is simply a rule-of-thumb expression. Sevin has long cited (as have many others) cases of more extreme concentration,

> One manufacturer found that 78 percent of his customers produced only slightly more than 2 percent of the sales volume, [and] . . . 76 percent of the number of products manufactured accounted for only 3 percent of the sales volume.[10]

On the other hand, Wolfe and Albaum found a lesser degree of concentration than the 80–20 principle suggests, but concentration nevertheless. They turned the 80–20 principle around and tested the 20–80 principle: 20% of the sales volume and net profit of a firm comes from 80% of the territories, customers, and so on. Their findings were that 33% of the sales and profit in a sample of well-managed firms came from:[11]

---

[9] J. H. Heckert and R. Miner, *Distribution Costs*. New York: Ronald, 1953, p. 24.
[10] Charles H. Sevin, *Marketing Productivity Analysis*. New York: McGraw-Hill, 1965, p. 8. (Originally cited by Sevin in a 1946 publication issued by the U.S. Department of Commerce.)
[11] Harry D. Wolfe and Gerald Albaum, "Inequality in Products, Orders, Customers, Salesmen, and Sales Territories," *Journal of Business*, July 1962, pp. 298–301.

61% of the territories
74% of the customers
58% of the salesmen
74% of the products
71% of the orders

Although the fundamental explanation of the ubiquity of the 80–20 principle is to be found in the principle of economies of scale, Sevin and, more recently, Stanton and Buskirk have contended that,

> ... most marketing programs and distribution systems typically have some misplaced efforts. That is, marketing efforts and costs follow the number of territories, products, customers, or other units rather than the actual or potential sales volume or profit.[12]

They are therefore arguing that "misdirected marketing effort" is the basic explanation for the 80–20 principle. Whatever the basic explanation may be, there seems to be no question that marketing activities have contributed to the presence of the 80–20 principle in many firms.

One of the primary thrusts of every sales analysis program therefore should be the identification of the extent and nature of sales concentration. Consideration may then be given to redirecting marketing effort through: (1) territory realignment, (2) product abandonment, (3) changing sales call patterns, (4) installing a minimum order charge, and other actions that will change the concentration pattern. Alternatively, the firm may decide to increase its degree of concentration by emphasizing its marketing efforts to a selected set of territories, customers, and products.

Setting Sales Standards

Planning a comprehensive sales analysis program also requires that various sales standards be set as a basis for measuring performance and for control purposes. The most important standards involve time and targets. Time standards are usually of two types: (1) previous periods, and (2) year-to-date measures. Target standards include: (1) plans, (2) budgets, and (3) quotas. Figure 5–2 illustrates a monthly customer performance report that includes two information segments (customer and product) and three standards:

---

[12] William J. Stanton and Richard H. Buskirk, *Management of the Sales Force*, 3rd ed. Homewood, Ill.: Irwin, 1969, p. 579.

Customer _____   Territory _____

Customer Number _____

		Month			Year-to-Date			
Product		Current Month	Over (Under) Plan	Over (Under) Last Yr.	Current Period	Over (Under) Plan	Over (Under) Last Yr.	% Customer Purchases
0120	Units	10,000	100	350	35,750	(6,500)	1,520	8.4
	$(000)	25,640	250	1,040	90,400	(18,400)	4,210	
0187	Units	2,400	150	250	7,000	(150)	—	2.3
	$(000)	6,240 →	450 →	700 →	20,150 →	(450) →	520 →	→
All Others	$(000)	19,020	(1,200)	(500)	44,000	(240)	1,000	4.0
Total	$(000)	240,000	(21,600)	1,520	862,000	4,200	8,700	100.0

Adapted from: Kurt H. Schaffir and H. George Trentin, *Marketing Information Systems*. New York: AMACOM (American Management Association), 1973, p. 52.

Figure 5-2 Monthly customer performance report.

1. *Previous period*—Current month sales are compared with the same month last year.
2. *Year-to-date*—Sales in the current year-to-date are compared with sales in the same year-to-date period for the last year.
3. *Plans*—Current month and year-to-date sales are compared with sales plans for these periods.

The use of an exception reporting system for monitoring sales performance is shown in Figure 5–3, using two information segments (territory and salesman) and two standards:

1. *Budgets*—Current month sales are compared with the budget for the month.
2. *Year to date*—Year-to-date sales are compared with the budget for the period.

Additional Data Sources for Sales Analysis

Complete sales analysis programs generally include data from sources other than the internal accounting system of the firm. Among the most important data sources in this category are sales call reports and customer profiles. The nature and extent of sales call report data that are incorporated into sales analysis programs were reported to vary widely among firms surveyed in a Conference Board study, ranging from ". . . the number of calls the salesmen have made in some specified period" to the "nature of the calls, customer reactions, reasons for sales success or failure . . ."[13] Figure 5–4 shows a copy of the weekly sales call report used by the Industrial Products Group of the Goodyear Tire & Rubber Company. Goodyear produces five sales information reports from the call reports, including tabulations of the number of calls made by district, by salesman, by type of customer, and by type of products discussed. Sales call data are also combined with sales data in other reports.

Many industrial firms rely heavily on customer profile data to provide background information for sales analysis programs. Perhaps the best published example of the use of customer profile data in an integrated marketing information system is given in a case study of a manufacturer of industrial refractories.[14] Figure 5–5 shows an example of the customer profile data collected by this firm. The profile contains data on customer facilities and equipment, product usage, future plans, competitive posi-

[13] Stanley J. Po Kempner, *op. cit.*, p. 9.
[14] Schaffir and Trentin, *op. cit.*, p. 249.

Territory		Current Month				Year-to-Date		
Salesman	Salesman number	Actual sales	Over (under) Budget	Budget variance %		Actual sales	Over (under) budget	Budget variance %
Smith	01020	$ 42,000	($ 8,000)	(16.0)		$ 142,000	($ 18,000)	(12.0)
Jones	03041	34,000 →	(5,000) →	(12.5)		121,000 →	(3,000) →	(2.4) →
Subtotal		1,246,000	(240,000)	(16.8)		5,245,000	(578,000)	(9.9)
Other performance (≥ Budget)		1,824,000	120,000	7.0		5,940,000	240,000	4.2
Territory Total		3,070,000	(120,000)	(3.6)		11,185,000	(338,000)	(3.2)

Adapted from: Kurt H. Schaffir and H. George Trentin, *Marketing Information Systems*. New York: AMACOM (American Management Association), 1973, p. 55.

Figure 5–3 Monthly budget performance exception report.

GOODYEAR (Product sales group) Weekly call report

Salesman ______

Salesman no. ______ Dist. no. ___

Week of ______ to ______

Dept. contacted
1. Gen. mgm't.
2. Purchasing
3. Sales
4. Merchandising
5. Production
6. Engineering
7. Research

Products

01 Truck tires
02 Aviation W & B
03 Vitafilm
04 Neolite
05 Videne
06 Pillow tanks
07 Air hose
08 Molded & ext. goods
09 V–Belts
10 Studded snow tires
11 Chemicals

Class	Number	Date	Customer/Prospect Name and Address (Use two lines if necessary)	Dept. con–tacted	Person interviewed	Type account C or P	Products Discussed (Fill in column using proper above numbers)	Remarks

Figure 5–4 Weekly sales call report, Industrial Products Group, Goodyear Tire & Rubber Company.

PAGE 1

CUSTOMER PROFILE

CUSTOMER NAME *American Steel*   LOCATION *South Chicago*   DEPT. *Blast Furnace*
PERSONS CONTACTED *Charles Jones (Supervisor), Frank Brown (Purchasing Agent)*   DATE PREPARED *5/6/7X*
NUMBER AND DIAMETER OF FURNACES *Two (#11, #12) #11-30' #12-29'2" at Bosh*
CAST CYCLE *#11-8.16 #12-7.12* HRS.   CAST SIZE *#11-510, #12-495* TONS
19X9 PRODUCTION *#11-349-7 #12-315-3* 000 TONS; 19X0 PLANS *#11-301-0 #12-328-0* 000 TONS 19X1 FORECAST *#11-360-0, #12-330-0* 000 TONS

PRODUCT USAGE

ROW	PRODUCT LINE	HEARTH	HEARTH WALLS	BOSH	STACK	STOVES	TRANSFER LADLES
1	SELAG I	#11, #12	#11, #12	#11, #12			
13	FLUXITE						#11, #12

TRANSFER LADLE TYPE *Pugh*   LADLE LIFE *150,000* TONS HAULED
LADLE MAINTENANCE DESCRIPTION: *Scanned by crew after each heat; reviewed by foreman weekly; minor maintenance every 100 casts; major overhaul at 600 casts*
INSTALLATION _____ LB./TON PRODUCED; MAINTENANCE *.0012* LB./TON PRODUCED; TOTAL *.0124* LB./TON
COMMENTS (ANTICIPATED PRACTICE CHANGES THROUGH 19X5): *Will phase Blast Furnace #12 (built 1941) out in 19X3. Replacement not determined.*
COMPETITORS *Maxwell Chemical, Inter-American;*
REASONS *Nearby warehouse and faster delivery*

PAGE 2

DEPARTMENT *Blast Furnace*

ROW	PRODUCT	$ OF CHEMICALS USED PER TON PRODUCED
1	SELAG I	.0040
2	SELAG – CASTABLE	
3	CLAY CASTABLE	.0387
4	H. T. FIRE CLAY – BRICK	.0775
39	HIGH ALUMINA	

DEPARTMENT TOTAL REFRACTORIES CONSUMPTION *.0124* S/TON

Figure 5–5 Customer profiles, industrial refractories manufacturer. Source: Kurt H. Schaffir and H. George Trentin, Marketing Information Systems. New York: AMACOM (American Management Association), 1973, p. 249.

tions, and buying influences. Some of these data may be incorporated directly into the sales analysis program; other data will be used primarily for marketing planning purposes. Although the preparation of such detailed profiles is time-consuming and costly, its importance may be recognized more easily upon noting that the average salesman of the industrial refractories manufacturer had only *five* major accounts for which the profile was to be prepared and maintained. The dependence of the salesmen and the firm on each account in concentrated market requires and permits intensive data collection from each account. The information is provided by the customer and the salesman through extended and continued communications.

COST AND PROFITABILITY ANALYSIS

Although sales analysis is a very important element in a comprehensive industrial marketing research program, it is also important that cost and profitability analysis of the information segments (territories, customers, etc.) be conducted as well. Unfortunately there are many industrial firms that do not conduct them properly. It is a moot question as to whether it is worse to do nothing or to do the wrong thing, but neither is right. Firms that do not conduct cost and profitability analyses are very likely to run afoul of the "iceberg" principle.[15] The small, visible part of an iceberg is comparable to the total net sales and profit figures that appear on a firm's operating statement, while the dominant, unseen part of an iceberg is comparable to the sales and profit data for the territories, customers, and products of the firm. Favorable total net sales and profit figures often conceal dangerous, unseen performances among the information segments of the firm, just as the invisible portion of the iceberg threatens the seaman.

Sevin has noted that many manufacturers erroneously conduct marketing cost and profitability analyses with three widespread types of errors:[16]

1. Marketing costs are generally allocated to individual products, customers, territories, etc., on the basis of their dollar sales volumes, [which is] completely erroneous.
2. General and administrative costs are arbitrarily and erroneously allocated to segments, also on the basis of dollar sales volume.

---
[15] Stanton and Buskirk, *op. cit.*, p. 580.
[16] Sevin, *op. cit.*, p. 12.

3. Many marketing costs are not allocated at all to segments, not being identified as marketing costs but, rather, being classified otherwise, i.e., as manufacturing or as general and administrative costs.

Having condemned the practices of many, if not most, industrial firms, Sevin proceeds to offer the solution:

1. Classify all marketing expenditures into "functional-cost" groups.
2. Allocate the "functional-cost" groups of marketing expenditures to segments on the basis of measurable factors.[17]

These measurable factors are selected on the basis of being characteristics of the segments being analyzed and being related to the marketing expenditures to be allocated. Figure 5-6 presents a listing of functional cost groups and bases of allocation. Additional information about the groups and bases is found in Chapter 2 of Sevin's book.

Alternative Approaches to Profitability Analysis

In addition to the question of *how* to allocate marketing costs to information segments, another important issue in cost and profitability analysis is whether to use a full-cost or direct-cost approach. The full-cost or net profit approach assigns all costs, both direct and indirect, to segments in order to determine profitability. The direct cost or contribution margin approach assigns only the direct costs to segments, and thereby measures their respective contribution to the overhead and net profit of the total firm. Figure 5-7 illustrates the difference between the two approaches. There seems to be rather widespread agreement that the contribution margin approach is superior for marketing decision-making purposes, primarily because it avoids the problems of assigning indirect costs to segments.[18] Stanton and Buskirk however contend that, ". . . both approaches have a place in marketing cost analysis."[19] They suggest that the net profit approach is best suited for long-range studies of segment profitability and the formulation of long-range marketing plans and policies. The contribution margin approach, in their view, is best for short-run marketing decisions, such as territory realignment, product line changes, and promotional expenditure decisions. Beik and Buzby have

---

[17]*Ibid.*, pp. 12, 16.
[18]V. H. Kirpalani and Stanley J. Shapiro, "Financial Dimensions of Marketing Management," *Journal of Marketing*, Vol. 37, July 1973, pp. 40–47.
[19]Stanton and Buskirk, *op. cit.*, p. 603.

| | Basis of Allocation | |
Functional Cost Group	To products	To customers
1. Investment	Average inventory value	(Not allocated)
2. Storage	Floor space occupied	(Not allocated)
3. Inventory control	Number of invoice lines	(Not allocated)
4. Order assembly (handling)	Number of standard handling units	Number of invoice lines
5. Packing and shipping	Weight or number of shipping units	Weight or number of shipping units
6. Transportation	Weight or number of shipping units	Weight or number of shipping units
7. Selling	Work-measurement studies	Number of sales calls
8. Advertising	Cost of space, etc., of specific-product advertising	Cost of space, etc., of specific-customer advertising
9. Order entry	Number of invoice lines	Number of orders
10. Billing	Number of invoice lines	Number of invoice lines
11. Credit extension	(Not allocated)	Average amount outstanding
12. Accounts receivable	(Not allocated)	Number of invoices posted

Source: Charles H. Sevin, *Marketing Productivity Analysis*. New York: McGraw-Hill, 1965, p. 25.

Figure 5-6 Functional cost groups and bases of allocation.

shown how the contribution margin approach may be applied to multiple segments including territories, customer class, and products, with the principal limitation to the extensiveness of the segmentation analysis being the availability of assignable sales revenue and cost data for less tangible segments.[20]

Incorporating Investment in Profitability Analysis

Since the term "profitability" implies a measure of the relation of profits to assets employed, it is to be expected that cost and profitability analysis

[20] Leland L. Beik and Stephen L. Buzby, "Profitability Analysis by Market Segments," *Journal of Marketing*, Vol. 37, July 1973, pp. 48-53.

Contribution Margin Approach

(000 Omitted)

	Total	Eastern territory	Western territory
Net sales	$ 90,000	$ 64,000	$ 26,000
Less cost of goods sold	60,000	41,000	19,000
Gross margin	$ 30,000	$ 23,000	$ 7,000
Less direct expenses:			
Selling	10,000	7,000	3,000
All other	6,000	4,000	2,000
Total direct exp.	$ 16,000	$ 11,000	$ 5,000
Contribution margin	$ 14,000	$ 12,000	$ 2,000
Less indirect expenses:			
Selling	3,000		
All other	6,000		
Total indirect exp.	$ 9,000		
Net profit before income taxes	$ 5,000		

Net Profit Approach

(000 Omitted)

	Total	Eastern territory	Western territory
Net sales	$ 90,000	$ 64,000	$ 26,000
Less cost of goods sold	60,000	41,000	19,000
Gross margin	$ 30,000	$ 23,000	$ 7,000
Less direct expenses:			
Selling	10,000	7,000	3,000
All other	6,000	4,000	2,000
Total direct exp.	$ 16,000	$ 11,000	$ 5,000
Contribution margin	$ 14,000	$ 12,000	$ 2,000
Less indirect expenses:			
Selling	3,000	2,000	1,000
All other	6,000	4,000	2,000
Total indirect exp.	$ 9,000	$ 6,000	$ 3,000
Net profit before income taxes	$ 5,000	$ 6,000	($ 1,000)

Figure 5-7 Alternative approaches to profitability analysis.

in marketing would incorporate measures of assets employed. Traditionally however this has not been done in most organizations, but there is a growing volume of recommendations and publications extolling the virtues of such an approach. As early as 1963 Schiff proposed that return-on-investment concepts be employed in sales management decisions.[21] He suggested, for example, that the profitability of a territory be measured by relating the contribution margin of territories to the working capital assets employed in doing business in the territories, specifically the value of the inventory and accounts receivable associated with the accounts in the territories. There have been subsequent calls for the use of return-on-investment measures for marketing decisions in the areas of a variety of other segments, including customers[22] and products.[23]

An alternative approach to the return-on-investment method that incorporates the costs of assets employed in a contribution margin framework has been proposed by a special committee of the American Accounting Association.[24] They propose, for example, that in a contribution margin approach to territory profitability analysis as shown in Figure 5–7, the cost of capital and user costs for fixed assets depreciation should be included to obtain a better measure of the actual contribution of the segments being analyzed. Regardless of the approach used, it seems clear that investment measures should be and increasingly will be employed in marketing cost and profitability analysis.

Marketing Cost Ratios

Another dimension of marketing cost analysis of interest to many manufacturers is that of cost comparison: there is often a need to know whether marketing expenditures are "in line" with competition. Marketing cost data were nonexistent or very limited and old, until the publication of a study conducted in 1972 by the Conference Board with 511 marketing units of United States manufacturing companies or their operating divisions.[25] The study reported the ratio of marketing costs to

---

[21] Michael Schiff, "The Use of ROI in Sales Management," *Journal of Marketing,* Vol. 27, July 1963, pp. 70–73.
[22] Edward C. Bursk, "View Your Customers as Investments," *Harvard Business Review,* Vol. 44, May–June 1966, pp. 91–94.
[23] Philip A. Scheuble, Jr., "ROI for New Product Policy," *Harvard Business Review,* Vol. 47, November–December 1969, pp. 110–120.
[24] "Report of the Committee on Cost and Profitability Analyses for Marketing," *Accounting Review,* Supplement to Vol. 47, 1972, pp. 574–615.
[25] Earl L. Bailey, *Marketing-Cost Ratios of U.S. Manufacturers.* New York: National Industrial Conference Board, 1975.

SALES, COST AND PROFITABILITY ANALYSIS

net sales in 1971 for the total and eleven categories of marketing costs, together with a marketing profile for each product class studied. A total of 39 product classes were developed, 8 consumer goods and 31 industrial goods, from the 1239 specific product lines studied (246 consumer lines and 992 industrial lines). A special feature of the study was the attempt to explain the variance in the ratios on the basis of product-class grouping and marketing profile variables. For industrial goods, the explained variance was about 50%, with almost 30% of the variance explained by the 31 product class groupings. Among the 31 groups, office equipment manufacturers had the highest marketing costs, averaging 29% of sales. The lowest group in terms of the ratio of total marketing costs to net sales was that of pulp and unconverted paper products which averaged only 3% of net sales.

The study showed that there were a number of characteristics of industrial goods that were statistically significant in explaining differences in marketing cost ratios:

1. *Size of the sales force*—Large sales forces resulted in higher marketing cost ratios.
2. *Frequency of product purchase*—Products purchased more than once a year had higher marketing costs than those purchased less frequently.
3. *Sales volume of the individual product line relative to others in the same product class*—Product lines with the highest sales volume had the lowest marketing cost ratios.
4. *Channel of distribution used*—It was more costly to distribute industrial goods through manufacturers' representatives, agents, or brokers than through the manufacturer's own sales force direct to users.
5. *Service support required*—Product lines that require the most frequent service support have higher marketing cost ratios.
6. *Size of the geographic market*—The larger the geographic area in which products are sold and serviced, the higher the marketing cost ratio.
7. *Method of filling orders*—Product lines for which orders were filled from inventory had higher marketing cost ratios than lines in which products were manufactured to order.
8. *Importance of product purchase to users*—The more important the product purchase was to the user, the lower the marketing cost ratio for the manufacturer.
9. *Importance/uniqueness of the manufacturer's marketing unit*—The

marketing cost ratio of the largest division (or the only marketing unit) in a firm was lower than that of smaller divisions.
10. *Number of accounts served*—The larger the number of accounts served (beyond a threshold level of 1000 accounts), the greater the marketing cost ratio.
11. *Number of competitive firms.*—When there were more than 15 competing manufacturers of a product line, the marketing cost ratios of these manufacturers tended to be lower than for lines with 15 or less suppliers.
12. *Focus of the marketing effort*—Marketing cost ratios tended to be higher when marketing effort was directed primarily to users, as compared to resellers or outside specifiers.[26]

In addition to these general findings, the study also presents detailed statistics for each of the 31 product groups of industrial goods. Industrial marketing researchers will find a great deal of useful information in this report, and it is hoped that the study will be replicated in the future.

This chapter has focused on sales and cost and profitability analysis for the individual firm, with primary emphasis on the manufacturer or distributor of industrial goods and services. Our concern has therefore been with the individual seller and the relationships of these sellers with various market segments in terms of sales and cost and profitability. In Chapter 6, we turn to a consideration of industry and market analysis, focusing on *all* sellers of given industrial products and services (the industry) and *all* buyers of the same goods and services (the market or markets).

SUMMARY

Sales analysis probably ranks at the top of the list of industrial marketing research activities. Sales analysis is a subdivision of marketing research activity which involves the systematic study and comparison of sales data of the individual firm. It owes its preponderance to its reliance on internal data to its being relatively inexpensive and easy to apply and to its being a basic first step of analysis.

Ramond's rules for identifying marketing problems listed in Chapter 1 are the basis of three rules for identifying marketing opportunities:

1. Look for situations of comparatively high sales results.

[26]*Ibid.*, pp. 11, 15.

2. Compare sales with relevant information along geographic, customer, product line, time, and sales performance measures.
3. Narrow the choice of opportunities, based on appropriate choice criteria.

Exception reporting is the basis of those rules. Exception reporting requires standards for comparison and the ability to aggregate and disaggregate data for detecting opportunities. A consistent definition of sales is also required, whether orders or shipments, dollars or units.

Sales must be broken down by territories, customers, and products. The preferred territorial alignment is by county. Customers should be classified by size, due to the high degree of demand concentration that prevails among industrial markets. This high demand concentration makes it possible to keep detailed profiles of larger customers.

"Sales" analysis should also include an examination of costs and profiles. It appears that for most marketing decision purposes, contribution cost analysis is to be preferred to full-cost analysis. Full cost is preferable for the evaluation and formulation of long-term marketing plans and policies. A problem with the full-cost approach is that allocations have tended to be either gross or arbitrary. The key to solving this problem is to classify marketing expenditures into functions and to allocate functional costs according to measurable activity factors.

Investment measures and marketing cost ratios are receiving increasing attention in marketing sales analysis. Recent studies by the American Accounting Association and the National Industrial Conference Board give important insights into both topics.

SUGGESTED READINGS

Bailey, Earl L., *Marketing-Cost Ratios of U.S. Manufacturers*. New York: National Industrial Conference Board, 1975.

Beik, Leland L., and Stephen L. Buzby, "Profitability Analysis by Market Segments," *Journal of Marketing,* Vol. 37, July 1973, pp. 48–53.

Bursk, Edward C., "View Your Customers as Investments," *Harvard Business Review,* Vol. 44, May–June 1966, pp. 91–94.

Crisp, Richard D., *Marketing Research*. New York: McGraw-Hill, 1957.

Heckert, J. H., and R. Miner, *Distribution Costs*. New York: Ronald, 1953.

Kirpalani, V. H., and Stanley J. Shapiro, "Financial Dimensions of Marketing and Management," *Journal of Marketing,* Vol. 37, July 1973, pp. 40–47.

Po Kempner, Stanley J., *Information Systems for Sales and Marketing Management*. New York: National Industrial Conference Board, 1973.

Ramond, Charles, *The Art of Using Science in Marketing*. New York: Harper & Row, 1974, pp. 156–161.

Schaffir, Kurt H., and H. George Trentin, *Marketing Information Systems*. New York: AMACOM (American Management Association), 1973.

Scheuble, Philip A., Jr., "ROI for New Product Policy," *Harvard Business Review*, Vol. 47, November–December 1969, pp. 110–120.

Schiff, Michael, "The Use of ROI in Sales Management," *Journal of Marketing*, Vol. 27, July 1963, pp. 70–73.

Sevin, Charles H., *Marketing Productivity Analysis*. New York: McGraw-Hill, 1965.

Stanton, William J., and Richard H. Buskirk, *Management of the Sales Force*, 3rd ed. Homewood, Ill.: Irwin, 1969, pp. 579–580.

CHAPTER SIX
Market and Industry Analysis

How big is the market for polyethylene? Which firms dominate the gate valve industry? What is our share of the integrated circuit market? These and related questions require market and industry analysis.

In Chapter 5 the focus was on sales analysis, dealing with the evaluation of the demand for the goods and services of the individual seller. We now shift to a consideration of market and industry analysis, examining the demand for closely substitutable goods and services of a *group* of sellers who supply a common *group* of buyers. We shall refer to a group of buyers as a market, a group of sellers as an industry. Thus the sellers of cold-rolled steel sheet comprise an industry and the "Big Four" automobile companies comprise a market; it is assumed that the market demand for cold-rolled steel sheet is equivalent to the industry supply.

MARKET DEMAND AND ITS RELATIONSHIP TO MARKET POTENTIAL AND FORECAST

The market demand for a product is a concept that requires detailed specification if it is to be measured in a meaningful way. Continuing with the previous example of cold-rolled steel sheet and adapting a definitional framework proposed by Kotler,[1] we obtain the following:

> The market demand for cold-rolled automotive steel sheet in 1976 was the total dollar volume that was shipped to the four largest United States automobile manufacturers in the period.

This definition stipulates that market demand refers to the volume of a specific product bought in a previous period by a defined customer group in a particular geographic area. As such market demand refers to a single number, not a function as usually defined. If we add the elements of the marketing programs employed by the steel producers (which are controllable) and the marketing environment that they faced (uncontrollable), it becomes apparent that the market demand could have been higher or lower in 1976, depending on the nature of the marketing programs used and the state of the environment. In this case the marketing programs used by the steel manufacturers and the environment they faced in 1976 can be specified, resulting in a market demand of a single number. At the same time we note that the market demand would have taken on other values if the marketing programs had been changed or if the environment had been different, so in fact there was a market demand function as well.

The importance of recognizing that market demand is a function becomes readily apparent when it is related to the concepts of market potential and market forecast. Figure 6–1 illustrates the relationship between the three concepts. Market demand is shown to be a function of the level of industry marketing effort and the actual marketing environment. A market forecast is shown to be the level of market demand, given an *expected* level of industry marketing effort and an *assumed* marketing environment. Market potential then becomes the *limit* approached by market demand within an assumed marketing environment, as industry marketing effort approaches infinity. Market potential therefore establishes an upper limit to market demand, while a market forecast specifies the expected level of market demand for a particular time period. Chapter 7 will be devoted to further examination of the concepts and methodologies associated with market and sales potentials; Chapter 8 will consider market and sales forecasting in some detail.

What Is a Market?

The concept of market demand has been shown to be complex, based on many elements, and systematically related to other complex market mea-

---

[1] Philip Kotler, *Marketing Management,* 3rd ed. Englewood Cliffs, N.J.: Prentice-Hall, 1976, pp. 118–120.

MARKET AND INDUSTRY ANALYSIS

Figure 6-1 Market demand and its relationship to market potential and a market forecast. Source: Philip Kotler, Marketing Management, *3rd ed. Englewood Cliffs, N.J.: Prentice-Hall, 1976, p. 121.*

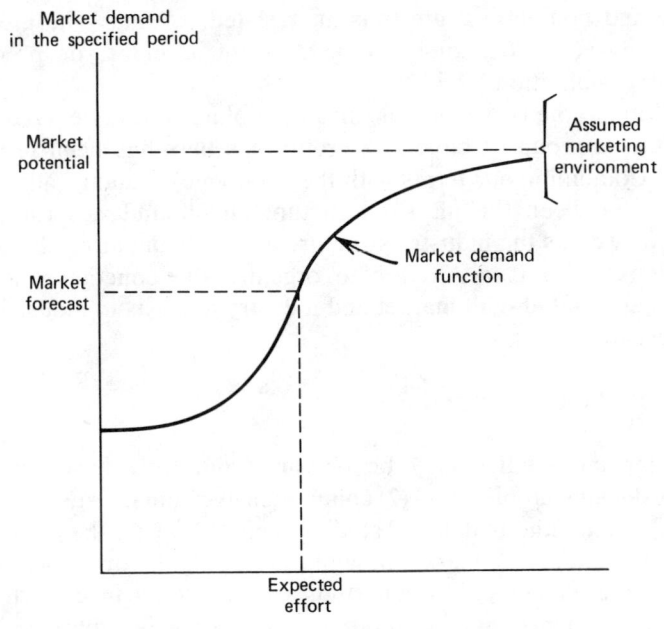

sures. As complicated as it may be, the concept of demand is not as knotty and elusive as that of a market. Steiner has noted that, "Economists use the word 'market' in two substantially different senses."[2] This often produces confusion. The first meaning encompasses the conditions under which exchange takes place between buyers and sellers, with the *conditions* summarized in the form of models of market structure. The second meaning refers to the *boundaries* that serve to identify particular groups of sellers, buyers, and products, with the boundaries setting the extent of the market. Models of market structures, such as perfect competition and oligopoly, are essentially based on the number of buyers and sellers of a given commodity in a defined market. The defined market however depends on the market boundaries, so that a change in the boundaries results in a change in the number of buyers and sellers within the market. The two economic meanings of a market,

[2] Peter O. Steiner, "Markets and Industries," in D. L. Sills, Ed., *International Encyclopedia of the Social Sciences.* New York: Free Press, 1968, p. 576.

structure and boundaries, are thus interrelated, so that "the great hazard in analyses of economic markets is the circular, or prediction-determining, definition."[3]

In addition to the two economic meanings of a market, we have defined a market as a group of buyers; a group of sellers has been termed an industry. Combining our terms with the economic meanings allows us to distinguish between the market structure and boundaries for a given product, as well as the industry structure and its boundaries. The following sections use this distinction to organize the concepts and methodologies associated with market and industry analysis in industrial marketing research.

Types of Market Demand Studies

Market demand studies may be classified into two basic types: (1) minimum demand studies, and (2) comprehensive demand studies. Wilson has noted that minimum demand studies begin ". . . with the premise that there is a minimum size market now or developing, below which the firm will not make an entry."[4] Such studies have grown in importance as researchers recognize that traditional, comprehensive market demand studies produce more information than was needed to make an entry decision, particularly decisions of a "go/no go" type. Minimum demand studies are particularly useful in making new product and new market decisions, and often involve the sequential examination of a series of market segments until a fairly clear "go/no go" decision point is reached. The information focus is usually on market size only, although limited data on other market characteristics may be collected simultaneously.

Comprehensive market demand studies, in contrast, usually involve the simultaneous development of market data for multiple markets or segments, and include data on market size, shares, structure, and trends. The relationship between minimum and comprehensive demand studies in industrial marketing research practice may therefore be measured in terms of time, cost, and scope factors. At the outset and during the new product development process in a firm, minimum demand studies should be undertaken to establish and monitor the "go/no go" decision on each product under development. Each product selected for addition to the product line should then have a comprehensive market demand study prepared prior to market entry.

---

[3] *Ibid.*
[4] Aubrey Wilson, "Industrial Marketing Research in Britain," *Journal of Marketing Research,* Vol. 6, February 1969, p. 17.

Minimum Demand Studies

Published examples of minimum demand studies are rare, for they usually contain proprietary data. Wilson provides an example of one study in which a firm was considering whether to obtain the licensing rights to manufacture chassis dynamometers.[5] The firm established that they required a minimum demand level of 75 units per year, and that a market share of 20% was available and desirable. Thus the "go/no go" decision to accept or reject the licensing rights depended on the existence of a minimum demand level of 375 units per year. After identifying six principal market segments for the product, survey research was conducted in each segment to determine: (1) the number of chassis dynamometers currently being used, and (2) the annual rate of replacement and expansion demand for the product. After completing the surveys of the six market segments, it was concluded that the annual demand was far less than the required minimum. A "no go" decision was therefore made to reject the licensing rights. There was a significant savings in marketing research costs, to say nothing of the potential losses that would have been incurred if no research had been done.

Minimum demand studies may also be conducted entirely with secondary data sources, or by an exploratory research approach that uses secondary data and a survey of knowledgeable persons. Several years ago a manufacturer of materials handling equipment was considering the possible addition of a crane and hoist product line. The firm had identified several potential acquisition candidates and was also engaged in a feasibility study regarding internal development of a product line. To narrow their range of choices with respect to specific crane and hoist products that would form the product line, the firm commissioned a minimum demand study of the United States crane and hoist market. The study was designed to provide data on the market size and sales trend for cranes and hoists based on the research procedure and data sources shown in Figure 6–2. Within two weeks the minimum demand study was completed and comprehensive market demand studies were undertaken for the specific products that the management of the firm selected on the basis of the findings of the minimum demand study.

[5]*Ibid.*, p. 18.

1. **Identify industries and products**—the *Standard Industrial Classification Manual* (1972) indicated that cranes and hoists were classified in industry SIC 3536, Hoists, industrial cranes, and monorail systems.

2. **Review secondary data sources:**

    a. Internal sources—since the proposed product line would be new to the firm, no internal accounting data were available. The prospective acquisitions had no data on market sizes and trends.

    b. External sources:

    (1) Marketing research organizations—the fastest and most economical sources of market size and trends data are organizations that offer industry studies for approximately $500 each. These organizations include: Frost and Sullivan, Morton Research Corp., and Predicasts, Inc.

    (2) U.S. Department of Commerce publications:

    U.S. Industrial Outlook—an annual review of more than 200 industries with current and trend data. Useful for an overview of materials handling equipment, and cranes and hoists specifically (SIC 3536), but lacks product detail.

    Census of Manufactures—provides detailed data on product shipments. For example, the *Census of Manufactures—1972. Industry Series: Construction, Mining, and Materials Handling Machinery and Equipment* (MC 72(2)-35B) shows that 1972 shipments of (SIC 35362 12) electric overhead traveling cranes [bridge type] were $104 million.

    (3) Trade associations—usually provide statistics only to members. This is the case with the Crane Manufacturers of America and the Hoist Manufacturers Institute.

    (4) Trade and business publications—often have statistics and surveys of the markets they serve. Both *Materials Handling* and *Materials Handling Engineering* provide useful data in this case.

3. **Contact knowledgeable persons**—marketing personnel in firms currently engaged in the industry were willing to provide estimates of market size and trends, as were personnel of construction engineering firms. Trade publication editors were also helpful in terms of data and contacts.

Figure 6-2 Research procedure and data sources for minimum demand studies (based on a crane and hoist example).

MARKET AND INDUSTRY ANALYSIS

ELEMENTS OF COMPREHENSIVE MARKET DEMAND STUDIES

Comprehensive market demand studies, which usually involve the simultaneous development of data on multiple markets and/or segments, should always include four basic elements of information:

1. *Market size*—The size of the total market, submarkets, and market segments should be measured in dollars and units (where appropriate).
2. *Market trends*—The growth rates of markets and market segments should be specified for periods preceding the period for which market size estimates are provided.
3. *Market share*—After the market sizes for various markets and market segments are established, market shares for the client firm may be specified.
4. *Industry and market structure*—The number of sellers and buyers and the size distribution of each should be determined. Profiles of the leading firms in the industry are useful, and may include information on the number of plant locations, number of employees, engineering and manufacturing evaluations, and marketing emphasis in terms of markets, channels of distribution, and so on.

Some firms also include other elements of information in their comprehensive market demand studies. These elements include:

1. *Buying behavior*—May include information on bidding/sourcing procedures, buying influences, source loyalty patterns, frequency of purchase, and timing of purchases.
2. *Technical standards and government regulations*—Industrial products and services must meet a growing number of standards and regulations. These include industry standards set by sellers, state and local codes, and federal government regulations.

Each of the basic elements of comprehensive market demand studies will now be examined. The elements and their relationships are specifically examined with the use of a model study, see the Appendix.

Market Size and Boundary Setting

Any attempt to measure the size of a market must contend with two primary factors: (1) the size of a market is a function of the specified boundaries that are used to identify particular groups of buyers, sellers, and products; and (2) measurement of the size of a market is usually conducted by measuring the output of the sellers within specified industry boundaries. The specification of boundaries presents problems at every turn: How to define a product market and segments within the market? How to define geographic boundaries? In addition there are a host of other questions regarding functional, time, and unit of measurement dimensions of markets.

For years many economists defined product markets in terms of industries, which were considered to be

> ... a group of firms closely related in the competitive process by reason of the great substitutability of their respective products, and distinguished from other firms by a 'gap' in the range of substitute products.[6]

This typical definition combined the Marshallian concept of an industry with Joan Robinson's notion of a gap in the chain of substitute products. It was generally suggested that the degree of substitutability of products could be measured by the cross-elasticity of demand. While theoretically useful, cross-elasticity measures have rarely been computed empirically, limiting the value of this approach to setting industry boundaries.

However the establishment of bases for market definition and boundary setting is much more than an issue in economic theory and analysis, for it is at the center of all manner of legal issues regarding competition. Massel has noted,

> The evaluation of the general state of competition, prospective statutory developments, industry studies, public utility regulation, tariffs, and price control are all affected by relevant market definitions.[7]

The term "relevant market" has been developed and applied in particular in merger cases since 1950, but the meaning of a "relevant market" for merger cases may not be the same as for monopoly cases. Thus,

> Any definition depends on the purposes of, and the setting for, the

---

[6] Kenneth E. Boulding, *Economic Analysis*, 3rd ed. New York: Harper & Row, 1955, p. 629.
[7] Mark S. Massel, *Competition and Monopoly*. Garden City, N.Y.: Anchor Books, 1964, p. 246.

analysis. There appears to be no fixed boundaries for industries or markets.[8]

Nevertheless there is a growing body of legal opinion in which the setting of market, industry, and product boundaries has been a central issue and useful insights have been developed therein.

One of the earliest cases that dealt with the problem of boundaries was *United States* v. *ALCOA* (1941, 1950) in which Judge Learned Hand offered guidelines for assessing whether a monopoly exists,

> ... if a company occupies 90 per cent of the relevant market, that situation is enough to constitute a monopoly; it is doubtful whether 60 or 64 per cent would be enough; and certainly 33 per cent is not.[9]

Massel points out:

> ... Judge Hand could have defined the market to match each of the three percentages he used as bench marks. Alcoa's production of virgin aluminum ingots represented 90 percent of the ingots used by all fabricators of aluminum products in the United States. On the other hand, Alcoa's production accounted for two-thirds of all aluminum available—including secondary and scrap aluminum as well as virgin ingots. Further, if the market definition covered ingots which are available for purchase, plus secondary and scrap, and if Alcoa's percentage was based solely on its sale of ingots to others (excluding its own use of the ingots it produced), Alcoa's share would be approximately one-third of the market.[10]

The Alcoa case (with Massel's commentary) illustrates the dilemma involved in establishing wide versus narrow boundaries, but there is also the question of which and how many dimensions to consider in setting boundaries. Many dimensions have been applied by the courts as a result of their recognition that no single dimension is sufficient to set boundaries: physical characteristics and end uses of products, geographic boundaries of industries and markets, units of economic measurement, and the relative separation of production facilities, customers, channels of distribution, and prices. In addition to the valuable insights provided by

[8]*Ibid.*, p. 247.
[9]*Ibid.*
[10]*Ibid.*

Massel, there is another important resource book that is helpful in understanding the problems of setting boundaries.[11] Ultimately the industrial marketing researcher must make some hard judgments about boundaries. Steiner has suggested that:[12]

> ... any particular buyer or seller has a definable set of alternative sources of supply or demand which he considers available to him.

After admitting that there are many different ways to define sets of alternatives, he recommends two that are particularly useful:[13]

> ... [identify the] real alternative sources of supply available to a defined group of buyers.
> ... [identify the] group of relevant rivals to a particular seller.

Steiner would therefore set industry boundaries by first defining a given group of buyers for a specific product or product line, next identifying the group of sellers from whom they may buy, and then determining the rivals to these sellers. Product boundaries would be established by identifying the range of products which would be substitutable or interchangeable with the specific product or product line. Finally, market boundaries would be determined by examining four considerations that influence the buyer's choice of a seller:[14]

1. Portability of the product
2. Cost of transportation of the product
3. Information about the availability and conditions of supply of the product
4. Acceptability of the customer to the seller

Steiner notes that if any one of these considerations creates a dominant limitation on the sources of supply, the setting of market boundaries is relatively simple, but the absence of any dominant limitations will make it virtually impossible to establish market boundaries.

[11] Betty Bock, *Mergers and Markets*, 3rd ed. New York: National Industrial Conference Board, 1964.
[12] Steiner, *op. cit.*, p. 577.
[13] *Ibid.*, p. 578.
[14] *Ibid.*, p. 579.

MARKET AND INDUSTRY ANALYSIS

Researchers may be able to establish industry, market, and product boundaries in part through observation and analysis of secondary data, but at least some of the needed information may require surveys among buyers to determine their perceptions of different sources of supply and substitute products.

After the boundaries of relevant groups of buyers, sellers, and products, have been set, measurement of the size of a market may be initiated. Since the measurement of market size is one of the elements of a comprehensive market demand study and since we defined the concept of market demand as the volume of a product (service) bought in a *previous* period, it is expected that secondary data on market size will be available. In the United States and other industrial nations published economic statistics tend to emphasize the output of sellers. There are relatively few statistics available on the consumption of buyers. We begin our search of external secondary sources by searching for measures of industry output classified by product, seller locations, and time. To make the process of conducting a comprehensive market demand study as clear as possible, a model is presented in the Appendix. It is presented in outline and is specifically prepared for a United States manufacturer of cranes. The format is sufficiently general however so that it can be used as a model for any seller of industrial goods and services. It contains actual estimated data on output, data sources, and a host of market information, thereby suggesting to researchers how to conduct comparable studies for any other industry. Further discussion of the elements of a comprehensive market demand study will center on the model study with variations in research methodology noted where appropriate.

We shall assume that the firm commissioning the model study is a United States manufacturer of cranes, that it has been engaged in crane manufacture for more than 20 years, and that internal sources of secondary data are of little value in determining market size. If the firm is interested only in the size of the crane market in which it has already participated, it could measure market size by determining the shares of the crane market and its segments that it has held. In this case, as in general, internal data on market shares are either unavailable or unreliable. Consequently we must start with external secondary data. Further, let us assume that no industry studies of sufficient detail are available for purchase from an external marketing research organization. We start therefore with United States government data and information sources. Crane products and the producing industry are classified in SIC 3536, Hoists, industrial cranes, and monorail systems which are defined in the *1972 Standard Industrial Classification Manual* as:

Establishments primarily engaged in manufacturing overhead traveling cranes, hoists, and monorail systems for installation in factories, warehouses, and other industrial and commercial establishments.

The model study examines the crane market for 1975 and assumes that it was initiated in December 1975, thereby establishing the external secondary data that were available at that time.

Determining Market Size by Market Trend Analysis

Studies of market size are usually commissioned for the current year or the preceding year period. This delay in publishing United States government data sharply limits the availability of information for the desired period. Therefore it is often necessary to begin to determine market size for the desired period through the use of market trend analysis. Three United States government publications provide the basic data available for market trend analysis:

1. *U.S. Industrial Outlook*—The 1975 volume provided data on the value of shipments for SIC 3436 for 1967 and 1970–1975 as well as 1973–1975 estimates and actual data for earlier years.
2. *Annual Survey of Manufactures*—The 1973 survey was available and provided shipment data for 1973 at the 5-digit product level.
3. *Census of Manufactures*—The 1972 *Industry Series: Construction, Mining, and Materials Handling Machinery and Equipment* (MC 72(2)-35 B) was available in March 1975 and included detailed data on output for 1972 and 1967 as well as shipments figures for 1968–1971, 1963, and 1958.

The 1975 estimate for the value of shipments for SIC 3536 was set at $620 million based on the estimate presented in the *1975 U.S. Industrial Outlook*. At the 5-digit SIC product level the primary industry of interest was SIC 35362, overhead traveling cranes and monorail systems. Value of shipments data for this industry for the years 1967–1973 were drawn from the *Census of Manufactures* and the *Annual Survey of Manufactures*, and a trend analysis program was used to produce a market size estimate for 1975. The trend analysis was conducted with a standard least squares linear regression routine on a calculator—a procedure which is crude statistically, but sufficient for the purpose. According to the trend analysis, the 1975 market size for SIC 35362 was $254.5 million, indicating essentially no growth between 1972 and 1975.

MARKET AND INDUSTRY ANALYSIS

Before accepting the results of the trend analysis, the researcher should attempt to verify the results by using ratio-estimate techniques to obtain independently an estimate of market size. Table A-1 shows the ratio of the value of shipments for SIC 35362 as a percent of SIC 3536. Taking the arithmetic mean of these ratios for 1967–1973 period gives an average ratio of 51%. This ratio-estimate when applied to the 1975 estimate of $620 million for SIC 3536 gives a 1975 estimate of $316 million for SIC 35362. Since this estimate is substantially higher than the trend analysis estimate of $254.5 million, further investigation is required.

The ratio-estimate technique produced a higher estimate ($316 million) than the trend analysis method, and the data were of more recent origin, suggesting that perhaps a shift in trend was occurring during the 1972–1975 period. Assuming that no other external secondary data were available, the next step would be to contact a group of knowledgeable persons. A good starting point would be with those serving on the crane industry desks at the U.S. Department of Commerce and the Bureau of the Census. Additional calls might be made to editors of the crane industry journals, personnel in construction engineering firms, and other sources of information noted previously in Chapter 2.

After checking with these knowledgeable persons, these findings emerged: (1) the crane industry experienced a rapid growth from 1972–1975 as a result of a sharp increase in new plant construction, and (2) there seemed to be a general agreement that United States government data tends to underestimate the size of the crane market. As a result the final 1975 estimate of the size of the market for SIC 3536 was $760 million, the ratio of SIC 35362 to SIC 3536 was 55% and the consequent 1975 estimate of the size of the market for SIC 35362 was set at $418 million.

Finding the Size of Market Segments by Ratio/Estimate Techniques

Assume that the firm commissioning the study is primarily interested in the size of the market for electric overhead traveling cranes (SIC 35362 11–14), and not interested in the other products within SIC 35362: hand powered overhead traveling cranes (SIC 35362 15); automatic stacking machines (SIC 35362 41); monorail systems, powered and manual (SIC 35362 52,54); parts and attachments for overhead traveling cranes, monorail systems, and automatic stacking machines (SIC 34362 55,57); and overhead traveling cranes and monorail systems not clearly classified (SIC 35362 00). Table A-2 shows that shipments of electric overhead traveling cranes in 1967 accounted for 75% of the shipments for SIC 35362, falling to 68% in 1972. If we assume that the rapid growth of crane demand in the 1972–1975 period brought the ratio back to 75% in 1975, the market size for electric overhead traveling cranes was $314 million.

Table A–2 indicates that there are four major classifications of electric overhead traveling cranes, providing an opportunity to estimate market size for each classification (product type). Assuming that the 1972 ratios of each product type to the total hold for 1975, the respective market sizes would be:

Total—Electric overhead traveling cranes	$314 million
SIC 35362 11 Gantry type	$189 million (60.3%)
35362 12 Bridge type	85 million (27.2%)
35362 13 Stacker/storage type	24 million (7.5%)
35362 14 Others, including jib type	16 million (5.0%)

Data are also available on the number of cranes shipped in 1972 within each product type classification, thereby permitting the calculation of average prices within each classification. By assuming that the ratios of the numbers shipped within each product type stayed constant between 1972–1975 and estimating the change in the price index for electric overhead traveling cranes during the period, additional insight into the market size of the product type segments may be obtained.

There is another segmentation dimension of interest in the market for cranes lift capacity, for which United States government data are not available. Trade association data on lift capacity of cranes shipped are available to association members, but nonmembers must rely on surveys of knowledgeable persons for such information. Assume that these sources provided a 1975 breakdown of crane shipments in units by lift capacity and average prices along the following lines:

Capacity	Number Shipped (Units)	Average Price ($)	Value of Shipments
Under 5 tons	3,000	$ 5,000	$ 15 million
5–10 tons	4,400	15,000	66 million
11–30 tons	3,500	35,000	123 million
31–50 tons	675	90,000	61 million
Over 50 tons	350	140,000	49 million
Totals	11,925		314 million

Insight into the geographic segmentation of the overhead traveling crane and monorail system market (SIC 35362) may be gained from Table

MARKET AND INDUSTRY ANALYSIS

A-3. The value of shipments in 1967 and 1972 for SIC 35362 are shown for regions, divisions, and states within the United States. Again ratio estimate techniques may be used to develop 1975 estimates for specific products within these geographic areas.

Market Growth Rates as a Measure of Market Trends

Although market size is certainly a critical element in comprehensive market demand studies, market trends are of significant interest too. Market trends, as defined here, are concerned with changes in the sizes of markets and market segments, particularly with the *rate* of such changes. One of the most common signs of present or potential marketing problems is a declining or stable market growth rate; increasing market growth rates tend to signal market opportunities. Thus a major indicator of market and industry attractiveness is the market trend, measured by the market growth rate.

We are interested in the growth rates of the crane market and its various market segments. The market data in Tables A-1 and A-2 provide the basis for determining numerous growth rates. Since industrial marketing researchers are often called upon to calculate growth rates and generally have access to a hand calculator, the following compound growth formula and calculation procedure provides a simple guide to the calculation of market growth rates:

$$g = \left(\frac{LV}{EV}\right)^{1/n} - 1$$

where:
- g = compound growth rate (per period)
- LV = latest value in a time series (= FV, future value)
- EV = earliest value in a time series (= PV, present value)
- n = number of periods in a time series

On a Texas Instruments 51A calculator, the calculation procedure is as follows:

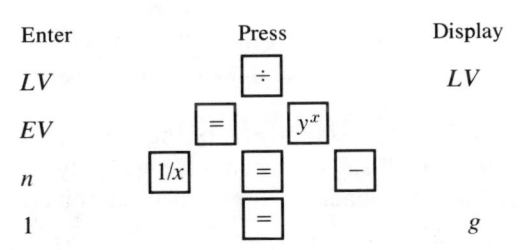

Enter	Press	Display
LV	÷	LV
EV	= , y^x	
n	1/x , = , −	
1	=	g

Some illustrative market growth rates for SIC 35362 are:

Period	Compound Annual Growth Rates
1958–1967	+ 7.3%
1958–1973	+ 5.6
1963–1967	+13.2
1963–1973	+ 7.4
1967–1973	+ 2.4
1967–1975(c)	+ 8.0
1973–1975(c)	+19.2

These widely varying market growth rates for various periods dramatically illustrate the volatility of the larger industry classification (SIC 35362); even greater volatility is evident for the more specific industry classification of SIC 35362 11–14, electric overhead traveling cranes:

Period	Compound Annual Growth Rates
1967–1972	+ 1.2%
1967–1975(c)	+ 7.7
1972–1975(c)	+22.1

Similar calculations could be developed for each of the market segments of the electric overhead traveling crane market as an aid in spotting either marketing problems or opportunities.

Determining Market Share

Based on the definitions of the electric overhead traveling crane market and its various market segments, the data in Tables A–6, A–2, and A–3 establish the levels of market demand for 1975. The market share of an individual firm may be determined by the following formula:

$$\text{Market share} = \frac{\text{Individual firm sales for period}}{\text{Market demand for period}}$$

Assume that the 1975 sales (shipments) of the Midwest Crane Company totaled $20 million, that all units shipped were bridge type cranes, and that all units shipped had lift capacities in excess of 30 tons. As shown in the

MARKET AND INDUSTRY ANALYSIS

following tabulation, the market shares of the firm varied considerably, depending on the boundaries of the market or market segments:

Market/Market Segment	Market Share—Midwest Crane Company
Electric overhead traveling cranes	$6.4\% = \dfrac{\$20}{\$314}$
Bridge type cranes	$10.6\% = \dfrac{\$20}{\$189}$
Over 30 tons capacity	$18.2\% = \dfrac{\$20}{\$110}$

It is apparent therefore that literally each seller in an industry will have an infinite number of market share positions with each market share figure determined by industry, market, and product boundaries.

Industry Structure

Market and industry analysis relies heavily on the availability of external secondary data, particularly United States government data which tends to be oriented toward output measures of economic activity. Thus the Standard Industrial Classification (SIC) system of classifying economic activity assigns SIC numbers to establishments on the basis of their output rather than their consumption. As a result we know much more about industry structure than market structure for virtually every product and service, simply because so much data on industry output are available.

The major determinants of industry structure are the number of sellers, their size distribution, and their interaction in serving a specified product/market. A good place to start a study of industry structure is with the *Census of Manufactures*. The usefulness of the census data is very much a matter of the level of product homogeneity within the 4- and 5-digit SIC levels, with the most detailed statistics being available at the 4-digit industry level. In the case of the electric overhead traveling crane industry (SIC 35362 11–14), its value of shipments in 1972 accounted for less than one-third of the total shipments of establishments classified in SIC 3536 (Hoists, cranes, and monorails). Table A–4 illustrates these relationships for the value of shipments at the 4- and 5-digit SIC level, starting with SIC 3536.

In Chapter 3, we examined the use of the primary product specialization ratio and the coverage ratio as means of adjusting some of the problems associated with the census practice of assigning multi-product establishments to a single industry. Table A-5 shows that establishments classified in SIC 3536 shipped only 78% of their output in primary (SIC 3536) products, and that 84% of all shipments of SIC 3536 products were made by establishments classified in that industry. Relative to other industries, SIC 3536 contains establishments that are more diversified with regard to product lines. This results in a comparatively low primary product specialization ratio of 78%. In addition the coverage ratio of 84% is also relatively low, indicating that a higher-than-average proportion of SIC 3536 products (hoists, cranes, and monorails) were shipped by establishments not classified in SIC 3536.

Moving to analysis of industry structure at the 5-digit SIC level, Table A-6 shows that the primary product specialization ratio for SIC 35362 in 1972 was 71%, so that establishments classified in this industry were even more product-diversified than those in SIC 3536. The coverage ratio for SIC 35362 was 88% however. This was higher than that for SIC 3536, indicating that a higher proportion of the total shipments of overhead traveling cranes and monorail systems (SIC 35362) were made by establishments specializing in such products than in a broader industry classification (SIC 3536) in which hoists were included. Further insight into the components of the coverage ratio is provided by Table A-7, which shows the extent to which various related industries (SIC 3531, 3532, 3534, 3535, and 3537) accounted for the primary product shipments made by other industries (line H in Tables A-5 and A-6).

Another dimension of industry structure that can be investigated with the aid of the *Census of Manufactures* is the size distribution of establishments in terms of the number of establishments, value of shipments per establishment, and the value of shipments per employee. We have noted that the Midwest Crane Company had estimated shipments in 1975 of $20 million. In 1975 the average number of employees at Midwest was 675. In order to compare these data against those shown in Table A-8 however it is necessary to obtain a consistent time frame: the value of shipments per establishment and employee in Table A-8 are from the *1972 Census*. In 1972 Midwest had sales (shipments) of $12 million, one establishment, and 390 employees: placing these data within the context of Table A-8 shows that Midwest in 1972 was in the top 10% of the establishments in the SIC 3536 industry and was significantly larger than the average establishment in SIC 35362. If 1975 comparisons were desired, Midwest could obtain data on individual firm's shipments and number of employees for 1973 and 1974 (with estimates for 1975); com-

MARKET AND INDUSTRY ANALYSIS

pare the data with the industry estimates in Table A–1 for 1975; and calculate expected size distributions for shipments per establishment and employee in 1975.

Additional insight into industry structure is provided by a publication developed from the *Census of Manufactures* entitled *Concentration Ratios in Manufacturing*.[15] Table A–9 shows that concentration, measured by the share of value of shipments accounted for by the largest companies in both SIC 3536 and 35362, remained stable from 1958 to 1967 and then decreased considerably from 1967 to 1972. These data may be used to determine the size distribution of establishments also by combining them with data from Table A–8. Table A–8 indicates that there were 66 establishments classified in SIC 35362 in 1972. Since total shipments for the industry were $253.5 million, the average value of shipments per establishment was $3.8 million. Taking the data on the shares of total shipments accounted for by the largest establishments in the industry, we obtain the following:

Establishment Group	Value of Shipments per Establishment
4 largest	$20.9
5–8 largest	10.8
9–20 largest	5.3
21–50 largest	1.6
51–66 largest	1.0

In order to bring these data up to date in 1975, there is a need for detailed information about the individual firms and establishments that make up the SIC 35362 industry. The following section responds to this need.

Competitive Profiles and Industry Structure Analysis

Profiles should be prepared for each major manufacturer in an industry as a vital part of a comprehensive market demand study and as an important source of information in industry structure analysis. As usual the competitive profiles should be assembled initially from secondary data sources. Assuming that Midwest Crane Company had no internal secondary data of relevance, external sources would be the starting place. Although there

---

[15]U.S. Bureau of the Census, *Census of Manufactures—1972. Special Report Series: Concentration Ratios in Manufacturing* (MC 72(SR)–2, Washington: U.S. Government Printing Office, 1975.

are numerous possible sources, three are selected because of their general availability in corporate and public libraries:

1. *Dun and Bradstreet directories*—the *Million Dollar, Middle Market*, and *Metalworking* directories (where appropriate).
2. *Standard and Poor's Register of Corporations*—Volume 3 indexes corporations by SIC number.
3. *Thomas Register of American Manufacturers*—One of the volumes in the multivolume directory contains an index of firms by SIC number.

Using the index of firms by SIC number in each source will produce a list of firms classified in the industry. The Dun and Bradstreet directories and Standard and Poor's *Register* will also provide information on sales, number of employees, and principle products.

After a comprehensive list of firms classified in the industry of interest has been developed, the major firms should be separated for more intensive investigation. There are three major sources of information:

1. *Moody's Industrial Manual*—contains detailed information on sales, products, and plants of major firms.
2. *F & S Indexes*—published by Predicasts, Inc., contains information on industries and firms drawn from key periodicals.
3. *SEC (Securities and Exchange Commission) 10–K Reports*—a 10-K report (Part I, Items 1–3) should be ordered for each major firm in the industry.

Another source that is often of value is Standard and Poor's Industry Surveys, which frequently identifies the leading firms in an industry and provides sales and financial data on the leading firms within many major industries.

Additional information is needed for comprehensive competitive profiles, and is available primarily from surveys of knowledgeable persons. Among the most important items of information that is needed and available are:

1. Relative size and market shares of leading firms in the industry
2. Major markets and market segments for each major firm
3. Technical and performance information on products of each major firm
4. Plans for increasing capacity, dropping products, and so on, for each major firm
5. Marketing and distribution practices for each major firm

MARKET AND INDUSTRY ANALYSIS

Names and titles of all persons contacted in a survey of knowledgeable persons should be listed in the study report, but attributed quotations are generally not used. It should also be noted that persons are generally not asked to supply information about their own firm (such information is usually proprietary), but instead about the industry and other firms in the industry.

Table A–10 shows the estimated sales and market shares of the major firms in the electric overhead traveling crane industry in 1975. Only the two leading firms in the industry are identified specifically; the Midwest Crane Company is among the four firms shown as Firms A, B, C, D. Table A–11 illustrates the type of information presented in a competitive profile by using the Harnischfeger Corporation as an example. A partial list of persons contacted in the survey of knowledgeable persons is given in Table A–14 but without names to perserve confidentiality.

Market Structure

The weakest element in comprehensive market demand studies is usually market structure, basically because there is so little external secondary data on consumption patterns for industrial goods and services. It is obviously important to know: *which* markets are purchasing and consuming industrial goods and services; *when* they are purchasing and the rate of consumption; *where* they are purchasing and consuming; and *how much* they are purchasing and consuming. In addition the same information is needed for individual firms within the markets. The paucity of data is due to the tendency of governmental and private statistical agencies to measure economic activity primarily in terms of output (shipments, and so on) rather than input (consumption, and so on).

An examination of market structure should therefore show the nature, number, and size distribution of markets and firms, and contain some indication of the trends therein. Again the starting point should be with internal secondary data. Since Midwest Crane Company had been serving the crane market for 20 years and assuming that internal sales records for at least several years past were available, an analysis of prior sales should be conducted. Each customer should be assigned an SIC number based on the output of its principal products, and then sales analysis should proceed by SIC group at the 2-, 3-, and 4-digit levels. The primary focus of the sales analysis should be to establish usage factors for each major SIC group at both the firm and market levels. The most common usage factors are based on the number of employees, then purchases (or sales) per employee ratios are developed for the firm and the market. Thus in the case of electric overhead traveling cranes, usage factors might be established for the SIC 3312 (Blast furnace) market on the basis of one crane per 100 employees. Demand would be divided into replacement and expansion demand, and then demand at the firm level allocated on the basis of observed replacement and expansion practices.

A major limitation in determining market structure on the basis of internal data is that few, if any, industrial firms have sales patterns that are truly representative of their industry. As a result there is a need for external secondary data against which internal data can be checked. There are two basic sources of external secondary data for these purposes: input-output data and periodical surveys.

Some gross estimates of which markets are purchasing cranes and the relative size of these markets may be obtained from input-output data, developed by the U.S. Department of Commerce from economic census data. Table A-12 presents the best available information from input-output statistics, but it should be emphasized that the information is really not very useful. Chapter 9 presents a detailed examination of input-output analysis. For now we can identify three severe limitations to the data shown in Table A-12:

1. The data are old, based on the *1967 Census of Manufactures*.
2. Only limited detailed data are available (those dealing with Intermediate Outputs), and the categories are too broad to be useful.
3. The portion of the output that goes into the Final Demand category (as capital equipment in specific industries) can only be identified at the materials handling industry level (SIC 3534–3537) of which cranes are only a small part.

With these caveats, examination of Table A-12 reveals that the major portion of the intermediate output of hoists, cranes, and monorails goes into (is consumed by) new construction. Within the final demand category, the major consumers are: (1) wholesale and retail trade, and (2) the food industry.

A second potential source of external secondary data is that of periodicals serving the industry. For example, a survey of the crane and hoist market was conducted in 1971 by *Material Handling Engineering* among those receiving that periodical. The survey revealed that the major markets for cranes were:

SIC 32 Stone, clay, glass products
    33 Primary metal industries
    34 Fabricated metal products
    35 Machinery, except electrical

MARKET AND INDUSTRY ANALYSIS

36 Electrical machinery
37 Transportation equipment

Assume that Midwest's shipments corresponded with the findings of the survey, and that more than 70% of its sales in recent years have been made to the six SIC 2-digit market groups identified in the survey. We are now in a position to indicate the major markets for electric overhead traveling cranes and their estimated size by means of market structure analysis.

Determining Major Markets and Market Sizes by Market Structure Analysis

A relatively crude yet workable approach to the determination of major market segments and their estimated sizes within a market is provided by a combination of the methods just described. Based on the finding that Midwest's shipments tended to be concentrated within six SIC 2-digit market groups (SIC 32–37), assume that the usage factors per customer employee in 1975 for Midwest Crane were as shown in Appendix Table 13. These usage factors were developed by determining Midwest sales to each major SIC group and by dividing those sales by the number of employees in customer accounts within each SIC group. By estimating Midwest's market share within each SIC group and dividing the sales of Midwest by its market share, we obtain the 1975 market demand for each SIC group. If desired, the calculations may be carried further to SIC 3- and 4-digit groups. Demand can be separated into replacement and expansion demand, and the demand levels of individual customer accounts estimated, assuming that appropriate additional data are available for such tasks.

Surveys of knowledgeable persons and market surveys may also be used to determine major markets and market sizes. Since surveys tend to be relatively expensive, time-consuming, and highly perishable, they should be viewed primarily as means of supplementing and improving market estimates developed first from secondary data sources. A continuing program of measuring market sizes and market shares will also provide estimates of market trends and growth rates, thereby providing a valuable data base for marketing planning and control.

SUMMARY

Market and industry analysis examines the demand for closely substitutable goods and services of a group of sellers who supply a common group of buyers. A group of buyers is referred to as a market; a group of sellers as an industry. Market demand is both a specific figure and a function of the level of industry marketing effort and of the actual marketing environment.

The term market encompasses both structure (defined in terms of the numbers of buyers and sellers) and boundaries. Setting the boundaries directly affects structure of market and industry. Many bases for boundary setting have been suggested. Following Steiner, boundaries can be defined by first identifying a group of buyers and sellers for a specific product or product line, next identifying the group of sellers from whom they buy, and then identifying the rivals to those sellers. Product boundaries would be established by identifying the range of interchangeable or substitutable products for the product or product line being studied. Primary data collection may be necessary for the purpose of establishing the range of interchangeability and substitutability.

Minimum demand studies usually focus on the size of total market demand for "go/no go" decisions concerning entry into new products or markets. Comprehensive demand studies on the other hand involve the simultaneous development of data on market size, trends, market share, and industry and demand structure for submarkets and market segments. Comprehensive market demand studies would be conducted after the "go" decision for new products was reached.

The starting point of data gathering for comprehensive demand studies is with the *Standard Industrial Classification Manual* for industry and product definitions. Initial estimates of market size based on the *U.S. Industrial Outlook* and on trend analysis based on data from the *Annual Survey of Manufactures* are verified with ratio estimates of the relationship between 5-digit product figures to 4-digit industry figures. A further check with knowledgeable persons is recommended before the final demand figures are set.

Market size by segment can be estimated by means of the *Census of Manufactures* data for value of shipments and number of units by product classes within product type classifications. Once the market size is determined, market share measures can be obtained for a variety of market segment boundaries using the ratio of company sales to the segment size figures.

Industry structure data are far more extensive than demand structure data because of the emphasis of government and private data agencies on output rather than consumption. Primary product ratios, industry specialization ratios, and concentration ratios—followed by a search through appropriate directories—will produce a list of firms as well as their key rivals, approximate sales, the number of their employees, and

MARKET AND INDUSTRY ANALYSIS

other data. However information on their key market segments, shares, products, plans, and practices must come for the most part from surveys of knowledgeable individuals.

Market structure data are less extensive. However internal secondary data on shipments to customers classified by SIC groups can be tied to the number of production employees or other statistical series to develop estimates of market size and market share. The estimates can be supplemented with surveys of knowledgeable persons.

SUGGESTED READINGS

Bock, Betty, *Mergers and Markets*, 3rd ed. New York: National Industrial Conference Board, 1964.

Boulding, Kenneth E., *Economic Analysis*, 3rd ed. New York: Harper & Row.

Massel, Mark S., *Competition and Monopoly*. Garden City, N.Y.: Anchor Books, 1964.

Steiner, Peter O., "Markets and Industries," in D. L. Sills, Ed., *International Encyclopedia of the Social Sciences*. New York: Free Press, 1968.

Wilson, Aubrey, "Industrial Marketing Research in Britain," *Journal of Marketing Research*, Vol. 6, February 1969, pp. 17–18.

CHAPTER SEVEN

Market and Sales Potentials

A distinction was drawn between three concepts of demand measurement: demand, potential, and forecast. Figure 6–1 illustrated the relationships between these three concepts, and Chapter 6 examined demand analysis. We now turn to the concept of potentials. The concept itself is basically very simple, for it deals with the *maximum* level of demand for a product or service in a given environment. Beneath the simplicity of the concept of potentials however lies some of the greatest confusion and misunderstanding in all of marketing research. The problem appears to result from a need and desire to translate an abstract concept into a practical measure.

The idea that there exists some maximum level of demand for a product or service that is reached when it is purchased by all possible buyers up to their limits of satiation is indeed an abstraction. It is also a convenient and useful abstraction, for it serves as a primary indication of marketing opportunity. However translating the abstraction into a useful and practical measure requires a definition of terms, and it is here that the problems begin. First, and perhaps most importantly, potentials differ from both demand and forecasts by being independent of a finite level of marketing effort, either actual or expected. Kotler has defined potential in terms of, ". . . the limit approached by demand as marketing effort goes to

MARKET AND SALES POTENTIALS

infinity."[1] Philosophers and mathematicians have long debated the concept and measurement of infinity with little resolution, so marketing researchers are unlikely to be very interested or successful in pursuing such an abstruse matter. Thus the term potential is often used as being synonomous with demand and forecast, in that it is related to a finite, rather than infinite, level of marketing effort.

A second problem with the definition of potentials is that of recognizing the meaning of the phrase, ". . . in a given environment." The dynamic nature of potentials is reflected by noting that a change in environment will usually result in a change in potential. Further the term "environment" includes the following dimensions:

1. A specified time period
2. Stage of the business cycle, industry life cycle, and product/service life cycle
3. Industry structure
4. Industry, market, and product boundaries

Figure 7–1 illustrates the dynamic character of potentials by portraying the effect of a change in one dimension of the environment (stage of the business cycle) on the level of market potential. If you then envision the effect of the stage of the industry life cycle (a new, emerging industry or a stable, mature one); product life cycle stage (introduction, growth, and so on); industry structure (degree of concentration); and the effects of changing industry, market, and product boundaries, it becomes evident that the definition and measurement of potentials is indeed a challenge. It is a worthy challenge also because of the importance of potentials in planning, executing, and controlling marketing strategy and programs.

Uhl and Schoner note that there has also been disagreement over the distinction between market and sales potential, leading them to reject the distinction and discuss only potentials.[2] Their "potentials" are actually market potentials, in that they include the demand available to all industry sellers of a product or service. Sales (company) potentials then refer to the *share* of the market potential that is available to an individual firm within the industry. There is very good reason to maintain the distinction between market and sales potentials, and the term "sales potential" should be distinguished from both "market share" and "sales forecast."

---

[1] Philip Kotler, *Marketing Management,* 3rd ed. Englewood Cliffs, N.J.: Prentice-Hall, 1976, p. 121.
[2] Kenneth P. Uhl and Bertram Schoner, *Marketing Research.* New York: Wiley, 1969, p. 475.

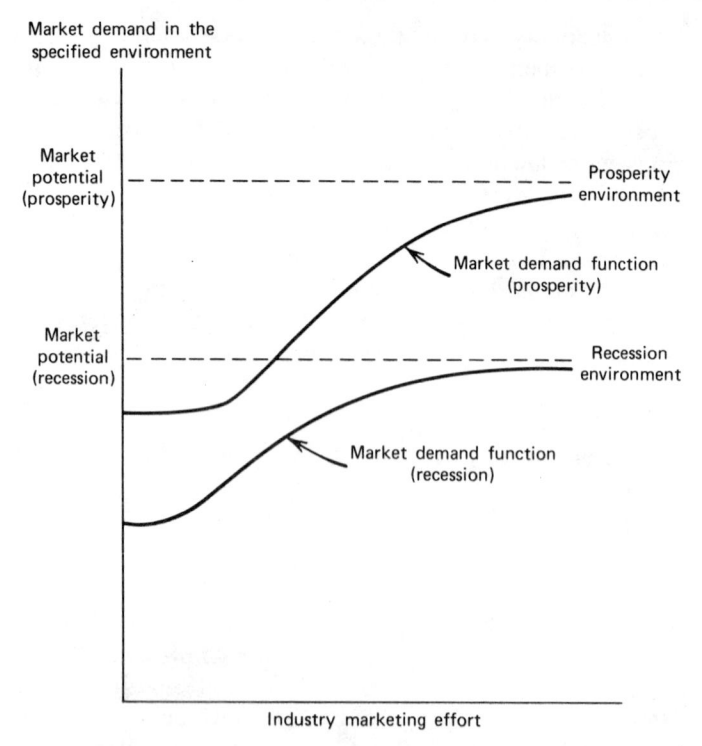

Figure 7-1 Environmental effects on potential and demand levels. Source: Philip Kotler, Marketing Management, *3rd ed. Englewood Cliffs, N.J.: Prentice-Hall, 1976, p. 121.*

Consequently both market and sales potentials are measured and illustrated in this chapter.

Uses of Market and Sales Potential Data

The important role that market and sales potentials may play in marketing planning and strategy is well-illustrated by reviewing the variety of uses for potentials data, as suggested by Hummel.[3] Assume that the St. Joe Minerals Corporation, a leading producer of zinc oxide, has just completed a study of the market and sales potential for zinc oxide in the United States and is now considering the various possible uses for the potentials in marketing planning and strategy:

1. *Sales territories*—The determination of the market and sales potential for each control unit (county) for zinc oxide will allow St. Joe to

---

[3]Francis E. Hummel, *Market and Sales Potentials.* New York: Ronald, 1961, pp. 9–10.

aggregate control units into sales territories of equal sales potential, one of the generally accepted practices for territory design.[4]
2. *Sales quotas*—Salesmen's goals, in the form of sales quotas, should be established for each territory on the basis of the sales potential of the territory and St. Joe's territory sales of zinc oxide in the preceding period.[5]
3. *Distribution strategy*—St. Joe may decide to use a direct sales force in those territories that are concentrated and compact, and on the basis of the equal potential principle rely on manufacturer's representatives or distributors to serve those territories which encompass several states. Departing from the equal potential principle, such territories might be reduced in size and assigned to outside organizations to ensure better account coverage.[6]
4. *Allocating advertising and sales promotion efforts*—Zinc oxide is used in a variety of products (rubber, paint, pharmaceuticals, and so on), and St. Joe could determine how much advertising expense should be incurred in each end-use market segment by using the MEDIAC model which is based on the sales potentials of each segment.[7]
5. *Locating new plants and warehouses*—A decision on where to locate new plants or warehouses for the distribution of zinc oxide should be based on sales potentials rather than demand, as suggested in the literature.[8]
6. *Sales compensation*—Sales potential may serve as one of the bases for determining the compensation levels of St. Joe's sales force, although some have argued that profit potential is a superior measure.[9]
7. *Salesmen's performance*—Perhaps the most important factor to consider in evaluating the performance of the St. Joe sales force is territory potential (market and sales),[10] although the distributors for St. Joe could use potentials to measure the performance of their salesmen.[11]

---

[4]Richard D. Crisp, *Sales Planning and Control*. New York: McGraw-Hill, 1961, p. 241.
[5]Philip Kotler, *Marketing Decision-Making:* A Model Building Approach. New York: Holt, Rinehart and Winston, 1971, pp. 407–419.
[6]Ibid., pp. 290–298.
[7]John D. C. Little and Leonard M. Lodish, "A Media Planning Calculus," *Operations Research*, January–February 1969, pp. 1–35.
[8]M. L. Gerson and R. B. Maffei, "Technical Characteristics of Distribution Simulators," *Management Science*, Vol. 10, October 1963, pp. 62–69.
[9]Ralph L. Day and Peter D. Bennett, "Should Salesmen's Compensation Be Geared to Profits?," *Journal of Marketing*, Vol. 26, October 1962, pp. 6–9.
[10]*Measuring Salesmen's Performance*, Studies in Business Policy, no. 114. New York: National Industrial Conference Board, 1965, p. 9.
[11]*Sales Analysis*, Studies in Business Policy, no. 113. New York: National Industrial Conference Board, 1965, pp. 18–23.

The cited National Industrial Conference Board studies provide case examples of the use of potentials to measure sales performance.

8. *Finding prospect accounts*—St. Joe could use a system developed by the Air Reduction Company for finding prospect accounts. This is based on a procedure for estimating the potential volume of purchases from any account.[12] Another very useful source of information on finding prospects is Hummel's article on pinpointing prospects in which he presents four different methods for identifying prospects.[13] For selected industrial products, another approach available is based on the *Census of Manufactures* consumption data.[14]

9. *New product introduction*—St. Joe has recently developed a new product, zinc dust, and should determine the market and sales potential for the product as one of the primary bases for a "go/no go" decision on market entry. A comprehensive study of methods for estimating the market and sales potentials for new industrial products with nine case studies is available and will be reviewed in this chapter.[15]

ESTIMATING POTENTIAL FOR ESTABLISHED PRODUCTS

Prior to considering various methods that may be used to estimate potentials for industrial products and services, it should be noted that different methods are required for new versus established products and services. In this case the distinction between new and established products is based on whether the product is new to the industry, rather than to the individual seller. Estimates of potentials for new products require different research methods and tend to be much more subjective than those for established products.

Methods for estimating potentials for established products may be classified into two groups, based on contrasting approaches: (1) breakdown methods: these begin with aggregate industry or market data and break down the data into segments of interest to the firm, and (2) buildup methods: these start with individual accounts (customers and prospects) and aggregate the data to the industry or market level. Uhl and Schoner

---

[12]*Ibid.*, p. 31.
[13]Francis E. Hummel, "Pinpointing Prospects for Industrial Sales," *Journal of Marketing*, Vol. 25, July 1960, pp. 26–31.
[14]Alfred Lieberman, "Further Pinpointing of Prospects for Industrial Sales," *Journal of Marketing*, Vol. 25, April 1961, pp. 64–68.
[15]Morgan B. McDonald, Jr., *Appraising the Market for New Industrial Products*, Studies in Business Policy no. 123, New York: National Industrial Conference Board, 1967, Chap. 3.

MARKET AND SALES POTENTIALS

have termed these approaches macro and micro methods respectively. There are numerous other synonyms employed in the literature.[16]

Breakdown Methods

Basically there are two approaches to the use of breakdown methods for estimating potentials. The first—termed the "Total Market Measure" method by Hummel, the "Direct Data" method by Boyd and Westfall, and the "Sales Index" method by Uhl and Schoner—is characterized by the use of available total industry or market data to estimate market and sales potentials. The second—named the "Statistical Series" method by Hummel, the "Corollary Data" method by Boyd and Westfall, and the "Single/Multiple-Variable Indexes" method by Uhl and Schoner—is based on the determination of observed statistical relationships between industry and market (sales and consumption) data on the one hand and on the other one or more socio-economic variables descriptive of the industry and market (such as employment). Hummel's terminology will be used, and each approach will be illustrated with one or more examples of how market and sales potentials may be derived.

Total Market Measure Method. The Total Market Measure method for calculating market and sales potentials is distinguished by its reliance on total industry or market data (usually shipments or consumption) as the basis for calculating potentials. A critical factor to consider in evaluating the applicability of this method is: (1) the availability of data on total industry shipments, or (2) total market consumption for the specific product or service in question, broken down by control units or segments of interest. It is rare indeed to have access to such data, especially on a time series basis that may permit the setting of different levels of potentials for varying environmental conditions. One usually settles for more general product or service data at the 4-digit SIC level, rather than 5- or more SIC digits, provided that even those data are available.

Since the primary application of the Total Market Measure method is at the control unit or segment level, the usual approach is to establish a sales or consumption index based on the available total industry or market data. If these data are reasonably accurate and current, Hummel suggests that the potentials based on such data are, "theoretically the most accurate."[17] Two examples will serve to indicate the development and application of the Total Market Measure method.

Hummel provides an example of the industry (shipments) data approach with a case study of the Bassick Company, the largest caster

[16]Uhl and Schoner, *op. cit.*, Chap. 15.
[17]Hummel, *Market and Sales Potentials, op. cit.*, p. 126.

manufacturer in the United States. Bassick wanted a market potential index for its line of industrial truck casters.[18] The company sold their products through several marketing channels, but wanted an index developed specifically for casters sold through industrial distributors and material handling distributors. Trade associations are a primary source for total industry (shipments) data in many industries. The American Supply and Machinery Manufacturers Association (ASMMA) issues a yearly report on sales made through industrial distributors by its members. Shipments are classified into six product categories, with United States totals for each category and breakdowns for each state, Size by Market Structure Analysis (SMSA), and major city.

The six product categories and their 1956 United States shipment totals are as follows:

Class I—Abrasives and cutting tools	$147,976,525
Class II—Other tools and accessories	93,710,443
Class III—Iron, steel, non-ferrous products, threaded products wire rope, chain, fittings	68,515,930
Class IV—Pipe fittings and valves, pumps and compressors	189,548,263
Class V—Power transmission equipment, industrial rubber goods, materials handling equipment	21,268,051
United States Total	$584,397,404

Hummel then shows how the index (Mill Supply Index) was determined for the Bridgeport, Connecticut area:

	% of U.S. in 1956
Class I—Abrasives and cutting tools	.872%
Class II—Other tools	.633
Class III—Iron, steel, etc.	.655
Class IV—Pipe fittings, pumps, etc.	.529
Class V—Power transmissions, rubber goods, materials handling equipment	.193
Misc.	.508
Total, All Products	.538

[18]Ibid., pp. 127–132.

MARKET AND SALES POTENTIALS   151

The Mill Supply Index for Bridgeport, Connecticut for industrial truck casters would be .193%, while the "all products" Mill Supply Index would be .538%. In order to illustrate the use of the Index, Hummel shows the relationship between Bassick sales in several areas and the Index figures:

	Trading Area and City of Bridgeport (% of U.S.)	State of Connecticut (% of U.S.)
Bassick caster sales	1.1	2.9
ASMMA Index		
Class V	0.3	1.2
Total, all products	0.8	2.4

Since Bassick was located in Bridgeport, it would be expected that its performance in Bridgeport and Connecticut would be relatively good and this is shown by the tabulation. After running similar comparisons for all other states and major marketing areas, Bassick concluded that there was a very high correlation between its caster shipments by market areas and the Mill Supply Index for Class V products. They therefore used the Index as a measure of market potential and were able to identify strong and weak market areas as well as detect sales trends in these areas.

Another approach to the Total Market Measure method is based on the use of total market consumption data, as illustrated by Tull and Hawkins.[19] They provide an example of establishing market potentials for printing ink by user segment for the San Francisco–Oakland SMSA area. The approach utilizes data on materials consumed by manufacturing establishments drawn from the *Census of Manufactures*. Although all products are not specifically covered in the *Census* data, it is usually possible to construct a Consumption Index that is sufficiently accurate for use as a measure of market potential.

Figure 7–2 is developed from the example provided by Tull and Hawkins. It shows the market potentials for printing ink for six user market segments and the data used to calculate the potentials. Taking the manifold business forms (SIC 2761) user segment as an example, establishments classified in this segment consumed a total of $348.9 million in materials and supplies nationally in 1967, of which $4.4 million was spent for printing inks, amounting to 1.3% of the total. In the San Francisco–Oakland SMSA area, establishments classified in SIC 2761 spent a total of

---

[19]Donald S. Tull and Del I. Hawkins, *Marketing Research*. New York: Macmillan, 1976, pp. 579–581.

		Materials Consumed, United States			San Francisco–Oakland SMSA	
Industry	SIC code	All materials and supplies ($000,000)	Printing inks ($000,000)	Proportion of printing inks to All M & S	All materials and supplies ($000,000)	Market potential ($)
Newpapers	2711	$1,438.2	$ 25.6	.018	$35.9	$ 646,200
Periodicals	2721	510.3	18.2	.035	7.6	266,000
Book Publishing	2731	252.4	3.5	.014	3.8	53,200
Book Printing	2732	224.4	11.5	.051	2.6	132,600
Commercial Printing	275	2,112.3	139.3	.066	67.0	4,422,000
Manifold Business Forms	2761	348.9	4.4	.013	13.0	169,000
				Total		5,689,000

Note: Data on materials consumed, United States, drawn from *1967 Census of Manufactures—Vol. I, Summary and Subject Statistics*; data on materials consumed in San Francisco–Oakland SMSA drawn from Vol. III, Part I of same *Census—Area Statistics*.
Source: Adapted from: Donald S. Tull and Del I. Hawkins, *Marketing Research*. New York: Macmillan, 1976, p. 581.

Figure 7-2   Market potential for printing ink in the San Francisco–Oakland SMSA area.

MARKET AND SALES POTENTIALS

$13.0 million for all materials and supplies in 1967. Applying the 1.3% proportion spent nationally for printing inks to the local area figure for total consumption of materials and supplies, the market potential for the SIC 2761 user segment in the San Francisco–Oakland SMSA area was estimated to be $169,000 ($13 million × .013 = $169,000). The total market potential for all six user segments was estimated at $5.689 million.

Both approaches to the Total Market Measure method have dealt only with market potentials, sales potentials have not been mentioned. Breakdown methods are characterized in part by their initial focus on the measurement of market potentials; sales potentials must be derived by estimating the share of the market potential available to the individual firm. The usual approach is: (1) determine the market shares held by the firm in segments and areas where performance is judged to be superior under relevant environmental conditions, and (2) use these shares to establish sales potentials. To illustrate this approach, assume that the Western Printing Ink Company has determined that it holds a 40% share of the manifold business form market in several SMSA's where it is well-established with excellent sales and distribution support. Applying the 40% share to the market potential of $169,000 for SIC 2761 in the San Francisco-Oakland SMSA area, the sales potential would be $67,600. If the 40% market share also held for the other five market segments, the sales potential for Western in the San Francisco–Oakland SMSA area would be $2,275,600 ($5.689 million × .40).

Statistical Series Method. The Statistical Series method for determining market and sales potentials is based on the development of an index of potential from one or more statistical series related to the consumption or purchasing power for the industrial product or service being studied. Although the distinction between the Statistical Series and Total Market Measure methods is often blurred in practice, indexes based on the total sales or consumption of a product/service are termed Total Market Measures and indexes based on all other statistical series are considered to represent the Statistical Series method. Both methods are primarily used to estimate potentials for geographic areas or market segments within the total market, but the Statistical Series method (unlike the Total Market Measure method) requires an independent estimate of *total* market/sales potential in absolute terms. More specifically, the Statistical Series method assumes that the total market equals 100% and develops indexes of potential for geographic areas or market segments expressed in percentages of the total market. In order to determine the dollar/unit potential for an area or segment, it is necessary to have an estimate of total potential in dollars or units.

Hummel has suggested that a five-step process be used in calculating potentials by means of the Statistical Series method:[20]

1. Assembly of market research data
2. Estimate factors affecting the market
3. Establishment of weights
4. Selection of statistical series
5. Calculation of the index

These steps will be illustrated by the use of a case study of the Bryant Chucking Grinder Company, prepared by Hummel.[21] Bryant wished to establish market potentials for precision internal grinding machines in each state and major industrial area in the United States. The first step, assembly of market research data, began with a sales analysis designed to identify past sales or quotations to industry (SIC 4-digit) groups. Bryant also examined data on: (1) number and size of metalworking establishments using internal grinding machines (using *Census of Manufactures* and trade publication data); (2) need for new original equipment, based on the relationship between machinery sales and capital expenditures; (3) need for replacement equipment; and (4) available funds for new equipment.

After identifying the primary using industries, the second step was to determine the factors that were most influential in affecting the sales of grinding machines to each primary industry. Next weights were assigned subjectively to each industry by Bryant executives, based on their judgement as to the combined effect of such factors as usage level of grinding machines by industry, business trends and their probable effects on grinder sales, and the availability of funds for the purchase of new equipment.

A number of statistical series were considered for use in establishing indexes of potential, including:

1. Number of total employees
2. Number of production employees
3. Value added by manufacture

---

[20] Hummel, *Market and Sales Potentials*, *op. cit.*, p. 84.
[21] Hummel, *Ibid.*, pp. 98–102. This case was originally published in: "Market Potentials in the Machine Tool Industry—A Case Study," *Journal of Marketing*, Vol. 19, July 1954, pp. 34–41.

MARKET AND SALES POTENTIALS

4. Expenditures for new plant and equipment
5. Value of products shipped
6. Value of materials consumed

After experimentation with a number of single and multiple-series indexes, Bryant opted to use a single series based on the number of production employees in each using industry. Indexes were then determined for each state and major industrial area, and relative market potentials calculated as shown in Figure 7–3. In this example for Illinois, the market potential for internal grinding machines was estimated to be 7.6% of the United States total. If we assume that the total United States market had been estimated to be $80 million, the market potential for Illinois would have been $6.1 million.

Another widely used approach to the Statistical Series method is based on *Sales and Marketing Management's Survey of Industrial Purchasing Power*. This annual survey provides data on the value of shipments of manufactured products by SIC industry groups and geographic areas. With this approach it is assumed that the value of shipments of an industry is a reliable indicator of the purchasing power of the industry, and thus suitable as a single factor index of market potential. As an example assume that the Whiting Corporation (listed in Table A–10 as a leading producer of overhead traveling cranes) is interested in establishing the market potential for its cupolas and ladle handlers that are sold to the iron and steel industry. A simple 1975 index of market potential for Whiting could be established for the state of Maryland by noting that the state accounted for an estimated 1.5326% of the United States total of manufacturing shipments in 1975.[22] More specifically however the *Survey of Industrial Purchasing Power* indicated that there are two plants classified in SIC 3312 (Blast furnaces and steel mills) and that their estimated 1975 shipments were $1.53 billion, accounting for 5.5% of the United States shipments in that industry. Accordingly the market potential for cupolas and ladle handlers in SIC 3312 establishments in Maryland would be estimated at 5.5% of the United States total.

Certain industrial products and services have been shown to display high correlations between their sales (shipments) and specific statistical series of particular relevance to the product or service. Telfer has noted that shipments of building materials tend to be closely related to the level of construction contract activity, measured in terms of the floor area in

[22] "Survey of Industrial Purchasing Power," *Sales and Marketing Management*, April 1976, p. 82.

SIC Code	Industry	Number of production employees in industry	Proportion of U.S. employees in industry	Weights for industries	Weighted proportion U.S. employees in industry
3541	Machine tools	4,117	.05013	3	.15039
3521	Tractors	41,153	.53410	1	.53410
3531	Mining equipment	8,079	.10330	2	.20660
3532	Oil well equipment	157	.00541	1	.00541
etc.	etc.		etc.	etc.	etc.

Totals 100 = 7.58446%
Market potential, Illinois = 7.6%

Source: Francis E. Hummel, *Market and Sales Potentials*. New York: Ronald, 1961, p. 102.

Figure 7-3 Estimation of market potentials for internal grinding machines, Illinois, 1954.

square feet for total residential and non-residential buildings, within specified geographic areas.[23] This observed relationship permitted an eastern firm to calculate the market potential for its products in its three geographic markets and use the potentials as a basis for evaluating sales performance in the markets.

Relationships between the consumption of selected industrial products and services and certain statistical series have been used to establish area market potentials for chemical process raw materials.[24] Aries and Copulsky have shown how market potentials for the United States and each state, by end-use market segments, could be calculated for refined soybean oil. Piersol has used consumption data from the *Census of Manufactures* for 10 industrial products to attempt to validate estimates of area market potentials based on a number of statistical series.[25] His finding was that,

> . . . 44 percent of all area estimates for the ten products were at least 50 percent higher or lower than the actual market shares.[26]

Despite the relatively large errors associated with the method, Piersol concludes that it is better than using hunches and suggests various ways to improve the accuracy. In view of the probable errors in the consumption data used to validate the shipments data, the actual magnitude of the errors associated with the Statistical Series method remain unknown. The use of various correction procedures suggested by Piersol, as well as the use of all available market data, should help to control the errors inherent in such estimating techniques.

Buildup Methods

Buildup methods for estimating market and sales potentials involve the aggregation of data from the individual account level to the industry or market level. Three approaches to the use of buildup methods will be examined: (1) the Census method, in which all users and prospective users of a product or service are asked to estimate their requirements; (2) the Market Survey method, in which a sample of firms are asked the same

---

[23] Kenneth R. Telfer, "How to Measure Sales against Market Potential in the Construction Industry," *Journal of Marketing*, Vol. 26, January 1962, pp. 35–41.
[24] Robert S. Aries and William Copulsky, "Determination of Area Market Potentials for Chemical Process Raw Materials," *Journal of Marketing*, Vol. 14, April 1950, pp. 730–732.
[25] Robert J. Piersol, "Accuracy of Estimating Markets for Industrial Products by Size of Consuming Industries," *Journal of Marketing Research*, Vol. 5, May 1968, pp. 147–154.
[26] *Ibid.*, p. 149.

questions; (3) Secondary Data methods, which develop estimates of potentials from secondary, rather than primary, data sources.

Census Method. Hummel, in his review of the Census method, has noted that it involves a separate appraisal of every user or prospective user in a market. The market potential is derived from a summation of the individual potentials.[27] The Census method is therefore most applicable to industrial goods and services characterized by: (1) very concentrated markets, (2) direct sales contract, (3) relatively high value of orders, and (4) relatively low unit volume. An example of such a situation regarding a manufacturer of industrial refractories is presented in Chapter 5. Figure 5–5 provides an example of the customer profile data collected by the firm for each major account. By summing the total refractories consumption for each account, the firm was able to estimate total market potential.

A case study of the use of the Census method to estimate potentials shows the ways in which the Wire Rope Division of the John A. Roebling's Sons Corporation proceeded.[28] This case is particularly interesting because it illustrates that the method can be applied to both OEM and distributor accounts. The firm designed a one-page "Customer and Prospect Rating Report" to be completed by the salesman for each user and prospective user of wire rope products in his territory. For each type of wire rope product, the form called for data on the account's annual requirements, Roebling's share of these requirements, and the principal competitors supplying the requirements. Salesmen were assigned the responsibility of obtaining the data and received a monthly report based on the data listing each account, its annual wire rope requirements (market potential), Roebling's sales to the account, and its share of the market potential. Management at Roebling's checked the estimates of aggregate potential against shipments data in the *Annual Survey of Manufactures* (U.S. Bureau of the Census) and against trade association data. They also checked the lists of accounts against lists of industry participants in directories of manufacturers and trade associations to ensure that their coverage was complete.

Another perspective on the use of the Census method is provided by Hummel in the form of a case study relating the use of the method by the U.S. Steel Corporation.[29] This case relates how U.S. Steel shifted from a program of recording the future tonnage requirements of customers to

---

[27] Hummel, *Market and Sales Potentials*, Chap. 9, pp. 137–151.
[28] Harry Leopold, Jr., "Sales Potentials by Customers," *Marketing Research in Action*, Studies in Business Policy no. 84. New York: National Industrial Conference Board, 1964, pp. 78–82.
[29] Hummel, *Market and Sales Potentials, op. cit.*, pp. 149–151.

MARKET AND SALES POTENTIALS

their total requirements for steel products during the past year. They discovered that consumer expected demands for steel products were consistently in error, and that much better, useful data on market movements and trends could be obtained by collecting data on *past* requirements. Thus instead of having the salesmen produce short-term forecasts of requirements, the emphasis was shifted to the development of estimates of market and sales potentials with far better results for all concerned.

There are numerous other examples of the application of the Census method among industrial goods and services, and opportunities for additional uses will grow as sellers and buyers discover the advantages of data sharing. The automobile industry, for example, provides its steel suppliers with detailed estimates of its requirements for steel; injection molders work closely with the suppliers of plastic resins to ensure a continuing supply.

Market Survey Method. In contrast to the Census method of appraising each user and potential user of an industrial good or service, the Market Survey method is based on a *sample* of such accounts. This method tends to be used for those industrial goods and services which have relatively unconcentrated markets, thus ruling out the Census method because of cost and time considerations.

The basic approach to the Market Survey method involves the collection of data on past purchases or probable requirements for the product or service being studied, together with classification data on the principal products/services produced, number of employees (total and production), and other relevant statistical series. For capital equipment, data may be obtained on the stock of equipment stock sources and applications of the equipment. Hummel has noted that the most difficult problem in using this method is determining who to contact to obtain the required data.[30] Although the purchasing department of the users might be expected to have the required data on purchases, they may not be in a position to provide information on probable requirements for products not previously purchased by the firm. Manufacturing and engineering personnel would more likely be able to estimate probable requirements, but getting access to the right individuals is often a difficult matter. The best approach is usually to start the inquiry with the manager of engineering or manufacturing and ask to be referred to the appropriate individual(s) within the unit.

Data required for the use of the Market Survey method may be ob-

---

[30] Hummel, *Ibid.*, p. 106.

tained, by any of the three survey techniques (personal interview, telephone, or mail), but the personal interview technique is generally best. It is essential to use personal interviews to obtain data from prospective users and in cases involving highly technical products or services. Telephone and mail surveys are most applicable for data collection from users when respondents can be identified by name and title and factual data on past purchases and classification data only are sought. Even under these restrictive conditions, mail surveys may be dangerous.

Cox and Havens have reported the results of a mail survey conducted among purchasing agents in a sample of buyers of quick-connective couplings in 1974.[31] Each buyer, as a known customer of the Hansen Manufacturing Company, a Cleveland manufacturer of couplings, was asked to provide data on their firm's total purchases of quick-connective couplings from all sources. Total reported purchases from the survey were to be matched against known purchases of Hansen couplings to obtain market shares for Hansen products. The results of the survey proved to be worthless, more than three-fourths of the respondents reported that their total purchases were less than their known purchases of Hansen couplings alone. The respondents simply did not know how much their firms had spent for couplings in 1973, and their estimates were considerably lower than their actual purchases. In a personal interview, the interviewer has an opportunity to determine whether the respondent examines records in answering questions, mail and telephone techniques do not permit such checks. Theoretically mail surveys provide the best opportunity to obtain accurate data, as a result of the absence of time pressures to answer. However most respondents in the couplings study did not take the opportunity to examine their records. Telephone surveys are also risky, for they do not provide the time required to consult necessary records. Consequently, personal interviews are the preferred medium for collecting data for the use of the Market Survey method.

There is a similarity between the Market Survey and Statistical Series methods for estimating potentials. Both methods seek to establish a relationship between the purchases of a given industrial product or service by firms within market groups, such as SIC 4-digit industries, and one or more statistical series, such as the number of production employees in the buying firms. We can illustrate the use of the Market Survey method with an example based on tapered roller bearings. Assume that Timken, the largest producer of such bearings, is interested in determining the

---

[31] William E. Cox, Jr., and George N. Havens, "Determination of Sales Potentials and Performance for an Industrial Goods Manufacturer," *Journal of Marketing Research*, Vol. 14, November 1977, pp. 574–578.

MARKET AND SALES POTENTIALS

market and sales potentials for these products. Using their internal sales records and general market knowledge, they can define the major using industries as well as prospective users. Within these industries they can also identify the firms using, or most likely to use, tapered roller bearings. Personal interviews would then be conducted with a sample of the firms.

Assume that the survey produced the data shown in Figure 7–4 for four market segments. Each firm in the sample was asked to provide both data on their total purchases of tapered roller bearings from all sources for the preceding calendar year and data on the average number of production employees in the firm during the year. From these data the average purchases per employee was calculated for each of the four market segments (user industries). The total employment for each user industry during the preceding year was estimated from data available in the latest *Annual Survey of Manufactures*. It should be emphasized that these employment data are for *all* firms in the universe from which the sample survey is drawn. The United States market potential may then be estimated by multiplying the average purchases per employee by the total number of production employees in all firms in the market segment (user industry). Market potentials for states, counties, and smaller geographic areas may be derived by substituting the employment data for these areas in place of the United States figures. Sales potentials may be determined for each market segment by estimating the market share held by Timken in each sample account and calculating a weighted average market share for each segment. Multiplying this weighted market share by the market potential will give the sales potential for Timken in each market segment.

Hummel has suggested that prospective users of an industrial product or service, as opposed to users, be classified separately and a "possible-use" approach be employed to calculate market and sales potentials for such firms and industries.[32] We shall examine this approach in the discussion on determining potentials for new products, but it should be noted that the approach may also be used for established products that have not been purchased by certain segments of a market.

Secondary Data Methods. A third approach among the Buildup methods for determining market and sales potentials may be termed Secondary Data methods. These are distinguished from the other two methods (Census and Market Survey) by reliance on internal sales data rather than survey data on product purchases. Two variations of the Secondary Data method will be examined: the first is basically the same as the Market Survey method, except that sales per employee ratios are calculated from

---

[32] Hummel, *Market and Sales Potentials*, pp. 105–107, 111–114.

Market Survey Data

SIC Code	Industry	Product purchases	Number of production employees	Average purchases per employee	U.S. total, production employees	Estimated U.S. market potentials
3573	Computers and related equipment	$201,627	8,736	$23.08	78,000	$1,800,240
3585	Refrigeration and heating equipment	851,552	15,720	54.17	120,000	6,500,400
3721	Aircraft industry	292,692	20,020	14.62	130,000	1,900,600
3811	Engineering and scientific inst.	178,200	4,950	36.00	25,000	900,000

Notes: "Market survey data" are based on personal interviews with known users of roller bearings. "Product purchases" are totals purchased from all suppliers in previous calendar year. "Number of production employees" is the average employment during previous calendar year in user sample firms. "Average purchases per employee" is obtained from product purchases by the number of production employees. "U.S. total, production employees" data are estimated from the latest U.S. Bureau of the Census, *Annual Survey of Manufactures—General Statistics for Industry Groups and Industries*. "Estimated U.S. market potentials" are derived by multiplying "U.S. total production employees" by "average purchases per employee."
Source: Francis E. Hummel, "Market Potentials in the Machine Tool Industry—A Case Study," *Journal of Marketing*, Vol. 19, July 1954, pp. 34–41.

Figure 7–4 Market potentials for roller bearings based on the market survey method.

MARKET AND SALES POTENTIALS

internal sales records in place of the purchases per employee ratios obtained from a survey.[33] The second, developed by IBM, is based on a two-factor model for assessing growth opportunities for established products.[34]

Cox and Havens were interested in developing measures of potential for use in evaluating the relative performance of industrial distributors of the Hansen Manufacturing Company. Hansen, a Cleveland manufacturer of quick-connective couplings for air and fluid power transmission systems, distributed its products through a national network of 31 industrial distributors. A sales analysis was conducted on a sample of 178 accounts of 7 distributors who made lists available of all accounts that purchased $2,000 or more of Hansen products from the distributors in 1973. Results of the sales analysis are shown in Figure 7–5. Sales per employee ratios were developed for six SIC 2-digit groups (4-digit groups could not be used because of insufficient sample sizes) and a miscellaneous group. Figure 7–6 shows how the sales potential for Distributor A was calculated. Sales per employee ratios for each group were multiplied by the total employment in all establishments classified within the group (data from *County Business Patterns*) to obtain the sales potential for each group and the total for the territory. It should be noted that this approach, unlike all the previously described approaches and methods for determining potentials, produces the *sales* potential first rather than the market potential. The reason for this difference is the initial emphasis on company sales rather than industry sales or market consumption. Market potentials can be estimated by obtaining the estimated market share held by Hansen in each account in the sample (by means of a market survey using personal interviews) and dividing the sales potentials by the weighted average market share for each group.

The IBM approach described by Stern is based on the observation that there are two ways in which the sales of an established product can grow: (1) by selling more to present customers, and (2) by converting potential users into users. The approach therefore determines market and sales potentials by establishing two factors that measure these two growth paths. The opportunity to sell more to present customers is measured by a

> depth of penetration factor [that takes the form of] . . . a goal of raising the average sales revenue obtained from all customers to the level of the average revenue that the best x percent yield.[35]

---

[33]Cox and Havens, *op. cit.*
[34]Mark E. Stern, *Marketing Planning*. New York: McGraw-Hill, 1966, pp. 23–37.
[35]*Ibid.*, p. 24.

2-digit SIC group	Number of accounts	1973 sales	Number of employees	Sales per employee
33 Primary metal industries	14	$ 116,551	74,625	$1.56
34 Fabricated metal products	22	152,412	60,169	2.53
35 Machinery, except electrical	57	503,929	153,670	3.28
36 Electrical machinery	24	155,903	80,807	1.93
37 Transportation equipment	36	316,878	185,784	1.71
38 Professional, scientific and controlling instruments	9	76,883	22,122	3.48
Miscellaneous firms	16	89,708	60,177	1.49
Totals	178	1,412,264	637,354	2.21

Source: William E. Cox, Jr., and George N. Havens, "Determination of Sales Potentials and Performance for an Industrial Goods Manufacturer," *Journal of Marketing Research*, Vol. 14, November 1977, p. 575.

Figure 7–5 Analysis of quick-connective coupling sales by customer groups, 1973, Hansen Manufacturing Company.

2-digit SIC group	1973 Hansen sales per employee	Total employees	Sales potential
33	$1.56	4,113	$ 6,416
34	2.53	14,792	37,424
35	3.28	15,907	52,175
36	1.93	32,677	63,067
37	1.71	2,024	3,461
38	3.48	409	1,423
Total	—	69,922	163,966

Source: William E. Cox, Jr., and George N. Havens, "Determination of Sales Potentials and Performance for an Industrial Goods Manufacturer," *Journal of Marketing Research*, Vol. 14, November 1977, p. 575.

Figure 7–6 Secondary data method for estimating sales potentials for the Hansen Manufacturing Company.

MARKET AND SALES POTENTIALS

Depth of penetration factor	Number of customers	Total revenue	Average revenue per customer	Total potential[a]
Current level	117	$481,000	$ 4,100	$ 481,000
Top 5%	6	118,000	19,700	2,304,000
Top 10%	12	167,000	14,000	1,638,000
Top 25%	29	261,000	9,000	1,053,000

Note:[a] Total potential is the quotient of total revenue and all (117) customers. If total revenue is based on one seller's revenues, sales potentials are obtained; if total revenue is based on all seller's (industry) revenues, market potentials are obtained.
Source: Adapted from Mark E. Stern, *Marketing Planning*. New York: McGraw-Hill, 1966, pp. 26–28.

Figure 7-7 Market/sales potentials based on depth of penetration factors in the insurance industry, SIC 63.

The opportunity to convert potential users into users is measured by the

> market occupancy factor [which Stern defines as] . . . the ratio of the company's actual customers to the total potential customers for the product.[36]

As in other approaches to the calculation of potentials, the IBM approach classifies customers on the basis of SIC group and size, measured by the total number of employees. Stern's examples are based on 2-digit SIC groups and nine employee size groups. He illustrates the calculation of potentials based on depth of penetration factors with an example from the insurance industry (SIC 63), size group 7 (1000–2499 employees), in measuring the potentials for copying machines within the firms in SIC 63. Figure 7-7 shows how potentials may be calculated for the 117 customers making up size group 7 in the insurance industry. If sales analysis is used to measure past reveneues of the seller (IBM), the resulting potentials would be sales potentials, and market share estimates would be needed to determine market potentials. If past revenues are based on the total purchases of copying machines from all sellers (from trade association or government sources, for example), the potentials would be market potentials, and estimates of sales potentials would have to be developed on the basis of past or expected market shares held by IBM.

The average revenue for the 117 customers in SIC 63, size group 7, is shown in Figure 7-7 to be $4100. Stern suggests that three "depth of penetration" goals may be established:

[36]*Ibid.*

Highly optimistic—potential based on increasing the average revenue for all 117 accounts to the level of the top 5%.

Optimistic—potential based on raising the average revenue for all 117 accounts to the level of the top 10% of the present accounts.

Less optimistic—potential based on raising the average revenue for all 117 accounts to the level of the top 25% of all accounts.[37]

The choice of a "depth of penetration" goal should be based on an evaluation of the degree of homogeneity of the average revenues across the size groups. The more similar the average revenues are between groups, the more optimistic the goal may be, since the average revenue figure is less likely to be dominated by a few large firms. SIC 63 appears to be relatively heterogeneous and concentrated, so that the best choice would appear to be a 25% depth of penetration goal, resulting in a potential of $1.053 million.

Stern uses the textile industry (SIC 23) to illustrate the determination of potentials by the use of market occupancy factors. Figure 7-8 shows how estimates of the potential may be developed, based on current and expected market occupancy ratios, estimates of the number of potential customers in each size group, and an assumed penetration factor. Data on the number of establishments in the United States by size group are available from *County Business Patterns*; Stern uses 1962 data and these are retained in Figure 7-8 for ease in comparing these calculations with the original materials presented by Stern.[38] The number of company customers may be determined by an analysis of internal sales records; the number of industry customers would have to be collected by market survey. Current market occupancy factors can then be calculated for each size group as the quotient of the number of establishments and the number of customers. Following Stern,

> It is assumed that if a 10 percent or greater current ratio has been reached in a given size group, then 100 percent of the establishments in this group will become customers for the product.[39]

Thus all firms in size groups 6-9 (500 or more employees) are treated as potential customers. Expected market occupancy ratios for size groups 1-5 are derived from fitting a trend line to a scatter diagram (log-log

---

[37] *Ibid.*, p. 26.
[38] *Ibid.*, pp. 28-30.
[39] *Ibid.*, pp. 28-29.

Size group	No. of establishments in the U.S.[a]	No. of company (industry) customers	Current market occupancy factor	Expected market occupancy factor	Number of potential customers	Average revenue per customer[b]	Total potential[c] ($ revenue)
1 (1–19)	16,000	1	.00006	.00031	5	$ 160	$ 800
2 (20–49)	7,200	6	.00083	.00330	24	220	5,280
3 (50–99)	3,590	5	.00139	.01350	48	550	26,400
4 (100–249)	2,140	24	.01121	.06500	139	900	125,100
5 (250–499)	518	44	.08494	.27500	142	1,400	198,800
6 (500–999)	161	37	.22981	1.00000	161	2,200	354,200
7 (1,000–2,499)	24	18	.75000	1.00000	24	7,300	175,200
8 (2,500–4,999)	9	9	1.00000	1.00000	9	11,000	99,000
9 (5,000 & over)	1	1	1.00000	1.00000	1	18,500	18,500
Totals	29,643	145			553		$1,003,280

Notes: [a]No. of establishments in the U.S. by size group may be obtained from *County Business Patterns*.
[b]Average revenue per customer data are hypothetical.
[c]Total revenue is the quotient of the number of potential customers and the average revenue per customer.
Source: Adapted from Mark E. Stern, *Marketing Planning*. New York: McGraw-Hill, 1966, pp. 28–30.

Figure 7–8 Market/sales potentials based on market occupancy factors and assumed penetration factors in the textile industry, SIC 23.

scale) of size group data on the number of establishments and current market occupancy ratios. The resulting trend line is then shifted so that

> the smallest size group (6) with a current ratio of 10 percent or more shows a 100 percent potential.[40]

Expected market occupancy ratios may be estimated from the shifted trend line estimates for each size group.

The number of potential customers in each size group may be estimated by multiplying the total number of establishments in the size group by the expected market occupancy ratio for the group. To obtain total potentials for each size group, it is necessary to have data on average revenue per customer in each group. If internal sales data are used, the resulting potentials will be sales potentials; the use of data on industry revenue will provide estimates of market potentials. Hypothetical internal sales data are provided in Figure 7–8, with the result that sales potentials are presented for each size group. Market potentials could be derived for each size group by estimating the firm's actual or desired market share in each group and obtaining the quotient of these shares and the sales potentials for each size group.

The IBM approach to the development of market and sales potentials is examined in considerable detail here because of: (1) its general applicability to all industrial goods and services, using secondary data available to all sellers, and (2) its additional value in assessing the feasibility of various marketing objectives and goals. Stern illustrates this application by assuming that

> a company has a current annual revenue of $35 million and . . . has a five-year marketing objective of attaining an annual revenue of $150 million.[41]

Taking various combinations of market occupancy and depth of penetration factors, and specifying that market occupancy factors may not exceed 35% and depth of penetration factors may not be higher than the top 10%, Stern is able to show that the $150 million revenue objective may be reached by a combination of factors within the limits of 30–35% market occupancy and 15–25% depth of penetration.[42] This approach to marketing and strategic planning provides an excellent opportunity to link mar-

---

[40]*Ibid.*, p. 29.
[41]*Ibid.*, p. 31
[42]*Ibid.*, pp. 34–35.

ket and sales analysis, potentials, and planning into a comprehensive, integrated program for identifying and pursuing growth opportunities for the firm.

ESTIMATING POTENTIALS FOR NEW PRODUCTS

In contrast to the methods and approaches available for estimating market and sales potentials for established products, the task of estimating potentials for new products tends to be much more subjective and speculative in nature. McDonald, in the best available review of methods for estimating potentials for new industrial products, has suggested that the magnitude of the task is affected primarily by four factors:

1. *Availability of secondary data*—Finding data that are relevant to the product and reliable is generally difficult but the availability varies considerably between products.
2. *Degree of precision required or obtainable*—Minimum demand studies often require a relatively low level of precision with respect to data on demand or potential. Comprehensive studies typically require higher levels of precision.
3. *Market structure and situation*—Concentrated and relatively stable markets are much easier to measure regarding new product potentials than those that are fragmented, new, and changing.
4. *Degree of product newness*—The greater the degree of newness that the product represents, the more difficult it is to determine the potential demand for the product, in terms of both the level and the rate of substitution of product demand.[43]

Although it might seem that the best approach to estimating the potential demand for a new industrial product service would be to identify potential users and ask them whether they would buy the product/service, and if so, how much, this is actually the *worst* possible approach. The primary danger in this approach is that respondents either do not know whether they would buy, or they recognize that it is in their best interest to indicate interest as a way of maximizing their future choice at little or no cost. Some authors have suggested that test marketing is the best approach to determining potentials for new products, but estimates of potentials are usually required long before product/services are developed

[43]McDonald, *op. cit.*, pp. 66–67.

to the point that they are ready for test marketing.[44] In order to obtain timely, relevant, and reliable estimates of market and sales potentials, relatively objective measures of possible demand for a new product or service are needed. There are basically three methods that meet this requirement: (1) Usage Factor method, (2) Possible Use method, and (3) Analogy/Substitution method.

Usage Factor Method

The Usage Factor method of estimating the potential for new industrial products and services is based on a multi-step process:

1. Identify the possible end-use situations for the proposed product service.
2. Identify the principal market segments in which these situations will be found.
3. Determine the level of economic activity for each principal market segment, such as its end-product output, size, and number of establishments.
4. Calculate usage factor ratios for each segment, based on the expected use of the new product/service per unit of economic activity.
5. Estimate market potential for each segment by multiplying the usage factor ratio by the economic activity of the segment.
6. Estimate sales potential by means of a market survey of possible users in each segment or by obtaining market share estimates from the firm's sales force.[45]

A number of specific examples of the development of usage factors ratios to measure new product potential are provided by McDonald in the National Industrial Conference Board study of member practices:

1. *Weyerhaeuser Company*—estimated the market potential for movable partitions by calculating the average number of lineal feet of movable partitions per 1000 square feet of floor space for specific types of buildings, such as hospitals, offices, and factories.
2. *Norton Company*—determined the market potential for a new grinding fluid from a market survey of its customers. From this usage factor, ratios were developed relating the number of gallons of grinding fluid

---

[44] Uhl and Schoner, *op. cit.*, p. 490.
[45] McDonald, *op. cit.*, pp. 70–71.

MARKET AND SALES POTENTIALS

used per dollar of grinding wheels sold within different applications of grinding wheels.
3. *Pharmaseal Laboratories*—measured the market potential for disposable trays for patient care in hospitals by developing a usage factor ratio relating the total number of trays used per year in each hospital in a sample to the total number of beds in the hospital.[46]

Possible Use Method

Hummel has suggested that the Possible Use method is appropriate for determining the potential for a new industrial product.[47] He notes that the method is based on a market survey of prospective users to

> determine whether a given industrial plant can use a specific product as a component part or as part of its manufacturing operations, and if so, to what extent.[48]

Questions are designed to provide information on the nature and level of manufacturing activity in each plant, particularly with respect to the factors that determine the use or non-use of the product. Classification data on the principal products of the plant (SIC number), the number of employees, and other measures of economic activity are also collected in the market survey. The marketing researcher must assess whether a given plant is a prospect for the product. An estimate of the potential must be developed for each plant with total potentials calculated in accordance with the procedures described in the Market Survey method for established products.

The types of questions employed in the Possible Use method are illustrated in a survey designed to measure the potential for optical projectors in metalworking plants.[49] Non-users of optical projectors were asked:

1. Does the work of this plan require:
    A. Precision measurements (thousandths of an inch or less, degrees of an arc, and so on)   Yes___ No___
    B. Quality comparison inspection   Yes___ No___

---

[46]*Ibid.*, Chaps. 2, 3.
[47]Hummel, *Market and Sales Potentials*, p. 106.
[48]*Ibid.*, p. 105.
[49]*Ibid.*, p. 106.

2. Do you perform either of the above operations in:
   A. Your receiving room   Yes___ No___
   B. Your production line   Yes___ No___
   C. Your final inspection   Yes___ No___
   D. Your tool room   Yes___ No___

Analogy/Substitution Method

Perhaps the weakest of the three methods available for estimating potentials for new industrial products and services by relatively objective procedures is the Analogy/Substitution method. This method is based on the hypotheses that: (1) past diffusion processes of similar or related products are analogous to and a useful guide to the market growth process for new products and services, or (2) virtually all new products and services are basically substitutes for existing products and services, so that the estimation of the potential for new products and services is simply a matter of determining the rate of substitution of the new for the old. The Sprague Electric Company used this method to estimate the extent and rate of substitution of integrated circuits for transistors and vacuum tubes, based on the earlier substitution of transistors for receiving tubes.[50] The author has used life cycle studies of early ethical drug products to determine the market potential for new products.[51] It has been shown by deKluyver that the potential demand for steering gears in the heavy-duty truck and farm equipment markets may be estimated by analyzing the product life cycles of previous types of steering gears.[52] In spite of these and other reported applications of the Analogy/Substitution method, many individuals and firms have not been successful in their attempts to use the method and have concluded that the method is of little value.[53] It appears that at least some of the disenchantment on the part of the critics of the method is due to unrealistic expectations regarding the precision of the estimates derived by the method. It should be emphasized that the Analogy/Substitution method is at best relatively crude and should be used primarily in minimum demand studies in which "go/no go" decisions may be made on the basis of relatively rough estimates of market and sales potential.

---

[50] McDonald, Jr., *op. cit.*, pp. 91–92.
[51] William E. Cox, Jr., "Product Life Cycles as Marketing Models," *Journal of Business*, October, 1967, pp. 375–384.
[52] Cornelis A. de Kluyver, Innovation and Industrial Product Life Cycles: A Heuristic Classification Study (Ph.D. diss., Case Western Reserve University, 1975).
[53] McDonald, *op. cit.*, pp. 74–75; N. K. Dhalla and S. Yuspeh, "Forget the Product Life Cycle Concept," *Harvard Business Review*, January–February 1976, pp. 102–110.

Other Methods

There is a place for test marketing, even though it is not considered one of the primary methods for determining potentials for new industrial products and services, because of the need to have a marketable product. Where new products involve relatively high risks and the stakes are large in the market place, the firm may wish to obtain more precise estimates of market and sales potential before committing itself to a program of national introduction. Test marketing may be a very effective means of obtaining precise, reliable data—indeed it may be the method of choice in many situations.

Another interesting method for estimating potentials for new industrial products involves the use of Bayesian analysis to decide whether to market, for example, a new type of welding torch. Harris describes how the product planning committee of a firm assessed: (1) a distribution of the proportion of new users who might purchase the new product, and (2) a distribution chosen to specify the mean and mode of the prior distribution.[54] Based on a prior analysis, the committee decided to recommend that the product be marketed, but the president was skeptical and asked for a determination of the cost of uncertainty. Following this calculation, the president approved the recommendation and ordered ten new torches. A sample of 100 potential customers were contacted and 8 torches were sold. On the basis of this finding, the prior probabilities were modified and a posterior distribution was obtained. Since the resulting expected value for the proposition of new users who might buy the product significantly exceeded the minimum proportion required to market the product, it was decided to market the new type of welding torch nationally. While this method uses relatively sophisticated analysis to obtain estimates of the market potential, the input data are subjective and therefore the method is not included among the primary methods based on more objective input data. This method could be used in conjunction with the other methods however and would accordingly increase the power of those methods.

SUMMARY

Potential refers to the level of demand for a product or service in a given environment. Market potential plays an important role in marketing planning and strategy decisions. The challenge however is to turn the concept into a useful and practical measure.

Methods of estimating potential for establishing products differ from

---

[54] Lawrence Harris, "New Product Marketing: A Case Study in Decision-Making Under Uncertainty," *Applied Statistics*, Vol. 16, no. 1, 1967, pp. 39–42.

those used for new products. For established products there are Breakdown and Buildup methods. There are two types of Breakdown methods: (1) the Total Market Measure method—relies on total industry shipments or consumption data from which a measure of market potential is derived; and (2) sales potential—estimated by applying market shares held by the firm in segments and areas where performance is judged to be superior.

The Statistical Series method is the other Breakdown approach. It equates the total market to 100% and indexes each market segment as a percent of total demand. The percentages are based on a statistical proven relationship between one or more variables and market size. A widely used version uses Sales and Marketing Management's *Survey of Industrial Purchasing Power*. The total size of market potential must be estimated separately with Statistical Series methods.

Market Buildup methods aggregate individual account data to market or industry level data. The Census method, as the name implies, counts all users and prospective users. It is feasible only in highly concentrated high value/low volume markets where direct selling is involved. The Market Survey method, as the name implies, relies on a survey rather than a census of buying firms. It employs past purchases or probable requirements for the product being studied, together with account characteristics. Like the Statistical Series method, it relies on a relationship between one or more statistical series, such as number of employees and purchases. To obtain reliable data, the use of personal interviewing of sampled firms is judged to be essential.

Secondary data methods rely on internal sales data. One variant uses sales per employee for the firm's customers. From this figure it extrapolates directly to sales potential, without having to estimate market potential first. Another variant is the IBM approach in which sales are the results of the percentage of potential customers being sold (occupancy) and the percentage of their purchases that the firm accounts for (penetration). As with other approaches, it relies on SIC groupings by product or industry and customer size. By specifying the range of occupancy and penetration rates required to satisfy sales objectives, this approach directly links strategy analysis and measurement of potential demand.

Potential estimation for new products is far more subjective than for established products. This is particularly true where demand is not highly concentrated, secondary data are scarce, the product is rather new, and the required estimates must be very precise. The Usage Factor method and the Possible Use method are the preferred alternatives. The Analogy/Substitution method is generally thought to be less precise. Other approaches include Bayesian estimation and, of course, test marketing.

MARKET AND SALES POTENTIALS

SUGGESTED READINGS

Aries Robert S., and William Copulsky, "Determination of Area Market Potentials for Chemical Process Raw Materials," *Journal of Marketing*, Vol. 14, April 1950, pp. 730–732.

Cox, William E., Jr., and George N. Havens, "Determination of Sales Potentials and Performance for an Industrial Goods Manufacturer," *Journal of Marketing Research*, Vol. 14, November 1977, pp. 574–578.

Cox, William E., Jr., "Product Life Cycles as Marketing Models," *Journal of Business*, October 1967, pp. 375–384.

Crisp, Richard D., *Sales Planning and Control*. New York: McGraw-Hill, 1961.

Dhalla, N. K., and S. Yuseh, "Forget the Product Life Cycle Concept," *Harvard Business Review*, January–February 1976, pp. 102–110.

Hummel, Francis E., "Market Potentials in the Machine Tool Industry—A Case Study," *Journal of Marketing*, Vol. 19, July 1954, pp. 34–41.

Hummel, Francis E., "Pinpointing Prospects for Industrial Sales," *Journal of Marketing*, Vol. 25, July 1960, pp. 26–31.

de Kluyver, Cornelis A., Innovation and Industrial Product Life Cycles: A Heuristic Classification Study (Ph.D. diss., Case Western Reserve University, 1975).

Leopold, Harry, Jr., "Sales Potentials by Customers," *Marketing Research in Action*, Studies in Business Policy no. 84. New York: National Industrial Conference Board, 1964, pp. 78–82.

Lieberman, Alfred, "Further Pinpointing of Prospects for Industrial Sales," *Journal of Marketing*, Vol. 25, April 1961, pp. 64–68.

Little, John D. C., and Leonard M. Lodish, "A Media Planning Calculus," *Operations Research*, January–February 1969, pp. 1–35.

McDonald, Morgan B., Jr., *Appraising the Market for New Industrial Products*, Studies in Business Policy no. 123, New York: National Industrial Conference Board, 1967, Chap. 2, 3.

National Industrial Conference Board, *Measuring Salesmen's Performance*, Studies in Business Policy, No. 114. New York: NICB, 1965.

National Industrial Conference Board, *Sales Analysis*, Studies in Business Policy, no. 113. New York: NICB, 1965, pp. 18–23.

Piersol, Robert J., "Accuracy of Estimating Markets for Industrial Products by Size of Consuming Industries," *Journal of Marketing Research*, Vol. 5, May 1968, pp. 147–154.

Stern, Mark E., *Market Planning*. New York: McGraw-Hill, 1966, pp. 23–37.

Telfer, Kenneth R., "How to Measure Sales against Market Potential in in the Construction Industry," *Journal of Marketing*, Vol. 26, January 1962, pp. 35–41.

Tull, Donald S., and Del I. Hawkins, *Marketing Research*. New York: Macmillan, 1976.

Uhl, Kenneth P., and Bertram Schoner, *Marketing Research*. New York: Wiley, 1969, Chap. 13, 15.

CHAPTER EIGHT
Market and Sales Forecasting

Forecasting is one of the most critical functions in business organizations—it serves implicitly or explicitly as the basis for all planning and decision-making activities in the organization. Industrial marketing researchers usually assume the responsibility for preparing formal market and sales forecasts for the firm and, in many firms, they are responsible for economic and business forecasting as well. The planning process usually begins with market and sales forecasts. On the other hand business decisions ". . . are based implicitly and explicitly on forecasts of the consequences of alternative courses on action."[1] Thus forecasting and planning are different functions: (1) *forecasting* tries to describe ". . . what will happen for a set of decisions and events in a given situation," assuming that no changes are made by management; (2) *planning* is "based on the notion that by taking certain actions the decision maker can affect the subsequent events relating to a given situation."[2]

There are three elements that are common to all forecasts: (1) a focus on the future and a specific time in the future, (2) the future is characterized by uncertainty, and (3) a reliance on historical information to

---
[1] Nicholas A. H. Stacey and Aubrey Wilson, *Industrial Marketing Research*. London: Hutchinson and Co., 1963, p. 192.
[2] Steven C. Wheelwright and Spryos Makridakis, *Forecasting Methods for Management*, 2nd ed. New York: Wiley, 1977, p. 4.

develop the forecast.[3] Accordingly, forecasting has been defined as ". . . the art of making maximum use of available knowledge to derive a set of probabilities concerning future events."[4] In Chapter 6 we noted (following Kotler) that forecasts are related to the concepts of demand and potential. We defined a market forecast as the level of market demand, given an expected level of industry marketing effort and an assumed marketing environment. Figure 8-1 shows the relationship between the concepts of demand, potential, and forecast (as did Figure 6-1). It also illustrates the difference between nonconditional and conditional forecasts. Modifying the distinction suggested by Theil, nonconditional forecasts are defined as those based on an assumption of unknown change in the level of industry marketing effort and the marketing environment.[5] Conditional forecasts are then based on known or assumed changes in the level of industry marketing effort and the marketing environment. Market forecasts refers to the level of demand by a group of buyers for total industry output or shipments, whereas sales forecasts refers to the level of demand for the output or shipments of an individual seller. At the outset of the planning process in a given period for an industrial firm, nonconditional market and sales forecasts would be prepared. These forecasts would be based on the best information available at that time, often specifying no change from the most recent period. As a result of the planning process, it would be anticipated that newer and better information would be developed with respect to the expected level of industry marketing effort and market potential (based on changes in the marketing environment). Revisions would be made in the levels of expected industry marketing effort, market potential, and the market demand function. The result would be a conditional market forecast based on these revisions. Similar procedures would be used to develop nonconditional and conditional sales forecasts.

FORECASTING PROCEDURES

Most discussions on forecasting focus upon the methods for forecasting, leaving the marketing researcher with the task of trying to decide which of many choices is most appropriate in a given situation. There are two books available that offer valuable guidance in the choice task. They will

---

[3] Adapted from Wheelwright and Makridakis, p. 3.
[4] Chester R. Wasson, *The Strategy of Marketing Research*. New York: Appleton-Century-Crofts, 1964, p. 517.
[5] H. Theil, *Economic Forecasts and Policy*. Amsterdam: North Holland Publishing Co., 1958, p. 6.

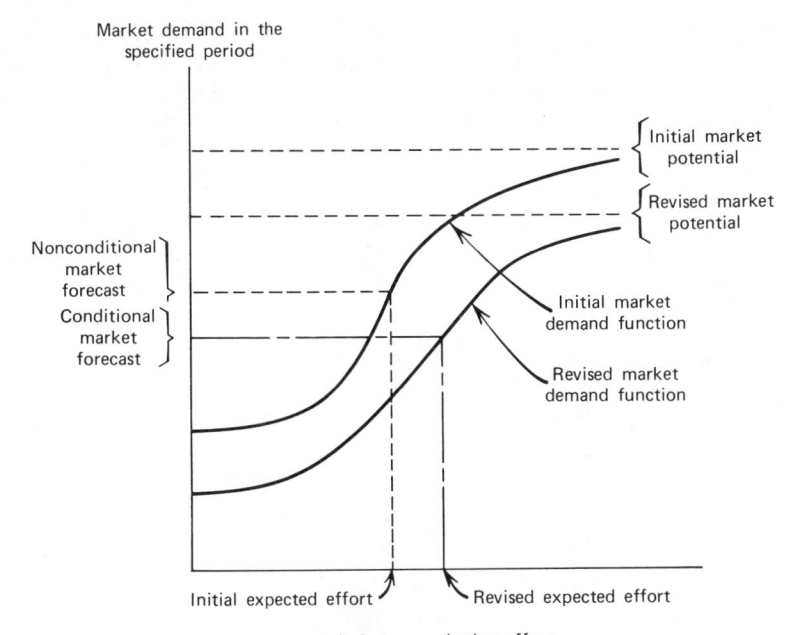

MARKET AND SALES FORECASTING

Figure 8-1 Conditional and nonconditional market forecasts based on alternative market demands and potentials. Source: Philip Kotler, Marketing Management, *3rd ed. Englewood Cliffs, N.J.: Prentice-Hall, 1976, p. 121.*

be utilized heavily in this discussion. Wolfe has written a practical, concise guide to business forecasting that is particularly useful in providing a straight-forward approach to forecasting procedure.[6] Wheelwright and Makridakis have produced the best current guide to the many forecasting methods available. They offer many suggestions for selecting among the methods on the basis of various decision-making situations.[7]

Wolfe has suggested that there are four basic steps in forecasting procedure:

1. Obtaining adequate and accurate bench-mark data
2. Preparing the data properly
3. Applying more than one forecasting method to the data
4. Applying sound judgment and intuition to the forecasts[8]

---
[6] Harry D. Wolfe, *Business Forecasting Methods*. New York: Holt, Rinehart, and Winston, 1966.
[7] Wheelwright and Makridakis, *op. cit.*
[8] Wolfe, *op. cit.*, p. 2.

The first step requires some clarification. Bench-mark data are defined as "... a guide, a barometer, which can be depended upon to assist in making accurate forecasts."[9] Wolfe's examples suggest that bench-mark data are statistical series related to the object being forecast (company sales, product shipments, and so on). Although a number of important forecasting methods, such as regression models, do rely on such bench-mark data, there are others that do not (smoothing techniques and qualitative techniques). Therefore this step has only limited application.

Preparing data properly for forecasting is vital to success, yet it is often overlooked in practice even by experienced forecasters. Wolfe describes eight techniques of data preparation, including the most common technique of doing nothing:

1. Leaving data in its original (raw) form
2. Leaving data in its original form, but combining several series arithmetically or statistically into one series
3. Drawing graphs to determine relationships between forecast object data and bench-mark data, or object data and time
4. Developing lead, lag, or coincidental relationships by graphical or statistical analysis
5. Putting data into percentage form or index numbers and developing ratios and first differences in dollars or percentage terms
6. Separating the data for each recognizable cycle and determining recurrent cycles and cycle stage by analogy
7. Establishing critical levels for a number of series by setting upper and lower limits of historical cyclical variation
8. Putting data into statistical form for use in various quantitative analysis methods[10]

Pursuing this important step further, Wolfe also offers some general rules for preparing data:

1. Use sticky data wherever possible—sticky data are defined as data that do not fluctuate widely or frequently.
2. Use the most macro-level data available—data at the economy level are preferred to industry data which, in turn, are preferred to company data.
3. Use shares or ratios to express relationships among micro-level

[9]*Ibid.*, p. 13.
[10]*Ibid.*, pp. 19–20.

data—shares and ratio data tend to be more sticky than absolute data in dollars or units.
4. Eliminate seasonal influence in the data, if possible.
5. Eliminate dollar and inflation influence by converting data into constant dollars while forecasting, then convert back to current dollars through price adjustments.
6. Eliminate population influence by reducing data to a per capital basis, such as sales per establishment or per employee.
7. Make graphic analyses (free-hand or with a computer plotter) before using advanced forecasting methods.[11]

In the pursuit of accurate forecasts, Wolfe believes that there is some safety in numbers. He recommends that more than one forecasting method should be used and that each method should be applied to an independent data base. Even the use of multiple methods however does not insure against the acceptance of poor forecasts. There is a need for good judgement and intuition on the part of all concerned with forecasting, with forecast data used basically to improve the judgement of those having responsibility for developing accurate forecasts. Figure 8–2 illustrates two approaches to forecasts differing primarily in the process of reconciling the grass-roots and staff forecasts. The right-angle approach places the responsibility for reconciliation on a conference of corporate executives; the I approach places this responsibility on the professional staff forecaster. Each approach has merit: the right-angle approach is best for industrial firms in unstable market situations where a variety of inputs is essential; the I approach is best for relatively stable situations.

The Four-Stage Approach to Forecasting

Both approaches to forecasting illustrated in Figure 8–2 utilize buildup and breakdown procedures analogous to those described in the chapter on market and sales potentials. Grass-roots forecasts are developed by aggregating the forecasts for individual accounts into successively larger segments and thus utilize a buildup procedure. Forecasts prepared by professional staff members of the marketing department are usually based on a breakdown procedure, perhaps the best-known one being the four-stage approach described by Wolfe.[12]

In the four-stage approach to forecasting an initial forecast is prepared

---

[11] *Ibid.*, p. 20.
[12] *Ibid.*, p. 17.

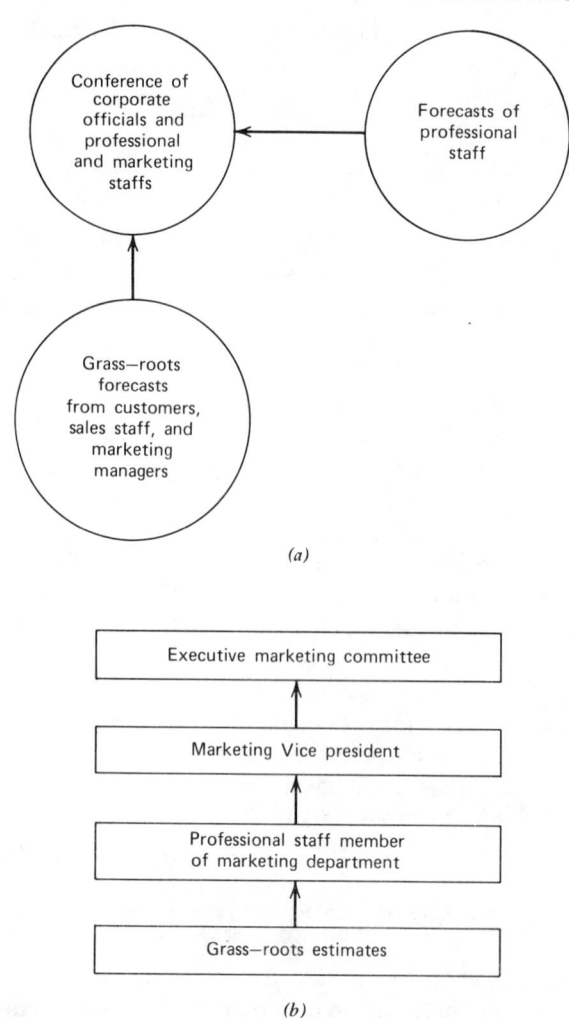

Figure 8-2 Two approaches to reconciling different forecast estimates. (a) Right-angle approach to forecasting. (b) I approach to forecasting. Source: Harry D. Wolfe, Business Forecasting Methods. *New York: Holt, Rinehart, and Winston, 1966, pp. 28-29.*

for the economy (stage 1); then for the industry (stage 2); next for the company (stage 3); and finally for the product/service of the company (stage 4). The usual procedure is to forecast each succeeding stage as a percentage or ratio of the preceding stage forecast. Each stage is thereby linked to all other stages, and changes in any stage can then be introduced and traced with respect to impact on the other stages. The four-stage

MARKET AND SALES FORECASTING

approach will be used in this chapter to organize and illustrate the issues and choices regarding forecasting procedures in the industrial firm.

Forecasting of the Economy. The state of the economy is a powerful influence on the demand for industrial goods and services, so the four-stage approach to forecasting begins with forecasts of changes in general business conditions. The time period to be forecast has a significant effect on the choice of forecasting methods, with long-term forecasts (more than two years ahead) based on trend analysis to a much greater extent than short-term forecasts. Long-term forecasts of general business conditions usually involve trend projections of gross national product (GNP) and its components, such as personal consumption expenditures (PCE) and changes in inventories. Such projections utilize relatively simple arithmetic and statistical calculations of historical growth rates, growth curve fitting with Pearl-Reed and Gompertz curves, and ratio-estimate techniques to relate GNP components to GNP levels. These projections are not likely to be very accurate but that is usually not a problem, since ball-park estimates are generally sufficient for long-term forecasts.

Figure 8-3 shows several long-term forecasts for gross national product and producers' durable equipment, with the forecasts developed by the use of trend analysis and from estimates of federal government agencies and private firms. The researcher has the choice of developing the forecasts internally by trend analysis and other methods, adopting the forecasts developed by others, or a combination of approaches. Most business forecasters seem to favor a combination approach that produces composite forecasts based on both internal and external sources.

Econometric Models for Short-Term Forecasts

Shorter-term forecasts of general business conditions, in contrast to long-term forecasts, increasingly are being based on highly sophisticated economic and statistical analysis. Two of the most important approaches are based on: (1) econometric models, and (2) lead-lag statistical series. Large-scale econometric models have gained acceptance by businesses during the last decade after twenty years of development following the end of World War II. Business acceptance has taken the form of subscription to the continuing services of the major developers of large-scale models, such as the Economics Research Unit of the Wharton School at the University of Pennsylvania, Data Resources Incorporated of Cambridge, Massachusetts, and Chase Econometrics of New York. These models, based on complex systems of simultaneous equations, will be illustrated by examining briefly *The Wharton Quarterly Econometric Forecasting Model (Mark III)*. Figure 8-4 shows a simplified flow chart of

Year	Gross National Product ($)	Producers' durable equipment ($)
1967	1007.7	62.4
1968	1051.8	66.1
1969	1078.8	70.3
1970	1075.3	67.2
1971	1107.5	66.3
1972	1171.1	74.3
1973	1235.0	85.5
1974	1214.0	86.5
1975	1191.7	74.7
1976	1265.0	77.6
1980[a]	1400.0	92.7
1980[b]	1481.0	105.0

[a] 1980 forecasts based on trend analysis of 1967–1976 data.
[b] Forecasts are composites prepared by Predicasts, Inc., and are based on numerous independent forecasts.
Source: 1967–1976 data, *Economic Report of the President*. Washington: U.S. Government Printing Office, 1977, p. 188.

Figure 8–3 Long-Term forecasts of Gross National Product and producers' durable equipment. (billions of 1972 dollars)

Wharton Model. Since the Model is not recursive, it is possible to start at any point in the flow chart and trace the relationships between the factors included in the Model. Starting on the left side of the flow chart, the boxes labeled C, IP, IH, EX and IM, and G represent the various demands within the economy. Lines from these boxes lead to the boxes labeled MNO, XMF, K, XR, and XC, representing the capital stock and the output of the various sectors of the economy. McCarthy then notes that:

> Given sector outputs and available stocks of capital (equipment and structures), we obtain labor requirements (E, MH, and H).[13]

Labor requirements and the labor force participation rate (an exogenous variable) combine to provide a measure of unemployment (UN). The level of unemployment has a lagged effect on wage rates (WR), shown by the

[13] Michael D. McCarthy, *The Wharton Quarterly Econometric Forecasting Model Mark III*. Philadelphia: Economics Research Unit, University of Pennsylvania, 1972, p. 6.

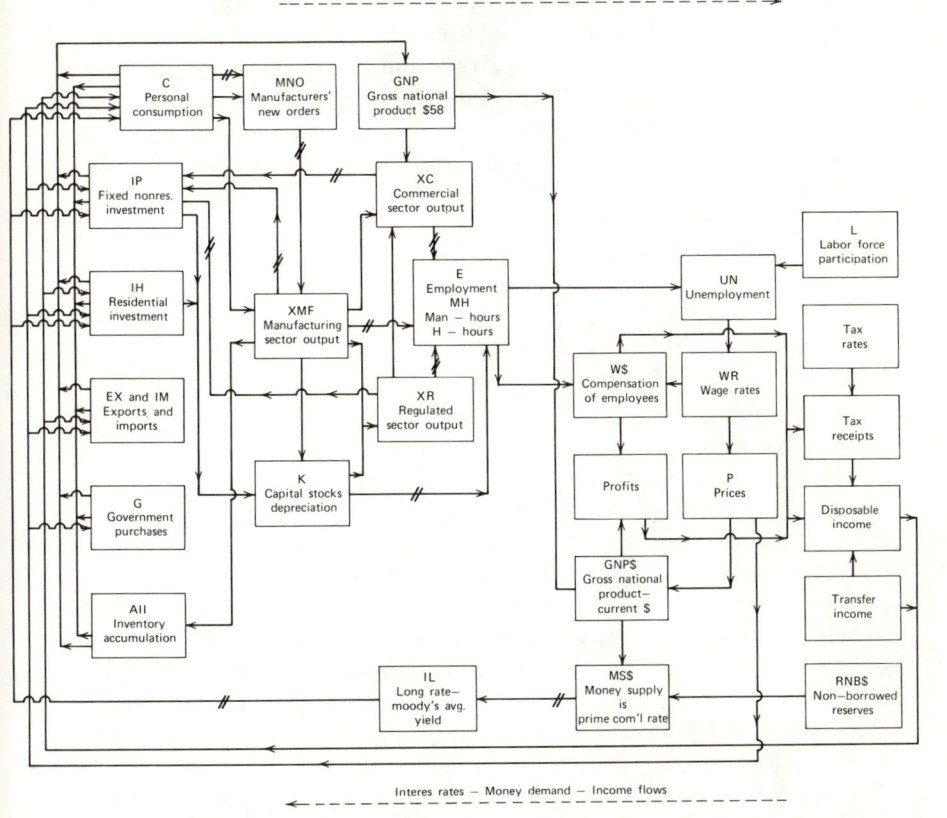

Figure 8–4 Simplified flow chart of The Wharton Quarterly Econometric Forecasting Model Mark III. *Source: Michael D. McCarthy,* The Wharton Quarterly Econometric Forecasting Model Mark III. *Philadelphia: Economics Research Unit, University of Pennsylvania, 1972, p. 7.*

two slashes on the line connecting the two boxes. Wages rates affect the prices of goods and services (P), and prices together with the combined demands for goods and services expressed through GNP in 1958 dollars determines the gross national product in current dollars (GNP$).

The Wharton Model produces quarterly forecasts for the gross national product and its components in current and constant dollars, along with forecasts of the unemployment rate, capacity utilization, percentage change in the money supply, interest rates, and corporate profits. In terms of performance during the 1960s, the Wharton Model did well, predicting each downturn in GNP (in constant dollars), but showing less ability to forecast the timing of upturns in activity. Its record in the 1970s has continued to be good, with the result that businesses have come to rely increasingly on econometric models for short-term economic forecasts.

Lead-Lag Series for Short-Term Forecasts

A second approach to short-term forecasting of general business conditions is based on the concept of cyclical indicators. Stemming from the belief that general business activity is marked by business cycles of alternating periods of expansion and contraction, the cyclical indicators concept seeks to identify those economic time series that tend to lead, coincide, or lag changes in general business activity.

The National Bureau of Economic Research (NBER) has been engaged in research on cyclical indicators since 1938. By 1966 it had identified a list of 73 indicators related to short-term changes in general business activity. Current values of these indicators are readily available in a monthly U.S. Department of Commerce publication, *Business Conditions Digest*. Many business forecasters prefer to use a "short list" of 26 indicators, drawn from the full list and divided into 12 leading series, 8 coincident series, and 6 lagging series. Figure 8–5 shows the composition of the "short list," broken down into the three cyclical timing groups. Forecasters are primarily interested in the leading indicators, which tend to reach their turning points (peaks or troughs) prior to turns in business activity. The coincident and lagging indicators are used by forecasters primarily to confirm or reject the signals received earlier from the leading indicators.

Industrial marketing researchers may find that business activity in their industries and markets tends to be associated with specific leading indicators including and in addition to those in the NBER "short list." Figure 8–6 lists 10 leading series associated with fixed capital investment and 7 leading series associated with inventory investment and purchasing. Historical orders and shipments of the industry and firm may be compared with these indicators to discover which, if any, of the leading series have

MARKET AND SALES FORECASTING

Leading indicators (12 series)

    Average workweek, production workers, manufacturing
    Average weekly initial claims, state unemployment insurance
    Net business formation
    New orders, durable goods industries
    Contracts and orders, plant and equipment
    New building permits, private housing units
    Stock prices, 500 common stocks
    Change in book value, manufacturing and trade inventories
    Industrial materials prices
    Corporate profits after taxes
    Ratio, price to unit labor cost, manufacturing
    Change in consumer installment debt

Roughly coincident indicators (8 series)

    Employees on nonagricultural payrolls
    Unemployment rate, total
    GNP in current dollars
    GNP in 1958 dollars
    Industrial production
    Personal income
    Manufacturing and trade sales
    Sales of retail stores

Lagging indicators (6 series)

    Unemployment rate, persons unemployed 15 weeks and over
    Business expenditures, new plant and equipment
    Book value, manufacturing and trade inventories
    Labor cost per unit of output, manufacturing
    Commercial and industrial loans outstanding, weekly reporting large commercial banks
    Bank rates on short-term business loans

Source: U.S. Department of Commerce, *Business Conditions Digest*. Washington: U.S. Government Printing Office.

Figure 8-5 National Bureau of Economic Research "Short List" of cyclical indicators of general business activity.

tended to reach turning points prior to turns in the industry and firm measures.

Forecasting by the lead-lag approach can involve large-scale data acquisition, maintenance, and handling activities that become very costly and time-consuming. As a result there are a growing number of organizations that offer access and maintenance services together with statistical packages on time-shared computer systems. One of the largest and oldest of these services is MAPCAST, offered by the Information Services Division of the General Electric Company. MAPCAST provides time-

Fixed capital investment series (10 leading indicators)

Formation of business enterprises series

Net business formation
New business incorporations

New investment commitments series

New orders, durable goods industries
Construction contracts, total value
Contracts and orders, plant and equipment
New capital appropriations, manufacturing
Manufacturers' new orders, capital goods industries, nondefense
Construction contracts, commercial and industrial
New private housing units started, total
New building permits, private housing units

Inventory investment and purchasing series (7 leading indicators)

Change in business inventories
Change in book value, manufacturing and trade inventories
Purchased materials, percent of companies reporting higher inventories
Change in book value, manufacturers' inventories of materials and supplies
Buying policy, production materials, percent of companies reporting commitments 60 days or longer
Vendor performance, percent of companies reporting slower deliveries
Change in unfilled orders, durable goods industries

Source: U.S. Department of Commerce, *Business Conditions Digest*. Washington: U.S. Government Printing Office.

Figure 8-6 Selected cyclical indicators that tend to lead industrial business activity.

shared computer access to all of the NBER cyclical indicators as well as some 2000 additional time series from *Business Conditions Digest* and the *Survey of Current Business*. A primary advantage of these services is that each time series is regularly updated and readily accessible along with statistical programs for data analysis. The cost of such services is modest compared to the benefits and their acceptance may be expected to grow accordingly.

Industry and Market Forecasting. In the four-stage approach to forecasting, industry and market forecasts are based on relationships between measures of activity for the industry and market on the one hand and the economy on the other. As in the case of demand and potential estimation, forecasts are generally developed for industries rather than markets because of the quantitative and qualitative superiority of industry data.

Initially historical relationships are sought between general or specific measures of business activity (such as GNP or new capital appropriations by manufacturers) and industry orders or shipments. Once these historical relationships are discovered, the measures of activity at the level of the economy are forecast (internally, from external sources, or both) and forecasts of industry activity are derived on the assumption that the historical relationships will continue in the future. There are times and situations however when historical relationships change expectably or unexpectedly. For industrial goods and services, a major cause of such shifts is technological change.

Forecasting Technological Change

During the past decade there has been a growing interest in technological forecasting. This refers to the process and methods used to evaluate the probability and significance of future technological conditions. Although a number of large industrial organizations such as TRW, General Electric, and Westinghouse have used technological forecasting for ten years or more, there is much less acceptance than of long-range economic forecasting. My experience and that of some others engaged in consulting practice is that most industrial firms are unconvinced that forecasting of technological change is either feasible or practical; both managerial and technical personnel believe that virtually all long-range (over five years) forecasts of technological change would be so imprecise to render them useless. Yet in these same firms, as Isenson has noted,

> The economic forecast is accepted as and expected to be imprecise. It is meant to tell the planner only what might be achieved under the assumed set of conditions.[14]

Similarly organizations and individuals continue to utilize weather forecasts in their planning despite the universal recognition that they are imprecise.

Contrary to widespread opinion, there is continuity in the development of technology and its applications:

> Virtually any technology has a wide and relatively continuous range of characteristics in various applications over a given time period, . . .

---

[14]Raymond S. Isenson, "Technological Forecasting in Perspective," *Management Science*, Vol. 13, October 1966, p. B73.

and it is this relative continuity in a technology's technical and economic characteristics and potential applications which makes technological forecasting possible.[15]

A variety of techniques have been developed for technological forecasting and they may be broadly classified into three groups:[16]

1. *Exploratory techniques*—these capability-oriented techniques are based on extrapolations of historical technological trends.
2. *Normative techniques*—these needs-oriented techniques are based on assessments of the future and technology requirements for the future.
3. *Dynamic techniques*—these techniques combine exploratory and normative elements into a feedback cycle in computer-based models.

EXPLORATORY TECHNIQUES

Exploratory techniques based on trend extrapolation have tended to dominate much of the more recent literature on technological forecasting. They all rely on quantitative historical data as a basis for forecasting. The techniques may be grouped into the following categories:

1. *Systematic curve fitting*—A number of various empirical equations may be fitted to historical data, such as first-, second-, and third-degree polynomials; exponential, power, logistic, and Gompertz curves. Mohn applied each of these types of equations to data on justified typesetting capability as a basis for forecasting typesetting technology.[17]
2. *Diffusion process models*—Anthropologists and sociologists have long been interested in measuring the rate at which innovations spread through a culture and have used logistic curves to portray the process. More recently, economists have adopted these models to explain the spread of industrial innovations. Chapter 9 reviews some of the large body of literature on diffusion models. For another example of these models applied to the United States petroleum refining industry, see

---

[15]James B. Quinn, "Technological Forecasting," *Harvard Business Review*, Vol. 45, March–April 1967, p. 90.
[16]Edwin B. Roberts, "Exploratory and Normative Technological Forecasting: A Critical Appraisal," *Technological Forecasting and Social Change*, Vol. 1, 1969, pp. 113–127.
[17]N. Carroll Mohn, Jr., "Application of Trend Concepts in Forecasting Typesetting Technology," *Technological Forecasting and Social Change*, Vol. 3, 1972, pp. 225–253.

the article by Bundgaard-Nielsen and Fiehn.[18] Rosegger has reviewed the literature and makes a number of useful suggestions for future research in industrial diffusion processes.[19]

3. *Step-wise growth models*—Simmonds[20] has found that plant sizes in the chemical industry tend to constitute a relatively constant proportion of total industry plant capacity. Thus the number of plants tends to be constant with individual plant sizes growing at the same rate as industry capacity and market demand.

Women market demand exceeds industry capacity, one industry producer will build the largest, technically feasible plant possible. Competitors will follow by building comparable plants and closing their older and smaller plants. This process results in a stairstep pattern of plant size growth. Simmonds also found that the principle of a constant relationship between maximum single unit capacity and total industry capacity also applies to a variety of other industries: jet engines, computers, oil tankers, and phosphorous furnaces are some of those identified as adhering to the principle.[21] Martino and Conver have shown that steam and hydroelectric turbines also follow a pattern of step-wise growth. They suggest that the principle appears to be applicable to all technologies characterized by economies of scale.[22]

4. *Technological progress functions*—The three previous exploratory techniques have all been based on plots of a technical capability parameter against time on arithmetic scales. In a technological progress function, a technical capability parameter is plotted against cumulative production output on logarithmic scales. Figure 8–7 shows the plot of the technological progress function representing the development of typesetting technology. Thus the technological progress function is shown to be closely related to the "experience curve" concept developed by the Boston Consulting Group.[23]

---

[18]M. Bundgaard-Nielson and Peter Fiehn, "The Diffusion of New Technology in the U.S. Petroleum Refining Industry," *Technological Forecasting and Social Change*, Vol. 6, 1974, pp. 33–39.
[19]Gerhard Rosegger, "Diffusion Research in the Industrial Setting: Some Conceptual Clarifications," *Technological Forecasting and Social Change*, Vol. 9, 1976, pp. 401–410.
[20]W. H. C. Simmonds, "The Analysis of Industrial Behavior and Its Use in Forecasting," *Technological Forecasting and Social Change*, Vol. 3, 1972, pp. 205–224.
[21]*Ibid.*
[22]Joseph P. Martino and Stephen K. Conver, "The Step-wise Growth of Electric Generator Size," *Technological Forecasting and Social Change*, Vol. 3, 1972, pp. 465–471.
[23]William E. Cox, Jr., "Product Portfolio Strategy: A Review of the Boston Consulting Group Approach to Marketing Strategy," in R. Curhan, Ed., *Marketing's Contributions to the Firm and to Society*. Chicago: American Marketing Association, 1975, pp. 465–470.

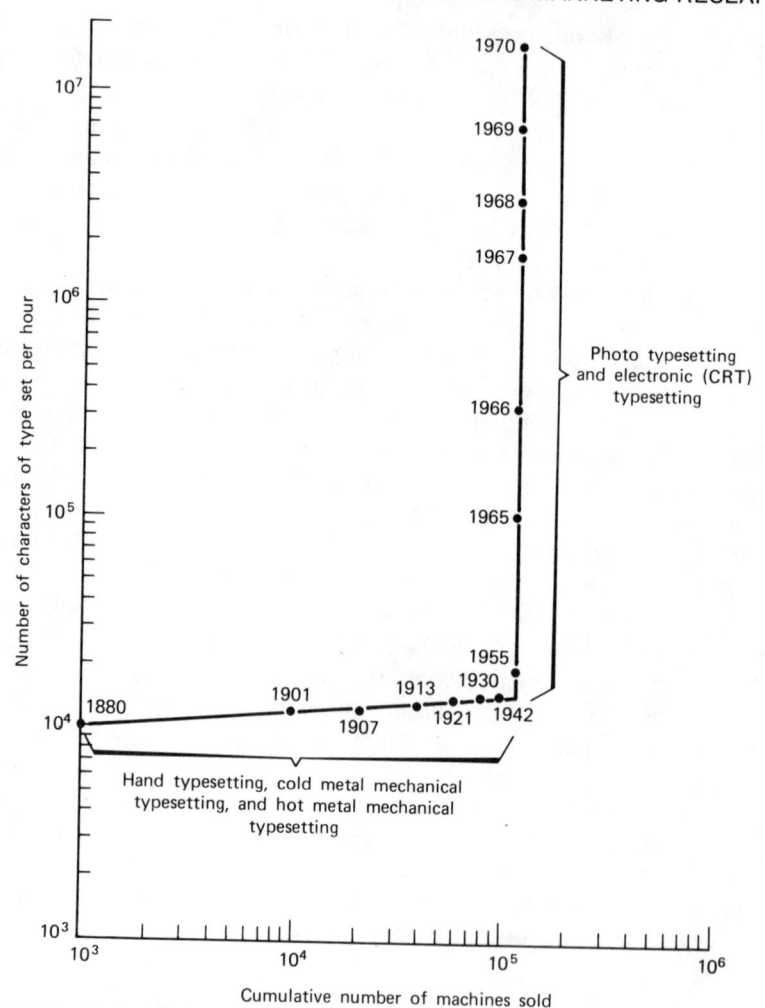

Figure 8-7 Technological progress function: typesetting technology. Source: N. Carroll Mohn, Jr., "Application of Trend Concepts in Forecasting Typesetting Technology," Technological Forecasting and Social Change, Vol. 3, P. 247.

Applications of technological progress functions to turbojet engines and electric lamps has been reported by Fusfeld,[24] and to typesetting technology by Mohn.[25] Sahal has reformulated the technological prog-

[24] Alan R. Fusfeld, "The Technological Progress Function: A New Technique for Forecasting," *Technological Forecasting and Social Change*, Vol. 1, March 1970, pp. 301–312.
[25] Mohn, *op. cit.*

MARKET AND SALES FORECASTING

ress function to correct a variety of theoretical and empirical problems associated with it.[26]

5. *Substitution models*—The most popular exploratory technique currently appears to be substitution models, which seek to measure the rate at which new technologies will be substituted for old. Mansfield developed the first substitution model in which he measured the extent of substitution by the cumulative number of firms adopting the new technology and applied the model successfully to the railroad, steel, coal, and brewery industries.[27] Bass developed a new product growth model similar to Mansfield's and applied it to consumer durables;[28] Nevers extended the Bass model to other sectors, including industrial goods.[29] The models developed by Mansfield, Bass, and Nevers are classified here as substitution models, but they are also generally considered to be diffusion models and will be reviewed in that context in Chapter 9.

Credit for the first substitution model to carry that title goes to Fisher and Pry, who apparently developed their model without knowledge of the Mansfield and Bass models.[30] Their model contains two key assumptions: (1) once the new technology has replaced a few percent of the old technology, it will proceed to 100%, and (2) the fractional rate of substitution of new for old technology is proportional to the remaining amount of old technology-based consumption or output.

Fisher and Pry observed that substitutions tended to follow an S-shaped curve, with two constants:[31]

(1) the early growth rate, and (2) the time at which the substitution is half complete. The corresponding fraction substituted is given by the relationship:

$$f = \frac{1}{2} 1 + \tan h \, \alpha \, (t - t_0)$$

---

[26] Davendra Sahal, "A Reformulation of the Technological Progress Function," *Technological Forecasting and Social Change*, Vol. 8, 1975, pp. 75–90.

[27] Edwin Mansfield, "Technical Change and the Rate of Imitation," *Econometrica*, Vol. 29, October 1961, pp. 741–766.

[28] Frank M. Bass, "A New Product Growth Model for Consumer Durables," *Management Science*, Vol. 15, January 1969, pp. 215–227.

[29] John V. Nevers, "Extensions of a New Product Growth Model," *Sloan Management Review*, Vol. 13, Winter 1972, pp. 77–91.

[30] J. C. Fisher and R. H. Pry, "A Simple Substitution Model of Technological Change," *Technological Forecasting and Social Change*, Vol. 3, 1971, pp. 75–88.

[31] *Ibid.*, p. 76.

where α is half the annual fractional growth in the early years and where t_0 is the time at which $f = 1/2$.

They elected to measure a substitution in terms of its takeover time, defined as the time required to go from $f = 0.1$ to $f = 0.9$. This time is shown to be inversely proportional to α,

$$t = t_{0.9} - t_{0.1} = \frac{2.2}{\alpha}$$

Fisher and Pry next pointed out that[32]

A more convenient form of the above substitution expression (1) is:

$$f/(1 - f) = \exp 2\alpha(t - t_0)$$

This expression allows one to plot the substitution data in the form of $f/(1-f)$ as a function of time on semilog paper and fit a straight line through the resulting points. The slope of the line is 2α, the time t_0 is found at $f/(1-f) = 1$, and the takeover time is easily measured as the time between $f/(1-f) = 0.11$ and $f/(1-f) = 9$.

They applied their substitution model with impressive results to 17 cases, such as the substitution of synthetic for natural rubber.

Lenz and Lanford then demonstrated that the Fisher-Pry model can be successfully applied once a substitution of 2% has been reached. They noted the following uses of substitution forecasts:[33]

To determine the advisability of remaining in a technology that is being displaced;

[To] assist in the decision of investing in a new technology that may expect a long period of severe competition; and

[To] assess when a new technology may be expected to prevail, when to enter a new technology, when to leave an old technology, and anticipated dates of general usage.

Subsequently a number of modifications to the Mansfield and Fisher-Pry models have been reported for a variety of industrial products and

---

[32] *Ibid.*, p. 77.
[33] Ralph C. Lenz, Jr. and H. W. Lanford, "The Substitution Phenomenon," *Business Horizons*, Vol. 14, February 1972, pp. 63–68.

processes: Blackman,[34] Stern, et al.,[35] and Sharif and Uddin[36] are examples of this growing literature.

NORMATIVE TECHNIQUES

Normative techniques for technological forecasting share the common characteristics of being based on assessments of the future by experts, being essentially qualitative in nature, and being relatively free of historical influence. All of these characteristics serve to differentiate these techniques sharply from exploratory techniques. As such, normative techniques are particularly useful for very long-range forecasting and in situations generally where discontinuities in technology may be anticipated. Two broad classifications of normative techniques may be established: (1) scenario generation, and (2) morphological analysis. Scenario generation techniques, in turn, may be further classified into two categories:

1. *Delphi method*—Originally developed as a short-term forecasting method, the Delphi method has become the most popular normative technique for technological forecasting. It pools the opinions of a group of experts, based on the proposition that group opinion will be more accurate than that of any individual expert. Fusfeld and Foster have noted that the technique

    . . . will include anonymity of experts (to eliminate bias); controlled feedback (to develop consensus); and an estimator of group opinion (to extrapolate a forecast).[37]

Their article also includes brief reviews of the use of the Delphi method

---

[34] A. Wade Blackman, "The Rate of Innovation in the Commercial Aircraft Jet Engine Market," *Technological Forecasting and Social Change*, Vol. 2, 1971, pp. 269–276; Blackman, "A Mathematical Model for Trend Forecasts," *Technological Forecasting and Social Change*, Vol. 3, 1972, pp. 441–452; Blackman, "The Market Dynamics of Technological Substitutions," *Technological Forecasting and Social Change*, Vol. 6, 1974, pp. 41–63.

[35] M. O. Stern, R. U. Ayres, and A. Shapanka, "A Model for Forecasting the Substitution of One Technology for Another," *Technological Forecasting and Social Change*, Vol. 7, 1975, pp. 57–79.

[36] M. N. Sharif and G. A. Uddin, "A Procedure for Adapting Technological Forecasting Models," *Technological Forecasting and Social Change*, Vol. 7, 1975, pp. 99–106.

[37] Alan R. Fusfeld and Richard N. Foster, "The Delphi Technique: Survey and Comment," *Business Horizons*, Vol. 14, June 1971, p. 65.

by LTV, TRW, and Goodyear Tire & Rubber Corporation, as well as an examination of various studies on the behavior and accuracy of forecasts developed by the Delphi method.

One of the most widely publicized applications of the Delphi method for the purposes of technological forecasting has been the PROBE studies conducted by TRW.[38] These studies were begun in the early 1960s. PROBE 1 identified 401 technical events that a panel of 27 experts believed would occur by 1986 and have a significant impact on the future of TRW.

2. *Cross-impact analysis*—An extension of the Delphi method is provided by cross-impact analysis, which seeks to examine the interrelationships between the forecasted events and items. Many of the 401 technical events identified in PROBE 1 by TRW would be interrelated. Cross-impact analysis would proceed by establishing a matrix of the cross-effects of the various events, specifying linkages among events, the strength of the relationships, and the nature of the relationships: positive, negative, and precursor events. A recent article by Helmer (.who was the codeveloper of both the Delphi method and cross-impact analysis) reviews both methods of scenario generation and proposes a new method for conducting cross-impact analysis.[39]

Another class of normative techniques for technological forecasting is morphological analysis. This is generally mentioned in any listing of technological forecasting techniques, but apparently rarely applied in practice. Morphological analysis seeks to

> ... visualize all possible solutions to any given problem and point the way toward the general performance evaluation of these solutions.[40]

This cited article by O'Neal and another by Wissema[41] provide illustrations of how the technique might be applied to technological forecasting, but case studies of actual applications are needed to demonstrate the usefulness of the technique.

---

[38] Harper Q. North and Donald L. Pyke, " 'Probes' of the Technological Future," *Harvard Business Review*, Vol. 47, May–June 1969, pp. 68–76.
[39] Olaf Helmer, "Problems in Futures Research: Delphi and Causal Cross-Impact Analysis," *Futures*, Vol. 9, February 1977, pp. 17–31.
[40] Charles R. O'Neal, "Morphological Analysis," *Business Horizons*, Vol. 13, December 1970, p. 49.
[41] Johan G. Wissema, "Morphological Analysis: Its Application to a Company TF Investigation," *Futures*, Vol. 8, April 1976, pp. 146–153.

DYNAMIC TECHNIQUES

In recent years there has been a great deal of public attention drawn to the several studies of the future sponsored by the Club of Rome. These studies have used dynamic techniques to forecast technological change, using both exploratory and normative elements in a computer-based model. While these studies have had a global perspective, Blackman has shown that the techniques can be applied to industry-level forecasts.[42]

A survey of technological forecasting practices in 29 firms (largely industrial goods producers) revealed that 15 firms were preparing formal technological forecasts.[43] Firms with the largest numbers of products and markets (considered to be in complex environments) were most likely to use formal techniques for technological forecasting. No clear pattern of technique use appeared in the study. Most respondents indicated that technological forecasting had not been integrated into their firm's planning and decision-making activities. Thus this potentially valuable management tool appears to have had limited acceptance to date among industrial firms, but there are signs that technological forecasting is becoming accepted among firms that face complex, rapidly changing technical environments.

Selecting Appropriate Techniques for Industry Forecasts

In addition to considering the impact of technological change on industry forecasts, the forecaster must also take into account a number of other characteristics of the situation. Wheelwright and Makridakis suggest six major characteristics that should be considered in selecting the most appropriate techniques for forecasting:

1. *Time horizon*—Forecasts may be prepared for the immediate term (less than one month), short term (one to three months), medium term (over three months and up to two years), and long term (more than two years).
2. *Level of detail*—Industry forecasts may range from relatively general levels such as an SIC 4-digit industry (SIC 3541, Metalworking

---

[42] A. Wade Blackman, "Forecasting through Dynamic Modeling," *Technological Forecasting and Social Change*, Vol. 3, 1972, pp. 291–307.

[43] James M. Utterback and Elmer H. Burack, "Identification of Technological Threats and Opportunities by Firms," *Technological Forecasting and Social Change*, Vol. 8, 1975, pp. 7–21.

machinery, metal cutting type) to specific products at the SIC 7-digit level (SIC 3541436, horizontal surface grinding machines, reciprocating table type).

3. *Number of items*—Firms requiring forecasts for hundreds of different products may have to use different forecasting techniques than the firm with a limited product or service line.
4. *Control versus planning requirements*—Forecasting techniques used for control purposes must be very responsive to sudden changes in the direction and magnitude of the data, while those used for planning must be capable of identifying complex historical patterns as a basis for extrapolation.
5. *Stability*—The historic level of stability in the situation being forecasted affects the choice of techniques, since they vary widely in their capacity to deal with variations in data.
6. *Existing planning procedures*—Since the acceptance of any forecasting technique will usually result in a change in planning and decision-making procedures in the firm, Wheelwright and Makridakis recommend that the initial choice of technique should be strongly influenced by existing procedures and that an evolutionary process of upgrading the techniques used be adopted.[44]

There is another characteristic that is very important in the choice of forecasting technique, the type of product or service produced by the industry. This characteristic is so important in choosing the right technique for forecasting activity in industrial goods and services that it has been adopted as the primary basis for organizing the following material on the available techniques. All industrial products and services may be classified into three groups:

1. *Major and accessory equipment*—used directly in the production process, such as machine tools and hoists.
2. *Component parts and materials*—incorporated directly into the products of the producer, such as compressor components and plastic resins.
3. *Operating supplies and services*—consumed in the process of production, such as oils, pens, and accounting services.

Three other considerations in the choice of appropriate forecasting techniques are: (1) the characteristics of the techniques, (2) the quality

---
[44]Wheelwright and Makridakis, *op. cit.*, pp. 6–8.

MARKET AND SALES FORECASTING

and quantity of available historical data, and (3) the time available for producing forecasts. Wheelwright and Makridakis have identified six major characteristics to consider in evaluating forecasting techniques:

1. *Time horizon*—Quantitative techniques tend to be better for shorter-term forecasts, qualitative techniques are best applied to long-term forecast situations. The number of future periods to be forecast is also a factor in the choice of techniques.
2. *Data patterns*—Techniques vary in their ability to detect seasonal, cyclical, and trend influences in data and should be matched appropriately with observed data patterns.
3. *Type of model*—Some techniques implicitly assume that time is the most important determinant of data variation, others are based on a search for relationships among variables.
4. *Cost*—The cost of using the various techniques differs considerably and thus may influence choice.
5. *Accuracy*—The level of accuracy required in the forecast may also influence the selection of a technique, for there are inherent differences between techniques that affect their probable level of accuracy.
6. *Ease of application*—Some forecasting techniques are very easy to understand and apply, others are extremely complex and difficult to apply. Managers are unlikely to use techniques which they do not understand or find difficult to apply.[45]

Another very useful guide to the various forecasting techniques available has been developed by Chambers, Mullick, and Smith.[46] They compare 18 techniques with the aid of six criteria: (1) accuracy, (2) turning point identification capability, (3) most appropriate applications, (4) data required, (5) cost, and (6) time required to develop the forecast. In the following section, these criteria and those suggested by Wheelwright and Makridakis will be employed within the three-group product and service classification scheme to suggest the most appropriate forecasting techniques to use in various situations.

Major and Accessory Equipment

Major equipment is characterized primarily by its relatively high unit price, with the result that buying firms generally treat such equipment as a

---
[45] Wheelwright and Makridakis, *op. cit.*, pp. 8–9.
[46] John C. Chambers, Satinder K. Mullick, and Donald D. Smith, "How to Choose the Right Forecasting Technique," *Harvard Business Review*, Vol. 49, July–August 1971, pp. 45–74.

capital expense for accounting purposes. These capital goods are often highly specialized, custom-built items, and thereby associated with very limited, well-defined markets. Accessory equipment in contrast tends to be characterized by lower unit prices, the items are charged to current expenses in most situations and tend to be more standardized. Markets for accessory equipment tend to be more numerous and diverse than those for major equipment, but they are sufficiently similar to permit us to treat them as a group for our purposes.

The demand for major and accessory equipment tends to be highly volatile, with "boom or bust" conditions prevailing most of the time. Short product lines mean that few forecasts have to be prepared and the limited markets make it possible to identify and contact potential buyers. Industry and market data are relatively volatile, so that problems of autocorrelation (relationship between successive values in a data series) are minimal. The primary techniques applicable to forecasting the demand for equipment are: (1) sales force composite method, (2) users' expectations method, and (3) regression analysis.

The sales force composite method is sometimes referred to as the grass-roots approach, since it is based on salesmen's estimates of future sales in their territories by customer and product class. Branch or regional sales managers generally review each salesman's estimates, preferably in consultation with the salesman, making any adjustments required and then forwarding the forecasts to the next level in the sales organization. A composite sales forecast is thereby developed that reflects the best available market information among all sales personnel. Historically most companies have only asked salesmen for forecasts of company sales, but the practice today is to ask for industry sales as well, so that salesmen take on additional responsibility for examining the company's opportunities from a larger perspective. A good example of how the Harris Corporation (formerly Harris-Intertype) used the sales force composite method to produce forecasts for printing presses and bindery equipment is provided in a publication of the National Industrial Conference Board.[47] A special feature of the Harris approach was that all district managers, within two to three weeks after the call for the semi-annual forecast, received a visit from a staff forecasting specialist, who reviewed the estimates in detail and examined any variations from historical patterns with particular care. This process not only helped the district managers prepare their own forecasts, but also gave the staff specialist (who had to

---

[47] National Industrial Conference Board, *Forecasting Sales*. New York: NICB, 1964, pp. 26–27.

MARKET AND SALES FORECASTING

prepare an independent forecast) important insights into market conditions necessary for accurate aggregate forecasts.

Another qualitative technique used to forecast the demand for equipment is the users' expectations method. This technique is based on surveys of product users, who are asked to provide information on their expected purchases of given products during a specified future period. The surveys are generally conducted by marketing research personnel and focus on the users' expected purchases from all suppliers of the product. Phelps and Westing provide an example of the use of this technique to forecast the demand for radiation gauges.[48] These gauges are used in metal rolling mills to monitor deviations from specified thickness or weight in sheet and strip products and correct the rollers accordingly. The X-ray department of the General Electric Company wanted to forecast the demand for radiation gauges and initially sought to determine the relationship between gauge sales and capital expenditures. In the steel industry, as well as others, it was found that this approach would not work, because gauge sales were a very small fraction of the cost of a new or rebuilt rolling mill (although the average price of a gauge was approximately $50,000) and the number and size of the mills were changing continuously. After determining that there were only 10 builders of steel mills in the United States, it was decided to interview each of them. These firms were willing to disclose the number of mills they had completed and had contracts to build, allowing GE to develop reliable forecasts annually of radiation gauge sales.

Regression analysis involves the use of statistical techniques to develop a relationship between the forecast (dependent) variable and one or more independent variables. Ohis quantitative technique seeks to fit a model containing these variables to historical data, as a basis for forecasting future values of the dependent variable. Wheelwright and Makridakis show how regression analysis may be used in forecasting with simplified illustrations of applications of the technique.[49] A specific application of regression analysis to capital goods forecasting is provided in a series of articles dealing with the relationship between new orders and shipments of capital goods. All of these studies are based on models of the general form:

$$S_t = \sum_{i=0}^{n-1} W^t(i)\, N_{t-1}$$

---

[48] D. Maynard Phelps and J. Howard Westing, *Marketing Management*, 3rd ed. Homewood, Ill.: Irwin, 1968, pp. 477–479.
[49] Wheelwright and Makridakis, *op. cit.*, Chaps. 5 and 7.

where

S_t = shipments level in current period
$W_t(i)$ = variable weight coefficient
N_{t-1} = value of new orders at time $t-1$
n = maximum length of the lag between new orders and shipments

Each study of the orders-shipment relationship disclosed that the "... lag of shipments behind new orders lengthens as the ratio of accumulated unfilled orders to shipments increases."[50] As this ratio increases, the weights applied to earlier periods increases and the current period weight decreases. The Bodkin and Murthy study found that the maximum length of the lag is 5 (n = 5), so that shipments in the current period (quarter) are generated from new orders in the current period and the preceding four periods.[51] Earlier studies based on United States data examined shorter maximum lag periods, with Popkin using a two-period lag and Tinsley a four-period lag. The findings of all three studies are generally comparable.[52] This suggests that shipments of capital goods industries may be forecast by using data on new orders for up to five quarters ahead of the forecast period.

Another feature of forecasting the demand for equipment is that it may be useful to distinguish between expansion and replacement demand and prepare independent forecasts for each type of demand. For relatively mature industries and products, replacement demand is typically far larger and much more stable than expansion demand. Using data on the size of the stock and its age distribution, by consuming industry, longer-term forecasting of the replacement demand for equipment may be improved over aggregate forecasts of demand. The ability of consuming industries to accelerate or postpone purchases of equipment relative to an expected time of replacement often adversely affects the forecasts of equipment for a given year. Over a period of years however such forecasts are generally quite accurate. Forecasts of expansion demand must be grounded more on the level and expectations regarding general busi-

---

[50] Ronald G. Bodkin and K. S. R. Murthy, "The Orders-Shipments Mechanism in Canadian Producer Goods Industries," *Journal of the American Statistical Association*, Vol. 68, June 1973, p. 304.

[51] *Ibid.*, p. 303.

[52] Joel Popkin, "The Relationship Between New Orders and Shipments: An Analysis of the Machinery and Equipment Industries," *Survey of Current Business*, March 1965, pp. 24–32; Peter A. Tinsley, "An Application of Variable Weight Distributed Lags," *Journal of the American Statistical Association*, Vol. 62, December 1967, pp. 1277–1289.

ness conditions, the availability of tax incentives, and the growth of end-product markets. Since expansion demand for equipment is also subject to acceleration or postponement as well as the other factors mentioned, it tends to be much more volatile than replacement demand with accompanying reduction in forecast accuracy.

Forecasting the demand for *new* equipment requires that other techniques be adopted. Variations on the S-curve approach used in technological forecasting are the most common techniques reported in the literature. Wentz and Eyrich suggest a three-step process: (1) construct a general model of the determinants of demand for the product, (2) estimate the parameters of each demand determinant (independent variable) and specify the explicit equation for the market potential for the product, and (3) estimate the rate of market penetration by using a Gompertz or logistic function to describe an S-shared demand curve.[53] Root and Klompmaker recommend a similar approach based on the following model:[54]

$$S(t) = \sum_{i=1}^{n} Q_i(t) M_i(t) F_i(t) - \sum_{j=1}^{t-1} S(j)$$

where

$S(t)$ = total estimated unit sales in period t for all n customers
$Q_i(t)$ = total potential usage
$M_i(t)$ = maximum fraction of the business obtainable from customer (market segment) i in period t
$F_i(t)$ = proportion of the total potential converted to the generic new product by period t
$S(j)$ = total estimated sales in period j for all n customers
i = index for a particular customer or market segment
t = index for the time period

It will be noted that the $F_i(t)$ variable is the rate of market penetration expected by period t, and the authors suggest using a Weibull distribution rather than a Gompertz or logistic function to describe the growth (S-shaped) curve because of the inherent flexibility of the distribution. The model also includes a maximum market share variable, $M_i(t)$, that results

---

[53] W. B. Wentz and G. I. Eyrich, "Product Forecasting without Historical, Survey, or Experimental Data," in R. L. King, Ed., *Marketing and the New Science of Planning.* Chicago: American Marketing Association, 1968, pp. 215–221.

[54] H. Paul Root and Jay E. Klompmaker, "A Microanalytic Sales Forecasting Model for New Industrial Products," in Fred C. Allvine, Ed., *Marketing in Motion.* Chicago: Marketing Association, 1972, pp. 474–477.

in $S(t)$ denoting sales rather than industry forecasts. Industry forecasts could of course be derived from the model.

Component Parts and Materials

We have noted that component parts and materials are characterized by their incorporation into the final products of the producer. The principal distinction of component parts is that they retain their identity in the final product whereas most materials do not. There is consequently a replacement demand for component parts. For some products the replacement demand may be larger than the OEM (original equipment manufacturer) demand. In this regard component parts resemble major and accessory equipment, but there are important differences (and similarities with materials) that argue for treating component parts and materials as a separate group. The most important difference between parts and materials as compared to equipment is the importance of inventory levels on period demand. Inventory adjustment (both input and output inventories of consuming industries) can have a profound effect on short-term demand for component parts and materials. While not absent as an effect on equipment, particularly accessory equipment, inventories generally have a lesser impact on the demand for such goods.

Additional factors that distinguish component parts and materials as a separate group of industrial goods are: (1) a larger number of potential customers, and (2) a lower average sales transaction per customer than that associated with equipment. As a result the forecasting techniques most applicable to component parts and materials are those based on analysis of historical data (time series) for the forecast variable. The primary basis for concentrating on the statistical analysis of one variable (the forecast variable) rather than several variables is economic; it is expensive to develop multivariate demand models and the benefit/cost ratio of such models for most component parts and materials would be unfavorable.

There are reported uses of such qualitative techniques as the sales force composite and users' expectations methods for forecasting the demand for component parts and materials. In each case however the focus is on key accounts with limited coverage of the remaining accounts to produce total industry forecasts.[55] By concentrating on forecasting the demand by

---

[55] For a case study on the application of the sales force composite method to materials, see: Pennsalt Chemicals Corporation in National Industrial Conference Board, *Forecasting Sales*. New York: NICB, 1964, pp. 25–26. A case study on the users' expectations method to forecast material sales is provided in the same source: National Lead Company, pp. 31–32.

key accounts, the costs of using these methods may be controlled and useful information may be developed. The regression analysis example (presented in the section on major and accessory equipment), which used new orders as a leading indicator for shipments, has its analogue in an example to be discussed next on forecasting steel consumption with the aid of a very simple model based on anticipated sales and capital spending by using industries. Thus all of the forecasting techniques that are assigned to one group of industrial products may, with appropriate modification, be used with other groups. Nevertheless there are preferred forecasting techniques that should be considered for each product and service group prior to adapting other techniques to fit the specific situation.

A four-year forecast of steel consumption by consuming industry was developed using the following equation:[56]

$$\hat{Y}_k, t+h = \sum_j a'_{kj} S^*_j, t+h + \sum_j b'_{kj} I^*_j, t+h$$

where

$\hat{Y}_k, t+h$ = the forecast of sales by industry k (steel industry, in the example) in period $t+h$

$S^*_j, t+h$ = anticipated sales of industry j (consuming industry) in period $t+h$

$I^*_j, t+h$ = anticipated capital spending of industry j in period $t+h$

h = forecast horizon, number of periods

The authors obtained data on steel consumption by consuming industry from American Iron and Steel Institute (AISI) data on steel shipments, adjusting the shipments data to transform them to consumption data, and then assigning the consuming industry into two groups: (1) those purchasing steel on capital account (and thus not directly related to their output), and (2) current account industries (that purchase steel directly in relation to their output). The coefficients, a'_{kj} and b'_{kj}, were estimated from consumption data for 1969 together with actual data on sales and capital spending for 1969. Forecasts for the years 1970–1973 were developed by combining the coefficients with data from McGraw-Hill's *Business Plans for New Plants and Equipment* on anticipated sales and capital spending for those years by consuming industry. The resulting forecasts are shown in Figure 8–8, and it will be observed that while the 1970 forecast was substantially in error, the forecasts were reasonably

[56] Richard Rippe, Maurice Wilkinson, and Donald Morrison, "Industrial Market Forecasting with Anticipations Data." *Management Science.* Vol. 22, February 1976, pp. 639–651.

Industry	1969 Actual	1970 Fore.	1970 Act.	1971 Fore.	1971 Act.	1972 Fore.	1972 Act.	1973 Fore.	1973 Act.
Capital account									
Mining	670	711	762	656	756	901	806	807	810
Petroleum	3,124	3,172	2,911	3,000	3,190	3,248	3,337	2,760	4,141
Other industries	23,822	24,499	23,014	23,620	22,913	25,717	23,046	28,794	27,088
Current account									
Automobiles	26,001	26,520	21,490	24,596	26,856	28,563	28,319	31,723	34,070
Other transport equipment	4,862	5,138	4,479	4,313	4,854	3,997	3,927	4,678	4,678
Machinery except electrical	9,619	10,234	9,169	9,319	9,001	9,551	10,207	11,652	11,381
Electrical machinery	7,456	7,940	7,445	7,981	7,498	7,998	8,326	8,528	9,242
Fabricated metals and instruments	20,351	22,313	20,386	20,555	19,406	20,945	19,180	23,252	21,167
Other manufacturing industries	6,777	7,273	7,444	7,090	8,041	7,391	9,415	8,024	9,951
Total	102,682	107,800	97,100	101,130	102,515	108,311	106,613	120,218	122,528

Note: Fore. = Forecast; Act. = Actual
Source: Richard Rippe, Maurice Wilkinson, and Donald Morrison, "Industrial Market Forecasting with Anticipations Data," *Management Science*, Vol. 22, February 1976, pp. 647–648.

Figure 8–8 *Actual and forecast steel consumption by industry 1969–1973 (in 000 tons)*.

close to the actual results for 1971-1973. It is especially interesting that this simple model out-performed two naive forecasting models (no change and same change between the two most recent years) in terms of accuracy. It will be observed that the actual data tend to be relatively horizontal. Thus little further improvement in forecasting accuracy could be expected by applying more advanced techniques to these data. The most likely source of improvement in this simple model would be to treat explicitly the effect of inventory changes—the authors did not do this in their use of adjustment procedures to transform shipments data to consumption data. At this point it is appropriate to consider an approach to handling inventory changes.

Kuehn and Day have suggested that the acceleration principle of macroeconomic theory may be useful in forecasting factory shipments of basic industrial products, where historical shipments data have shown relatively large fluctuations over time.[57] Applied to inventory investment, the acceleration principle results from a tendency for holders of inventory to maintain inventory levels at a constant ratio to sales, thereby accelerating or amplifying the magnitude of changes in their orders on suppliers. Kuehn and Day provide an example of a firm producing a special purpose alloy that wished to forecast industry shipments of the product for a coming year. Using survey and other data, consumption of the alloy was expected to increase by 20% in the coming year and current inventory levels were considered normal. At the end of the year consumption was up almost exactly 20% and inventories were still normal, but factory shipments had increased by 33%. The difference between consumption and shipments was due to the presence of the acceleration effect and their example shows how this effect may be measured. In this industry manufacturers sold to fabricators who attempted to maintain inventory levels on a 9-week supply basis (equal to 15-weeks sales); jobbers bought the week supply basis (equal to 15-weeks sales); jobbers bought the alloy from fabricators and tried to maintain a 15-weeks supply; end-users bought from jobbers and sought to maintain a 5-weeks supply.

The cumulative effect on a 20% increase in consumption may be traced through the channel of distribution as shown in Figure 8-9, resulting in a final increase of 33.1% in manufacturers' sales. Decreases in consumption have a similar cumulative effect, indicating the importance of measuring the acceleration effect on forecasts of shipments of industrial goods subject to inventory-holding in their channels of distribution.

The influence of inventory adjustment on short-term demand for com-

---

[57] Alfred A. Kuehn and Ralph L. Day, "The Acceleration Effect in Forecasting Industrial Shipments," *Journal of Marketing*, January 1963, pp. 25-28.

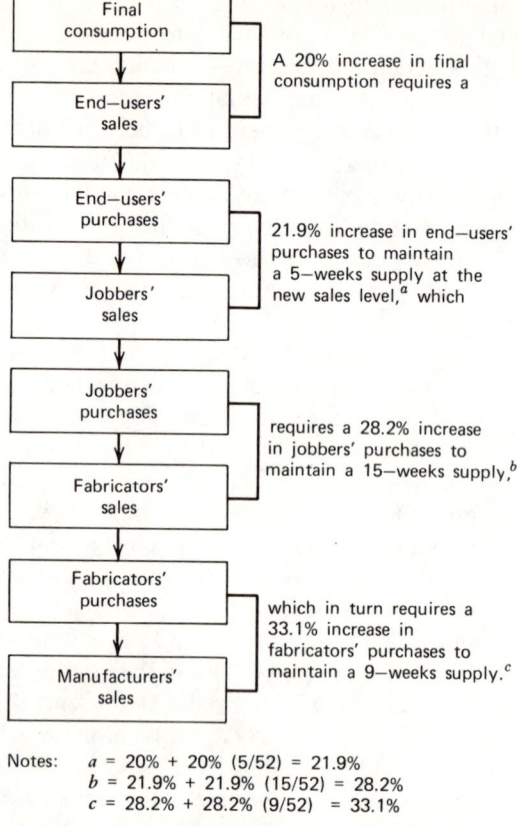

```
┌─────────────────┐
│      Final      │
│   consumption   │
└────────┬────────┘
         ▼                    A 20% increase in final
┌─────────────────┐           consumption requires a
│   End—users'    │
│      sales      │
└────────┬────────┘
         ▼
┌─────────────────┐
│   End—users'    │
│    purchases    │
└────────┬────────┘           21.9% increase in end—users'
         ▼                    purchases to maintain
┌─────────────────┐           a 5—weeks supply at the
│    Jobbers'     │           new sales level,$^a$ which
│      sales      │
└────────┬────────┘
         ▼
┌─────────────────┐
│    Jobbers'     │
│    purchases    │
└────────┬────────┘           requires a 28.2% increase
         ▼                    in jobbers' purchases to
┌─────────────────┐           maintain a 15—weeks supply,$^b$
│   Fabricators'  │
│      sales      │
└────────┬────────┘
         ▼
┌─────────────────┐
│   Fabricators'  │
│    purchases    │
└────────┬────────┘           which in turn requires a
         ▼                    33.1% increase in
┌─────────────────┐           fabricators' purchases to
│  Manufacturers' │           maintain a 9—weeks supply.$^c$
│      sales      │
└─────────────────┘
```

Notes: $a = 20\% + 20\% (5/52) = 21.9\%$
         $b = 21.9\% + 21.9\% (15/52) = 28.2\%$
         $c = 28.2\% + 28.2\% (9/52) = 33.1\%$

Figure 8-9 Acceleration effects of changes in final consumption on demand in a channel of distribution. Source: Alfred A. Kuehn and Ralph L. Day, "The Acceleration Effect in Forecasting Industrial Shipments," Journal of Marketing, January 1963, p. 26.

ponent parts and materials has been noted, and the application of the acceleration principle examined as a basis for improving the forecasts of shipments of such products. There may be however other factors contributing to the traditional volatility of historical time series for component parts and materials. Seasonal and cyclical factors, as well as random influences, may have significant impacts on the demand for these products and historical time series should be examined to determine these impacts. The general forecasting technique applicable in such situations is what Wheelwright and Makridakis have called the "classical decomposition" method.[58]

[58] Wheelwright and Makridakis, *op. cit.*, Chap. 6.

MARKET AND SALES FORECASTING

Applying the decomposition method to historical time series data results in a separation of three factors that compose the basic pattern of the time series together with the random variation within the pattern. The equation generally used to portray the decomposition method in multiplicative, although some authors prefer an additive relationship:

$$O = T \times C \times S \times R$$

where

O = original time series data
T = trend factor, to measure long-run linear pattern
C = cyclical factor, to measure periodic variation of one year or more
S = seasonal factor, to measure periodic variation of less than one year
R = random variation, to account for unexplained variation in pattern.

Figure 8–10 presents monthly time series data on industry shipments of Malleable Iron Castings Shipments for sale. Inspection of these data indicates that: (1) seasonality appears to be a factor, October tends to be a high-shipment month and December appears to be a low-shipment month; (2) a trend factor seems to be present, 1975 shipments were lower than 1969 values; and (3) a cyclical factor may also be present because of the rising and falling pattern during the period.

The seasonal factor is determined by calculating a 12-month moving average for each month (Figure 8–11), and deriving the seasonal index for each month as shown in Figure 8–12. Next, the trend factor is determined by fitting a simple regression equation ($Y = a + b\ X$) to the moving average values and obtaining a trend value for each monthly value in the time series. Finally, the cyclical factor may be estimated for each month by dividing the moving average value by the trend value for the month.

Forecasts may then be prepared for any desired future month or set of months by: (1) applying the appropriate seasonal factor(s), (2) calculating the trend factor by substituting the month(s) value of x_i in the regression equation ($Y = 48.408 - .067\ x_i$), and (3) computing the cyclical factor. The forecasts are computed by using the equation

$$F = T \times C \times S$$

with the random variation removed through the use of moving averages.

Year	Jan.	Feb.	Mar.	Apr.	May	June	July	Aug.	Sept.	Oct.	Nov.	Dec.
1969	56	64	59	60	54	54	50	56	58	63	49	49
1970	45	45	45	47	44	45	41	42	44	42	44	42
1971	42	37	45	44	43	46	33	42	46	46	40	42
1972	42	45	49	46	49	54	45	48	49	52	53	47
1973	52	52	56	51	57	52	49	51	48	57	49	42
1974	51	47	50	46	52	46	43	47	46	50	42	33
1975	37	33	34	37	36	35	29	36	39	44	35	35

Source: *Current Industrial Reports: Iron and Steel Castings*, Series 33A. Washington: U.S. Bureau of the Census, July 1976.

Figure 8-10 Monthly time series data—malleable iron castings shipments for sale, 1969–1975 (1,000 short tons).

Year	Jan.	Feb.	Mar.	Apr.	May	June	July	Aug.	Sept.	Oct.	Nov.	Dec.
1969							56	54	53	52	51	50
1970	49	48	47	46	45	44	44	43	43	43	43	43
1971	42	42	42	42	42	42	42	43	43	43	44	44
1972	45	45	46	46	47	48	48	49	50	50	51	51
1973	51	51	51	52	52	51	51	51	50	50	51	49
1974	48	48	48	47	47	46	45	44	43	42	41	40
1975	39	38	37	36	36	35						

Source: Developed from Figure 8–10.

Figure 8–11 Centered 12-month moving average data—malleable iron castings shipments for sale 1969–1975 (1,000 short tons).

Year	Jan.	Feb.	Mar.	Apr.	May	June	July	Aug.	Sept.	Oct.	Nov.	Dec.	Total
1969	91.8	93.8	95.7	102.2	97.8	102.3	89.3	103.7	109.4	121.2	96.1	98.0	
1970	100.0	88.1	107.1	104.8	102.4	109.5	93.2	97.7	102.3	97.7	102.3	97.7	
1971	93.3	100.0	106.5	100.0	104.3	112.5	78.6	97.7	107.0	107.0	90.9	95.5	
1972	102.0	102.0	109.8	98.1	109.6	102.0	93.8	98.0	98.0	104.0	103.9	92.2	
1973	106.3	97.9	104.2	97.9	110.6	100.0	96.1	100.0	96.0	114.0	100.0	85.7	
1974	94.9	86.8	91.9	102.8	100.0	100.0	95.6	106.8	107.0	119.0	102.4	82.5	
1975													
Media[a] Averages	97.6	95.0	103.4	100.8	104.1	103.5	93.0	99.9	103.6	111.0	100.2	92.8	1204.9
Seasonal Index[b]	97.2	94.6	103.0	100.4	103.7	103.1	92.6	99.5	103.2	110.5	99.8	92.4	1200.0

[a]The column average excluding the highest and lowest value.
[b]Adjustment factor = 1200/1204.9 = .9959
Source: Calculated from data in Figures 8–10 and 8–11.
Methodology: Steven C. Wheelwright and Spyros Makridakis, *Forecasting Methods for Management*, 2nd ed. New York: Wiley, 1977, pp. 93–97.

Figure 8–12 Seasonal index factors—malleable iron castings shipments for sale 1969–1975

MARKET AND SALES FORECASTING

Month	Trend value	×	Seasonal factor	×	Cyclical factor	=	1976 forecast
January	43		.972		.909		38
February	43		.946		.932		38
March	43		1.030		.955		42
April	43		1.004		.977		42
May	43		1.037		1.000		45
June	43		1.031		1.023		46
July	43		.926		1.045		42
August	43		.995		1.068		46
September	43		1.032		1.044		46
October	42		1.105		1.067		50
November	42		.998		1.067		45
December	42		.924		1.067		41

Figure 8-13 1976 Forecast worksheet—malleable iron castings shipments for sale

Figure 8–13 shows the forecasts for 1976 developed by the use of the decomposition method.

Wheelwright and Makridakis provide a detailed review of the decomposition method and also discuss two additional techniques that represent significant improvements over the classical decomposition methods.[59] The Census II technique was developed by Julius Shiskin of the U.S. Bureau of the Census to deseasonalize government time series, but it has been widely used by business forecasters during the past 20 years as a decomposition method.[60] Computer programs for the Census II technique are generally available from computer hardware and software firms. Most users believe that Census II is superior to the classical methods in identifying seasonal factors and random variation within time series. The Foran system technique was developed by Robert McLaughlin of Scovill Manufacturing Company and builds on the foundation of the Census II technique.[61] Foran has the advantage of being able to handle any independent variable (while Census II is limited to time), it provides a series of forecasts based on the prior 12 periods, and it allows the forecaster to select any combination of preliminary forecasts as the basis for a final forecast.

[59]*Ibid.*, Chap. 6.
[60]Julius Shiskin, *Electronic Computers and Business Indicators*, Occasional Paper 57. Washington: National Bureau of Economic Research, 1968.
[61]Robert L. McLaughlin and J. J. Boyle, *Short-Term Forecasting*. Chicago: American Marketing Association, 1968.

There is one additional technique that should be mentioned in a review of decomposition methods of forecasting. The Box-Jenkins method, unlike the classical, Census II, and Foran techniques is well-suited to the analysis of complex time series in which no underlying pattern is evident.[62] It is a complicated, powerful system that requires a high level of analytical and statistical capability on the part of the user. The Box-Jenkins method is costly to use, but its accuracy has caused many business forecasters to consider it as the best available technique for short term forecasting. Computer programs for using the Box-Jenkins technique are available from many hardware and software organizations.

New product forecasting for component parts and materials is limited basically to the same approaches described in the section on major and accessory equipment, although products and markets may have to be aggregated for component parts and materials to control the cost of these approaches.

Operating Supplies and Services

The third group of industrial goods and services to be considered includes operating supplies, which are distinguished by their characteristic of being consumed in the production process, and services, which also support the production process. These types of goods and services are treated as current expenses, the average purchase order is relatively small in value, and demand tends to be widespread among industries. Demand also tends to be relatively steady with a long-term relationship to the level of general business activity. Firms tend to offer relatively standardized supplies and services with multiple product and service lines, and in the case of supplies, large numbers of individual products. The characteristic of widespread demand among industries and firms results in most firms dealing with hundreds or thousands of accounts, either directly with users or through distributors and dealers. Finally time series data for operating supplies and services tend to be autocorrelated, in that successive values in a time series are correlated rather than independent. All of these characteristics of the demand for operating supplies and services suggest that two types of forecasting techniques are applicable: (1) input-output analysis and (2) exponential smoothing and adaptive filtering techniques. Input-output forecasting would be most applicable in situations whereby forecasts are required for multiple industry demands of a particular product or product line. Exponential smoothing and adaptive filtering tech-

---

[62] George E. P. Box and G. M. Jenkins, *Time Series Analysis*, San Francisco: Holden-Day, 1970.

MARKET AND SALES FORECASTING

niques would be most applicable when large numbers of short-term forecasts must be made regularly such as industry light bulb shipments by consuming industry.

Input-output analysis has been an important tool for macroeconomic analysis for many years and increasingly is being applied by industrial firms. Its basic value lies in its ability to portray the structural relationships of an economy so that the flows of goods and services among industries may be traced. Input-output data are now integrated with the national income and product accounts of the United States, so that Gross National Product and Census of Manufactures data, for example, are used to develop input-output tables. The use of input-output analysis is of considerable importance in industrial marketing research, and thus a separate chapter (Chapter 9) is devoted to the subject. Our interest at this point is limited to the use of input-output concepts for forecasting purposes. Based on a review of the literature, there appear to be a number of industrial firms that have used input-output analysis for forecasting, with a concentration among firms producing component parts, materials, and supplies; Western Electric Co.,[63] Celanese Corporation,[64,65] Glass Containers Corporation,[66] and Combustion Engineering, Inc.[67] Since our primary interest is in applications to operating supplies and services in this section, the latter example (Combustion Engineering, Inc.) will be examined here. Combustion Engineering offers a large variety of industrial products and services to many industries, including 24 major refractory products to 19 different industries (market segments). Figure 8-14 illustrates how Combustion Engineering views its forecasting task as a hierarchy of forecasts with the information inputs and outputs noted for each step in the hierarchy. Figure 8-15 then shows how an input/output table may be constructed for refractories with the rows listing the 24 refractory products and the columns the 19 market segments. Forecasts are prepared by substituting forecast values of the output for each market segment for the historical values shown in the diagram.

[63] Robert E. Johnson, "The Application of Input/Output Analysis in Industrial Marketing Management," *Proceedings*, 1965 Fall Conference. Chicago: American Marketing Association, 1966, pp. 309-320.
[64] Elisabeth K. Rabitsch and J. M. Fuerst, "Input/Output as a Planning Tool," in Reed Moyer, Ed., *Changing Marketing Systems*, Chicago: American Marketing Association, 1968, pp. 307-312.
[65] Elisabeth K. Rabitsch, "Input-Output Analysis and Business Forecasting," *Technological Forecasting and Social Change*, Vol. 3, 1972, pp. 453-463.
[66] "How Input-Output Helped to Map the Marketing Strategy of Glass Containers Corporation," *Industrial Marketing*, Vol. 55, January 1970, pp. 21-25.
[67] Elliot D. Ranard, "Use of Input/Output Concepts in Sales Forecasting," *Journal of Marketing Research*, Vol. 9, February 1972, pp. 53-58.

Figure 8-14

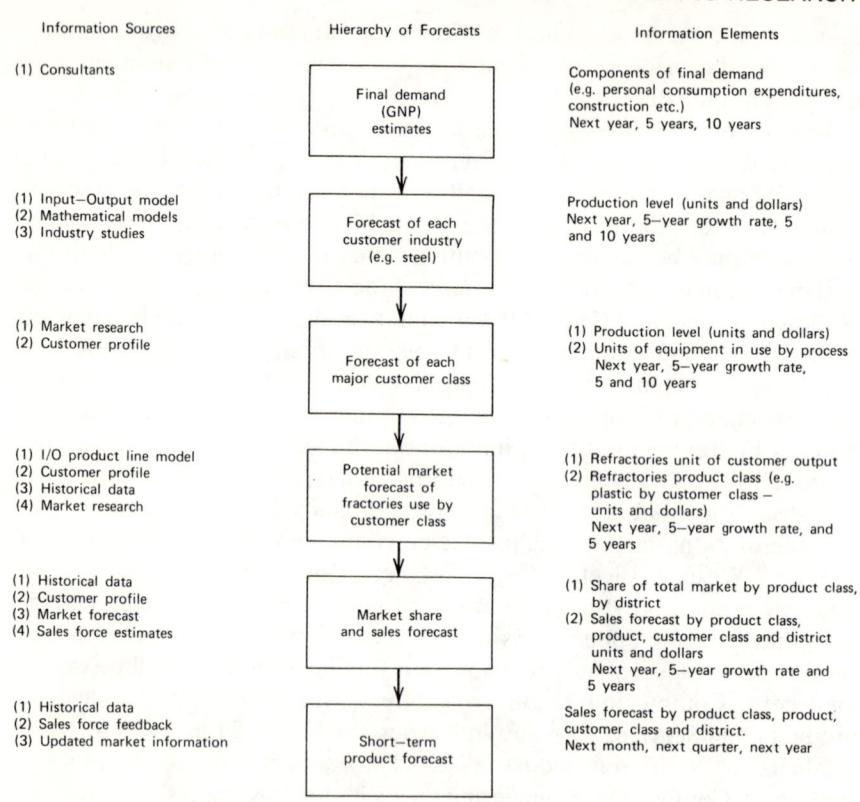

Information Sources	Hierarchy of Forecasts	Information Elements
(1) Consultants	Final demand (GNP) estimates	Components of final demand (e.g. personal consumption expenditures, construction etc.) Next year, 5 years, 10 years
(1) Input–Output model (2) Mathematical models (3) Industry studies	Forecast of each customer industry (e.g. steel)	Production level (units and dollars) Next year, 5-year growth rate, 5 and 10 years
(1) Market research (2) Customer profile	Forecast of each major customer class	(1) Production level (units and dollars) (2) Units of equipment in use by process Next year, 5-year growth rate, 5 and 10 years
(1) I/O product line model (2) Customer profile (3) Historical data (4) Market research	Potential market forecast of fractories use by customer class	(1) Refractories unit of customer output (2) Refractories product class (e.g. plastic by customer class – units and dollars) Next year, 5-year growth rate, and 5 years
(1) Historical data (2) Customer profile (3) Market forecast (4) Sales force estimates	Market share and sales forecast	(1) Share of total market by product class, by district (2) Sales forecast by product class, product, customer class and district units and dollars Next year, 5-year growth rate and 5 years
(1) Historical data (2) Sales force feedback (3) Updated market information	Short-term product forecast	Sales forecast by product class, product, customer class and district. Next month, next quarter, next year

Figure 8-14 Forecasting procedures for refractory products at Combusion Engineering, Inc. Source: Elliot D. Ranard, "Use of Input/Output Concepts in Sales Forecasting," Journal of Marketing Research, Vol. 9, February 1972, p. 54.

Industry forecasting by means of input-output analysis requires that the coefficients of the interindustry tables be examined and possibly adjusted as the result of technological and price changes. A detailed study of the stability of the coefficients over time for individual industries showed varying patterns regarding the relative accuracy of current and constant dollar data.[68] Suggestions for handling changing technical coefficients have been offered in other sources.[69]

[68] Roger H. Bezdek and Robert M. Wendling, "Current- and Constant-Dollar Input-Output Forecasts for the U.S. Economy," *Journal of the American Statistical Association*, Vol. 71, September 1976, pp. 543–551.
[69] Anne P. Carter, "How to Handle Changing Technical Coefficients in Input-Output Tables," in Keith Cox and Ben Enis, Eds., *A New Measure of Responsibility for Marketing*. Chicago: American Marketing Association, 1968, pp. 306–309.

MARKET AND SALES FORECASTING

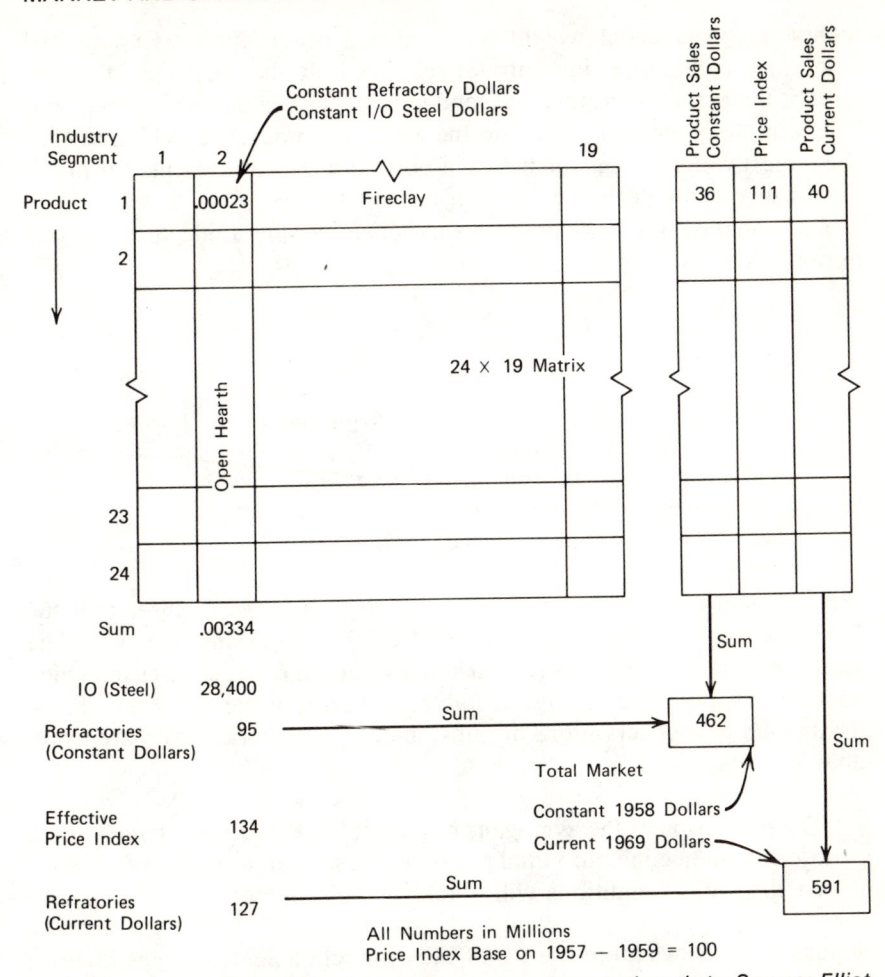

Figure 8–15 Input/output matrix for refractory products and markets. Source: Elliot D. Ranard, "Use of Input/Output Concepts in Sales Forecasting," Journal of Marketing Research, *Vol. 9, February 1972, p. 57.*

In situations where (1) large numbers of short-term forecasts must be made frequently and (2) the characteristics of the demand for operating supplies and services are in force, exponential smoothing is comparable to the use of moving averages to eliminate random variation in a historical data series. However exponential smoothing is superior to the moving averages technique which requires that all relevent data be stored, so that a 12-month moving average would require that 12 observations be stored in a computer file, leading to high costs. In addition the moving average technique gives equal weight to all stored observations. Exponential smoothing techniques, in contrast, requires only the most recent observation, the most recent forecast, and a value for the smoothing constant. The term "exponential" refers to the weighting procedure, which assigns the largest weight to the most recent observation, with weights for previous observations declining geometrically over time.

The equation for developing an exponential smoothing forecast one period ahead is:[70]

$$S_{t+1} = S_t + \alpha (x_t - S_t)$$

where

S_{t+1} = smooth forecast one period ahead
α = smoothing constant
x_t = most recent observed value
s_t = most recent forecast
$(x_t - S_t)$ = error in most recent forecast

Successful use of exponential smoothing techniques requires that the forecaster select appropriate values of α, the smoothing constant. The values may range from 0 to 1, with small values of α (.1, .2, .3) used when past observations are relatively stable, and large values of α (.7, .8, .9) used when past observations are unstable. If no historical data are available,

> ... a prediction of the average is required, [and] ... if you have very little confidence in your initial prediction, use a larger value (of α), so that the initial conditions will quickly be discounted.[71]

Figure 8–16 shows a time series of the production acetylene gas in 1976, together with the exponential smoothing forecasts for the series one period ahead based on different values of α.

The forecast for May 1976, with $\alpha = .5$, was calculated as follows:

$$S_t + 1 = S_t + \alpha (x_t - S_t)$$
$$S_{\text{May '76}} = S_{\text{April '76}} + \alpha (x_{\text{April '76}} - S_{\text{April '76}})$$
$$S_{\text{May '76}} = 593 + .5 (617 - 593)$$
$$= 593 + .5 (24)$$
$$= 593 + 12$$
$$S_{\text{May '76}} = 605$$

[70] Wheelwright and Makridakis, op. cit., p. 36.
[71] Robert G. Brown, *Smoothing, Forecasting, and Prediction of Discrete Time Series*. Englewood Cliffs, N.J.: Prentice-Hall, 1963, pp. 102–103.

MARKET AND SALES FORECASTING

1976 Month	Production (mil. cu. ft.)	Exponential smoothing forecasts		
		$\alpha = .1$	$\alpha = .5$	$\alpha = .9$
January	582	—	—	—
February	588	582	582	582
March	601	583	585	587
April	617	585	593	600
May	605	588	605	615
June	622	589	605	606
July	603	592	614	620
August	639	593	608	605
September	626	598	624	636
October	583	601	625	627
November	563	599	604	587
December	542	595	583	565

Data Source: *Current Industrial Reports: Industrial Gases,* Series (M 28C(77)–1). Washington: U. S. Bureau of the Census, March 1977.
Methodology: Steven C. Wheelwright and Spyros Makridakis, *Forecasting Methods for Management,* 2nd ed. New York: Wiley, 1977, p. 37.

Figure 8–16 Forecasting the production of acetylene gas by exponential smoothing.

When time series data are basically horizontal in character (displaying no growth or variation), the simple form of exponential smoothing just presented is sufficient. If growth in the form of a trend is evident, double exponential smoothing should be used, and if a seasonal factor is also present, Winters' linear and seasonal exponential smoothing technique will handle both trend and seasonal factors.[72]

In cases where exponential smoothing techniques seem appropriate, but the data patterns are too complex to permit the use of Winters' technique, the adaptive filtering technique should be considered.[73] Adaptive filtering is very similar to exponential smoothing except that it contains a procedure for determining the *best* weights α to fit an historical time series, whereas exponential smoothing techniques must determine the best α value through trial and error. Although adaptive filtering techniques are more powerful than exponential smoothing and are simpler to understand and use than the Box-Jenkins technique, they do not provide confidence intervals and significance tests for the forecasts as does Box-Jenkins. Adaptive filtering therefore offers an additional choice to the

---

[72] Peter R. Winters, "Forecasting Sales by Exponentially Weighted Moving Averages," *Management Science*, Vol. 6, April 1960, pp. 324–342.
[73] Wheelwright and Makridakis, *op. cit.*, Chap. 4.

forecaster seeking ways to enhance the forecasting capabilities of the organization.

The demand for *new* operating supplies and services may be forecast, as noted previously, by predicting an expected average value for early demand and using a relatively large α value to allow for rapid adjustment to forecast error. In addition the techniques suggested for other groups of industrial goods and services may be used for operating supplies and services by aggregating the data to economically viable and statistically viable levels.

Sales Forecasting at the Company Level. The third stage in the four-stage approach to forecasting is the company level, and once again the basic procedure is to forecast sales (shipments or other measures of output) of the company as a percentage or ratio of the preceding stage forecast. The industry forecasts therefore serve as the base for company forecasts with market share as the linking element between the stages. Although the concepts of conditional and nonconditional forecasts were discussed at the outset of the chapter, they are important at every stage and bear repeating at this point. Nonconditional forecasts of company market share for the firm's markets and market segments may be prepared, assuming unknown (and thus no) change in the level of industry marketing effort and the marketing environment. The nonconditional forecast would then be that portion of the market share which would remain constant. Conditional forecasts of company market share would next be prepared, based on expected changes in the level of industry and firm marketing effort, together with expected changes in the marketing environment. Such forecasts require specification of market and company demand functions for the products and services in question. At this point, our position will be summarized by stating that these functions can and should be estimated as an integral part of the forecasting process.

Sales Forecasting at the Product/Service Level. In the fourth and final stage of the four-stage approach to forecasting, the demand for products/services is forecast, as a percentage or ratio of the preceding stages. The plural "stages" is used deliberately, because product/service demand forecasts are often implicitly combined with the company forecasts to determine the firm's share of a given product/service demand at the industry level. Thus we might find Federal Mogul forecasting its demand for tapered roller bearings directly as a market share of the industry demand for such products. Alternatively Federal Mogul might forecast its company market share of the total industry demand for roller and ball bearings, and then forecast its demand for tapered roller bearings as a percentage or ratio of the total company forecast for bearings demand.

MARKET AND SALES FORECASTING

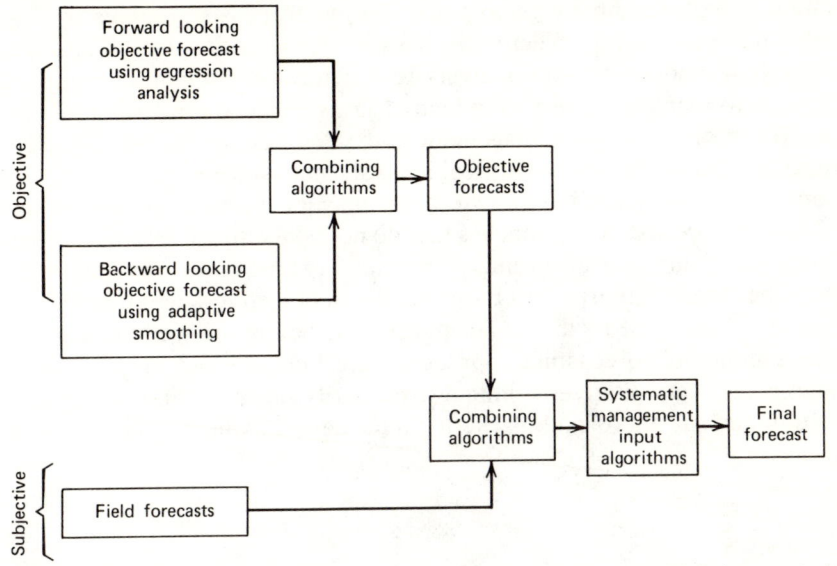

Figure 8-17 A compound approach to forecasting. Source: Arnold Reisman et al., "Forecasting Short-Term Demand," Industrial Engineering, *May 1976, p. 38.*

The former approach is recommended, for it avoids the temptation to allocate mechanically the company forecast across the product/service line. As in the case of company forecasts, there is a need to prepare both nonconditional and conditional forecasts of product/service demand, based on an analysis of market and company demand functions for the products/services.

Compound Approaches to Forecasting. Many industrial companies have adopted the evolutionary approach to forecasting improvement suggested by Wheelwright and Clarke, in that they have evolved from primary reliance on relatively qualitative techniques (such as the sales force composite method) to greater use of the quantitative techniques emphasized in this chapter.[74] In the evolutionary process, they have not discarded the qualitative techniques however, but have retained them in what we shall call a "compound" approach to forecasting. An excellent example of a compound approach is provided by Reisman, et al., in a case study describing a forecasting system for a manufacturer of residential and light commercial air conditioners and heating units.[75] Figure 8–17

---

[74] Steven C. Wheelwright and Darral G. Clarke, "Corporate Forecasting: Promise and Reality," *Harvard Business Review*, Vol. 54, November–December 1976, p. 64.
[75] Arnold Reisman, et. al., "Forecasting Short-Term Demand," *Industrial Engineering*, May 1976, pp. 38–45.

shows how the company combines subjective forecasts prepared by field sales personnel with objective forecasts based on the use of adaptive smoothing and regression analysis techniques. A compound approach appeals to many managers of industrial firms because it incorporates the market information of management and sales personnel with objective measures based on both historical analysis and future expectations. Our consulting experience has shown that managers are often inherently suspicious of forecasting approaches that do not explicitly include managerial judgement, and are accordingly far more receptive to compound approaches than to approaches based solely on objective, quantitative techniques. It also appears that the managers' suspicions are well founded and that compound forecasting approaches are indeed often more accurate than purely quantitative techniques, primarily because they do incorporate important microlevel marketing information explicitly into the forecasts.

SUMMARY

Forecasting is one of the most critical functions in business organizations, for it serves explicitly or implicitly as the basis for all planning and decision-making activities. Forecasts are conditional or nonconditional, depending upon whether or not they employ known or assumed changes in the level of industry marketing effort and the marketing environment.

Grassroots forecasts are developed by aggregating forecasts for individual accounts into successively larger segments through a buildup procedure. Forecasts of professional staff members are based on a breakdown procedure. The best-known one starts with a forecast for the economy, then for the industry, next for the company and finally, for the product/service of the company. The usual procedure is for each succeeding forecast to be a ratio of the preceding forecast. Differences in buildup and breakdown procedures can be reconciled by a conference of corporate executives or by the professional staff forecaster.

Short- and long-term economic forecasts differ methodologically. Long-term forecasts usually rely on fairly simple extrapolations of GNP and GNP components. Although they are not terribly accurate, those forecasts are sufficient as ballpark estimates. For shorter-term forecasts, econometric models and lead-lag indicator models are widely used with good results.

Industry forecasts are more commonplace than market forecasts because of the qualitative and quantitative superiority of supply data. The usual approach is to relate industry to economic data. However this relationship may have to be adjusted for technological change and for a variety of characteristics of the forecasting problem. A principal factor in the choice of forecasting procedure is whether the products or services produced by the industry in question are major or accessory equipment, component parts and materials, or operating supplies and services.

Technological forecasting may be exploratory or normative. Exploratory procedures rely on past information. They include simple curve fitting, diffusion models, step-wise models of gradual growth, technological progress and "experience curve" models, and substitution models. Normative procedures involve expert judgments. The most widely used technique is the Delphi method with cross-impact analysis as a further followup.

Demand for major and accessory equipment is highly specialized, volatile, and associated with well defined markets. Commonly used methods are grassroots forecasting, users' expectations, and regression analysis of the relationship between current shipments and past orders. For established industries the age of existing stock is an important factor. For new products an S-shaped growth curve for penetration of existing markets by the new product is recommended.

Shipments of component parts and materials are affected by fluctuations in inventory levels. Seasonal, cyclical, and random variation in demand are adjusted for by decomposition models. Box-Jenkins methodology can also be applied where the data have no apparent underlying time-series pattern.

For operating supplies and services the techniques in widest use are exponential smoothing, adaptive filtering, and Input-Output analysis. Company and product sales forecasting are the next to be prepared. Both conditional and nonconditional forecasts should be prepared. It is urged that product sales forecast not be mechanically based on the ratio of that product to other company products.

Many industrial companies have gradually evolved from primary reliance on relatively qualitative techniques to greater use of quantitative techniques without discarding qualitative techniques. Experience has shown that managers are inherently suspicious of forecasting approaches and are more receptive to compound approaches that incorporate their judgements. It also appears that compound approaches tend to be more accurate.

SUGGESTED READINGS

Bass, Frank M., "A New Product Growth Model for Consumer Durables," *Management Science*, Vol. 15, January 1969, pp. 215–227.

Bezdek, Roger H., and Robert M. Wendling," Current- and Constant-

Dollar Input-Output Forecasts for the U.S. Economy," *Journal of the American Statistical Association*, Vol. 71, September 1976, pp. 543–551.

Blackman, A. Wade, "Forecasting through Dynamic Modeling," *Technological Forecasting and Social Change*, Vol. 3, 1972, pp. 291–307; Blackman, "The Market Dynamics of Technological Substitutions," *Technological Forecasts and Social Change*, Vol. 6, 1974, pp. 41–63; Blackman, "The Rate of Innovation in the Commercial Aircraft Jet Engine Market," *Technological Forecasting and Social Change*, Vol. 3, 1972, pp. 441–452.

Box, George E. P., and G. M. Jenkins, *Time Series Analysis*. San Francisco: Holden-Day, 1970.

Brown, Robert G., *Smoothing, Forecasting, and Prediction of Discrete Time Series*. Englewood Cliffs, N.J.: Prentice-Hall, 1963.

Bundgaard-Nielson, M., and Peter Fiehn, "The Diffusion of New Technology in the U.S. Petroleum Refining Industry," *Technological Forecasting and Social Change*, Vol. 6, 1974, pp. 33–39.

Carter, Anne P., "How to Handle Technical Coefficients in Input-Output Tables," in Keith Cox and Ben Enis, Eds., *A New Measure of Responsibility for Marketing*. Chicago: American Marketing Association, 1968, pp. 306–309.

Chambers, John C., Satinder K. Mullick, and Donald D. Smith, "How to Choose the Right Forecasting Technique," *Harvard Business Review*, Vol. 49, July–August 1971, pp. 45–74.

Cox, William E., Jr., "Product Portfolio Strategy: A Review of the Boston Consulting Group Approach to Marketing Strategy," in R. Curham, Ed., *Marketing's Contributions to the Firm and to Society*. Chicago: American Marketing Association, 1975, pp. 465–470.

Fusfeld, Alan R., and Richard N. Foster, "The Delphi Technique: Survey and Comment," *Business Horizons*, Vol. 14, June 1971.

Fusfeld, Alan R., "The Technological Progress Function: A New Technique for Forecasting," *Technological Forecasting and Social Change*, Vol. 1, March 1970, pp. 301–312.

Helmer, Olaf, "Problems in Futures Research: Delphi and Causal Cross-Impact Analysis," *Futures*, Vol. 9, February 1977, pp. 17–31.

Industrial Marketing, "How Input-Output Helped to Map the Marketing Strategy of Glass Containers Corporation," Vol. 55, January 1970, pp. 21–25.

Johnson, Robert E., "The Application of Input/Output Analysis in Industrial Marketing Management," *Proceedings, 1965 Fall Conference*, Chicago: American Marketing Association, 1966.

Kuehn, Alfred A., and Ralph L. Day, "The Acceleration Effect in Forecasting Industrial Shipments," *Journal of Marketing*, January 1963, pp. 25–28.

McCarthy, Michael D., *The Wharton Quarterly Econometric Forecasting Model Mark III*. Philadelphia: Economics Research Unit, University of Pennsylvania, 1972, pp. 6–7.

McLaughlin, Robert L., and J. J. Boyle, *Short-Term Forecasting*. Chicago: American Marketing Association, 1968.

Martino, Joseph P., and Stephen K. Conver, "The Step-wise Growth of Electric Generators Size," *Technological Forecasting and Social Change*, Vol. 3, 1972, pp. 465–471.

Mohn, N. Carroll, Jr., "Application of Trend Concepts in Forecasting Typesetting Technology," *Technological Forecasting and Social Change*, Vol. 3, 1972, pp. 225–253.

Nevers, John V., "Extensions of a New Product Growth Model," *Sloan Management Review*, Vol. 13, Winter 1972, pp. 77–91.

North, Harper Q., and Donald L. Pyke, " 'Probes' of the Technological Future," *Harvard Business Review*, Vol. 47, May–June 1969, pp. 68–76.

North, Harper Q., and Donald L. Pyke, " 'Probes' of the Technological Future," *Harvard Business Review*, Vol. 47, May–June 1969, pp. 68–76.

Phelps, D. Maynard, and J. Howard Westing, *Marketing Management*, 3rd ed. Homewood, Ill.: Irwin, 1968, pp. 477–479.

Rabitsch, Elisabeth K., "Input-Output Analysis and Business Forecasting," *Technological Forecasting and Social Change*, Vol. 3, 1972, pp. 453–463.

Rabitsch, Elisabeth K. and J. M. Fuerst, "Input/Output as a Planning Tool," in Reed Moyer, E. *Changing Marketing Systems*. Chicago: American Marketing Association, 1968, pp. 307–312.

Ranard, Elliot D., "Use of Input/Output Concepts in Sales Forecasting," *Journal of Marketing Research*, Vol. 9, February 1972, pp. 53–58.

Reisman, Arnold, et al., "Forecasting Short-Term Demand," *Industrial Engineering*, May 1976, pp. 38–45.

Rippe, Richard, Maurice Wilkenson, and Donald Morrison, "Industrial Market Forecasting with Anticipations Data," *Management Science*, Vol. 22, February 1976, pp. 639–651.

Roberts, Edwin B., "Exploratory and Normative Technological Forecasting: A Critical Appraisal," *Technological Forecasting and Social Change*, Vol. 1, 1969, pp. 113–127.

Rosegger, Gerhard, "Diffusion Research in the Industrial Setting: Some Conceptual Clarifications," *Technological Forecasting and Social Change*, Vol. 9, 1976, pp. 401–410.

Root, H. Paul and Jay E. Klompmaker, "A Microanalytic Sales Forecasting Model for New Industrial Products," in Fred C. Allvine, Ed., *Marketing in Motion*. Chicago: American Marketing Association, 1972, pp. 474–477.

Sahal, Davendra, "A Reformulation of the Technological Progress Function," *Technological Forecasting and Social Change*, Vol. 8, 1975, pp. 79–90.

Sharif, M. N., and G. A. Uddin, "A Procedure for Adapting Technological Forecasting Models," *Technological Forecasting and Social Change*, Vol. 7, 1975, pp. 99–106.

Shiskin, Julius, *Electronic Computers and Business Indicators*, Occasional Paper 57, Washington, D.C.: National Bureau of Economic Research, 1968.

Simmonds, W. H. C., "The Analysis of Industrial Behavior and Its Use in Forecasting," *Technological Forecasting and Social Change*, Vol. 3, 1972, pp. 205–224.

Stacey, Nicholas A. H., and Aubrey Wilson, *Industrial Marketing Research*. London: Hutchinson and Co., 1968.

Stern, M. O., R. U. Ayres, and A. Shapanka, "A Model for Forecasting the Substitution of One Technology for Another," *Technological Forecasting and Social Change*, Vol. 7, 1975, pp. 57–79.

Wasson, Chester R., *The Strategy of Marketing Research*. New York: Appleton-Century-Crofts, 1964.

Wentz, W. B., and G. I. Eyrich, "Product Forecasting without Historical, Survey or Experimental Data," in R. L. King, Ed., *Marketing and the New Science of Planning*. Chicago: American Marketing Association, 1968, pp. 215–221.

Wheelwright, Steven C., and Darral G. Clarke, "Corporate Forecasting: Promise and Reality," *Harvard Business Review*, Vol. 54, November–December 1976.

Wheelwright, Steven C., and Spyros Makridakis, *Forecasting Methods for Management*, 2nd ed. New York: Wiley 1977, Chaps. 4–7.

Winters, Peter R., "Forecasting Sales by Exponentially Weighted Moving Averages," *Management Science*, Vol. 6, April 1960, pp. 324–342.

Wissema, Johan G., "Morphological Analysis: Its Application to a Company TF Investigation," *Futures*, Vol. 8, April 1976, pp. 146–153.

Wolfe, Harry D., *Business Forecasting Methods*. New York: Holt, Rinehart, and Winston, 1966.

CHAPTER NINE
Input-Output Analysis

Input-Output (I-O) analysis is a technique for examining the relationships between all industries within an economy, based on the simple proposition that the purchases (input) of one industry are the sales (output) of another industry. Since industrial marketing research is vitally concerned with interindustry relationships, input-output analysis would seem to be of major importance and value. Although the potential value of input-output analysis is indeed high, there appears to be very limited use of the technique in marketing applications to date. There are a number of possible explanations for the limited use of input-output analysis in industrial marketing research, but perhaps the most important is a lack of awareness and knowledge among marketing academicians and practitioners as to the characteristics and benefits of the technique for marketing analysis. In this chapter the background, characteristics, applications, and limitations of input-output analysis will be presented in order to stimulate consideration and wider adoption of the technique in industrial marketing research.

Background and Characteristics

Dr. Wassily Leontieff, a long-time professor of economics at Harvard University and a Nobel Prize winner in economics, produced the first input-output tables in the early 1930s for the years 1919 and 1929. These tables divided the United States economy into 42 sectors with 37 industries comprising the intermediate demand portion of the table and 5 sectors representing final demand. Intermediate demand refers to the sales of one industry to itself and all other industries; final demand refers to the consumption of industry outputs by markets other than industries, such as ultimate consumers and governments. The tables were set up as a matrix with 42 rows and columns, with each sector represented therefore in both the rows and columns of the tables. Within the matrix, the rows show how the output of each sector are distributed (sold) to all other sectors; the columns show the inputs (purchases) required by each sector from all other sectors. Each cell in the matrix, created by the intersection of a row and a column, therefore contains one figure that is both an input and an output.

Since 1939 federal statistical agencies have developed input-output tables from the *Census of Manufactures* and national economic accounts data, thereby providing estimates for 1939, 1947, 1958, 1963, 1967, and 1968 through 1970. The 1967 and 1963 input-output studies provide detailed data on 484 and 367 industries, respectively, while the 1968 through 1970 annual studies cover 87 aggregated industries. In each study input-output data are presented in three tables:[1]

1. *Transactions table*—shows:

    . . . the dollar value of the transactions among the various industries, the sales of each industry to final markets, and the value added originating in each industry. Each row of the table displays the distribution of the output of goods and services of the industry named at the beginning of the row to each of the industries and final users named across the top of the table. The columns show the value of each industry's current consumption (input) of raw materials, semi-finished products and services, and its value added in production.

2. *Direct requirements table*—relates:

    . . . each of the inputs of an industry to its total output. Each column in the table shows the inputs that the industry named at the head of the column required from each of the industries named at the beginning of the rows to produce a dollar of its output.

3. *Total requirements table*—shows:

    . . . the direct and indirect effects of final demand on the output of each industry. Each column in the table shows the amount of

[1]U.S. Department of Commerce, *Input-Output Structure of the U.S. Economy*. Vol. 1. Washington: U.S. Government Printing Office, 1074, p. i.

INPUT-OUTPUT ANALYSIS

output required both directly and indirectly from each of the industries named at the beginning of the rows for a dollar of deliveries to final demand by the industry named at the head of the column.

Interpreting Input-Output Tables Data

In order to illustrate the nature and use of input-output data, Figures 9-1, 9-2, and 9-3 have been developed from the 1967 study, covering two general and six detailed intermediate industries (Industry Numbers 41 and 47), and the final demand sector. The intermediate industries are:

Industry number	Industry title	Related census-SIC codes
41	Screw machine products, bolts, nuts, etc., and metal stampings	
41.01	Screw machine products and bolts, nuts, rivets, and washers	345
41.02	Metal stampings	3461
47	Metalworking machinery and equipment	
47.01	Machine tools, metal cutting types	3541
47.02	Machine tools, metal forming types	3542
47.03	Special dies and tools and machine tool accessories	3544, 3545
47.04	Metalworking machinery, not elsewhere classified	3548

Figure 9-1, a transactions table, shows that Industry/Number I/N 41.02, Metal stampings, sold $2.2 million of its output to I/N 47.01, Machine tools, metal cutting types; the industry also sold $245.9 million of its output to I/N 47.03, Special dies and tools and machine tool accessories. These output figures are found by reading across the row headed I/N 41.02. In order to determine the inputs required by I/N 41.02, read down the column: the industry purchased $61.1 million from I/N 47.03 and $42.5 million from I/N 41.01, Screw machine products, and so on.

Figure 9-1 also shows that the total output of I/N 41.02 in 1967 was $6,384 million, with $5,765 million of the output going to intermediate industries and $619 million to final demand categories. The total input of I/N 41.02 is, of course, also $6,384 million, composed of $3,576 million of intermediate inputs (goods and services consumed by the industry) and $2,808 million in value added by the industry (including corporate profits, employee compensation, and depreciation allowances.)

	Industry number[b]								
Industry number[b]	41.01	41.02	47.01	47.02	47.03	47.04	88.00	92.00	99.02	99.03
41.01	37.8	42.5	13.4	9.7	16.2	15.3	2,663	—	267	2,929
41.02	9.8	107.2	2.2	0.6	245.9	2.4	5,765	—	619	6,384
47.01	5.2	2.9	96.8	22.6	151.9	6.5	583	1,584	1,943	2,526
47.02	2.2	4.5	24.1	29.5	46.6	15.1	241	492	623	864
47.03	88.7	61.1	136.3	36.6	253.6	51.8	3,523	645	839	4,362
47.04	3.5	0.9	7.4	17.5	24.1	34.3	295	741	972	1,267
I	1,476	3,576	1,324	500	2,147	679	—	—	—	—
V.A.	1,454	2,808	1,202	364	2,215	588	—	—	—	795,388
T.	2,929	6,384	2,526	864	4,362	1,267	—	110,443	795,388	—

[a] For the distribution of output of an industry, read the industry row. For the composition of inputs to an industry, read the industry column.

[b] Industry Number 41.01 = Screw machine products and bolts, nuts, rivets, and washers
   41.02 = Metal stampings
   47.01 = Machine tools, metal cutting types
   47.02 = Machine tools, metal forming types
   47.03 = Special dies and tools and machine tool accessories
   47.04 = Metalworking machinery, not elsewhere classified
   88.00 = Total intermediate output
   92.00 = Gross private fixed capital formation
   99.02 = Total final demand
   99.03 = Total output
      I. = Total intermediate output
    V.A. = Value added
      T. = Total input

Figure 9–1 Interindustry transactions, 1967[a] (in millions of dollars at producer's prices).

Source: U.S. Department of Commerce, *Input-Output Structure of the U.S. Economy*: Vol. 1, *Transactions Data for Detailed Industries*. Washington: U.S. Government Printing Office, 1974.

INPUT-OUTPUT ANALYSIS

Industry number[b]	Industry number[b]					
	41.01	41.02	47.01	47.02	47.03	47.04
41.01	.01290	.00666	.00531	.01123	.00371	.01208
41.02	.00335	.01679	.00087	.00069	.05637	.00189
47.01	.00178	.00045	.03832	.02615	.03482	.00513
47.02	.00075	.00070.	.00954	.03414	.01068	.01192
47.03	.03028	.00957	.05396	.04236	.05814	.04090
47.04	.00119	.00014	.00293	.02025	.00553	.02708
V.A.	.49621	.43984	.47597	.42102	.50778	.46403
T.	1.00000	1.00000	1.00000	1.00000	1.00000	1.00000

[a] For the composition of inputs to an industry, read the column for that industry.
[b] Industry Number 41.01 = Screw machine products and bolts, nuts, rivets, and washers
          41.02 = Metal stampings
          47.01 = Machine tools, metal cutting types
          47.02 = Machine tools, metal forming types
          47.03 = Special dies and tools and machine tool accessories
          47.04 = Metalworking machinery, not elsewhere classified
          V.A. = Value added
          T = Total inputs

Source: U.S. Department of Commerce, *Input-Output Structure of the U. S. Economy*: Vol. 2, *Direct Requirements for Detailed Industries*. Washington: U.S. Government Printing Office, 1974.

Figure 9-2   Direct requirements per dollar of gross output, 1967[a] (producers' prices).

The relationships between the inputs to an industry and its total output are shown in Figure 9-2, the direct requirements table. The entires in each cell in the table are called "technical coefficients," and are calculated directly from the data in the transactions table (Figure 9-1). It was noted previously that I/N 41.02 purchased $61.1 million from I/N 47.03, and $42.5 million from I/N 41.01. Relating each of these inputs to the total inputs for I/N 41.02 ($6,384 million), the resulting technical coefficients are:

I/N 47.03

$$\frac{\$61.1}{\$6,384} = .00957$$

I/N 41.01

$$\frac{\$42.5}{\$6,384} = .00666$$

Similarly, the value added coefficient for I/N 41.02 in Figure 9-2 is derived from data in Figure 9-1:

$$\frac{\$2{,}808}{\$6{,}384} = .43984$$

Figure 9–3, the total requirements table, is also developed from the transactions table (Figure 9–1), based on the impact of a specified change in final demand on the various supplying industries and producing industry in question. The total requirements table includes both direct requirements (using the technical coefficients in Figure 9–2) and the indirect requirements of a specified change in final demand. Assume that personal consumption expenditures for automobiles rise sufficiently to create an increase in the final demand for metal stampings (I/N 41.02) in the amount of $1 million. Figure 9–2 indicates that the direct requirements for I/N 41.02 include technical coefficients of .01679 from its own industry (I/N 41.02) and .00957 for I/N 47.03. Thus an increase of $1 million in the final demand for metal stampings requires that the industry produce at least $1,016,790 ($1 million × 1.01679). This level of output will also require $9,731 ($1,016,790 × .00957) of Special dies and tools and machine tool accessories from I/N 47.03. Next the indirect requirements of the increase in final demand may be illustrated by tracing the impact of the direct

Industry number[b]	Industry number[b]					
	41.01	41.02	47.01	47.02	47.03	47.04
41.01	1.02654	.01154	.00893	.01628	.00770	.01642
41.02	.00823	1.03776	.00704	.00710	.06587	.00771
47.01	.00378	.00147	1.04405	.03141	.03994	.00889
47.02	.00143	.00114	.01133	1.03739	.01257	.01369
47.03	.03762	.01604	.06644	.05673	1.07241	.05355
47.04	.00187	.00053	.00441	.02299	.00686	1.03041

[a]Each entry represents the output required, directly and indirectly, from the industry named at the beginning of the row for each dollar of delivery to final demand by the industry named at the head of the column.
[b]Industry Number 41.01 = Screw machine products and bolts, nuts, rivets, and washers
    41.02 = Metal stampings
    47.01 = Machine tools, metal cutting types
    47.02 = Machine tools, metal forming types
    47.03 = Special dies and tools and machine tool accessories
    47.04 = Metalworking machinery, not elsewhere classified
Source: U.S. Department of Commerce, *Input-Output Structure of the U.S. Economy*: Vol. 3, *Total Requirements for Detailed Industries*. Washington: U.S. Government Printing Office, 1974.

Figure 9–3 Total requirements (direct and indirect) per dollar[a] of delivery to final demand, 1967 (producers' prices).

INPUT-OUTPUT ANALYSIS

requirements on the supplying industries. Thus I/N 41.02 placed direct requirements of $9,731 on I/N 47.03. To meet this requirement, I/N 47.03 requires an output of $566 ($9,731 × .05814) from its own industry (technical coefficient shown in Figure 9-2 for I/N 47.03). The new level of output, $10,297 ($9,731 + $566), requires an output of $580 ($10,297 × .05637) from I/N 41.02, increasing the total output of that industry to $1,017,370. If one traced all of the indirect requirements effects for all industries, the total requirements coefficients shown in Figure 9-3 would be obtained. These show, for example, that the total requirements impact of a $1 million increase in final demand for metal stampings requires that the industry (I/N 41.02) produce $1,037,760 ($1 million × 1.03776) and $16,040 ($1 million × .01604) in output will be required from I/N 47.03. The calculation of indirect requirements is thus facilitated by using the coefficients in Figure 9-3 (total requirements—direct requirements from Figure 9-2), rather than tracing the chain of relationships as illustrated here.

MARKETING RESEARCH APPLICATIONS

Applications of input-output analysis for manufacturers of industrial goods are many and varied, subject primarily to the limitations of the technique itself and the imaginations of those who would use it. Reported uses have ranged from studies of market identification, size, potential, and growth rates to sales forecasting to the creation of individual firm input-output tables. The most common application appears to be based on a comparison of the market distribution of sales of an individual firm with the market distribution of its industry as indicated in the transaction table. This application draws heavily upon one of the most important features of the input-output tables: they are one of the very few (and often the only) sources of secondary data on industrial consumption (input). Most industrial statistics pertain to production (output) and a source that relates production and consumption has considerable potential value. For many firms the potential value is only partially realized because of various limitations.

Limitations of Input-Output Analysis

First, input-output classifications of industries and markets are usually too aggregated in comparison with the product mix of the individual firm, so that direct firm-industry comparisons are only rough approximations at best. Second, the delayed availability of input-output data (1967 data are the most recent comprehensive tables available in 1977) raises questions about the relevance of the technical coefficients, especially in industries marked by rapidly changing technology. Third, the practice of assigning capital goods output to final demand rather than intermediate output poses special problems for potential users among capital goods producers. Each of these limitations can be reduced or minimized with the result that input-output analysis offers valuable insights for all producers of industrial goods.

Fabricated Parts Markets

Returning to the earlier examples in this chapter, the metal stampings industry (I/N 41.02) in 1967 had total output of $6,384 million. Figure 9-4 shows the top ten markets for metal stampings in 1967. More than one-third of the total output went to establishments in consuming industry I/N 59.03, composed of manufacturers of motor vehicles and parts (which includes SIC 3711, 3714). Another one-seventh (14.8%) of the total output was sold to establishments in I/N 75.00, composed of automotive service firms. In total, more than 90% of the output of metal stampings was consumed as intermediate output. The descriptions of the top ten markets in Figure 9-4 demonstrates that many of the consuming industries are highly aggregated, particularly the largest market, motor vehicles and parts.

The pivotal role of the automobile industry (part of I/N 59.03) as the primary consumer of metal stampings output was recognized in the *1972 Census of Manufactures*, with the division of the 1967 SIC 3461 (metal stampings) industry classification into three industry classifications: SIC 3465 (automotive stampings), SIC 3466 (crowns and closures), and SIC 3469 (metal stampings, n.e.c.). In the years prior to the release of the 1972 I-O study, the 1972 Census of Manufactures data could be used to adjust the available 1967 I-O data. This disaggregation of metal stampings output will help to make input-output analysis partially more useful, but it would be desirable to subdivide the motor vehicle and parts industry (I/N 59.03) also, so that automotive stampings could be linked with the various consuming segments of I/N 59.03.

The problem of the delayed availability of I-O data has been reduced somewhat by the development of interim summary I-O tables for the years between the *Census of Manufactures*. Summary tables for 1968, 1969, and 1970 were published in 1975. It is planned to provide other interim tables on an annual basis in the future.[2]

---

[2] U.S. Department of Commerce, *Summary Input-Output Tables of the U.S. Economy: 1968, 1969, 1970*. BEA Staff Paper No. 27. Springfield, Va.: National Technical Information Service, 1975.

INPUT-OUTPUT ANALYSIS

Consuming industry (Industry number and description)	Millions of dollars	Percentage
59.03—Motor vehicles and parts	$2,150.5	33.7%
75.00—Automobile repair and services	944.4	14.8
47.03—Special dies and tools and machine tool accessories	245.9	3.9
41.02—Metal stampings	107.2	1.7
60.01—Aircraft	106.7	1.7
56.04—Radio and TV communication equipment	93.1	1.5
57.03—Electronic components, n.e.c.	90.7	1.4
56.01—Radio and TV receiving sets	67.7	1.1
73.01—Miscellaneous business services	6.2	1.0
52.03—Refrigeration machinery	58.2	0.9
Other industries—total	1,838.5	28.8
88.00—Total intermediate output	5,765.1	90.3
91.00—Personal consumption expenditures	340.3	5.3
92.00—Gross private fixed capital formation	—	—
93.00—Net inventory change	29.0	0.5
94.00—Net exports	219.3	3.4
97&98—Government purchases	30.7	0.5
99.02—Total final demand	619.3	9.7
99.03—Total output	6,384.4	100.0

Source: U.S. Department of Commerce, *Input-Output Structure of the U. S. Economy*: Vol. 1, Transactions Data for Detailed Industries. Washington: U.S. Government Printing Office, 1974.

Figure 9–4 Distribution of output to consuming industries, 1967 Industry Number 41.02—Metal stampings.

Capital Goods Markets

Figure 9–5 shows that the total output in 1967 of I/N 47.01, manufacturers of metal cutting types of machine tools, was $2526 million, with only 23.1% of the output consumed by intermediate industries. More than three-fourths of the output of these machine tools passed directly into final demand with most of the total in I/N 92.00, gross private fixed capital formation. The basic input-output tables are thus of limited value to firms producing capital goods such as machine tools, since the majority of the output cannot be related to consuming intermediate industries.

In recent years, the U.S. Department of Commerce has prepared capi-

Consuming industry (Industry number and description)	Millions of dollars	Percentage (%)
47.03—Special dies and tools and machine tool accessories	$ 151.9	6.0
47.01—Machine tools, metal cutting types	96.8	3.8
47.02—Machine tools, metal forming types	22.6	0.9
42.02—Hand and edge tools including saws	20.1	0.8
48.06—Special industry machinery, n.e.c.	18.8	0.7
50.00—Machine shop products	17.9	0.7
59.03—Motor vehicles and parts	17.7	0.7
37.02—Iron and steel foundries	16.1	0.6
69.01—Wholesale trade	16.0	0.6
48.03—Woodworking machinery	12.2	0.5
Other industries—total	192.7	7.6
88.00—Total intermediate output	528.8	23.1
91.00—Personal consumption expenditures	27.3	1.1
92.00—Gross private fixed capital formation	1,583.8	62.7
93.00—Net inventory change	38.4	1.5
94.00—Net exports	195.4	7.7
97&98—Government purchases	98.1	3.9
99.02—Total final demand	1,943.0	76.9
99.03—Total input	2,525.8	100.0

Source: U.S. Department of Commerce, *Input-Output Structure of the U.S. Economy*: Vol. 1, *Transactions Data for Detailed Industries*. Washington: U.S. Government Printing Office, 1974.

Figure 9-5 *Distribution of output to consuming industries, 1967 Industry Number 47.01—Machine Tools, metal cutting types.*

tal flow tables that provide data on interindustry transactions in new structures and equipment, thereby allowing analysts to trace the development of gross private fixed capital formation by individual industries. Figure 9-6 presents a capital flow table for I/N 47.01 for 1967, indicating that the top ten markets for metal cutting types of machine tools accounted for more than one-half (56.9%) of the total purchases of these machine tools in 1967. The leading purchasers were the aircraft (I/N 60) and motor vehicle (I/N 59) industries, which accounted for a combined 18% of total purchases in 1967.

Forecasting and Planning Applications

The use of input-output analysis in forecasting was examined in the previous chapter. Although there are some skeptics regarding the validity

INPUT-OUTPUT ANALYSIS

Capital using industry (Industry number and description)	Millions of dollars	Percentage
60 Aircraft and parts	$ 149.4	9.4%
59 Motor vehicles and equipment	135.6	8.6
47 Metalworking machinery and equipment	124.5	7.9
50 Machine shop products	82.9	5.2
41 Stampings, screw machine products, and bolts	75.1	4.7
49 General industrial machinery and equipment	74.8	4.7
42 Other fabricated metal products	70.7	4.5
37 Primary iron and steel manufacturing	66.3	4.2
45 Construction, mining, and oilfield machinery	63.8	4.0
48 Special industry machinery and equipment	58.6	3.7
Subtotals	901.7	56.9
All other capital using industries	682.1	43.1
Totals	1,583.8	100.0

Source: U.S. Department of Commerce, *Interindustry Transactions in New Structures and Equipment, 1963 and 1967.* Washington: U.S. Government Printing Office, 1975.

Figure 9–6 *Interindustry transactions in new structures and equipment, 1967 Industry Number 47.01—Machine tools, metal cutting types.*

of using input-output analysis as a basis for forecasting, there are a number of industrial firms that have reported successful use: Western Electric, Celanese, National Steel, and Combustion Engineering.

It appears that firms that have utilized input-output analysis for forecasting have generally applied the technique to planning tasks as well. Thus several articles have described the use of I-O analysis for planning at the Celanese Corporation.[3] An article by Gols describes some of the extensive experiences that Arthur D. Little, Inc., management consultants, have in using input-output analysis to assist their industrial clients in their planning activities.[4]

---

[3] Elisabeth K. Rabitsch and J. M. Fuerst, "Input/Output as a Planning Tool," in Reed Moyer, Ed., *Changing Marketing Systems*. Chicago: American Marketing Association, 1967, pp. 307–312; Rabitsch, "Input-Output Analysis and Business Forecasting," *Technological Forecasting and Social Change*, Vol. 3, 1972, pp. 453–463.
[4] A. George Gols, "The Use of Input-Output in Industrial Planning," *Business Economics*, Vol. 20, May 1975, pp. 19–27.

	(1) 1963	(2) 1963	(3)	(4)
Top Six Markets	Purchases (Millions)	User Output (Millions)	1963 Employment	Output per Employee
Meat Products	$145.1	18,526	316,500	$58,530
Fluid Milk	282.7	7,443	210,600	35,342
Paperboard Containers & Boxes	136.3	4,798	189,700	25,028
Converted Paper Products	236.1	3,615	91,000	39,725
Wholesale Trade	144.4	48,440	3,104,000	15,600
Retail Trade	435.7	72,173	8,675,000	8,319

Source: Adapted from James T. Rothe, "The Reliability of Input/Output Analysis for Marketing," *California Management Review*, Vol. 14, Summer 1972, pp. 77–78.

Figure 9-7 Determination of 1970 market potentials for paperboard containers and boxes.

A Balanced Review of Input-Output Analysis

Many of the articles extolling the virtues of input-output analysis gloss over some of the major problems associated with the application of the technique. Perhaps the clearest and most balanced evaluation of the application of input-output analysis to marketing problems has been offered by Rothe.[5] His article shows how to use input-output data to determine the market potential for paperboard containers and boxes in ten user industries. Figure 9–7 shows how market potential was calculated for the top six markets (user industries in Rothe's terms). Data in columns (1) and (2) on 1963 purchases and user output were obtained from the transactions table (Volume 1) of the *1963 Input-Output Structure of the U.S. Economy* publication of the U.S. Department of Commerce. Employment data for each market were taken from *Employment and Earnings Statistics of the U.S.: 1909–1968*, and entered in column (3). Output per employee column (4) was then calculated by dividing data in column (2) by data in column (3): for the meat products market, output per employee of $58,530 was determined by dividing $18,526 million (1963 user output) by 316,500 (1963 employment).

1970 employment data in column (5) were obtained by projecting historical employment data for each market. Estimated output in 1970 for each market column (6) was determined by multiplying output per employee column (4) by 1970 employment column (5). For the meat products

[5]James T. Rothe, "The Reliability of Input/Output Analysis for Marketing," *California Management Review*, Vol. 14, Summer 1972, pp. 75–81.

INPUT-OUTPUT ANALYSIS

(5) 1970 Employment	(6) 1970 Estimated Output (Millions)	(7) Direct Technical Coefficient	(8) Demand 1970 (in 1963$) (Millions)	(9) Demand 1970 (after Inflation Adjustment, 1.12) (Millions)
339,100	$19,847	.00784	$155.6	$174.3
179,860	6,356	.03803	241.7	270.7
235,242	5,887	.02871	169.0	189.0
127,205	5,053	.06529	329.9	369.5
3,921,507	61,176	.00298	182.3	204.2
11,341,700	94,359	.00604	569.9	638.3

market, the 1970 estimated output of $19,847 million was developed by multiplying $58,530 by 339,100. The direct technical coefficients in column (7) for each market may be taken from the direct requirements table (Volume 2) of the *1963 Input-Output Structure of the U.S. Economy* publication of the U.S. Department of Commerce. The coefficients may also be calculated from the data in Figure 9–7 by dividing column (1) data by column (2) data: for the meat products market, the direct technical coefficient of .00784 can be obtained by dividing $145.1 million by $18,526 million.

The 1970 demand (market potential) for paperboard containers and boxes in each market can be estimated by multiplying the 1970 estimated output of the market column (6) by the direct technical coefficient column (7) for the market. Thus for the meat products market, the 1970 demand (market potential), in 1963 dollars, for paperboard containers and boxes was estimated to be $155.6 million, obtained by multiplying the 1970 estimated output of meat products ($19,847 million) by the direct technical coefficient (.00784). The 1970 demand (market potential) figure of $155.6 million was expressed in 1963 dollars column (8) and may be adjusted for inflation to a 1970 base by using an adjustment factor (1.12) obtained from the *Wholesale Price Index* for 1970. The resulting 1970 demand (market potential) for paperboard containers and boxes by the meat products market was estimated to be $174.3 million column (9), based on multiplying $155.6 million by 1.12.

After developing these market potential estimates, Rothe proceeds to show that there are significant reliability problems in two areas: (1) the direct technical coefficients for a number of markets were not constant as generally assumed, but varied by as much as 40% between 1958 and 1963, and (2) productivity (output) per employee estimates varied significantly over the five year period from 1958 to 1963, thus exerting strong influence on estimates of demand/market potential.

Input-output analysis can be of considerable value in industrial marketing research when used judiciously, and it is particularly useful in situations where: (1) consumption, rather than production, studies are required, and (2) there are a large number of products and markets to be studied with little other secondary data available.

This chapter concludes Part II and our review of the principal responsibilities of industrial marketing research. In Part III, the role of surveys in industrial marketing research will be examined.

SUGGESTED READINGS

Gols, A. George, "The Use of Input-Output in Industrial Planning," *Business Economics*, Vol. 20, May 1975, pp. 19–27.

Rabitsch, Elisabeth K., and J. M. Fuerst, "Input/Output as a Planning Tool," in Reed Moyer, Ed., *Changing Marketing Systems*. Chicago: American Marketing Association, 1967, pp. 307–312.

Rabitsch, "Input-Output Analysis and Business Forecasting," *Technological Forecasting and Social Change*, Vol. 3, 1972, pp. 453–463.

Rothe, James T., "The Reliability of Input/Output Analysis for Marketing," *California Management Review*, Vol. 14, Summer 1972, pp. 75–81.

U. S. Department of Commerce, *Input-Output Structure of the U.S. Economy*, Vol. 1., *Transactions for Detailed Industries*. Washington: U. S. Government Printing Office, 1974; Vol. 2, *Direct Requirements of Detailed Industries*. Washington: U. S. Government Printing Office, 1974; Vol. 3, *Total Requirement for Detailed Industries*. Washington: U.S. Government Printing Office, 1974.

U.S. Department of Commerce, *Interindustry Transactions in New Structures and Equipment, 1963 and 1967*. Washington: U.S. Government Printing Office, 1975.

U.S. Department of Commerce, *Summary Input-Output Tables of the U.S. Economy: 1968, 1969, 1970*. BEA Staff Paper No. 27. Springfield, Va.: National Technical Information Service, 1975.

CHAPTER TEN
The Place of Surveys in Industrial Marketing Research

Part II dealt with the principal responsibilities of industrial marketing research, and the analytical methods presented relied almost entirely on secondary data. Is there a place for primary data obtained by survey research methods? The answer of course is yes, although survey research may be less important in industrial marketing research practice than in consumer marketing research. The reason for this situation is not entirely clear. One explanation is that the need for survey research is a direct function of the channel length between the seller and buyers with the short, often direct, channels for industrial products allegedly resulting in little need for survey research. Another possible explanation is that industrial marketing research budgets are too small to permit the use of survey research in anything more than a perfunctory way.

The place of survey research in the marketing research activities of firms is somewhat enigmatic however, for there are apparently no systematic studies available on its frequency of use. A review of the contents of marketing research textbooks suggests that survey research methodology is the core of marketing research activity in firms. Survey methods and analysis receive the largest coverage (in terms of pages) of all forms of research methodology. Examination of the periodic surveys of marketing research practice conducted by the American Marketing Association, as well as my consulting experience with many firms, suggests that survey research is less important in practice than its textbook coverage would indicate. If textbook coverage and content were a reliable guide to marketing research practice, one would also have to conclude that there is little marketing research activity in industrial firms and virtually no use of survey research methods. We examined the level of industrial marketing research activity in Chapter 1, but found no indication in the American Marketing Association surveys regarding the use of survey research. Personal experience indicates that the level of use is relatively low in industrial firms, and the use level is directly related to the size of the marketing research budget. There is *sufficient use* and *opportunity for the use* of survey research methods in industrial marketing research to warrant our attention. The abundant coverage of survey research in most books on marketing research also permits us to focus on the differences in survey research and analysis as applied to industrial goods and services. We rely on the reader's use of one or more of other available books as a basis for general understanding and comparison.

Our review of survey methods emanates from the framework established in Chapter 4, in which the selection of the survey method is made from the set of primary data methods. This choice in turn depends on the type of research design and the research objectives.

Types of Survey Data Obtained

Lorie and Roberts suggested years ago that the place of surveys in marketing research could be understood by examining the types of data to be obtained.[1] We shall use an amended classification scheme from their approach to review the place of surveys in industrial marketing research. Six types of data may be obtained by surveys:

1. Awareness and knowledge
2. Attitudes and opinions
3. Intentions
4. Motivations
5. Demographic characteristics
6. Behavior

Assume that the General Electric Company wished to improve its mar-

[1] James H. Lorie and Harry V. Roberts, *Basic Methods of Marketing Research*. New York: McGraw-Hill, 1951.

keting information on power and distribution transformers. By conducting surveys among electric utilities, the primary buyers of transformers, General Electric could collect each of the types of data listed above. The primary reason for collecting such data and improving its marketing information is the same for General Electric as any other firm: the first five types of data are valuable primarily in terms of being useful in: (1) understanding present and past buying behavior and (2) predicting future behavior. Improved understanding and prediction of behavior should lead in turn to better performance in terms of the objectives and goals of the firm.

It is important to stress that General Electric *could and should* seek to attain the highest feasible ability to understand and predict behavior through the collection and analysis of secondary data. The collection of primary data by the use of the survey method is dictated by the need to *supplement* the secondary data available in order to understand and predict behavior effectively.

Suppose that General Electric has evaluated its market share position for distribution transformers in the electric utility market and finds that the market shares show considerable variance between regions of the United States. What accounts for this variance? Insight may be gained by conducting a survey among a sample of utilities incorporating questions dealing with awareness and knowledge, attitudes and opinions, motivations, and demographic characteristics of the utilities and their buying influentials.

Awareness and knowledge should be ascertained regarding the sellers (GE and competitors), products and product lines, and product attributes to determine if the levels of awareness and knowledge are systematically related to GE's market share. The attitudes and opinions of buying influentials with respect to the same stimuli (sellers, products, and product attributes) may also be related to market share position, while an understanding of the motivations involved in the purchase of transformers (combined with awareness and attitudes) may provide additional insight into the reasons for variations in market shares. Finally the demographic characteristics of the utilities (size, location, nature of the area served) and the characteristics of the buying influentials (age, experience, buying center structure, and roles) may also explain part of the variation in market shares. This information, with the possible exception of certain demographic data, would not be available as secondary data, so that a survey would be the only means of acquiring the data required to examine and determine the basis for the observed variations in market share position.

General Electric might also be interested in predicting the future behavior of market share positions in the various regions of the United States, and a survey of buying intentions could be valuable in this regard. Utilities, as with most other industrial organizations, annually announce their capital spending plans for the coming year and they are generally quite willing to respond to surveys regarding their detailed plans. These plans do not usually specify the distribution of orders among competing vendors, but define the opportunity. This leaves the task of market share estimation to General Electric on the basis of its ability to influence the determinant buying attributes.

Surveys may be used to collect information on the purchase and use behavior of electric utilities for power and distribution transformers. Schreier has suggested that behavior questions may include a number of elements: (1) what? (2) how much? (3) how? (4) where? (5) when? (6) in what situation? and (7) who?[2] Again most of these elements of purchase and use behavior information are available only from surveys.

Our review of the types of survey data that might be obtained by General Electric in a study of power and distribution transformers purchased by electric utilities suggests that there are no basic differences between consumer and industrial goods and services. The same types of survey data may be collected for all goods and services. The evident differences appear to be associated primarily with the methods of collecting data.

Methods of Collecting Survey Data

Boyd, Westfall, and Stasch offer three bases for classifying methods of collecting survey data: (1) degree of structure or standardization, (2) degree of disguise regarding survey objectives, and (3) type of communication.[3] Following the practice suggested by Campbell[4] of combining the first two bases, four approaches to collecting survey data emerge:

1. *Structured-Nondisguised approach*—Other marketing research books appear to be unanimous in agreeing that the structured-nondisguised survey is the most common. Such surveys are characterized by prescribed wording and sequence of questions together with an openness with respect to the purpose of the survey. Although this approach dominates certain types of communications (mail and, to a lesser

---

[2] Fred T. Schreier, *Modern Marketing Research*. Belmont, Cal.: Wadsworth, 1963, p. 251.
[3] Harper W. Boyd, Jr., Ralph Westfall, and Stanley F. Stasch, *Marketing Research*, 4th ed. Homewood, Ill.: Irwin, 1977, p. 109.
[4] Donald T. Campbell, "The Indirect Assessment of Social Attitudes," *Psychological Bulletin*, Vol. 47, January 1950, p. 15.

extent, telephone) in industrial surveys, it is not the method of choice for personal interviews and therefore plays a limited role in industrial marketing research.

2. *Nonstructured-Nondisguised approach*—Industrial survey research is often designed to examine the awareness, attitudes, intentions, motivations, and behavior of a limited number of knowledgeable persons in considerable depth. In such situations the individual depth and (focused) group interview is the preferred approach. Such interviews are marked by their relative lack of structure with the interviewer seeking to encourage the respondent(s) to express freely ideas and thoughts about the subject. This survey approach is the cornerstone of industrial survey research because of its inherent flexibility and effectiveness, but it is also a major challenge because of its requirement for skilled interviewers, sophisticated analysts, and relatively high time and costs demands.

3. *Nonstructured-Disguised approach*—There are times and situations in industrial survey research when respondents are unable or unwilling to reveal their attitudes and motivations. A variety of projective techniques (word association, sentence completion, story telling, and role playing) have been used in consumer marketing research practice but there are very few reported applications of projective techniques in industrial surveys.[5] There are no inherent reasons why such techniques would not be used in industrial surveys, and greater familiarity with these techniques among industrial marketing researchers would reveal many opportunities for their wider use.

4. *Structured-Disguised approach*—There are numerous problems associated with the large-scale use of the *unstructured*-disguised approach, and consequently there has been some interest in developing *structured*-disguised techniques for marketing research.[6] Although scale is generally of little concern in industrial survey research, there are certain situations in which relatively large samples may be used. One such situation occurs in corporate image research. Cohen has shown how a structured-disguised approach was used to avoid the sterotyped answers often received in image studies.[7] Potential purchasers of con-

---

[5] For an application of a storytelling technique to an industrial buying situation, see: G. M. Robertson, "Motives in Industrial Buying," in R. S. Hancock, Ed., *Dynamic Marketing for a Changing World*. Chicago: American Marketing Association, 1960, pp. 266–276.

[6] Ralph Westfall, Harper W. Boyd, Jr., and Donald T. Campbell, "The Use of Structured Techniques in Motivation Research," *Journal of Marketing*, Vol. 31 October 1967, pp. 134–139.

[7] Louis Cohen, "The Differentiation Ratio in Corporate Image Research," *Journal of Advertising Research*, Vol. 4, September 1967, pp. 32–36.

trol instruments were asked to select five characteristics (from a list of 28) "... which a control instruments manufacturer must have if he wants your business."[8] Respondents were also asked to rank the client manufacturer and six competitors as sources for control instruments, using three questionnaires each of which listed the client and two competitors. The ten most important characteristics of control manufacturers as ranked by respondents are shown in Column 1 in Figure 10–1. Column 2 shows the rankings of characteristics based on the use of the "differentiation ratio," determined by the following calculation:

$$\text{Differentiation Ratio} = \frac{\text{Percent Selecting Characteristic for No. 1 Source}}{\text{Percent Selecting Characteristic for No. 2–7 Source}}$$

The differentiation ratio is based on the rank of the characteristics that respondents associate with their No. 1 source; they are expected to be the most important in source selection. Further it appears that direct questions did indeed produce stereotype responses that did not differentiate between key and secondary sources. In contrast the differentiation ratio produced a very different ranking of factors having primary influence on source selection. The results were verified in subsequent depth interviews with respondents. The use of this analytic technique based on a disguised approach provides "... useful information because it does not ask the respondent to give information which he does not have."[9]

Survey Methods Classified by Type of Communication. The third basis for classifying methods of collecting survey data is the type of communication involved. Three methods are available: (1) personal interview, (2) telephone, and (3) mail. Each method will be examined in the context of its characteristics, advantages, and disadvantages from an industrial marketing research perspective.

A personal interview survey is characterized by a face-to-face meeting in which an interviewer seeks to obtain information from a respondent. We have noted that the "Nonstructured-Nondisguised Approach" is the cornerstone of industrial survey research, and this approach to the collection of primary data must rely almost entirely on the personal interview method. Personal interview surveys are therefore the most important of

[8]*Ibid.*, p. 34.
[9]*Ibid.*, p. 35.

SURVEYS IN INDUSTRIAL MARKETING RESEARCH

	Column 1	Column 2
Rank	Most important characteristics	Best differentiators
1	Quality products	Diversified line
2	Dependable	Leader
3	Cooperative	Pioneer
4	Quality conscious	Dependable
5	Accurate	Accurate
6	Able personnel	Flexible
7	Ethical	Alert
8	Good values	Aggressive
9	Diversified line	Quality conscious
10	Helpful	Constructive

Source: Louis Cohen, "The Differential Ratio in Corporate Image Research," *Journal of Advertising Research*, Vol. 4, September 1967, pp. 32–36.

Figure 10-1 Comparative results of nondisguised and disguised approaches to corporate image research.

the three methods available, but there are situations where the other methods singly or in combination are preferred.

Telephone and mail surveys are named and classified by the type of communication involved so there is no problem with regard to definition. Their special advantages and disadvantages, as well as those of personal interviewing, suggest that it is useful to apply a number of criteria to each of the three methods for collecting survey data as a basis for evaluation and comparison. The criteria may be classified into three groups as suggested by Churchill:[10] (1) information control, (2) sample control, and (3) administrative control. Additional specific criteria are used in the first and third groups, resulting in a total of six criteria by which to evaluate each method.[11]

Information Control

The information control group of criteria includes three specific criteria:

1. *Information complexity*—The greater the complexity of the informa-

---

[10] Gilbert A. Churchill, Jr., *Marketing Research*. Hinsdale, Ill.: Dryden, 1976, p. 177.
[11] These six criteria are suggested by Donald S. Tull and Del I. Hawkins, *Marketing Research*. New York: Macmillan, 1976, p. 377.

tion to be collected, the stronger the case for using personal interviews in industrial marketing research. If technical concepts and data are to be presented and visual stimuli (models, prototypes, drawings, graphs) used, personal interviews may be the only choice. Telephone surveys may be used for complex information collection only when prior contact and shared vocabulary limit or eliminate any problems of mutual understanding. Mail surveys can only handle moderately complex information when coupled with telephone survey followup to minimize ambiguity.

2. *Information amount*—There seems to be general agreement among marketing researchers that personal interview surveys can obtain more information than telephone or mail surveys. The primary reason is that social pressures on respondents to respond actively and complete the questioning process are stronger in the personal interview. Laurent has found that an effective way to increase the amount of information obtained in a personal interview is to double the length of the question (contrary to the usual warning to be brief and to the point) by adding introductory statements and redundant explanations to each question.[12] This technique may also be successful in producing more information in telephone surveys because it serves to reduce tension by introducing a conversational mode while stimulating respondents to provide more information in essentially the same length of time. The amount of information that may be collected by mail surveys depends primarily on the respondent's interest in the topic (which also affects personal interview and telephone surveys) and the degree of effort required of the respondent. Several studies have found that the length of the mail questionnaire does not affect the response rate.[13]

3. *Information accuracy*—The method of communication does not appear to affect the accuracy of the information collected[14] with the exception of certain sensitive data which are best collected by mail

---

[12] Andre Laurent, "Effects of Question Length on Reporting Behavior in the Survey Interview," *Journal of the American Statistical Association*, Vol. 67, June 1972, pp. 298–305.

[13] For a review of these studies, see: Leslie Kanuk and Conrad Berenson, "Mail Surveys and Response Rates: A Literature Review," *Journal of Marketing Research*, Vol. 12, November 1975, pp. 440–453; Arnold S. Linsky, "Stimulating Responses to Mailed Questionnaires: A Review," *Public Opinion Quarterly*, Vol. 39, Spring 1975, pp. 82–101; Christopher Scott, "Research on Mail Surveys," *Journal of the Royal Statistical Society*, Series A, Vol. 124, Part 2, 1961, pp. 143–205.

[14] Del I. Hawkins, Gerald Albaum, and R. Best, "Stapel Scale or Semantic Differential in Marketing Research," *Journal of Marketing Research*, Vol. 11, August 1974, pp. 318–322; Don Cahalan, "Measuring Newspaper Readership by Telephone: Two Comparisons with Face-to-Face Interviews," *Journal of Advertising Research*, Vol. 1, December 1960, pp. 1–6.

surveys.[15] Personal interview and telephone surveys present problems of detecting and controlling interviewer error and bias,[16] while mail surveys are affected by their inability to clarify confusion among respondents. Thus there are trade-offs among the three methods regarding accuracy and the choice of method will largely rest on other factors, assuming that the surveys are equally well designed and administered. There is also a need for methodological research on information accuracy in industrial surveys to determine if there are significant differences from current knowledge which is based almost entirely on consumer surveys.

Sample Control

Among the many differences between the three survey methods, some of the greatest are those associated with sample control. Boyd, Westfall, and Stasch have suggested that there are two elements involved in sample control: (1) sample designation and (2) obtaining data from the sample.[17] In industrial surveys sample designation initially requires the determination of the organizations to be included in the sample. Defining and identifying the universe of organizations from which a sample is drawn is a much more demanding task in industrial survey research than in most consumer surveys, and is considered in detail in Chapter 11. Sample designation also involves the determination of the individuals within the organizations to be included in the sample, and again the presence of multiple buying influences within organizations makes this task challenging. Sample designation is clearly an important and complex issue in industrial surveys but there are no real differences between the three survey methods, in contrast to consumer surveys in which telephone and mail samples are often more difficult to develop than personal interviews.

In industrial surveys the principal differences between the three methods of communication stem from the problem of obtaining data from the sample. There is an analogue to the "not-at-home" problem of consumer surveys, since organization employees may be away from the firm for extended periods and refusals to cooperate in surveys do occur. As with

---

[15] William F. O'Dell, "Personal Interviews or Mail Panels," *Journal of Marketing*, Vol. 26, October 1962, pp. 34–39.

[16] P. B. Case, "How to Catch Interviewer Errors," *Journal of Advertising Research*, Vol. 11, April 1971, pp. 39–43; M. J. Shapiro, "Discovering Interviewer Bias in Open-Ended Survey Responses," *Public Opinion Quarterly*, Vol. 34, Fall 1970, pp. 412–415; Harper W. Boyd, Jr., and Ralph Westfall, "Interviewer Bias Once More Revisited," *Journal of Marketing Research*, Vol. 7, May 1970, pp. 249–253.

[17] Boyd, Westfall, and Stasch, *op. cit.*, p. 120.

consumer surveys the personal interview method is superior in dealing with nonresponse problems and is often selected as the method of choice in industrial surveys for this reason. Industrial telephone surveys must cope with the "gatekeeper" problem of gaining access to an executive zealously protected by secretaries. The nonresponse problem is most severe with industrial mail surveys, especially among large firms.[18] Even if the mail questionnaires are returned, they are often completed by employees other than the designated respondent thereby reducing or eliminating sample control.

Administrative Control

Two criteria comprise the administrative control group for the purpose of evaluating the three survey methods:

1. *Time requirements*—Telephone surveys are clearly the fastest method for collecting information. When time is an important criterion, and it frequently is in industrial marketing research, this factor alone may make the telephone survey the method of choice. The continuing association between industrial buyers and sellers, as well as the heavy reliance on outside expert opinion, has led many firms to establish a universe of firms and individuals from which a sample may be quickly drawn and surveyed as an aid to management decisionmaking.

    Industrial mail surveys require more time than telephone surveys primarily because of: (1) the need to develop a structured, standardized questionnaire and (2) a limited ability to control the response rate and pattern. The author has demonstrated that two-wave mail surveys may be conducted in a two-week period by determining the optimum mailing interval (about 7 days), thereby exerting some control over the response pattern.[19] The same study indicated that ". . . up to the seventh day after mailing, the cumulative response to the industrial surveys was substantially higher than the response to the consumer surveys."[20] Response rates generally tend to be much lower for industrial surveys than for consumer surveys, and relatively few industrial surveys attain the 80% response rate considered desirable by the Advertising Research Foundation. Among the dozens of articles deal-

---

[18] For a discussion of the growing resistance of firms to mail surveys, see: T. L. Renschling and M. J. Etzel, "The Disappearing Data Source," *Business Horizons,* vol. 16, April 1963, p. 17.

[19] William E. Cox, Jr., "Response Patterns to Mail Surveys," *Journal of Marketing Research,* Vol. 3, November 1966, pp. 392–397.

[20] *Ibid.*, p. 394.

ing with methods for improving the response rate to mail surveys, a review failed to disclose any articles that were based on an industrial sample. Research is needed on the most effective and efficient ways to increase the response rate to industrial mail surveys to that researchers can realistically aim for 80% or higher response rates.

Personal interviews are the most time-consuming method, due primarily to the time required to plan, execute, and control the field interviews. Appointments must be made with busy managers and executives, substantial travel is often required, and a maximum of two interviews per day is the standard for each interviewer if more than one organization is involved. These and all the other dimensions of personal interview surveys involve substantial commitments of time for each completed interview, and thus rule out the use of the method for large samples. Even small samples (≤ 10) require substantially more time to conduct however than telephone and mail survey samples that are 10–50 times larger.

2. *Cost factors*—The high costs of field interviewing tends to be the primary influence in making personal interview surveys the most expensive of the three methods. Lower interviewing costs result in telephone surveys ranking second in terms of cost per respondent, while mail surveys are the least expensive method. The basis for this ranking is intuitive however, in the absence of information on the actual costs of industrial surveys.

Interview Guide and Questionnaire Design. Every general marketing research book now in print emphasizes the design and development of standardized questionnaires as an integral part of the survey research process. Yet standardized questionnaires play only a minor role in industrial marketing research in which nonstructured approaches dominate among the methods used to collect primary data. The use of standardized questionnaires in industrial surveys is basically limited to mail surveys and the occasional large-scale telephone survey. Recognition of these limits helps to explain the virtual absence of industrial examples and illustrations in these general books and serves to highlight one of the major differences between industrial and consumer marketing research. The dominance of nonstructured approaches in industrial personal interview and telephone (small-scale) surveys leads to reliance on two types of nonstructured interviews: (1) nondirective interviews and (2) focused interviews. Wilson has defined nondirective interviews as

> . . . a free discussion between interviewer and respondent orientated towards, but not directed along certain channels, [and states that

they are] . . . by far the commonest and most useful method used in interviewing in industrial marketing research.[21]

Schreier however has commented that the use of nondirective interviews is rare because interviewers find it difficult to avoid directing the interview toward certain directions and topics.[22] In a pure nondirective interview, the interviewer does not ask substantive questions after introducing the subject, but uses a variety of techniques to encourage the respondent to continue to provide information. These techniques range from repeating the final words or phrase of the respondent's comments with a "questioning" inflection, to commenting: "Please tell me more about that," "How do you mean?," or "Is that right?" Pure nondirective interviews *are* rare in marketing research practice, in that it is too risky to use them in decision-oriented research situations, since they are too likely to produce irrelevant and incomplete responses.

The Focused Interview

The most important type of nonstructured interview in industrial marketing research is focused interviews, sometimes called depth interviews which are frequently associated with motivation research. The focused interview is used to collect all types of survey data, not just motivations, and may be used to collect quantitative as well as qualitative data. In introducing the term "focused interview," Merton, Fisk, and Kendall[23] noted that effective focused interviews should meet four criteria:

1. *Range*—The interview should enable interviewees to maximize the reported range of evocative elements and patterns in the stimulus situation as well as the range of responses;
2. *Specificity*—The interview should elicit highly specific reports of the aspects of the stimulus situation to which the interviewees have responded;
3. *Depth*—The interview should help interviewees to describe the affective, cognitive, and evaluative meanings of the situation and the degree of their involvement in it;
4. *Personal context*—The interview should bring out the attributes and

---

[21] Aubrey Wilson, *The Assessment of Industrial Markets*. London: Hutchinson and Co., 1968, p. 168.
[22] Schreier, *op. cit.*, p. 65.
[23] Robert K. Merton, Marjorie Fisk, and Patricia L. Kendall, *The Focused Interview*. Glencoe, Ill.: Free Press, 1956.

1. What trends do you foresee (in % terms) in the use of contract packagers by manufacturers of blister-packaged items over the next four years (through 1980)? (Percentages should be based on dollar volumes and expressed as an annual change rate.)

2. What are the most important conditions *favoring* the use of a contract packager? (We are interested in blister-packaged items only. Rank the identified conditions in order of importance. Probe such conditions as: introductions of new products; limitations of packaging capacity in plant; required investment in packaging machinery; economic climate and expectations; complexity of packaging job. Probe: any trends in these conditions that favor the future use of contract packagers.)

3. What are the most important conditions *limiting* the use of contract packagers? (Same directions as for Question 2, except probe for *opposite* conditions as well as: quality control, prices, and transportation costs.)

4. What are the most important attributes that you look for in a contract packager? (Rank the attributes named; probe for attributes such as: ability to deliver on contract terms, packaging equipment availability and capability, previous experience with packager.)

Figure 10-2 Interview guide—contract packaging study (excerpt).

prior experience of interviewees which endow the situation with these distinctive meanings.[24]

In the focused interview, the interviewer should be briefed as to the management and research problem/opportunity, research objectives, and interview objectives. It is critical that the interviewer have this background information because the interviewer must continually adjust the interview situation towards the fulfillment of the objectives. An interview guide should be prepared to ensure that the objectives and major topics are covered in the interviews. A portion of an interview guide prepared for a personal interview survey of users of industrial contract packaging services is shown in Figure 10-2. The interview guide provides suggested wording of questions, probes, reminders regarding data needs, but permits the interviewer to modify the wording and order of the questions, ask additional questions, and pursue any potentially interesting topics.

Extracts from a focused interview to determine the nature of the market for butterfly valves are provided in Figure 10-3 to illustrate the type and variety of information produced in a focused interview. These extracts

[24] *Ibid.*, p. 12.

The chemical industry in this area is a potential user of butterfly valves. This is the inorganic segment of the industry—many of the applications involve the handling of high-temperature corrosive gases. Pressures are low—gases like SO_2. Valves must shut off, but not necessarily give a tight shut-off. We do not have synthetic fiber plants in our district, but the valves for Dupont's plants are bought here. Butterflies are used in the acid reclaim sections of viscose rayon production process—nmot ours—they do buy from competitors. They use metal seat valves—tight shut-off is not required.

Dupont could give a lot of information on the use of butterfly valves in many areas of the chemical industry. You could talk to a number of people, but the instrumentation people would be best—they buy most of the butterfly valves. They are part of the plant design group at Dupont. Dupont builds most of its own plants, and this is typical of the larger producers of chemicals. They usually buy valves of small sizes.

(Asked about a valve which might go as high as 400–500 psi pressure:) Can't get too excited about a high-pressure valve. If you said degrees, I would be more interested. The big problem in the industrial field is designing for corrosion and for higher temperatures.

Source: Chester R. Wasson, *The Strategy of Marketing Research*. New York: Appleton-Century-Crofts, 1964, pp. 101–102.

Figure 10-3 Focused interview extracts—butterfly valve study.

emphasize qualitative data, which predominate in such focused interviews, but quantitative data on the demand for butterfly valves also may be collected in the same interview.

Successful focus interviews depend heavily on the interviewer's ability to select and use various techniques to focus and control the interaction following a question. Kahn and Cannell have suggested two useful techniques:[25]

1. Supplement the question:
    (a) Use a brief assertion of understanding and interest, such as "I see" and "um-hm."
    (b) Pause and wait for the respondent to answer further.

[25] Robert L. Kahn and Charles F. Cannell, The Dynamics of Interviewing. New York: John Wiley & Sons, 1957.

SURVEYS IN INDUSTRIAL MARKETING RESEARCH

   (c) Use a neutral phrase to indicate interest and communicate to the respondent that more information is desired:

     . . . How do you mean?
     . . . I'd like to know more about your thinking on that.
     . . . What do you have in mind there?
     . . . Why do you think that is so?
     . . . What do you think causes that?
     . . . Anything else?

2. Summarize the response:

     . . . The interviewer attempts to summarize briefly the response as accurately as possible in order to convey both understanding and acceptance.

These probing techniques serve two primary purposes: to motivate the respondent and to focus the response on question objectives. A high order of skill is required to conduct focused interviews that produce complete and unbiased responses. Much of the skill lies in the appropriate selection and use of the probing techniques described.

Recording the Interview

Focused interviews involve wide-ranging, nonstructured dialogues that tax the recall capacity of the most skilled interviewers. Most interviewers need to take notes during the interview, and it is good practice to tell the respondent that notes will be taken for the sake of both accuracy and completeness. Note-taking should be as unobtrusive as possible, using key words and phrases, and should never be allowed to interfere with the dialogue flow.

Tape recorders are extremely valuable adjuncts in the focused interview and should be used whenever possible. The interviewer should explain the importance of obtaining a full and accurate record of the interview, assure the respondent of the confidentiality of the record, and offer to turn off the recorder at any time the respondent wishes to speak off the record. The use of a battery-powered recorder, with a built-in microphone and high tape capacity, will minimize the obtrusive effects of the instrument. The use of a tape recorder does not eliminate the need and importance of note-taking during the interview; note-taking helps the interviewer to concentrate on responses, aids in formulating probes, helps in subsequent analysis of tape content, and provides backup for inaudible and blank tape situations.

Sales Personnel as Interviewers

One of the more controversial issues in industrial marketing research practice deals with the advisability of using sales personnel as interviewers in industrial surveys. Wilson states that the practice is

> highly undesirable. Salesmen are trained to persuade, not to report objectively on factors which may both reflect on their own performance or which might be against their personal interest and aspirations.[26]

Webster, in contrast, has observed:

> By limiting, either explicitly or implicitly, the salesman's role to that of a promotional agent, the company minimizes his opportunity to function as a source of market information.[27] [and] Use of the salesman for gathering information can be much more critical than his use for promotion.[28]

There is an increasing tendency for industrial firms to regard their direct sales personnel as "marketing managers," with responsibilities ranging far beyond the narrow bounds of the selling function. Sales personnel also have the advantages of: (1) having relatively well-developed interpersonal skills, (2) being familiar with respondents and their operations, (3) having a "shared vocabulary" with respondents, and (4) being familiar with the firm's products and services. Their drawbacks as potential interviewers are: (1) lack of interviewing skills; (2) vested interests in responses, particularly those that are critical of the sales person, products, or the seller; and (3) reluctance of respondents to provide objective answers. There are very strong arguments for using direct sales personnel as interviewers in industrial surveys; the drawbacks can be largely controlled or eliminated by training.

Direct sales personnel however may not be required in many industrial surveys in which the total number of focused interviews will be less than ten. In such cases it is preferable to use the firm's marketing research personnel exclusively and thereby minimize the training and potential bias problems associated with the use of direct sales personnel. Larger sample surveys should be conducted in two stages with marketing research per-

---

[26] Wilson, *op. cit.*, p. 192.
[27] Frederick E. Webster, Jr., "The Industrial Salesman as a Source of Market Information," *Business Horizons*, Vol. 8, Spring 1965, p. 77.
[28] *Ibid.*, p. 78.

sonnel conducting the first stage interviews and using the results then to assist in the training of the direct sales personnel as interviewers in the second and larger sample stage.

Industrial manufacturers and wholesalers may both use their direct sales personnel as interviewers but it is usually inappropriate for manufacturers to attempt to use wholesaler sales personnel as interviewers. The manufacturer's general lack of control over these individuals tends to rule out this possible option. Manufacturers who distribute through wholesalers must rely on their own marketing research personnel or use an independent marketing research agency.

A recent article in *Industrial Distribution* reports that industrial distributors are increasingly becoming involved in marketing research activities, particularly in customer surveys.[29]

Outside Research Agencies as Interviewer Sources

The use of direct sales personnel as interviewers in industrial surveys works out best in customer surveys; surveys that involve interviews with relatively large numbers of noncustomers are best carried out with the assistance of outside marketing research agencies. Most major cities in the United States have one or more agencies specializing in industrial marketing research, and they usually have access to skilled executive interviewers. These experienced interviewers are usually quick to pick up the required product/service background vocabulary and respond well to briefing sessions on the situation and research objectives. They also bring a sense of objectivity to issues that involve complex value judgments. The major disadvantages associated with the use of outside agencies are: (1) potentially higher costs per interview and (2) inability to capitalize on the learning that accrues to interviewers as a result of their exposure to buyers and markets. These disadvantages are sufficiently important to cause most industrial firms to rely primarily on internal personnel and to view outside agencies as supplemental sources of interviewers.

Technical and Nontechnical Interviewers

Wilson has stated that

> The greatest single problem of industrial interviewing and, indeed, perhaps the fundamental difficulty of industrial marketing research is

---

[29] "Do You Know Your Market? If Not, Try Market Research," *Industrial Distribution*, April 1977, pp. 37–41.

how far technical knowledge of the product is necessary or indeed useful to the researcher.[30]

There are two opposing views, as Wilson notes, with one view being that an industrial interviewer must have a degree of technical knowledge as large as the respondents and preferably larger. The other view is that interviewing skills and techniques are far more important than technical and product knowledge, and that technical knowledge may be more harmful than useful because it results in technical biases. Wilson suggests that the best solution is a compromise, with expert technical briefing of skilled interviewers. The briefing should be conducted by qualified technical personnel within the firm, although Wilson maintains that independent marketing research agencies usually have links with technical organizations that

> . . . employ researchers of a far higher calibre in relation to the technology being researched, than will be available in the operating management of the sponsor's firm.[31]

Regardless of who conducts the technical briefing, it is true that technical marketing research personnel, skilled in interviewing techniques, can absorb technical and product information rapidly and should always be responsible for the exploratory interviews in industrial survey research. These personnel, in conjunction with the technical experts, can then brief the sales personnel or agency interviewers as required.

Although nonstructured approaches are of primary interest in industrial surveys, there is a role for structured approaches and standardized questionnaires.

Structured Approaches and Standardized Questionnaires

The need for structured approaches and standardized questionnaires in industrial surveys arises when the population to be surveyed is relatively large, market demand is relatively unconcentrated, and the types of survey data to be collected fall into three categories:

1. Awareness and knowledge
2. Attitudes and opinions
3. Prior and present behavior

---

[30] Wilson, *op. cit.*, p. 193.
[31] *Ibid.*, p. 196.

Selecting the appropriate survey method by type of communication depends upon the application of the criteria of information, sample, and administrative control. In the situations just described, the choice will usually be either telephone and mail surveys or a combination of the two methods. There are also a number of other important decisions that must be made with respect to questionnaire design, regardless of the method selected. These questions have been summarized by Tull and Hawkins and are listed in Figure 10-4. Each decision, where appropriate, should be supported by a review of the literature. Although the literature is almost totally based on issues and products apart from industrial goods and services, the findings appear to have general applicability in most instances.[32]

Despite the general applicability of the literature on questionnaire design and the availability of rules-of-thumb to support many of the decisions on the list developed by Tull and Hawkins, the virtual absence of industrial examples in the literature leaves many industrial marketing researchers in a very uncertain state when they are charged with the responsibility of drafting a standardized questionnaire. Many have asked me for specimen questions to illustrate various types of questions, just to get them started, and so a sampling of questions has been prepared from a variety of surveys conducted by the author and his associates over a twenty-year period. The questions are shown in Figure 10-5 and are organized by type of data to be collected. Although some of the company and product names are disguised, the questions are not edited and most readers will be able to make improvements in the questions. It is literally impossible to design the perfect question, but the pursuit of this elusive objective provides some of the challenge, satisfaction, and frustration associated with survey research.

In addition to the need to collect the types of primary data covered in Figure 10-5, it is common practice to obtain secondary data on the demographic characteristics of the responding firm and the industry. Such data may be used to stratify the population as a basis for sampling, as check data against the validity of the survey data, and as a basis for weighting responses in the analysis of survey data. These data may be on file in customer records internally and are often available in the various directories discussed in Chapter 3. These data include such measures as SIC numbers, size of the firm and establishment in terms of the number of

---

[32] Comprehensive discussions of questionnaire design from a marketing research perspective are available in: Tull and Hawkins, *op. cit.*, Chaps. 8-10; and Boyd, Westfall, and Stasch, *op. cit.*, Chaps. 7-8. For a social research perspective see: Claire Selltiz, Lawrence S. Wrightsman, and Stuart W. Cook, *Research Methods in Social Relations*, 3rd ed. New York: Holt, Rinehart and Winston, 1976, Chap. 9, 10, 12.

I. **Preliminary Decisions**
   A. Exactly what information is required?
   B. Exactly what are the target respondents?
   C. What method of communication will be used to reach these respondents?

II. **Decisions about Question Content**
   A. Is this question really needed?
   B. Is this question sufficient to generate the needed information?
   C. Can the respondents answer the question correctly?
   D. Will the respondents answer the question correctly?
   E. Are there any external events that might bias the response to the question?

III. **Decisions concerning Question Phrasing**
   A. Do the words used have but one meaning to all the respondents?
   B. Are any of the words or phrases loaded or leading in any way?
   C. Are there any implied alternatives in the question?
   D. Are there any unstated assumptions related to the question?
   E. Will the respondents approach the question from the frame of reference desired by the researcher?

IV. **Decisions about the Response Format**
   A. Can this question best be asked as an open-ended, multiple-choice, or dichotomous question?

V. **Decisions concerning the Question Sequence**
   A. Are the questions organized in a logical manner that avoids introducing errors?

VI. **Decisions on the Layout of the Questionnaire**
   A. Is the questionnaire designed in a manner to avoid confusion and minimize recording errors?

VII. **Decisions about the Pretest**
   A. Has the final questionnaire been subjected to a thorough pretest using respondents similar to those that will be included in the final survey?

Source: Donald S. Tull and Del I. Hawkins, *Marketing Research*. New York: Macmillan, 1976, p. 242.

Figure 10–4 Summary of the major decisions on questionnaire design.

employees, number and size of plants, prior sales history, and a variety of other factors.

The use of mail questionnaires presents certain specific requirements not associated with the other methods of collecting data. A cover letter is needed to accompany the mail questionnaire. It should describe the purpose and content of the survey and present a request for cooperation. Figure 10–6 presents a cover letter with disguised names that accompanied a self-mailer questionnaire and produced more than an 80% return with two follow-up mailings.

All three types of data collection methods must deal with the problem of nonresponse, but mail surveys pose a special problem. The identity of nonrespondents is known for personal interviews and telephone surveys as a matter of course, but in mail surveys it is necessary to code all questionnaires so that nonrespondents may be identified and sent follow-up questionnaires. It is generally considered unethical to resort to hidden code marks (under the stamp on a stamped return envelope; disappearing ink, and so on), while the absence of a code number and the failure to followup with nonrespondents destroys the value of a mail survey. It is customary to ask respondents in industrial surveys to sign the completed questionnaire with their name and title, but many fail to do this. It is therefore necessary to code all questionnaires and the code should be evident to the respondent without being overly conspicuous. Some researchers prefer to mention the code in the cover letter and assure respondents that it will be used only to determine nonrespondents to the questionnaire. Do not fall prey to the all-too-common temptation to guarantee the mail survey respondent anonymity in return for the hope of obtaining a higher response rate; the inability to determine whether the respondents are representative of the total sample and population makes such a survey worthless.

SUMMARY

Survey research plays less important a role in industrial marketing research than in consumer marketing research. Part of the reason may be that the need for survey research is diminished by the short, often direct channels for industrial products. Another factor is that industrial marketing research budgets tend to be too small to permit extensive survey research activity.

Personal interviews and nonstructured-nondisguised research of a limited number of respondents is by far the most prevalent survey approach in industrial marketing research. Structured-nondisguised studies that are

I. Questions to Measure Awareness and Knowledge

    A. Have your hear of the following:

Chicago "Stak-o-matic"	( ) Yes ( ) No
Triax "Retriever"	( ) Yes ( ) No
Eaton "StackSystem"	( ) Yes ( ) No

    B. Which of the paper products listed are offered by each of the following companies? (Check where applicable)

Name of Company	Business Communication Papers	Linerboard and Corrugating Medium
Boise Cascade	____	____
Great Northern Nekoosa	____	____
Mead	____	____
Potlatch	____	____
Union Camp	____	____
Westvaco	____	____

II. Questions to Measure Attitudes and Opinions

    A. Which manufacturers of plastic injection molding machines do you associate with the following characteristics:

	Name of Manufacturer(s)
Lowest machine prices	_____
Best engineering service	_____
Highest quality machines	_____

    B. Please check your evaluation of the quality of the bearings offered by the following firms:

Name of Firm	Excellent	Good	Average	Fair	Poor	Not Familiar With Quality
American Toyo	__	__	__	__	__	__
Barden	__	__	__	__	__	__
Federal Mogul	__	__	__	__	__	__
Hoover NSK	__	__	__	__	__	__
SKF Industries	__	__	__	__	__	__
Timken	__	__	__	__	__	__
Torrington	__	__	__	__	__	__

III. Questions to Measure Past and Present Behavior (Use)

    A. How many circular cut-off saws are installed in your plant? Saws used to cut-off billets, rods, structurals, or plates—(Please do not include "scalper" saws used to trim the sides of shapes)

                                                                                              Number

        12– 23" outside diameter saws   —
        24–116" outside diameter saws   —

    B. How frequently have you requested immediate delivery (with 2 hours) on packaged industrial petroleum products in the past six months?

        None ____   2–5 times ____
        Once ____   More than 5 times ____

IV. Questions to Measure Demographic Characteristics

    A. What is your title?_____
    B. How many employees (full-time) do you now have? ____
    C. Please list the principal products of your firm: ____

Figure 10-5 *Specimen questions from structured questionnaires.*

---

so prevalent in consumer marketing research have a limited role in industrial marketing research.

Churchill suggests applying the criteria of information control, sample control, and administrative control to the choice among telephone, mail, and personal survey approaches. It appears that the more information needed or the more complex the information, the more desirable it is to employ personal interviewing techniques. Personal interviewing is also to be preferred for reaching executives who are often away, hard to see, or who may delegate questionnaire filling to subordinates. However personal interviewing is the costliest and most time consuming approach and requires considerable interviewing skills. Focus interviews are the most common type of personal interviewing technique in industrial marketing research.

With proper training sales personnel may be used as interviewers. However for the small samples typically required in surveys of knowledgeable persons, it is best to use marketing research personnel from within the company or from professional research agencies. Interviewers should have technical training or briefing on the topic being studied so that they can absorb technical and product information rapidly and probe the right issues during exploratory interviews.

CROWN CORPORATION
14 State Street
Detroit, Michigan

May 1977

Good Morning:

The Crown Corporation is interested in your opinions and suggestions on the most effective way to present information in equipment catalogs. Will you help us?

To help you express your thoughts concerning catalogs, we are enclosing a form which requires a minimum of writing. Your individual reply is important to us. We will appreciate your completing the form and sending it to us. When folded and sealed, it becomes a postage-paid, self-addressed envelope.

You need not sign your name, but we would appreciate having your title.

Thank you for your cooperation.

Sincerely,

CROWN CORPORATION

Edward S. King

Edward S. King, Manager
Marketing Research Department

Enclosure

Figure 10-6 Specimen cover letter to accompany a mail questionnaire.

Structured approaches and standardized questionnaires are desirable when the population to be surveyed is large; demand is relatively unconcentrated; and the types of data to be collected primarily focus on awareness, knowledge, attitudes, opinions, and behavior. Demographic information should also be collected for validation against company records and for survey analysis as well. Mail, telephone, or a combination of both approaches is usually employed with a cover letter and a follow-up questionnaire mailing advisable to ensure adequate response to mail surveys.

SUGGESTED READINGS

Boyd, Harper W., Jr., and Ralph Westfall, "Interviewer Bias Once More Revisited," *Journal of Marketing Research*, Vol. 7, May 1970, pp. 249–253.

Boyd, Harper W., Jr., Ralph Westfall, and Stanley F. Stasch, *Marketing Research*, 4th ed. Homewood, Ill.: Irwin, 1977, Chap. 4.

Cahalan, Don, "Measuring Newspaper Readership by Telephone: Two Comparisons with Face-to-Face Interviews," *Journal of Advertising Research*, Vol. 1, December 1960, pp. 1–6.

Campbell, Donald T., "The Indirect Assessment of Social Attitudes," *Psychological Bulletin*, Vol. 47, January 1950.

Case, P. B., "How to Catch Interviewer Errors," *Journal of Advertising Research*, Vol. 11, April 1971, pp. 39–43.

Churchill, Gilbert A., Jr., *Marketing Research*. Hinsdale, Ill.: Dryden, 1976.

Cohen, Louis, "The Differentiation Ratio in Corporate Image Research," *Journal of Advertising Research*, Vol. 4, September 1967, pp. 32–36.

Cox, William E., Jr., "Response Patterns to Mail Surveys," *Journal of Marketing Research*, Vol. 3, November 1966, pp. 392–397.

Hawkins, Del I., Gerald Albaum, and R. Best, "Staple Scale or Semantic Differential in Marketing Research," *Journal of Marketing Research*, Vol. 11, August 1974, pp. 318–322.

Industrial Distribution, "Do You Know Your Market? If not, Try Market Research," April 1977, pp. 37–41.

Kanuk, Leslie, and Conrad Berenson, "Mail Surveys and Response Rates: A Literature Review," *Journal of Marketing Research*, Vol. 12, November 1975, pp. 440–453.

Laurent, Andre, "Effects of Question Length on Reporting Behavior in the Survey Interview," *Journal of American Statistical Association*, Vol. 67, June 1972, pp. 298–305.

Linsky, Arnold S., "Stimulating Responses to Mailed Questionnaires: A Review," *Public Opinion Quarterly*, Vol. 39, Spring 1975, pp. 82–101.

Lori, James H., and Harry V. Roberts, *Basic Methods of Marketing Research*. New York: McGraw-Hill, 1951.

Merton, Robert K., Majorie Fisk, and Patricia L. Kendall, *The Focused Interview*. Glencoe, Ill.: Free Press, 1956.

O'Dell, William F., "Personal Interviews or Mail Panels," *Journal of Marketing*, Vol. 26, October 1962, pp. 34–39.

Renschling, T. L., and M. J. Etzel, "The Disappearing Data Source," *Business Horizons*, Vol. 16, April 1963.

Robertson, G. M., "Motives in Industrial Buying," in R. S. Hancock, Ed., *Dynamic Marketing for a Changing World*. Chicago: American Marketing Association, 1960, pp. 266–276.

Schreier, Fred T., *Modern Marketing Research*. Belmont, Calif.: Wadsworth, 1963.

Scott, Christoper, "Research on Mail Surveys," *Journal of the Royal Statistical Society*, Series A, Vol. 124, Part 2, 1961, pp. 143–205.

Selltiz, Claire, Lawrence S. Wrightsman, and Stuart W. Cook, *Research Methods in Social Relations*, 3rd ed. New York: Holt, Rhinehart and Winston, 1976, Chaps. 9, 10, 12.

Shapiro, M. J., "Discovering Interviewer Bias in Open-Ended Survey Responses," *Public Opinion Quarterly*, Vol. 34, Fall 1970, pp. 412–415.

Tull, Donald S., and Del I. Hawkins, *Marketing Research*. New York: Macmillan, 1976, pp. 579–581.

Wasson, Chester R., *The Strategy of Marketing Research*. New York: Appleton-Century-Crofts, 1964.

Webster, Frederick E., Jr., "The Industrial Salesman as a Source of Market Information," *Business Horizons*, Vol. 8, no. 1, Spring 1965, pp. 77–82.

Westfall, Ralph, Harper W. Boyd, Jr., and Donald T. Campbell, "The Use of Structured Techniques in Motivation Research," *Journal of Marketing*, Vol. 31, October 1967, pp. 134–139.

Wilson, Aubrey, *The Assessment of Industrial Markets*. London: Hutchinson and Co., 1968, Chap. 1.

CHAPTER ELEVEN
Sampling in Industrial Survey Research

One of the basic objectives of this book is to identify and develop those areas of marketing research activity in which there are significant differences between consumer and industrial products and services. A number of these differences were discussed in Chapter 10. In this chapter the emphasis is on sampling in industrial surveys. Wilson has noted,

> It is perhaps in sampling procedures where the greatest and most fundamental divergence occurs between consumer and industrial marketing research.[1]

The abundance of resource material on sampling techniques in general marketing research books again makes it possible to focus on the specific areas and issues in which industrial marketing research requirements are different. Surveys have been identified as the principal method for collecting primary data in industrial marketing research. Industrial surveys involve the collection of data from respondents in industrial markets. Chapter 1 outlined a number of differences between industrial and consumer products and services markets. One critical difference was

---

[1] Aubrey Wilson, *The Assessment of Industrial Markets*. London: Hutchinson and Co., 1968, p. 109.

identified as the level of demand concentration, particularly with respect to industrial and purchasing concentration. Concentration in industrial markets has several important consequences for sampling:

1. Industrial concentration indicates that the markets are relatively limited in terms of the number of actual and potential buying firms. Secondary data sources may be used to identify and classify market members, thereby specifying the individual members of a market population to a degree rarely possible for consumer products and services.
2. Purchasing concentration occurs in many industrial markets whereby a few large firms account for a high proportion of total market demand. This situation requires that industrial surveys explicitly reflect the inequality of the members of the population in the choice of sampling and analytical methods. Consumer surveys generally implicitly assume approximate equality among market populations.

Universe Definition

Industrial concentration does indeed make it possible to identify the individual members of a market population to a large degree but as noted in Chapter 6, the definition of a relevant market is often difficult. There are five steps in the sampling process in industrial survey research as shown in Figure 11–1, the first step involves universe (and market) definition. The definition of an industrial market requires that industry, product, and market boundaries be established, based on a prescribed process.[2] A group of actual and potential buying firms for a specific product or product line, along with a series of limitations on supply sources, serve to define market boundaries. These firms within the market boundaries then become the universe (population) for sampling purposes in many industrial surveys. The research objectives of the survey will actually determine the definition of the universe, and since research objectives vary widely, the sampling units that may comprise a universe will also vary widely. Wilson has noted that the universe in a study to determine the demand for vitreous enamel pipes could be defined in terms of four different sampling units: (1) buyers (construction companies), (2) outside purchasing influences (architects and consulting engineers), (3) end-user specifiers (municipal governments and regional authorities), and (4)

---

[2] Peter O. Steiner, "Markets and Industries," in D. L. Sills, Ed., *International Encyclopedia of the Social Sciences*. New York: Free Press, 1968, pp. 577–579.

SAMPLING IN INDUSTRIAL SURVEY RESEARCH

1. **Universe definition**—population to be surveyed is defined in terms of (a) sampling units, (b) elements, (c) extent, and (d) time.
2. **Sampling frame development**—a list of universe members is developed as a basis for sampling.
3. **Sampling unit and element specification**—universe members may be sampling units (such as firms or establishments) with individuals within the sampling units designated as sampling elements (purchasing agents, engineers), or the sampling units and elements may be identical (presidents of firms).
4. **Sampling method selection**—the method for selecting sampling units must be determined.
5. **Sample size determination**—the number of sampling units (and elements) to be included in the sample must be determined.

Source: Adapted from: Donald S. Tull and Del I. Hawkins, *Marketing Research*. New York: Macmillan, 1976, p. 154.

Figure 11-1 Steps in the sampling process of industrial surveys.

suppliers (pipe manufacturers).[3] In addition to sampling units, a definition of a universe should also include the: (1) sampling element (purchasing agents, presidents), (2) sampling extent (product and geographic boundaries), and (3) time (buyers of fork-lift trucks in the last six months).[4] Research objectives may also direct that the universe be defined on the basis of attributes for which no secondary data are available, such as establishments with five or more copying machines. In such cases correlates for the attributes may be used or an exploratory survey may be conducted to aid in the definition of the universe.

Sampling Frame Development

A sampling frame is a

> means of access to the universe, . . . made up of sampling units, and . . . every sampling unit in a frame will bear a serial number, or will have a prescribed way of getting one.[5]

---
[3] Wilson, *op cit.*, p. 115.
[4] Tull and Hawkins, *op. cit.*, p. 154.
[5] W. Edwards Deming, *Sample Design in Business Research*. New York: Wiley, 1960, pp. 39-40.

Co de Koning has suggested that there are two approaches available for building an industrial sampling frame: (1) formal frame building in which a complete list of sampling units is developed prior to data collection and (2) sequential frame building whereby the frame is developed during the process of data collection.[6] Sequential frame building is generally used in the absence of secondary data on important universe characteristics. An alternative is to use double sampling in which a large initial sample is used to screen sampling units for a smaller sample, which is stratified on the basis of the distribution of the universe characteristics in the initial sample.[7]

It would be ideal if the sampling frame and universe proved to be identical, but this is a rare event. There is almost always a gap between the sampling frame and the universe. The relationship between the universe, sampling frame, and gap can be illustrated with an example drawn from the ceramics industry. Suppose that a manufacturer was interested in conducting a survey of United States establishments now engaged in manufacturing porcelain electrical supplies. This definition of the universe is relatively simple and straight-forward but the measurement of universe characteristics and development of a sampling frame is not so easy.

A first step in the development of a sampling frame is to determine the SIC number for establishments primarily engaged in manufacturing porcelain electrical supplies (SIC 3264). The next step is to determine how many establishments were so classified in various U.S. government sources, including the *Census of Manufactures*, *Annual Survey of Manufacturers*, *Current Industrial Reports*, and *County Business Patterns*. All of these sources will be out of date, thus creating a gap due to publication delay. Another gap is created by the practice of assigning multiproduct establishments to a single SIC 4-digit category based on its primary activity. All establishments producing porcelain electrical supplies as a secondary activity will not be included in the establishment count, resulting in a gap due to secondary product classification. These gaps indicate that there is little likelihood that an accurate count of the number of establishments can be obtained for the present universe, and that similar or greater problems would be encountered in trying to measure any other characteristic of the universe. Since the universe characteristics cannot be measured accurately, the gap must usually be estimated by using the available secondary data as the basis for the estimates.

[6] Co de Koning, "Effective Techniques in Industrial Marketing Research," *Journal of Marketing*, Vol. 28, no. 2, April 1964, p. 59.
[7] Robert Ferber, *Statistical Techniques in Market Research*. New York: McGraw-Hill, 1949, pp. 80–81.

Most industrial sampling frames are developed from directories, most notably those from Dun and Bradstreet, Standard and Poor's, and the Thomas Register. It is best to use all available sources in building the list; they offer the advantage of including firms and establishments manufacturing a product as a secondary activity. All directories are out of date before they appear in print however and they all contain errors of omission and classification. Purchased lists obtained from list brokers usually have all of the shortcomings of directories (often the source of the lists); tend to be too general for any particular sampling frame requirement; and frequently are unavailable to the researcher for examination, followup, and validity checks.

McIntosh warns about two other sources of sampling frames: (1) internal customer lists are often partial and biased with incomplete coverage of key market segments and (2) circulation lists of business and trade magazines may not be reaching expected audiences and markets. He cites the case of a

> ... survey of the use of hydraulic and cutting oils in machine shops. The original intention of the survey was to obtain readers' reaction to a publication issued to machine shop managers by a leading oil company. Sampling from the circulation list revealed that fully 50% of the copies were sent to individuals or establishments which did not exist, had no machine shops, or where the individuals named had no connection with a machine shop. A high proportion of the remaining 50% were either unread, or read by machine shop managers who, despite their job title, had no say in the choice of brand of hydraulic or cutting oil.[8]

Sampling frames in industrial surveys often tend to have substantial deficiencies with gaps that are uncomfortably large. The *1972 Census of Manufactures* indicates that there were 83 establishments and 75 companies classified in SIC 3264, while a review of the latest available directories from Dun and Bradstreet, Standard and Poor's, and the Thomas Register revealed 74 establishments and 72 companies. It is quite likely that the time difference between the *Census* and the directories could account for the discrepancy in this case. The use of multiple sources helped to minimize the discrepancy. The small gap also helps to assure

---

[8] Andrew R. McIntosh, "Improving the Efficiency of Sample Surveys in Industrial Markets," *Journal of the Marketing Research Society*, Vol. 17, no. 4, 1976, pp. 225–226.

that most, if not all, of the largest establishments and companies would be included in both the counts of the *Census* and the directories.

Sampling Unit and Element Specification

Industrial surveys usually specify an establishment or company as the sampling unit with the members of the decision-making unit (DMU) within the organization designated as sampling elements. There are occasions when the sampling units and elements are identical, notably when a complete sampling frame is available, listing for example the presidents of all Fortune "500" companies. Specification of the sampling unit however is usually an initial and independent event. Wilson's study of the demand for vitreous enamel pipes provides a good illustration of the choice decision. If the research objectives included assessment of installation problems, pipe buyers (construction companies) would be selected as sampling units. If the study sponsor was a clay products firm interested in the pipe market, suppliers (pipe manufacturers) might be chosen as sampling units. The sampling units might be architects and consulting engineers (outside buying influences) if the research objectives included a study of the buying decision. A buying decision study would also require the designation of end-user specifiers (municipal governments and regional authorities) as sampling units. A comprehensive study of the demand for vitreous enamel pipes might therefore include all four groups as sampling units, each within a designated sampling frame.

The specification of sampling elements is also directed primarily by the research and survey objectives. Members of the DMU in each sampling unit will vary widely by job titles and degrees of influence. Purchasing agents for example may have significant influence in establishing specifications and qualified suppliers for vitreous enamel pipes in some buying firms; in others the chief engineer may have dominant influence. One of the major advantages of personal interview methods in industrial surveys is that they provide the greatest degree of flexibility for identifying and collecting data from the most appropriate sampling elements within the sampling units. The key point is that the industrial survey researcher must first assess in general terms the decision-making environment within the sampling units and also be open to the need to adapt the choice of sampling elements within certain sampling units. Thus purchasing agents may be designated as the primary sampling elements in the sampling units in a frame, while screening questions and probes will be included in the interview and questionnaire to aid in spotting the need to include other sampling elements such as design engineers in certain sampling units.

Sampling Method Selection

After the sampling units and elements are specified, the next step in the sampling process is to select the sampling method. The term "sampling method" refers to the procedure for selecting sampling units and elements from the sampling frame. In selecting sampling methods, the first and most important decision is whether to use probability or nonprobability sampling methods. Probability sampling is marked by the random selection of sampling units and elements with each sampling unit and element in a sampling frame having a known chance of being selected. Nonprobability sampling involves the arbitrary, nonrandom choice of sampling units and elements without knowledge of the chance that any particular sampling unit or element will be selected.

Within the broad categories of probability and nonprobability sampling methods, there are a number of specific methods available for selecting sampling units and elements. These choices are outlined in a diagram in Figure 11-2. The initial choice between probability and nonprobability methods depends primarily on: (1) the importance of making inferences about sampling frame and universe characteristics on the basis of sample findings and (2) the probability and expected costs of making erroneous inferences. If inferences are important and being wrong is both likely and costly, probability sampling methods should be used.

Judgment Sampling

Judgment samples are widely used in industrial survey research, most notably in surveys of knowledgeable persons. Such persons are selected on the judgment of the survey researcher who recognizes that only certain sampling elements possess the requisite information. In addition not all persons possessing the information are willing to provide it. This again requires that the sample be selected on the basis of judgment. Firms and establishments too are often selected on a judgment sampling basis because they possess certain characteristics or information. Frequently the industrial survey researcher does not know or care about the distribution of the characteristic or the information within the sampling frame or universe, and has no interest in making inferences from the sample to frame or universe. In all of these cases the judgment sample is superior to a probability sample in terms of both value and cost.

Convenience and Quota Sampling

Exploratory research is almost always conducted with either judgement or convenience samples. Convenience samples are usually drawn on the

```
Nonprobability       ┌── Judgement sampling
sampling        ─────┼── Convenience sampling
methods              └── Quota sampling

                     ┌── Simple random sampling
                     │                          ┌── Multistage cluster sampling
Probability          ├── Cluster sampling ─────┼── Systematic sampling
sampling        ─────┤                          └── Area sampling
methods              │
                     │                          ┌── Proportionate stratified sampling
                     └── Stratified sampling ──┤
                                                └── Disproportionate stratified sampling
```

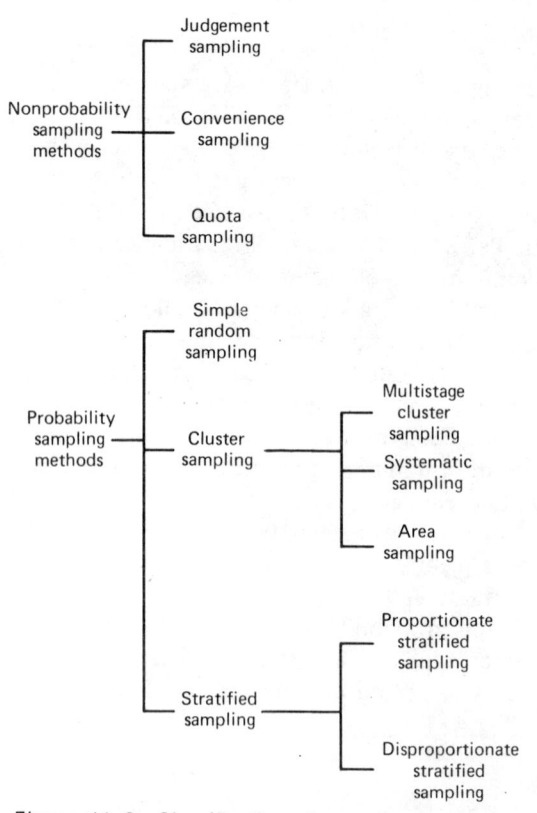

Figure 11-2   Classification of sampling methods.

basis of accessibility, as in the case of a Chicago based machine manufacturer who conducts most of his concept and product tests with Chicago firms and personnel. If there is no concern with the representativeness of the sample and no need for making inferences from the sample to the frame and universe, convenience samples may be useful as a means of: (1) initiating research on a product, (2) testing an interview guide or questionnaire, or (3) gaining background information. Convenience samples may be transformed into quota samples by placing quotas (controls) on the selection of a sampling units and elements. An example would be a preliminary survey to determine various buying influence patterns among firms in a market in which quotas might be specified on firm-size and end-use markets. There are, in summary, numerous situations in which nonprobability sampling methods are preferable, and industrial survey researchers should not hesitate to use these methods when appropriate.

Nonprobability sampling methods are no less "scientific" than probability methods and often produce findings that are superior in terms of both accuracy and cost.

Simple Random Sampling

Among the probability sampling designs available, Kish has noted that

> Simple random sampling is the basic selection process, and all other procedures can be viewed as modifications of it, introduced to provide more practical, economical, or precise designs.[9]

Suppose that a sampling frame of all United States manufacturers of cap screws was available with the sampling units composed of establishments of these manufacturers. A simple random sample of establishments could be drawn by assigning a list number to each establishment, obtaining a list of random numbers equivalent to the desired sample size from a table of random numbers or a random number generator (available on most computers and calculators), and matching the random number list with the establishment list numbers. As each random number was matched with an establishment list number, the establishment selected would be assigned to the sample, so that each remaining establishment would have a known and equal probability of being selected. If the same random number appeared more than once, it would be disregarded so that sampling would be without replacement. Kish also suggests that the term "simple random sampling" be limited to sample designs in which the sampling units and elements are the same or in which elements are drawn individually.[10] Sample designs in which sampling units and elements are both drawn and are different are called cluster samples. Although simple random sampling is at the focal point of sampling theory, it is rarely used in sample surveys. The basic reason is that it is a statistically inefficient design in comparison with other probability sampling methods that provide greater reliability for the same sample size and cost.

Cluster Sampling

If a sample survey of purchasing agents *and* design engineers was conducted among establishments of United States cap screw manufacturers, the establishment sample might be termed a cluster sample. The total

---

[9] Leslie Kish, *Survey Sampling*. New York: Wiley, 1965, p. 21.
[10] *Ibid.*, p. 38.

sampling design would be a multistage, cluster sample. The first stage sample would be the group of establishments selected from the sampling frame, while the second stage would be the sample of elements (purchasing agents and design engineers) drawn from the first stage establishments. Such a design is generally more statistically and cost efficient than simple random sampling of individual elements.

Another type of cluster sampling method is systematic sampling, in which a sample of cap screw establishments might be drawn from the frame by selecting every Nth establishment. If there were 300 establishments listed in the frame and a sample size of 60 was to be selected, every 5th establishment would be selected. Drawing a random number between 1 and 5 would determine which of the 5 clusters in the frame was to serve as the sample; if the random number was 2, the 2nd, 7th, 12th, and so on, establishment on the frame list would be selected. Systematic sampling has the primary advantage of being easy to administer, but periodicities in the frame may pose a potential danger in the use of this method.[11]

Area sampling is still another form of cluster sampling and may be adopted to reduce personal interview travel time and costs. The establishments could be grouped into geographic clusters and a three-stage design adopted: in the first stage draw a sample of, let us say, four clusters from a total of ten; in the second stage, a sample of establishments would be drawn from the four clusters selected in the first stage; the third stage would involve selecting a sample of elements within the establishments drawn in the second stage.

In each of the various types of cluster sample methods emphasis is placed on forming the clusters so that the sampling units within the clusters are as heterogeneous as possible, while seeking the maximum degree of homogeneity among clusters.

Stratified Sampling

The most important method of probability sampling in industrial survey research is stratified sampling, which is based on the division of the sampling frame into mutually-exclusive groups (strata) with independent probability samples drawn from each stratum. Stratified sampling is the dominant method in industrial surveys because it provides the: (1) most effective means of explicitly reflecting the presence of industrial and purchasing concentration among sampling units and (2) it is often the most statistically efficient method available.

[11] Harper W. Boyd, Jr., Ralph Westfall, and Stanley F. Stasch, *Marketing Research*, 4th ed. Homewood, Ill: Irwin, 1977, pp. 353–354.

Assume that a sampling frame has been established for United States establishments now manufacturing porcelain electrical supplies (SIC 3264), with the frame listing 75 establishments. Examination of the latest available *Census of Manufactures: Concentration Ratios in Manufacturing* report discloses that the 4 largest companies in 1972 (74 companies operated 83 establishments, with the 8 largest companies responsible for all of the multiple establishment firms in the industry) accounted for 46% of the value of shipments.[12] The top 8 companies accounted for 70% of the shipments, the top 20 companies shipped 88% of the industry total, while the largest 50 companies accounted for 99% of the value of shipments for the entire industry. In addition the largest 50 companies accounted for 98% of all employees, production employees, and new capital expenditures in the industry. Industrial concentration is indicated by the relatively small number of establishments that make up the industry, while purchasing concentration is shown by the disproportionate share of total industry shipments ($) accounted for by the larger companies in the industry. The sampling frame should therefore be stratified by size of establishment, measured in terms of the number of all employees or production employees in each establishment. If additional bases for stratification are desired, geographic location as well as specific product output and major end-user markets may be considered, but the impact of industrial concentration is such that it would preclude the use of more than one base for this industry. Kish has also suggested that poststratification may be used by using the sample survey data to stratify a sampling frame following the completion of the survey but prior to survey analysis.[13]

Sudman has observed that

> It is a general (although not universal) rule that, as elements (and sampling units) become larger and more complex, the variability between them increases.... This suggests that institutions and firms be stratified by size and that larger samples be taken from the strata consisting of the larger-sized institutions.[14]

In the largest stratum, in particular, the number of firms is often very small while the variance between firms may be large. The solution in these cases is to take a 100% sample (census) of the firms (sampling units or

---

[12] U.S. Bureau of the Census, *1972 Census of Manufactures: Concentration Ratios in Manufacturing*, Special Report Series MC 72(SR)-2. Washington: U.S. Government Printing Office, 1975, p. 205.
[13] Kish, *op. cit.*, pp. 90–92.
[14] Seymour Sudman, *Applied Sampling*. New York: Academic Press, 1976, p. 115.

elements) in the largest stratum, thereby eliminating any possibility of sampling error in the stratum.[15]

Next a decision must be made on the number of strata to use. The objective of stratification is to develop the strata boundaries in such a way as to make the sampling units (elements) within each stratum as homogeneous as possible, while striving for heterogeneity among the strata. Subject to these constraints Cochran has recommended that no more than 6 strata be used if analysis will be limited to data for all strata combined.[16] If analysis is to be conducted on findings for individual strata, it may be desirable to allocate a given sample size among as few strata as possible in order to obtain adequate sample sizes for the individual strata. The data on concentration ratios for the porcelain electrical supplies industry suggests that the first stratum might be composed of the 10 establishments owned by the top 4 companies. A second stratum could contain the 7 establishments owned by the 5th through the 8th largest companies; alternatively the first stratum might be composed of the 17 establishments owned by the top 8 companies. The next two strata might be composed of the 18th through the 29th largest establishments and the 30th through the 59th largest establishments, respectively. The final stratum would be composed of all remaining establishments (60th through 83rd).

A final decision regarding stratified sampling must be made as to the use of proportionate or disproportionate stratified sampling. Proportionate stratified sampling provides that each stratum be represented in the sample proportionate to its share of the total sampling frame. If we assume that the top 10 establishments in SIC 3264 should constitute the first stratum in the sampling frame of 75 establishments, and the desired sample size is 50, a proportionate stratified sample would contain 7 (10/75 · 50) establishments from the first stratum. The decision to include all 10 establishments in the first stratum in the sample would result in a disproportionate stratified sample. This in fact is the decision that is usually made in industrial surveys. The reason, of course, is that a simple random sample of 7 establishments drawn from a stratum of 10 could result in the omission of the 3 largest establishments, an outcome which would be unacceptable in view of the degree of purchasing concentration in the industry.

Sample Size Determination

Determination of sample sizes for industrial surveys requires that a number of statistical concepts be used, all of which are more or less

[15] *Ibid.*, p. 117.
[16] William G. Cochran, *Sampling Techniques*, 2nd ed. New York: Wiley, 1963, p. 134.

SAMPLING IN INDUSTRIAL SURVEY RESEARCH

familiar to industrial marketing researchers. A brief review of the most important concepts may be useful however to provide a common base of understanding. In addition the concepts will be examined within the context of the proposed survey of establishments in the porcelain electrical supplies industry (SIC 3264). Initially the concepts will be developed within the framework of simple random sampling to aid in understanding, followed by consideration of stratified sampling designs. The initial examples will focus on sample size determination based on variables data measured by arithmetic means and standard errors of the mean, followed by the calculation of sample sizes based on attribute data measured by the proportion of the sampling frame (population or universe also) having the attribute.

Most of the vital concepts of sampling theory for our purposes can be illustrated within the framework of three statistical distributions shown in Figure 11-3.[17] Assume that one of the major objectives of the survey of SIC 3264 establishments is to determine the size of the last order for refractory brick placed by them with any supplier during the past year. The universe distribution (as estimated by the sampling frame distribution) pictured in Figure 11-3 indicates the frequency distribution that would be obtained from a census (100% sample) of all establishments listed in the sampling frame. A single random sample of 30 establishments drawn from the sampling frame produced the sample distribution shown, while the distribution of sample means illustrates the distribution generated by drawing 15 samples of 30 establishments from the sampling frame, calculating the mean for each sample, and replacing the establishments in the sampling frame after each draw so that each establishment has a known and equal chance of being included in the sample on every draw.

Figure 11-3 also depicts a number of symbols that represent statistical concepts and measures:

- μ = mu, the arithmetic mean of the universe distribution. (Greek letters are used to denote measures of the universe, which are termed *parameters*.)
- σ = sigma, the standard deviation of the universe, used to measure the dispersion of the individual observations around the mean.
- σ^2 = sigma-squared, the *variance* of the universe.
- $\sigma_{\bar{x}}$ = sigma X-bar, the standard error of the mean, used to measure the dispersion of the distribution of sample means and thus serving as the standard deviation of this distribution.

[17] Figure 11-3 and much of the following discussion are adapted from: C. William Emory, *Business Research Methods*. Homewood, Ill.: Irwin, 1976, pp. 142-153.

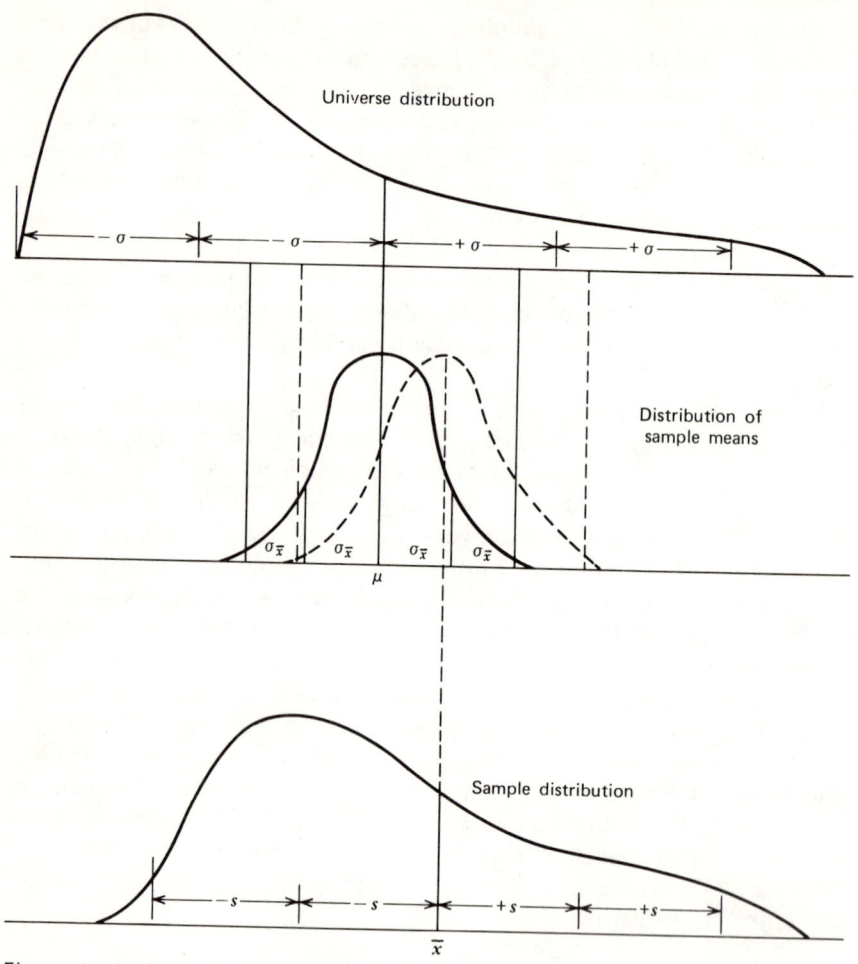

Figure 11-3 Statistical distributions used in sampling theory and practice. Source: Adapted from C. William Emory, Business Research Methods. *Homewood, Ill.: Irwin, 1976, p. 143.*

$\overline{X}$ = X-bar, the arithmetic mean of the sample distribution. (A measure of a sample is called a statistic.)

s = small ess, the standard deviation of the sample.

A number of statistical concepts may now be illustrated with the use of the distributions portrayed in Figure 11-3, together with the distribution measures just defined:

SAMPLING IN INDUSTRIAL SURVEY RESEARCH

1. The mean (μ) and standard deviation (σ) of the universe distribution are generally not known; the basic objective of most sample surveys is to make *point and interval estimates* about universe parameters from sample statistics; $\overline{X}$ is a point estimate of μ.

2. The point estimate of the one sample distribution shown in Figure 11-3 differs from the universe parameter μ as expected. Accuracy of the point estimate relative to the universe parameter can be determined and expressed as an *interval estimate*, based on the relationship between the universe distribution and the distribution of sample means.

3. The relationship between the universe distribution and the distribution of sample means is the single most important concept in statistics and sampling theory, for it serves as the foundation for making inferences regarding universe parameters from sample statistics. This relationship is known as the Central Limit Theorem: If simple random samples of size n are drawn from any universe with mean μ and variance σ^2, the sampling distribution of X will be approximately normally distributed with mean μ and variance σ^2. Cases in which $n < 30$ require special treatment, to be discussed later.

4. The relationship shown in the Central Limit Theorem may be expressed as:

$$\sigma_{\bar{x}}^2 = \frac{\sigma^2}{n} \text{ or } \sigma_{\bar{x}} = \frac{\sigma}{\sqrt{(n)}}$$

where n = sample size, and other terms are defined as previously.

5. The Central Limit Theorem makes it possible to use the properties of the normal distribution to develop interval estimates. Using both tails in a normal distribution, 68.27% of the area under a normal curve will be within one standard deviation (plus or minus) of the mean, and 95.45% of the area will be within two standard deviations.

Assume that the firm conducting the sample survey of SIC 3264 establishments is a supplier of refractory brick and therefore has access to secondary data in its own files on the average size of an order. A review of these data indicated that the arithmetic mean of the sample distribution ($\overline{X}$) might be estimated at $650, with the standard deviation of the sample (s) estimated to be $475. Using these data and the statistical concepts and measures just developed, our point estimate of the population mean would be $650. The accuracy of this estimate can be calculated by initially considering the relationship derived from the Central Limit Theorem:

$$\sigma_{\bar{x}}^2 = \frac{\sigma^2}{n}$$

At this point, we have neither the standard deviation of the universe (σ) nor the sample size (n). Let us arbitrarily assume that the sample size will be 30 establishments with one sampling element (purchasing agent) per establishment. The standard deviation of the universe is not available (as usual), but the standard error of the mean can be computed by substituting the standard deviation of the sample (s) for (σ) and ($n-1$) for (n) to make (s) an unbiased estimate of ($\hat{\sigma}$):

$$\hat{\sigma}_{\bar{x}} = \frac{s}{\sqrt{(n-1)}} = \frac{\$475}{\sqrt{(29)}} = \$88$$

One further adjustment is required in this case because of the large size of the sample relative to the universe (sampling frame) size. When a sample comprises 5% or more of the sampling frame, a finite universe adjustment factor should be included:

$$\hat{\sigma}_{\bar{x}} = \frac{s}{\sqrt{n-1}} \times \sqrt{\left(\frac{N-n}{N-1}\right)} = \frac{\$475}{\sqrt{(29)}} \times \sqrt{\left(\frac{45}{74}\right)} = \$69$$

where:

N = size of the sampling frame (universe).

For a given sample size, use of the finite adjustment factor increases the precision of the point estimate. Since industrial survey samples often comprise more than 5% of the sampling frame (in total or within particular strata), use of the finite adjustment factor should be considered routinely rather than as a rare and somewhat esoteric statistical technique.[18]

One standard error of the mean ($\hat{\sigma}_{\bar{x}}$) has been estimated to be \$69; suppose that we wanted to be 95% confident that the universe mean (μ) was within two standard errors of the sample mean ($\overline{X}$). If 1 $\hat{\sigma}_{\bar{x}} = \$69$, 2 $\hat{\sigma}_{\bar{x}} = \$138$, so the interval estimate is that there is a 95% chance that the universe mean of refractory brick orders is $\$650 \pm \$138$, or between \$512 and \$788.

Instead of assuming that the sample size will be 30 establishments, suppose that the primary question is how big the sample should be, given a desired confidence level and an acceptable interval estimate. If we establish a 95% confidence level (1.96 standard errors) and specify that the interval estimate should be $\pm \$100$, the required sample size will be

---

[18] Kish, *op. cit.*, p. 432 notes a number of situations in which the finite adjustment factor is important.

SAMPLING IN INDUSTRIAL SURVEY RESEARCH

$$\hat{\sigma}_{\bar{x}} = \frac{s}{\sqrt{(n-1)}} \times \sqrt{\left(\frac{N-n}{N-1}\right)} = \$51 = \frac{\$475}{\sqrt{(n-1)}} \times \sqrt{\left(\frac{75-n}{75-1}\right)}$$

where: $1.96\, \hat{\sigma}_{\bar{x}} = \pm \$100$

$\hat{\sigma}_{\bar{x}} = \pm \$51$

The required sample size *without* the use of finite adjustment factor would be 88, which is larger than the sampling frame (75) and the universe (83). This example clearly shows how the required sample size is overstated when the sample constitutes a relatively large proportion of the universe. The actual required sample size may be determined by using the formula:

$$n' = \frac{n}{1 + \frac{n}{N}} = \frac{88}{1 + \frac{88}{75}} = \frac{88}{2.1173} = 42 \text{ establishments}$$

where: n = unadjusted sample size requirement.

N = size of the sampling frame (universe).

With a sample of 42 establishments, the interval estimate is that there is a 95% chance that the universe mean of refractory brick orders is $650 ± $100, or between $550 and $750.

Sample Size Determination with Attribute Data

Many industrial surveys are concerned wholly or partly with attribute data in which the focus is on the proportion of the sampling frame (universe) having a particular attribute. Assume that the proposed survey of establishments manufacturing porcelain electrical supplies (SIC 3264) includes a question designed to estimate the percentage of establishments interested in a guaranteed maintenance program for their refractory furnaces.

The Central Limit Theorem also applies to proportions since they are merely special cases of the mean. Consequently the sampling distribution of a proportion will be approximately normally distributed (when $n = 30$), with the universe variance measured by ($p \times q$) rather than the σ^2 used with variables data. The proportion of the universe (sampling frame) having an attribute is designated as p, while q (which $= 1 - p$) is the proportion not having the attribute. The dispersion of the distribution of sample proportions is measured by the standard error of the proportion,

σ_p, such that with a simple random sample, the estimated standard error ($\hat{\sigma}_p$) would be computed by:

$$\hat{\sigma}_p = \sqrt{\left(\frac{p\,q}{n-1}\right)}$$

In our example using variables data, it was possible to estimate the arithmetic mean of the sample distribution and the standard deviation of the sample from secondary data, but there is often no secondary data available for estimating proportions. In such cases, p should be arbitrarily set at 0.5, also resulting in $q = 0.5$. If we assume that the sample size has been set at $n = 42$, the estimated standard error of the proportion may be estimated as follows:

$$\hat{\sigma}_p = \sqrt{\left(\frac{p\,q}{n-1}\right)} = \sqrt{\left(\frac{(0.5)\,(0.5)}{41}\right)} = \sqrt{(.0061)} = 0.078 = 7.8\%$$

The 95% confidence interval could be specified by:

$$p \pm 1.96\,\hat{\sigma}_p = 50\% \pm 1.96\,(7.8\%) = 34.7\% \text{ to } 65.3\%$$

There is a need to introduce the finite universe adjustment factor again in this case because the sample comprises 56% (42/75) of the sampling frame (universe), far in excess of the threshold level of 5% specified for its use. The procedure is the same as that used with variables data:

$$\hat{\sigma}_p = \sqrt{\left(\frac{p\,q}{n-1}\right)} \times \sqrt{\left(\frac{N-n}{N-1}\right)} = \sqrt{\left(\frac{0.25}{41}\right)} \times \sqrt{\left(\frac{33}{75}\right)} = 0.052 = 5.2\%$$

With a sample size of 42 and using the finite adjustment factor, the 95% confidence interval would be:

$$p \pm 1.96\,\hat{\sigma}_p = 50\% \pm 1.96\,(5.2\%) = 39.8\% \text{ to } 60.2\%$$

Thus we can state that there is a 95% chance that the universe (sampling frame) proportion of establishments interested in a guaranteed maintenance program for their refractory furnaces will be between 39.8% and 60.2%.

Instead of assuming that the sample size is 42, suppose that the major question is the sample size required to be 95% confident that the interval estimate would be ± 5%. Letting $1.96\,\hat{\sigma}_p = \pm 5\%$, $\hat{\sigma}_p = \pm 0.0255$, or ±

SAMPLING IN INDUSTRIAL SURVEY RESEARCH 285

2.55%. Solving for the sample size (n) needed without the use of the finite adjustment factor we obtain:

$$\sigma_p = \sqrt{\left(\frac{p\,q}{n-1}\right)} = .0255 = \sqrt{\left(\frac{(0.5)\,(0.5)}{n-1}\right)}$$

$$n = 100$$

The required sample size is larger than the sampling frame and universe without the use of the finite adjustment factor; the actual sample size required may be determined by using the same formula applicable to variables data:

$$n' = \frac{n}{1 + \frac{n}{N}} = \frac{100}{1 + \frac{100}{75}} = \frac{100}{2.333} = 43 \text{ establishments}$$

This analysis demonstrates that by increasing the sample size by only 1 establishment (from 42 to 43), the confidence interval could be reduced by more than 50%:

$$p \pm 1.96\,\hat{\sigma}_p = 50\% \pm 1.96\,(2.55\%) = 45.0\% \text{ to } 55.0\%$$

There is a 95% chance that the universe proportion of establishments interested in a guaranteed maintenance program for their refractory furnaces will be between 45% and 55%. It should also be noted that the arbitrary use of a p value of 0.5 leads to the largest sample size required to obtain a given confidence level and interval estimate. Any value of p obtained in the survey other than 0.5 will result in a higher degree of precision in the sample estimate.

Sample Size Determination for Stratified Samples

We have previously noted that the most important method of probability sampling in industrial survey research is stratified sampling. The example of the proposed survey of United States establishments now manufacturing porcelain electrical supplies (SIC 3264) was introduced to illustrate some of the statistical concepts and methods associated with stratified sampling. This same proposed survey was also used to develop the previous section on sample size determination in simple random samples. Now this same example will be used to determine the sample sizes required for several types of stratified samples, thereby providing a basis for comparing the sample sizes under a variety of different sampling designs.

Previously in this chapter it was noted that the user of stratified sampling must choose between proportionate and disproportionate sampling designs. The basis for choice is discussed in two articles on stratified sampling in industrial survey research,[19] and may be summarized as follows: Prior knowledge regarding the standard deviation of the sampling units in each stratum, as well as the size of each stratum:

1. If only the sizes of the strata are known, proportionate stratified sampling should be used.
2. If the standard deviations of each stratum can be estimated from prior information and they are believed to be approximately equal, use proportionate sampling. If the standard deviations are believed to vary, use disproportionate sampling.

When both the strata sizes and standard deviations can be estimated from prior information,

> ... allocation of a total sample size among strata is said to be the *optimal allocation* if, for that sample size, it provides the smallest possible standard error of the estimated mean.[20]

Optimal sampling designs therefore may be proportionate stratified samples (when the strata standard deviations are equal) or disproportionate stratified samples (when the strata standard deviations are not equal). Purchasing concentration in industrial markets usually results in unequal standard deviations among strata so that disproportionate samples are most likely to be optimal in industrial surveys.

Optimal allocation of total sample size among strata may also depend on the *costs* of data collection among strata, where such costs are known, significant, and different among strata. Industrial surveys often use combined methods of data collection, such as personal interviews with large firms and telephone interviews or mail questionnaires with small firms. The costs of each method can be estimated in advance, personal interviews are generally much more costly per unit than other methods of data

---

[19] J. G. VanBeeck and J. B. Vermetten, "Application of the Theory of Sampling with Stratification Proportional to Size on Industrial Surveys," *Applied Sampling*, Vol. 15, June 1966, pp. 74–93; and Andrew R. McIntosh and Roger J. Davies, "The Sampling of Non-Domestic Populations," *Journal of the Marketing Research Society*, Vol. 12, October 1970, pp. 217–232.
[20] Boyd, Westfall, and Stasch, *op. cit.*, p. 345.

SAMPLING IN INDUSTRIAL SURVEY RESEARCH

collection, thereby resulting in different costs among strata. As a result there are three types of stratified sampling designs:

1. Proportionate stratified sampling
2. Disproportionate stratified sampling
3. Cost optimal disproportionate stratified sampling

Each of the three types of stratified sampling designs may result in different allocations of total sample size among strata, while stratified sampling designs in general will result in smaller total sample sizes than required by simple random sampling. These relationships may be examined by using the proposed survey of United States establishments now manufacturing porcelain electrical supplies (SIC 3264). Figure 11-4 shows the worksheet used to estimate the required total sample sizes under specified assumptions for simple random sampling and for proportionate and disproportionate stratified sampling. Figure 11-5 then illustrates how a given total sample size (for disproportionate stratified sampling from Figure 11-4) would be allocated among the strata for each of the three types of stratified sampling designs, given some estimates of the strata means, standard deviations, and data collection costs.[21]

Determining Total Sample Size

Determination of the total sample size requires that the desired level of confidence in the results be specified as well as the interval estimate. Assume that we wish to be 95% confident with an interval estimate for the total sample of $40. Let $1.96\, \hat{\sigma}_{\bar{x}} = \$40$, then $\hat{\sigma}_{\bar{x}} = \$20$. The required sample sizes for each type of sampling design may be calculated then by substituting the appropriate data from Figure 11-4 on the total weighted variance and standard deviation ($\Sigma W_i S_i, \Sigma W_i S_i^2$) along with the estimated standard error of the mean ($\hat{\sigma}_{\bar{x}}$), in the formulas below. It will be observed in Figure 11-4 that the "Large plant" stratum contains no entry in the "Stratum Weight" column or in a number of other columns. The reason is that the decision was made to take a 100% sample (census) of the establishments in the "Large plant" stratum because of: (1) the industrial and purchasing concentration (the 17 establishments are estimated to account for about 75% of the industry shipments) and (2) the high estimated standard deviation ($1,318) of the orders associated with the establish-

---

[21] The worksheets in Figure 11-4 and 11-5 and the associated statistical procedures have been adapted from: C. William Emory, *Business Research Methods*. Homewood, Ill.: Irwin, 1976, pp. 157-159.

Strata	Universe size (N)	Mean $\bar{X}_i$	Standard deviation s_i	Stratum weight W_i	$W_i s_i$	$W_i s_i^2$	$(\bar{X}_i - \bar{X})^2$	$W_i(\bar{X}_i - \bar{X})^2$
Large plants (#1)	17	$2,961	$1,318	—	$ —	$ —	$ —	$ —
Medium plants (#2)	42	292	160	.64	$102	16,384	220,900	141,376
Small plants (#3)	24	73	115	.36	41	4,761	549,081	197,669
Totals (All 3 strata)	83	650	475	—	—	—	—	—
Totals (Strata #2 and 3)	66	—	—	1.00	$143	21,145	—	339,045

Note: $\bar{X} = (W_i \bar{X}_i) = \$187 \div \$26 = \$213$.

Adapted from: C. William Emory, *Business Research Methods*. Homewood, Ill.: Irwin, 1976, p. 159.

Figure 11–4 Total sample size worksheet for SIC 3264 stratified sampling design study.

SAMPLING IN INDUSTRIAL SURVEY RESEARCH

				Sample Allocation		
Strata	$W_i s_i$	Cost $\sqrt{(C_i)}$	$W_i s_i / \sqrt{(C_i)}$	Proportionate	Disproportionate	Cost optimal
Large plants (#1)	$—	$—	$—	17	17	17
Medium plants (#2)	102	6.32	16.14	19	21	18
Small plants (#3)	41	4.24	9.67	10	8	11
Totals	143	—	25.81	46	46	46

Adapted from: C. William Emory, *Business Research Methods*. Homewood, Ill.: Irwin, 1976, p. 158.

Figure 11-5 Allocation of sample size worksheet for SIC 3264 stratified sampling design study.

ments in the stratum. By taking a 100% sample there will be no sampling error associated with the "Large plant" stratum. The acceptable sampling error of the mean ($20) can be distributed among the two strata that will contain sampling errors, thereby reducing the sample size required in disproportionate stratified sampling.

Disproportionate Stratified Sample Size

$$\hat{\sigma}_{\bar{x}}^2 = \frac{\Sigma(W_i \sigma_i)^2}{n} = \frac{\Sigma(W_i S_i)^2}{n-1} \quad (\$20)^2 = \frac{(\$143)^2}{n-1} \quad n = 52$$

Finite Adjustment Factor: $n' = \dfrac{n}{1 + \dfrac{n}{N}} = \dfrac{52}{1 + \dfrac{52}{66}} = \dfrac{52}{1.788}$

$$n' = 29$$

Proportionate Stratified Sample Size

$$\hat{\sigma}_{\bar{x}}^2 = \frac{\Sigma(W_i \sigma_i)^2}{n} = \frac{\Sigma(W_i S_i)^2}{n-1} \quad (\$20)^2 = \frac{\$21{,}145}{n-1} \quad n = 54$$

Finite Adjustment Factor: $n' = \dfrac{n}{1 + \dfrac{n}{N}} = \dfrac{54}{1 + \dfrac{54}{64}} = \dfrac{54}{1.818}$

$$n' = 30$$

Simple Random Sample Size

$$\hat{\sigma}_{\bar{x}} = \frac{\Sigma\, W_i\, \sigma_i^2 + \Sigma\, W_i\, (\bar{X}_i - \bar{X})^2}{n} = \frac{\Sigma\, W_i\, S_i^2 + \sigma\, W_i\, (\bar{X}_i - \bar{X})^2}{n - 1}$$

$$(\$20)^2 = \frac{\$21{,}145 + \$339{,}045}{n - 1}; \quad n = 901$$

Finite Adjustment Factor: $\quad n' = \dfrac{n}{1 + \dfrac{n}{N}} = \dfrac{901}{1 + \dfrac{901}{66}} = \dfrac{901}{13.65}$

$$n' = 66$$

After the Finite Universe Adjustment Factor is applied to this type of sampling design, the advantage of using stratified sampling is dramatically illustrated: a simple random sample would have to be a 100% sample and even that would result in a far higher degree error than specified. Stratified sampling results in much smaller sample sizes, but the usual reduction in sample size possible from disproportionate sampling is only minimally evident with 29 establishments required versus 30 for proportionate sampling. The primary reason for the similarity in required sample sizes is the relatively small deviation in the expected standard deviation between the "Medium plant" and "Small plant" strata.

Allocation of Total Sample Size to Strata

In determining the allocation of the total sample size to the three strata, the specified sample size for a disproportionate stratified sample ($n = 29$) will be used. Data collection costs are estimated to be $75 each for personal interviews and $18 each for telephone interviews. All interviews in the "Small plant" stratum will be conducted by telephone only; a combination of personal and telephone interviews will be used in the "medium plant" stratum with an average cost per interview of $40. Based on this information and the data presented in Figure 11–5, the allocations of total sample size to each stratum based on each of the three types of stratified samples are shown in Figure 11–5, and calculated as follows:

PROPORTIONATE STRATIFIED SAMPLE ALLOCATION

$n_1 = W_1\, N$

$n_2 = W_2\, N = (.64) \times (29) = 19$

$n_3 = W_3\, N = (.36) \times (29) = 10$

DISPROPORTIONATE STRATIFIED SAMPLE ALLOCATION

$$\mu_1 = \frac{W_1 \sigma_1}{\Sigma (W_1 \sigma_1)} N = \frac{W_1 S_1}{\Sigma (W_1 S_1)} N$$

$$\mu_2 = \frac{\$102}{\$143} (29) = 21$$

$$\mu_3 = \frac{\$41}{\$143} (29) = 8$$

COST OPTIMAL DISPROPORTIONATE STRATIFIED SAMPLE SIZES

$$\mu_1 = \frac{W_1 \sigma_1/\sqrt{(C_1)}}{\Sigma (W_1 \sigma_1/\sqrt{(C_1)})} N = \frac{W_1 S_1/\sqrt{(C_1)}}{\Sigma (W_1 S_1/\sqrt{(C_1)})} N$$

$$\mu_2 = \frac{\$16.14}{\$25.81} (29) = 18$$

$$\mu_3 = \frac{\$ 9.67}{\$25.81} (29) = 11$$

A review of the sample size allocations among the two eligible strata (Medium and Small) reveals that the "Small plant" Stratum received a smaller allocation than the "Medium plant" stratum in all three designs. The allocation among the three types of stratified sampling designs indicates that shifting from a proportionate to a disproportionate design results in an increase of two establishments in the "Medium plant" stratum and a corresponding decrease in the "Small plant" stratum. The small total sample size masks the usual strong effects of using disproportionate designs: a heavy shift in favor of larger establishments with their customary higher variances. Introduction of lower data collection costs for the "Small plant" stratum results in a shift back towards a larger sample size for that stratum.

A Bayesian Approach to Sample Size Determination

Our approach to sample size determination until now has been based on classical statistical methods. These methods allowed us to specify a confidence interval associated with a point estimate, thereby specifying the possible range of sampling error involved in making inferences from a point estimate statistic to a universe parameter. In order to use these methods however it was necessary to estimate the mean (or proportion) and the standard deviation, which in our examples was done by the use of secondary data. Suppose that no secondary data were available for estimation. A researcher must then draw on experience and intuition to specify the probabilities that a given outcome will occur. These subjective probabilities are at the heart of the Bayesian approach which is marked by the estimation of probabilities when the *outcome* is known, in contrast to classical methods which ". . . predict the outcome when the *probabilities* are known."[22] Thus we previously stated that there is a 95% chance that the universe mean of refractory brick orders is $650 ± $100 (when $n = 42$, with simple random sampling); a Bayesian approach might find that the probability is 0.85 that the mean is $650.

Tull and Hawkins have indicated that the Bayesian approach to sample size determination involves the selection of

> . . . the sample size that results in the greatest positive difference in the expected monetary value of the information to be obtained from the sample minus the cost of taking it.[23]

The attempt to specify the expected value of perfect information and the expected cost of errors introduces a consideration of factors not included in the classical approach, and suggests that one of the major advantages of the Bayesian approach is its utilization of more information that may be known to the researcher. The principal limitation of the Bayesian approach is the inability to specify an interval estimate that indicates the possible range of sampling error. The choice of the classical or the Bayesian approach to sample size determination should be based on the nature of the sampling problem and the information available.

Sample Size Determination in Nonprobability Sampling

There is widespread use of nonprobability sampling in industrial marketing research, in situations where it is superior to probability sampling and also in situations where it would be preferable to use probability sampling methods. These latter situations often involve the estimation of universe parameters from sample statistics, with the consequent inability to specify sampling errors. This limitation apparently has had little influence on the

---

[22] W. B. Wentz, and G. I. Eyrich, "Product Forecasting without Historical, Survey or Experimental Data," in H. L. King, Ed., *Marketing and the New Science of Planning*. Chicago: American Marketing Association, 1968, p. 217.
[23] Tull and Hawkins, *op. cit.*, p. 708.

willingness of researchers to use nonprobability methods, but it does mean that they have no objective basis for determining sample size.[24]

Classical statistical methods also do not provide for the incorporation of nonsampling errors into the determination of sample size, even though it is generally acknowledged that nonsampling errors frequently are more significant than sampling errors in survey research practice. Kish provides a comprehensive discussion of the total error concept, in which sampling (variable) errors and nonsampling (bias) errors are combined in one model.[25] Brown[26] and Mayer[27] have been shown how the total error concept may be applied to sampling in marketing research studies with a specific approach to the estimation of the magnitude of the combined error in a survey. Tull and Hawkins recommend that a Bayesian-type approach be adopted for determining sample size in nonprobability sampling with the choice based on the relationship between the value and cost of information for various sample sizes.[28]

Our review of the five steps in the sampling process in industrial survey research is now complete, and we turn in the following chapter to a consideration of the analysis of survey data.

SUMMARY

Sampling in industrial marketing research differs markedly from sampling in consumer marketing research. One critical reason for this is the greater level of industrial demand concentration which makes it more feasible to identify and classify market members from secondary data. The greater level of industrial demand concentration also means that a few firms account for a large proportion of total market demand.

Despite these advantages the researcher must use considerable care in defining the universe to be studied. Product, geographic, and time period boundaries must be defined. Sampling units that make up the sampling frame must be obtained from the various directories available for the SIC

---

[24] For an interesting discussion of the problem of estimating the variance of a distribution obtained by quota sampling, see: Frederick J. Stephan and Philip J. McCarthy, *Sampling Opinions*. New York: Wiley, 1963, Chap. 10.
[25] Kish, *op. cit.*, Chap. 13.
[26] Rex V. Brown, *Research and the Credibility of Estimates*. Cambridge, Mass.: Harvard University Press, 1969.
[27] Charles S. Mayer, "Assessing the Accuracy of Marketing Research," *Journal of Marketing Research*, Vol. 7, August 1970, pp. 285–291.
[28] Tull and Hawkins, *op. cit.*, pp. 199–203.

codes of interest. Care must be taken not to exclude unwittingly establishments for whom the activity of interest is a secondary SIC code. Despite such precautions the sampling frame will almost never encompass the entire universe. However it will almost surely include all the larger establishments.

Industrial surveys usually designate within each sampling unit the decision-making units within each organization as the sampling elements to be surveyed. Personal interviewing methods are very desirable in industrial marketing research since they allow the researcher to adapt the choice of sampling element according to the decision-making environment in each firm.

Once sampling units and sampling elements are specified, the next step is to select the sampling method. The three types of nonprobability sampling are judgement, convenience, and quota sampling. Judgement samples are widely used in industrial survey research, most notably in surveys of knowledgeable persons, where sampling distributions and statistical inference are of no interest. Exploratory research is almost always conducted with judgement, convenience, or quota sampling.

Simple random sampling is the basic sampling method from which all other methods depart. Cluster sampling is generally more statistically and cost efficient than simple random sampling. Its variants include systematic sampling, in which every Nth sampling unit is selected after the initial random selection is made, and area sampling in which the clusters are geographic.

Whereas in cluster analysis efficiency is greater the more heterogeneous the clusters are, in stratified sampling efficiency is gained by stratification which usually proceeds according to organization size. Cochran recommends no more than six strata if the analysis is to be limited to the measurement of the combined characteristics of the entire sample. However if the individual strata are to be analyzed, fewer strata are desirable to assure adequate sample size in each stratum. The usual strategy also calls for a complete census of all sampling units in the stratum containing the largest organizations.

Stratified random sampling generally results in smaller sample sizes than with simple random sampling. Sample size is optimally allocated on a proportional basis when within-stratum variances are equal and disproportionately when they are not. If it is advisable to employ different survey approaches for different strata, cost-optimal allocation would be recommended. The result would be to reduce the required sample size among the strata where survey cost per unit are higher and to increase sample size for the other strata.

In recent years new approaches to sampling design have introduced

Bayesian considerations and the estimation of nonsampling as well as sampling error.

SUGGESTED READINGS

Boyd, Harper W., Jr., Ralph Westfall, and Stanley F. Stasch, *Marketing Research*, 4th ed. Homewood, Ill.: Irwin, 1977.

Brown, Rex V., *Research and Credibility of Estimates*. Cambridge, Mass.: Harvard University Press, 1969.

Cochran, William G., *Sampling Techniques*, 2nd ed. New York: Wiley, 1963.

Deming, W. Edwards, *Sample Design in Business Research*. New York: Wiley, 1960.

Emory, C. William, *Business Research Methods*. Homewood, Ill.: Irwin, 1976, pp. 142–153, 157–159.

Ferber, Robert, *Statistical Techniques in Market Research*. New York: McGraw-Hill, 1949.

Kish, Leslie, *Survey Sampling*. New York: Wiley, 1965, Chap. 13.

Koning, Co de, "Effective Techniques in Industrial Marketing Research," *Journal of Marketing*, Vol. 28, no. 2, April, 1964, pp. 57–61.

McIntosh, Andrew R., "Improving the Efficiency of Sample Surveys in Industrial Markets," *Journal of the Marketing Research Society*, Vol. 17, no. 4, 1976, pp. 219–231.

McIntosh, Andrew R., and Roger J. Davies, "The Sampling of Non-Domestic Populations," *Journal of the Marketing Research Society*, Vol. 12, October 1970, pp. 217–232.

Mayer, Charles S., "Assessing the Accuracy of Marketing Research," *Journal of Marketing Research*, Vol. 7, August 1970, pp. 285–291.

Stephan, Frederick J., and Philip J. McCarthy, *Sampling Opinions*. New York: Wiley, 1963, Chap. 10.

Sudman, Seymour, *Applied Sampling*. New York: Academic Press, 1976.

Tull, Donald S., and Del I. Hawkins, *Marketing Research*. New York: Macmillan, 1976, pp. 579–581.

VanBeeck, J. G., and J. B. Vermettern, "Application of the Theory of Sampling with Stratification Proportional to Size on Industrial Surveys," *Applied Sampling*, Vol. 15, June 1966, pp. 74–93.

Wentz, W. B., and G. I. Eyrich, "Product Forecasting without Historical, Survey, or Experimental Data," in H. L. King, Ed., *Marketing and the New Science of Planning*. Chicago: American Marketing Association, 1968, pp. 215–221.

Wilson, Aubrey, *The Assessment of Industrial Markets*. London: Hutchinson and Co., 1968.

CHAPTER TWELVE
Analysis of Survey Data

All of our attention in Chapter 11 was directed toward questions of sample design with the expectation that the eventual outcome would be a set of survey data that are representative of the universe from which they are drawn. Our discussion of probability sampling methods included a very brief review of some of the principles of statistical inference, designed to illustrate how to assess the relationships between sample and universe data. Statistical inference is a highly technical, complex matter that comprises one part of the subject called statistics; another part is descriptive statistics which deals with methods for summarizing and analyzing sample data. This chapter emphasizes the use of descriptive statistics to summarize and analyze industrial survey research data. As in chapter 11, it is assumed that the reader has some familiarity with statistical concepts and methods, access to general books on marketing research, and a primary interest in survey data pertaining to industrial products and markets.

The raw survey data contained in data collection instruments must be processed prior to analysis. This processing step includes editing the instrument, coding the responses, and establishing response categories. These are general marketing research functions with no special adaptations required for industrial surveys and are discussed in all general books. The only real issue associated with pre-analysis processing of survey data from industrial surveys is whether machine tabulation is

ANALYSIS OF SURVEY DATA

warranted. This *is* an issue because of the relatively small sample sizes of many industrial surveys, raising the question as whether the costs and time involved in keypunching data into Hollerith cards is worth the effort. For very small samples ($n < 10$), the answer is clearly that manual tabulation is preferred. Small sample ($10 \leq n < 30$) use of machine tabulation depends on the number of cross-tabulations and the degree of structured responses; larger numbers of tabulations and structured responses indicate the choice of machine tabulation. When the sample size exceeds 30, machine tabulation should be used.

When the data have been assembled and a decision made with respect to the form of tabulation, the steps in the analytical process shown in Figure 12-1 are followed, starting with "Ordering the data." Luck, Wales, and Taylor note a

> . . . primitive form in which data can be brought into quantitative order is an *array* that lists all of them in numerical sequence, . . . but usually this would be inefficient.[1]

Instead the data should be classified into groups and Luck, Wales, and Taylor suggest that four principles should be followed in setting classifications:

1. Class intervals should be initially set with relatively narrow intervals so that data patterns are not obscured.
2. Class intervals should be the same width, where possible.
3. Open-end class intervals should not be used.
4. Class intervals should be designed so that tendencies to round off answers will place the data at the midpoints of the class intervals.[2]

The next step in the analytical process involves summarizing the data. The technique for doing this is to construct a frequency distribution for each data set by assigning individual observations to the class intervals determined in the preceding step. Additional techniques for summarizing data include the calculation of various measures of central tendency, such as the arithmetic mean, and the median. If machine tabulation is used, the researcher should consider using a statistical analysis package such as the Statistical Package for the Social Sciences (SPSS).[3] The SPSS package

---

[1] David J. Luck, Hugh G. Wales, and Donald A. Taylor, *Marketing Research*, 4th ed. Englewood Cliffs, N.J.: Prentice-Hall, 1974, p. 259.
[2] *Ibid.*, pp. 259-260.
[3] Norman H. Nie, C. Hadlai Hull, Jean G. Jenkins, Karin Steinbrenner, and Dale H. Bent, *SPSS*, 2nd ed. New York: McGraw-Hill, 1975.

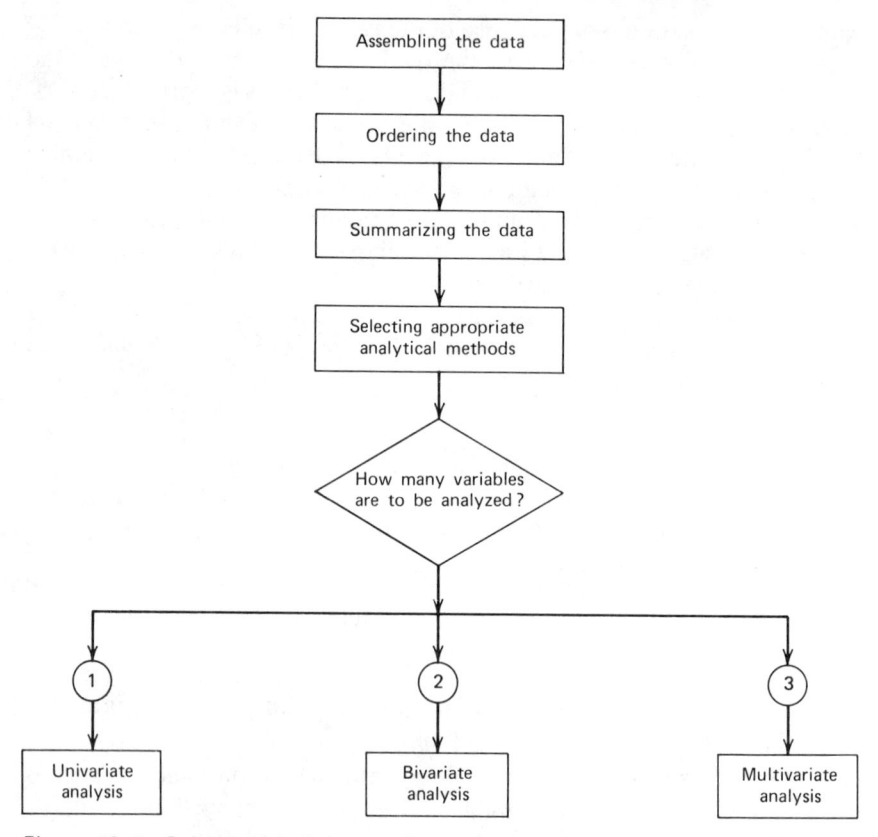

Figure 12-1 Process chart for analyzing survey data. Source: David J. Luck, Hugh G. Wales, and Donald A. Taylor, Marketing Research, 4th ed. Englewood Cliffs, N.J.: Prentice-Hall, 1974, p. 257.

includes programs for summarizing data, scatter diagrams, crosstabulations, and many of the analytical methods to be discussed in this chapter.

One of the major challenges in the analysis of survey data is the selection of the appropriate analytical methods. Figure 12-1 shows that the initial choice is based on the number of variables to be analyzed, with the selection to be made from three categories: (1) univariate analysis for one variable, (2) bivariate analysis for two variables and (3) multivariate analysis for more than two variables. Each of these categories will be examined in following sections, and the principal analytical methods in each category will be illustrated by an industrial marketing research example. This form of organization should not only be of interest and value, but also may serve to inspire those who have disdained the use of analytical methods in the mistaken belief that such methods are not applicable to industrial marketing research. Emphasis in each example is placed on the application of the analytical method; detailed statistical methodology is omitted. References are provided for each example so that those interested in their use may obtain the requisite background materials.

UNIVARIATE ANALYSIS

A number of analytical procedures may be used to examine a single variable, such as measures of dispersion (standard deviation) and trend (method of least squares), but we shall limit our review to tests of statistical significance. These tests are conducted within the framework of testing statistical hypotheses about universe parameters, based on sample statistics. Statistical hypotheses are generally stated in two forms: (1) null hypotheses which state that the universe parameter is equal to a specified value and (2) alternative hypotheses which state that the universe parameter is different from the null hypothesis value. In testing statistical hypotheses, the researcher wishes to avoid two types of error: (1) Type I errors (rejecting a null hypothesis when it is true) and (2) Type II errors (accepting a null hypothesis when it is false). Type I errors may be minimized by setting a high level significance (95% or 99% confidence levels), but this increases the possibility of committing a Type II error. This dilemma is often partially resolved by using a one- rather than a two-tail test. This refers to the areas under the normal curve (generated by the premises of the Central Limit Theorem) in which the rejection region is placed on only one side of the curve rather than both.

We shall consider two types of tests of statistical hypotheses: (1) tests of the difference between two means and (2) tests of the difference between two proportions. In tests of the difference between two means, the procedure will vary depending on a series of considerations:

1. Whether the universe variances are known
2. Whether the variances may be considered equal if known
3. Whether the samples are independent or related
4. The size of the samples

In industrial marketing research surveys the universe variances are almost always unknown and may, or may not, be equal. The samples are generally independent and the sample sizes will vary widely. A study of the role perceptions of various members of the "buying centers" of 75 industrial firms provides an opportunity to illustrate the application of a test of the difference between two means.[4] Purchasing agents for a sample of customers and prospective customers for three chemical products of a large firm were asked to complete a mail questionnaire. They were also asked to distribute questionnaires to the scientist and the manager most closely involved with the purchase decision for one of the products. Each of these "buying center" members was asked to evaluate his involvement in the vendor selection process and that of the other two members as well. The study findings are presented in Figure 12–2, showing in Figure 12–2(a) the means and standard deviations of the perceptions of each buying center member. It is evident that buying center members consistently rate themselves higher in both influence and responsibility than did their peers, while scientists received the highest ratings on both dimensions of involvement.

Figure 12–2(b) provides statistical comparisons of the differences between various means in Figure 12–2(b), with a t value and the level of significance for each test of the difference between two means. In order to demonstrate the derivation of the statistics in Figure 12–2(b), we shall test the significance of the difference between the managers' mean perception of their own influence on the vendor selection decision (3.20) against the scientists' mean perception of the managers' influence (2.34). The appropriate test statistic is:

$$t = \frac{\bar{X}_m - \bar{X}_{sc}}{S_{\bar{x}_m - \bar{x}_s}}$$

where t = "student" t value, based on the t distribution, which depends on the number of degrees of freedom ($= n - 1$) in each sample. This test statistic is appropriate when the universe variances are not known and also in situations where they are known but the sample sizes are less than 30.

$\bar{X}_m, \bar{X}_{sc}$ = sample means for managers and scientists, respectively.

$S_{\bar{x}_m - \bar{x}_s}$ = estimated standard error of the difference between the two means.

The estimated weighted average of the standard deviations of the two samples is:

---

[4]James R. McMillan, "Role Differentiation in Industrial Buying Decisions," in Thomas V. Greer, Ed., *1973 Combined Conference Proceedings*. Chicago: American Marketing Association, 1974, pp. 207–211.

ANALYSIS OF SURVEY DATA

$$s_{m+sc} = \sqrt{\left(\frac{\Sigma x_m^2 + \Sigma x_{sc}^2}{n_m - 1 + n_{sc} - 1}\right)}$$

where $\Sigma x_m^2 = n_m s_m^2$ and $s_m = \sqrt{\left(\frac{\Sigma x_m^2}{n_m}\right)}$

$\Sigma x_{sc}^2 = n_{sc} s_{sc}^2$ and $s_{sc} = \sqrt{\left(\frac{\Sigma x_{sc}^2}{n_{sc}}\right)}$

Figure 12–2(a) provides the data necessary to calculate the estimated standard error of the difference:

$n_m = 46$, $n_{sc} = 43$, $s_m = 1.28$, $s_{sc} = 1.28$ (Note that although the sample standard deviations are identical, there is no basis for assuming that the universe values are also identical.)

After substituting these data in the equation, we obtain:

$s_{m+sc} = 1.2184$. Now the estimated standard error of the difference between the two means can be calculated:

$$S_{\bar{x}_m - \bar{x}_{sc}} = s_{m+sc} \sqrt{\left(\frac{1}{n_m} + \frac{1}{n_{sc}}\right)} = .2583$$

We are now prepared to obtain the t ratio:

$$t = \frac{\bar{X}_m - \bar{X}_{sc}}{S_{\bar{x}_m - \bar{x}_{sc}}} = \frac{3.20 - 2.34}{.2583} = 3.33$$

The probability of obtaining a t value of 3.33 by chance with 87 degrees of freedom ($n_m - 1 + n_{sc} - 1 = 45 + 42$) can be found from a table of the t distribution (in any general statistics book) to be less than .01; the difference between the two means is therefore statistically significant at the 99% level. Consequently we can state that the mean perception of managers of their own influence on the vendor selection decision is significantly greater than scientists' mean perception of the influence of managers, and we can reject the null hypothesis that there is no difference in the mean perceptions of the two groups. Each of the other statistical comparisons in Figure 12–2(b) have been calculated in a similar manner, thereby providing a basis for evaluating the role perceptions and expectations among members of an industrial buying center.

	Perception by[a]						
	Purchasing agent		Scientist		Manager		Average of all[b]
Perceptual Variable	Mean[b]	Std. dev.	Mean[b]	Std. dev.	Mean[b]	Std. dev.	
In the vendor selection decision, how much *influence* was exerted by the:							
Purchasing agent	3.26	1.47	2.60	1.39	3.13	1.41	3.00
Scientist	3.53	1.37	4.00	1.07	3.76	1.45	3.76
Manager	2.02	1.39	2.34	1.28	3.20	1.28	2.52
If later events show that the current source is not the best, how much of the *responsibility* will belong to:							
Purchasing agent	3.49	1.40	2.49	1.31	2.72	1.19	2.90
Scientist	3.53	1.36	3.70	1.28	3.98	0.86	3.74
Manager	2.20	1.51	2.60	1.25	3.67	1.08	2.82
	$N = 49$		$N = 43$		$N = 46$		

[a] A mean perception of 1 indicates "not at all influential" while 5 indicates "very influential."
[b] All means were significantly greater than 1 at the 0.01 level using one-tailed t test.

(*a*)

	Comparison for												
	Purchasing agent				Scientist				Manager			
	Scientists' perception compared to purchasing agents'		Managers' perception compared to purchasing agents'		Purchasing agents' perception compared to scientists'		Managers' perception compared to scientists'		Purchasing agents' perception compared to managers'		Scientists' perception compared to managers'	
Perceptual variable	t val.	Level of sig.	t val.	Level of sig.	t val.	Level of sig.	t val.	Level of sig.	t val.	Level of sig.	t val.	Level of sig.
Influence	2.33	98	0.44	n.s.	1.92	90	0.93	n.s.	4.31	99	3.33	99
responsibility	3.72	99	2.89	99	0.65	n.s.	1.29	n.s.	5.48	99	4.57	99

n.s. = not significant at 80% level using two-tailed *t* test.

(*b*)

Source: James R. McMillan, "Role Differentiation in Industrial Buying Decisions," in Thomas V. Greer, Ed., *1973 Combined Conference Proceedings.* Chicago: American Marketing Association, 1974, p. 209.

Figure 12-2 Application of a test of the difference between two means. (a) Buying center members' perceptions of their respective influences and responsibilities. (b) Statistical comparison of influence and responsibility perceptions.

Testing the Difference between Two Proportions

One of the most common assignments in industrial marketing research practice is that of determining the proportion or percentage of a universe that possesses a given attribute or characteristic and those that do not. Thus we may be interested in the proportion of firms buying one or more units of a product and/or the proportion of purchasing agents indicating an awareness of a promotional program: in each case the variable being investigated is dichotomized into two categories of haves and have-nots. Often the next assignment is to determine whether the difference between two proportions is statistically significant. Hughes has reported a study of corporate images held by prospective buyers of adding machines in which geographic variations in awareness and attitudes were measured.[5] This study will be used to illustrate the procedure for testing the significance of difference between two proportions.

On one of the dimensions used to measure corporate image, 76% of the survey respondents in City Y were judged to be aware of Company A, while 40% of the respondents in City X were considered to be aware of Company A. All of the sample proportions that *might* be obtained in such a study constitute a sampling distribution of proportions with a mean p_u and a standard deviation $\sqrt{\left(\frac{p_u q_u}{n}\right)}$ in a binomial distribution. We can use the normal curve to approximate the binomial distribution if the sample size (n) and proportion (p) are large enough so that $np > 5$.

The null hypothesis is that there is no difference between the proportions aware of Company A in Cities X and Y, and the confidence level is set at 95% ($\alpha = .05$). We can test whether the difference between the proportions for the two cities ($P_y - P_x = 76\% - 40\% = 36\%$) is significant by converting the difference to a z score:

$$z = \frac{P_y - P_x}{\sigma_{p_y - p_x}} = \frac{P_y - P_x}{\sqrt{\left(p\, q\left(\frac{1}{n_y} + \frac{1}{n_x}\right)\right)}}$$

$$z = \frac{.76 - .40}{\sqrt{\left((.33)(.67)\left(\frac{1}{21} + \frac{1}{133}\right)\right)}}$$

---

[5] G. David Hughes, "A New Tool for Sales Managers," *Journal of Marketing Research*, Vol. 1, May 1964, pp. 32–38.

where $p = \dfrac{(p_y n_y + p_x n_x)}{n_y + n_x}$ and $q = 1 - p$

$$z = \frac{.36}{.11} = 3.27$$

Since the critical value of t is 1.96 (based on a 95% confidence level), and the z score is 3.27 is larger than the critical value, the null hypothesis is rejected. There is a statistically significant difference between the proportions aware of Company A in the two cities: respondents in City Y were significantly more aware of Company A than those in City X.

BIVARIATE ANALYSIS

Although univariate analysis methods are useful in extracting statistical information about a single variable, most industrial marketing research studies are concerned with more than one variable. Rather than limiting the analysis to each variable individually, additional insight may be gained through bivariate analysis in which the relationships between two variables are examined. There are a number of bivariate methods available, but we shall limit our review to three of the most widely used methods:

1. Cross-classification analysis.
2. Chi-square analysis.
3. Simple correlation and regression analysis.

Cross-Classification Analysis

Finding and examining relationships between two variables may be initiated by classifying data for each variable into two or more categories. We shall use a dichotomous classification for each variable to illustrate the method, with an example drawn from a study of opinion leadership in institutional markets.[6] A mail survey of nursing home administrators in the northeast region of the United States was conducted to determine the relationship between the frequency with which the administrators were *asked* for advice and the frequency with which they *sought* advice. The responses served as measures of opinion leadership.

A major question associated with the use of cross-classification analysis

---

[6]Leon G. Schiffman and Vincent Gaccione, "Opinion Leaders in Institutional Markets," *Journal of Marketing*, Vol. 38, April 1974, pp. 49–53.

Frequency with which others ask for advice	Frequency with which information is sought			Base (N)
	Infrequently	Frequently	Total	
Infrequently (nonleaders)	89%	11% ↕	100%	57
Frequently (leaders)	49	51	100	59

(a)

Frequency with which others ask for advice	Frequency with which information is sought		Base (N)
	Infrequently	Frequently	
Infrequently (nonleaders)	64%	17%	80
Frequently (leaders)	36 ←———→	83	36
Total	100	100	

(b)

Source: Leon G. Schiffman and Vincent Gaccione, "Opinion Leaders in Institutional Markets," *Journal of Marketing*, Vol. 38, April 1974, p. 52.

Figure 12-3 Relationship between the frequency of being asked and seeking advice. (a) Percentages calculated horizontally. (b) Percentages calculated vertically.

is the appropriate direction to calculate percentages. Figure 12–3(a) shows the percentages calculated horizontally, indicating that opinion leaders were more likely to seek information from others (51%) than nonleaders (11%). Figure 12–3(b), using percentages calculated vertically, indicates that 83% of those who *frequently* sought information were opinion leaders, while 36% of those who *infrequently* sought information were opinion leaders.

The hypothesis being tested with the data in Figure 12–3 was: opinion leaders seek information from others more often than nonleaders. Frequency of information-seeking was thus hypothesized to be "caused" by the frequency of being asked for advice by others (opinion leaders = high frequency of being asked for advice). A basic rule for deciding which direction to calculate percentages is to determine the "causal" factor and develop the percentages in that direction. Figure 12–3(a) is based on

ANALYSIS OF SURVEY DATA

calculating the percentages in the direction of the causal factor—the degree of leadership, which corresponds to the hypothesis and is therefore correct. Figure 12–3(*b*) is not appropriate because it assumes that the frequency of seeking advice from others "causes" the degree of opinion leadership and therefore does not test the hypothesis. Although cross-classification analysis can be a useful method for exploring relationships between pairs of categorial variables, it does not specify the degree of relationships between the variables. Two methods for doing this are now examined.

Chi-Square Analysis

In relating two variables with cross-classification analysis, the focus was on the choice and interpretation of pairs of percentages. Additional insight into the relationship between the variables may be gained by using chi-square analysis. The cross-classification data may be prepared for chi-square analysis by using a 2 × 2 (fourfold; 2 columns, 2 rows) contingency table with 4 cells and marginal totals. The hypothesis of the previous cross-classification analysis may be restated as a null hypothesis:

> There is no association between the frequency of seeking advice from others and the degree of opinion leadership.

A chi-square analysis of the data in the contingency table in Figure 12–4 seeks to test the significance of any difference between the *observed* frequency distribution and an *expected* frequency distribution based on the null hypothesis of no association between the variables. This difference between the two frequency distributions will follow a chi-square distribution if the variables are independent and thus not associated. The sampling distributions of chi-square vary with the degrees of freedom (similar to the t distribution in this regard), where the number of degrees of freedom in a contingency table is based on the formula $(r - 1) \times (c - 1)$. In Figure 12–4 with two rows (r) and two columns (c) in the contingency table, there is one degree of freedom.

Figure 12–4 shows that the chi-square (X^2) value is 23.2, and with one degree of freedom, the probability (p) of obtaining such a value is less than one chance in a thousand ($p < .001$). If we set our confidence level at 95% or even 99%, we must reject the null hypothesis of no relationship between the variables. The determination of the probability associated with the chi-square value and the number of degrees of freedom is based on the use of a table of the chi-square distribution, found in any general statistics book.

Frequency of others seeking advice	Frequency off Seeking Advice from Others		
	Infrequently	Frequently	Total
Infrequently (nonleaders)	39 / 51	18 / 6	57
Frequently (leaders)	41 / 29	18 / 30	59
Total	80	36	116

$$\chi^2 = \Sigma \frac{(f_o - f_e)^2}{f_e}$$ shown as $\begin{array}{c} f_e \\ f_o \end{array}$

where χ^2 = chi-square value
f_o = observed frequency value
f_e = expected frequency value

$$f_e = \frac{57 \times 80}{116}, \quad \frac{59 \times 80}{116}, \quad \frac{57 \times 36}{116}, \quad \frac{59 \times 36}{116}$$

f_e = 39, 41, 18, 18

$$\chi^2 = \frac{(51 - 39)^2}{39} + \frac{(29 - 41)^2}{41} + \frac{(6 - 18)^2}{18} + \frac{(30 - 18)^2}{18}$$

$\chi^2 = $ 3.7 + 3.5 + 8.0 + 8.0

$\chi^2 = 23.2$, 1 df, $p < .001$

Source: Adapted from: Leon G. Schiffman and Vincent Gaccione, "Opinion Leaders in Institutional Markets," *Journal of Marketing*, Vol. 38, April 1974, p. 52.

Figure 12-4 Chi-square analysis of opinion leadership.

In applying chi-square analysis to industrial survey data, it should be noted that this method can also be used with larger contingency tables than the 2 × 2 example. There are some minimum *expected* cell frequency requirements that should be noted:

1. No more than 20% of the cells should have an expected frequency of less than 5 (and therefore *none* in a 2 × 2 table.)
2. None of the cells, regardless of table size, should have an expected frequency of less than 1.

ANALYSIS OF SURVEY DATA

Simple Correlation and Regression Analysis

Another analytical approach to the measurement of association between two variables is that of simple correlation and regression analysis. The adjective "simple" refers to the measure of association between *two* variables; if more than two variables are involved, the appropriate term is "multiple" correlation and regression analysis. Correlation analysis refers to the degree of closeness of the relationship between the variables. Regression analysis seeks to develop an equation that will show: (1) the functional relationship between the variables or (2) how variations in one variable are related to the second variable.

The application of simple correlation and regression analysis to industrial survey data may be illustrated by a study designed to show how to measure the efficiency with which a manufacturer provides industrial technical product services.[7] Simon defined technical product services as

> . . . those activities which the manufacturer engages in, besides sale of a product, to produce for the purchaser of his product the expected utility or end values in terms of product performance for which the product is obtained.[8]

Five elements of technical product service were identified, and one element (completeness) was selected for illustration here. Completeness was defined as ". . . the scope, range, or number of technical services provided for customers," and respondents in three industries (our example is limited to the chemicals industry) were asked to indicate their degree of satisfaction with various levels of performance for the element.[9] A correlation coefficient (r) of + .761 was obtained as a measure of the degree of relationship between customer satisfaction and the level of performance on the completeness element of technical product services among respondents in the chemicals industry. This value of r indicates that there is a moderately high, positive relationship between the variables.

Although the correlation coefficient is a useful summary measure of the relationship between two variables, regression analysis is also usually carried out in order to specify the functional relationship between the variables and thereby gain further insight into the relationship. Simon used the following regression equation to represent the relationship be-

---

[7]Leonard S. Simon, "Measuring the Market Impact of Technical Services," *Journal of Marketing Research*, Vol. 2, February 1965, pp. 32–39.
[8]*Ibid.*, p. 32.
[9]*Ibid.*, p. 35.

tween satisfaction and performance on the completeness element in the chemicals industry:[10]

$$Y = a + bX = 8.90 - .83X$$

where Y = degree of customer satisfaction
a = constant
b = slope of the linear relationship between Y and X
X = the performance level of the completeness element

Performance on the completeness element was measured by the percentage of requests for service that were refused, so that an 8.3% decrease in refusals would be associated with a 10% increase in the degree of customer satisfaction according to the regression equation. Thus regression analysis does provide additional information regarding the nature of the relationship between the two variables.

MULTIVARIATE ANALYSIS

The rapid adoption and widespread diffusion of multivariate analysis in marketing research has been attributed by Sheth to three factors:

1. Computer availability and utilization
2. Development of survey research methods and consequent survey data availability
3. Market complexity that results in many intervening factors that mediate between marketing activities and market responses[11]

Multivariate analysis methods are thus distinguished from univariate and bivariate methods by their focus on: (1) more variables (three or more) and (2) the simultaneous, complex relationships between these multiple variables. Figure 12–5 illustrates a classification of multivariate analysis methods used in marketing research generally, and in industrial marketing research specifically as our examples show. In developing this classification scheme, Sheth has noted that:

> . . . It is based on three judgments the marketing researcher must make about the nature and utilization of his data:

---

[10]*Ibid.*, p. 38.
[11]Jagdish N. Sheth, "The Multivariate Revolution in Marketing Research," *Journal of Marketing*, Vol. 35, January 1971, pp. 13–15.

ANALYSIS OF SURVEY DATA

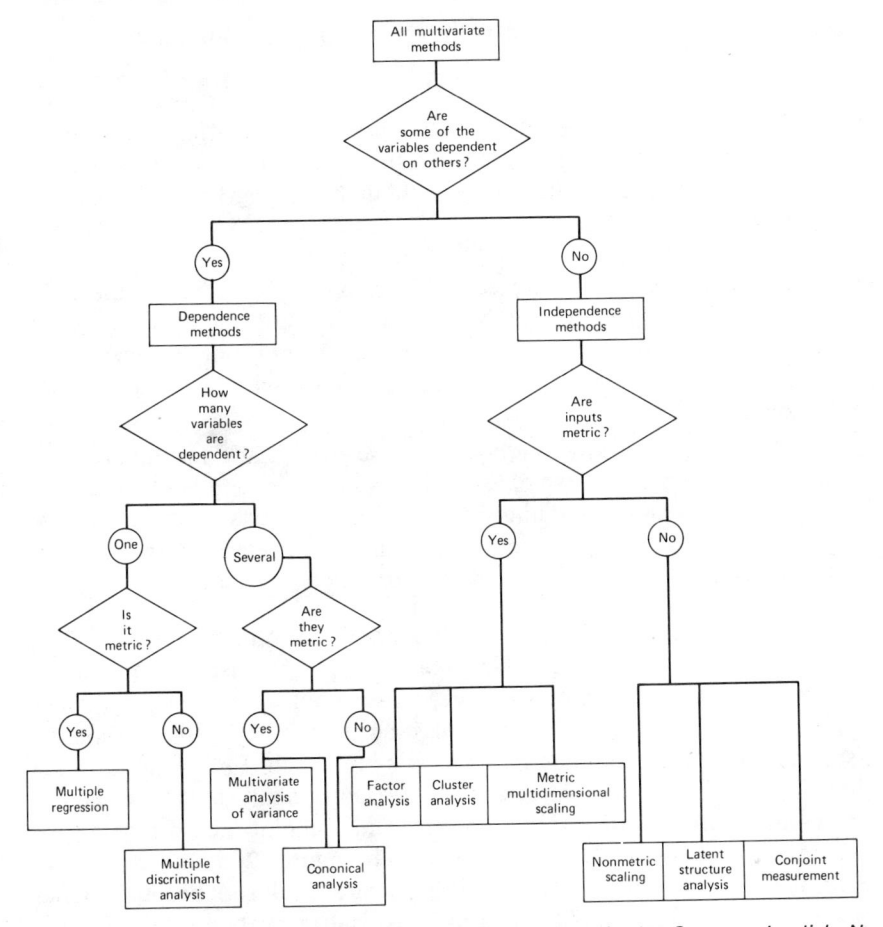

Figure 12-5 Classification of multivariate analysis methods. Source: Jagdish N. Sheth, "The Multivariate Revolution in Marketing Research," Journal of Marketing, Vol. 35, January 1971, p. 15. (Conjoint measurement has been added to the original diagram.)

1. Are some of the variables dependent upon others, thereby requiring special treatment?
2. If yes, how many are to be treated as dependent in a single analysis?
3. What are the presumed properties of the data? Specifically, are the data *qualitative* (nonmetric) in that marketing reality is scaled on nominal or ordinal scales, or *quantitative* (metric) and scaled on interval or ratio scales?

The technique to be utilized will depend upon the answer to these three questions.[12]

A recent survey article on the application of multivariate analysis in marketing by Sheth has provided additional insight into the bases for choice among various multivariate methods by noting that they may be categorized into two types:

1. *Functional multivariate methods*—These methods are ". . . most appropriate for building predictive models . . ." of market behavior in which the objective is to forecast or explain one or more "dependent" variables on the basis of their relationships with a set of "independent" variables.[13]
2. *Structural multivariate methods*—These are ". . . essentially data reduction techniques which simplify complex and diverse relationships . . ." among seemingly "independent" variables with the objective of gaining insight into the structure of the relationships between the variables.[14]

Four types of functional multivariate methods are shown in Figure 12–5 (multiple correlation and regression analysis, multiple discriminant analysis, multivariate analysis of variance, and canonical analysis) and each method will be examined briefly regarding its characteristics, basis for use, and application to industrial marketing research. Following this section, four structural multivariate methods (factor analysis, cluster analysis, nonmetric multidimensional scaling, and conjoint measurement) are presented, with two of the methods shown in Figure 12–5 omitted (metric multidimensional scaling and latent structure analysis) because of an absence of published applications in industrial marketing research.

FUNCTIONAL MULTIVARIATE METHODS

Multiple Correlation and Regression Analysis

Among the functional multivariate methods which all share the common characteristic of having some variables dependent on others, multiple correlation and regression analysis is the most frequently used method in

---

[12]*Ibid.*, p. 14.
[13]Jagdish N. Sheth, "What is Multivariate Analysis?", in Jagdish N. Sheth, Ed., *Multivariate Methods for Market and Survey Research*. Chicago: American Marketing Association, 1977, p. 3.
[14]*Ibid.*, p. 5.

industrial marketing research. Figure 12-5 indicates that this method is used when the objective is to find the optimum simultaneous relationship between one metric dependent variable and two or more independent variables. As such the primary difference between simple and multiple correlation and regression analysis is the introduction of one or more *additional* independent variables in the multiple analysis. This results in a need to explore the simultaneous, more complex relationships created by the additional variables. The example selected to illustrate the application of multiple correlation and regression analysis is a study of the purchase of industrial components by a West Coast electronics firm by Wind.[15] Four dependent variables that measured various dimensions of source loyalty were related, one at a time, with 45 independent variables initially. The 45 independent variables were reduced to 11 and then to 6 in the measure of source loyalty considered here. In the multiple regression equations developed for each measure of source loyalty, Wind computed standardized parameter estimates so that the partial correlation coefficients for each independent variable could be compared. The equation for one measure of source loyalty was:

$$SL_1 = a - bP_2 + cA_2 - dDLV_1 + eCS_1 + fORG_1 + gWS_2$$

$$SL_1 = a - \underset{(-3.078)}{.3154\,P_2} + \underset{(3.734)}{.1910\,A_2} - \underset{(-2.681)}{.2235\,DLV_1} + \underset{(4.535)}{.3429\,CS_1}$$

$$+ \underset{(3.815)}{.2036\,ORG_1} + \underset{(2.593)}{.1310\,WS_2}$$

where SL_1 = number of purchases from favorite sources as percentage of total number of purchases from all sources.
a = constant (value not given in article).
b, c, d, e, f, g = standardized parameter estimates or adjusted partial regression coefficients (t values are shown in parentheses under each coefficient).
P_2 = price at time t relative to previous price.
A_2 = attitude toward a given source relative to other sources.
DLV_1 = dollar value of an order.
CS_1 = divisional cost savings relative to cost savings of other divisions.
ORG_1 = recommendation of brand by user.
WS_2 = previous purchase history.

[15] Yoram Wind, "Industrial Source Loyalty," *Journal of Marketing Research*, Vol. 7, November 1970, pp. 450–457.

The relative explanatory power of each independent variable was indicated by the size of the partial correlation coefficients; the most important determinants of source loyalty were therefore cost savings (CS_1), price (P_2), and the dollar value of an order (DLV_1). A further matter of importance is that the direction of the hypothesized relationship of each independent variable with source loyalty was exactly as predicted, providing some assurance that the equation was correctly specified. The primary indication that the equation was correctly specified was that the coefficient of determination (R^2 = correlation coefficient, squared) was .94, so that 94% of the variation in source loyalty was explained by and associated with the variation in the six independent variables.

Multiple Discriminant Analysis

In his study of industrial source loyalty, Wind was also interested in determining the ability of the independent variables to distinguish or "discriminate" between two categories of source loyalty: perfect source loyalty ($SL = 1$) and relative source loyalty ($SL = < 1$).[16] When the dependent variable is nonmetric as in a dichotomous treatment of the data, and there are multiple independent variables involved, multiple discriminant analysis is the appropriate multivariate method. Multivariate discriminant analysis was used to classify sampling units (purchases of electronic components in the Wind study) into two or more (dichotomous or multichotomous) categories, on the basis of the values of the independent variables. The prediction of the category classification for each sampling unit was compared with its actual classification to determine the ability of the independent variables to discriminate effectively between the categories of the dependent variable. Wind obtained a discriminant function for $SL = 1$ and $SL < 1$ with a D^2 value of 10.746 and an F-value of 29.781, thereby indicating a highly statistically significant difference between the two categories.[17] In addition the function was shown to be a very effective predictor of category membership by correctly classifying approximately 85% of the purchases studied.

Multivariate Analysis of Variance

The application of multivariate analysis of variance (MANOVA) to marketing research data tends to be associated with experimental rather than

---

[16]*Ibid.*, pp. 453–454. Another analysis was conducted with a second dichotomy ($SL > .5$ and $SL < .5$) with less effective results.

[17]*Ibid.*, p. 454. The F value is obtained by the use of analysis of variance (discussed in the following section) and tested for significance by reference to a table of the F distribution. D^2 is the discriminant score obtained for the specified function.

ANALYSIS OF SURVEY DATA

survey data, in which there are two or more metric dependent variables. Actually, analysis of variance methods may be used with any type of data provided that certain assumptions regarding the nature of the data are met. A search of the industrial marketing research literature failed to reveal any use of MANOVA, but a univariate (ANOVA) example will be presented to illustrate the basic characteristics of the method. A study by Walker, Churchill, and Ford examines the relationships between two dependent variables (role conflict and role ambiguity) and six independent variables:[18]

O = Number of organization departments affecting the salesman's activities
C = Salesman's perception of the closeness of supervision of his performance
I = Salesman's perception of the amount of influence he has in determining the performance standards used to evaluate him
N = Amount of innovativeness required by the sales job
F = Salesman's frequency of contact with his sales manager
T = Length of time in the present sales job

In a multiple regression analysis of the relationship between role conflict and the six independent variables, the R^2 value was .02 but the authors maintained that emphasis ". . . should be on the statistical significance of the overall equation . . . ,"[19] which was done by using analysis of variance methods. The F ratio of 0.997 shown in Figure 12-6 was not statistically significant (any F value of 1.00 is nonsignificant, regardless of the number of degrees of freedom involved), indicating that the regression equation was not adequately specified. Use of analysis of variance methods therefore provides a means for testing for significant differences in one (ANOVA) or more (MANOVA) dependent variables as a result of variations in three or more independent variables.

Figure 12-6 also shows the results of an analysis of variance with role ambiguity as the dependent variable. In this case, the F ratio of 6.516 was statistically significant at the .01 level. While this suggests that the regression equation may have been correctly specified, the R^2 value of .13 indicated that only 13% of the variation in role ambiguity was associated with variations in the six independent variables. Further examination of the regression equation revealed that three of the regression (beta) coefficients were statistically significant (C, N, T) and that the predicted

---

[18] Orville C. Walker, Jr., Gilbert A. Churchill, Jr., and Neil M. Ford, "Organizational Determinants of the Industrial Salesman's Role Conflict and Ambiguity," *Journal of Marketing*, Vol. 39, January 1975, pp. 32-39.
[19] *Ibid.*, p. 37.

	Sum of squares	Degrees of freedom	Mean square	F ratio
Due to regression	596.2	6	99.366	0.997
Due to residuals	25713.6	258	99.665	
Total	26309.8	264		

(a)

	Sum of squares	Degrees of freedom	Mean square	F ratio
Due to regression	3466.9	6	577.8	6.516
Due to residuals	22879.7	258	88.7	
Total	26346.6	264		

(b)

Source: Orville C. Walker, Jr., Gilbert A. Churchill, Jr., and Neil M. Ford, "Organizational Determinants of the Industrial Salesman's Role Conflict and Ambiguity," *Journal of Marketing*, Vol. 39, January 1975, pp. 37–38.

Figure 12-6 *Analysis of variance methods.* (a) *With role conflict as the dependent variable.* (b) *With role ambiguity as the dependent variable.*

direction of association was correct for all six variables. Analysis of variance methods are thus shown to be complementary to correlation and regression methods, providing additional analytical power and insight into simultaneous relationships among variables.

Canonical Analysis

The fourth and final functional multivariate method to be considered here is canonical analysis in which the objective is to:

> . . . simultaneously predict a *set* of dependent variables from their joint covariance with a *set* of independent variables.[20]

There is no restriction on the type of data that are acceptable in canonical analysis (both metric and nonmetric data may be used) and, most importantly for industrial marketing research purposes, the method provides

[20] Jagdish N. Sheth, "The Multivariate Revolution in Marketing Research," *op. cit.*, p. 15.

the opportunity to obtain a variety of information useful in exploratory research:

1. The number of significant relationships between the sets of variables, as indicated by the number of significant canonical correlations.
2. The strengths of the relationships between the variable sets, as revealed by the magnitude of the canonical roots (root = R_c^2).
3. The nature of the significant relationships as suggested by the magnitude of the individual canonical weights and respective variable-variate correlations.[21]

Application of canonical analysis in industrial marketing research will be illustrated by a study of 91 West Coast building materials salesmen, in which the objective was to examine the relationship between the personality attributes of the salesmen (the set of independent variables) and their sales performance and job satisfaction (the set of dependent variables).[22] Since there were two dependent and five independent variables in the two sets, a maximum of two canonical correlations could be computed (based on the number of variables in the smaller of the two sets). The two correlation coefficients (R_c) were .47 and .14, with the first found to be significant at the .002 level, while the second was nonsignificant. The strength of the one significant coefficient was given by the canonical root ($R_c^2 = (.47)^2 = .22$), indicating ". . . the proportion of shared variance in the two sets due to the first canonical relationship."[23]

Five independent variables (power, social interest, marginality, identification, and openness) were used to represent the personality attributes of the salesmen and comprised the independent variable set. Figure 12–7 shows: (1) the simple correlation coefficients among all of the individual independent and dependent variables, and (2) the correlation coefficients between the independent variables and the independent variable set (independent canonical variate). The coefficients between the dependent variable set and the individual dependent variables are also shown, as is the coefficient between the two dependent variables. Finally in the last row of Figure 12–7 the individual canonical weights are presented with the magnitude of the weight indicating the relative contribution of the variable to the canonical relationship.

---

[21] Henry O. Pruden and Robert A. Peterson, "Personality and Performance-Satisfaction of Industrial Salesmen," *Journal of Marketing Research*, Vol. 8, November 1971, p. 502.
[22] *Ibid.*, pp. 501–504.
[23] *Ibid.*, p. 503.

	Variables					
Variables	Power	Social interest	Marginality	Identification	Openness	Performance	Satis-faction
Power							
Social interest	−.13						
Marginality	.07	.08					
Identification	−.11	.00	−.03				
Openness	.05	−.04	−.07	−.23			
Performance	.25	.00	.22	.05	.11		
Satisfaction	.13	.16	.22	.10	.02	−.03	
Independent canonical variate	.59	.23	.67	.22	.19		
Dependent canonical variate						.74	.65
Canonical weights	.59	.26	.61	.36	.29	.75	.66

Source: Henry O. Pruden and Robert A. Peterson, "Personality and Performance-Satisfaction of Industrial Salesmen," *Journal of Marketing Research*, Vol. 8, November 1971, p. 502.

Figure 12-7 Intercorrelation matrix and weights for canonical analysis.

ANALYSIS OF SURVEY DATA

The canonical weights show that both sales performance and job satisfaction contributed to the canonical relationship (.75 and .66 respectively), although they were only minimally related to each other (−.03). Marginality (noncommitment, neutrality, and openness to new information) and power (perceived dominance over customers) contributed the most among the independent variables (.61 and .59 respectively) to the canonical relationship. Further the presence of marginality and power was associated with high sales performance and job satisfaction. Perhaps the most important finding from our perspective is that the use of canonical analysis suggests that the simultaneous examination of sales performance and job satisfaction provides more information than studying them independently. Thus canonical analysis may offer important additional insights into the nature of the relationships among variables and consequently should prove useful in many industrial marketing research studies.

STRUCTURAL MULTIVARIATE METHODS

Factor Analysis

A distinguishing characteristic of the *functional* multivariate methods reviewed in the preceding section is that they all separate the variables under investigation into "dependent" and "independent" classifications. This separation is consistent with the objective of seeking to predict or explain the values of one or more "dependent" variables from their relationships with two or more "independent" variables. In our discussion emphasis will be on *structural* multivariate methods, which are used when all of the variables being studied are considered to be "independent" and the focus is on the structure of the relationships among all variables. Factor analysis is probably the most widely applied structural multivariate method and is characterized by its objective of summarizing ". . . a large number of original variables into a small number of synthetic variables, called factors."[24] A factor is a linear combination of variables, and there are a number of different factor analysis techniques distinguished primarily by their different approaches to determining factor weights.

One of the major purposes of factor analysis is data reduction, in that the factors obtained from a large number of original variables presumably

---

[24] Donald S. Tull and Del I. Hawkins, *Marketing Research*. New York: Macmillan, 1976, p. 542.

contain the "important" information contained in those variables. A second major purpose is data analysis and interpretation, and ". . . interpretation of a factor solution focuses on the identification of the construct or constructs that underlie the observed (original) variables."[25] Each factor therefore is presumed to result from the common characteristics shared by the original variables comprising the factor with the common characteristics forming one or more constructs. In this way factor analysis may reveal interrelationships among variables that are complex, unexpected, and counter-intuitive.

Application of factor analysis to an industrial marketing research situation may be shown by a study of the risk reducing strategies used by industrial buyers.[26] Based on the proposition that

> . . . an industrial buyer can reduce perceived risk by striving to reduce the uncertainty surrounding the situation or by minimizing the possibility of serious negative consequences . . . ,[27]

a sample of 134 purchasing personnel responded to a hypothetical purchasing problem and ten risk reducing strategies. The problem dealt with a color television manufacturer (Tube Tec) that wanted to buy electronic components and

> . . . faced the risk of a delay in production at an estimated cost of twelve to fifteen hundred dollars for each day that the shipments of components was late. . . . Participants were asked to evaluate two suppliers: (1) a supplier (Draper Manufacturing) who represented a greater cost saving to the buyer by offering a lower price, but could not guarantee delivery when needed; and (2) a supplier (Eddington, Inc.) who quoted a higher price, but guaranteed delivery of the product when needed.[28]

Each of the ten risk reducing strategies were rated on seven-point scales by the respondents and a factor analysis of the resulting data was conducted. Four factors were identified, and Figure 12–8 shows the factor correlation matrix for the four factors and ten strategies. Figure 12–9

---

[25]Gilbert A. Churchill, Jr., *Marketing Research*. Hinsdale, Ill.: Dryden, 1976, p. 553.
[26]Timothy W. Sweeney, H. Lee Mathews, and David T. Wilson, "An Analysis of Industrial Buyers' Risk Reducing Behavior: Some Personality Correlates," in Thomas V. Greer, Ed., *1973 Combined Conference Proceedings*. Chicago: American Marketing Association, 1974, pp. 217–221.
[27]*Ibid.*, p. 218.
[28]*Ibid.*, p. 219.

Risk reducing strategy	Factor I	Factor II	Factor III	Factor IV
1. Consult with buyers in other firms about their experience with Draper.	−.12716	−.17931	.67257[b]	.31446
2. Arrange for a visit to Draper plant.	.67957[b]	−.21523	.22097	.21339
3. Investigate possible means of expediting Draper's delivery commitment.	.66338[b]	.08123	.13160	−.19998
4. Seek top management commitment from Draper.	.72031[b]	.10307	−.15767	.07726
5. Search for additional published information.	.45030	.12990	.50296[b]	−.12550
6. Consult with Tube Tec's top management before decision.	−.14710	.75396[b]	.36137	.00280
7. Negotiate a penalty clause in the Draper contract.	.17524	.11137	.63960[b]	−.20047
8. Consult with Tube Tec's manufacturing people about rescheduling production.	.18397	.75257[b]	−.20859	.02220
9. Negotiate with Eddington for a better price.	−.02730	.09510	−.20507	.75920[b]
10. Split the order between Draper and Eddington at some acceptable level.	.03933	−.04847	.11564	.62892[b]

Notes: [a]These results are based upon an "orthogonal" rotation as opposed to "oblique" rotation. As a general rule, unless the researcher suspects high intercorrelations among the factors, orthogonal rotation is acceptable. The factor correlation matrix of these four factors revealed only slight intercorrelations. See Figure 12–9 for an interpretation of each factor.
[b]Loadings greater than an absolute value of .50.

Source: Timothy W. Sweeney, H. Lee Mathews, and David T. Wilson, "An Analysis of Industrial Buyers' Risk Reducing Behavior: Some Personality Correlates," in Thomas V. Greer, Ed., *1973 Combined Conference Proceedings*. Chicago: American Marketing Association, 1974, p. 219.

Figure 12–8 Factor analysis of 10 risk reduction strategies: 4 factors rotated.[a]

Factor	Dominant strategies	Interpretation	Label
I	2. Arrange for a visit to Draper plant. 3. Investigate possible means of expediting Draper's delivery commitment. 4. Seek top management commitment from Draper.	These strategies require the industrial buyer to go outside of his own organization in order to reduce the uncertainty in the buying situation.	External uncertainty reduction
II	6. Consult with Tube Tec's top management before decision. 8. Consult with Tube Tec's manufacturing people about rescheduling production.	A high score on this factor would indicate that the buyer would prefer trying to reduce the seriousness of negative consequences by taking action within his own firm.	Internal consequence reduction
III	1. Consult with buyers in other firms about their experience with Draper. 5. Search for additional published information. 7. Negotiate a penalty clause in the Draper contract.	These strategies tend to reduce the uncertainty perceived in the buying situation and can be initiated within the buyer's organization or purchasing community.	Internal uncertainty reduction
IV	9. Negotiate with Eddington for a better price. 10. Split the order between Draper and Eddington at some acceptable level.	This factor refers to negotiation activity with the suppliers where price is the main consideration. A better price would mean less at stake or, less serious negative consequences. Both strategies loading on this factor entail price negotiation outside of the buyer's organization.	External consequence reduction

Source: Timothy W. Sweeney, H. Lee Mathews, and David T. Wilson, "An Analysis of Industrial Buyers' Risk Reducing Behavior: Some Personality Correlates," in Thomas V. Greer, Ed., *1973 Combined Conference Proceedings*, Chicago: American Marketing Association, 1974, p. 220.

Figure 12–9 Interpretation of factor—variable associations.

ANALYSIS OF SURVEY DATA

provides an interpretation of the associations between each factor and the variables (dominant strategies), together with a label for the construct underlying the factor. The labels indicate that the industrial buyers use both uncertainty reduction and consequence reduction methods and that these methods may be further classified into internal and external methods.

Cluster Analysis

We have noted that one of the major purposes of factor analysis is data reduction, which has the objective of reducing a large number of original variables into a small number of factors. Cluster analysis is another structural multivariate method, which shares this major purpose of data reduction but the focus shifts from variables to objects. Cluster analysis therefore seeks to separate objects (persons, products, organizations) into groups marked by relative homogeneity within the groups and relative heterogeneity among groups. An application of cluster analysis to industrial marketing research has been provided by Green and Tull, using an example of 102 different computer models introduced between 1955 and 1968.[29] The computer models were divided into two classes: Class I, comprised of the 55 models introduced between 1955 and 1963; Class II, made up of 47 models introduced from 1964 to 1968. Separate analyses were conducted for each class, using the computer models as objects and 22 performance measures as variables. Figure 12-10 shows the cluster composition for Class II computer models. Eight clusters were developed from the data and

> . . . the resulting clusters indicated which manufacturers competed with which other manufacturers in terms of similarity in the overall performance profiles on their machines.[30]

In *Cluster 5*, the IBM 360 series (with one omission) was shown to be most similar to selected RCA models, while *Cluster 6* shows that the remaining IBM 360/20 model was similar to two RCA Spectra models (70/15 and 70/25) as well as models offered by GE, Honeywell, and Univac. Green and Tull also applied factor analysis to the performance measures (as appropriate for the analysis of variables) and

> . . . found that four 'factors' explained the similarities and dif-

---
[29] Paul E. Green and Donald S. Tull, *Research for Marketing Decisions*, 3rd ed. Englewood Cliffs, N.J.: Prentice-Hall, 1975, pp. 579–587.
[30] *Ibid.*, p. 587.

Cluster 1	Cluster 5
Burroughs B2500	IBM 360/30
GE 415	IBM 360/40
GE 425	IBM 360/50
GE 435	IBM 360/65
Honeywell 1400	IBM 360/75
IBM 1130	IBM 360/44
	IBM 360/67
	RCA Spectra 70/35
	RCA Spectra 70/45
	RCA Spectra 70/55
	RCA 3301/3304

Cluster 2	Cluster 6
CDC 3100	GE 235
CDC 3200	Honeywell 200/120
CDC 3300	Honeywell 200/200
CDC 3400	IBM 360/20
Honeywell 1800	RCA Spectra 70/15
	RCA Spectra 70/25
	Univac 9200
	Univac 9300

Cluster 3	Cluster 7
CDC 6400	Honeywell 200/2200
CDC 6600	Honeywell 200/4200
CDC 6800	NCR 315 RMC
GE 625	
GE 635	
Honeywell 200/8200	
IBM 7092-2	
Univac 1108	

Cluster 4	Cluster 8
Burroughs B300	Burroughs B3500
GE 115	Honeywell 200/1200
IBM 1401—G	RCA 3301/3303

Source: Paul E. Green and Donald S. Tull, *Research for Marketing Decisions*, 3rd ed. Englewood Cliffs, N.J.: Prentice-Hall, 1975, p. 586.

Figure 12-10 Cluster composition—Class II computer models.

ferences among the computer models—total number of features, features pattern, speed, and machine capacity.[31]

This study therefore illustrates how both cluster analysis and factor analysis may be applied for the purposes of data reduction and determining relationships between and among objects and variables.

Nonmetric Multidimensional Scaling

There has been a growing interest in attitude measurement among marketing researchers during the past fifteen years, as attitudes have become recognized as the forerunners of purchase behavior. Since attitudes deal with the feelings, ideas, and predispositions of people toward specific objects (products, organizations), the most common method used to measure attitudes is to ask people to "self-report." A variety of scales and scaling methods have been developed to aid people in the task of self-reporting. There has also been a great deal of research in recent years on the measurement of the attributes of objects, since it is the attributes of an object rather than the object itself that is measured. The measurement of attributes depends on the properties of the attributes, and these properties determine the appropriate scales to use. Attributes can be measured on four types of scales:[32]

1. *Nominal scale*—used when the numbers that measure the attribute have the property of *identity*; large firms might be classed as "1" and small firms as "2".
2. *Ordinal scale*—used to measure the *order*, rank, or relative standing of an attribute; the "Fortune 500" uses an ordinal scale to rank the 500 largest corporations.
3. *Interval scale*—used to measure the *intervals* or differences between objects with respect to an attribute; indexes are often used to illustrate this property.
4. *Ratio scale*—used to measure the *absolute magnitude* of the differences between objects with respect to an attribute; market share is an example of a ratio scale measure, a firm with a market share of 40% is said to have twice the share of a firm with a 20% market share.

All of the attitude scales that have been widely applied in marketing

---
[31]*Ibid.*, p. 584.
[32]Churchill, *op. cit.*, pp. 208–210.

research (Guttman, Likert, Q-sort, Thurstone, semantic differential, and so on) are

> . . . based on one of two simplifying assumptions. Several scales, such as the Guttman scale, assume that only one attitude dimension such as like/dislike or high quality/low quality is relevant. Others, such as the semantic differential scale, assume that several dimensions may be relevant *and* that the researcher knows in advance what these attitude dimensions are (since he must provide the relevant adjectives).[33]

Multidimensional scaling has been developed to avoid these restrictive assumptions by using computer-based techniques that require no limits on the number or nature of the attitude dimensions. The objective of multidimensional scaling is: (1) to measure the perceptions and attitudes of respondents toward the attributes of one or more objects based on perceived similarities and preferences and (2) to represent these perceptions and attitudes in multidimensional space. Green and Carmone have identified three types of multidimensional scaling techniques:[34]

1. *Fully metric multidimensional scaling techniques*—Use metric (ratio-scale) input data of the distances between objects (in multidimensional space) and provide metric output.
2. *Fully nonmetric multidimensional scaling techniques*—Use nonmetric (ordinal) input data and provide nonmetric output. The rank order of the distances between the objects in multidimensional space constitutes the input, while the output is expressed in terms of the rank order of the objects on each dimension.
3. *Nonmetric multidimensional scaling techniques*—These techniques use nonmetric (ordinal scale) input data but provide metric (ratio scale) output. The ability of these techniques to transform nonmetric input data into metric output has resulted in their dominance in the marketing research literature to date, since metric (ratio scale) data have the most powerful properties for analytical purposes.

Nonmetric multidimensional scaling techniques therefore use nonmetric input data, derived from rank-ordered similarity judgements between each pair of objects being studied, to construct perceptual spaces in which the rank order of the distances (metric output data)

---

[33]Tull and Hawkins, *op. cit.*, p. 355.
[34]Paul E. Green and Frank J. Carmone, *Multidimensional Scaling and Related Techniques in Marketing Analysis*. Boston: Allyn and Bacon, 1970, pp. 10–11.

. . . maximally corresponds with the rankings of the pairwise similarity judgements.[35]

Day has suggested that

. . . a logical next step is to include locations of respondents (based on their preference judgments) within the perceptual space which represents the locations of the various stimulus objects. Preference information is summarized as an ideal point . . . ,[36]

with the combined mapping of perceptual and preference points known as joint space analysis.

An application of nonmetric multidimensional scaling (and joint space analysis) to industrial marketing research has been provided in a study of the potential demand in California for calcium-silicate bricks made from gold-mine tailings.[37] A joint space model was developed using 12 types of bricks varying in price, texture, color, and material as objects and the preference judgements of a sample of 44 persons with specifying influence in the choice of bricks as a building material, including builders, designers, and architects. Figure 12–11(a) shows a joint space map of the study findings, with 11 types of bricks collected within three categories: (1) calcium-silicate bricks, (2) common clay bricks, and (3) tan-brown bricks. Day noted that,

. . . the labels for the two-dimensional perceptual space, which fit the data very closely, were easy to infer . . . ,[38]

with one axis labeled "price" and the other a composite of "color/texture." In most applications of nonmetric multidimensional scaling, the location of an average ideal point for all respondents is obtained implicitly from preference rank orders, but Day has also shown the location of an explicit ideal point obtained by including an ideal object into the perceptual space of the respondents. He also depicted separate ideal points for 9 respondents on the joint space map, and isopreference circles centered on each average ideal point. The map indicates that the ideal (preference) points for the respondents corresponds most closely with the perceptual space location of common clay bricks, and that there is little resulting potential demand for calcium-silicate or tan-brown bricks.

[35]George S. Day, "Evaluating Models of Attitude Structure," *Journal of Marketing Research*, Vol. 9, August 1972, p. 282.
[36]*Ibid.*, p. 283.
[37]*Ibid.*, pp. 279–286.
[38]*Ibid.*, p. 283.

(a)

- Ⓟ Stimulus point
- ⊗ Average implicit ideal point
- □ Subjects ideal point
- • Average explicit ideal point

(b)

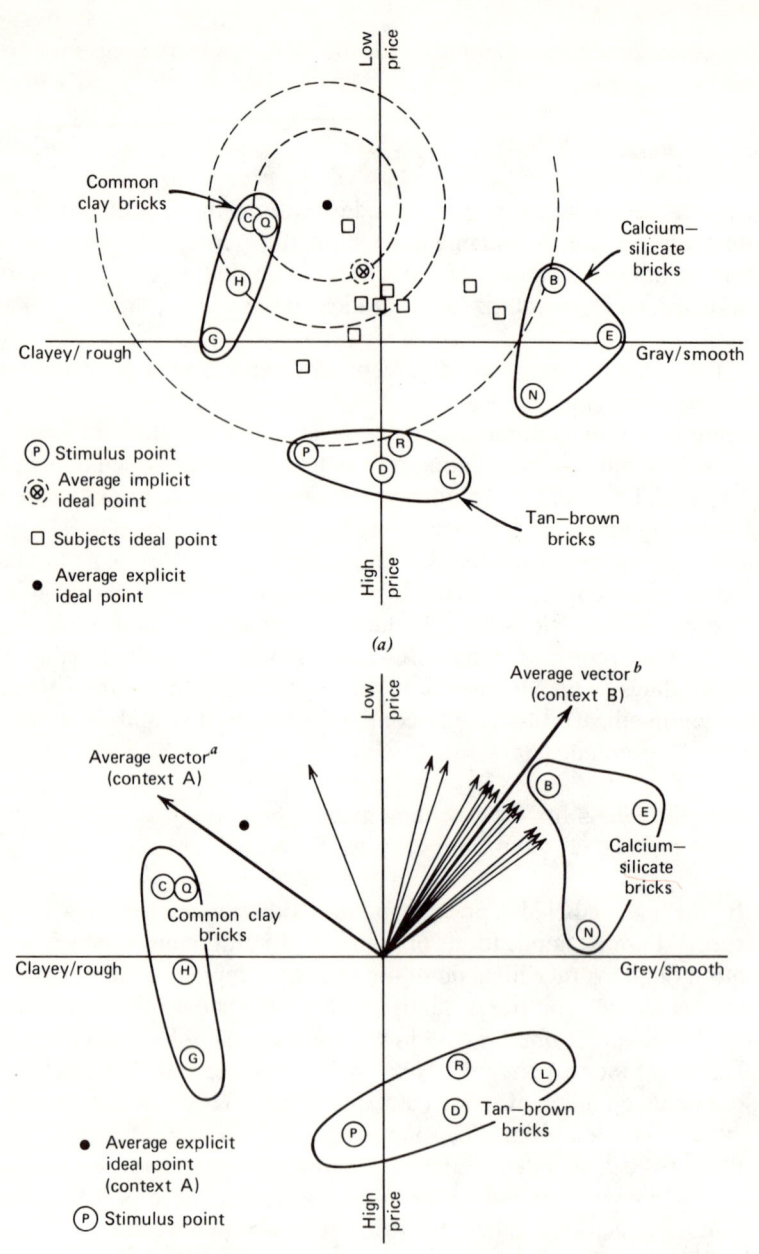

[a]Context A is decorative application of bricks in an average-priced house. Context B is use of bricks in the chimney and fireplace of an inexpensive house.

Day also tested the effect of a change in context on preference judgments with a subsample of 13 respondents who were

> ... asked which bricks they would prefer for the chimney and fireplace of an inexpensive house (Context B) after being asked about preferences for decorative applications in a more expensive house (Context A).[39]

Figure 12-11(*b*) shows that the change in context had a marked effect on preference judgments, with calcium-silicate bricks corresponding closely with the average (and individual) vectors representing preferences in context B. This joint space map therefore suggests that there is potential demand for calcium-silicate bricks if they are positioned in the market as being appropriate for the chimney and fireplace of inexpensive houses.

Conjoint Measurement

Sheth has described conjoint measurement as

> ... a very recent extension of nonmetric multidimensional scaling to the problems of measuring trade-offs between attributes ... based on the rank ordering of preferences expressed by an individual for all pairwise combinations of different levels of two or more attributes, the objective in conjoint analysis is to derive a quantitative measure of presumed utility underlying the individual's expressed preferences in terms of trade-offs.[40]

An application of conjoint measurement to industrial marketing research has been provided in a study of physicians' evaluation of the criteria used in the selection of clinical laboratories.[41] A sample of 51 physicians were involved in the study with a subsample of 36 of the physicians asked to

---

[39]*Ibid.*, p. 284.
[40]Jagdish N. Sheth, "What is Multivariate Analysis?", *op. cit.*, p. 7.
[41]Yoram Wind, "Recent Approaches to the Study of Organizational Buying Behavior," in Thomas V. Greer, Ed., *1973 Combined Conference Proceedings*. Chicago: American Marketing Association, 1974, pp. 203-206.

Figure 12-11 Application of nonmetric multidimensional scaling and joint space analysis to industrial marketing research. (a) Joint space representation of the ideal points. (b) Vector model of preferences, showing the effect of a change in context. Source: George S. Day, "Evaluating Models of Attitude Structure," Journal of Marketing Research, Vol. 9, August 1972, pp. 279-286.

rank 16 clinical laboratories in terms of their use intentions. The 16 profiles of the hypothetical laboratories were based on various combinations of laboratory attributes as derived by applying a fractional factorial experimental design to a group of 10 variables at 4 levels each. The 10 variables were:

1. Quality
2. Promptness and reliability
3. Pick up and delivery procedure
4. Convenience of location
5. Prices
6. Range of services (full line vs. partial)
7. Pleasantness of personnel
8. Billing procedures
9. 24-hour service
10. Turn around time

The other 15 physicians in the sample were asked to rank the 10 variables in order of their importance, producing a 15 × 10 matrix which was analyzed with a Thurstone Case V unidimensional scale. These results were then compared with the results from applying conjoint measurement analysis to the 36 × 16 matrix of nonmetric multidimensional scale scores. Wind found that,

> Overall, the most important factor in the selection of a clinical lab is quality. Secondary in importance are promptness and reliability, range of tests offered, and convenience of location.[42]

By comparing the results of the conjoint measurement analysis with those of the Thurstone Case V analysis, Wind found that the evaluation of single factors (using unidimensional scaling) lead to

> . . . an overestimation of the importance of the less important factors . . .[43]

such as prices and billing procedure.

Our review of the many analytical methods available for the analysis of survey data has used a variety of industrial marketing research studies to illustrate the application of the methods. These methods have also been

---
[42] *Ibid.*, p. 205.
[43] *Ibid.*

ANALYSIS OF SURVEY DATA

applied to many other industrial marketing research studies not included in this review; many of these studies are listed in the "Suggested Readings" for this chapter. This review and the cited references should serve to awaken many and remind others that the application of modern, sophisticated analytical methods to industrial marketing research management is expanding rapidly as a result of these research findings. Much remains to be done in the application of these and newer analytical methods.

SUMMARY

Once a set of survey data have been obtained that are representative of the universe from which they are drawn the next two steps are to prepare the data for analysis and to select the appropriate statistical techniques.

In many industrial surveys sample sizes are sufficiently small that machine tabulation is unnecessary. When sample size exceeds 30, machine tabulation should be used. Regardless the data should be ordered into narrow categories of approximately equal width. Open-ended categories should be avoided. Once the data have been ordered into categories, simple univariate data description through frequency distributions and measures of central tendency should be prepared prior to selection of analytical methods.

The data analysis can be univariate, bivariate, or multivariate. Univariate analysis is used for comparing a group mean or proportion to a null hypothesis or to other group means or proportions. Bivariate analysis looks at the interrelation among pairs of variables. Cross-classification data can be expressed as column or row percentages depending upon the direction of causality. Chi-square analysis may be used to test whether the row and column variables are significantly associated. Simple correlation analysis measures the degree of closeness of the relation between two variables while regression analysis looks at the functional relation between the independent variable and the dependent variable.

Multivariate analysis in marketing research has been sparked by the availability and use of computers, the development of new research techniques and the complexity of markets in which many intervening factors mediate between marketing activities and market responses. Multivariate methods are functional if they specify one or more independent variables, structural if they treat all variables as independent, focusing on their interrelationships.

As in the bivariate case multiple correlation and regression focus on the relationship between independent and dependent variables. The dependent variable is assumed to be metric. In contrast multiple discriminant analysis requires that the dependent variable be dichotomous or multichotomous. The results show the significance of differences among the categories of the dependent variable, the ability of the independent variables in correctly classifying objects into their categories, and the relative importance of each independent variable in separating the categories.

Multivariate analysis of variance and univariate analysis of variance may be regarded as complementary to correlation and regression methods providing additional analytic power and insight into simultaneous relationships among variables. Canonical analysis simultaneously predicts a set of dependent variables from their covariance with a set of independent variables. In so doing it sorts out the causal pattern between independent and dependent variables.

Structural methods for which industrial marketing research applications have been reported are factor analysis, cluster analysis, and nonmetric multidimensional analysis. Factor analysis is a method for data reduction and for the identification of the one or more constructs that underlie the observed variables. Cluster analysis principally differs from factor analysis in that it seeks to reduce objects, not variables. The resulting clusters are groupings of homogeneous sampling units. When factor analysis is applied to the characteristics of the objects being clustered, it becomes possible to interpret more clearly the dimensions on which the market segments or clusters differ from each other.

Nonmetric multidimensional scaling techniques are so designated because they use nonmetric input data from rank ordered similarity judgements to construct rank ordered perceptual spaces. The rank ordered position of objects along the resulting dimensions produced by the technique allows the researcher to cluster objects into groups and to interpret meaningfully the dimensions on which respondents implicitly made their comparisons among objects. Conjoint analysis is a further extension of nonmetric multidimensional scaling for the evaluation of individuals' preferences in terms of trade-offs among attributes of products, sellers, or other objects.

It is hoped that the review of data analysis methods and the cited references and readings will serve to awaken many, and remind others, that the application of sophisticated analytical methods to industrial marketing research is rapidly expanding.

SUGGESTED READINGS

Churchill, Gilbert A., Jr., *Marketing Research*. Hinsdale, Ill.: Dryden, 1976.

Day, George S., "Evaluating Models of Attitude Structure," *Journal of Marketing Research*, Vol. 9, August 1972, pp. 279–286.

Green, Paul E., and Frank J. Carmone, *Multidimensional Scaling and Related Techniques in Marketing Analysis*. Boston: Allyn and Bacon, 1970, pp. 10–11.

Green, Paul E., and Donald S. Tull, *Research for Marketing Decisions*, 3rd ed. Englewood Cliffs, N.J.: Prentice-Hall, 1975, pp. 579–587.

Hughes, G. David, "A New Tool for Sales Managers," *Journal of Marketing Research*, Vol. 1, May 1964, pp. 32–38.

Luck, David J., Hugh G. Wales and Donald A. Taylor, *Marketing Research*, 4th ed. Englewood Cliffs, N.J.: Prentice-Hall, 1974.

McMillan, James R., "Role Differentiation in Industrial Buying Decisions," in Thomas V. Greer, Ed., *1973 Combined Conference Proceedings*. Chicago: American Marketing Association, 1974, pp. 207–211.

Nie, Norman H., C. Hadlai Hull, Jean G. Jenkins, Karen Steinbrenner, and Dale H. Bent, *SPSS*, 2nd ed. New York: McGraw-Hill, 1975.

Pruden, Henry O., and Robert A. Peterson, "Personality and Performance-Satisfaction of Industrial Salesmen," *Journal of Marketing Research*, Vol. 8, November 1971, pp. 501–504.

Schiffman, Leon G., and Vincent Gaccione, "Opinion Leaders in Institutional Markets," *Journal of Marketing*. Vol. 38, April 1974, pp. 49–53.

Sheth, Jagdish N., "The Multivariate Revolution in Marketing Research," *Journal of Marketing*, Vol. 35, January 1971, pp. 13–15.

Sheth, Jagdish N., "What is Multivariate Analysis?" in Jagdish N. Sheth, Ed., *Multivariate Methods for Market and Survey Research*. Chicago: American Marketing Association, 1977.

Simon, Leonard L., "Measuring the Market Impact of Technical Services," *Journal of Marketing Research*, Vol. 2, February 1965, pp. 32–39.

Sweeney, Timothy W., H. Lee Mathews, and David T. Wilson, "An Analysis of Industrial Buyers' Risk Reducing Behavior: Some Personality Correlates," in Thomas V. Greer, Ed., *1973 Combined Conference Proceedings*. Chicago: American Marketing Association, 1974, pp. 217–221.

Tull, Donald S., and Del I. Hawkins, *Marketing Research*. New York: Macmillan, 1976.

Walker, Orville C., Jr., Gilbert A. Churchill, Jr., and Neil M. Ford, "Organizational Determinants of the Industrial Salesman's Role Conflict and Ambiguity," *Journal of Marketing*, Vol. 39, January 1975, pp. 32–39.

Wind, Yoram, "Industrial Source Loyalty," *Journal of Marketing Research*, Vol. 7, November 1970, pp. 450–457.

Wind, Yoram, "Recent Approaches to the Study of Organizational Buying Behavior," in Thomas V. Greer, Ed., *1973 Combined Conference Proceedings*. Chicago: American Marketing Association, 1974, pp. 203–206.

CHAPTER THIRTEEN
Product Analysis

Market and product choice are the most important strategic decisions for virtually all business organizations, and marketing research plays a vital role in providing information necessary to make these decisions wisely. Up to this point we have primarily focused on those marketing research activities that are directed towards the choice of markets to be served by industrial firms. In this chapter the role of industrial marketing research in improving product choice decisions will be emphasized. Although the choice of new products to be offered to selected markets is of central concern, product choice decisions must be made throughout the life of existing products. The concept of an extended product life cycle will be used to organize the materials with the extended cycle consisting of two phases: (1) the Development phase and (2) the Market phase.

The Development phase of the extended product life cycle includes the entire range of activities from searching for and screening new product ideas to the initial shipment of the finished product to the marketplace. Pessemier has portrayed the Development phase as being composed of three stages, marked by changing dominance among the activities performed:[1]

1. Product Development stage when technical research and development (R & D) activities are dominant.

[1] Edgar A. Pessemier, *Managing Innovation and New Product Development*. Cambridge, Mass.: Marketing Science Institute, 1975, p. 24.

2. Process Development stage when emphasis shifts from product to process development and production decisions dominate.
3. Marketing Development stage when time marketing decisions dominate the phase.

Within the three stages of the Development phase, Pessemier has shown that eight functional activities tend to follow cyclical patterns in terms of the allocation of total effort in the firm dedicated to the development of the product.[2] These eight activities appear in approximately the following order:

1. Product research
2. Marketing strategy and planning
3. Marketing research
4. Technical development
5. Customer trials
6. Process development
7. Construction engineering
8. Applications engineering

Our interest is primarily in the marketing research activity and its relationship to the other activities on the list. More specifically we shall examine the role of industrial marketing research at four decision points within the Development phase:

1. *Product Feasibility decision*—Marketing research should be utilized in searching for and screening new product ideas.
2. *Product Specification decision*—The characteristics of the product should be determined by marketing research studies of prospective buyers.
3. *Product Testing decision*—The evaluation of pilot samples and prototypes through product-use tests should be directed by marketing research personnel.
4. *Market Testing decision*—Final market tests involving product, promotion, and distribution strategy issues should be designed and evaluated by marketing research personnel.

Figure 13–1 illustrates the three stages of the Development phase, the

[2]*Ibid.*

PRODUCT ANALYSIS

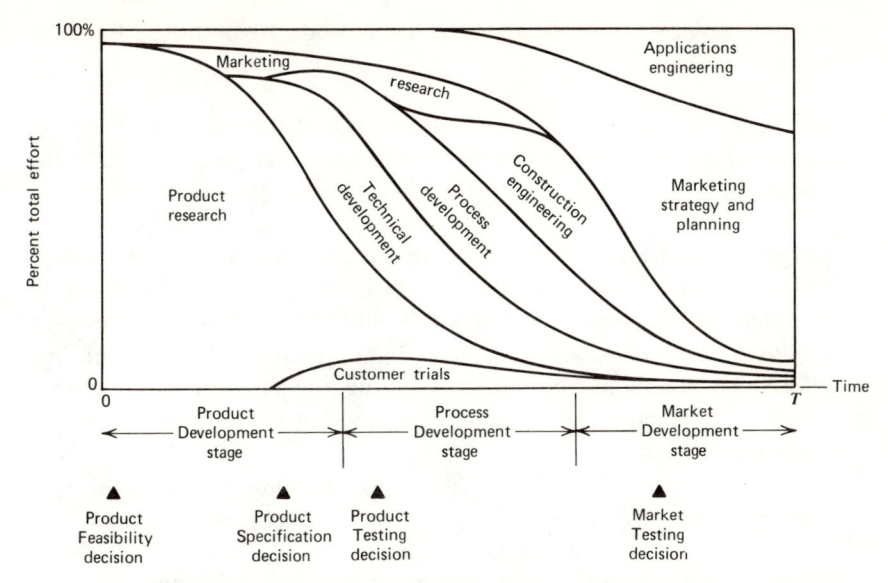

Figure 13-1 The Development phase of the product life cycle. Source: Edgar A. Pessemier, Managing Innovation and New Product Development. *Cambridge, Mass.: Marketing Science Institute, 1975, p. 24.*

cycles of the eight primary activities, and the time axis location of the four decision points requiring marketing research activity.

The Market phase of the product life cycle begins with the first shipment of the finished product to the marketplace and ends with the withdrawal of the product from the market. The standard four-stage model of the Market phase will be used:[3]

1. *Introduction stage*—The period between market (catalogue) birth, when the first shipment occurs, and commercial birth, when a threshold sales level is reached.
2. *Growth stage*—Defined as the period between commercial birth and maximum sales revenue.
3. *Maturity stage*—The period between the point of maximum sales revenue and commercial death, defined in terms of a fraction (10% or 20%) of maximum sales revenue.
4. *Decline stage*—The period between commercial death and market

---

[3] William E. Cox, Jr., "Product Life Cycles as Marketing Models," *Journal of Business*, Vol. 40, October 1967, pp. 375–384.

(catalogue) death, the point at which the product is removed from the market.

Within the four stages of the Market phase of the product life cycle, there are three types of decisions to be made that require marketing research activity:

1. *Commercial evaluation decision*—Initial acceptance of the new product should be evaluated in the Introduction stage through the use of tracking studies, new product models, and other research techniques.
2. *Product audit decisions*—Audits of the product and product line should be conducted periodically during the Growth and Maturity stages for the purposes of monitoring market response to the firm's products.
3. *Product elimination decision*—Products reaching the Decline stage must be evaluated in terms of retention or discontinuance.

Figure 13-2 portrays the Market phase of the product life cycle with the four stages and decision points illustrated on the time axis. With the framework for the chapter established, we turn to a consideration of the marketing research function.

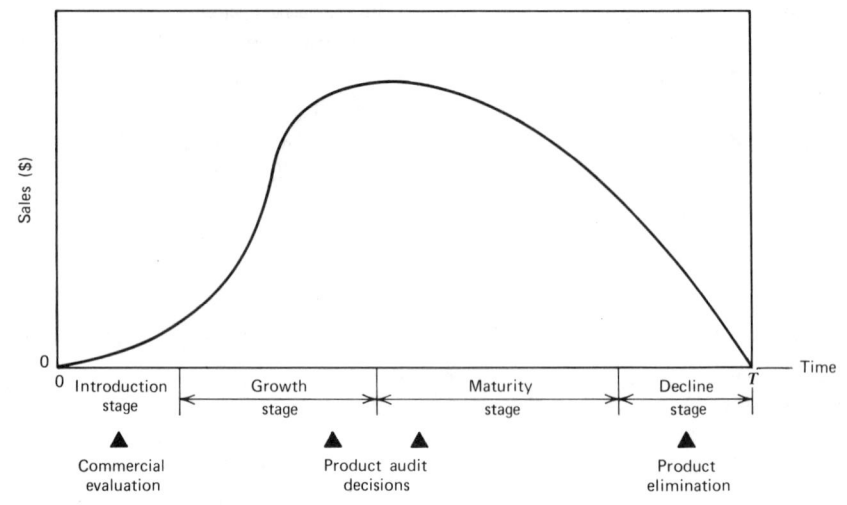

Figure 13-2 The Market phase of the product life cycle. Source: William E. Cox, Jr., "Product Life Cycles as Marketing Models," Journal of Business, Vol. 40, October 1967, p. 377.

PRODUCT ANALYSIS

THE DEVELOPMENT PHASE OF THE PRODUCT LIFE CYCLE

The importance of innovation and new product development as a principal basis for economic growth and improved social benefits has long been recognized, particularly in the United States where interest and responsiveness to innovation were recognized by de Tocqueville as a distinguishing characteristic of the American people. He was struck by the commitment of Americans to "the idea of indefinite perfectibility":

> I accost an American sailor and inquire why the ships of his country are built so as to last for only a short time; he answers without hesitation that the art of navigation is every day making such rapid progress that the finest vessel would become almost useless if it lasted beyond a few years. In these words, which fell accidentally, and on a particular subject, from an uninstructed man, I recognize the general and systematic idea upon which a great people direct all their concerns.[4]

During the past twenty-five years innovation and new product development has resulted in a flood of new products, but available evidence suggests that the new product failure rate remains high and that "most causes of failure are (or should be) amenable to marketing research."[5] There is mounting evidence to indicate that ". . . the creating of new products is moving from its traditional technology emphasis or phase into a much broader marketing phase."[6] The emerging recognition of the importance of marketing activities in the management of the new product process in industrial organizations, against an historical commitment to "indefinite perfectibility," provides the setting for our review of the role of marketing research in the Development phase of the product life cycle. This review will successively consider four decision points within the Development phase and the role of industrial marketing research at each decision point, starting with the product feasibility decision.

Product Feasibility Decision

Seemingly ideas for new products are never in short supply. That is fortunate indeed given the reported decay rate for new products. Booz, Allen, and Hamilton reported that even among large, well-managed com-

[4]Alexis de Tocqueville, *Democracy in America*. Edinburg: R & R Ltd., 1954, p. 108.
[5]C. Merle Crawford, "Marketing Research and the New Product Failure Rate," *Journal of Marketing*, Vol. 41, April 1977, p. 51.
[6]"New Products: The Push Is On Marketing," *Business Week*, March 4, 1972, p. 72.

panies the probability of an idea being translated into a successful new product is 2.4%—about one chance in 40.[7] Based on their six-stage model of new product evolution (exploration, screening, business analysis, development, testing, and commercialization), Booz, Allen, and Hamilton estimate that 50% of the ideas being considered at each stage are rejected (thus indicating the shape of the decay curve) and that each stage is progressively more costly and time-consuming. Effective and efficient management of the new product development process therefore requires that ideas be subjected to rapid, yet thorough examination. The type of examination however will depend on the nature and origin of the idea.

Ideas for innovations have been described as ". . . the fusion of a recognized demand and a recognized technical feasibility into a design concept."[8] There have been a number of studies of major innovations, primarily focused on industrial goods, which universally concluded that most such innovations originated outside the firms that eventually brought the innovations to the marketplace.[9] These studies have concentrated on technological breakthroughs however and most new products do not fall into this category. For this reason a study by Meyers and Marquis is of primary interest because it examined 567 industrial innovations introduced by 121 firms in 5 industries.[10] Although these innovations were nominated by the executives of the firms as their most important technical innovations in the past five or ten years and were presumed to be commercially successful, relatively few could be called "technological breakthroughs," and were therefore typical of most industrial innovations. The five industries in the study were: (1) railroad companies, (2) railroad suppliers, (3) housing product suppliers, (4) computer manufacturers, and (5) computer suppliers. Respondents in the 121 company sample in these industries were asked:

> What most immediately moved the firm to attempt to attain a specific objective and to undertake the innovation?

---

[7]*Management of New Products*. New York: Booz, Allen, and Hamilton, 1968.
[8]Summer Myers and Donald G. Marquis, *Successful Industrial Innovations*. Washington: U.S. Government Printing Office, 1969, p. 5.
[9]J. Jewkes, D. Sawers, and R. Stillerman, *The Sources of Invention*. London: Macmillan, 1958; Daniel Hamberg, "Invention in the Industrial Research Laboratory," *Journal of Political Economy*, Vol. 71, 1963, pp. 95–115; J. L. Enos, *Petroleum Progress and Profits*. Cambridge, Mass.: M.I.T. Press, 1962; M. J. Peck, "Inventions in the Post War American Aluminum Industry," in R. R. Nelson, Ed., *The Rate and Direction of Inventive Activity*. Princeton, N.J.: Princeton University Press, 1962, pp. 279–298; W. F. Mueller, "The Origins of the Basic Inventions Underlying DuPont's Major Product and Process Innovations, 1920–1950," in R. R. Nelson, Ed., *The Rate and Direction of Inventive Activity*. Princeton, N.J.: Princeton University Press, 1962, pp. 323–360.
[10]Myers and Marquis, *loc. cit.*

Answers were classified into four categories:

	Number	Percentage
Market factors	257	45%
Production factors	169	30
Technical factors	120	21
Administrative factors	21	4
Total	567	100

In reviewing the response data to the question, Myers and Marquis stated:

> ... the most striking finding was that the primary factor in only 21 percent of the successful innovations was the recognition of a technical opportunity. Market factors were reported as the primary factor in 45 percent of the innovations and manufacturing factors in 30 percent, indicating the three-fourths of the innovations could be classed as responses to demand recognition.[11]

A series of other studies in varying industrial settings have also concluded that about three out of every four industrial innovations originate from a recognition of need and demand in the marketplace.[12] Since there is such general agreement among the various studies regarding the dominance of demand recognition as the primary origin of industrial innovations, it might be expected that marketing research would be undertaken as a matter of course during the Development phase of the product life cycle. The literature of new product management however unanimously laments the absence or paucity of marketing research activity in the Development phase and condemns the tendency to conduct marketing research too late in the phase, even when it is conducted.

Pessemier has distinguished between the new product marketing research activity of companies that depend on market-based opportunities and those that depend on laboratory research and development to originate innovations.[13] He maintains that comprehensive marketing research

---

[11]*Ibid.*, p. 31.
[12]C. F. Carter and B. R. Williams, *Industry and Technical Progress: Factors Governing and Speed of Application of Science*. London: Oxford University Press, 1957; Materials Advisory Board, *Report on the Ad Hoc Committee on Principles of Research—Engineering Interaction*. Washington: National Academy of Sciences—National Research Council, 1966; N. R. Baker, J. Siegman, and A. H. Rubenstein, "The Effects of Perceived Needs and Means on the Generation of Ideas for Industrial Research and Development Projects," *IEEE Transactions on Engineering Management*, Vol. 14, 1967, pp. 156–163.
[13]Pessemier, *op. cit.*, pp. 26–35.

programs are conducted in market-oriented companies in this study, while technical R&D-oriented companies basically limit their marketing research activities to market screening. Our position is that comprehensive marketing research programs are needed in all industrial organizations, and that companies primarily dependent upon laboratory research and development as a source of innovations have the greatest need for formal marketing research programs, precisely because product ideas are not based on demand recognition.

All of the blame for the inadequate and inappropriate use of marketing research in the development of innovations and new products cannot be laid on scientific and technical personnel in industrial firms. Reynolds has noted that "market researchers have a professional bias against 'quick and dirty studies,'" while Bernard Kahn (a new product consultant to many firms) has observed "The nine-month market study is six months overdue."[14] Too often scientific and technical personnel, as well as general managers, decide to rely on their own market assessments after encountering resistance from marketing researchers unwilling to adapt their methodologies to the time and money available.

Managers, faced with the necessity to make their own market and product evaluations on the basis of previous experience, have often turned to various types of rating systems as an aid to decision-making.[15] The relative simplicity and apparent logic of these systems appealed to managers in the 1960s and considerable effort was expended in refining and correcting some of the inherent deficiencies of the early systems.[16] The continued failure of new products, the higher risks associated with new product innovation, and the multiplicity of problems associated with the management of new product development have resulted in the 1970s in far greater emphasis on marketing research studies as a basis for decision making.

Several marketing research techniques presented in earlier chapters are applicable to the product feasibility decision. The use of exploratory research, discussed in Chapter 2, is particularly important for product programs and projects in which time and money are severely constrained.

---

[14] William H. Reynolds, *Products and Markets*. New York: Appleton-Century-Crofts, 1969, p. 63; Kahn is quoted in: "New Products: The Push Is on Marketing," *op. cit.*, p. 72.

[15] Perhaps the most widely cited new product rating system is described in: John T. O'Meara, Jr., "Selecting Profitable Products," *Harvard Business Review*, Vol. 39, January–February 1961, pp. 83–89.

[16] Two examples of refined and amended systems are presented in: Edgar A. Pessemier, *New Product Decisions: An Analytical Approach*. New York: McGraw-Hill Book Co., 1966, 146–162; Marshall Freimer and Leonard S. Simon, "The Evaluation of Potential New Product Alternatives," *Management Science*, Vol. 13, February 1967, pp. B279–B292.

PRODUCT ANALYSIS

These "quick and dirty" studies should concentrate on developing measures of market size, including market potential and market demand. The basic approach should be to develop a minimum demand study, as outlined in Chapter 6. Revenue estimates should be derived from unit volume-price relationships within each major market segment, based on assessments of competitive positions in each segment. As noted minimum demand studies are based on evaluation of available secondary data and surveys of knowledgeable persons. An experienced marketing researcher should be able to complete a minimum demand study within two weeks or less.

It is particularly useful to present the findings of the minimum demand study in terms of expected revenues (and profits) of the product during the Market phase of the product life cycle. A Gompertz function is often used to represent a product life cycle, producing an S-shaped growth curve that depicts the cumulative sales of a product over time. The general form of the Gompertz function is:[17]

$$Y_t = K\ a^{b^t}$$

or

$$\log Y_t = \log K + (\log a) \cdot b^t$$

where Y_t = cumulative sales through period t
K = asymtotic limit of Y (market potential)
a, b = parameters
t = number of periods elapsed since the base period t_0

The product life cycle for magnetic bubble memories, a solid-state electronic device that may replace disc memories in computers as well as open new applications, can be estimated by intuitively specifying a Gompertz model. Texas Instruments introduced the bubble memories in March 1977 and estimates that annual industry sales of the devices will be $100 million in 1979 and $500 million in 1985.[18] Assume that the cumulative market potential in 1985 will reach $2.5 billion. The parameter K in the model is therefore $2.5 billion.

The estimates of total market demand and potential should be developed by first identifying the major market segments over the life cycle. Texas Instruments has identified a number of market segments, including some that will be important early in the life cycle: handheld, programm-

---

[17] Walter B. Wentz, *Marketing Research: Management and Methods.* New York: Harper & Row, 1972, p. 408.
[18] "The Bubble Memory Finally Arrives," *Business Week*, March 28, 1977, pp. 72, 74.

able calculators; portable computer terminals; word-processing systems; microprocessors; and minicomputers. The large-volume market segments, medium- and large-scale computers, will open as bubble memories replace fixed-head and floppy disk memories that now dominate those segments. Unit volume estimates should be prepared for each segment, with price/cost "experience curves" determined as a function of the growth in cumulative unit volume.[19]

If we designate 1977 as the base period ($t = 0$) and estimate that industry sales for 1977 will total $5 million, parameter a in the above equation may be determined by substituting 0 for t:

$$Y_0 = K\ a^{b^0} \quad \text{or} \quad Y_0 = K\ a$$

therefore,

$$a = \frac{Y_0}{K} = \frac{\$5 \text{ million}}{\$2.5 \text{ billion}} = 0.002$$

Wentz suggests that the remaining parameter b may be calculated and the specification of the Gompertz model completed by representing cumulative industry sales at maturity (we shall assume that 1985 represents maturity for bubble memories) by Y_t when $t = m - 1$, with m defined as the time required for the product to reach maturity. In this case $m = 8$ years.[20] Cumulative sales at maturity for Texas Instruments (Y_{m-1}) may be determined by multiplying its estimated market share at t_{m-1} by K. Texas Instruments expects to hold a dominant market share by that point (assume 40%), and given that K is estimated to be $2.5 billion in 1985 ($Y_{m-1}$ or Y_7), then Y_{m-1} or $Y_7 = \$1$ billion. By substitution and algebraic manipulation in equation (1), the value of parameter b may be obtained:

$$\text{Let } t = m - 1, \text{ then } Y_t = K\ a^{b^t} = Y_{m-1} = K\ a^{b^{m-1}}$$

By algebraic manipulation and logarithm transformation, then

$$b = \left[\frac{\log\ (Y_{m-1}/K)}{\log a}\right]^{1/m-1}$$

$$b = \left[\frac{\log \cdot 4}{\log \cdot 002}\right] \frac{1}{7}$$

$$b = 1.1336$$

---

[19]William E. Cox, Jr., "Product Portfolio Strategy: A Review of the Boston Consulting Group Approach to Marketing Strategy," in R. Curhan, Ed., *Marketing's Contributions to the Firm and to Society*. Chicago: American Marketing Association, 1975, pp. 465–470.
[20]Wentz, *op. cit.*, pp. 410–411.

PRODUCT ANALYSIS

Inserting the values for parameter K, a, and b in the equation, the product life cycle model for bubble memories produced by Texas Instruments is:

$$Y_t = (\$2.5 \text{ billion})(0.002)^{(1.1336)^t}$$

Values of t may be substituted in the model to develop sales estimates for any specific time period for Texas Instruments, and as new or better data become available, they may be used to respecify the model.

The product feasibility decision is a critical point in the Development phase of the product life cycle that requires a capacity to analyze the often profound effects of new products on the marketplace. Bubble memories, if successful, will be far more than a replacement for disk memories. While serving the same basic function, bubble memories will change these functions significantly as a result of their multiple advantages:[21]

1. *Size*—Bubble memories require 4-5% of the space needed by disks.
2. *Power usage*—Bubble memories use far less power.
3. *Speed*—Bubbles are 2-75 times as fast as disks.
4. *Nonvolatility*—Unlike disks, bubbles retain their stored data when power is cut off.
5. *Reliability*—Bubble memories have no moving parts and are thus far more reliable than disk memories.

The major potential disadvantages of bubble memories are price (now 10 times as high as disks) and slower speed than another new memory product, charge-coupled devices, which Texas Instruments introduced commercially simultaneously with bubble memories to compete with disk memories.

Zarecor has noted that optical scanners have failed to achieve their heralded impact on electronic data processing after more than 10 years.[22] He attributes their lack of promised success to superficial marketing research. This failed to indicate that for most users, optical scanning would be a more costly and complicated form of data entry than keypunching cards and entering data into computers with cards. Much of the higher costs of optical scanning come from "systems effects" of scanning: many scanners can only read certain type faces, thus requiring special typewriters and conversion of documents not prepared on special

---

[21]"The Bubble Memory Finally Arrives," *op. cit.*, p. 72.
[22]William D. Zarecor, "High-Technology Product Planning," *Harvard Business Review*, Vol. 53, January–February 1975, pp. 110–112.

typewriters; new forms and procedures are often required because scanners are limited to special paper sizes and line placements. The need to assess the "systems effects" of new products as well as both their impact on the functions they serve and on the behavior of those affected by the new product demands a keen understanding of market factors and influences. This understanding must be initially applied to support the product feasibility decision, but it must also be enhanced during the marketing research activities associated with each of the other decision points in the Development phase of the product life cycle. The complexity of the task has been illustrated by considering the probable impact of bubble memories on the marketplace. It seems clear that these new products will have significant systems effects, alter the functions they serve, and profoundly affect the behavior of everyone associated with computers and data memory systems.

Product Specification Decision

Following the decision that a new product idea appears feasible from both a demand and technical standpoint, marketing research studies should be undertaken to determine the product specifications. Zarecor suggests that specifications should be set in terms of minimum standards, recognizing that "Engineers are basically interested in exploiting the technology and, consequently, they overdesign."[23] The minimum standards should be established therefore, not by engineers, but on the basis of surveys of prospective buyers. Among the most important marketing research techniques useful in establishing product specifications are: (1) concept testing, (2) market structure analysis, (3) preference distribution analysis, and (4) product positioning studies.

Concept testing involves the assessment of prospective buyers with respect to new product ideas or concepts, prior to the availability of pilot samples or prototypes of the new product. Green and Tull have summarized the common characteristics of most concept testing procedures:[24]

1. A sample of potential buyers is presented with verbal or pictoral descriptions of the product—what its characteristics are, what functions it is designed to serve, its unique features compared to existing products. 'Control' concepts (describing existing, but unidentified, products) are often included as well.

---

[23]*Ibid.*, p. 114.
[24]Paul E. Green and Donald S. Tull, *Research for Marketing Decisions*, 3rd ed. Englewood Cliffs, N.J.: Prentice-Hall, 1975, p. 715.

PRODUCT ANALYSIS

2. Respondents are asked to rate each concept on various scales—degree of interest (attitudes), intentions to buy, etc.
3. Ratings may also be obtained on various prespecified attributes of the concept and respondents may be asked to list particular likes and dislikes about the concept, additional information that would be desirable to have about the concept, and so on.

Fred Gross, Manager of Marketing Research and Analysis for Xerox Corporation, provided some specific advice about concept testing for new industrial products:[25]

1. The concept statement should be expressed verbally and clarified with models, pictures, and so on.
2. Include optional equipment or accessories in the statement.
3. Price is part of the concept; test alternative concepts and prices in the same research project.
4. The most commonly used method is semistructured, informal personal interviews; group interviews may be used—customer interaction is valuable. Interviews are costly, difficult to quantify.
5. Obtain data on respondent's usage of product class, brands used, and attitudes toward them; future purchase plans.
6. Expose concept, obtain reactions without price. Then obtain customer likelihood of purchase when exposed to price; next expose accessories/options and determine their effect on sales of basic product. Obtain comparisons with available products.

Wind has proposed that concept testing should be considered as one part of an integrated procedure that includes market structure analysis, preference distribution analysis, and product positioning.[26] His presentation is detailed and persuasive, although limited to consumer goods examples. Our position agrees with that of Wind, and the independent treatment of the various techniques here should not obscure their principal roles as parts of an integrated procedure to support the product specification decision.

[25] Fred J. Gross, "Concept Testing and Screening—New Industrial Products." (Outline of paper delivered to the National Industrial Conference Board, New York, October 1969.)
[26] Yoram Wind, "A New Procedure for Concept Evaluation," *Journal of Marketing*, Vol. 37, October 1973, pp. 2–11.

MARKET STRUCTURE ANALYSIS

Market structure analysis seeks to describe the structure of various product-markets in terms of products, product attributes, and buyer/user preferences for products and product attributes.[27] Early market structure studies tended to focus on performance characteristics of competing products in specified markets, resulting in "performance space" maps. A market structure study of the market for numerically controlled milling machines examined 25 machine characteristics (divided into 60 variables) for 26 different machines produced by more than 10 firms.[28] The primary finding was that there was greater similarity between the machines of a given manufacturer than between competitors, so that each manufacturer catered to a different market segment in terms of performance space. Upon investigation it was found that this questionable marketing strategy resulted from the practice of each manufacturer producing one "frame," with machines in the product line varying only in terms of accessories. The frame determined the basic performance of the machines however, resulting in the surprising finding of the performance space map.

Those who scoff at industrial marketing research for its alleged lack of sophistication would do well to examine the market structure analyses conducted during the past decade by Green and his associates at the Wharton School. Many of these studies are focused on the computer market, drawing upon a data bank of 22 performance characteristics obtained for 102 computer models introduced between 1955 and 1968. A miniature data bank composed of 6 performance characteristics for 15 computer models has been drawn from the larger data bank and is shown in Figure 13-3. Green and Tull use the miniature data bank to illustrate the application of multivariate statistical techniques to market structure analysis, ranging from multiple regression to factor analysis, cluster analysis, and multidimensional scaling.[29] Although these applications cannot be reviewed here, they serve to demonstrate the feasibility of applying

---

[27] Market structure analysis appears to have originated with Volney Stefflre, "Market Structure Studies: New Products for Old Markets and New Markets (Foreign) for Old Products," in Bass, King, and Pessemier, Eds., *Applications of the Sciences in Marketing*. New York: Wiley, 1968, pp. 251–268; Green and his graduate students at the Wharton School were also pioneers in this area: Paul E. Green and Frank J. Carmone, "The Performance Structure of the Computer Market: A Multivariate Approach," *The Economic and Business Bulletin*, Vol. 21, Fall 1968, pp. 1–11.

[28] Richard D. Teach, Lester A. Neidell, and Robert E. Gibson, "Industrial Product Differentiation," in Fred C. Allvine, Ed., *Marketing in Motion*. Chicago: American Marketing Association, 1972, pp. 557–561.

[29] Green and Tull, *op. cit.*, Chap. 10, 14–16.

Computer number	Description	1	2	3	4	5	6
1	Philco 2000/210	−0.28	−0.36	−0.49	−0.52	−0.48	−0.27
2	Recomp II	3.51	3.61	−0.55	−0.60	−0.87	3.74
3	Honeywell 800	−0.39	−0.34	−0.55	−0.53	−0.59	−0.27
4	GE225	−0.06	−0.28	−0.55	−0.57	−0.83	−0.26
5	RPC 301/354, 355	0.38	−0.27	−0.46	−0.50	−0.88	−0.27
6	Burroughs B5500–B461	−0.43	−0.38	−0.55	−0.52	−0.48	−0.27
7	IBM 7040	−0.26	−0.37	−0.55	−0.52	−0.59	−0.27
8	Univac 1004–1	0.70	0.68	−0.60	−0.61	−0.92	−0.27
9	CDC 3400	−0.47	−0.39	−0.37	−0.52	−0.48	−0.27
10	RCA 3301/3303	−0.28	−0.23	−0.02	−0.14	−0.77	−0.27
11	GE 635	−0.49	−0.39	−0.13	0.16	1.71	−0.27
12	IBM 360/65	−0.50	−0.39	1.32	2.47	1.08	−0.27
13	Univac 1108	−0.51	−0.39	0.36	0.16	1.70	−0.27
14	IBM 360/75	−0.51	−0.39	3.26	2.47	1.08	−0.27
15	CDC 6800	−0.52	−0.12	−0.13	−0.23	1.33	−0.27

Characteristic number

Note: Each performance characteristic variable has been standardized to zero mean and unit standard deviation.

Key to Performance Characteristic Variables:
1—Execution time (a + b) in microseconds.
2—Execution time (a · b) in microseconds.
3—Minimum number of words in storage.
4—Maximum number of words in storage.
5—Maximum total storage.
6—Cycle time in microseconds.

Source: Paul E. Green and V. R. Rao, "A Note on Proximity Measures and Cluster Analysis," *Journal of Marketing Research*, Vol. 6, August 1969, p. 360.

Figure 13–3 Original data matrix for market structure analysis.

market structure analysis and multivariate statistical techniques to the analysis of industrial markets.

While the early market structure studies tended to emphasize the distribution of performance characteristics of competing brands and models within markets, preference distribution analysis was being developed independently to describe the distribution of preferences for products within specified markets.[30] Preference distribution studies seek to determine buyer preferences for various product characteristics by developing rating scales (based on ranking, paired comparison tests, or other procedures) for each significant characteristic. The distribution of buyers preferring various levels of the characteristic (as measured on the rating scale) can be estimated and compared against the positions of the available products on the rating scale. The primary focus of preference distribution analysis may be considered therefore to be the development of preference space maps.

The logical consequence of the development of separate space maps for product performance and personal preferences was the creation of joint space maps in which product perceptions and preferences are combined into one space map.[31] The analysis of joint space maps involves the use of multidimensional scaling techniques. A useful review of these techniques may be found in a recent article by Green.[32] Multidimensional scaling techniques are most useful in situations in which product perceptions and preferences are relatively well structured, product attributes are independent and well defined, and the product preferences are relatively clear. There are many situations in marketing however in which the relationships between product attributes and buyer preferences are relatively unstructured and ambiguous, especially when buyers must make trade-offs among product attributes. A recent study of the potential demand for electrically powered delivery vans in commercial fleet applications used conjoint measurement techniques (similar to multidimensional scaling) to analyze the trade-offs between the negative attributes (reduced technical capabilities and higher price) and the positive attributes (less pollution and lower operating costs) of electric delivery vans.[33] The principal finding

---

[30] Purnell H. Benson, "A Short Method for Estimating a Distribution of Consumer Preferences," *Journal of Applied Psychology*, Vol. 46, October 1962, pp. 307–313; Alfred A. Kuehn and Ralph L. Day, "Strategy of Product Quality," *Harvard Business Review*, Vol. 40, November–December 1962, pp. 100–110.

[31] Green and Tull, *op. cit.*, pp. 618–623.

[32] Paul E. Green, "Marketing Application of MDS: Assessment and Outlook," *Journal of Marketing*, Vol. 39, January 1975, pp. 24–31.

[33] George Hargreaves, John D. Claxton, and Frederick H. Siller, "New Product Evaluation: Electric Vehicles for Commercial Applications," *Journal of Marketing*, Vol. 40, January 1976, pp. 74–77.

PRODUCT ANALYSIS

was that the negative attributes outweighed the positive attributes and that electric delivery vans will be acceptable only after improvements in capability or lower prices take effect. This study is one of the first published applications of conjoint measurement techniques to industrial marketing, but the prevalence of situations requiring trade-offs among product attributes suggests that these techniques will find growing acceptance in industrial marketing research practice.

PRODUCT POSITIONING STUDIES

Product positioning studies have gained wide acceptance among consumer goods firms as a technique for determining the product specifications of primary interest to various market segments. Although there are very few published examples of industrial product positioning, the concept is equally applicable to industrial products and services. The technique is similar to the development of joint space maps in market structure analysis with a broader definition of product/company attributes than that of market structure studies. Green and Tull provide an example of a positioning study for a computer manufacturer that wanted to evaluate its position with respect to 15 attributes against 7 other firms.[34] It also wanted to know the relative importance of each attribute to selected key segments: customers, noncustomers, and its own sales personnel. The list of attributes and firms is shown in Figure 13-4. Each respondent in the study ranked the 8 firms on each attribute and classified the attributes (except overall preference) into 4 groups, based on their relative importance in choosing a computer supplier. The most important finding of the study was that the sponsoring firm "... tended to be rated highly on the *less important* attributes underlying supplier choice."[35] This appeared to result from the sales personnel's emphasis on these attributes as well as their failure to emphasize the strengths of the firm with more sophisticated computer users. By using the findings of the study to redirect its strategy, it could more effectively position itself in the computer market.

Based on the data obtained through concept testing, market structure analysis, and product position studies, optimum product characteristics may be determined and the product specification decision executed. Assuming that the decision is to proceed with development, the next milestone is the product testing decision.

---

[34] Green and Tull, *op. cit.*, pp. 690–696.
[35] *Ibid.*, p. 695.

ATTRIBUTES

1. Favorableness of performance/cost ratio
2. Provision for utilizing a large number of programming languages
3. Reliability of hardware
4. Extensiveness of software packages
5. Ease of change-over from other systems
6. Quality of education/training
7. Quality of technical back-up services
8. Quality of sales presentations
9. Most effective use of virtual memory
10. High acceptance by systems personnel
11. Innovativeness
12. Thoroughness and speed of service after the sale
13. Flexibility regarding price negotiation
14. Suitability for time sharing
15. Your over-all preference

FIRMS

1. Burroughs
2. Control Data Corporation (CDC)
3. Honeywell
4. International Business Machines (IBM)
5. National Cash register (NCR)
6. Radio Corporation of America (RCA)
7. Univac
8. Xerox (XDS)

Source: Paul E. Green and Donald S. Tull, *Research for Marketing Decisions*, 3rd ed. Englewood Cliffs, N.J.: Prentice-Hall, 1975, p. 691.

Figure 13–4 Attributes and firms in computer supplier positioning study.

Product Testing Decision

Product tests for industrial goods are basically use tests in which pilot samples of materials or prototypes of equipment, components, and supplies, are placed in service with potential buyers. These tests are conducted in close cooperation with representative potential buyers in each market segment and are primarily designed to measure performance under varying conditions of use. In most cases the new product to be tested is a modification of an existing product in the firm's line with one or more new characteristics or features. Since the new characteristics may have been suggested by or developed in cooperating with present customers of the firm, the customers involved are usually selected for product testing as well as other customers and noncustomers. There is little or no use of product comparison testing for industrial products in contrast to the common practice for consumer goods, but marketing research personnel should be responsible for administering product tests. Wherever possible the new product should be tested in direct comparison with existing products in comparable use situations and evaluations prepared on:

1. Overall customer reaction to the new product
2. Specific advantages and disadvantages of the new product in terms of measured performance as compared to existing products
3. Estimated value of the new product to customers

Product testing may go through a series of iterations as new products are modified in response to findings of the product tests. If and when a satisfactory product emerges, the final product testing decision must be made: should the new product be subjected to market testing? The results of the product tests should be evaluated in the context of *updated* minimum demand studies that assess current expected revenues and profits. Adler has shown that the time lag in new product development is often very long with the time for the Development phase of seven industrial products ranging from 20 months to 15 years.[36] Given the extended time frame for the development of most new products, it is important to periodically update the minimum demand studies of markets and market segments so that they reflect current conditions.

Market Testing Decision

Although the use of market testing is standard procedure in the development of many consumer goods, it is relatively rare for industrial goods. The primary reason appears to be that "creeping commitment" is such a powerful influence in the development of new industrial products that there is extreme reluctance to truncate the process once the new product survives the product testing decision. The nature of the product test for industrial products often requires such a high degree of cooperation from prospective buyers that a market test is in fact conducted simultaneously with the product test. Once the new product emerges from a successful

---

[36] Lee Adler, "Time Lag in New Product Development," *Journal of Marketing*, Vol. 30, January 1966, pp. 17–21.

product test, it is implicitly assumed by both seller and buyer that the product will be produced.

Market tests are usually designed to offer new products to a limited part of the market for a limited time for the purpose of (1) deciding whether to offer the new product to the entire market and (2) determining the appropriate "marketing mix" for the new product. For industrial products market testing may take the form of offering the new product initially only to the firms participating in product testing, or only to those market segments that appear to offer the greatest opportunity for the new product. Ideally the market testing should last long enough to permit the assessment of repeat purchasing behavior, but for many industrial products this is impractical. The decision to offer the new product to other customers and segments must usually be made on the basis of careful analysis of the response of relatively few firms to the initial offering. Unless there are significant surprises and problems associated with the early response to the new product, market testing for industrial products is concerned primarily with the development of the optimum marketing mix. Among the most important questions in the development of the marketing mix are:

1. Price
2. The selection of advertising appeals and media
3. Level and frequency of sales call activity
4. Need for education and training of customer personnel
5. Installation and service requirements
6. Outright sale versus lease and terms of sale
7. Channels of distribution—direct sales versus use of intermediaries

If the initial customers and market segments for a new industrial product are utilized as settings for the market testing of various price, promotion, and distribution strategies, effective market testing may be accomplished within the context of a program of gradual roll-out of the new product. It may not be possible to conduct the market tests with the scientific rigor associated with consumer goods testing, but important insights may be gained by exploring different marketing mixes for industrial goods.

Perhaps the most important output of the marketing research studies undertaken to support the market testing decision is contained in the response functions that may be generated by considering different marketing mixes. The impact of changes in marketing variables on revenue and profits, as shown by the response functions, may be used to improve the economic and financial analysis of proposed new products. The importance of conducting minimum demand studies and updating them regularly has been discussed, but the market testing decision requires that the data from these studies be placed in the context of a comprehensive demand study along with data gained from studies supporting the product specification and testing decisions. Since a positive market testing decision may involve the allocation of significant investments in new plant and equipment to provide the required capacity to serve the total markets for new products, it is important to have the best possible marketing information available as a basis for decision. Two analytical models have been proposed to aid in this decision process for industrial goods and each model has been empirically validated.

Urban has developed a mathematical model for evaluating new products that is composed of four submodels dealing with demand, cost, profit, and uncertainty.[37] The demand submodel uses the best available estimates of the industry life cycle, the firm's market share, and various response functions (price, advertising, distribution) for the new product. Given the quantity demanded for the new product, the cost submodel provides the minimum cost of production. The profit submodel combines the demand and cost models to determine the differential profit associated with adding the new product to the firm's line. Differential profits for each year over the firm's planning horizon are discounted at the firm's rate of return and summed to give the total differential profit for the new product. The uncertainty associated with the new product is modeled on the basis of the variances of the old product line profits (with the new product) together with the covariance of the old and new line profits.

A case study that applied the new product model to a proposed new plastic product revealed that the firm's Board of Directors had conditionally approved the product on the basis of a preliminary estimate of sales and profits. On the basis of a $8 million investment, the new product considered independently of other products in the line (the usual approach in such studies) showed $18.5 million of undiscounted profits and $8.35 million of discounted cash flow profits. Assuming certainty in the estimates and no interdependencies with other products, the decision would be to introduce the new product (a "GO" decision) since the target rate of return (15%) would have been achieved. Interdependencies with other products reduced the total discounted profit to $6 million however. This would have required a "NO" decision became a failure to achieve the

---

[37] Glen L. Urban, "A New Product Analysis and Decision Model," *Management Science*, Vol. 14, April 1968, pp. 490–517. Also the critique by Benjamin Lipstein in the same issue, pp. 518–519.

target rate of return. By exploring various marketing mixes however, it was found that lower prices for the new product could produce higher profits, as could increasing the size of the sales force. These findings persuaded the firm to make an "ON" decision to study the new product situation further, particularly with respect to the feasibility of a lower price, higher capacity approach.

Root extended the new product simulation model for analyzing the financial impact of new products developed by Pessemier[38] and applied the model to the financial analysis of new industrial products in six large firms.[39] The basic thrust of Root's study was to determine if the formal development of subjective probability estimates (SPE's) of expected sales, costs, investments, and profits from several people in a firm could improve the new product decision process. His findings were that the model served to identify the many assumptions in the input data that had not been made explicit previously, and it allowed the analysis to be structured so that it could produce more choices and make better use of available information.

The presumed need for strict and explicit critieria for new product decisions has led to greater advocacy for the use of economic and financial models as an aid to decision making. It was reported for example that Gould, Inc. specified for its new energy systems that,

> ... development to market introduction can take no longer than three to five years, the total market for the product must run $50 million and be growing at least 15% per year, the product must be capable of producing a pretax return of 30% on sales and 40% on investment, and it must establish Gould as either a technical or market leader in the product's field.[40]

The Gould criteria and the Urban and Root models all invoke capital budgeting and return on investment concepts as a primary basis for new product decision. It might be presumed therefore that industrial firms would use these concepts as a basis for new products decision making. Studies have shown that managers and executives are aware of the concepts and may use them, but they tend to rely primarily on managerial

---

[38]Pessemier, *New Product Decisions: An Analytical Approach*, op. cit., pp. 146–162.
[39]H. Paul Root, "The Use of Subjective Probability Estimates in the Analysis of New Products," in P. R. McDonald, Ed., *Marketing Involvement in Society and the Economy*. Chicago: American Marketing Association, 1970, pp. 200–207.
[40]*Business Week*, "The Breakdown of U.S. Innovation," February 16, 1976, p. 60.

PRODUCT ANALYSIS

judgment as a basis for decision making.[41] The basic reason for this situation is that managers and executives recognize the problems associated with the estimation of the cost of capital, future demand and prices, and the many problems associated with decision theory analysis. Such models are viewed therefore as aids to new product decisions and not as substitutes for decision. They provide useful inputs but are only part of the complex decision process that determines whether a new product should be introduced to the market.

THE MARKET PHASE OF THE PRODUCT LIFE CYCLE

At the beginning of this chapter, the Market phase of the product life cycle was said to begin with the first shipment of the finished product to the market place and end with the withdrawal of the product from the market. If we assume that the products placed with customers and prospects in connection with the product and market testing decisions in the Development phase were either prototypes or pilot samples, then the finished products shipped in the Market phase refer to the first output of the full-scale production facilities for the new product. We have also noted that the Market phase of the product life cycle encompasses the familiar life cycle of a product with its four stages: introduction, growth, maturity, and decline. Within these four stages of the product life cycle there are three major decisions which should be supported by marketing research studies. The first decision occurs in the Introduction stage.

Commercial Evaluation Decision

Following the first shipment of the new product, the firm must evaluate the commercial success of the product by measuring the initial acceptance of the product. The commercial evaluation decision determines whether the new industrial product will be actively supported and added to the firm's product line, added to the line but modestly supported, studied carefully for possible abandonment, or discontinued from the product line. This decision should be made on the basis of expected and actual market response to the new product, drawn from marketing research studies on the adoption and diffusion of new industrial products. A large

---

[41] Bela Gold, "The Shaky Foundations of Capital Budgeting," *California Management Review*, Vol. 19, Winter 1976, pp. 51–60; Herbert E. Kierulff, "Return on Investment and the Fatal Flaw," *California Management Review*, Vol. 19, Winter 1976, pp. 61–70.

and growing body of research is available on adoption and diffusion processes in industrial markets and should serve as the framework within which marketing research and subsequent decisions may be conducted.

Ozanne and Churchill have defined the industrial adoption process as

> ... that set of activities and decisions through which decision makers in an individual firm move from awareness of the industrial innovation to its final adoption or rejection.[42]

This definition is developed around the traditional five stage model of the adoption process developed by rural sociologists:[43]

1. *Awareness*—Decision-makers in the prospect firm are exposed to the innovation (new industrial product) for the first time.
2. *Interest*—Decision-makers seek more information about the innovation.
3. *Evaluation*—Decision-making group in the firm assess the benefits and costs of the innovation.
4. *Trial*—New industrial product (innovation) is purchased on a limited basis to test its value in use.
5. *Adoption*—Firm decides to continue the full use of the new industrial product (innovation).

Published studies on the industrial adoption process include: Ozanne and Churchill (machine tools);[44] Webster (various industrial manufacturers);[45] Ness (building materials, design forms, and construction techniques among architects);[46] Martilla (paper converters);[47] Baker (shoe

---

[42] Urban B. Ozanne and Gilbert A. Churchill, "Adoption Research: Information Sources in the Industrial Purchasing Decision," in R. L. King, Ed., *Marketing and the New Science of Planning*. Chicago: American Marketing Association, 1968, p. 352.
[43] *Ibid.*, p. 354.
[44] *Ibid.*, pp. 352–359.
[45] Frederick E. Webster, Jr., "New Product Adoption in Industrial Markets: A Framework for Analysis," *Journal of Marketing*, Vol. 33, July 1969, pp. 35–39.
[46] Thomas E. Ness, "Innovation in the Building Industry: The Architectural Innovator," in P. R. McDonald, Ed., *Marketing Involvement in Society and the Economy*. Chicago: American Marketing Association, 1969, pp. 353–356.
[47] John A. Martilla, "Word-of-Mouth Communication in the Industrial Adoption Process," *Journal of Marketing Research*, Vol. 8, May 1971, pp. 173–178.

manufacturing machines and numerically controlled machine tools);[48] Peters and Venkatesan (small computers);[49] and Czepiel (continuous casting process in the steel industry).[50]

Although understanding of the industrial adoption process may improve the quality of the commercial evaluation decision and provide vital input into marketing mix decisions, the new industrial diffusion process concept is far more important in terms of supporting the commercial evaluation decision.

The diffusion process has been variously compared to a learning process and a contagion process (from epidemiology) in that it seeks to describe the adoption of an innovation by a population over time. Rogers has proposed a general model of the diffusion process in which there are five categories of adopters, based on their relative time of adoption, displaying a frequency distribution approximating a normal curve and an S-shaped cumulative frequency distribution.[51]

The five categories are:

1. *Innovators*—the first 2.5% of all adopters.
2. *Early adopters*—the next 13.5% of all adopters.
3. *Early majority*—the next 34%.
4. *Late majority*—the next 34%.
5. *Laggards*—the final 16% of all adopters.

There are some empirical studies on the diffusion of industrial innovations, including studies by Brown (machine tools);[52] Enos (petroleum refining);[53] Sutherland (cotton spinning);[54] Mansfield (bituminous coal,

---

[48] Michael J. Baker, "The Adoption of Industrial Products," Working Paper no. P-64, Cambridge, Mass.: Marketing Science Institute, 1971.

[49] Michael P. Peters and M. Venkatesan, "Exploration of Variables Inherent in Adopting an Industrial Product," *Journal of Marketing Research*, Vol. 10, August 1973, pp. 312-315.

[50] John A. Czepiel, "Decision Group and Firm Characteristics in an Industrial Adoption Decision," in K. L. Bernhardt, Ed., *Marketing: 1776-1976 and Beyond*. Chicago: American Marketing Association, 1976, pp. 340-343.

[51] Everett M. Rogers, *Diffusion of Innovations*. New York: Free Press, 1962, p. 162.

[52] William H. Brown, "Innovation in the Machine Tool Industry," *Quarterly Journal of Economics*, Vol. 71, August 1957, pp. 406-425.

[53] John L. Enos, "A Measure of Rate of Technological Progress in the Petroleum Refining Industry," *Journal of Industrial Economics*, Vol. 6, June 1958, pp. 180-197.

[54] Alister Sutherland, "The Diffusion of an Innovation in Cotton Spinning," *Journal of Industrial Economics*, Vol. 7, March 1959, pp. 118-135.

iron and steel, brewing, and railroad industries);[55] Bernhardt (petroleum refining);[56] Gold, Peirce, and Rosegger (iron and steel);[57] and Czepiel (steel industry).[58]

There are numerous methodological and analytical problems associated with measuring the rate and effect of the diffusuion of industrial products. Bernhardt and Mackenzie illustrate a number of these problems[59] as does Gold.[60] Despite these difficulties analysis of the diffusion of new industrial products is useful in providing a better basis for commercial evaluation decisions.

Several models that have been developed and applied to new industrial products and processes may be used to determine the expected rate of diffusion of the new product (process) and thereby provide a benchmark against which initial purchases of the new product may be compared for purposes of deciding whether to add it to the product line or discontinue it. Bass has developed a new product growth model designed to measure the sales (S) of a new product at time (T), distinguishing between sales to innovators (category 1 in Rogers' model) and sales to "imitators" (categories 2–5 in Rogers' model).[61] The influence of sales to these two groups is captured by the parameters p and q, the coefficients of innovation and imitation respectively. The parameter m estimates the number of initial purchases (repeat purchases are not measured) of the new product over the life cycle. These parameters are incorporated into a model in which time is the only variable:

$$S(T) = (m\,(p+q)^2/p)\,\frac{e^{-(p+q)T}}{(1+(q/p)\,e^{-(p+q)T})^2}$$

[55] Edwin Mansfield, *Industrial Research and Technological Innovation*, New York: Norton, 1968, Chap. 7.
[56] Irwin Bernhardt, "Diffusion of Catalytic Techniques through a Population of Medium-Size Petroleum Refining Firms," *Journal of Industrial Economics*, Vol. 19, November 1970, pp. 50–65.
[57] Bela Gold, William S. Peirce, and Gerhard Rosegger, "Diffusion of Major Technological Innovations in U.S. Iron and Steel Manufacturing," *Journal of Industrial Economics*, Vol. 19, July 1970, pp. 218–241.
[58] John A. Czepiel, "Word-of-Mouth Processes in the Diffusion of a Major Technological Innovation," *Journal of Marketing Research*, Vol. 11, May 1974, pp. 172–180.
[59] Irwin Bernhardt and Kenneth Mackenzie, "Some Problems in Using Diffusion Models for New Products," *Management Science*, Vol. 19, October 1972, pp. 187–200.
[60] Bela Gold, "Tracing Gaps Between Expectations and Results of Technological Innovations: The Case of Iron and Steel," *Journal of Industrial Economics*, Vol. 25, September 1976, pp. 1–28.
[61] Frank M. Bass, "A New Product Growth Model for Consumer Durables," *Management Science*, Vol. 15, January 1969, pp. 215–227.

By differentiating S, the maximum value and predicted time of maximum $S(T)$ may be obtained. Bass tested the model by developing regression estimates of the parameters from annual time series data for 11 consumer durables. Nevers applied the Bass model to a variety of other market data, including 3 time series for industrial products and processes.[62] Two of the series dealt with textile bleaching processes introduced by Dupont while the third dealt with Shell Chemical's innovation of 70% hydrogen peroxide deliveries. The Bass model has shown an impressive capacity to model actual sales on an *ex post* basis for a variety of industries and products, and it appears that it should be possible to estimate the parameters p, q, and m from other marketing research data. The parameter m may be estimated from studies of market potential, while p and q might be estimated from studies of adoption behavior among innovators and imitators for previous new products.

Nevers has pointed out that the Bass model closely resembles an early growth model introduced by Mansfield to predict diffusion rates of industrial innovations.[63] The two models produce similar results when the ratio q/p exceeds 10, which appears to be the case for almost all of the applications reported to date. The Bass model however has the advantage of being expressed in terms of product sales in contrast to Mansfield's use of the number of adopting firms as the dependent variable. It appears that the Bass model could provide a useful framework for making commercial evaluation decisions for new industrial products in the Introduction stage of the product life cycle.

Product Audit Decisions

Assuming that the new product has been retained in the product line as the result of a positive commercial evaluation decision, there is a need to conduct product audits periodically during the Growth and Maturity stages of the market phase of the product life cycle. These product audits should result in a series of decisions to retain or discontinue the product. If the Bass model is used to support the commercial evaluation decision, it also may be of some value in making product audit decisions, but its restriction to initial sales (adoptions) limits its usefulness as repeat sales account for higher proportions of total sales of the new product.

Product audits require an assessment of the firm's objectives, goals,

---

[62] John V. Nevers, "Extensions of a New Product Growth Model," *Sloan Management Review*, Vol. 13, Winter 1972, pp. 77–91.
[63] Edwin Mansfield, "Technological Change and the Rate of Imitation," *Econometrics*, Vol. 29, October 1961, pp. 741–766.

and strategies for the new product; evaluation of the product's contributions as measured by gross margins, contribution to profits, and return on investment; and changes in competitive behavior and market postion over the life cycle.[64] Marketing research information of course provides the basis for such product audits as well as for the subsequent development of strategies designed to stretch the maturity stage of the product life cycle. A number of studies of the product life cycle have focused on the importance of strategy development over the life cycle of a product: Patton,[65] Levitt,[66] Kotler,[67] and Cox[68] all contain material and examples applicable to industrial products.

A detailed case study of the use of a product audit within the context of product life cycle analysis is provided by Cunningham and Hammouda.[69] Their study examined an engineering company with four main product groups, comprising products for the measurement of gaseous fluids, water, industrial liquids, and telecommunication systems. The case outlines the development of a product plan; reviews the procedures and outcomes of a product line analysis for power distribution instruments; discusses the development of product objectives, policies, and strategy; and appraises the effects of product planning on the performance of the firm. The use of marketing research data in the product audit is well illustrated throughout the case study.

A demonstration of the feasibility of determining product life cycles for industrial products and developing appropriate marketing strategies therein was provided in a doctoral dissertation by de Kluyver.[70] This study of steering gears for heavy-duty trucks and farm equipment showed that a strategy of identifying "progressive" customer firms and concentrating efforts on securing adoption of the new products by these firms resulted in a rapid movement of the product into the growth and maturity stages of the life cycle, which in turn provided a higher present value of

[64] Donald K. Clifford, Jr., "Leverage in the Product Life Cycle," *Dun's Review*, May 1965, pp. 62–70.
[65] Arch Patton, "Stretch Your Product's Earning Years: Top Management's Stake in the Product Life Cycle," *The Management Review*, Vol. 18, June 1959, pp. 9–14, 67–71, 76–79.
[66] Theodore Levitt, "Exploit the Product Life Cycle," *Harvard Business Review*, Vol. 43, November–December 1965, pp. 81–94.
[67] Philip Kotler, "Competitive Strategies for New Product Marketing over the Life Cycle," *Management Science*, Vol. 12, December 1965, pp. B104–B119.
[68] William E. Cox, Jr., "Product Life Cycles as Marketing Models," *op. cit.* pp. 375–384.
[69] M. T. Cunningham and M. A. A. Hammouda, "Product Strategy for Industrial Goods," *Journal of Management Studies*, Vol. 6, May 1969, pp. 223–242.
[70] Cornelis A. de Kluyver, "Innovation and Industrial Product Life Cycles: A Heuristic Classification Study" (Ph.D. diss., Case Western Reserve University, 1975).

PRODUCT ANALYSIS

the contribution stream for the new product and a lower sensitivity to the discount factor employed. It was also found by de Kluyver that the first generation products of a new steering gear design (such as the link valve and power cylinder type) tend to be perceived as highly innovative and display a distinct life cycle form (Type 1, innovative maturity form), while successive generations of improved or modified products of the same type take on different life cycle forms (Type 2, growth maturity; or Type 3, decline maturity).

Mansfield has also formulated a simple mathematical model to describe the *rate* of diffusion among firms in an industry adopting new industrial products and processes.[71] The model is based on four hypotheses:

1. Increases in the number of firms in an industry adopting an innovation leads to higher probabilities of its adoption by non-users.
2. The expected profitability of an innovation is directly related to its probability of adoption.
3. For equally profitable innovations, innovations requiring relatively large investments will have lower probabilities of adoption.
4. The industry in which the innovation is introduced will affect the probability of adoption.

The resulting model is:

$$\beta = a + bp + cS$$

where

β = a measure of the rate of diffusion of the innovation
a = Y-intercept of the equation, which varies among industries
b, c = regression coefficients
p = profitability of the innovation, measured by the average payout period to justify investments divided by average payout period for investment in the innovation
S = average initial investment in the innovation divided by the average total assets for the period

Mansfield applied this model to data on 12 innovations in 4 industries (bituminous coal, iron and steel, brewing, and railroads) resulting in the following equation:

[71] Edwin Mansfield, *Technological Change*. New York: Norton, pp. 88–92.

$$\beta = \begin{Bmatrix} -0.57 \\ -0.52 \\ -0.29 \\ -0.59 \end{Bmatrix} + 0.53\ P - 0.027\ S$$

This model appeared to explain almost all of the observed variation in the rate of diffusion of the 12 innovations among firms in the 4 industries. The model does not deal with intrafirm rates of diffusion however and this requires a separate study. In a study of the diffusion of diesel locomotives in 30 railroads, Mansfield used an econometric study to explain about two-thirds of the diffusion rate of dieselization among railroads.[72] The primary explanatory variables were:

1. Profit expectation of the investment in diesel locomotives
2. The date when a firm began to dieselize
3. Size of the firm
4. The age distribution of its steam locomotives
5. A firm's intitial liquidity

These models of the rate of diffusion of industrial products and processes, as well as product life cycle models, provide a valuable analytical foundation for the product audit decisions that must be made in the growth and maturity stages of the Market phase of the product life cycle. Although additional work is needed to refine these models, it has been demonstrated that they are already valid and useful tools for industrial marketing research.

Product Elimination Decision

As products reach the decline stage of the product life cycle, it is important to note that by definition these products are commercially dead. Their sales have dropped to a fraction (say 10–20%) of the earlier maximum sales level, yet the products are still part of the product line and available to the market. Such products are not necessarily the oldest or least profitable items in the product line either; Sevin cites the case of a firm with some 300 products in its line: 6 products accounted for 58% of the sales volume and 86% of the net operating profit contribution, yet all were old products ranging in age from 10 to 25 years in the product line.[73]

---

[72]*Ibid.*, p. 95–97.
[73]Charles H. Sevin, *Marketing Productivity Analysis*. New York: McGraw-Hill, 1965, pp. 55–57.

PRODUCT ANALYSIS

Although 3 of the 6 products each accounted for more than 10% of the total sales volume of the firm and were thus probably still in the maturity stage of the life cycle, 2 of the remaining products had smaller sales volumes (3% or less of the total), yet produced proportionately high profits.

Despite the continual flow of new products in the economy, many firms seem reluctant to drop products from the product line. Under such conditions product proliferation reigns and management problems abound; Kotler has observed that ". . . as products and product lines increase numerically, the range of management problems seems to grow geometrically."[74] The 80-20 principle applies with perhaps 80% of the sales and profits accounted for by 20% of the products in the line, or an even higher concentration as illustrated in the cited Sevin example. Under these conditions inventory costs grow, small order problems become severe, short production runs drive up manufacturing costs, executive time becomes dispersed across the product line, and excess capital is tied up with many of the costs being hidden.[75] Although it might be argued that products should be reviewed for elimination prior to reaching the decline stage, the attainment of commercial death appears to be a logical benchmark at which to initiate a system of product review. Experience with the system may indicate the need for an earlier review as well as when the review should be scheduled. Alexander has suggested that five other indicators may be used to select products for review and possible elimination:

1. Declining price trend
2. Declining profit trend
3. Availability of substitute products
4. Loss in product effectiveness
5. Rapid increase in executive time required to solve problems[76]

Kotler has suggested that the product elimination decision may be cast in the framework of a weak-product review system.[77] An outline of this system is shown in Figure 13-5. In Step 1, the product review committee should be composed of representatives from manufacturing, marketing,

---

[74] Philip Kotler, "Phasing Out Weak Products," *Harvard Business Review*, Vol. 43, March-April 1965, p. 107.
[75] Ralph S. Alexander, "The Death and Burial of Sick Products," *Journal of Marketing*, Vol. 28, April 1964, p. 1.
[76] *Ibid.*, p. 2.
[77] Kotler, *op. cit*, p. 111.

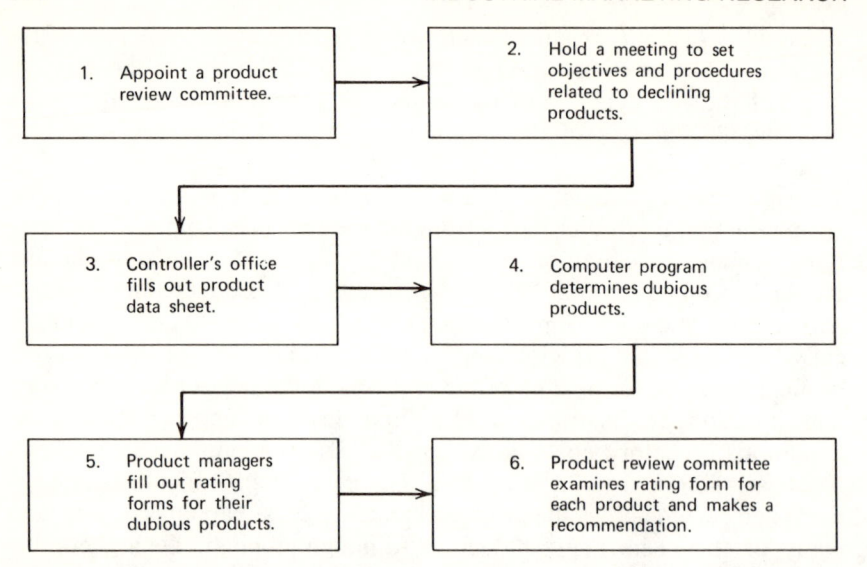

```
┌─────────────────────────┐      ┌─────────────────────────────┐
│ 1. Appoint a product    │─────▶│ 2. Hold a meeting to set    │
│    review committee.    │      │    objectives and procedures│
│                         │      │    related to declining     │
│                         │      │    products.                │
└─────────────────────────┘      └─────────────────────────────┘
                                              │
              ┌───────────────────────────────┘
              ▼
┌─────────────────────────┐      ┌─────────────────────────────┐
│ 3. Controller's office  │─────▶│ 4. Computer program         │
│    fills out product    │      │    determines dubious       │
│    data sheet.          │      │    products.                │
└─────────────────────────┘      └─────────────────────────────┘
                                              │
              ┌───────────────────────────────┘
              ▼
┌─────────────────────────┐      ┌─────────────────────────────┐
│ 5. Product managers     │─────▶│ 6. Product review committee │
│    fill out rating      │      │    examines rating form for │
│    forms for their      │      │    each product and makes a │
│    dubious products.    │      │    recommendation.          │
└─────────────────────────┘      └─────────────────────────────┘
```

Figure 13–5 A review system for weak products. Source: Philip Kotler, Marketing Management, *3rd ed. Englewood Cliffs, N.J.: Prentice-Hall, 1976, p. 243. (Adapted by Kotler from his "Phasing Out Weak Products,"* Harvard Business Review, *Vol. 43, March–April 1965, pp. 107–118).*

and controller functions in the firm; in Step 2, the committee should establish criteria for the review of weak products, as well as determine the objectives and procedures for conducting the review. In Step 3, the controller provides data on product sales (industry and firm), prices, and costs over the life cycle. A computer program is prepared in Step 4 to apply the selected criteria to the weak products and thereby identify candidates for further review. Kotler has suggested such criteria as:

1. Number of years of sales decline
2. Market-share trends
3. Gross profit margin
4. Return on investment[78]

Alexander reports that a manufacturer of electric motors used five criteria:

1. Profitability
2. Position on growth curve

[78]*Ibid.*, p. 114.

PRODUCT ANALYSIS

3. Product leadership
4. Market position
5. Marketing dependence of other products[79]

In step 5 of Kotler's system, the very weak product candidates identified in Step 4 are brought to the attention of the product (market) manager responsible for the product. The product manager completes a rating form that indicates the expected sales and profit trend for the product if no changes in marketing strategy are adopted, as well as any recommended changes in strategy. In Step 6, the product review committee evaluates the rating form prepared in Step 5 and recommends that: (1) the product be retained with no changes in strategy, (2) the product be retained with specified strategy changes, or (3) that the product be eliminated. If the recommendation is to eliminate the product, the decision is usually made by the chief marketing executive of the firm. This decision must take into account a number of ramifications of the decision. Alexander has identified four key considerations:

1. Timing, with the elimination of the old product managed to coincide with the transfer of resources to new products where possible.
2. Parts and replacement, requiring forecasts of the need for repair parts and replacement items.
3. Inventory liquidation.
4. Holdover demand, which may lead to a decision to sell the product to another firm in order to assure customers of a continuing source of supply.[80]

The weak-product review system advocated by Kotler required marketing research data as input to the process, particularly for the criteria used to screen the weakest products from among those reaching commercial death.

SUMMARY

Up to Chapter 12 we have focused primarily on marketing research activities that are directed toward the choice of market. Chapter 13 has focused on the role of industrial marketing in improving product decisions during both the Development phase and the Market phase.

[79] Alexander, *op. cit.*, p. 6.
[80] *Ibid.*, p. 6–7.

The Development phase involves Product Feasibility, Product Specification, Product Testing, and Market Testing decisions. Booth, Allen and Hamilton estimated that the chance of an idea being translated into a successful product is about 1 in 40 and that 50% of the ideas being considered at each stage of the new product development process are rejected with the evaluation becoming more expensive at each succeeding stage.

In reviewing 567 industrial innovations introduced by 121 firms in 5 industries, Myers and Marquis concluded that about three-fourths of the innovations could be classed as responding to demand recognition rather than outright technological innovation. Unfortunately research activity in the Development phase tends to be little, nonexistent, or late in the process. Part of the problem is the excessive time that research studies tend to take. A response to this problem was a movement to rating devices. However in the face of higher new-product risks and the continued high new-product failure rates, there has been a return to market demand studies, particularly minimum demand studies coupled with product growth curves.

Following Product Feasibility testing come Product Specification tests. Wind has proposed that product concept testing become closely integrated with market structure analysis, preference distribution analysis, and product positioning studies. In this regard nonmetric multidimensional scaling has shown much promise. By combining product performance and preference analysis into a common space or utilizing conjoint analysis, it becomes possible for the researcher to segment a product market at once and find the determinant characteristics involved in product choice, thereby gaining important insights for product positioning strategy.

Product Testing is the third stage of the Development Phase. It focuses on overall customer reaction to the product, perception of specific advantages and disadvantages compared to performance characteristics of existing products and the estimated value of the new product to customers.

After successive product improvements, a decision is made whether or not to continue testing. The final stage of the Development phase is Market Testing, an activity that is relatively rare for industrial goods. A primary reason for the paucity of testing is a "creeping commitment" to the new-product idea. However models by Urban and Pessemier have been successfully applied in several industrial marketing situations. There has also been a growing emphasis on the application of economic and financial decisions. However all formal tests are viewed as inputs to the decision process rather than as the sole decision-making criteria.

The Market phase begins with the first shipment of the product. In early stages of the product life cycle the objective is to determine whether the product should be actively or moderately supported or discontinued. Diffusion models, particularly that of Bass, have had an impressive capacity to model actual sales of a variety of new products.

If a new product remains in the product line, there will be a need to conduct periodic audits as it reaches the Growth and Maturity stages of the product life cycle. Marketing research information provides the basis for such product audits. As for product elimination decisions, it appears that the problem is that unproductive products are allowed to linger too long. Alexander offers criteria for identifying candidates for elimination and candidates for more intensive evaluation as well as criteria for evaluating the consequences of product elimination. Kotler has suggested a weak-product review system that is conducted by representatives of the manufacturing, marketing, and controller functions as well as product managers for the products involved. Marketing research provides key inputs into the weak-product elimination decision process.

SUGGESTED READINGS

Adler, Lee, "Time Lag in New Product Development," *Journal of Marketing*, Vol. 30, January 1966, pp. 17–21.

Alexander, Ralph S., "The Death and Burial of Sick Products," *Journal of Marketing*, Vol. 28, April 1964.

Baker, Michael J., "The Adoption of Industrial Products," Working Paper no. P–64. Cambridge, Mass.: Marketing Science Institute, 1971.

Baker, N. R., J. Siegman, and A. H. Rubenstein, "The Effects of Perceived Needs and Means on the Generation of Ideas for Industrial Research and Development Projects." *IEEE Transactions on Engineering Management*, Vol. 14, 1967, pp. 156–163.

Bass, Frank M., "A New Product Growth Model for Consumer Durables," *Management Science*, Vol. 15, January 1969, pp. 215–227.

Benson, Purnell N., "A Short Method for Estimating a Distribution of Consumer Preferences," *Journal of Applied Psychology*, Vol. 46, October 1962, pp. 307–313.

Bernhardt, Irwin, "Diffusion of Catalytic Techniques through a Population of Medium-Size Petroleum Refining Firms," *Journal of Industrial Economics*, Vol. 19, November 1970, pp. 50–65.

Bernhardt, Irwin, and Kenneth Makenzie, "Some Problems in Using Diffusion Models for New Products," *Management Science*, Vol. 19, October 1972, pp. 187–200.

Management of New Products. New York: Booz, Allen and Hamilton, 1968.

Business Week, "The Breakdown of U.S. Innovation," February 16, 1976, p. 60.

Business Week, "The Bubble Memory Finally Arrives," March 28, 1977, pp. 72, 74.

Business Week, "New Products: The Push Is on Marketing," March 4, 1972, p. 72.

Brown, William H., "Innovation in the Machine Tool Industry," *Quarterly Journal of Economics*, Vol. 71, August 1957, pp. 406–425.

Carter C. F., and B. R. Williams, *Industry and Technical Progress: Factors Governing and Speed of Application of Science*. London: Oxford University Press, 1957.

Clifford, Donald K., Jr., "Leverage in the Product Life Cycle," *Dun's Review*, May 1965, pp. 62–70.

Cox, William E., Jr., "Product Life Cycles as Marketing Models," *Journal of Business*, Vol. 40, October 1967, pp. 375–384.

Cox, William E., Jr., "Product Portfolio Strategy: A Review of the Boston Consulting Group Approach to Marketing Strategy," in R. Curham, Ed., Marketing Contributions to the Firm and to Society. Chicago: American Marketing Association, 1975, pp. 465–470.

Crawford, C. Merle, "Marketing Research and the New Product Failure Rate," *Journal of Marketing*, Vol. 41, April 1977.

Cunningham, M. T., and M. A. A. Hammouda, "Product Strategy for Industrial Goods," *Journal of Management Studies*, Vol. 6, May 1969, pp. 223–242.

Czepiel, John A., "Decision Group and Firm Characteristics in an Industrial Adoption Decision," in K. L. Bernhardt, Ed., *Marketing: 1776–1976 and Beyond*. Chicago: American Marketing Association, 1976, pp. 340–343.

Czepiel, John A., "Word-of-Mouth Processes in the Diffusion of a Major Technological Innovation," *Journal of Marketing Research*, Vol. 11, May 1974, pp. 172–180.

Enos, John L., "A Measure of Rate Technological Progress in the Petroleum Refining Industry," *Journal of Industrial Economics*, Vol. 6, June 1958, pp. 180–197.

Enos, John L., *Petroleum Progress and Profits*. Cambridge, Mass. M.I.T. Press, 1962.

Freimer, Marshall, and Leonard S. Simon, "The Evaluation of Potential New Product Alternatives," *Management Science*, Vol. 13, February 1967, pp. B279–B292.

Gold, Bela, "The Shaky Foundations of Capital Budgeting," *California Management Review*, Vol. 19, Winter 1976, pp. 51–60.

Gold, Bela, "Tracing Gaps Between Expectations and Results of Technological Innovations: The Case of Iron and Steel," *Journal of Industrial Economics*, Vol. 25, September 1976, pp. 1–28.

Gold, Bela, William S. Pierce, and Gerhard Rosegger, "Diffusion of Major Technological Innovations in U.S. Iron and Steel Manufacturing," *Journal of Industrial Economics*, Vol. 18, July 1970, pp. 218–241.

Green, Paul E., "Marketing Applications of MDS: Assessment and Outlook," *Journal of Marketing*, Vol. 39, January 1975, pp. 24–31.

Green, Paul E., and Frank J. Carmone, "The Performance Structure of the Computer Market: A Multivariate Approach," *The Economic and Business Bulletin*, Vol. 21, Fall 1968, pp. 1–11.

Green, Paul E., and V. R. Rao, "A Note on Proximity Measures and Cluster Analysis," *Journal of Marketing Research*, Vol. 6, August 1969.

Green, Paul E., and Donald S. Tull, *Research for Marketing Decisions*, 3rd ed. Englewood Cliffs, N.J.: Prentice-Hall, 1975.

Gross, Fred J., "Concept Testing and Screening—New Industrial Products." (Outline of paper delivered to the National Industrial Conference Board, New York, October 1969.)

Hamberg, Daniel, "Invention in the Industrial Research Laboratory," *Journal of Political Economy*, Vol. 71, 1963, pp. 95–115.

Hargreaves, George, John D. Claxton, and Frederick H. Siller, "New Product Evaluation: Electric Vehicles for Commercial Applications," *Journal of Marketing*, Vol. 40, January 1976, pp. 74–77.

Jewkes, J., D. Sawers, and R. Stillerman, *The Sources of Invention*. London: Macmillan, 1958.

Kierulff, Herbert E., "Return on Investment and the Total Flaw," *California Management Review*, Vol. 19, Winter 1976, pp. 61–70.

Kluyver, Cornelius A. de, "Innovation and Industrial Product Life Cycles: A Heuristic Classification Study" (Ph.D. diss., Case Western Reserve University, 1975).

Kotler, Philip, "Competitive Strategies for New Product Marketing over the Life Cycle," *Management Science*, Vol. 12, December 1965, pp. B104–B119.

Kotler, Philip, "Phasing Out Weak Products," *Harvard Business Review*, Vol. 43, March–April 1965, pp. 107–118.

Kuehn, Alfred A., and Ralph L. Day, "Strategy of Product Quality," *Harvard Business Review*, Vol. 40, November–December, 1962, pp. 100–110.

Levitt, Theodore, "Exploit the Product Life Cycle," *Harvard Business Review*. Vol. 43, November–December 1965, pp. 81–94.

Lipstein, Benjamin, critique of Glen L. Urban, "A New Product Analysis and Decision Model," *Management Science*, Vol. 14, April 1968, 518–519.

Mansfield, Edwin, *Industrial Research and Technological Innovation*. New York: Norton, 1968, Chap. 7.

Mansfield, Edwin, *Technological Change*. New York:. Norton, pp. 88–92.

Mansfield, Edwin, "Technological Change and the Rate of Imitation," *Econometrics*, Vol. 29, October 1961, pp. 741–766.

Martilla, John A., "Word-of-Mouth Communication in the Industrial Adoption Process," *Journal of Marketing Research*, Vol. 8, May 1971, pp. 173–178.

Materials Advisory Board, *Report of the Ad Hoc Committee on Principles of Research-Engineering Interaction*. Washington: National Academy of Sciences—National Research Council, 1966.

Mueller, W. F., "The Origins of the Basic Inventions Underlying DuPont's Major Product and Process Innovations, 1920–1950," in R. R. Nelson, Ed., *The Rate and Direction of Inventive Activity*. Princeton, N.J.: Princeton University Press, 1962, pp. 323–360.

Myers, Summer, and Donald G. Marquis, *Successful Industrial Innovations*. Washington: U.S. Government Printing Office, 1965.

Nelson, R. R., Ed., *The Rate and Direction of Inventive Activity*. Princeton, N.J.: Princeton University Press, 1962.

Ness, Thomas E., "Innovation in the Building Industry: The Architectural Innovator," in P. R. McDonald, Ed., *Marketing Involvement in Society and the Economy*. Chicago: American Marketing Association, 1969, pp. 353–356.

Nevers, John V., "Extensions of a New Product Growth Model," *Sloan Management Review*, Vol. 13, Winter 1972, pp. 77–91.

O'Meara, John T., Jr. "Selecting Profitable Products," *Harvard Business Review*, Vol. 39, January–February, 1961, pp. 83–89.

Ozanne, Urban B., and Gilbert A. Churchill, "Adoption Research: Information Sources in the Industrial Purchasing Decision," in R. L. King, Ed., *Marketing and the New Science of Planning*. Chicago: American Marketing Association, 1968, p. 352–359.

Patton, Arch, "Stretch Your Product's Earning Years: Top Management's Stake in the Product Life Cycle," *The Management Review*, Vol. 18, June 1959, pp. 9–14, 67–71, 76–79.

Peck, M. J., "Inventions in the Post War American Aluminum Industry," in R. R. Nelson, Ed., *The Rate and Direction of Inventive Activity*. Princeton, N.J.: Princeton University Press, 1962, pp. 279–298.

Pessemier, Edgar A., *Managing Innovation and New Product Development*. Cambridge, Mass.: Marketing Science Institute, 1975, 26–35.

Pessemier, Edgar A., *New Product Decisions: An Analytical Approach*. New York: McGraw-Hill, 1966, pp. 146–162.

Peters, Michael P., and M. Venkatesan, "Exploration of Variables Inherent in Adopting an Industrial Product," *Journal of Marketing Research*, Vol. 10, August 1973, pp. 312–315.

Reynolds, William H., *Products and Markets*. New York: Appleton-Century-Crofts, 1969, p. 63.

Rogers, Everett M., *Diffusion of Innovations*. New York: Free Press, 1962.

Root, H. Paul, "The Use of Subjective Probability Estimates in the Analysis of New Products," in P. R. McDonald, Ed., *Marketing Involvement in Society and the Economy*. Chicago: American Marketing Association, 1970, pp. 200–207.

Sevin, Charles H., *Marketing Productivity Analysis*. New York: McGraw-Hill, 1965, pp. 55–57.

Simon, Leonard S., "Measuring the Market Impact of Technical Services," *Journal of Marketing Research*, Vol. 2, February, 1965, pp. 32–39.

Stefflre, Volney, "Market Structure Studies: New Products for Old Markets and New Markets (Foreign) for Old Products," in Frank Bass, Charles King, and Edgar Pessemier, Eds., *Applications of the Sciences in Marketing*. New York: Wiley, 1968, pp. 251–268.

Sutherland, Alister, "The Diffusion of an Innovation in Cotton Spinning," *Journal of Industrial Economics*, Vol. 7, March 1959, pp. 118–135.

Teach, Richard D., Lester A. Neidell, and Robert E. Gibson, "Industrial Product Differentiation," in Fred C. Allvine, Ed., *Marketing in Motion*. Chicago: American Marketing Association, 1972, pp. 557–571.

Urban, Glen L., "A New Product Analysis and Decision Model," *Management Science*, Vol. 145, April 1968, pp. 490–517.

Webster, Frederick E., Jr., "New Product Adoption in Industrial Markets: A Framework for Analysis," *Journal of Marketing*, Vol. 33, July 1969, pp. 35–39.

Wentz, Walter B., *Marketing Research: Management and Methods*. New York: Harper & Row, 1972.

Wind, Yoram, "A New Procedure for Concept Evaluation," *Journal of Marketing*, Vol. 37, October 1973, pp. 2–11.

Zarecor, William D., "High-Technology Products Planning," *Harvard Business Review*, Vol. 53, January–February 1975, pp. 110-112.

CHAPTER FOURTEEN
The Buying/Selling Interface: Purchasing and Promotion Analysis

In an eminently readable book review, Wilson lamented the failure of most marketing books to examine or even mention the vitally important concept of the buying/selling interface.[1] Wittily conceding his inability to create a memorable word or phrase to describe the interface, Wilson paid homage to the pioneering contribution of *Industrial Buying and Creative Marketing* toward greater awareness and understanding of the concept.[2] The BUYGRID model that served as the focus of this influential book provides useful insights into the organizational buying process, but it had several limitations. Responding to these limitations as well as those of other models of organizational buying behavior, Webster and Wind have developed an integrative model of organizational buying behavior as a guideline for marketing decisions that offers a complex, yet pragmatic,

[1]Aubrey Wilson, *Journal of Marketing Research*, Vol. 11, August 1974, pp. 351–353.
[2]Patrick J. Robinson, Charles W. Faris, and Yoram Wind, *Industrial Buying and Creative Marketing*. Boston: Allyn & Bacon, 1967.

framework for examining the buying/selling interface.[3] This chapter will use the integrative model of Webster and Wind as the framework for scrutinizing the buying/selling interface from an industrial marketing research perspective.

We have repeatedly stressed that the basic purpose of industrial marketing research activity in the individual firm is to improve marketing decisions. Webster and Wind shared this view in their development of their model:

> ... effective marketing strategy for organizational markets requires accurate information about buyers as the basis for understanding and predicting their response to marketing effort. ... Information about buyer behavior then helps the decision-maker reduce his uncertainty about alternative strategic actions and choose those most likely to produce buyer response consistent with company objectives.[4]

A framework for collecting and analyzing the required information about buyers is provided in their model of organizational buying behavior, and we shall use their model as a basis for assessing current knowledge regarding industrial buying behavior. At the same time we shall examine the role of industrial marketing research in collecting and analyzing the data needed to develop the information needed for marketing decision making at the level of the firm. In order to further illustrate the importance of an integrated framework that combines both a buying behavioral model and a marketing decision perspective, promotional strategy (price and communications) will be examined as a decision area requiring detailed and accurate information about buying behavior. Our treatment of the buying/selling interface therefore also deals with the relationships between industrial buying behavior and promotional strategy, with an emphasis on the information needed to make price and communications strategy decisions.

MODELS OF ORGANIZATIONAL AND INDUSTRIAL BUYING BEHAVIOR

A simplified diagram of the Webster and Wind model of organizational (industrial and institutional) buying behavior is shown in Figure 14–1,

---

[3] Frederick E. Webster, Jr., and Yoram Wind, *Organizational Buying Behavior*. Englewood Cliffs, N.J.: Prentice-Hall, 1972.
[4] *Ibid.*, p. 108

```
                    ┌──────────────┐
                    │Environmental │───┐
                    │   factors    │   │
                    └──────┬───────┘   │
                           ▼           │
                    ┌──────────────┐   │
                    │Organizational│───┤
                    │   factors    │   │
                    └──────┬───────┘   │
                           ▼           │
                    ┌──────────────┐   │
                    │Interpersonal │───┤
                    │   factors    │   │
                    └──────┬───────┘   │
                           ▼           │
                    ┌──────────────┐   │
                    │  Individual  │   │
                    │   factors    │   │
                    └──────┬───────┘   │
                           ▼           ▼
   ┌──────────┐     ┌──────────────┐
   │  Buying  │────▶│Buying decision│◀─┘
   │ situation│     │   process    │
   └──────────┘     └──────┬───────┘
                           ▼
                    ┌──────────────┐
                    │    Buying    │
                    │   decisions  │
                    └──────────────┘
```

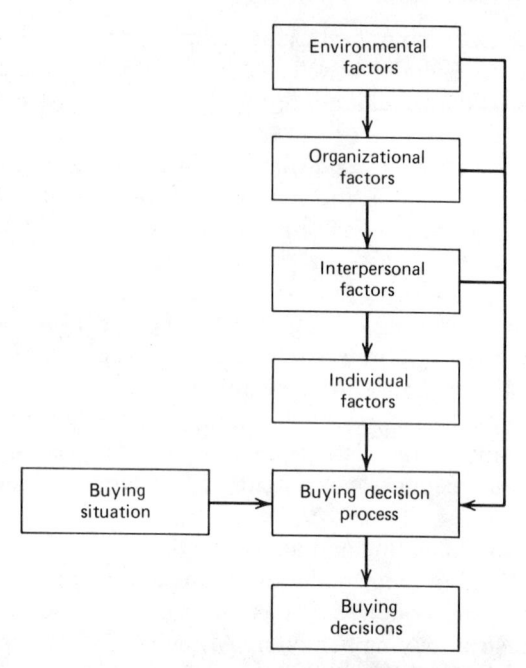

Figure 14-1 A model of organizational buying behavior. Adapted from Frederick E. Webster, Jr., and Yoram Wind, "A General Model for Understanding Organizational Buying Behavior," Journal of Marketing, Vol. 36, April 1972, p. 15.

indicating that there are four classes of variables influencing the buying decision process: environmental, organizational, interpersonal, and individual factors. The buying decision process is also influenced by the nature of the buying situation with the outcome of the process depicted as a set of buying decisions.

Each of the four classes of variables influencing the buying decision process contains two categories of variables,

> Those directly related to the buying problem, called *task* variables; and those that extend beyond the buying problem, called *nontask* variables.[5]

Combining the four classes and two categories of variables produces a 4 × 2, 8-cell matrix, and Figure 14-2 provides an example for each cell in the matrix. In the following pages, each of the four classes of variables are

---

[5]Frederick E. Webster, Jr., and Yoram Wind, "A General Model for Understanding Organizational Buying Behavior," *Journal of Marketing,* Vol. 36, April 1972, p. 13.

THE BUYING/SELLING INTERFACE

Source of influence	Task variables	Nontask variables
Individual factors	Desire to obtain lowest price	Personal values
Interpersonal factors	Meetings to set product specifications	Off-the-job interactions among company employees
Organizational factors	Company policies with respect to product quality	Company policies regarding community relations
Environmental factors	Expected trends in business conditions	Political factors in an election year

Source: Frederick E. Webster, Jr., and Yoram Wind, *Organizational Buying Behavior*. Englewood Cliffs, N.J.: Prentice-Hall, 1972, p. 29.

Figure 14-2 Determinants of organizational buying behavior.

examined along two lines: (1) a review of the literature on the subject and (2) information requirements on the subject for promotion decisions and the role of industrial marketing research in collecting and analyzing the information for the individual firm.

Environmental Factors

Webster and Wind have identified six sets of environmental influences that affect organizational buying behavior:[6]

1. *Physical*—These factors include climate, geographic location of the organization and its suppliers, existing plant and equipment of the organization, and the ecological impact of and on buying decisions.
2. *Technological*—Scientific and engineering developments influence buying behavior through their effects on the goods and services that are bought and sold, and influence the buying/selling process itself through computers, management science systems, and so on.
3. *Economic*—The general economic conditions of a country as well as level of specific economic indicators have a profound effect on organizational buying behavior.
4. *Political*—There are a variety of governmental actions that influence

[6]Webster and Wind, *Organizational Buying Behavior, op. cit.*, Chap. 4.

industrial buying behavior, including government expenditures, tariff and trade agreements, and so on.

5. *Legal*—Regulations at all levels of government exert influence by affecting the availability and quality of products available, product specifications, and competitive practices of both industrial buyers and sellers.

6. *Cultural*—The value systems of individuals and organizations is strongly influenced by society, and these values affect organizational buying behavior.

Webster and Wind have portrayed the six sets of environmental influences exerting influence on the organizational buying decision process through a series of institutions as shown in Figure 14-3. These influences take shape in four ways:

1. By determining the availability of goods and services
2. By defining the general business conditions in which buying takes place
3. By establishing the values and norms for individual and organization behavior
4. By providing information to buying organization members on the other three influences: availability of goods and services, general business conditions, and values and norms of society[7]

Although there is general agreement that environmental influences do affect organizational buying behavior, there is a paucity of research evidence to support the contention. Meanwhile the business press has repeatedly documented the effects of the oil crisis, materials shortages, inflation, and recession on the buying behavior of individual firms. Frequently these reports have noted that the firms were not prepared for these environmental changes, resulting in disruptions in operations, higher costs, and lower efficiency. Perrow has observed that

> Most organizations attempt to stabilize and control these environmental influences. That is, they attempt to deal with changes in the environment by setting up rules and positions which can make it possible to deal with the environment on a routine, predictable basis.[8]

[7]*Ibid.*, p. 41.
[8]Charles B. Perrow, *Organizational Analysis: A Sociological View.* Belmont, Cal.: Brooks/Cole, 1970, p. 55.

THE BUYING/SELLING INTERFACE

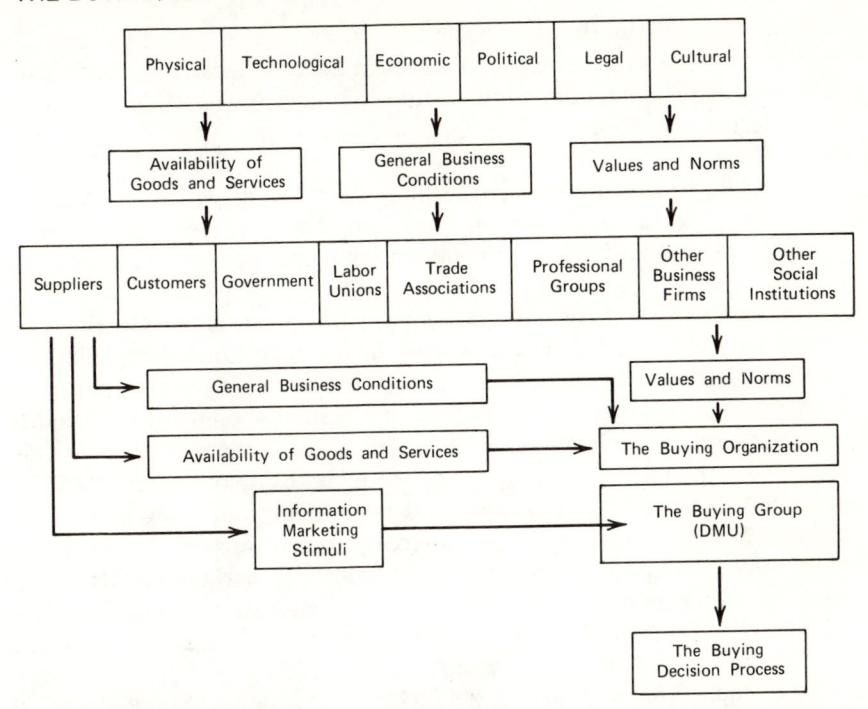

Figure 14-3 A model of environmental effects on the organizational buying process. Source: Frederick E. Webster, Jr., and Yoram Wind, Organizational Buying Behavior. *Englewood Cliffs, N.J.: Prentice-Hall, 1972, p. 42.*

These corporate responses implicitly assume continuity in environmental change and most organizations have managed continuous change reasonably well. The major challenge however is in dealing with "future shock" and "the age of discontinuity," marked by accelerating and discontinuous environmental changes.[9] A number of organizations have turned to strategic planning systems as a means of managing environmental change. A few large organizations are now exploring the broader concept of strategic management, including strategic issues analysis, as an approach to managing environmental surprises.[10]

Some organizations, such as the General Electric Company, have established special units with a primary responsibility for forecasting the environment; virtually all large industrial firms have one or more indi-

[9] Alvin Toffler, *Future Shock.* New York: Random House, 1970; Peter F. Drucker, *The Age of Discontinuity: Guidelines to Our Changing Society.* New York: Harper & Row, 1969.
[10] H. Igor Ansoff, "Managing Strategic Surprise by Response to Weak Signals," *California Management Review,* Vol. 18, Winter 1975, pp. 21-33.

viduals assigned to this responsibility on at least a part-time basis.[11] Interest in futures research has exploded in the past decade and interest in technological and economic forecasting continues to rise.[12] Despite all of this interest and effort,

> ... little has been done concerning the ways in which managers perceive the environment, in classifying these perceptions, or in explaining how different perceptions influence their decisions.[13]

The assessment of relationships between organizations and their environments has occupied a central role in the literature of organization theory, business and management policy, and strategic planning for more than a decade, yet there has been little or no progress on many of the most important issues facing industrial organizations. When viewed in this light, the lack of knowledge regarding the relationship of the environment and organizational buying behavior takes on a different perspective. The general absence of information on many dimensions of organization-environment relationships suggests that industrial marketing researchers have an opportunity to make significant contributions toward understanding environmental influences on the firm as well as the ways in which the firm influences the environment.

Two studies that explore limited facets of environmental influences on organizational buying behavior have been published:

1. Hakansson and Wootz dealt with physical environmental influences and found that supplier location was the most important determinant of source selection in a multinational setting.[14]
2. Gronhaug found that economic and legal environmental factors influenced the buying behavior of 48 Norwegian organizations that had recently purchased a minicomputer.[15]

---

[11]Ian H. Wilson, "Reforming the Strategic Planning Process: Integration of Social and Business Needs," *Long Range Planning,* Vol. 7, October 1974, pp. 2–6.

[12]David T. Kollat, "Environmental Forecasting and Strategic Planning: Perspectives on the Methodology of Futurology," in Fred C. Allvine, Ed., *Marketing in Motion.* Chicago: American Marketing Association, 1972, pp. 210–213.

[13]George A. Steiner and John B. Miner, *Management Policy and Strategy.* New York: Macmillan, 1977, p. 53.

[14]Hakan Hakansson and Bjorn Wootz, "Supplier Selection in an International Environment—An Experimental Study," *Journal of Marketing Research,* Vol. 12, February 1975, pp. 46–51.

[15]Kjell Gronhaug, "Exploring Environmental Influences in Organizational Buying," *Journal of Marketing Research,* Vol. 13, August 1976, pp. 225–229.

THE BUYING/SELLING INTERFACE

Further studies of industrial buying behavior should: (1) consider the opportunity to meet total organization needs for information on environmental influences as well as particular marketing needs, (2) specifically recognize the mutual interest of strategic planning and marketing units in determining and measuring environmental influences on the organization, and (3) utilize the abundant literature on environmental-organizational relationships in the fields of organization theory, business and management policy, and strategic planning in preparation for developing research designs for assessing environmental influences on industrial buying behavior.[16]

Organizational Factors

One of the distinguishing characteristics of organizational buying behavior is that it takes place within a formal organization and is thereby shaped by the purposes, objectives, and constraints of that organization. In order to examine the effects of organizational factors on organizational buying behavior, Webster and Wind have adopted Leavitt's perspective on organizations: they are

> . . . multivariate systems composed of four sets of interacting variables:
>
> *Tasks*—the work to be performed in accomplishing the objectives of the organization
> *Structure*—systems of communication, authority, status, rewards, and work flow
> *Technology*—problem-solving inventions used by the firm, including plant and equipment and programs for organizing and managing work
> *People*—the actors in the system[17]

Applying this perspective of the industrial buying organization within a larger corporate organization suggests that each set of variables should be analyzed both independently and interdependently within the buying organization itself as well as in relation to the same set of variables in the corporate organization. Zaltman and Bonoma have offered a four-cell buying grid that recognizes that there is both a corporate and buying

---
[16] For a brief, recent review of this literature, see: Steiner and Miner, *op. cit.*, Chap. 4.
[17] Webster and Wind, *Organizational Buying Behavior, op. cit.*, p. 53.

	Corporate Locus	
	Intrafirm influences	Interfirm (environmental) influences
Intradepartmental influences	**I** The P.A.:[a] Intraindividual factors Decision models Decision types Risk analyses	**III** Professionalism Trade shows Journals Diffusion of innovation models Communication nets and patterns
Interdepartmental influences	**II** Purchasing vis-a-vis other departments Organizational structure Conflict models Who decides?	**IV** Environmental constraints Legal, governmental factors Value and cultural analyses Business and society

(Departmental locus)

Note: (a) Purchasing Agent
Source: Gerald Zaltman and Thomas V. Bonoma, "Organizational Buying Behavior: Hypotheses and Directions," *Industrial Marketing Management*, Vol. 6, 1977, p. 55.

Figure 14-4 Industrial buying locus of influence grid.

department locus of influence, as shown in Figure 14-4.[18] Cell I, dealing with intradepartmental/intrafirm influences, focuses on the purchasing agent and department.

Interdepartmental/intrafirm influences are emphasized in Cell II, thereby spotlighting the concept of the "buying center" and its central place in the analysis of organizational buying behavior. We shall defer examination of the "buying center" concept until the discussion on Interpersonal Factors. Cell III contains interfirm (environmental)/(intradepartmental) influences on the purchasing agent and department, such as the impact of external contacts and information on the behavior of purchasing personel. In Cell IV, interfirm (environmental)/(interdepartmental) influences are recognized and comprise the environmental factors affecting organizational buying behavior that were discussed earlier.

The impact of organizational factors on buying behavior is thus cen-

[18] Gerald Zaltman and Thomas V. Bonoma, "Organizational Buying Behavior: Hypotheses and Directions," *Industrial Marketing Management*, Vol. 6, 1977, pp. 53-60.

tered on Cell II in Figure 14–4, and in the context of the Leavitt organization typology, virtually all of the published research to date focuses on two of the four sets of variables: structure and people. Research on the influence of organization structure on industrial buying behavior has tended to focus on buying center membership and responsibility[19] and the effects of centralized/decentralized structures.[20] Zaltman and Bonoma have offered a series of hypotheses regarding the effects of various structures on industrial buying behavior such as:

Perhaps decentralized purchasing authority is best when the changing technical environment for products is changing rapidly.[21]

Steiner and Miner have noted that

... recent research shows that the appropriate response to rapidly changing environments is decentralization, flatter organization structures (for example, wider span of control), dominance of organizational goal orientation, participation in decision making, and interpersonal managerial styles ... but that there was no one 'right' way to respond to changing environments. Organizational design must be tailored to each situation ...[22]

The influence of people on organizations and organizational buying behavior has been studied by Webster[23] and Wind[24] within the framework of *"the behavioral theory of the firm,"* developed at Carnegie Institute of Technology in the 1950s[25] and endorsed by Webster and Wind as "... one of the richest and most realistic frameworks for understanding the nature of organizational buying behavior."[26] Much of the work on Interpersonal Factors in the following section is also applicable here, with the result that

---

[19]Robert E. Wiegand, "Identifying Industrial Buying Responsibility," *Journal of Marketing Research*, Vol. 3, February 1966, pp. 81–84.
[20]Yoram Wind, "Industrial Buying Behavior: Source Loyalty in the Purchase of Industrial Components" (Ph.D. diss., Graduate School of Business, Stanford University, 1966).
[21]Zaltman and Bonoma, *op. cit.*, p. 57.
[22]Steiner and Miner, *op. cit.*, p. 52.
[23]Frederick E. Webster, Jr., "Modeling the Industrial Buying Process," *Journal of Marketing Research*, Vol. 2, November 1965, pp. 370–376.
[24]Yoram Wind, "Applying the Behavioral Theory of the Firm to Industrial Buying Decisions," *The Economic and Business Bulletin* (Temple University), Vol. 20, Spring 1968, pp. 22–28.
[25]Richard M. Cyert and James G. March, *A Behavioral Theory of the Firm*. Englewood Cliffs, N.J.: Prentice-Hall, 1963.
[26]Webster and Wind, *Organizational Buying Behavior, op. cit.*, p. 68.

there is a small, but growing body of literature emerging on the influence of organizational factors on industrial buying behavior.

Industrial marketing researchers interested in applying these findings to the individual firm should find that a review of the organization and management theory literature will provide valuable background and insights for analyzing industrial buying processes and decisions.

Interpersonal Factors

Another important set of factors that affect organizational buying behavior are those characterized as interpersonal influences, which can be defined as

> ... the influence of one person on another. When several individuals interact simultaneously and are guided by a shared set of objectives, norms, expectations, and so on, interpersonal influences become 'group' influences.[27]

As noted in the discussion on organizational influences, the concept of the buying center occupies a central position in the analysis of organizational buying behavior and will be used as the principal vehicle for examining the place of interpersonal influences. All of the individuals in an organization who are involved in the buying decision process comprise the buying center, which is composed of five roles:

1. *Users*—those members of the organization who use the purchased products and services.
2. *Buyers*—those who influence the decision process directly or indirectly by providing information and criteria for evaluating alternative buying actions.
3. *Influencers*—those who influence the decision process directly or indirectly by providing information and criteria for evaluating alternative buying actions.
4. *Deciders*—those with authority to choose among alternative buying actions.
5. *Gatekeepers*—those who control the flow of information (and materials) into the buying center.[28]

Contributing to the complexity of the buying center concept are the following: (1) the same individual may occupy several roles; (2) several

---
[27]Webster and Wind, *Organizational Buying Behavior, op. cit.,* p. 75.
[28]Webster and Wind, "A General Model for Understanding Organizational Buying Behavior," *op. cit.,* p. 17.

THE BUYING/SELLING INTERFACE

	Users	Influencers	Buyers	Deciders	Gate-keepers
Identification of need	X	X			
Establishing specifications and scheduling the purchase	X	X	X	X	
Identifying buying alternatives	X	X	X		X
Evaluating alternative buying actions	X	X	X		
Selecting the suppliers	X	X	X	X	

Source: Frederick E. Webster, Jr., and Yoram Wind, *Organizational Buying Behavior*. Englewood Cliffs, N.J.: Prentice-Hall, 1972, p. 80.

Figure 14-5 Decision stages and roles in the buying center.

individuals may fill the same role; (3) role influence varies at different stages of the buying process, as shown in Figure 14-5, by type of purchase (new vs. repeat), by size of purchase, and so on; and (4) the number of individuals comprising a buying center varies widely from one to fifty.[29] Although it is generally conceded that the buying center concept is valid and that there are multiple roles and buying influences involved, relatively little is known about the relationships among the various roles. One of the major problems has been that researchers have been unable to develop methodologies to measure accurately role influence. Weigand,[30] McMillan,[31] and Grashof and Thomas[32] have all reported that buying center members tend to inflate their own influence relative to the perceptions of others. Thus Zaltman and Bonoma concluded that there is "... a need for developing new methodologies which will facilitate our studying buying centers as units of analysis rather than individuals."[33]

Another approach to studying the interactions between the members of buying centers was suggested by Strauss, who focused on the relationships among purchasing agents and other members of the buying center

---

[29]Murray Harding, "Who Really Makes the Purchasing Decision?," *Industrial Marketing*, Vol. 51, September 1966, p. 76; Mary R. O'Rourke, James M. Shea, and William M. Solley, "Survey Shows Need for Increased Sales Calls, Advertising, and Updated Mailing Lists to Reach Buying Influences," *Industrial Marketing*, Vol. 58, April 1973, p. 38.
[30]Weigand, *op. cit.*
[31]James R. McMillan, "Role Differentiation in Industrial Buying Decisions," *1973 Combined Conference Proceedings*, Thomas V. Greer, Ed. Chicago: American Marketing Association, 1974, pp. 207-211.
[32]John F. Grashof and Gloria P. Thomas, "Industrial Buying Center Responsibilities: Self versus Other Member Evaluations of Importance," in K. L. Bernhardt, Ed., *Marketing: 1776-1976 and Beyond*. Chicago: American Marketing Association, 1976, pp. 344-347.
[33]Zaltman and Bonoma, *op. cit.*, p. 59.

on approximately the same level in the organization.[34] He found that purchasing agents tended to use tactics in their relationships that would enhance their own power and status in the organization while attempting to reduce the power and influence of other members of the buying center. The interaction between purchasing agents and salesmen has been examined in several studies using a dyadic interaction model that emphasizes the effect of role expectations on organizational buying behavior. Tosi found that the role expectations of the purchasing agent with respect to the salesman were important, but that a role consensus between the parties regarding their own role was not important.[35] Farrer[36] and Sweitzer[37] have confirmed the importance of the role expectations of the purchasing agent with respect to the salesman. Sweitzer has also noted that role consensus is not necessary if the salesman demonstrates empathy for the role and task of the purchasing agent.

Sheth, in considering the implications of his model of industrial buying behavior for marketing research, began by calling for additional research on all members of the buying center.[38] While purchasing agents are the most accessible and studied members of the buying center, they frequently have relatively little influence on the industrial buying decision process. It is important to begin to identify these situations. In the development of theory and models that will explain and predict the choice of industrial suppliers, the inclusion of measures of interpersonal influences among all members of the buying center must rank among the highest priorities for further industrial marketing research activity.

Individual Factors

The fourth and final class of variables influencing the organizational buying decision process are individual factors; these are important because, "In the final analysis, all organizational buying behavior is indi-

---

[34]George Strauss, "Tactics of Lateral Relationship: The Purchasing Agent," *Administrative Science Quarterly*, Vol. 7, September 1962, pp. 161–186; George Strauss, "Work-Flow Frictions, Interfunctional Rivalry, and Professionalism: A Case Study of Purchasing Agents," *Human Organization*, Vol. 23, Summer 1964, pp. 137–149.

[35]Henry L. Tosi, "The Effects of Expectation Levels of Role Consensus on the Buyer-Seller Dyad," *Journal of Business*, Vol. 39, October 1966, pp. 516–529.

[36]Dean G. Farrer, "Life of a Salesman: Value and Attitude Hierarchies," *Atlanta Economic Review*, Vol. 20, March 1970, pp. 4–7, 33–35.

[37]Robert W. Sweitzer, "Interpersonal Information Processing of Industrial Buyers," in K. L. Bernhardt, Ed., *Marketing: 1776–1976 and Beyond*. Chicago: American Marketing Association, 1976, pp. 334–339.

[38]Jagdish N. Sheth, "A Model of Industrial Buyer Behavior," *Journal of Marketing*, Vol. 37, October 1973, p. 56.

THE BUYING/SELLING INTERFACE

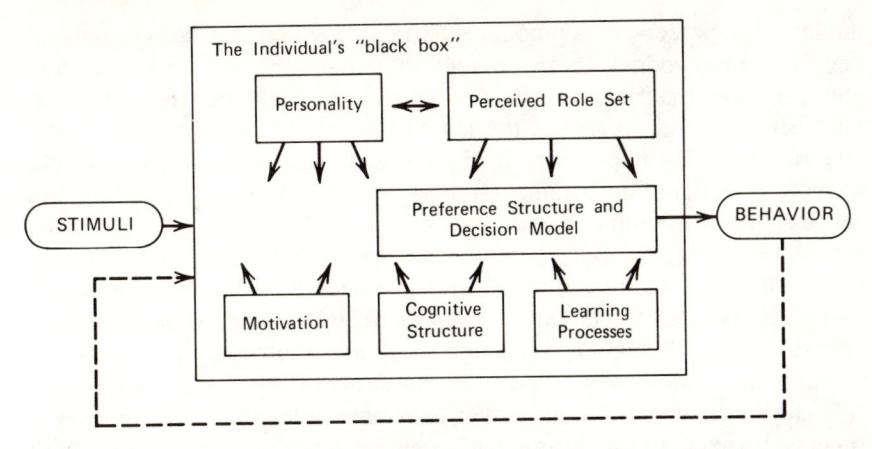

Figure 14-6 A simplified model of individual behavior. Source: Frederick E. Webster, Jr. and Yoram Wind, Organizational Buying Behavior. *Englewood Cliffs, N.J.: Prentice-Hall, 1976, p. 341.*

vidual behavior."[39] Figure 14-6 portrays a simplified model of individual behavior developed by Webster and Wind. This model suggests that a variety of psychological processes interact and influence the individual's preference structure and decision model within a "black-box" framework. This model is shown to be directly related to behavior. Webster and Wind contend that:

> Focusing on the individual's preference structure and decision model as the central explanatory and predictive variable of buyer behavior has considerable implications for organizational buying research inasmuch as it allows one to focus on this operationally measured variable and to avoid the need to measure a large number of abstract constructs (such as motivation and cognition) and to assess their interrelationships.[40]

Most researchers appear to have followed this path and have concentrated on the decision models of individuals, particularly purchasing agents.

A review of the research literature on individual behavior within the framework of organizational buying behavior reveals that research has been concentrated on two types of decision models: (1) dominant dimension models, particularly the perceived risk model and (2) multiattribute

---
[39] Webster and Wind, "A General Model for Understanding Organizational Buying Behavior," *op. cit.*, p. 18.
[40] Webster and Wind, *Organizational Buying Behavior, op. cit.*, p. 89.

models. The perceived risk model is based on the premise that virtually all decisions involve risk to the extent that they embrace outcomes and consequences that are uncertain at the time of decision. The individual will therefore seek to reduce the level of perceived risk by reducing the uncertainty or the importance of the consequences. One of the principal means of reducing uncertainty and perceived risk is by collecting and processing information. Levitt conducted a study of communications effects on industrial buying behavior and found that the reputation of the source of the communications affected behavior.[41] His research indicated that both "source effects" and "sleeper effects" were present: (1) source effects refer to the tendency for high credibility sources to induce greater changes in opinion than low credibility sources and (2) sleeper effects refer to the tendency for the effect of source credibility to decline over time as the result of the disassociation of the source and the message with the passage of time. Specifically Levitt found that company reputation affected the response of industrial buying center members to sales presentations, that company reputation had greater impact on higher risk decisions, and that the effect of company reputation decreased over time. Subsequent studies by Cardozo and Cagley[42] and McMillan[43] confirmed Levitt's findings that the source credibility of the seller was an important influence on uncertainty and perceived risk reduction. Two other studies however failed to support Levitt's findings: Capon, Holbrook, and Hulbert[44] and Sweitzer[45] found little evidence of a "source effect" and suggested that the source credibility of the individual salesman was more important than company reputation in reducing uncertainty and perceived risk among members of industrial buying centers. These mixed results suggest the need for further research on the matter, since it appears that situational effects have had a significant impact on the results in all of the studies on source credibility to date.

Another approach to the use of the perceived risk model has been Wilson's work on the relationship between personality characteristics and risk reduction behavior among industrial buyers. His initial study used an expected monetary value (EMV) model as the basis for judging the deci-

---

[41]Theodore Levitt, "Industrial Purchasing Behavior: A study of Communications Effects" (Ph.D. diss., Graduate School of Business Administration, Harvard University, 1965).
[42]Richard N. Cardozo and James W. Cagley, "Experimental Study of Industrial Buyer Behavior," *Journal of Marketing Research*, Vol. 8, August 1971, pp. 329–334.
[43]James R. McMillan, "The Role of Perceived Risk in Industrial Marketing Decisions," in Boris and Helmut Becker, Eds., *1972 Combined Conference Proceedings*. Chicago: American Marketing Association, 1973, pp. 412–417.
[44]Noel Capon, M. Holbrook, and J. Hulbert, "Industrial Buying Behavior: A Reappraisal," *Journal of Business Administration*, Vol. 4, Fall 1972, pp. 69–77.
[45]Sweitzer, *op. cit.*

sions of purchasing agents and classifying their decision-making styles.[46] Purchasing agents who generally made choices on five simulated purchasing problems that produced the largest expected values (in accord with the EMV model) were considered to have *normative* decision styles; purchasing agents who made nonnormative choices generally were considered to have *conservative* decision styles. Three personality traits were studied: (1) need for certainty, (2) generalized self-confidence, and (3) need to achieve. Only one of the three traits, need for certainty, was found to be significantly related to decision-making style, with low need for certainty related to a conservative style. Purchasing agents with normative styles also perceived less risk in a high uncertainty, high potential payoff problem than did conservatives. A second study examined the relationship between risk reducing behavior and two other personality characteristics: need for cognitive clarity and cognitive style. It also attempted to classify patterns of risk reducing behavior.[47] Using a hypothetical purchasing problem with ten suggested risk reducing strategies, it was found that four patterns of risk reducing behavior were used by purchasing agents: two forms of uncertainty reduction (external and internal) and two forms of consequence reduction (external and internal). Although the study found a significant relationship between risk reducing behavior and the personality variables, the authors urged caution in interpreting the results.

The second type of decision model used to examine individual behavior within the context of organizational buying behavior has been multiattribute models, which in turn may be categorized into: (1) cognitive consistency theory models, which require ". . . highly structured judgments about specific attributes . . . ,"[48] and (2) preference and perceptual mapping models, which require less complex data from respondents but use multidimensional scaling and conjoint measurement techniques to extract the maximum information from the data. All of the consistency theory models reported in the industrial buying literature to date have been compensatory models, in which the scores on the multiple attributes are considered to be linear and additive, with or without weights, so that high scores on one attribute may offset low scores on others. The earliest

---

[46]David T. Wilson, "Industrial Buyers' Decision-Making Styles," *Journal of Marketing Research*, Vol. 8, November 1971, pp. 433–436.

[47]Timothy W. Sweeny, H. Lee Mathews, and David T. Wilson, "An Analysis of Industrial Buyers' Risk Reducing Behavior: Some Personality Correlates," in Thomas V. Greer, Ed., *1973 Combined Conference Proceedings*. Chicago: American Marketing Association, 1974, pp. 217–221.

[48]George S. Day, "Evaluating Models of Attitude Structure," *Journal of Marketing Research*, Vol. 9, August 1972, p. 285.

application of these models appears to be based on a study of the determinants of vendor selection.[49] Scott and Bennett[50] used a compensatory model to predict preferences for 5 brands of fixed-value resistors based on 21 product attributes. Wildt and Bruno[51] demonstrated the application of linear compensatory models (with and without weights) to the prediction of preferences for various brands in two categories of capital equipment. Subsequently, Lehmann and O'Shaughnessy[52] analyzed differences in the importance of attributes for four types of products among industrial buyers in the United States and Great Britain. They found that perceived attribute importance depended heavily on product type and the cultural backgrounds of the buyers. This was reinforced by a study conducted by Kelly and Coaker[53] regarding the attributes (choice criteria) used to evaluate vendors by buyers in five large manufacturing firms in Virginia. These researchers found significant differences in perceived attribute importance between the five firms and thus were led to question whether it is useful to attempt to generalize about attribute importance across industrial firms.

The stringent data requirements of the consistency theory models have led some researchers to explore the possibility of using preference and perceptual mapping models to examine individual behavior. Day[54] used joint-space analysis to examine the perceptions and preferences of 44 architects, designers, and builders for 12 types of building bricks with a wide range of product attributes. Wind[55] applied conjoint measurement

---

[49]Yoram Wind, Paul E. Green, and Patrick J. Robinson, "The Determinants of Vendor Selection: The Evaluation Function Approach," *Journal of Purchasing,* Vol. 4, August 1968, pp. 29–41.

[50]Jerome E. Scott and Peter D. Bennett, "Cognitive Models of Attitude Structure: 'Value Importance' *Is* Important," in Fred C. Allvine, Ed., *Marketing in Motion.* Chicago: American Marketing Association, 1972, pp. 346–350.

[51]Albert R. Wildt and Albert V. Bruno, "The Prediction of Preference for Capital Equipment Using Linear Attitude Models," *Journal of Marketing Research,* Vol. 11, May 1974, pp. 203–205.

[52]Donald R. Lehmann and John O'Shaughnessy, "Difference in Attribute Importance for Different Industrial Products,"*Journal of Marketing,* Vol. 38, April 1974, pp. 36–42. Also see: Thomas T. Semon, "A Cautionary Note on Difference in Attribute Importance for Different Industrial Products'," *Journal of Marketing,* Vol. 39, January 1975, p. 80.

[53]J. Patrick Kelly and James W. Coaker, "Can We Generalize about Choice Criteria for Industrial Purchasing Decisions?," in K. L. Bernhardt, Ed., *Marketing: 1776–1976 and Beyond.* Chicago: American Marketing Association, 1976, pp. 330–333.

[54]Day, *op. cit.,* pp. 279–286.

[55]Yoram Wind, "Recent Approaches to the Study of Organizational Buying Behavior," in Thomas V. Greer, Ed., *1973 Combined Conference Proceedings.* Chicago: American Marketing Association, 1974, pp. 203–206.

techniques to the attributes used by 51 physicians to select a medical/clinical laboratory.

This review of the research literature on individual behavior within the framework of organizational buying behavior shows that while a great deal has been accomplished in the past decade, much remains to be done, particularly in examining the interrelationships between individual factors and the other three classes of variables that influence the organizational buying decision process.

Buying Situation

In the model of organizational buying behavior presented in Figure 14–1, the buying decision process was portrayed as being affected by the buying situation, in addition to the four classes of variables examined previously discussed. The BUYGRID model has been widely used to describe industrial buying situations and recognizes three classes of buying situations (BUYCLASSES):[56] (1) new task, (2) straight rebuy, and (3) modified rebuy. Webster and Wind have suggested that "Every buying situation can be characterized by three interrelated factors . . . ,"[57] and Figure 14–7 has been prepared to show how these three factors can be used to define the three classes of buying situations.

DEVELOPING PROMOTIONAL STRATEGIES

As previously noted, information about organizational buying behavior is considered valuable and relevant primarily on the basis of its ability to explain and predict buying decisions. Among the environmental factors that affect buying decisions are marketing decisions of sellers, which are unlike the other environmental factors in that they are controllable variables. Some of the most important marketing decisions therefore *affect and are affected by* organizational buying behavior. Two of these decisions have been singled out to illustrate the importance of utilizing an integrated framework for assessing the information requirements of marketing decision makers in the individual firm. We shall examine the decision involving the identification of market segments among industrial buyers first, and then we shall review the promotional mix decision for the industrial seller, emphasizing the development of promotional (price

---

[56] Robinson, Faris, and Wind, *op. cit.*
[57] Webster and Wind, *Organizational Buying Behavior, op. cit.,* p. 115.

	Factors Affecting Buying Situations		
Buyclasses	Newness of buying problem; level of past buying experience among buying center members	Information requirements of buying center members	Number of new sources of supply likely to be considered
New task situations	Totally new problem; little or no experience	High	Many
Moderate rebuy situations	Some new/changed problems; some experience	Moderate	Some
Straight rebuy situations	Routine problem; high experience	None	None

Adapted from: Patrick J. Robinson, Charles W. Faris, and Yoram Wind, *Industrial Buying and Creative Marketing*. Boston: Allyn and Bacon, 1967; Frederick E. Webster, Jr., and Yoram Wind, *Organizational Buying Behavior*. Englewood Cliffs, N.J.: Prentice-Hall, 1972, p. 115.

Figure 14-7 Classification of industrial buying situations.

communications and distribution) strategies designed to influence the industrial buying decision.

Identification of Industrial Market Segments

The process of identifying appropriate market segments for an individual seller is basically the same for consumer and industrial products/services, but the relevant bases for segmentation vary. Cardozo reported that most of the industrial buying literature up to 1968 seldom carried a discussion of market segmentation bases ". . . further than stating that, for any particular industrial product, purchasing behavior varies according to geography and end use of the commodity purchased."[58] After reviewing the various other bases, Cardozo concluded that five additional bases might be considered for industrial market segmentation:[59]

[58]Richard N. Cardozo, "Segmenting the Industrial Market," in Robert L. King, Ed., *Marketing and the New Science of Planning*. Chicago: American Marketing Association, 1969, p. 433.
[59]*Ibid.*, p. 440.

1. Industrial buyers' purchasing strategies
2. Buyers' risk preferences, role types, and cognitive styles
3. The problems and risks perceived by different buyers
4. Differences among purchase requisitions
5. Differences in the environmental forces affecting different buyers

The next significant contribution to the task of identifying industrial market segments was offered in a comprehensive book on the concept and practice of market segmentation that viewed organizational markets as being divided into macro and micro segments.[60] Macro segments were defined as those based on organizational characteristics, while micro segments were based on the characteristics of the decision-making units (DMU) in the organization. The DMU's are the individual buying center members associated with the purchase of a particular industrial product or service. A number of industrial market segmentation bases were suggested earlier, organized into a classification scheme shown in Figure 14-8. In addition to introducing new bases for segmentation, this classification scheme distinguished between segmentation bases that were intrinsic to an organization (general) and situation-specific characteristics regarding products, suppliers, and particular buying situations.

The most recent comprehensive approach to the identification of industrial market segments has been developed by Wind and Cardozo, including both an "ideal" segmentation model and a report on industrial segmentation practices in 30 industrial companies.[61] The "ideal" model used the distinction between macro and micro segments introduced by Frank, Massy, and Wind but added the idea that segmentation be construed as a two-stage process. In the first stage, macro segments would be identified, screened, and selected on such bases as: size of the buying firm, usage rate of the product, SIC categories and product end-uses, location, new versus repeat purchase, and so on. Evaluation of the macro segments may reveal that there is no need to proceed further and that segments may be drawn at the macro level. Otherwise micro segments would be identified on the basis of DMU characteristics as well as their organizational characteristics that served as the bases for the macro-level segmentation. The report of a survey of segmentation practices in 30 industrial companies indicated that organization characteristics were used

[60]Ronald E. Frank, William F. Massy, and Yoram Wind, *Market Segmentation*. Englewood Cliffs, N.J.: Prentice-Hall, 1971, Chap. 5.
[61]Yoram Wind and Richard Cardozo, "Industrial Market Segmentation," *Industrial Marketing Management*, Vol. 3, 1974, pp. 153–166.

Type of measure by level (object) of segmentation		Nature of characteristics	
		General	Situation-specific
Organizational characteristics	Objective measures	Organization demographics Organization structure and technology	Product Usage Loyalty pattern The buying center Buying situation
	Inferred measures	Buying tasks and purchasing decision rules	Attitudes, perception and preference The determinants of the purchase decision and their relative importance
Decisionmaking unit (DMU) characteristics	Objective measures	Demographic characteristics: age, sex, education	Loyalty pattern
	Inferred measures	Personality and life style	Attitudes, perceptions, and preferences

Source: Ronald E. Frank, William F. Massy, and Yoram Wind, *Market Segmentation.* Englewood Cliffs, N.J.: Prentice-Hall, 1971, p. 95.

Figure 14–8 A classification scheme of bases for organizational segmentation.

most frequently as bases for segmentation, with the bases for segmentation grouped into three clusters:

1. Organization characteristics of buying firms: type of industry (SIC category), size of firm, geographic location.
2. Product characteristics of buying firms: frequency and size of purchase, end use of the product, product specifications.
3. Decision-making unit (DMU) characteristics of buying firms: buyer's identity (job title), source loyalty patterns, buyer's personality.

Wind and Cardozo found that

Segmentation appears to be largely an after-the-fact explanation of why a marketing program did or did not work, rather than a carefully thought-out foundation for marketing programs.[62]

The authors contend (with our total endorsement) that market segmentation should play a major role in industrial marketing planning and strategy

[62]*Ibid.*, p. 155.

formation and provide a useful guide to a number of bases that have been found to be appropriate for industrial products and services.

Promotional Mix Decisions

Following the identification of appropriate industrial market segments, a series of promotional mix decisions must be made. The promotional mix is a subset of the marketing mix and refers to those controllable variables designed to influence buyer response to the product/service offering of the seller. Specifically, the promotional mix includes: price and communications. The latter is subdivided into (1) personal selling, (2) advertising, (3) sales promotion and publicity, and (4) distribution channel variables. Primary emphasis is placed on the development of a comprehensive, coordinated promotional strategy for each market segment, recognizing that there are

> ... a number of requirements which must be met at the interface of the marketing and buying systems if viable relationships are to develop and be maintained between the systems.[63]

These requirements focus on the *information* needs of both parties at the buying/selling interface:[64]

1. *Mutual or complementary awareness*—Both the buyer and the seller must have a mutual awareness of a buyer's problem situation amenable to a given product concept solution.
2. *Complementarity of data dissemination and acquisition patterns*—Recognizing that buying systems are basically information and decision systems supports the idea that buyers search for data (not information) to solve their problems and that marketers have the task of providing the required data.
3. *Complementarity of goals*—"The essence of the marketing concept is the creation and maintenance of a relationship between buyers and sellers which takes into account the goals of both systems."[65]
4. *Complementarity of product concepts*—There are often wide differences among buyers with respect to their knowledge and perception

---
[63]Patrick J. Robinson and Bent Stidsen, *Personal Selling in a Modern Perspective*. Boston: Allyn and Bacon, 1967, p. 189.
[64]These requirements are discussed in some detail by Robinson and Stidsen, *op. cit.*, pp. 189–198.
[65]*Ibid.*, p. 195.

of a particular product. One of the major tasks of promotional strategy is to produce greater complementarity of product concepts among and between buyers in conjunction with appropriate segmentation as well as greater complementarity between the marketing and the buying systems.

5. *Mutuality of values*—Data credibility requires that both marketing and buying systems recognize their mutual responsibility for truth and the maintenance of moral values.

Levitt has expressed a similar view of the importance of problem definition:

> The marketing concept views the customer's purchasing activities as being problem-solving activities. This view of what the consumer does can have a profound effect on how the supplier or seller conducts his affairs. It affects more than how he does business and how much business he does. It affects what business he tries to do and what his product line should be. By looking at what the customer is actually trying to do, the seller will see that his problem as a seller is quite different from what it is usually assumed to be. Only after he defines his problem properly can the seller decide what is proper for him to do.[66]

One of the major questions surrounding industrial promotional mix decisions is whether they differ from those required for consumer goods and services. Webster and Wind think not:

> Not only is there conceptually no difference between the type of organizational and consumer marketing decisions and the approach that should be utilized in making them, but a comparison of existing industrial marketing texts with general marketing management texts reveals few idiosyncratic 'industrial' characteristics in any of the industrial texts. Actually, if one were to delete the word industrial from the chapters in industrial marketing texts dealing with product, price, promotion, and distribution decisions, the chapters could very well be ascribed to any general marketing management text.[67]

Wilson, in his review of the Webster and Wind book, took umbrage with this statement specifically, contending that ". . . their study of later texts

---

[66]Theodore Levitt, *Marketing for Business Growth*. New York: McGraw-Hill, 1974, p. 12.
[67]Webster and Wind, *Organizational Buying Behavior, op. cit.*, p. 120.

THE BUYING/SELLING INTERFACE

has been cursory and less than objective."[68] Since one of his own books had been included in the Webster and Wind list, Wilson had some reason to disagree. In balance it appears that the similarities between industrial and consumer promotional strategy are far greater than the differences; nevertheless there are differences that are worth noting.

Pricing Strategy

After acknowledging that,

> Many intelligent and well-informed persons maintain that price-setters need to know very different kinds of things and should behave quite differently according to the type of product for which they are responsible.[69] [Oxenfeldt found that] The product characteristics that have marketing and pricing significance are those that affect the actions of ultimate customers, rivals, resellers, colleagues, suppliers, government, and possibly other parties to the business process. In other words, it is not the product characteristics themselves that are important; instead it is the fact that the product characteristics affect the parties involved in the production, sale, purchase, and logistics of the product. The factors that matter most to price-setters may be related to product characteristics, but certainly not directly or in any simple way. . . .[70] We thus conclude that price-setters need not know different things according to whether they are responsible for pricing industrial rather than consumer products.[71]

A review of the meager number of journal articles on industrial pricing strategy generally supports Oxenfeldt's contention (as well as that of Webster and Wind): Moyer and Boewadt[72] urge that industrial pricing strategists examine the effects of price on several parties (both intermediate and end-users) and consider the use of test marketing and simulation techniques. Frederick[73] and Stobaugh and Townsend[74] applied selected

---

[68] Aubrey Wilson, *op. cit.*, p. 353.
[69] Alfred R. Oxenfeldt, *Pricing Strategies*. New York: AMACOM (Division of the American Management Association), 1975, p. 241.
[70] *Ibid.*, p. 243.
[71] *Ibid.*, p. 244.
[72] Reed Moyer and Robert J. Boewadt, "The Pricing of Industrial Goods," *Business Horizons*, Vol. 14, June 1971, pp. 27–34.
[73] Donald G. Frederick, "An Industrial Pricing Decision Using Bayesian Multivariate Analysis," *Journal of Marketing Research*, Vol. 8, May 1971, pp. 199–203.
[74] Robert B. Stobaugh and Philip L. Townsend, "Price Forecasting and Strategic Planning: The Case of Petrochemicals," *Journal of Marketing Research*, Vol. 12, February 1975, pp. 19–29.

techniques to industrial goods that can or have been applied also to consumer goods. Although pricing strategies under situations of competitive bidding are often associated with industrial goods and services,[75] there is in fact no particular association between the two. Public agencies use competitive bidding generally for all large contracts, regardless of the product/service type.

Communications Strategy: Personal Selling

A comprehensive study of the role of personal selling found:

> The strategic significance of the personal selling function derives from its potential role in the development and maintenance of intercommunicative relationships between selling and buying systems. . . . In the context of the marketing mix, the unique characteristic of the personal selling function is that it is a two-way communicative medium. Consequently, if properly integrated into the marketing function the salesman can serve both as an information disseminator and an information acquirer.[76]

There is actually no significant difference in the concepts and methods of personal selling between industrial and consumer products, but scale differences between industrial and consumer accounts result in significant differences in the place of personal selling in the promotional mix. The large number of buying influences and large dollar volume purchases associated with industrial buyers combine to require and permit a primary reliance on personal selling as the primary element in the promotional mix for most industrial marketers. Webster and Wind have identified three reasons for the primacy of personal selling:[77]

1. The salesman has the capacity to identify the members of the buying center in a particular buying situation, the nature of the buying problem, and the goals of the buying center members.
2. The salesman can provide the data required by buying center members to solve a particular buying problem and also collect data required by others in the organization to help solve the buyer's problem.

---

[75]James E. Reinmuth and Jim D. Barnes, "A Strategic Competitive Bidding Approach to Pricing Decisions for Petroleum Industry Drilling Contractors," *Journal of Marketing Research*, Vol. 12, August 1975, pp. 362–365; Murphy A. Sewall, "A Decision Calculus Model for Contract Bidding," *Journal of Marketing*, Vol. 40, October 1976, pp. 92–98.
[76]Robinson and Stidsen, *op. cit.*, p. 288.
[77]Webster and Wind, *Organizational Buying Behavior, op. cit.*, pp. 122–123.

3. The salesman receives immediate feedback on the adequacy and appropriateness of his data dissemination and communication efforts and may adapt his behavior accordingly.

Research on the personal selling function in industrial marketing has been concentrated largely on: (1) matters pertaining to individual salesmen and their relationship to the marketing organization and (2) the allocation of sales effort to industrial markets. The research on salesmen and their marketing organization relationships has tended to be based on behavioral science concepts, while research on the allocation of sales effort has drawn heavily upon operations research and statistical models. Conspicuously missing from the literature are studies of the role of personal selling at the buying/selling interface—two rare exceptions are Pruden's study of the salesmen of a national manufacturer and distributor of wood building materials and Brand's study of British firms.[78]

A large-scale study of 265 industrial salesmen from ten companies and seven industries serves as a prototype of research on individual salesmen and their organizational relationships that draws upon behavioral science concepts. Churchill, Ford, and Walker have published a number of articles that were developed from this data base.[79] There are a few studies of individual salesmen and their organizational relationships that combine behavioral concepts and quantitative models; Darmon's articles on the response of industrial salesmen to financial incentives are a good example of this category.[80]

---

[78]Henry O. Pruden, "Interorganizational Conflict, Linkage and Exchange: A Study of Industrial Salesmen," *Academy of Management Journal*, Vol. 12, September 1969, pp. 339–350; Pruden, "The Outside Salesman: Interorganizational Link," *California Management Review*, Vol. 12, Winter 1969, pp. 57–66; Gordon T. Brand, *The Industrial Buying Decision*. New York: Wiley, 1972.

[79]Gilbert A. Churchill, Jr., Neil M. Ford, and Orville C. Walker, Jr., "Measuring the Job Satisfaction of Industrial Salesmen," *Journal of Marketing Research*, Vol. 11, August 1964, pp. 254–260; Walker, Churchill, and Ford, "Organizational Determinants of the Industrial Salesman's Role Conflict and Ambiguity," *Journal of Marketing*, Vol. 39, January 1975, pp. 32–39; Ford, Walker, and Churchill, "Expectation-Specific Measures of the Intersender Conflict and Role Ambiguity Experienced by Industrial Salesmen," *Journal of Business Research*, Vol. 3, April 1975, pp. 95–111; Churchill, Ford, and Walker, "Organizational Climate and Job Satisfaction in the Salesforce," *Journal of Marketing Research*, Vol. 13, November 1976, pp. 323–332; Walker, Churchill, and Ford, "Motivation and Performance in Industrial Selling: Present Knowledge and Needed Research," *Journal of Marketing Research*, Vol. 14, May 1977, pp. 156–168.

[80]Rene Y. Darmon, "Salesmen's Response to Financial Incentives: An Empirical Study," *Journal of Marketing Research*, Vol. 11, November 1974, pp. 418–426; Darmon, "Alternative Models of Salesmen's Response to Financial Incentives," *Operational Research Quarterly*, Vol. 28, no. 1, 1977, pp. 37–49.

Models of the allocation of personal selling effort to industrial markets based on operations research and statistical techniques have begun to appear regularly during the past decade, following years of almost total neglect. After a notable early effort to allocate sales effort was reported by Waid, Clark and Ackoff,[81] as well as an unsuccessful attempt to allocate experimentally sales effort in the industrial distributor market by the author,[82] industrial marketing applications of management science models to sales effort allocation began to appear with increasing frequency in the 1970s.

Many of the models of sales effort allocation have concentrated on issues of sales territory design. Early studies focused on the entire sales force and generally sought to equalize potential[83] or workload.[84] Subsequent articles by Fogg and Rokus [85] and Hess and Samuels[86] showed how territories could be designed for individual salesmen or groups of salesmen using potentials and workloads respectively. Early work on the use of sales response functions to design sales territories was conducted by Lambert[87] followed by more complex models developed by Lodish[88] and Montgomery, et al.[89] Davis and Farley[90] introduced another dimension by suggesting that sales quotas be used to design territories, and their

---

[81]Clark Waid, Donald F. Clark, and Russell L. Ackoff, "Allocation of Sales Effort in the Lamp Division of the General Electric Company," *Operations Research*, Vol. 4, December 1956, pp. 629–647.

[82]William E. Cox, Jr., "An Experimental Study of Promotional Behavior in the Industrial Distributor Market," in Raymond M. Haas, Ed., *Science, Technology, and Marketing*. Chicago: American Marketing Association, 1967, pp. 578–586.

[83]Walter J. Semlow, "How Many Salesmen Do You Need?," *Harvard Business Review*, Vol. 37, May–June 1959, pp. 126–132.

[84]Walter J. Talley, Jr., "How to Design Sales Territories," *Journal of Marketing*, Vol. 25, January 1961, pp. 7–13.

[85]C. Davis Fogg and Josef W. Rokus, "A Quantitative Method for Structuring A Profitable Sales Force," *Journal of Marketing*, Vol. 37, July 1973, pp. 8–17.

[86]Sidney W. Hess and Stuart A. Samuelds, "Experience with a Sales Districting Model: Criteria and Implementation," *Management Science*, Vol. 18, December 1971 (Part 2), pp. P41-P54.

[87]Zarrel V. Lambert, "Determining the Number of Salesmen to Employ: An Empirical Study," in Reed Moyer, Ed., *Changing Marketing Systems*. Chicago: American Marketing Association, 1967, pp. 338–341.

[88]Leonard M. Lodish, "CALLPLAN: An Interactive Salesman's Call Planning System," *Management Science*, Vol. 18, December 1971 (Part 2), pp. P25–P40.

[89]David B. Montgomery, Alvin J. Silk, and Carlos E. Zaragoza, "A Multiple-Product Sales Force Allocation Model," *Management Science*, Vol. 18, December 1971 (Part 2), pp. P3–P24.

[90]Otto A. Davis and John U. Farley, "Allocating Sales Force Effort with Commissions and Quotas," *Management Science*, Vol. 18, December 1971 (Part 2), pp. P55–P63.

model was tested experimentally by Winer,[91] who found that further research was needed to validate the model.

Lodish stated that:

Three interrelated questions are at the crux of efficient sales force allocation: (1) How frequently should each account or prospect be called upon? (2) How should territory boundaries be defined? and (3) Should people be added to or deleted from the sales force?[92]

That article responded to all three questions. Subsequent articles by Lodish,[93] Shanker, et al.,[94] and Zoltners[95] have reflected the need for an integrated approach to the allocation problem.

Communications Strategy: Advertising

The role of advertising in the promotional mix of the industrial firm has been the subject of a variety of studies during the past fifteen years—with varying results. Kotler has contrasted the view that advertising is relatively unimportant for industrial goods, as shown in Figure 14-9, with results of a study conducted by IBM, which indicated that advertising and selected other elements in the promotion mix had different roles at different stages of buyer readiness, as shown in Figure 14-10.[96] IBM discovered that advertising and publicity were the most important elements in the awareness stage when introducing new computers, and other industrial firms and studies have confirmed this primary role for advertising, adding that publicity releases are often phased ahead of advertising and new product introduction.

IBM and other high-technology companies have found that education of the prospective buyer is the critical element in the comprehension stage

---

[91] Leon Winer, "The Effect of Product Sales Quotas on Sales Force Productivity," *Journal of Marketing Research,* Vol. 10, May 1973, pp. 180–183.

[92] Leonard M. Lodish, " 'Vaguely Right' Approach to Sales Force Allocations," *Harvard Business Review,* Vol. 52, January–February 1974, pp. 119–124.

[93] Leonard M. Lodish, "Sales Territory Alignment to Maximize Profit," *Journal of Marketing Research,* Vol. 12, February 1975, pp. 30–36; Lodish, "Assigning Salesmen to Accounts to Maximize Profits," *Journal of Marketing Research,* Vol. 13, November 1976, pp. 440–444.

[94] Roy J. Shanker, Ronald E. Turner, and Andris A. Zoltners, "Sales Territory Design: An Integrated Approach," *Management Science,* Vol. 22, November 1975, pp. 309–320.

[95] Andris A. Zoltners, "Integer Programming Models for Territory Alignment to Maximize Profit," *Journal of Marketing Research,* Vol. 13, November 1976, pp. 426–430.

[96] Philip Kotler, *Marketing Management,* 3rd ed. Englewood Cliffs, N.J.: Prentice-Hall, 1976, p. 342.

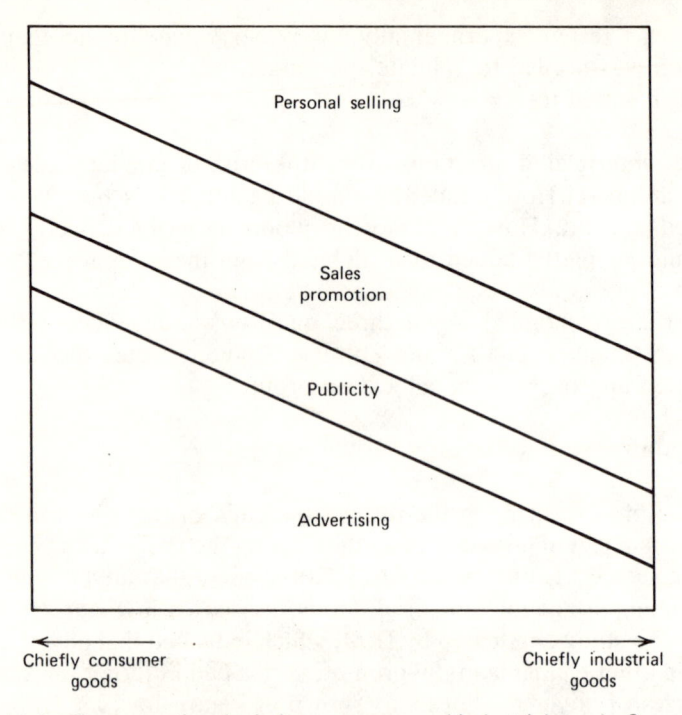

Figure 14-9 The promotional mix for consumer and industrial goods. Source: Philip Kotler, Marketing Management, *3rd ed. Englewood Cliffs, N.J.: Prentice-Hall, 1976, p. 341.*

with advertising taking a lesser role. The role of advertising increases again at the conviction stage, following up on the reduction of education's role but still playing a secondary role to the rising importance of personal selling. In the final stage of ordering, in which the buyer takes action, industrial advertising plays a very minor role.

Another major area of research interest has been the relationship between the use of industrial advertising and the level of personal selling effectiveness. In 1963 Kolliner reported that as industrial firms spend proportionately more of their marketing budget on advertising and sales promotion, their marketing expenses as a percent of sales tended to decline.[97] Levitt's study of industrial purchasing behavior suggested that a company's reputation had a positive effect on buyers, making it easier for salesmen from well-known firms to be favorably received.[98] Since indus-

[97] Sim A. Kolliner, Jr., "New Evidence of Ad Values," *Industrial Marketing*, Vol. 48, August 1963, pp. 81–84.
[98] Levitt, *Industrial Purchasing Behavior, op. cit.*

THE BUYING/SELLING INTERFACE

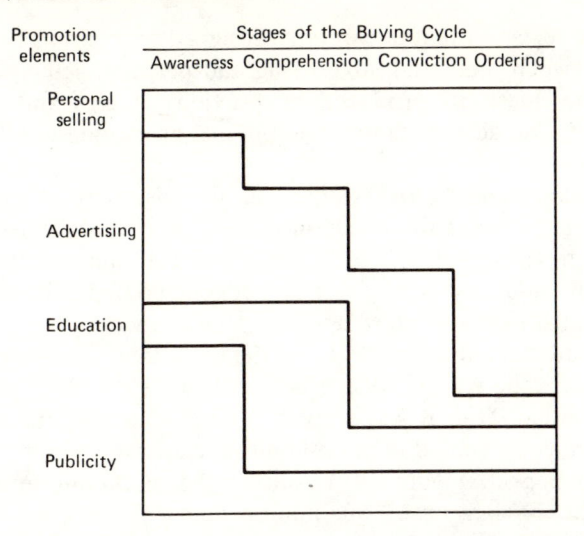

Figure 14-10 The promotion mix over the buying cycle. Source: Philip Kotler, Marketing Management, *3rd ed. Englewood Cliffs, N.J.: Prentice-Hall, 1976, p. 343.*

trial advertising is often used to promote the awareness and reputation of a seller, the findings indicated that industrial advertising could be of considerable help to larger, well-known companies, while smaller companies would be better off spending their limited funds on sales training in the hope that a superior sales presentation would give them an edge over their larger competitors. Two later studies have questioned the validity of Levitt's findings and additional research is needed to clarify the issue.[99]

Morrill has reported findings that support Kolliner's claim that the use of industrial advertising leads to a reduction in marketing expenses as a percent of sales and that

> . . . exposure to a manufacturer's industrial advertising improves the buyer's opinion of the manufacturer, and that this improvement in opinion means a larger share of the market for the manufacturer.[100]

Both the Kolliner and Morrill studies raise some disturbing methodological issues however and their findings must be cautiously interpreted.[101]

---

[99] Capon, Holbrook, and Hulbert, *op. cit.* 69–77: Sweitzer, *op. cit.* 334–339.
[100] John E. Morrill, "Industrial Advertising Pays Off," *Harvard Business Review,* Vol. 48, March–April 1970, pp. 4ff.
[101] Gary L. Lilien, Alvin J. Silk, Jean-Marie Choffray, and Murlidhar Rao, "Industrial Advertising Effects and Budgeting Practices," *Journal of Marketing,* Vol. 40, January 1976, pp. 16–24.

Additional research that is carefully designed to measure the interactive effects between industrial advertising and personal selling is needed to resolve the questions produced by previous studies and provide new insights into the determinants of an optimal promotion mix for industrial marketers.

The Kolliner and Morrill studies, as well as many others, have also been directed toward the question of how much to spend for industrial advertising. Lilien, et al., have reviewed the literature on budgeting practices in industrial advertising and concluded that percent of sales (as well as similar heuristic rules) and task methods were the most commonly used methods for budgeting.[102] To fill the information gap in this important decision area, the ADVISOR project has been initiated by M.I.T. and the Association of National Advertisers.[103] The initial data base for the ADVISOR project included data on 66 products from 12 companies for the 1972-1973 period. Figure 14-11 shows the marketing and advertising budgets for the data base firms and products. Each of the three budget ratios shown in Figure 14-11 were then related to 46 independent variables, with six variables identified as exerting primary influence on the ratios:

1. *Stage in the product life cycle*—In general ratios were highest in early stages, declining as the products matured.
2. *Frequency of purchase*—Products with relatively high frequency of purchase tended to be associated with high advertising/sales ratios.
3. *Product quality, uniqueness, and identification with company*—There tended to be a positive relationship between this factor and the A/S ratio.
4. *Market share*—There appeared to be an inverse relationship between market share and the A/S ratio, with higher shares linked with lower A/S ratios.
5. *Concentration of sales*—High sales concentration (over 24% of product sales from top 3 customers) resulted in a lower M/S ratio, but this also led to a higher A/M ratio so that the A/S ratio was minimally affected.
6. *Growth of customers*—An increase in the number of customers (over 1% annually) tended to be associated with an increase in each of three ratios.

---

[102]*Ibid.*, p. 24.
[103]Gary L. Lilien and John D. C. Little, "The ADVISOR Project: A Study of Industrial Advertising Budgets," *Sloan Management Review,* Vol. 17, Spring 1976, pp. 17-31.

THE BUYING/SELLING INTERFACE

	Advertising	Advertising/ Sales (A/S)	Marketing/ Sales (M/S)	Advertising/ Marketing (A/M)
Median:	$ 92,000	0.6%	6.9%	9.9%
Range:	0 1,100,000	0–68	0–340	0–95
Range for 50% of products	16,000- 272,000	0.1–1.8	3–14	5–19

Source: Gary L. Lilien and John D. C. Little, "The ADVISOR Project: A Study of Industrial Advertising Budgets," *Sloan Management Review*, Vol. 17, Spring 1976, p. 21.

Figure 14-11 Marketing and advertising budgets in the advisor data base.

Once an advertising budget is determined, the media to be used must be determined. The Morrill study found that

> ... lack of frequency of advertising is the single most common cause of program failure. Out of several hundred failures I have studied, more than 90% ran fewer than 5 pages of advertising in 1 magazine in a 12-month period.[104]

After this threshold level is reached, two models have been suggested for selecting industrial media. Aaker has proposed a relatively sophisticated, complex model comparable in many respects to those used for consumer goods and services,[105] while Boyd, et al., have proposed a much simpler model that uses marketing data on each individual in the sample as a basis for the media schedule.[106]

Communications Strategy: Sales Promotion

Sales promotion is treated here as a residual category to encompass all forms of advertising and sales promotion efforts other than space adver-

---

[104] Morrill, *op. cit.*, p. 168.
[105] David A. Aaker, "A Probabilistic Approach to Industrial Media Selection," *Journal of Advertising Research*, Vol. 8, September 1968, pp. 46–54.
[106] Harper W. Boyd, Jr., Henry J. Claycamp, and Charles W. McClelland, "Media Models for the Industrial Goods Advertiser—A Do-It-Yourself Opportunity," *Journal of Marketing*, Vol. 34, April 1970, pp. 23–27.

tising in trade, technical, and business publications. The category therefore includes:

1. Direct mail advertising
2. Catalogues, brochures, and other product-oriented materials
3. Trade shows, exhibits, and displays
4. Specialty advertising
5. Miscellaneous forms of sales promotion

There is relatively little research-based information available on the role of these sales promotion elements in the industrial promotion mix, with the exception of the early report on the findings of the ADVISOR project. This study found that the advertising and promotion budget was allocated among four categories as follows:[107]

	(Median amounts)
Space advertising	41%
Sales promotion	24
Direct mail and product materials	24
Trade shows, exhibitions	11
Total	100

Four firm and product characteristics were found to be related to the advertising and sales promotion budget allocation:

1. *Sales volume*—Expenditures on sales promotion and trade shows was found to be positively related to sales volume; direct mail expenditures showed a negative relationship with sales volume. A slightly negative relationship between space advertising expenditures and sales volume was explained as being due to spending a greater proportion on other forms of advertising and promotion after a given level of space advertising was reached.
2. *Stage in the product life cycle*—Products in the later stages of the life cycle tended to have higher expenditures for direct mail advertising; products in the early stages tended to have higher expenditures for sales promotion.
3. *Concentration of sales*—Firms with highly concentrated sales spent proportionately more for sales promotion.

[107] Lilien and Little, *op. cit.*, p. 27.

4. *Number of customers*—Firms with many customers were found to be less likely to use direct mail advertising with no effects on other forms of advertising and sales promotion.

Distribution Channel Strategy

Although the dominant channel of distribution for industrial goods and services is a direct, one-stage channel between the manufacturer and the industrial customer, the industrial distributor plays a key role in the distribution of many industrial products. A recent study by Webster is the first research-based study of these important intermediaries to appear in more than a decade.[108] Among the more important findings of this study were:

1. Among firms using industrial distributors, the distributors have taken on a broader set of marketing responsibilities and provided a growing proportion of the manufacturer's total sales.
2. Firms relying heavily on industrial distributors did not show any single dominant marketing strategy.
3. Industrial distributors have been of little value in gathering marketing data for their suppliers.
4. Manufacturers must be prepared to supplement the weaknesses of industrial distributors with strong "missionary" salesmen of their own who will help the distributor improve his effectiveness.

SUMMARY

This chapter has applied the Webster and Wind model of organizational buying behavior to assess the current state of knowledge concerning industrial buying behavior and to examine the role of industrial marketing research in marketing decision making with particular emphasis on promotional strategy.

In addition to the nature of the buying situation, four classes of variables influence the buying decision process: environmental, organizational, interpersonal, and individual factors. Each of the four classes of variables can be divided into task and nontask influences. A fifth class of influence is the buying situation, widely portrayed through the BUYGRID model.

[108] Frederick E. Webster, Jr., "The Role of the Industrial Distributor in Marketing Strategy," *Journal of Marketing,* Vol. 40, July 1976, pp. 10–16.

Environmental factors determine the availability of goods and services, the general conditions in which buying takes place, and the values and norms for individual and organizational behavior. Most organizations have attempted to deal with environmental changes in a manner that implicitly assumes continuity in those changes. Little progress has been made in dealing with discontinuous and accelerated change. This is an area in which industrial marketing researchers have an opportunity to make significant contributions toward a better understanding of environmental influences on the firm as well as of the ways in which the firm influences the environment.

Much of the research on the impact of organizational influences on buying behavior has centered on the effects of organization structure, particularly emphasizing buying center membership and responsiblity. Although decentralization is one of several ways of responding to environmental change, it is evident that there is no one "right" response except to tailor organizational design to each situation.

A study of interpersonal factors in organizational buying behavior starts with recognition of the differential roles of users, buyers, influencers, deciders, and gatekeepers, the overlapping roles of individuals in the buying process, and the differences in the influences exerted by those roles at different stages in the buying process. One of the remaining issues is that a methodology has as yet to be devised that can accurately measure role influence. Another research need calls for further study of all members of the buying group beyond the purchasing agent.

Individual factors play an important role in organizational buying behavior. Research on individual factors has been of the dominant dimension type, focusing for the most part on perceived risk and risk reduction strategies, or of the multiattribute decision type. Most multiattribute decision models have been of the linear compensatory type but there has been increasing reliance on perceptual and preference mapping models.

Information about organizational buying behavior can be classified from the point of view of promotional strategy into two topics: identification of promotional strategy and promotional mix decisions. Wind and Cardozo concluded that in industrial marketing, market segmentation at present is used largely as an after-the-fact explanation of marketing plan success or failure. Industrial market segmentations are largely based on geography and end use. However empirical research has suggested that other bases exist and have been used. It has been proposed that segmentation proceed according to a two-stage process wherein the first stage concentrates on macro (organizational) characteristics and the second stage, if needed, proceeds according to micro (decision-making unit) characteristics. Industrial market segmentation is another area in which further research is needed and which should play a major role in planning and strategy formulation.

On balance it appears that the similarities between industrial and consumer promotional strategy are far greater than the differences. However there are a number of important differences. Greater demand concentration of industrial markets permits and requires primary reliance on personal selling. Research on personal selling has paid considerable attention to individual salesman characteristics and allocation of sales effort but relatively little research has been conducted on the role of personal selling in the buyer/seller interface.

Despite the pivotal importance of personal selling in industrial marketing, advertising plays an important role in the early stages of the buying cycle, particularly in high-technology markets where customer education is necessary. In addition empirical studies show that industrial advertising can lead to a significant increase in personal selling effectiveness, a reduction in marketing expenses as a percent of sales and larger share of market. However some of these conclusions have been called into question. The ADVISOR project studies concluded that lack of advertising is the single most common cause of industrial marketing program failure. It is hoped that research of this type will continue and expand, particularly for its normative implications for corporate marketing strategy.

Little research data are available on sales promotion and distribution. It has been noted that sales promotion expenditures are generally proportionally higher among larger firms and in markets where products are in the late stages of the product life cycle or that experience high demand concentration. Distribution has received comparatively little attention partly because a direct, one-stage channel is the dominant form of distribution for most industrial goods. A recent study has noted several trends in industrial goods distribution, including broader responsibilities, greater percentage of industrial marketers' sales and more use of missionary selling.

SUGGESTED READINGS

Aaker, David A., "A Probabilistic Approach to Industrial Media Selection," *Journal of Advertising Research*, Vol. 8, September 1968, pp. 46–54.

Ansoff, H. Igor, "Managing Strategic Surprise by Response to Weak Signals," *California Management Review*, Vol. 18, Winter 1975, pp. 21–33.

Boyd, Harper W., Jr., Henry J. Claycamp, and Charles W. McClelland,

"Media Models for the Industrial Goods Advertiser—a Do-It-Yourself Opportunity," *Journal of Marketing*, Vol. 34, April 1970, pp. 23–27.

Brand, Gordon T., *The Industrial Buying Decision*. New York: Wiley, 1972.

Capon, Noel, M. Holbrook, and J. Hulbert, "Industrial Buying Behavior: A Reappraisal," *Journal of Business Administration*, Vol. 4, Fall 1972, pp. 69–77.

Cardozo, Richard N., "Segmenting the Industrial Market," in Robert L. King, Ed., *Marketing and the New Science of Planning*. Chicago: American Marketing Association, 1969, pp. 433–440.

Cardozo, Richard N., and James W. Cagley, "Experimental Study of Industrial Buyer Behavior," *Journal of Marketing Research*, Vol. 8, August 1971, pp. 329–334.

Churchill, Gilbert A., Jr., Neil M. Ford, and Orville C. Walker, Jr., "Measuring the Job Satisfaction of Industrial Salesmen," *Journal of Marketing Research*, Vol. 11, August 1964, pp. 254–260.

Churchill, Gilbert A., Jr., Neil M. Ford, and Orville C. Walker, Jr., "Organizational Climate and Job Satisfaction in the Salesforce," *Journal of Marketing Research*, Vol. 13, November 1978, pp. 323–332.

Cox, William E., Jr., "An Experimental Study of Promotional Behavior in the Industrial Distributor Market," in Raymond M. Haas, Ed., *Science, Technology and Marketing*. Chicago: American Marketing Association, 1966, pp. 578–586.

Cyert, Richard M., and James G. March, *A Behavioral Theory of the Firm*. Englewood Cliffs, N.J.: Prentice-Hall, 1963.

Darmon, Rene Y., "Alternative Models of Salesmen's Response to Financial Incentives," *Operational Research Quarterly*, Vol. 28, no. 1, 1977, pp. 37–49.

Darmon, Rene Y., "Salesmen's Response to Financial Incentives: An Empirical Study," *Journal of Marketing Research*, Vol. 11, November 1974, pp. 418–426.

Davis, Otto A., and John U. Farley, "Allocating Sales Force Effort with Commissions and Quotas," *Management Science*, Vol. 18, December 1971 (Part 2), pp. P55–P63.

Day, George S., "Evaluating Models of Attitude Structure," *Journal of Marketing Research*, Vol. 9, August 1972, pp. 279–286.

Farrer, Dean G., "Life of a Salesman: Value and Attitude Hierarchies," *Atlanta Economic Review*, Vol. 20, March 1970, pp. 4–7, 33–35.

Fogg, C. Davis, and Josef W. Rokus, "A Quantitative Method for Structuring a Profitable Sales Force," *Journal of Marketing*, Vol. 37, July 1973, pp. 8–17.

Ford, Neil M., Gilbert A. Churchill, Jr. and Orville C. Walker, Jr.,

"Expectation-Specific Measures of the Intersender Conflict and Role Ambiguity Experienced by Industrial Salesmen," *Journal of Business Research*, Vol. 3, April 1975, pp. 95–111.

Frank, Ronald E., William F. Massy, and Yoram Wind, *Market Segmentation*. Englewood Cliffs. N.J.: Prentice-Hall, 1971. Chap. 3, 5.

Frederick, Donald G., "An Industrial Pricing Decision Using Bayesian Multivariate Analysis," *Journal of Marketing Research*, Vol. 8, May 1971, pp. 199–203.

Grashof, John F., and Gloria P. Thomas, "Industrial Buying Center Responsibilities: Self versus Other Member Evaluations of Importance," in K. L. Bernhardt, Ed., *Marketing: 1776–1976 and Beyond*. Chicago: American Marketing Association, 1976, pp. 344–347.

Green, Paul E., and Donald S. Tull, *Research for Marketing Decisions*, Third Edition, Englewood Cliffs, N.J.: Prentice-Hall, 1975.

Gronhaug, Kjell, "Exploring Environmental Influences in Organizational Buying," *Journal of Marketing Research*, Vol. 13, August 1976, pp. 225–229.

Hakansson, Hakan, and Bjorn Wootz, "Supplier Selection in an Industrial Environment—An Experimental Study," *Journal of Marketing Research*, Vol. 12, February 1975, pp. 46–51.

Harding, Murray, "Who Really Makes the Purchasing Decisions?" *Industrial Marketing*, Vol. 51, September 1966, pp. 76–81.

Hess, Sidney W., and Stuart A. Samuelds, "Experience with a Sales District Model: Criteria and Implementation," *Management Science*, Vol. 18, December 1971 (Part 2), pp. P41–P54.

Kelley, J. Patrick, and James W. Coaker, "Can We Generalize about Choice Criteria for Industrial Purchasing Decisions?" in K. C. Bernhardt, Ed., *Marketing: 1776–1976 and Beyond*. Chicago: American Marketing Association, 1976, pp. 330–333.

Kollat, David T., "Environmental Forecasting and Strategic Planning: Perspectives on the Methodology of Futurology," in Fred C. Allvine, Ed., *Marketing in Motion*. Chicago: American Marketing Association, 1972, pp. 210–213.

Kolliner, Sim A., Jr., "New Evidence of Ad Values," *Industrial Marketing*, Vol. 48, August 1963, pp. 81–84.

Lambert, Zarrel V., "An Approach to Evaluating Competitive Effects and Selling Behavior in an Industrial Market," in B. R. McDonald, Ed., *Marketing Involvement in Society and the Economy*. Chicago: American Marketing Association, 1970, pp. 226–311.

Lambert, Zarrel V., "Determining the Number of Salesmen to Employ: An Empirical Study," in Reed Moyer, Ed., *Changing Marketing Systems*, Chicago: American Marketing Association, 1967, pp. 338–341.

Lehmann, Donald R., and John O'Shaughnessy, "Difference in Attribute Importance for Different Industrial Products," *Journal of Marketing*, Vol. 38, April 1974, pp. 36–42.

Levitt, Theodore, "Industrial Purchasing Behavior: A Study of Communications Effects" (Ph.D. diss., Graduate School of Business Administration, Harvard University, 1965).

Levitt, Theodore, *Marketing for Business Growth*. New York: McGraw-Hill, 1974.

Lilien, Gary L., and John D. C. Little, "The ADVISOR Project: A Study of Industrial Advertising Budgets," *Sloan Management Review*, Vol. 17, Spring 1976, pp. 17–31.

Lilien, Gary L., Alvin J. Silk, Jean-Marie Choffray, and Murlidhar Rao, "Industrial Advertising Effects and Budgeting Practices," *Journal of Marketing*, Vol. 40, January, 1976, pp. 16–24.

Lodish, Leonard M., "Assigning Salesmen to Accounts to Maximize Profits," *Journal of Marketing Research*, Vol. 13, November, 1976, pp. 440–444.

Lodish, Leonard M., "CALLPLAN: An Interactive Salesman's Call Planning System," *Management Science*, Vol. 18, December 1971 (Part 2), pp. P25–P40.

Lodish, Leonard M., "Sales Territory Alignment to Maximize Profit," *Journal of Marketing Research*, Vol. 12, February 1975, pp. 30–36.

Lodish, Leonard M., " 'Vaguely Right' Approach to Sales Force Allocations," *Harvard Business Review*, Vol. 52, January–February, 1974, pp. 119–124.

McMillan, James R., "Role Differentiation in Industrial Buying Decisions," in Thomas V. Greer, Ed., *1973 Combined Conference Proceedings*. Chicago: American Marketing Association, 1974, pp. 207–211.

McMillan, James R., "The Role of Perceived Risk in Industrial Marketing Decisions," in Boris and Helmut Becker, Eds., *1972 Combined Conference Proceedings*. Chicago: American Marketing Association, 1973, pp. 412–417.

Montgomery, David B., Alvin J. Silk, and Carlos E. Zaragoza, "A Multiple-Product Sales Force Allocation Model," *Management Science*, Vol. 18, December 1971 (Part 2), pp. P3–P24.

Morrill, John E., "Industrial Advertising Pays Off," *Harvard Business Review*, Vol. 48, March–April 1970, pp. 4ff.

Moyer, Reed, and Robert Boewadt, "The Pricing of Industrial Goods," *Business Horizons*, Vol. 14, June 1971, pp. 27–34.

O'Rourke, Mary R., James M. Shea, and William M. Solley, "Survey Shows Need for Increased Sales Calls, Advertising, and Updated

Mailing Lists to Reach Buying Influences," *Industrial Marketing*, Vol. 58, April 1973, pp. 32–43.

O'Shaughnessy, John, and Donald R. Lehmann, "A Reply to 'A Cautionary Note on Difference in Attribute Importance for Different Industrial Products'," *Journal of Marketing*, Vol. 39, January 1975.

Oxenfeldt, Alfred R., *Pricing Strategies*. New York: AMACOM (Division of the American Management Association), 1975, pp. 241–244.

Perrow, Charles B., *Organizational Analysis: A Sociological Point of View*. Belmont, Cal.: Brooks/Cole, 1970.

Pruden, Henry O., "Interorganizational Conflict, Linkage and Exchange: A Study of Industrial Salesmen," *Academy of Management Journal*, Vol. 12, September 1969, pp. 339–350.

Pruden, Henry O., "The Outside Salesman: Interorganizational Link," *California Management Review*, Vol. 12, Winter 1969, pp. 57–66.

Reinmuth, James E., and Jim D. Barnes, "A Strategic Competitive Bidding Approach to Pricing Decisions for Petroleum Industry Drilling Contractors," *Journal of Marketing Research*, 1975, pp. 362–365.

Robinson, Patrick J., Charles W. Faris, and Yoram Wind, *Industrial Buying and Creative Marketing*. Boston: Allyn and Bacon, 1967.

Robinson, Patrick J., and Bent Stidsen, *Personal Selling in a Modern Perspective*, Boston: Allyn and Bacon, 1967, pp. 189–198.

Scott, Jerome E., and Peter D. Bennett, "Cognitive Models of Attitude Structure: 'Value Importance' *Is* Important," in Fred C. Allvine, Ed., *Marketing in Motion*. Chicago: American Marketing Association, 1972, pp. 346–350.

Semlow, Walter J., "How Many Salesmen Do You Need?" *Harvard Business Review*, Vol. 37, May–June 1959, pp. 126–132.

Semon, Thomas T., "A Cautionary Note on 'Difference in Attribute Importance for Different Industrial Products'," *Journal of Marketing*, Vol. 39, January 1975, p. 79.

Sewell, Murphy A., "A Decision Calculus Model for Contract Bidding," *Journal of Marketing*, Vol. 40, October 1976, pp. 92–98.

Shanker, Roy J., Ronald E. Turner, and Andris A. Zoltners, "Sales Territory Design: An Integrated Approach," *Management Science*, Vol. 22, November 1975, pp. 309–320.

Sheth, Jagdish N., "A Model of Industrial Buyer Behavior," *Journal of Marketing*, Vol. 37, October 1973, pp. 50–56.

Steiner, George A., and John B. Miner, *Management Policy and Strategy*. New York: Macmillan, 1977.

Stobaugh, Robert B., and Philip L. Townsend, "Price Forecasting and Strategic Planning: The Case of Petrochemicals," *Journal of Marketing Research*, Vol. 12, February 1975, pp. 19–29.

Strauss, George, "Tactics of Lateral Relationship: The Purchasing Agent," *Administrative Science Quarterly*, Vol. 7, September 1962, pp. 161–186.

Strauss, George, "Work-Flow Frictions, Interfunctional Rivalry and Professionalism: A Case Study of Purchasing Agents," *Human Organization*, Vol. 23, Summer 1964, pp. 137–149.

Sweeney, Timothy W., H. Lee Mathews, and David T. Wilson, "An Analysis of Industrial Buyers' Risk Reducing Behavior: Some Personality Correlates," in Thomas V. Greer, Ed., *1973 Combined Conference Proceedings*. Chicago: American Marketing Association, 1974, pp. 217–221.

Sweitzer, Robert W., "Interpersonal Information Processing of Industrial Buyers," in K. L. Bernhardt, Ed., *Marketing: 1776–1976 and Beyond*. Chicago: American Marketing Association, 1976, pp. 334–339.

Talley, Walter J., Jr., "How to Design Sales Territories," *Journal of Marketing*, Vol. 25, January 1961, pp. 7–13.

Tosi, Henry L., "The Effects of Expectation Levels of Role Consensus on the Buyer-Seller Dyad," *Journal of Business*, Vol. 39, October 1966, pp. 516–529.

Waid, Clark, Donald F. Clark, and Russel L. Ackoff, "Allocation of Sales Effort in the Lamp Division of the General Electric Company," *Operations Research*, Vol. 4, December 1956, pp. 629–647.

Walker, Orville C., Jr., Gilbert A. Churchill, Jr., and Neil M. Ford, "Motivation and Performance in Industrial Selling: Present Knowledge and Needed Research," *Journal of Marketing Research*, Vol. 14, May 1977, pp. 156–168.

Walker, Orville C., Jr., Gilbert A. Churchill, Jr., and Neil M. Ford, "Organizational Determinants of the Industrial Salesman's Role Conflict and Ambiguity," *Journal of Marketing*, Vol. 39, January 1975, pp. 32–39.

Webster, Frederick E., Jr., "A General Model for Understanding Organizational Buying Behavior," *Journal of Marketing*, Vol. 36, April 1972, p. 13.

Webster, Frederick E., Jr., "The Industrial Salesman as a Source of Market Information," *Business Horizons*, Vol. 8, no. 1, Spring 1965, pp. 77–82.

Webster, Frederick E., Jr., "Modeling the Industrial Buying Process," *Journal of Marketing Research*, Vol. 2, November, 1965, pp. 370–376.

Webster, Frederick E., Jr., "The Role of the Industrial Distributor in Marketing Strategy," *Journal of Marketing*, Vol. 40, July 1976, pp. 10–16.

Webster, Frederick E., Jr., and Yoram Wind, *Organizational Buying Behavior*. Englewood Cliffs, N.J.: Prentice-Hall, 1972.
Wiegand, Robert E., "Identifying Industrial Buying Responsibility," *Journal of Marketing Research*, Vol. 3, February 1966, pp. 81–84.
Wildt, Albert R., and Albert V. Bruno, "The Prediction of Preference for Capital Equipment Using Linear Attitude Models," *Journal of Marketing Research*, Vol. 11, May 1974, pp. 203–205.
Wilson, Aubrey, book review in the *Journal of Marketing Research*, Vol. 11, August 1974, pp. 351–353.
Wilson, David T., "Industrial Buyers' Decision-Making Styles," *Journal of Marketing Research*, Vol. 8, November 1971, pp. 433–436.
Wilson, Ian H., "Reforming the Strategic Planning Process: Integration of Social and Business Needs," *Long Range Planning*, Vol. 7, October 1974, pp. 2–6.
Wind, Yoram, "Applying the Behavioral Theory of the Firm to Industrial Buying Decisions," *The Economic and Business Bulletin* (Temple University), Vol. 20, Spring 1968, pp. 22–28.
Wind, Yoram, "Industrial Buying Behavior: Source Loyalty in the Purchase of Industrial Components" (Ph.D. diss., Graduate School of Business, Stanford University, 1966).
Wind, Yoram, "Recent Approaches to the Study of Organizational Buying Behavior," in Thomas V. Greer, Ed., *1973 Combined Conference Proceedings*. Chicago: American Marketing Association, 1974, pp. 203–206.
Wind, Yoram, and Richard Cardozo, "Industrial Marketing Segmentation," *Industrial Marketing Management*, Vol. 3, 1974, pp. 153–166.
Wind, Yoram, Paul E. Green, and Patrick J. Robinson, "The Determinants of Vendor Selection: The Evaluation Function Approach," *Journal of Purchasing*, Vol. 4, August 1968, pp. 29–41.
Winer, Leon, "The Effect of Product Sales Quotas on Sales Force Productivity," *Journal of Marketing Research*, Vol. 10, May 1973, pp. 180–183.
Zaltman, Gerald, and Thomas V. Bonoma, "Organizational Buying Behavior: Hypotheses and Directions," *Industrial Marketing Management*, Vol. 6, 1977, pp. 53–60.
Zoltners, Andris A., "Integer Programming Models for Territory Alignment to Maximize Profit," *Journal of Marketing Research*, Vol. 13, November 1976, pp. 426–430.

CHAPTER FIFTEEN
Overview of Industrial Marketing Research

Industrial marketing research was defined at the outset of this book as the systematic gathering, recording, and analyzing of information about problems and opportunities relating to the marketing of industrial goods and services. Industrial marketing research has failed to receive its due attention in marketing texts and journals, even though the volume of transactions in industrial goods and services is more than twice that of consumer goods and services. This book has responded to the need for a systematic and wide ranging review of the procedures, issues, and opportunities found in industrial marketing research.

The Differential Characteristics of Industrial Marketing Research

An overview of industrial marketing research must begin with a discussion of the factors that impart industrial marketing research its unique character. First and foremost is the high degree of concentration of industrial market demand.[1] In most industrial markets a relatively small

---

This chapter was coauthored with Luis V. Dominguez, Associate Professor of Marketing, Case Western Reserve University.

[1] Aubrey Wilson, *The Assessment of Industrial Markets*. London: Hutchinson and Co., 1968, pp. 8–9.

OVERVIEW OF INDUSTRIAL MARKETING RESEARCH

number of customers account for most of the demand. Industrial market demand also tends to concentrate geographically and by industry. Demand concentration impacts significantly on the nature of data sources and research procedures that are most effective in industrial marketing research.

Industrial market demand is derived demand. As such it is more volatile than consumer demand. As a result industrial marketing research exhibits a greater concern with business and economic conditions and expectations, prices, and inventory levels.[2] Industrial market demand also results from group buying decisions to a greater extent than does consumer demand. Organizational factors play a key role in industrial buying. Consequently industrial buying behavior research tends to focus on different issues and to employ different research procedures from those that typify consumer research.

The industrial marketing researcher has less money and time to spend on each project.[3] Faced with smaller research budgets and staff, industrial marketing researchers rely to a smaller extent on external consultants and conclusive research and to a greater extent on expert judgements, secondary data, and exploratory studies than do marketing research departments of consumer firms.

As a consequence there are important differences in the emphasis that industrial and consumer marketing research place on various aspects of the marketing process. For example industrial marketing research pays a great deal of attention to market size and potential estimation and relatively little attention to market segmentation. There are also important differences in the relative development of research techniques, as noted in the preceding paragraph. In summary industrial marketing research entails more than the application of consumer research techniques in an industrial marketing context.

Given the differential characteristics of industrial marketing research, the discussion then focused on four key areas:

1. Data sources and basic research procedures (Chapters 2–4)
2. The principal areas of responsibility of industrial marketing (Chapters 5–9)
3. The use of survey methods in industrial marketing research (Chapters 10–12)
4. The contributions of industrial marketing research to product, pricing, and promotional strategy (Chapters 13–14)

[2]*Ibid.*, Chap. 1.
[3]*1973 Survey of Marketing Research.* Chicago, Illinois: American Marketing Association, 1973, pp. 28–30.

The state of the art, problems, and trends in those key areas are highlighted in the discussion that follows. It is hoped that the discussion will stimulate a continuing interest in bringing research sophistication to the identification and solution of industrial marketing problems and to the formulation of guidelines for industrial marketing strategy.

DATA SOURCES AND BASIC RESEARCH PROCEDURES

Surveys of Knowledgeable Persons

As already stated industrial marketing research tends to rely heavily on exploratory studies and secondary data or expert judgemental data. The high degree of demand concentration that characterizes industrial markets spells a high concentration of market information among a few knowledgeable persons. Surveys of knowledgeable persons are especially attractive when the time or cost factors make representative sampling infeasible, when respondents lack the requisite information, or when precise estimates are not needed. Today however there is an increasing interest in more rigorous procedures for expert data gathering that combine three key elements:

1. Sociogram analysis and "key informant" techniques for identifying knowledgeable experts[4]
2. Techniques for bounding expert assessments of the marketing environment including the Delphi method[5]
3. Cross-impact techniques for estimating the combined, interacting effects of anticipated environmental conditions on whose expected occurrence knowledgeable experts agree[6]

In an era of "future shock" and of discontinuities in the marketing

---

[4]Michael J. Houston, "The Key Informant Technique: Marketing Applications," in *Conceptual and Methodological Foundations of Marketing*, in Thomas V. Greer, Ed. Chicago: American Marketing Association, 1974, pp. 306–307; John Seidler, "On Using Informants: A Technique for Collecting Quantitative Data and Controlling Measurement Error in Organization Analysis," *American Sociological Review*, Vol. 39, December 1974, pp. 816–831.
[5]Philip Kotler, "A Guide to Gathering Expert Estimates." *Business Horizons,* October 1970, pp. 79-87; Alan R. Fusfeld and Richard N. Foster, "The Delphi Technique: Survey and Comments," *Business Horizons,* June 1971, pp. 63-74.
[6]Olaf Helmer, "Problems in Futures Research: Delphi and Causal Cross-Impact Analysis," *Futures,* Vol. 9, February 1977, pp. 17–31.

environment it can be expected that surveys of knowledgeable persons will become increasingly important. The development and application of more formalized and sophisticated techniques for identifying experts and obtaining precise expert estimates should be a high priority of industrial marketing researchers. Increasingly it is found that subjective estimates are part and essential ingredients of sophisticated decision models.[7]

Secondary Data Studies

Secondary data for exploratory or conclusive research are the principal sources of industrial marketing information. Secondary data are obtained from the firm's internal reporting systems or from external sources, chiefly from published reports of government agencies, trade associations, commercial directories, and commercial research services. Most secondary data are organized according to the Standard Industrial Classification (SIC) system. A combination of internal and external secondary data plus interviews with knowledgeable persons will usually provide most of the information typically needed for sales and market potential studies.

Extensive as secondary data are, there are a number of important limitations:[8]

1. *Timeliness*—Much of the data are collected only every five years although intercensus reports for many key industries are available.
2. *Need for finer classification*—The individual firm may be interested in industry or product data broken down to a level of detail not available in published reports.
3. *Multiproduct establishments*—An establishment that produces two or more products will be classified into the single industry that constitutes its primary activity.
4. *Inaccuracies*—These are caused by captive plants and varying production and purchasing methods.
5. *Most data reported at the establishment, not the company level*—Classified as establishments are corporate headquarters as well as individual factory sites. Thus in a study of sales potential for manufacturing raw materials based on the sales-per-employee relationship, the sales potential of territories that house corporate headquarters will be overestimated unless specific allowances for headquarters are made in the study.

---

[7]Kotler, *op. cit.*, p. 87.
[8]Francis E. Hummel, *Market and Sales Potentials*. New York: Ronald, 1961, pp. 74–76.

It is often possible to overcome or minimize the effects of the above limitations. Otherwise it becomes necessary to conduct primary data studies.

Primary Data Studies

Primary data studies are conducted for the most part when conclusive research is needed or the limitations of secondary data are too severe. Primary data studies are of three types: survey, observational, and experimental. Survey methods are by far the most common while observational and experimental methods are rarely, if ever, employed in industrial marketing research. The chief reason is that survey methods are the best suited to collecting most of the kinds of information sought in marketing research studies. Observational methods, especially panels and audits, are well suited to consumer goods studies for reasons that are largely inapplicable to most industrial marketing studies.[9] Field experimental analysis can be costly and complex. It will be useful only if the forecast error of market response is small in relation to the causal impact of the independent variables.[10] Experimental analysis however would be ideally suited to test marketing for marketing strategy selection. Laboratory experimentation has been used with some success in the study of organizational buyer behavior.[11]

THE PRINCIPAL RESPONSIBILITIES OF INDUSTRIAL MARKETING RESEARCH

Following the review of the sources and uses of industrial marketing data, the next topic concerns the principal uses to which research data are put. The principal responsibilities of industrial marketing research departments reported by at least 90% of industrial firms in an American Marketing Association survey included:

1. Development of market potentials

---

[9] Nicholas A. H. Stacey and Aubrey Wilson, *Industrial Marketing Research*. London: Hutchinson and Co., 1963, pp. 167–168.

[10] William E. Cox, Jr., "An Experimental Study of Promotional Behavior in the Industrial Distributor Market," in Raymond M. Haas, Ed., *Science, Technology and Marketing*. Chicago; Ill.: American Marketing Association, 1966, pp. 578–586.

[11] For example, Lowell E. Crow, "An Information Processing Approach to Industrial Buying: The Search and Choice Process" (Ph.D. diss. Graduate School of Business, Indiana University, 1974).

OVERVIEW OF INDUSTRIAL MARKETING RESEARCH

2. Market share analysis
3. Determination of market characteristics
4. Sales analysis
5. Short-term forecasting
6. Long-term forecasting
7. Studies of business trends
8. New product acceptance and potential
9. Competitive product studies
10. Determination of sales quotas and territories[12]

Sales, Cost, and Profitability Analysis

Sales, cost, and profitability analysis is the basic first step in any management-oriented analysis of marketing data. Its widespread usage stems from its almost exclusive reliance upon internal secondary data, its low cost, and its ease of application. Sales, cost, and profitability analysis requires four key elements:

1. *Definition of sales units*—whether orders or shipments, units sold or dollar revenue, in constant or current dollars.
2. *Definition of information segments*—From the point of view of availability of published secondary data, territories are best defined according to county lines. Since the 80-20 principle is particularly true of industrial demand,[13] it is advisable to classify customers into A, B, C accounts according to size.
3. *Setting sales standards*—for comparison with actual performance. The most common standards are last period, year to date, and plans.
4. *Specifying bases for profitability analysis*—This involves two separate issues:
    a. *Method of cost allocation*—As noted in Chapter 5, Stanton and Buskirk contend that direct costing is best suited to short-term analysis while full costing is best applied to long-term analysis.[14] Sevin has suggested that all functional costs be allocated to market segments on

---

[12]*1973 Survey of Marketing Research, op. cit.*
[13]Charles H. Sevin, *Marketing Productivity Analysis*. New York: McGraw-Hill, 1965, p. 8; Harry D. Wolfe and Gerald Albaum, "Inequality in Products, Orders, Customers, Salesmen, and Sales Territories," *Journal of Business*, July 1962, pp. 298–301.
[14]William J. Stanton and Richard H. Buskirk, *Management of the Sales Force*, 3rd ed. Homewood, Ill.: Irwin, 1969, p. 603.

activity bases. He has provided lists of possible activities to which various functional expenses might be apportioned.[15]

b. *Use of ratios for productivity analysis*—The two key issues are determining a basis for measuring segment return on investment[16] and determining the proper ratios, other than ROI, that might be used for productivity analysis.[17]

Two important recent developments merit the continuing attention of marketing research professionals. One is the work of the American Accounting Association on guidelines for measuring return on investment in marketing activity.[18] The other is the systematic analysis of marketing cost ratios pioneered by the Industrial Conference Board.[19] The Conference Board study identified 12 significant strategic determinants of marketing cost ratios. The potential implications of such a study are far reaching. Consider for example a firm that plans to expand its geographic markets to rely increasingly on intermediaries and to increase the number of accounts served. The Conference Board study would suggest that the combined effect of all these steps will be to increase the cost of marketing. If so, corporate planners should revise downward the firm's expected profit and payback rate from investment into marketing expansion.

Three salient implications result from the preceding discussion:

1. Continued, rigorous statistical analysis of the cost impact of market structure and marketing strategy across industries and over time is one of the most important and potentially productive areas of industrial marketing research. At the individual firm's level, the task of the industrial marketing researcher should be to verify whether findings such as those reported by the Conference Board are borne out by the firm's experience. If they are, his next task should be to determine possible strategies for minimizing cost pressures brought about by market structure or corporate strategy.

2. Industrial marketing researchers must become more actively involved

---

[15]Sevin, *op. cit.*, p. 25.

[16]For example: Edward C. Bursk, "View Your Customers as Investments," *Harvard Business Review*, Vol. 44, May–June 1966, pp. 91–94; Philip A. Scheuble, Jr., "ROI for New product Policy," *Harvard Business Review*, Vol. 47, November–December 1969, pp. 110–120.

[17]"Report of the Committee on Cost and Profitability Analyses for Marketing," *Accounting Review*, Supplement to Vol. 47, 1972, pp. 574–615.

[18]*Ibid.*

[19]Earl L. Bailey, *Marketing-Cost Ratios of U.S. Manufacturers*. New York: National Industrial Conference Board, 1975.

in the accounting of marketing costs. There is a need to determine more systematically and rigorously bases for cost allocation that make sense statistically as well as in marketing terms.

3. Measurement of marketing investment, incremental marketing investment, and return on marketing investment are critical to more systematic and quantitative analysis of market, product, and segment productivity analysis.

Market and Industry Analysis

Throughout this book "market" has referred to demand, "industry" has referred to supply. The first prerequisite to market or industry size measurement is to set boundaries based on the range of product substitutability for the needs of a specified group of buyers. Most published secondary data emphasize production and sales, hence most minimum demand studies and most comprehensive market demand studies actually rely primarily on industry as opposed to market data.

Minimum demand studies and comprehensive market demand studies[20] are among the most useful and common endeavors of industrial marketing research. Minimum demand studies are best suited to "go/no go" decisions on product/market feasibility. Comprehensive demand studies on the other hand look beyond market size to market trends, market share, industry structure and market structure analysis. Studies may even dwell on organizational buying procedures, industry technical standards, government regulation, and the characteristics of major customers. Some of that information will require primary data gathering.

Market and Sales Potential Estimation

Market and sales potential estimation rank along with market and industry analysis among the most common and useful endeavors of industrial marketing research.[21] Market potential was defined as the maximum level

---

[20]Aubrey Wilson, "Industrial Marketing Research in Britain," *Journal of Marketing Research*, Vol. 6, February 1969, p. 17.

[21]For a discussion of selected uses of sales and market potential, see: Hummel, *op. cit.*, pp. 9–10; Richard D. Crisp, *Sales Planning and Control*. New York: McGraw-Hill, 1961, p. 241; Philip Kotler, *Marketing Decision Making: A Model Building Approach*. New York: Holt, Rinehart & Winston, 1968, pp. 290–298, 407–419; M. L. Green and R. B. Maffei, "Technical Characteristics of Distribution Simulators," *Management Science*, Vol. 10, October 1963, pp. 62–69; National Industrial Conference Board, *Measuring Salesmen's Performance*, Studies in Business Policy No. 114. New York: 1965; Francis E. Hummel, "Pinpointing Prospects for Industrial Sales," *Journal of Marketing*, Vol. 25, July 1960, pp.

424   INDUSTRIAL MARKETING RESEARCH

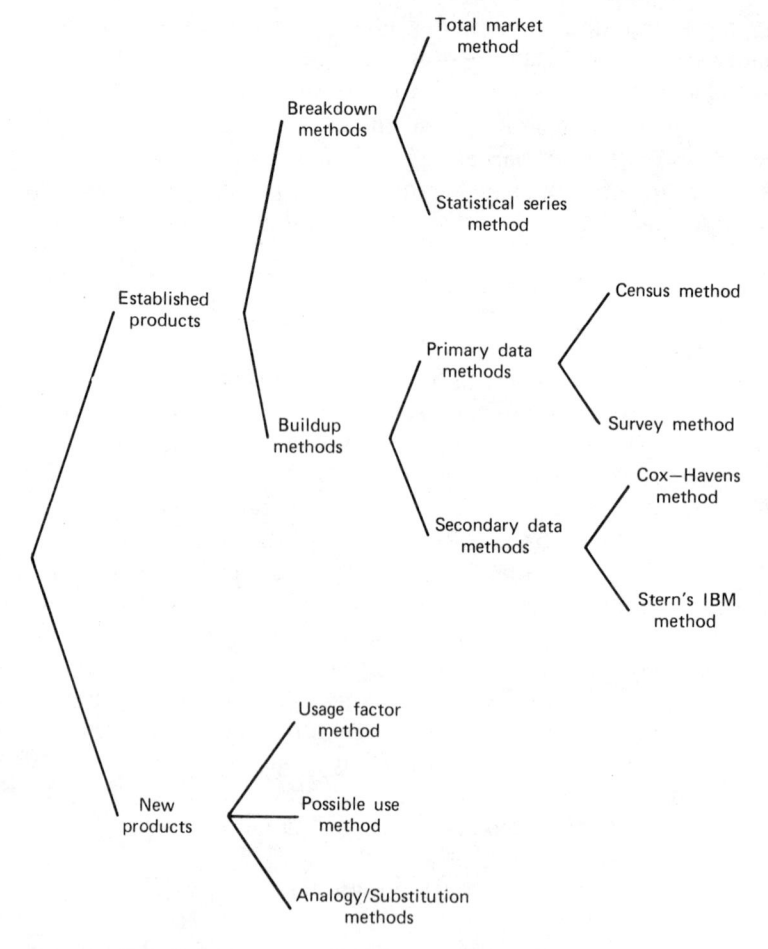

Figure 15-1 Methods of market and sales potential evaluation.

of demand for a product or service in a given environment. In practice this definition presents many difficulties. The result is that the line of distinction between actual and potential sales becomes blurred.

Figure 15–1 shows the taxonomy of potential estimation techniques. Potential estimation for new products is far more difficult than for estab-

---

26–31; Francis E. Hummel, "Further Pinpointing of Prospects for Industrial Sales," *Journal of Marketing*, Vol. 26, April 1961, pp. 64–68; Morgan B. McDonald, *Appraising the Market for New Industrial Products,* Studies in Business Policy No. 123. New York: National Industrial Conference Board, 1967, Chap. 3.

lished products where an existing sales data base can be tapped. The degree of difficulty and the complexity of the task of potential estimation increases with five factors:

1. Level of precision required
2. Lack of availability of secondary data
3. Lack of demand concentration
4. Demand volatility
5. Product newness[22]

Potential estimation for established products is generally much more straightforward. Regardless of whether one applies breakdown or buildup approaches, the cost and precision of potential estimates depends on finding a useful relationship between company or market sales and target market characteristics.

Our view is that precision can be achieved cost effectively by following four key guidelines:

1. Classify customers by SIC or product application. Often the structural relationship between sales and customer characteristics, such as number of employees, will vary by SIC number or by the type of application (automotive, medical, and so on) to which a product might be put.[23] Greater precision will be achieved if the sales-to-characteristic ratio is specific to that industry or application type.
2. Verify that there is a statistically reliable relationship between sales and the customer characteristic. If there are several available customer characteristics, pick the best one and explore the possibility of using more than one as the independent variable.
3. Whenever possible arrange all territorial data by county. This is because of the greater availability of data by counties.
4. When using a ratio of sales-to-customer characteristics as the basis of an estimate of market potential, verify wherever possible that achieved sales do not exceed market potential or do not exceed the firm's reasonably expected share of market potential. Whenever sales exceed potential, attempt to determine whether the inconsistencies are due to data errors or to poor model fit.

[22]Morgan B. McDonald, *op. cit.*, pp. 66–67.
[23]For example, see William E. Cox, Jr., and George N. Havens, "Determination of Sales Potentials for an Industrial Goods Manufacturer," *Journal of Marketing Research*, Vol. 14, November 1977, pp. 574–578.

The objective of these safeguards of course is to assess critically and improve the believability of the potential estimating procedure being used. The added costs of those safeguards is minor in comparison to total project cost.

Market and Sales Forecasting

The pivotal role of forecasting in the business planning process demands not only accuracy but management's confidence as well. That virtually requires management participation in the forecasting process. Reisman recommends blending objective, quantitative forecasts with qualitative forecasts.[24] Along the same lines Wolfe recommends using more than one forecasting procedure, each relying on a different data base. He advises that in unstable market situations, where a variety of inputs would be desirable, reconciliation of forecasts be delegated to a conference of executives.[25] The importance of subjective judgements as inputs to forecasting and planning models is expected to continue to rise.

Four types of forecasts must be linked together in order to produce a sales forecast:

1. Economic forecast
2. Industry forecast
3. Company sales forecast
4. Company product sales forecast[26]

The most salient aspects of market and sales forecasting can be summarized as follows:

1. An increased acceptance of econometric forecast services provided by several specialist organizations.[27] These economic forecasts have built a credible record in recent years.
2. The long-term relationship between economic activity and industry sales can be altered by a variety of factors, a major one being techno-

---

[24] Arnold Reisman, et al., "Forecasting Short-Term Demand," *Industrial Engineering*, May 1976, pp. 38–45.
[25] Harry D. Wolfe, *Business Forecasting Methods*. New York: Holt, Rinehart Winston, 1966, pp. 28–29.
[26] *Ibid.*, p. 17.
[27] For example, Michael D. McCarthy, *The Wharton Quarterly Econometric Forecasting Model Mark III*. Philadelphia: Economics Research Unit, University of Pennsylvania, 1972.

logical change.[28] There is increasing interest in systematic statistical modeling of the adoption of new products and technology, including the construction of new technology plants and installations and the substitution of new technology.[29] There is also an increased interest in subjectively based approaches utilizing Delphi[30] and cross-impact techniques[31] as well as hybrid models incorporating quantitative and qualitative inputs. Nevertheless a recent survey of technological forecasting practices found that most firms had not incorporated technological forecasting into their planning and decision making.[32]

3. The choice of forecasting technique depends in no small part on the nature of the product being studied. The demand for major accessories and equipment is volatile, with booms and busts. Like the demand for component parts and materials, forecasting must take cognizance of additions and replacements demand. Operating supplies and services however are directly tied to current output.

The overall theme of our discussion is that successful market and sales forecasting depends on cross validation of forecasts by alternative techniques and data bases, on management's participation in making judgmental adjustments to numerical forecasting and on in-house or purchased technology for dealing with the complexities of economic and technological forecasting. The starting point of forecasting should be a close examination of industry and product characteristics and management's forecasting objectives and requirements against the characteristics of the forecasting techniques being considered. Wheelwright and Makradikis and others have offered lists of those factors.[33]

---

[28] For a review of methods of technological forecasting, see Edwin B. Roberts, "Exploratory and Normative Technological Forecasting: A Critical Appraisal," *Technological Forecasting and Social Change*, Vol. 1, 1969, pp. 113–127. For an empirical survey of the extent of use and of the role of technological forecasting in corporate planning see James M. Utterback and Elmer H. Burack, "Identification of Technological Threats and Opportunities by Firms," *Technological Forecasting and Social Change*, Vol. 8, 1975, pp. 7–21.

[29] W. H. C. Simmonds, "The Analysis of Industrial Behavior and Its Use in Forecasting," *Technological Forecasting and Social Change*, Vol. 3, 1972, pp. 205–224; Joseph P. Martino and Stephen K. Conver, "The Step-wise Growth of Electric Generator Size," *Technological Forecasting and Social Change*, Vol. 3, 1972, pp. 465–471.

[30] See for example the PROBE studies conducted at TRW. Harper Q. North and Donald L. Pyke, " 'Probes' of the Technological Future," *Harvard Business Review*, Vol. 47, May–June 1969, pp. 68–76.

[31] Olaf Helmer, *op. cit.*

[32] Utterback and Burak, *op. cit.*

[33] Steven C. Wheelwright and Spyros Makradikis, *Forecasting Methods for Management*, 2nd ed. New York: Wiley, 1977, pp. 6–9.

Input-Output Analysis

Input-output analysis[34] remains a promising but little used technique for forecasting and potential estimation. Lack of awareness and knowledge among researchers of the characteristics and benefits of the technique, delayed availability of tables, the reported year-to-year instability of many input-output relationships, and excessive aggregation of industries and markets have limited its application.[35] It remains useful as a technique that provides one of the few secondary sources of demand rather than production data.

THE USE OF SURVEY METHODS IN INDUSTRIAL MARKETING RESEARCH

The collection of primary data through survey methods is dictated by the need to *supplement* secondary data in order to understand the purchase behavior of target customers. Limited research budgets and short channels are among the reasons why survey research activity is far less extensive among industrial goods marketers than among consumers goods marketers. Nevertheless surveys are the principal method for collecting primary data in industrial marketing research.

Survey methods can be classified according to survey structure or standardization, degree of disguise of survey objectives, and method of communication.[36] Structured nondisguised studies and mail questionnaires that are so prevalent in consumer research play a limited role in industrial marketing research. Structured and mail questionnaires are largely confined to large universes and to markets with relatively unconcentrated demand.

Personal interviews and nonstructured-nondisguised research of a limited number of respondents constitute by far the most prevalent survey approach in industrial marketing research. Personal interviewing of executives is to be preferred to other methods when target respondents

---

[34] John C. Chambers, Satinder K. Mullick, and Donald D. Smith, "How to Choose the Right Forecasting Technique," *Harvard Business Review,* Vol. 49, July–August 1971, pp. 45–74; National Industrial Conference Board, 1964.

[35] For a concise review of the methods and problems of application of input-output analysis to industrial marketing, see James T. Rothe, "The Reliability of Input/Output Analysis for Marketing," *California Management Review,* Vol. 14, Summer 1972, pp. 75–81.

[36] Harper W. Boyd, Jr., Ralph L. Westfall, and Stanley F. Stasch, *Marketing Research,* 4th ed. Homewood, Ill.: Irwin, 1977, p. 109; Donald T. Campbell, "The Indirect Assessment of Social Attitudes," *Psychological Bulletin,* Vol. 47, January 1950, p. 15.

may be away often, may tend to otherwise delegate questionnaire response to subordinates, or may simply tend to not respond. Interviewers should have technical training or briefing in the respondents' industry in order to both absorb respondents' insights and to probe the right issues.[37]

It has been said that some of the greatest differences between consumer and industrial marketing concern sampling procedures. The principal differentiating factor is the higher degree of demand concentration for industrial goods. The chief distinguishing considerations in industrial marketing surveys can be summarized thus:

1. Prior to sampling design it is essential to arrive at a definition of industry, market and product boundaries based on principles of product substitutability.[38]
2. Developing a sampling frame is comparatively easier for industrial markets than for consumer markets. Commercial directories of firms and establishments provide reasonably (though not completely accurate) lists of sampling units.
3. The selection of sampling elements within each sampling unit depends on organization structure of each firm. For this reason personal interviewing plays a key role in industrial sampling with the interviewer having the flexibility to select the appropriate respondent(s) in each organization.
4. Demand concentration spells a degree of information concentration that makes judgement sampling in particular and nonprobability sampling in general more desirable than in consumer studies. Judgement sampling of knowledgeable persons is especially common.
5. Demand concentration strongly favors the use of stratified sampling with no more than six strata generally recommended, and fewer if analysis of individual strata will be conducted.
6. Cost optimal disproportionate stratified sampling is recommended whenever large-account strata are surveyed by more costly, personal interviewing methods with small strata being surveyed by mail or telephone.[39] Industrial surveys often use combined methods of data collection for different sized firms.

In recent years there has been an increased interest in the use of

[37] Aubrey Wilson, *The Assessment of Industrial Markets, op. cit.* pp. 193–196.
[38] For a discussion of boundary setting, see Peter O. Steiner, "Markets and Industries," in D. L. Sills, Ed., *International Encyclopedia of the Social Sciences*, New York: Free Press, 1968.
[39] For a discussion of the technique of cost optimal allocation of sample size see C. William Emory, *Business Research Methods*. Homewood, Ill.: Irwin, 1976, pp. 157–159.

techniques for incorporating nonsampling (bias) costs as well as the trade off between cost and value of information into the sampling procedure selection process.[40]

Analysis of Survey Data

With the increasing availability of computers and statistical analysis programs, it is not surprising that industrial marketing research has resorted increasingly to the use of multivariate statistical analysis techniques,[41] of which the following appear to be particularly promising:

1. Multiple regression analysis is the most frequently used technique. Its uses range from sales forecasting and potential estimation to prediction of customer preference and loyalty.
2. Multiple discriminant analysis is useful both as a predictive technique for selecting successful products and attractive accounts or for finding the characteristics that significantly differentiate various customer segments. In this latter sense discriminant analysis is but a type of multivariate analysis of variance.[42]
3. Factor analysis is particularly useful for grouping industry, market, or company characteristics into a smaller set of meaningful dimensions.[43]
4. Cluster analysis, like factor analysis, groups items together. However it groups objects, not variables. Among the best known industrial marketing applications is Green and Tull's segmentation of the computer market.[44]
5. Nonmetric multidimensional scaling and conjoint analysis are recent developments that are particularly suited to mapping products and

---

[40] Leslie Kish, *Survey Sampling*. New York: Wiley, 1965, Chap. 13; Charles S. Mayer, "Assessing the Accuracy of Marketing Research," *Journal of Marketing Research*, Vol. 7, August 1970, pp. 285–291; Donald S. Tull and Dell I. Hawkins, *Marketing Research*. New York: Macmillan, 1976, pp. 579–581.

[41] For a classification of multivariate techniques according to the characteristics of data and relationships, see Jagdish N. Sheth, "The Multivariate Revolution in Marketing Research," *Journal of Marketing*, Vol. 35, January 1971, p. 15.

[42] For an industrial marketing application, see Yoram Wind, "Industrial Source Loyalty," *Journal of Marketing Research*, Vol. 7, November 1970, pp. 450–457.

[43] For an industrial marketing application, see Timothy W. Sweeny, H. Lee Matthews, and David T. Wilson, "An Analysis of Industrial Buyers' Risk Reducing Behavior: Some Personality Correlates," in Thomas V. Greer, Ed., *1973 Combined Conference Proceedings*. Chicago: American Marketing Association, 1974, pp. 217–221.

[44] Paul E. Green and Donald S. Tull, *Research for Marketing Decisions,* 3rd ed. Englewood Cliffs, N.J.: Prentice-Hall, 1975, pp. 584–587.

OVERVIEW OF INDUSTRIAL MARKETING RESEARCH

customers in a joint space, thereby gaining insights into unsatisfied market segment needs.[45]

To the extent that budget limitations will permit it, industrial marketing research is certain to benefit from a steady increase in the use of these more insightful and sophisticated techniques for market segmentation and strategy selection. It is to those two and other related topics that we now turn.

Product Analysis

Most of the preceding discussion has revolved around the choice of markets for a firm's products. Product choice decisions are equally important strategically. An assessment of trends and opportunities in product decision making might follow the stages of the extended product life cycle. Within the Development Phase, four key decisions are found.[46]

Product Feasibility Decisions. Studies indicate that market rather than technical opportunity factors are the primary source of industrial innovations. Unfortunately technological R&D-oriented firms tend to limit marketing research to screening studies.[47] Part of the reason is management's reluctance to engage in lengthy and costly marketing research studies. Exploratory research and minimum demand studies coupled with product life cycle curves like the Gompertz function can be used to develop quantitative projections of management's subjective estimates of the rate of product acceptance over time.

Product Specification Decisions. Following satisfactory feasibility results, the next step is to blend customer desires and engineering specifications. The objective is to study the distribution of product performance characteristics and customer desires. Multidimensional scaling, conjoint analysis techniques, and product positioning studies enable researchers to map jointly customer desires and product characteristics in order to

---

[45] For an application of nonmetric multidimensional scaling to joint space modeling of industrial markets, see George S. Day, "Evaluating Models of Attitude Structure," *Journal of Marketing Research,* Vol. 9, August 1972, pp. 279–286. For an industrial marketing application of conjoint analysis, see Yoram Wind, "Recent Approaches to the Study of Organizational Buying Behavior," in Thomas V. Greer, Ed., *1973 Combined Conference Proceedings.* Chicago: American Marketing Association, 1974, pp. 203–206.
[46] Edgar A. Pessemier, *Managing Innovation and New Product Development.* Cambridge, Mass.: Marketing Science Institute, 1975, p. 24.
[47] *Ibid.,* pp. 26–35.

identify new product opportunities.[48] We look to the continued refinement and application of these techniques for customer-oriented industrial product design.

Market and Product Testing Decisions. The distinction between market and product testing of industrial products is often blurred by the fact that product testing for industrial products tends to require a high degree of cooperation from prospective buyers. The result is a "creeping commitment" to industrial products and a relative dearth of market testing. However the following testing strategies have been applied successfully:

1. Gradual roll-out of new products to selected market segments and customers in order to evolve an acceptable marketing mix
2. Use of models of demand response linked to cost, profit, and risk submodels[49]
3. Subjective probability estimate models of expected costs, sales, investment, and profit[50]

In practice, such models are viewed as aids to decision making even though they respond to the need for incorporating capital budgeting and return on investment concepts in new product decision making. The reason is that management recognizes the problems of estimating costs, demands and subjective probabilities. Part of the solution is to involve management in model design and implementation.

During the Market Phase of the product life cycle, three key decision areas involve marketing research inputs, arranged according to product life cycle stage.

Commercial Evaluation Decision. Here emphasis is on initial product acceptance. Models of diffusion processes have been applied with considerable success in industrial marketing. Bass' model has demonstrated accuracy and versatility.[51]

---

[48] For an industrial marketing application, see Green and Tull, *op. cit.*, pp. 618–623, 690–696.
[49] Glen L. Urban, "A New Product Analysis and Decision Model," *Management Science,* Vol. 14, April 1968, pp. 490–517.
[50] H. Paul Root, "The Use of Subjective Probability Estimates in the Analysis of New Products," in P. R. McDonald, Ed., *Marketing Involvement in Society and the Economy.* Chicago: American Marketing Association, 1970, pp. 200–207.
[51] Frank M. Bass, "A New Product Growth Model for Consumer Durables," *Management Science,* Vol. 15, January 1969, pp. 215–277. For industrial applications, see John V. Nevers, "Extensions of a New Product Growth Model," *Sloan Management Review,* Vol. 13, Winter 1972, pp. 77–91.

Product Audit Decision. Periodic updates of product performance during the Growth and Maturity stages of the product life cycle are necessary in order to decide whether to retain a product. Here modeling emphasis turns to repeat and replacement purchases as well as to the distinction between first generation products and successive generations of improved or modified products, with product life cycles that are distinct from those of first generation products. The validity and usefulness of such models to industrial marketing has been amply demonstrated empirically.[52]

Product Elimination Decision. The key is to anticipate product decay to the point where elimination is not delayed beyond the useful life of the product. Alexander has suggested five key indicators of product decline.[53] Kotler proposed a six-step procedure for product elimination decisions.[54] Central to the analysis are the specification of product performance criteria and the projection of future product sales. A useful application of elimination models is to separate the weakest products from others that are approaching but have not reached commercial death.

A final element of product evaluation decision is the development of a product portfolio evaluation framework.[55] An example is shown in Figure 15–2. When coupled with an equilibrium distribution of the market shares of competitors' products, a growth/share matrix alerts the firm to the need for new product developments, the need to eliminate some products, and the list of possible candidates for product modification. For example, a firm that wishes to achieve a greater profit rate may find that its problem is being overcommitted to "cash cows." The prescription would be to make a commitment to new products with substantial growth capacity. Cox illustrated the applicability of the product portfolio management scheme to the ready-to-eat cereal market.[56]

---

[52] Cornelius A. de Kluyver, "Innovation and Industrial Product Life Cycles" (Ph.D. diss., Case Western Reserve University, 1975); Edwin Mansfield, *Technological Change.* New York: Norton, p. 88.
[53] Ralph S. Alexander, "The Death and Burial of Sick Products," *Journal of Marketing,* Vol. 28, April 1964, pp. 1–7.
[54] Philip Kotler, "Phasing Out Weak products," *Harvard Business Review,* Vol. 43, March–April, 1965, pp. 107–118.
[55] William E. Cox, Jr., "Product Portfolio Strategy: A Review of the Boston Consulting Group Approach to Marketing Strategy," in R. Curham, Ed., *Marketing's Contribution to the Firm and to Society.* Chicago: American Marketing Association, 1975, pp. 465–470.
[56] William E. Cox, Jr., "Product Portfolio Strategy, Market Structure and Performance," in Hans B. Thorelli, Ed., *Strategy + Structure = Performance.* Bloomington: Indiana University Press, 1977, pp. 83–102.

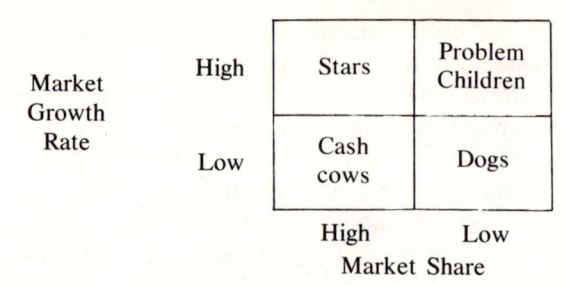

		High Market Share	Low Market Share
Market Growth Rate	High	Stars	Problem Children
	Low	Cash cows	Dogs

Source: William E. Cox, Jr., "Product Portfolio Strategy, Market Structure, and Performance," in Hans B. Thorelli, ed. *Strategy + Structure = Performance*. Bloomington: Indiana University Press, 1977, pp. 83–102.

Figure 15-2 Growth/Share matrix for product portfolio strategy.

PURCHASING BEHAVIOR

Webster and Wind's comprehensive model of the buying/selling interface provides a useful framework for appraising the state of the art in industrial buying behavior analysis and the role of industrial marketing research in advancing the current state of knowledge. Their model breaks the buying decisions process into six influence categories: environmental, organizational, interpersonal, individual, and buying decision factors as well as the nature of the decision process itself.[57] An appraisal of the buying/selling interface follows those six factors and concludes with some integrative remarks.

Environmental Factors

Although the list and nature of possible influences on organizational buying behavior are well documented,[58] there is a great paucity of research that would document those influences. The principal areas where research is sorely needed are now discussed:

Environmental change—It has been noted that organizations attempt to set up rules and postures that make it possible to deal with change in a predictable manner.[59] This raises two challenges however. One is the

[57] Frederick E. Webster, Jr., and Yoram Wind, *Organizational Buying Behavior*. Englewood Cliffs, N.J.: Prentice-Hall, 1972.
[58] *Ibid*.
[59] Charles B. Perrow, *Organizational Analysis: A Sociological View*. Belmont, Cal.: Brooks/Cole, 1970.

manner in which firms deal with abrupt, discontinued, and accelerated change.[60] Another is research on responses to discontinuity, which range from the expanding field of futures research and technological forecasting[61] to redefinition of the strategic planning process.[62]

The effects of organizational factors on industrial buying behavior— Most of the research to date has focused on just two issues: (1) buying center membership and responsibility and (2) the effects of centralization and decentralization. Zaltman and Bonoma's framework for classifying organizational influences points out a number of other research questions in need of empirical study.[63] The starting point of all such industrial marketing studies of organizational buying behavior should be a review of the literature of organizational behavior.

Buying decision centers—It has been widely noted that organizational buying behavior involves group influences and group decision making to a far greater extent than does consumer behavior. For all this interest in group processes there has been remarkably little research beyond the decision processes of purchasing agents[64] and the perception of buying group members' own role and power.[65] As Zaltman and Bonoma stated, there is ". . . a need for developing new methodologies which will facilitate our studying buying centers as units of analysis rather than individuals."[66]

---

[60] See Alvin Toeffler, *Future Shock*. New York: Random House, 1970; Peter F. Drucker, *The Age of Discontinuity: Guidelines to Our Changing Society*. New York: Harper & Row, 1969.
[61] David T. Kollat, "Environmental Forecasting and Strategic Planning: Perspectives on the Methodology of Futurology," in Fred C. Allvine, Ed., *Marketing in Motion*. Chicago: American Marketing Association, 1972, pp. 210–213.
[62] H. Igor Ansoff, "Managing Strategic Surprise by Response to Weak Signals," *California Management Review*, Vol. 18, Winter, 1975, pp. 21–33.
[63] Gerald Zaltman and Thomas V. Bonoma, "Organizational Buying Behavior: Hypotheses and Directions," *Industrial Marketing Management*, Vol. 6, 1977, pp. 53–60.
[64] Jagdish N. Sheth, "A Model of Industrial Buyer Behavior," *Journal of Marketing*, Vol. 37, October 1973, p. 56. For empirical studies, see Theodore Levitt, *Industrial Purchasing Behavior: A Study of Communication Effects*. Boston: Graduate School of Business, Harvard University, 1965; Richard N. Cardozo and James W. Cagley, "Experimental Study of Industrial Buyer Behavior," *Journal of Marketing Research*, Vol. 8, August 1971, pp. 329–334.
[65] Henry L. Tosi, "The Effects of Expectation Levels of ROI Consensus on the Buyer-Seller Dyad," *Journal of Business*, Vol. 39, October 1966, pp. 516–529; Dean G. Farrer, "Life of a Salesman: Value and Attitude Hierarchies," *Atlanta Economic Review*, Vol. 20, March 1970, pp. 4–7, 33–35; Robert W. Sweitzer, "Interpersonal Information Processing of Industrial Buyers," in Kenneth L. Bernhardt, Ed., *Marketing: 1776–1976 and Beyond*. Chicago: American Marketing Association, 1976.
[66] Zaltman and Bonoma, *op. cit.*, p. 59.

Modeling preference and decision-making structures—In recent years there has been an increasing interest in the modeling of individual buyer preference and decision-making structures. The principal research vehicle has been the linear compensatory model.[67] However its assumptions about underlying cognitive processes appear to be overly restrictive and unrealistic. Out of this dissatisfaction, two promising research strategies have emerged. One is the nonmetric multidimensional scaling[68] and conjoint analysis approaches.[69] The other, relatively new in marketing, involves the use of Newell and Simon's information processing theory and the development of micro-process simulations of individual behavior.[70] Crow's study of purchasing agent decisions demonstrated the feasibility and usefulness of the technique.[71] His findings on decision strategy agree with those of Lussier[72] and Payne[73] in other settings.

Before the ideal of an empirically based integrative model or set of general principles or organizational buying behavior can be stated it will be necessary to conduct extensive research in the areas outlined above. At present the state of the art in organizational buying behavior can best be characterized as one in which an adequate theoretical framework and taxonomies of behaviors and situations exist, but specific empirical research areas and linkages, as outlined, remain to be developed.

MARKET SEGMENTATION

It is commonly agreed that understanding of buyer behavior and market characteristics are prerequisites to the development of a comprehensive

---

[67] For instance, Yoram Wind, Paul E. Green, and Patrick J. Robinson, "The Determinants of Vendor Selection: The Evaluation Function Approach," *Journal of Purchasing*, Vol. 4, August 1958, pp. 29–41; Albert R. Wildt and Albert V. Bruno, "The Prediction of Preference for Capital Equipment Using Linear Attitude Models," *Journal of Marketing Research*, Vol. 11, May 1974, pp. 203–205; Donald R. Lehmann and John O'Shaughnessy, "Differences in Attribute Importance for Different Industrial Products," *Journal of Marketing*, Vol. 38, April 1974, pp. 36–42.

[68] Wind, Green, and Robinson, *op. cit.*

[69] Day, *op. cit.*

[70] Allen Newell and Herbert A. Simon, *Human Problem Solving*. Englewood, NJ: Prentice-Hall, 1972.

[71] For example, Crow, *op. cit.*

[72] Dennis A. Lussier, "An Information Processing Approach to the Study of Brand Choice Decisions" (Ph.D. diss., Graduate School of Business, Indiana University, 1976).

[73] John W. Payne, "Task Complexity and Contingent Information Processing in Decision Making: An Information Search and Protocol Analysis," *Organizational Behavior and Human Performance*, forthcoming.

OVERVIEW OF INDUSTRIAL MARKETING RESEARCH

marketing strategy. Market segmentation plays a pivotal role in strategy formulation. In practice industrial market segmentation seldom goes beyond geography and commodity end use. Frank, Massy, and Wind divided markets and market segmentation into macro (organizational) and micro (within-organization) decision-making unit characteristics.[74] One of the advantages of this approach is that it readily relates to Webster and Wind's theoretical framework for understanding organizational buying behavior.

Two observations concerning the state of the art in industrial market segmentation are in order at this point: (1) Ideally segmentation would begin at the macro level then proceed to the micro level if warranted. Unfortunately, that is not the case. There is little, if any, work reported on micro segmentation, and (2) It has been reported that industrial marketers tend to use segmentation as an after-the-fact explanation of results instead of as an element of forward planning and strategy formulation.[75] We wholeheartedly agree with Wind and Cardozo that segmentation should play a greater role in industrial marketing planning and strategy formulation.[76]

PROMOTIONAL MIX DECISIONS

One of the major questions surrounding industrial marketing mix decisions is whether they differ from those required for consumer good decisions. In balance it appears that the similarities are far greater than the differences. Here we shall concentrate on the points of difference as well as on those topics that are especially deserving of further research.

There is no question that personal selling plays a primary role in industrial marketing strategy. The reasons are the generally large volume of purchases per customer, the need to rely on salesmen to identify key decision makers in each buying situation, and the ability of salesmen to obtain and disseminate information needed by both the buying and selling organizations.[77] While much research on personal selling has been done, studies of the role of personal selling at the buyer/seller interface are sorely lacking. In contrast there is an abundance of models of salesforce size, call frequency and routing, and territory design.[78]

---

[74] Frank, Massy, and Wind, *op. cit.,* Chap. 5.
[75] *Ibid.,* p. 155
[76] Yoram Wind and Richard Cardozo, "Industrial Market Segmentation," *Industrial Marketing Management,* Vol. 3, 1974, pp. 153–166.
[77] Webster and Wind, *op. cit.* pp. 122–123.
[78] For some recent comprehensive mokdels, see Leonard M. Lodish, "'Vaguely Right' Approach to Sales Force Allocations," *Harvard Business Review,* Vol. 52, January–

Some of the most interesting research on industrial marketing has concerned the sales, cost, and profit impact of marketing strategy. Elsewhere we have already alluded to some of it. The following research topics however are particularly noteworthy:

1. Cost impact of the promotional mix. Studies by Kolliner,[79] Levitt,[80] and Morrill[81] suggest that as advertising and sales promotion outlays rise, marketing expenses as a percent of sales will decline. These findings should be taken only as suggestive. The work of some of the early operations researchers suggested saturation points that would reverse the relationship after a certain promotional level has been reached.

2. Finding the most effective promotional blend in relation to industry, market, and production characteristics. The results of the ADVISOR project would indicate that both the use and effectiveness of promotion varies with factors ranging from product newness and quality and product life cycle stage to the firm's market share and industry concentration.[82]

We firmly believe that the continued and systematic study of the effect of marketing strategy on market performance, conditioned by industry and market structure and product characteristics is one of the most promising fields of industrial marketing research. It is one where marketing research bears the potential for making direct inputs into strategy selection.

SUMMARY

Our point-by-point overview of the state of the art and opportunities for further study in industrial marketing research is now completed. Indus-

---

February 1974, pp. 119–124; Roy J. Shanker, Ronald E. Turner, and Andris A. Zoltners, "Sales Territory Design: An Integrated Approach," *Management Science,* Vol. 22, November 1975, pp. 309–320; Andris Zoltners, "Integer Programming Models for Territory Alignment to Maximize Profit," *Journal of Marketing Research,* Vol. 13, November 1976, pp. 426–430.

[79] Sim A. Kollimer, "New Evidence of Ad Values," *Industrial Marketing,* Vol. 48, August 1963, pp. 81–84.

[80] Theodore Levitt, *Industrial Purchasing Behavior: A Study of Communication Effects.* Boston, Massachusetts: Graduate School of Business Administration, Harvard University, 1965.

[81] John E. Morrill, "Industrial Advertising Pays Off," *Harvard Business School,* Vol. 48, March–April 1970, pp. 41ff.

[82] Gary L. Lilien and John D. C. Little, "The ADVISOR Project: A Study of Industrial Advertising Budgets," *Sloan Management Review,* Vol. 17, Spring 1976, pp. 17–31.

trial marketing research bears important distinctions from consumer products marketing research. Those differences stem in no small part from the greater degree of market demand concentration and the more direct channels of distribution that characterize industrial marketing.

Industrial marketing research was characterized by its smaller budgets and organizational staffs and its greater reliance on secondary data studies and informal designs. Yet at the same time we have seen that industrial marketing research offers a number of particularly important challenges and opportunities where breakthroughs will have considerable impact on marketing strategy. Briefly stated, they are:

1. The continued development of sophisticated yet economical-to-apply models and measures of market potential.
2. Development of comprehensive methodology for surveys of knowledgeable persons. Sociogram and key informant techniques, Delphi and cross-impact analysis techniques are some of the key ingredients.
3. Development of empirically based procedures for allocation of expenses to segments and territories.
4. Development of commonly agreed measures of marketing investment and of measures of investment productivity.
5. Application of nonmetric multidimensional scaling and conjoint analysis to the study of customer preferences and market segmentation.
6. Continued studies of product portfolio strategy for product life cycle and product/market growth strategy formulation.
7. Industry-wide and interindustry studies of the sales, cost, and profit impact of marketing strategy, market and industry structure, and product and product life cycle characteristics along the lines of the PIMS, ADVISOR and other major research programs.
8. Systematic research into organizational buying behavior, with special emphasis on: strategies for coping with and anticipating environmental discontinuities; research of the buying decision center itself rather than of the purchasing agent alone; information processing strategies of organizational buyers; and the buyer/seller interface.
9. Market segmentation studies that employ segmentation as a planning rather than *ex post facto* tool and which explore micro as well as macro segmentation.

We believe that industrial marketing research presents unusually exciting opportunities for practitioners and academicians alike to make valuable and important contributions to the development of contemporary thought on marketing and corporate strategy.

APPENDIX

A Model of a Comprehensive Market Demand Study For Cranes in the United States, 1975*

SUMMARY OF FINDINGS

Market Size Estimates

1. The United States market for electric overhead traveling cranes is estimated to be $314 million net sales volume, f.o.b. plant, in 1975. Tables A-1 and A-2, in which electric overhead traveling cranes (SIC 35362 11-14) are estimated to account for 75% of the shipments of SIC 35362: ($429 × .75 = $314).

---

*Prepared for the Midwest Crane Company, Inc., January 1976

Note: These summary statements are offered as examples for demonstration purposes in the model study. While all statements and supporting data are at least partly based on factual data, they should not be regarded as either complete or definitive.

APPENDIX

2. More than 70 % of the market demand for electric overhead traveling cranes is accounted for by customers in six SIC 2-digit groups (SIC 32-37). The largest market is SIC 35, Machinery manufacturers (other than electrical), with 1975 shipments of about $60 million (Table A-13).

Market Trends

3. During the period 1972-1975, the crane market showed a compound annual growth rate in shipments of 22.1%, a striking increase over the growth rate of 1.2% per annum from 1967-1972 (Tables A-1 and A-2).

Industry Structure

4. The overhead traveling crane industry is composed of more than 60 diversified firms (Tables A-6 to A-8) primarily located in the North Central Region of the United States (Table A-3), with average total shipments of under $5 million in 1972 (Table A-8).
5. Concentration in the crane industry remained relatively stable from 1958 to 1967, declined sharply from 1967 to 1972, and rose back to 1967 levels from 1972 to 1975 (Table A-9).

Market Shares

6. The dominant firm in the electric overhead traveling crane industry is the Harnischfeger Corporation, with estimated 1975 sales of $80 million and a 25% market share. The six largest firms in the industry account for 55% of the total market (Table A-10).
7. Midwest Crane Company holds a 6.4% market share of the electric overhead traveling crane market, 10.6% of the bridge type crane market, and 18.2% of the large crane market (over 30 tons lift capacity).

Table A-1 VALUE OF SHIPMENTS OF INDUSTRY AND PRODUCT CLASSES, 1958–1973 (millions of dollars)

Year	SIC 3536[a]	SIC 35362[b]	SIC 35362 as a % of SIC 3536
1958	$165.5	$106.1	64.1%
1963	224.2	115.7	51.6
1967	385.3	215.1	55.8
1968	428.2	227.2	53.1
1969	459.7	233.5	50.8
1970	475.7	221.7	46.6
1971	443.2	204.3	46.1
1972	446.0	253.5	56.8
1973	531.1	253.4	47.7
1975(a)	533.5	254.5	47.7
1975(b)	620.0	316.0	51.0
1975(c)	760.0	418.0	55.0

Notes: [a] SIC 3536—Hoists, industrial cranes, and monorail systems
[b] SIC 35362—Overhead traveling cranes and monorail systems
1975 (a)—Shipments figure for SIC 35362 based on trend analysis from 1967–1973; SIC 3536 estimate based on 35362/3536 ratio for 1973.
1975 (b)—Shipments figure for SIC 3536 taken from *U.S. Industrial Outlook* for 1975; 35362/3536 ratio is arithmetic mean of ratios for 1967–1973.
1975 (c)—Shipments figure for SIC 3536 and 35362/3536 ratio estimated from survey of knowledgeable persons.

Sources: 1958–1972: U.S. Bureau of the Census, *Census of Manufactures—1972. Industry Series: Construction, Mining, and Materials Handling Machinery and Equipment* (MC 72(2)-35B), Washington: U.S. Government Printing Office, March 1975. 1973: U.S. Bureau of the Census, *Annual Survey of Manufactures—1973: Value of Product Shipments* (M 73(AS)-2), Washington: U.S. Government Printing Office, September 1975.

Table A-2 VALUE OF SHIPMENTS OF SPECIFIC PRODUCTS, 1972 and 1967 (millions of dollars)

SIC #	Product Description	1972	1967	% of Total 1972	% of Total 1967
35362—	Overhead traveling cranes and monorail systems	$253.5	$215.1	100%	100%
	Overhead traveling cranes—				
	Electric	172.4	160.6	68.0	74.7
35362 11	Gantry type	46.8	—	27.2	[a]
35362 12	Bridge type	104.0	—	60.3	
35362 13	Stacker/storage type	13.0	—	7.5	
35362 14	Others, including jib type	8.6	—	5.0	
35362 15	Hand powered overhead traveling	0.9	2.3	0.4	1.1
35362 41	Automatic stacking machines	25.6	—	10.1	—
	Monorail Systems				
35362 52	Powered systems	21.1	23.7	8.3	11.0
35362 54	Manual systems	3.9		1.5	
35362 55	Parts and attachments for overhead traveling cranes and monorail systems (sold separately)	19.9	16.9	7.9	7.9
35362 57	Parts and attachments for automatic stacking machines	—	—	—	—
35362 00	Overhead traveling cranes and monorail systems, n.s.k.	9.7	3.8	3.8	1.8

Note: [a] Base = $172.4.

Source: U.S. Bureau of the Census, *Census of Manufactures—1972. Industry Series: Construction, Mining, and Materials Handling Machinery and Equipment* (MC 72(2)–35B), Washington: U.S. Government Printing Office, March 1975, Table 6A.

Table A-3 VALUE OF SHIPMENTS BY GEOGRAPHIC AREAS; 1972 and 1967
(millions of dollars)
SIC 35362—Overhead traveling cranes and monorail systems

Geographic Area	1972	1967
United States	$ 253.5	$ 215.1
Northeast Region	11.6	13.2
Middle Atlantic Division	(10.0–19.9)[a]	(10.0–19.9)
New York	(5.0–9.9)	(5.0–9.9)
Pennsylvania	4.7	6.2
North Central Region	145.5	170.0
East North Central Division	137.3	(50.0 & over)
Ohio	53.7	67.9
Illinois	(10.0–19.9)	(10.0–19.9)
Michigan	21.2	27.0
Wisconsin	44.4	(20.0–49.9)
West North Central Division	8.3	(10.0–19.9)
Minnesota	(1.0–1.9)	—
Iowa	(5.0–9.9)	(10.0–19.9)
South Region	31.4	6.6
South Atlantic Division	5.4	—
Virginia	(1.0–1.9)	—
South Carolina	(2.0–4.9)	—
East South Central Division	6.3	—
Tennessee	(1.0–1.9)	—
Alabama	(2.0–4.9)	—
Mississippi	(2.0–4.9)	—
West South Central Division	19.7	(5.0–9.9)
Texas	(10.0–19.9)	(5.0–9.9)
West Region	64.8	25.4
Mountain Division	(5.0–9.9)	—
Utah	(5.0–9.9)	—
Pacific Division	(50.0 & over)	25.4
Washington	(10.0–19.9)	(5.0–9.9)
California	39.7	(10.0–19.9)

Note: [a]Data in parentheses given in ranges to avoid disclosure.
Source: U.S. Bureau of the Census, *Census of Manufactures—1972. Industry Series: Construction, Mining, and Materials Handling Machinery and Equipment* (MC 72(2)–35B), Washington: U.S. Government Printing Office, March 1975, Table 6B.

Table A–4 VALUE OF SHIPMENTS 1972 (millions of dollars)

SIC 3536	Hoists, industrial cranes and monorail systems	$ 527.3
SIC 35361	Hoists	188.7
SIC 35362	Overhead traveling cranes and monorail systems	313.0
	Total—SIC 35361 & 35362	501.7

$$\text{Ratio: } \frac{35361 \ \& \ 35362}{3536} = 95.1\%$$

$$\text{Ratio: } \frac{35362}{3536} = 59.4\%$$

Note: Data for SIC 35361 and 35362 indicate total shipments for establishments that have these primary product class numbers—thus the data include primary *and* secondary product shipments *plus* miscellaneous receipts.

$$\text{Ratio: } \frac{35362 \ 11\text{-}14}{3536} = \frac{\$ 172.4}{\$ 527.3} = 32.7\%$$

Note: Shipments of electric overhead traveling cranes in 1972 accounted for less than one-third of the total shipments of establishments classified in SIC 3536.
Source: U.S. Bureau of the Census, *Census of Manufactures—1972. Industry Series: Construction, Mining, and Materials Handling Machinery and Equipment* (MC 72(2)–35B), Washington: U.S. Government Printing Office, March 1975, Table 5A.

Table A–5 INDUSTRY-PRODUCT ANALYSIS, 1972 INDUSTRY AND PRIMARY PRODUCT SHIPMENTS: SPECIALIZATION AND COVERAGE RATIOS

SIC 3536 Hoists, industrial cranes and monorail systems	Value of Shipments (*million dollars*)
A. Total shipments	$ 527.3
B. Primary products	375.9
C. Secondary products	103.8
D. Miscellaneous receipts	47.6
E. Primary product specialization ratio $\dfrac{\text{(Row B)}}{\text{(Rows B + C)}}$	78%
F. Total primary product shipments, made in all industries	446.0
G. Primary product shipments, made in SIC 3536 establishments	375.9
H. Primary product shipments, made in other industries	70.1
I. Coverage ratio $\dfrac{\text{(Row B or G)}}{\text{(Row F)}}$	84%

Note: An establishment is assigned to an industry based on the shipment values of products representing the largest amount considered as primary to an industry. Frequently the establishment shipments comprise mixtures of products assigned to an industry (primary products), those considered primary to other industries (secondary products of a given industry), and receipts for activities such as merchandising or contract work. This product pattern for SIC 3536 is shown in Rows A through D and the primary product specialization ratio in Row E. The extent to which the primary products of SIC 3536 are shipped by establishments classified in and out of SIC 3536 is summarized in Rows F through H and shown as a ratio in Row I.

Source: U.S. Bureau of the Census, *U.S. Census of Manufactures—1972. Industry Series: Construction, Mining, and Materials Handling Machinery and Equipment* (MC 72(2)–35B), Washington: U.S. Government Printing Office, March 1975, Table 5B.

Table A-6 INDUSTRY-PRODUCT ANALYSIS, 1972 INDUSTRY AND PRIMARY PRODUCT SHIPMENTS: SPECIALIZATION AND COVERAGE RATIOS

SIC 35362 Overhead traveling cranes and monorail systems	Value of Shipments (*million dollars*)
A. Total shipments	$ 313.0
B. Primary products	223.4
C. Secondary products	89.6
D. Miscellaneous receipts	—
E. Primary product specialization ratio $\dfrac{\text{(Row B)}}{\text{(Rows B + C)}}$	71%
F. Total primary product shipments, made in all industries	253.5
G. Primary product shipments, made in SIC 3536 establishments	223.4
H. Primary product shipments, made in other industries	30.1
I. Coverage ratio $\dfrac{\text{(Row B or G)}}{\text{(Row F)}}$	88%

Note: Explanation of this table is given in the note to Table 5.
Source: U.S. Bureau of the Census, *Census of Manufactures—1972. Industry Series: Construction, Mining, and Materials Handling Machinery and Equipment* (MC 72(2)-35B), Washington: U.S. Government Printing Office, March 1975, Tables 5A and 5C.

Table A-7 INDUSTRY-PRODUCT ANALYSIS, 1972 SHIPMENTS BY PRODUCT CLASS AND INDUSTRY

Producing Industry	Value of Shipments (*millions of dollars*) Industry and Product Classification	
	SIC 3536	SIC 35362
All industries	$446.0	$253.5
SIC 3536	375.9	223.4
SIC 3531—Construction machinery	12.2	6.8
SIC 3532—Mining machinery	(2–5)	—
SIC 3534—Elevators and moving stairways	(Under 2)	(Under 2)
SIC 3535—Conveyors and conveying equipment	5.8	5.6
SIC 3537—Industrial trucks and tractors	(Over 2)	(Over 2)
Other industries	42.8	14.6

Source: U.S. Bureau of the Census, *Census of Manufactures—1972. Industry Series: Construction, Mining, and Materials Handling Machinery and Equipment* (MC 72 (2)–35B), Washington: U.S. Government Printing Office, March 1975, Table 5C.

Table A-8 VALUE OF SHIPMENTS PER ESTABLISHMENT AND EMPLOYEE, 1972

Establishment Size	Number of Establishments	Value of Shipments per Establishment	Value of Shipments per Employee (All)
SIC 3536 Hoists, industrial cranes, and monorail systems			
All establishments	188	$ 2.80 million	$ 32,350
1–4 employees	32	69,000	22,000
5–9 employees	26	208,000	27,000
10–19 employees	38	616,000	39,000
20–49 employees	38	1.24 million	39,400
50–99 employees	23	2.55 million	36,600
100–249 employees	17	5.17 million	35,200
250–499 employees	6	12.27 million	30,700
500–999 employees	6	}	
1,000–2,499 employees	1	} 28.63 million	29,400
2,500 & Over	1	}	
SIC 35362 Overhead traveling cranes and monorail systems			
All establishments in primary product class	66	4.74 million	31,900

Note: Value of shipments data include primary products, secondary products, and miscellaneous receipts.
Source: U.S. Bureau of the Census, *Census of Manufactures—1972. Industry Series: Construction, Mining, and Materials Handling Machinery and Equipment* (MC 72(2)-35B), Washington: U.S. Government Printing Office, March 1975, Tables 4 and 5A.

Table A-9 CONCENTRATION RATIOS, SELECTED YEARS

Value of Industry Shipments

Year	Total (mil.$)	Percent Accounted for by 4 Largest Companies	8 Largest Companies	20 Largest Companies	50 Largest Companies
SIC 3536 Hoists, industrial cranes and monorail systems					
1972	$ 446.0	22%	34%	58%	80%
1967	385.3	31	45	65	85
1963	224.2	27	40	66	87
1958	165.5	33	50	72	91
SIC 35362 Overhead traveling cranes and monorail systems					
1972	$ 253.5	33%	50%	75%	94%
1967	215.1	47	67	86	99
1963	115.7	43	65	89	99+
1958	106.1	46	71	90	99

Note: Value of shipments data and ratios are based on shipments of primary products only.
Source: U.S. Bureau of the Census, *Census of Manufactures—1972. Special Report Series: Concentration Ratios in Manufacturing* (MC 72(SR)-2). Washington: U.S. Government Printing Office, 1975, Table 6.

Table A-10 ESTIMATED SALES AND MARKET SHARES OF THE MAJOR FIRMS IN THE ELECTRIC OVERHEAD TRAVELING CRANE INDUSTRY

Company	1975 Sales (Shipments $ Millions)	Market Share
Harnischfeger Corporation	$ 80	25%
Whiting Corporation	25	8
Firm A	20	6
Firm B	20	6
Firm C	15	5
Firm D	15	5
All others	139	45
	314	100

Table A-11 PROFILES OF MAJOR FIRMS IN THE ELECTRIC OVERHEAD TRAVELING CRANE INDUSTRY

Harnischfeger Corporation, Milwaukee, Wisconsin

Dominant firm in the industry with 1975 estimated crane shipments of $80 million and 25% market share.

Also the leading firm in the hoist industry; a leader in power cranes, shovels, and excavators in the construction and mining industry.

Electric overhead traveling cranes are manufactured at two locations: West Milwaukee, Wisconsin; Cudahy, Wisconsin. Plants have a total floor area of 1.86 million square feet.

Strong in all major market segments, but not the leader in all segments.

Uses the trademark "P & H" on all products which are considered by many as the best in the industry in terms of technical and performance characteristics.

Manufactures its own motors and controls which it also sells to other crane manufacturers. Also sells hoists to other crane manufacturers.

Sells through direct sales offices and distributors.

8000 employees in 1975; estimated sales of $350–400 million.

Expanding crane capacity in 1975 to meet sharp increase in demand.

Table A-12 INPUT-OUTPUT ANALYSIS OF INDUSTRY 46.03 (SIC 3536), 1967

Industry Number	Industry Description	Output (million $)	% Distribution
Intermediate outputs (consuming industries):			
11.02	New construction, nonresidential buildings	$ 158.2	42.8%
45.01	Construction machinery	34.6	9.4
11.03	New construction, public utilities	27.1	7.3
—	All other industries	148.8	40.2
	Total—termediate outputs	369.7	100.0
Final demand (based on industry 46—SIC 3534–3537):			
69	Wholesale and retail trade	$ 179.0	16.2%
14	Food and kindred products	133.6	12.1
24	Paper and allied products	47.4	4.3
15	Tobacco manufactures	45.1	4.1
59	Motor vehicles and equipment	44.3	4.0
36	Stone and clay products	43.9	4.0
—	Other industries	614.2	55.5
	Total—gross private fixed capital formation	1,107.5	100.0

Note: Gross Private Fixed Capital Formation for Industry 46.03 totals $121.2 million, while for Industry 46, the total is $1,107.5 million, or more than 9 times as large. Capital flows data were not available for Industry 46.03 with the result that the Final Demand figures are only very grossly comparable to the Intermediate Outputs.

Sources: "Interindustry Transactions in New Structures and Equipment, 1967," *Survey of Current Business*, September 1975, pp. 9–21. U.S. Department of Commerce, *Input-Output Structure of the U.S. Economy: 1967*, Volume I. Washington: U.S. Government Printing Office, 1974.

Table A-13 ESTIMATED DEMAND FOR CRANES IN MAJOR MARKET SEGMENTS, 1975
(Based on Midwest Crane Company position)

SIC Group	1975 Midwest Shipments per Customer Employee	Number of Employees in Customer Accounts	1975 Midwest Sales	1975 Midwest Market Share (Estimated)	1975 Market Demand
32	$ 26.19	42,000	$1.1 million	5.0%	$22 million
33	14.96	234,000	3.5	8.0	44
34	11.72	128,000	1.5	4.0	37
35	17.69	260,000	4.6	7.7	60
36	11.62	198,000	2.3	8.2	28
37	14.62	171,000	2.5	7.1	35
All others	5.63	800,000	4.5	5.1	88
			20.0 million		314 million

Table A-14 RESPONDENTS—SURVEYS OF KNOWLEDGEABLE PERSONS

Construction Engineering Firms

    Bechtel Corporation, San Francisco, California
    Fluor, Inc., Anaheim, California
    Arthur G. McKEE, Cleveland, Omio
      and so on.

Industry Periodicals

    Materials Handling, Boston, Mass.
    Materials Handling Engineering, Cleveland, Ohio

Firms in the Industry

    Harnischfeger Corporation, Milwaukee, Wisconsin
    Whiting Corporation, Harvey, Illinois
    Alliance Machine Company, Alliance, Ohio
    Cleveland Crane and Engineering, Cleveland, Ohio
    Euclid Crane Division, Kranco, Inc., Cleveland, Ohio
    Shepard Niles Division, Vulcan, Inc.,

Author Index

Aaker, D. A., 405
Achenbaum, A., 91
Ackoff, R. L., 400
Adler, L., 353
Aguilar, F., 18
Albaum, G., 103, 248, 421
Alexander, R., 5, 365, 367, 433
Ansoff, H. I., 379, 435
Aries, R., 157

Bailey, E., 114, 116, 422
Baker, M. J., 359
Baker, N. R., 341
Banks, S., 88
Barnes, J. D., 398
Bass, F., 193, 360, 432
Beik, L., 112
Bennett, P., 147, 390
Benson, P. H., 350
Bent, D. H., 297
Berenson, C., 248
Berhardt, I., 360
Best, R., 248
Bezdek, R. H., 216
Blackman, A., 195, 197
Block, B., 130
Bodkin, R. G., 202

Boewaldt, R. J., 397
Bonoma, T. V., 382, 383, 385, 435
Booz, Allen and Hamilton, 340
Boulding, K., 129
Box, E. P., 214
Boyd, H., 11, 12, 18, 72, 73, 77, 91, 244, 245, 249, 259, 276, 286, 400, 405, 425, 428, 433
Boyle, J. J., 213
Brand, G. T., 399
Britt, S., 74
Brown, R. G., 218
Brown, R. V., 293
Brown, W. H., 359
Bruno, A. V., 390, 436
Bundgaard, N., 191
Burack, E., 197, 427
Bursk, E., 114, 422
Buskirk, R., 104, 110, 111, 421
Buzby, S., 112

Cagley, J. W., 388, 435
Cahalan, D., 248
Campbell, D. T., 87, 242, 245, 428
Capon, N., 388, 403
Cardozo, R. N., 388, 392, 394, 435, 437
Carmone, F. J., 326, 348

455

AUTHOR INDEX

Carpenter, R., 74
Carter, A., 216
Carter, C. F., 341
Case, P. B., 249
Chambers, J., 199, 428
Choffray, J. M., 403
Churchill, G. A., Jr., 92, 247, 315, 320, 325, 358, 399
Clark, D. F., 400
Clarke, D. G., 221
Claxton, J. D., 350
Claycamp, H. J., 405
Cleland, D., 21
Clifford, D. K., 362
Coaker, J. W., 390
Cochran, W. G., 278
Cohen, L., 245, 246
Conver, S., 191, 427
Cook, S., 78, 259
Copulsky, W., 157
Cox, K., 4–24, 92
Cox, W. E., Jr., 14, 73, 89, 160, 163, 172, 191, 250, 337, 344, 362, 420
Crawford, C. M., 339
Crisp, R., 97, 101, 147, 423
Cross, J., 5
Crow, L., 420
Cunningham, M. T., 362
Cyert, R. M., 383
Czepiel, J. A., 359, 360

Darmon, R. Y., 399
Davies, R. J., 286
Davis, O. A., 400
Day, G. S., 207, 327, 329, 389, 431
Day, R., 147
DeKluyver, C., 172, 362, 433
Deming, W. E., 269
Dhalla, N. 172
Dirks, L. N., 72
Drucker, P., 379, 435

Emory, W., 78, 279, 286, 429
Enis, B., 92
Enos, J. L., 340, 359
Etzel, M. J., 250
Eyrich, G. I., 203, 292

Farley, J. U., 400
Farris, D. G., 386, 435

Farris, C. W., 374, 391
Ferber, R., 270
Fiehn, P., 191
Fisher, J. C., 193, 194
Fisk, M., 252, 253
Fogg, C. D., 400
Ford, N. M., 315, 399
Foster, R., 25, 195
Frank, N., 75
Frank, R. E., 393, 437
Frederick, D. G., 397
Freimer, M., 342
Fuerst, J. M., 215, 237
Fusefeld, A., 25, 192, 195

Gaccione, V., 305
Gerson, M., 147
Gibson, R. E., 348
Goeldner, C., 72
Gold, B., 357, 360
Gols, G., 237
Grashof, J. F., 385
Green, P. E., 12, 77, 323, 325, 326, 346, 348, 350, 351, 390, 423, 430, 432, 436
Gronhaug, K., 380
Gross, F. J., 347

Hakansson, H., 380
Hamberg, D., 340
Hammouda, M. A. A., 362
Harding, M., 385
Hargreaves, 350
Harris, L., 173
Havens, G., 160, 163, 425
Hawkins, D., 151, 247, 248, 259, 269, 293, 319, 326, 430
Heckert, J., 103
Helmer, Olaf, 196, 418, 427
Heskett, L. Jr., 19
Hess, S. W., 400
Hill, R. M., 5
Holbrook, M., 388
Holloway, R., 92
Horngren, C., 101
Houston, M., 24, 418
Hughes, G. D., 304
Hulbert, J. Jr., 388, 403
Hull, C. H., 291
Hummel, F. E., 35, 38, 48, 146, 148, 149, 150, 154, 158, 159, 161, 171, 419, 423, 424

AUTHOR INDEX

Isenson, R., 189

Jenkins, G. M., 214
Jenkins, J. G., 297
Jewkes, J. Jr., 340
Johnson, R. E., 215

Kahn, G., 254
Kanuk, L., 248
Kelly, J. P., 390
Kendall, P. L., 252, 253
Kierulff, H. E., 357
King, W., 21
Kirpalani, V. H., 111
Kish, L., 275, 277, 282, 293, 430
Klompmaker, J. E., 203
Kollat, D. T., 380, 435
Kollimer, S. A., 402, 438
Koning, C. de, 6, 270
Kotler, P., 3, 24, 25, 78, 145, 147, 362, 365, 366, 401, 418, 419, 423, 433
Kuehn, A. A., 207

Lambert, Z., 78, 79, 400
Lanford, H. W., 194
Laurent, A., 248
Lehmann, D. R., 390, 436
Lenz, R., 194
Leontieff, W., 227
Leopold, H., 158
Levitt, T., 362, 388, 396, 402, 435, 438
Lieberman, A., 148
Lilien, G. L., 403, 404, 405, 438
Linsky, A., 248
Lipstein, B., 355
Little, J. D. C., 147, 404, 405, 438
Lodish, L., 147, 400, 401, 437
Lorie, J., 242
Luck, D., 297
Lussier, D., 436

McCarthy, M., 184, 426
McCarthy, P. J., 293
McClelland, C. W., 405
McDonald, M., 90, 91, 148, 169, 170, 171, 172, 424, 425
McIntosh, A., 271, 286
Mackenzie, K., 360
McLaughlin, R. L., 213
McMillan, J. R., 300, 385, 388

Maffei, R., 147, 423
Makridakis, S., 177, 178, 179, 180, 181, 198, 199, 201, 208, 218, 219, 220, 427
Mansfield, E., 193, 360, 363, 364, 433
March, J. G., 383
Marketing Research, 1973 Survey of, 8, 9, 10, 29, 95, 417, 421
Marquis, D. G., 340
Martilla, J. A., 358
Martino, J., 191, 427
Massel, M., 128
Massy, W. F., 437
Mathews, H. L., 320, 389, 430
Mayer, C. S., 293, 430
Mead, R., 88
Merton, R. K., 252, 253
Miner, J. B., 103
Miner, R., 380, 381
Mohn, N., 190
Montgomery, D. G., 400
Morrill, J. E., 403, 405, 438
Morrison, D., 205
Moyer, R., 397
Mueller, W. F., 340
Mullick, S., 199, 428
Murthy, K. S. R., 202
Myers, J., 88
Myers, S., 340

National Industrial Conference Board, 100, 147, 148, 199, 204, 423
Neidell, L. A., 348
Nelson, R. R., 340
Newell, A., 436
Ness, T. E., 358
Nevers, J., 193, 361, 432
Nie, N. H., 297
North, H., 196, 427

O'Dell, W. F., 249
O'Meara, J. T., 342
O'Neal, C. R., 196
O'Rourke, M. R., 385
O'Shaughnessy, J., 390, 436
Oxenfeldt, A. R., 397
Ozanne, U. B., 358

Patton, A., 362
Payne, J. W., 436
Peck, M. J., 346

Perrow, C. B., 378, 434
Peirce, W. S., 360
Pessemier, E. A., 335, 341, 342, 356, 431
Peters, M. P., 359
Peterson, R. A., 317
Phelps, D. M., 201
Piersol, R., 157
Pinkerton, R., 19
PoKempner, S., 99, 106
Popkin, J., 202
Prince, T., 2
Pruden, A. O., 317, 399
Pry, R. H., 193, 194
Pyke, D., 196, 427

Quinn, J., 190

Rabitsch, E. K., 215, 237
Ramond, C., 12, 13, 80, 91, 97
Ranard, E. E., 215
Rao, M., 403
Reinmuth, J. E., 398
Reisman, A., 221, 426
Renschling, T. L., 250
Reynold, W. H., 342
Rippe, R., 205
Roa, V. R., 349
Roberts, E., 190
Roberts, H., 242, 427
Robertson, G. M., 245
Robinson, J., 128
Robinson, P. J., 374, 390, 391, 395, 398, 436
Rogers, E. M., 359
Rokus, J. W., 400
Root, H. P., 203, 356, 432
Rosegger, G., 191, 360
Rothe, J., 238, 428
Rothschild, W., 14
Rubenstein, A. H., 341

Sahal, D., 193
Samuelds, S. A., 400
Sawers, D., 340
Schaffir, K., 105, 106, 107, 109
Scheuble, P., 114, 422
Schiff, M., 114
Schiffman, L. G., 305
Schoner, 145, 149, 170
Schreier, 244, 252
Schwartz, R., 87

Scott, C., 248
Scott, J. E., 390
Sechrest, L., 87
Seidler, J., 25, 418
Selltiz, C., 78, 259
Semlow, W. J., 400
Semon, T. T., 390
Seven, C., 103, 110, 364, 421, 422
Sewall, M. A., 398
Shanker, R. J., 401, 438
Shankleman, E., 6
Shapanka, A., 195
Shapiro, I., 75
Shapiro, M. J., 249
Shapiro, S., 111
Sharif, M. N., 195
Shea, J. M., 385
Sheth, J. N., 310, 312, 316, 329, 386, 430, 435
Shiskin, J., 213
Siegman, J., 341
Silk, A. J., 400, 403
Siller, F. H., 350
Simmonds, W. H. C., 191, 426
Simon, H. A., 436
Simon, L. S., 309, 310, 342
Smith, D., 199, 428
Solley, W. M., 383
Stacey, N., 87, 177, 419
Stanton, W., 104, 110, 111, 421
Stasch, S., 11, 12, 18, 72, 73, 77, 242, 249, 259, 276, 286, 428
Stefflre, V., 348
Steinbrenner, K., 297
Steiner, G. A., 380, 381, 383
Steiner, P., 268, 429
Stephan, F. J., 293
Stern, L., 19
Stern, M. E., 163, 165, 166, 168
Stern, M. O., 195
Stidsen, B., 395, 398
Stillerman, R., 340
Stobaugh, R. B., 397
Strauss, G., 386
Sudman, S., 277
Sutherland, A., 359
Sweeney, T. W., 320, 389, 430
Sweitzer, R. W., 386, 388, 403, 435

Talley, W. J., 400

AUTHOR INDEX

Taylor, D., 297
Teach, R. D., 348
Telfer, K., 157
Theil, H., 178
Thomas, G. P., 385
Tinsely, P. A., 202
Tocqueville, A. de, 339
Toeffler, A., 379, 435
Tosi, H. L., 386, 435
Townsend, P. L., 397
Trentin, H. G., 105, 106, 107, 109
Tull, D., 12, 77, 151, 247, 259, 269, 292, 293, 319, 323, 325, 326, 346, 350, 430, 432
Turner, R., 25, 401, 438

Uddin, G. A., 195
Uhl, K., 145, 149, 170
Urban, G. L., 355, 432
Utterback, J., 197, 427

VanBeeck, J. G., 286
Vankatesan, M., 92, 359
Vermetten, J. B., 286

Waid, C., 400
Wales, H., 297
Walker, O. C., 315, 399
Wall, J., 21
Wasson, C., 178
Webb, E., 87
Webster, F., 19, 256, 358, 375, 376, 377, 378, 381, 383, 384, 387, 391, 396, 398, 407, 433

Weigand, R. E., 383, 385
Wendling, R. M., 216
Wentz, W. B., 203, 292, 343, 344
Westfall, R., 11, 12, 18, 72, 73, 77, 91, 242, 244, 245, 249, 259, 276, 286, 428
Westing, J. H., 201
Wheelwright, S., 177, 178, 179, 180, 181, 198, 199, 201, 208, 218, 219, 427
Wildt, A. R., 390, 436
Wilkinson, M., 205
Williams, B. R., 341
Wilson, A., 4, 7, 12, 86, 87, 90, 91, 177, 252, 256, 258, 267, 269, 320, 374, 389, 397, 416, 417, 420, 429
Wilson, D. T., 430
Wilson, I. H., 380, 423
Wind, Y., 313, 329, 330, 347, 374, 375, 376, 377, 378, 381, 383, 387, 387, 390, 391, 393, 394, 396, 398, 430, 431, 436, 437
Winer, L., 401
Winters, P. R., 219
Wissema, J., 196
Wolfe, H., 103, 179, 421, 426
Wootz, B., 380
Wrightsman, L., 78, 259

Yuspeh, S., 172

Zaltman, G., 382, 383, 385, 435
Zarecor, W. D., 345
Zarogoza, C. E., 400
Zoltners, A. A., 401, 438

Subject Index

Acceleration principle, 207
Advertising, 401-405
 budget allocation, 403
 see also Communications strategy
ADVISOR project, 404-405, 439
Analogy/Substitution method, 172-173. See also Potentials
Ansul Company, 19
Attitudes and opinions, 84, 242. See also Survey Research
Attribute scales, 325
 interval, 325
 nominal, 325
 ordinal, 325
 ratio, 325
 see also Nonmetric multidimensional scaling
Audits, 87
Awareness and knowledge, 242. See also Survey Research

Bassik Company, 35, 149-151
Bass model, 193, 360-361
Bayesian analysis, 173
Bench-mark data, 179-180
Bivariate analysis, 305-310
 Chi square analysis, 307-308
 cross classification analysis, 305-307
 simple correlation and regression analysis, 308-310
Boom-bust cycle, 4-5, 200. See also Demand, derived
Boston Consulting Group, 14, 191, 433
Boundary setting, 125-130. See also Market
Box-Jenkins method, 214
Breakdown methods, 149-157. See also Potentials
Bryant Chucking Grinder Company, 154-155

Buildup methods, 157-169. See also Potentials
Bureau of Labor Statistics, 65
BUYGRID model, 391
Buying behavior, see Organizational buying behavior and Industrial/institutional buying behavior
Buying/selling interface, 374-415. See also Purchasing analysis and Promotion analysis
Buying situation, 391

Canonical analysis, 316-319. See also Multivariate analysis
Caterpillar Corporation, 78
Celanese Corporation, 215, 237
Census, of Construction Industries, 53
 of Outlying Areas, 57
 of Retail Trade, 53
 of Selected Service Industries, 53
 of Transportation, 53
 of Wholesale Trade, 53
Census, U. S. Bureau of the, annual survey of manufacturers, 49, 52
 concentration ratios of manufacturing, 57
 County Business Patterns, 53
 Current Industrial Reports, 52-53
 enterprise statistics, 57
 foreign trade statistics, 57
 historical data, 1789–1954, 57
 Mini-Guide to the 1972 Economic Censuses, 62-64
 Statistical Abstract of the United States, 57
 U.S. Industrial Outlook, 65
Census method, 157-159. See also Potentials

460

SUBJECT INDEX

Census ratios, 38-41
  concentration, 40-41, 57
  coverage, 40
  primary product specialization, 40
Census II, 213
Central Limit Theorem, 281
Chase Econometrics, 183
Chi square analysis, 307-308. *See also* Bivariate analysis
"Classical decomposition method," 209-213
Cluster analysis, 323-325. *See also* Multivariate analysis
Cluster sampling, 275-276
Combustion Engineering, Inc., 215
Commercial evaluation decision, 357-361. *See also* Product analysis
Communications strategy, 398-407, 437-438
  advertising, 401-405
  ADVISOR, 404-405
  distribution channels, 407
  personal selling, 398-401
  personal selling models, 400-401
  sales promotion, 405-407
Competitive profiles, 137-139. *See also* Customer profiles
Component parts and materials, 198, 204-214. *See also* Forecasting, techniques
Comprehensive market demand studies, 125-141. *See also* Market demand
Concentration of industrial demand, 5
Concentration ratios, 40-41, 57. *See also* Census ratios
Concept testing, 346, 347. *See also* Product specification decision
Conclusive research, 77-78
  causal research, 80
  definition, 77
  descriptive research, 78-80
Conditional forecasts, 220-221. *See also* Forecasting
Conjoint measurement, 329-331.
Contribution margin approach, 111-112. *See also* Cost and Profitability analysis
Convenience sampling, 273-275. *See also* Sampling techniques
Cost and profitability analysis, 110-112, 421-423

alternative approaches, 112
contribution margin approach, 111-112
marketing cost ratio, 38, 40-41
net profit approach, 111
return on investment, 114, 422-423
types of error, 110-111
Coverage ratio, 38, 40-41. *See also* Census ratios
Cross classification analysis, 305-307. *See also* Bivariate analysis
Cross impact analysis, 196. *See also* Forecasting, procedures
Crown corporation, 264
Customer profiles, 106-110, 158. *See also* Competitive profiles

Data Resources, Inc., 183
Decision makers, 11, 384. *See also* Commercial evaluation decision
Decision making unit, 272
Decision matrix, 13-14
Decision models, conservative, 389
  multiattribute, 389-391
    cognitive consistency theory, 389-391
    compensatory, 389-391
    preference and perceptual mapping, 389
  normative, 389
Decision theory, 12
Delphi method, 24. *See also* Expert estimates *and* Forecasting procedures
Demand, concentration, 4, 6, 17, 22, 101-104, 417
  geographic, 4, 17
  industrial, 4, 6, 17
  purchasing, 4, 6, 17
  cross elasticity, 126-128
  definition of, 126
  derived, 4
    "boom-bust" cycle, 4-5
    chain of derived demand, 4-5, 417
  final, 227
  intermediate, 227-228
  industrial characteristics of, 4-5, 188-189
  market, 120-135
    comprehensive market demand studies, 122, 125-141
    definition of, 120
    Marshallian concept of, 126
    minimum demand studies, 123-124
    replacement and expansion, 140-141
    types of studies, 122-125

SUBJECT INDEX

variation, cyclical, 209
   random, 209
   seasonal, 209
   see also Market demand
"Depth of penetration," 163-165. See also IBM method
Distribution channel strategy, 102, 147, 407
Dun & Bradstreet, 66, 68, 271
   Dun's Market Identifiers, 66, 68
   Metalworking Directory, 66, 138
   Middle Market Directory, 66, 138
   Million Dollar Directory, 66, 138
DuPont deNemours, E. I., 254, 361

Early adopters, 359
Early majority, 359
Econometric models, 183-186. See also Forecasting, procedures
80–20 principle, 103-104
Estimates, interval, 281
   point, 281
Environment, 145
   effects on potential, 145-146
Environmental factors, 377-381
   economic, 377
   legal, 378
   model of, 378-379
   physical, 377
   political, 377-378
   technological, 377
Exception reporting systems, 98-100, 106
Expert estimates, 21-27, 195-196, 418-419
   Delphi method, 21, 195-196
   group discussion, 24
   key informant technique, 25-27
   nonmetric multidimensional scaling, 24-25
   pooling individual estimates, 24-25
   see also Key informant technique and Knowledgeable persons
Exploratory marketing research, 12, 17-28, 77-78
   definition, 17
Exploratory forecasting techniques, diffusion process, 190
   stepwise growth models, 191
   substitution models, 193-195
   systematic curve fitting, 190
   technological progress function, 191-193
   see also Forecasting

F & S Index of Corporations and Industries, 69, 71, 138
Factor analysis, 319-323. See also Multivariate analysis and Survey Research
Federal Mogul, 262
Federal Reserve Bulletin, 65
Ferry Cap and Set Screw Company, 89
Focused interview, 252-255
   interviewers, outside research agencies, 257
   salesmen, 256-257
   technical vs. nontechnical, 257-258
   see also Survey research
Foran system, 213. See also Survey research
Forecasting, 95-96, 177-226, 426-428
   compound approaches, 221-222
   conditional, 178, 220-221
   definition, 177
   nonconditional, 178, 220-221
   procedures, 177-222
      econometric model, 183-185
      four stage approach, 181-183, 220-221
      lead-lag statistical series, 186-189
   techniques, 190-226
      Box-Jenkins, 214
      Census II, 213
      "classical decomposition," 209-213
      exponential smoothing, 217-218
      input-output, 215-217
      moving average, 217
      regression analysis, 201-202, 204-205
      s-curve, 178-179, 190, 203, 343-346
      sales force composite, 200
      seasonal index, 209, 212
      time series, 213
      users expectation, 200-201, 205-207

General Electric Company, 14, 187-188, 196, 201
Glass Containers Corporation, 215
Goodyear Tire and Rubber Corporation, 189, 196
Gross National Product, 183-186

Hansen Manufacturing Company, 160-161, 163-164
Harnischfeger Corporation, 139
Harris Corporation, 200

SUBJECT INDEX

IBM Corporation, 25, 165-169
IBM Method, 165-169. *See also* Potentials
"Iceberg" principle, 110
Individual buying behavior factors, decision models, 387
  dominant dimension, 387
  multiattribute models, 386
  perceived risk, 388
  sleeper effects, 388
  source effect, 388
Industrial adoption process, 358-361. *See also* Commercial evaluation decision
Industrial Conference Board, 90, 114-116, 422
Industrial diffusion process, 358-361. *See also* Bass model *and* Commercial evaluation decision
Industrial/Institutional buying behavior, 374-391, 434-436. *See also* Organizational buying behavior
Industrial Marketing research, definition, 3
  determinants of its importance, 7
  organizing for, 7-8
Industrial Market segmentation, 392-395, 436-437
  macro segments, 393
  micro segments, 393
  organization characteristics for, 394
Industry, 119
  boundaries, 120-122, 125-130
  definition, 119
  structure, 135-137
Industry forecast, 188-189, 199-200
  technique selection criteria, 197-199
Industry structure analysis, 137-141
Information segments, 101-103
  definition, 101
  types, 101-103
Innovators, 359
Input/output analysis, 215-217, 227-240, 428
  direct requirements table, 228
  interpretation of coefficients, 229-233
  limitations, 216-217, 233-234, 238-240
  total requirements table, 228
  transaction table, 229
  see also Forecasting, techniques
International Harvester, 78-79

Judgement sampling, 273, 429

Kellogg Company, 2
Key informant technique, 25
  See also Expert estimates
Knowledgeable persons, 21-27, 195-196, 418-419, 429

Late majority, 359
Little, Arthurd D., 237
Loggards, 359

Macroeconomic theory, acceleration principle, 207
Mail surveys, 246-252. *See also* Survey research
Major and accessory equipment, 199-204. *See also* Forecasting
Market, 119-122, 423
  boundaries, 125-130
  definition, 120
  structure, 139-141
Market demand, 120-122
  definition, 120
  types of studies, 122-125
    comprehensive market demand studies, 125-141
    minimum demand studies, 123-124
  see also Demand *and* Market
Market forecast, 120, 177-178
  definition, 178
  see also Forecasting
Market growth rate, calculation of, 133
Marketing cost ratios, 114-116
Marketing information systems, 3
Marketing intelligence systems, 3, 18-21
Marketing management-science system, 3
Marketing research activities, industrial, 10-11
Marketing research budgets, 8-10
"Market occupancy" factor, 165
Market potential, *see* Potentials
Market segmentation, 78-79, 131-133, 392-395, 436-437
  buyer description, 79, 392-395
  end use, 79
  specific products, 79
Market share, formula to determine, 131-132
Market size, 125-133
Market structure, 139-141
Market survey method, 159-161. *See also* Potentials

SUBJECT INDEX

Market testing decision, 336, 353-357
Midwest Crane Company, 129-141, 440-454
Mill Supply Index, 150-151
Minimum demand studies, 123-124, 423. *See also* Demand *and* Market
Monopoly, definition of, 126-127
Moody's Industrial Manual, 138
Morphological analysis, 195-196. *See also* Forecasting
Moving average, 217-218. *See also* Forecasting
Multiple correlation and regression analysis, 201-202, 204-205. *See also* Multivariate analysis *and* Forecasting
Multiple discriminant analysis, 314. *See also* Multivariate analysis *and* Survey Research
Multivariate analysis, 310-331, 430-431
  classification of methods, 297-299, 310-312
  functional methods, 312-319
    canonical analysis, 316-319
    multiple correlation and regression analysis, 201-202, 204-205
    multiple discriminant analysis, 314
    multivariate analysis of variance, 314-316
  structural analysis, cluster analysis, 323-325
    conjoint measurement, 329-331
    factor analysis, 319-325
    nonmetric multidimensional scaling, 325-329

National Bureau of Economic Research (NBER), 186-188
National Industrial Conference Board, *see* Industrial Conference Board
National Steel Corporation, 237
Net profit approach, *see* Cost and profitability analysis
New products, 147-148, 169-173, 335, 339-347
  acceptance of, 147-148
  potential, 169-173
  evaluation of, 357-364
1973 Survey of Marketing Research, 7-11
Nonconditional forecast, *see* Forecasting
Nondirective interviews, 251-252

Nonmetric multidimensional scaling, 325-329, 430-431. *See also* Multivariate analysis *and* Survey Research
Nonstructured-disguised approach, 245. *See also* Survey research
Nonstructured-nondisguised research, 245. *See also* Survey research
Normative techniques, 190, 195-196
  morphological analysis, 196
  scenario generation, 195-196
  cross impact analysis, 196
  delphi method, 195-196
Norton Company, 170-171

Operating supplies and services, 214-220
Organizational buying behavior, 375-391
  buying situation, 391
  environmental factors, 377-381
  individual factors, 386-391
  interpersonal factors, 384-386
  model of, 376
Organizational factors, 381-384
  four-cell buying grid, 382
  people, 381
  structure, 381
  tasks, 381
  technology, 381

Panels, 87
Perceived risk model, 387-389. *See also* Organizational buying behavior, Individual factors
Personal interview surveys, 246-252. *See also* Survey research
Personal selling, 398, 401
  models of, 400-401
  see also Communications strategy
Pharmaseal Laboratories, 171
Possible use method, 171-172. *See also* Potentials
Potentials, 144-177, 423-426
  definition, 145
  development of, 144-145
  methods of estimating for established products, 148-169
    breakdown methods, 149-157
    statistical series, 153-157
    total market measure, 149-153
    buildup methods, 157-159
    census, 157-158

SUBJECT INDEX

market survey, 159-161
secondary data, 161-169
methods of estimating for new products, 169-174
analogy/substitution, 172-174
possible use, 171-172
usage factor, 169-171
Predicasts, Inc., 69-71
F/S Indexes, 69, 71, 138
Pricing strategy, 397-398
Primary data methods, 7, 12, 76-94, 420, 428-431
experimentation, 88-93
observation, 86-88
panels and audits, 86-87
procedure for selection, 81-82
sampling design, see Sampling techniques
Primary product specialization ratio, 38, 40. See also Census ratios
Problem/opportunity formulation, 11-14
Product analysis, 335-373, 431-434
development phase activities, 336, 339-347
development decision points, 336, 338
market testing, 353-357, 432
product feasibility, 339-346, 431
product specification, 346-347, 431-432
product testing, 352-353, 432
market phase, 336-338, 357-367
adoption process, 358-361
decline, 337
growth, 337
introduction, 337
maturity, 337
market phase activities, 357-367
commercial evaluation decision, 357-361, 432
product audit decision, 361-364, 432
product elimination decision, 364-367, 433
market structure analysis, 348-351
product life cycle, 536-538
Product portfolio strategy, 14, 433-434, 438
Product positioning studies, 351-352
Product specification decision, see Product analysis
Product testing decision, see Product analysis

Profitability analysis, 110-112, 421-423
contribution margin approach, 110-112, 421-422
net profit approach, 112, 421-422
see also Cost and profitability analysis
Promotion analysis, identification of industrial market segments, 392-395
mix decisions, 395-407
Purchasing agents, 386-391
Purchasing behavior analysis, 375-391. See also Organizational buying behavior

Questionnaires, 258-261
see also Survey research
Quota sampling, 244-249, 251-252, 258-261. See also Sampling techniques

Ratio-estimate techniques, see Market size
Regression analysis, see Forecasting, techniques
Republic Steel Corporation, 2
Roebling, John A., & Sons Corporation, 158

S-curve approach, 190, 193-195, 343-345. See also Forecasting, techniques
Sales analysis, 95-118, 421-422
additional data sources for, 106-110
concentration of, 103-104
defining information segments, 101-103
defining sales units, 100-103
definition, 96
identifying opportunities, 98-100
problem solving and opportunity analysis approach to, 96-100
scope of, 96
standards for, 104-106
Sales call reports, 106-110
Sales concentration, 103-104
Sales force composite method, 200
grass roots forecasting, 200
Sales forecast, see Forecasting, techniques
Sales promotion, 405-409
brochures, 406
budget allocation, 406-407
direct mail, 406
displays, 406
exhibits, 406
specialty, 406
trade shows, 406
see also Communication strategy

SUBJECT INDEX

Sampling Techniques, 267
Secondary data, 29-75, 98-102, 104-110,
    122-125, 130-141, 419-425
  external, 29-75, 130-141
  internal, 98-102, 104-110, 122-125
  see also Comprehensive market demand
    studies, Cost and profitability analysis, Input-output analysis, Minimum
    demand studies, *and* Sales analysis
Securities and Exchange Commission, 65
  Form 10-K reports, 65
Sequential analysis, 98-99
Simple correlation and regression analysis,
  see Forecasting techniques
Simple random sample, 275
Sleeper effect, 388
Source effect, 388
Sprague Electric Company, 172
Standard and Poor's Corporation, 69-71
  industry surveys, 71
  Register of Corporations, Directories and
    Executives, 69-71
Standard Industrial Classifications (SIC), 30
  classification system, 31
  establishments, 31
  limitations, 35-38
Statistical Package for the Social Sciences
    (SPSS), 297. *See also* Survey research
Statistical Series Method, 153-157. *See also*
    Potentials
Stepwise growth model, *see* Potentials
Stratified sampling, 276-278. *See also* Sampling techniques
Structured-disguised approach, 245
Structured-nondisguised approach, 244-245
Substitution models, 190. *See also* Forecasting, techniques
Survey research, 240-266, 428-431
  administrative control, 250-252
  analysis of data, *see* Multivariate analysis
  methods, nonstructured-disguised, 245
    nonstructured-nondisguised, 245
    structured-disguised, 245
    structured-nondisguised, 244-245
  questionnaire design, 251-255, 258-261

  types of communication, 246-247
    mail, 246-247
    personal, 246-247
    telephone, 246-247
  types of data, 242-244
    attitudes and intentions, 242
    awareness and knowledge, 242-243
    behavior, 242, 244
    demographic characteristics, 242
    intentions, 242
    motivations, 242
Systematic curve fitting, 190. *See also* Forecasting, techniques

Technological forecasting, 189-197
Technological progress function, 191-193
Telephone surveys, 246-247. *See also* Survey research
Test marketing, 89-92, 353-357
Texas Instruments Corporation, 343-345
Thomas Register of American Manufacturers, 66
Time series, *see* Forecasting, techniques
Timken Corporation, 160
Total market measure method, 149-153
TRW Corporation, 196

Universe definition, 268-269
U. S. Department of Commerce, *see* Census
U. S. Steel Corporation, 158
U. S. vs. ALCOA, 127
Usage factor method, 170-171
Users' expectations method, 200

Warner & Swasey Company, 81, 84
Weak product review, 365-367
Western Electric Company, 215, 237
Western Printing Ink Company, 153
Westinghouse Corporation, 189
Weyerhouser Corporation, 176
Wharton Econometric model, 183-184. *See also* Forecasting, techniques
Whiting Corporation, 155-156

Xerox Corporation, 347